REASON
AT WORK

Introductory Readings in Philosophy

STEVEN M. CAHN
*Graduate School and University Center,
  City University of New York*

PATRICIA KITCHER
University of Minnesota

GEORGE SHER
University of Vermont

Under the General Editorship of

Robert J. Fogelin
Dartmouth College

HARCOURT BRACE JOVANOVICH, PUBLISHERS
San Diego   New York   Chicago   Atlanta   Washington, D.C.
London   Sydney   Toronto

ISBN: 0-15-575990-6
Library of Congress Catalog Card Number: 83-82439
Printed in the United States of America

Copyrights and Acknowledgments

SAINT ANSELM/GAUNILO   "The Ontological Argument" by Saint Anselm and Gaunilo from *Proslogion, A Reply by the Author* and *A Reply on Behalf of the Fool*, translated by William Mann. Copyright © William E. Mann.

SAINT THOMAS AQUINAS   "Five Proofs for the Existence of God" from *The Basic Writings of St. Thomas Aquinas*, edited by Anton C. Pegis, copyright 1945. Reprinted by permission of Richard J. Pegis for the Estate of A. C. Pegis.

ARISTOTLE   "The Nature of Moral Virtue" from *The Ethics of Aristotle* by Aristotle, translated by J. A. K. Thomson. © 1953 by George Allen & Unwin Ltd. "The Functions of the Soul" from "De Anima" (selections) by Aristotle, translated by J. A. Smith from *The Oxford Translation of Aristotle*, edited by W. D. Ross (vol. 3, 1931). Reprinted by permission of Oxford University Press.

D. M. ARMSTRONG   "The Central-State Theory" from *A Materialist Theory of the Mind* by D. M. Armstrong Humanities Press, 1968. Reprinted by permission of Humanities Press, Inc., Atlantic Highlands, N.J. 07716.

NORMAN BOWIE/ROBERT SIMON   "Some Problems with Utilitarianism" from *The Individual and the Political Order: An Introduction to Social and Political Philosophy*, by Norman Bowie/Robert Simon. © 1977, pp. 48–51. Adapted by permission of Prentice-Hall, Inc., Englewood Cliffs, N.J.

FRANZ BRENTANO   "The Distinction Between Mental and Physical Phenomena" by Franz Brentano from *Psychology from an Empirical Standpoint*, Humanities Press, 1973. Reprinted by permission of Humanities Press, Inc., Atlantic Highlands, N.J. 07716.

Continued on page 725.

Preface

This book represents our attempt to introduce students to the best in contemporary and historical work in philosophy. In making our selections, we have been guided by several considerations. First, and most important, the readings are intended to illustrate our belief that philosophy is an essential tool for anyone who wishes to engage in serious intellectual work. Despite obvious limitations of space, we believe that our selections illuminate the presuppositions of many of the most important areas of human endeavor. In addition, the readings reflect our belief that, in the last twenty years, philosophers have made significant progress both on traditional questions and in newer interdisciplinary problem areas. Their findings are of interest to anyone who wants a contemporary version of a traditional liberal arts education. Finally, our selections are intended to capture what we find riveting about the discipline—the combination of rigor and imaginative genius that the best work often displays. Like much else, the success of these attempts is left for the reader to assess.

While editing the book, we incurred various debts of gratitude that we are pleased to acknowledge here. When the book was in the review stage, we received helpful comments and suggestions from Professors John Buckley of the University of South Alabama, Hugh Fleetwood of Western Washington University, Richard Arneson of the University of California, San Diego, Walter O'Briant of the University of Georgia, and James Doyle of the University of Missouri. We also wish to thank Harcourt Brace Jovanovich's series editor, Professor Robert Fogelin of Dartmouth College, and all the editors who collaborated with us on this project. At the University of Vermont, where the bulk of the editing was done, we would like to express special thanks to Hilary Kornblith for writing the introductory material for the epistemology section. We are also grateful to Philip Kitcher, Arthur Kuflik, and William Mann for frequent advice. However, our greatest debt is to Leslie Weiger. As with so many other philosophy department projects, she managed most of the difficult technical details of this work. We are, as always, deeply appreciative of her efforts.

Steven M. Cahn
Patricia Kitcher
George Sher

Contents

Preface   iii

INTRODUCTION
The Elements of Argument   1

I.   ETHICS   21
   1. Joel Feinberg, Psychological Egoism   25
   2. Paul Taylor, Ethical Relativism
      from *Problems of Moral Philosophy*, second edition   36
   3. Gilbert Harman, Ethics and Observation
      from *The Nature of Morality*   48
   4. John Rawls, Outline of a Decision Procedure for Ethics   54
   5. John Stuart Mill, Utilitarianism
      from *Utilitarianism*   62
   6. Norman Bowie and Robert Simon, Some Problems with
      Utilitarianism
      from *The Individual and the Political Order*   76
   7. R. M. Hare, Utilitarianism and Non-Utilitarian Intuitions
      from *Moral Thinking*   80
   8. Immanuel Kant, Morality and Rationality
      from *The Foundations of the Metaphysics of Morals*   87
   9. Philippa Foot, Morality as a System of Hypothetical
      Imperatives   107
  10. W. D. Ross, What Makes Right Acts Right?
      from *The Right and the Good*   116
  11. Aristotle, The Nature of Moral Virtue
      from *Nichomachean Ethics*   127
  12. Peter Singer, Famine, Affluence, and Morality   140

II. SOCIAL AND POLITICAL PHILOSOPHY   153
  13. Plato, What Do We Owe to Our Country?
      from the *Crito*   157
  14. Thomas Hobbes, Authority and Security
      from *Leviathan*   169
  15. John Locke, Limited Government as Defender of Property
      from *Second Treatise of Government*   181
  16. Robert Nozick, "The Principle of Fairness"
      from *Anarchy, State, and Utopia*   195
  17. John Stuart Mill, On Liberty
      from *On Liberty*   199

18. John Rawls, A Theory of Justice
from *A Theory of Justice* 213

19. Robert Nozick, Distributive Justice
from *Anarchy, State, and Utopia* 227

20. Karl Marx and Friedrich Engels, Communism
from *The Communist Manifesto* and *Critique of the Gotha Program* 239

21. Edward Nell and Onora O'Neill, On Justice Under Socialism 253

III. THEORY OF KNOWLEDGE 265

22. Plato, Knowledge as Justified True Belief
from the *Theaetetus* 269

23. Edmund L. Gettier III, Is Justified True Belief Knowledge? 280

24. René Descartes, Certain Knowledge
from *Meditations on First Philosophy* 283

25. John Locke, Empiricism
from *An Essay Concerning Human Understanding* 292

26. David Hume, The Problem of Induction
from *An Inquiry Concerning Human Understanding* 306

27. Nelson Goodman, The New Riddle of Induction
from *Fact, Fiction, and Forecast* 318

28. W. V. O. Quine, The Interdependence of Beliefs
from "Two Dogmas of Empiricism" 327

29. W. V. O. Quine, The Nature of Natural Knowledge 331

30. Alvin Goldman, Innate Knowledge 343

31. Michael Williams, The Appeal to the Given
from *Groundless Belief* 351

32. Friedrich Nietzsche, The Utility of Truth
from *Truth and the Lie, The Gay Science, Beyond Good and Evil, Genealogy of Morals,* and *The Will to Power* 356

33. T. S. Kuhn, Objectivity, Value Judgments, and Theory Choice
from *The Essential Tension* 371

34. Philip Kitcher, Believing Where We Cannot Prove
from *Abusing Science* 386

IV. METAPHYSICS 403

35. John Locke, Real and Nominal Essence
from *An Essay Concerning Human Understanding* 407

36. Gottfried Wilhelm Leibniz, On Possibility and Necessity 420

37. Saul Kripke, Metaphysical Necessity
from *Naming and Necessity* 424

38. John Locke, Personal Identity
from *An Essay Concerning Human Understanding* 436

39. Bernard Williams, The Self and the Future 451

40. Derek Parfit, Later Selves and Moral Principles 463

41. B. F. Skinner, Hard Determinism
   from *Walden Two*   477
42. Jean-Paul Sartre, Radical Freedom
   from *Being and Nothingness*   483
43. R. E. Hobart, Free Will as Involving Determinism   494
44. Gerald Dworkin, Acting Freely   509

V. PHILOSOPHY OF RELIGION   523
45. Plato, God and Morality
   from the *Euthyphro*   526
46. Saint Anselm and Gaunilo, The Ontological Argument
   from *Proslogion, A Reply on Behalf of the Fool,* and *A Reply
   by the Author*   540
47. Saint Thomas Aquinas, Five Proofs for the Existence of God
   from *Summa Theologica*   547
48. David Hume, The Teleological Argument
   from *Dialogues Concerning Natural Religion*   550
49. Ernest Nagel, A Defense of Atheism   569
50. Richard Swinburne, The Problem of Evil   581
51. Antony Flew, R. M. Hare, and Basil Mitchell, Theology and
   Falsification   596
52. Steven M. Cahn, Religion Reconsidered   605

VI. PHILOSOPHY OF MIND   611
53. Aristotle, The Functions of the Soul
   from *De Anima*   614
54. René Descartes, Dualism
   from *Meditations on First Philosophy*   625
55. Franz Brentano, The Distinction Between Mental and Physical
   Phenomena
   from *Psychology from an Empirical Standpoint*   635
56. B. F. Skinner, Behaviorism
   from *Science and Human Behavior*   648
57. Daniel C. Dennett, Skinner Skinned   665
58. Noam Chomsky, Linguistic Contributions to the Study of Mind
   from *Language and Mind*   679
59. D. M. Armstrong, The Central-State Theory
   from *A Materialist Theory of the Mind*   689
60. Jerry A. Fodor, Functionalism
   from *Psychological Explanation*   703
61. Daniel C. Dennett, Artificial Intelligence as Philosophy and as
   Psychology   712

INTRODUCTION

The Elements of Argument

We reason every day of our lives. All of us argue for our own points of view, whether the topic be politics, the value or burden of religion, the best route to drive between Boston and New York, or any of a myriad of other subjects. We are constantly barraged by the arguments of others, seeking to convince us that they know how to build a better computer or how to prevent a serious illness or whatever. When first approaching the subject of reasoning, a student is apt to feel like Molière's M. Jourdain, who suddenly realized that he had been speaking in prose for forty years. Just as prose can be elegant or ungrammatical, however, there are grades of reasoning, from the clear and compelling to the fallacious and sloppy. All scholars must engage in reasoning, but it is the mainstay of work in philosophy. A brief, but quite accurate, description of philosophical method is that we do not observe or experiment, we construct chains of reasoning. Because of its central role in their discipline, philosophers have tried to make their reasoning explicit and to discover the principles underlying good reasoning.

This introductory section of *Reason at Work* presents some basic principles of good reasoning. We hope to provide readers with some of the skills required for constructing good arguments of their own and for analyzing the reasoning of others. These two tasks—the constructive and the critical—are related. A good critic can reconstruct the best version of the argument under appraisal. Equally, a good reasoner is constantly playing critic, subjecting the developing argument to scrutiny. Besides the intrinsic value of improving the skill of reasoning, we hope that this section will also enable students to achieve a better understanding of the argumentation in the readings that follow.

1

Arguments

In ordinary parlance, an argument is a verbal dispute carried out with greater or less ferocity. The technical, philosophical notion is quite different. An argument is a collection of sentences consisting of *premises* and a *conclusion*. Arguments can have any number of premises, starting with as few as one. In reasoning, we often encounter a *chain of argumentation*, that is, a sequence of arguments. We begin with some premises and infer a conclusion. From this first conclusion, plus some other premises, we infer a second conclusion, and so on down the line until we reach the final conclusion of the entire chain of argumentation. The conclusions of the individual arguments in the chain are usually referred to as *subconclusions*, because although they function as premises for later arguments, they are not premises of the entire chain of argumentation. A statement functions as a *premise* in an argument, or in a chain of argumentation, if the truth of that statement is assumed and not established by the argumentation. *Conclusions* and *subconclusions* are the claims whose truth is supposed to be established and not assumed by the argumentation.

In the following chain of argumentation, 1, 2, and 4 are premises; 3 is a subconclusion, because it follows from 1 and 2 and because, along with 4, it supports 5; 5 is the final conclusion.

1. The people in the house would have been awakened the night the horse was stolen if the dog had barked.
2. Everyone slept peacefully the entire night the horse was stolen.
3. So, the dog must not have barked.
4. The dog would have barked if the individual or individuals leading the horse out of the stable had been strangers.
5. Therefore, the horse thief (or horse thieves) was (were) known to the dog.*

One crucial fact about philosophical arguments follows immediately from the recognition that arguments always have two basic parts: premises and conclusions. It is sometimes said that a true philosopher never assumes anything; every claim must be proved. Taken literally, this cannot be right. For if you are going to construct an argument at all, you must take some claim (or claims) as your premise(s). It would obviously be backwards to assume the truth of a very controversial claim in order to argue for something that is obvious to everyone. The direction of argumentation must always be, as above, from the more obvious to the less obvious. Ideally a reasoner will assume, as premises, claims that are very uncontroversial and argue that a much more controversial, perhaps even surprising, conclusion follows from those unproblematic assumptions.

A chain of argumentation is exactly as solid as the arguments it contains. If any link is weak, then the entire chain will break down. From a logical point

---

*Sherlock Holmes offers this chain of reasoning in "Silver Blaze," in *The Memoirs of Sherlock Holmes.*

of view, the crucial aspect of arguments is the relationship between the premises and the conclusion. Logic is that branch of philosophy which studies the inferential relations between premises and conclusion. The task of logic is to establish rules or guidelines about which claims can be inferred from which other claims. This task has been carried out with great success for *deductive inference*. Deductive logicians have provided clear and rich accounts of the standards of good deductive inference. Courses in deductive logic present these theories in detail. We will describe only those aspects of deductive logic that are particularly important for evaluating ordinary reasoning.

Deductive Arguments

The central concept of deductive logic is *validity*. An argument is valid if and only if the following relation holds between its premises and its conclusion: *It is impossible for the conclusion to be false if the premises are true.* Alternatively, in a valid argument, if the premises are true, that guarantees that the conclusion is also true. It is important to realize that logicians are not concerned with truth itself. Logicians will certify an argument as valid whether or not the premises are true. Their concern is only with the relation between the premises and the conclusion. Regardless of whether the premises are true, an argument is valid if, *if* the premises *happen* to be true, then the conclusion *must* be true. If all the arguments in a chain of argumentation are valid, then the entire chain will also be valid. Valid arguments are ideal, because if you start from true premises, true conclusions are guaranteed. Like a trolley car that is bound to follow the tracks, if you start with the truth and make only valid inferences, you will never veer away from the truth.

It is somewhat unfortunate that, in ordinary English, "valid" and "true" are often used as synonyms. Their technical, philosophical meanings are quite distinct. In the primary philosophical use of "valid," it makes no sense to say that a statement is "valid," for validity is a *relation among statements*. Statements can be true, but not valid; arguments can be valid, but not true. "True" and "valid" have distinct meanings, and truth and validity are independent properties; that is, each property can occur without the other. Arguments whose premises are all true can still be invalid and valid arguments can have false premises. Thus, a valid argument can have (i) true premises and a true conclusion, as in (1); (ii) one or more false premises and a false conclusion, as in (2); or (iii) one or more false premises and a true conclusion, as in (3). The only possibility ruled out by validity is that the argument have true premises and a false conclusion.

(1) P_1 Wombats belong to the order of marsupials.
     P_2 Koalas belong to the order of marsupials.
     C Wombats and Koalas belong to the same order.

(2) P_1 All philosophers lived in Ancient Greece. (false)
     P_2 Bertrand Russell was a philosopher.
     C Bertrand Russell lived in Ancient Greece. (false)

(3) P_1 All canaries are polar bears. (false)
           P_2 All polar bears have feathers. (false)
           C All canaries have feathers.

Finally, an argument can have true premises and a true conclusion and still be invalid, as in (4).

(4) P_1 Some roses are red.
           P_2 Some violets are blue.
           C Some flowers give some people hay fever.

The problem with argument (4) is that, while all the claims are true, the fact that P_1 and P_2 are true gives us no reason whatsoever to believe that C is true.

So far, we have been assuming that the reader can simply "see" when an argument is valid or invalid. But how can we actually test for deductive validity? In one sense, the test for validity comes right out of the definition of validity: A valid argument is one whose conclusion cannot be false if its premises are true. To test for validity, try negating the conclusion while assuming the truth of the premises.

(5) P_1 All Englishmen love the Queen. (false)
           P_2 Henry is English.
           C Henry loves the Queen.

In (5) we would negate the conclusion, yielding "Henry does not love the Queen." Now the queston is, can we still maintain the truth of the premises? Obviously not, for if we try to claim that Henry does *not* love the Queen, while holding to the truth of P_2, "Henry is English," then we shall have to give up the truth of P_1, "All Englishmen love the Queen." Conversely, if we claim that Henry does not love the Queen and try to maintain P_1 as well, then we will have to give up P_2. Since we cannot maintain the truth of both (or all) premises while negating the conclusion, this argument is valid. If it is possible to preserve the truth of the premises, while denying the conclusion, as in (6), then the argument is invalid.

(6) P_1 Only U.S. citizens vote in American elections.
           P_2 Jones is a U.S. citizen.
           C Jones votes in American elections.

Even though P_1 and P_2 are true, C could be false, if Jones is one of the citizens who does not bother to vote.

While the test just described is always sufficient to determine validity, sometimes it is difficult to tell whether an argument passes or fails this test, for example, argument (7).

(7) P_1 All Republicans are happy or handsome.
        P_2 No Republican is silly.
        P_3 All happy people are silly or hard-working.
Sub C All Republicans are hard-working or handsome.
        P_4 All hardworking people are silly or handsome.
        C All Republicans are handsome.

To simplify and systematize the task of determining validity, logicians have appealed to the notion of *logical form*. Since classical antiquity, philosophers have recognized that different arguments could share the same form. For example, arguments (8) and (9) have a common form.

(8) P_1 Either the Yankees or the Red Sox will win the pennant.
      P_2 The Yankees cannot win the pennant.
      C Therefore, the Red Sox will win the pennant.

(9) P_1 With the new Congress, taxes will either go down or up.
      P_2 Taxes never go down.
      C Therefore, taxes will go up.

This common form can be seen more clearly if we represent the claims contained in the arguments by letter variables. Both arguments have the following form:

F_1 P_1 A or B.
      P_2 Not A.
      C B.

Clearly, any argument of this form must be valid. For the first premise asserts that either A or B is true and the second premise claims that A is not true. Thus B must be true.

There are many, many valid argument forms. We list some of the more common forms alongside an example of each form.

(10) P_1 The 1960s were not a time of peace.
      C Therefore, the 1960s were not a time of peace and prosperity.

F_2 P_1 Not A.
      C Therefore, not both A and B.

(11) P_1 If interest rates come down, the stock market goes up.
      P_2 Interest rates have come down.
      C The stock market is going up.

F_3 P_1 If A, then B.
      P_2 A
      C B

(12) P₁ All Mozart compositions are melodious.
P₂ The "Window" aria
was composed by
Mozart.
C The "Window" aria is
melodious.

F₄ P₁ All A's are B.
P₂ a is an A.
C a is a B.

(13) P₁ Jones was an honest
politician.
C Some politicians are
honest.

F₅ P₁ a is A and a is B.
C Some A's are B's.

Finally, argument (7) above has the following form:

F₆ P₁ All A's are B or C.
P₂ No A is a D.
P₃ All B's are D or E.
Sub C All A's are E or C.
P₄ All E's are D or C.
C Therefore, all A's are C.

In an older tradition in logic, students would be expected to memorize numerous valid argument forms, many of which have special names. F_1 is called "constructive dilemma," F_3 "modus ponens," and F_4, a "syllogism in Barbara." A serious drawback of this system—aside from the archaic names—is that students simply cannot memorize all the valid forms, because there are too many of them. We suggest, instead, that students think of logical form as a tool to use in determining validity. When presented with an argument, it is extremely helpful to *schematize* that argument by using letter variables. Care must be taken in figuring out the correct schematic presentation of an argument. The first point to realize is that *one sentence* will often contain *two claims*. For example, (8) P_1, "Either the Yankees will win the pennant or the Red Sox will win the pennant" actually involves two distinct claims, "the Yankees will win the pennant" and "the Red Sox will win the pennant." It asserts a relation between these claims, namely, the relation that one of these two claims is true, so it should be represented as "Either A or B." Sometimes it is possible to schematize an argument adequately just by using letter variables to stand for *claims*. Of course, the same claim should always be represented by the same letter and each distinct claim must be represented by a different letter.

Other arguments have a more complex structure, because distinct claims share a common part and the shared part plays a role in the inference. In example (12), "All Mozart compositions are melodious" and "The 'Window' aria was composed by Mozart" share a common idea, "being composed by Mozart." Further, the fact that these two premises share this part is crucial in

6

allowing us to infer the conclusion. In such cases, distinct letters must be used for elements within claims. Otherwise, the schema would mask rather than reveal the logical interrelations between the claims. The standard procedure for assigning letter variables to elements within claims, is to replace attributes that different individuals can share—"being red," or "being composed by Mozart," for example—by capital letters, and names of individuals by lower case letters. So argument (12) should be represented as above:

F_4 P_1 All A's are B's.
    P_2 a is an A.
    C   a is a B.

To sum up: Where possible, schematize arguments by assigning letter variables only to distinct claims. When the inferential structure of the argument is hidden by this procedure, assign letter variables to elements within claims.

A compelling deductive argument should be valid. Otherwise, the premises should not lead us to accept the conclusion. However, validity is not enough. Even if the truth of a conclusion may be validly inferred from the truth of certain premises, that gives us no reason at all to accept the conclusion, unless we have good reason to believe that the premises are, in fact, true. Unfortunately, there is no magical device we can use to determine truth. For philosophers, as for anyone else, establishing the truth of claims is often a complex, difficult, and uncertain project. Still, through their explicit study of argumentation, philosophers have recognized that there is a general method that can be used to assess the worth of premises, even in the absence of a test of truth.

In analyzing arguments, philosophers noticed that the key terms in some premises were either so vague or so ambiguous that the premise ought to be rejected out of hand. For example,

(14) P_1 The Constitution requires that public education be theologically neutral.
    P_2 The theory of evolution is really just a religious doctrine.
    C   Therefore, since evolution is taught in schools, the Biblical account of creation should also be taught in order to ensure theological neutrality.

While P_2 is also highly questionable, we will just consider the terminology employed in P_1 and the conclusion. What is the key expression "theologically neutral" supposed to mean? Given a standard interpretation of the Constitutional doctrine of the separation of Church and State, if P_1 is to be true, then "theologically neutral" must be read as something like "devoid of theology." Notice, however, that this cannot be the intended reading of "theologically neutral" in the conclusion, or the conclusion would be self-contradictory, asserting that the way to make public education devoid of theology is to start teaching the Biblical account of creation. There, "theologically neutral" must be inter-

preted to mean something like "theologically balanced." In this example, the ambiguous terminology completely vitiates the argument. The only reason the premises even appear to support the conclusion is that the same phrase occurs in both P_1 and C. That connection is illusory, however, because the phrase is used ambiguously. In cases like this, the argument may be dismissed without trying to determine the *truth* of the premises. In fact, when a key term in a premise is either ambiguous or vague, there is no way to figure out whether the premise is true or not. For, if we are unsure about what the premise asserts, we are in no position to find out whether what the premise asserts is true.

Thus, when philosophers move from assessing the validity of an argument to assessing the plausibility of its premises, they make a preliminary inquiry into the *clarity* of the premises. Their two questions are: Are key terms used ambiguously? Is any key term too vague to be assigned a meaning? Sometimes, vagueness is very easy to spot as, for example, in the popular advertising claim, "Lipton tea is brisk." Here we are given no idea at all about what "brisk" is supposed to mean when applied to tea, as opposed to, say, a "brisk" walk. So we are in no position to weigh the plausibility, let alone the truth, of the claim. In other cases, it requires considerable practice and serious thought to figure out whether the claim made by a premise (or a conclusion) is acceptably clear. To take a contemporary example, most people believe in equality of opportunity for all. This superficial consensus can mask deep differences, however, because "equal opportunity" can mean many different things. To give just three possibilities, "equal opportunity" can mean "a right to equal consideration for all jobs," or "a right to equal education or training in the skills required by more prestigious jobs," or "a right to proportionate distribution of the actual jobs available." It will be easier or more difficult to defend the claim that the "equal opportunity" is correct, depending on which of these meanings is used. So when trying to assess the plausibility of a premise, the first step is to try to assign some clear meaning to its key terms. Often, different assignments will have to be tried, before it is possible to determine the best reading for the term or phrase in the argument. For, as we saw in (14), while one reading may work well in one premise, that reading may be disastrous in other parts of the argument. To avoid trading on any ambiguities, the same reading must be used for every occurrence of the term. As the example of "equal opportunity" suggests, thinking carefully about what the terms in an argument mean is just as important for constructing sound arguments as it is for criticizing the arguments of others.

Non-Deductive Arguments

We have looked briefly at one type of inferential relation between premises and conclusions—the relation of deductive validity. As noted above, the science of deductive logic has been worked out in great detail and with impressive precision. As we turn from deductive arguments to non-deductive arguments, matters look very different. Current theorizing about non-deductive inference

is much less certain, much less clear-cut than its counterpart in deductive reasoning. For reasons that we will touch on below, it may turn out that a rigorous and complete theory of non-deductive logic is not possible! Nevertheless, we must try to deal with non-deductive reasoning, because there are many good, but non-deductive inferences that we encounter in everyday and scientific discussions. Suppose, for example, that a particular drug is given 100,000 trials across a wide variety of people and it never produces serious side effects. Even the most scrupulous researcher would conclude that the drug is safe. Still, this conclusion cannot be validly inferred from the data.

(15) P_1 In 100,000 trials, drug X produced no serious side effects.
C Drug X does not have any serious side effects.

We can use our regular method of testing validity to show that this argument is invalid (see p. 4). Assuming the negation of the conclusion—drug X *has* a serious side effect—can we preserve the truth of premise P_1? It could turn out that a serious side effect only shows up on the 100,001st trial. Thus the premise, P_1, could be true, even though C is false, so the argument is valid.

There are many more good, but invalid arguments. Here is a mundane example.

(16) P_1 The dining room window is shattered.
P_2 There is a baseball lying in the middle of the glass on the dining room floor.
P_3 There is a baseball bat lying on the ground in the yard outside the dining room.
C The dining room window was shattered by being hit with a baseball.

Here is an example from a current scientific debate.

(17) P_1 The evolution of organisms depends on particular facts about environment and competitors.
P_2 Among many other facts, the development of mammals (and so, of human beings) probably depended on the accidental extinction of the dinosaurs, who had dominated the mammals.
C Since it is very unlikely that the sequence of facts which permitted the rise of human beings will ever be repeated, it is unlikely that we will encounter humanoid creatures on other planets.*

---

* Stephen Jay Gould offers this argument in *Discover* (March, 1983). Gould's main point is that while evolutionary considerations make the discovery of other humanoids unlikely, they do not tell against the possibility of discovering other forms of intelligent life.

If we cling to the standard of deductive validity, then all three of the above arguments—and all other arguments like these—will have to be dismissed as bad reasoning. That constraint on argumentation is unacceptable for three reasons. First, these arguments appear to be perfectly reasonable, at least at first glance. Second, it is hard to see how we could get by without engaging in the sorts of reasoning represented by these examples. Finally, and perhaps most critically, it seems unreasonable to demand that the truth of the premises must *guarantee* the truth of the conclusion. Very often it is reasonable to believe something that is merely very probable, given the evidence. To take a different example, given the number of traffic lights in Manhattan, it is reasonable to believe that, if you drive the entire length of the island in normal traffic, you will have to stop at some traffic light or other (and probably at several). At least, we would be willing to make a small wager on this point.

Logic has, therefore, a second task. It needs to provide criteria for evaluating good, but non-deductive, inferences. This work may never be carried out with the precision and detail found in theories of deductive inference. Still, philosophers have distinguished various types of non-deductive arguments and have offered suggestions about standards for evaluating these sorts of arguments.

Induction

Without any detailed knowledge of combustion, we know that if we place a dry piece of paper into the flame of a candle, the paper will burn. We know this because we have witnessed or heard about many similar events in the past. In the past, the paper has always burned, so we infer that the paper will burn in the present case. This common type of reasoning is called *induction*. In induction, one relies on similar, observed cases, to infer that the same event or property will recur in as yet unobserved cases. We reason that since paper has always burned when placed in a flame, the same thing will happen in the present case. In this example, we are using previous experience to make a single prediction. Inductive reasoning can also warrant general conclusions. Having determined that, in all the carbon atoms that have been tested, the atomic weight is 12, we infer that all atoms of carbon have an atomic weight of 12. As the reader can easily verify, neither a single-case induction nor inductive generalizations can be validly inferred from their premises.

(18) P_1 In all observed cases, paper burns when placed in a flame.
      C If the piece of paper in front of us is placed in a flame, it will burn.

(19) P_1 All the carbon atoms which have been tested have an atomic weight of 12.
      C All carbon atoms have an atomic weight of 12.

For different cases, we will have different amounts of evidence on which to draw. If only ten instances of a disease have been observed, then we will have much less confidence in predicting the course of the disease than if we had

observed 10,000 occurrences. Philosophers usually describe our "confidence" in a claim as our "strength of belief" in that claim. The obvious suggestion is that our strength of belief in a claim should vary with the amount of evidence supporting the claim. More precisely, our strength of belief should increase with the number of positive instances of the claim. In other words, the degree of *rational* belief *does* increase as positive instances increase. So, for example, if you arrive in a new town and notice that all the buses you see on your first day are green, then as the days pass and you continue to observe nothing but green buses, the degree of your rational belief in the claim that all the buses in town are green will continually go up. Each new instance of a green bus is said to "confirm" the generalization that all the buses are green. Another way to state this relationship is that the degree of rational belief in an inductive generalization should vary with the amount of confirmation that the generalization has received.

Positive instances gradually confirm an inductive generalization, making it more and more reasonable to accept the generalization. By contrast, a negative instance defeats the generalization in a single stroke. To take a dramatic twentieth-century example, with the splitting of the first atom, the long-standing claim that atoms are indivisible particles of matter had to be given up. Besides the sheer number of positive instances, another criterion for good inductive reasoning is that the evidence be varied. If you have observed buses in many different parts of town, then you are more justified in claiming that the town's buses are all green than if you only considered the buses on your street.

Hypothesis Testing

It is a commonplace that people—most notably scientists and detectives—test hypotheses and accept those hypotheses that pass the tests they have devised. The process of *hypothesis testing* (with consequent acceptance or rejection) is very similar to the process of inductive reasoning. For example, imagine that a problem has developed in a small rural town. Residents are falling sick, complaining of severe nausea, abdominal pains, and other symptoms. The local doctor hypothesizes that the trouble has been caused by the opening of a new chemical plant that is emptying waste within a mile of one of the lakes that yield the town's supply of drinking water. The hypothesis can be tested in a number of different ways. The residents might check the consequences of only drinking water from lakes that are not close to the chemical plant. Or they might examine the effects on laboratory animals of drinking water obtained shortly after large amounts of waste had been ejected from the plant. It is relatively easy to see how the doctor's hypothesis might fail such tests. The residents might find that using water from different lakes achieved nothing, and that the sickness continued to spread. Equally, it is evident how the hypothesis could pass the tests. One might discover, for example, that the health of laboratory animals was dramatically affected by providing them with water obtained shortly after an episode of waste disposal.

The case just described indicates the general way in which a hypothesis might be tested. Frequently we advance a claim—a hypothesis—whose truth or falsity we are unable to ascertain by relatively direct observation. We cannot just look and see what causes the sickness in the rural town (or what causes various forms of cancer); we cannot just look and see if the earth moves, or if the continents were once part of a single land mass, or if the butler committed the crime. In evaluating such hypotheses, we consider what things we would expect to observe if the hypothesis were true. Then we investigate to see if these expectations are or are not borne out. If they are, then the hypothesis passes the test, and its success counts in its favor. If they are not, then the failure counts against the hypothesis.

We can make our description of the process of hypothesis testing more precise as follows. For any hypothesis H, an *observational consequence* of H is a statement that meets two conditions: first, it must be possible to ascertain the truth or falsity of the statement by using observation; second, the statement must follow deductively from H. Then we can represent cases of success and failure with tests as follows. Suppose that O is an observational consequence of H. Then, as a matter of deductive logic, it is true that,

If H then O.

If we are fortunate to observe the truth of O, then we give the following argument:

F_7 If H then O
$\underline{\qquad O \qquad}$
  H

If experience is unkind to H, and we observe that O is false, we give the different argument:

F_8 If H then O
$\underline{\text{Not O}\quad}$
  Not H.

There is an important asymmetry between F_7 and F_8. The latter is conclusive in a way that the former is not. Notice that F_8 is a deductively valid form of argument. Hence, if we know that the premises are true, we have a guarantee that the conclusion is true. However, F_7 is not deductively valid: it is possible that the premises should be true and the conclusion false. Moreover, there are many instances of the form F_7 that we would not want to accept. However, as in the case of inductive generalization, we become ever more justified in accepting a hypothesis as we find that a numerous and varied collection of its obser-

vational consequences prove true. Although we may (reasonably) balk at accepting an argument of the form F_7, we find it hard to resist more elaborate arguments, taking such forms as

F_9 If H then O_1
    If H then O_2
      .
      .
      .
    If H then O_n
      O_1
      O_2
      .
      .
      .
      O_n
    _____
      H

where n is a large number and the O statements $O_1, \ldots, O_n$ form a varied collection of claims about what might be observed. For example, if Sherlock Holmes infers from the hypothesis that Moriarty was the culprit, observational consequences to the effect that the grandfather clock should have stopped at midnight, that a single goblet should be missing from the curio cabinet, that the rug in the hallway should show traces of clay on its underside ..., and if we discover that all of these effects are to be found, then we may justifiably conclude that the hypothesis is correct. Here again, arguments of form F_9, like those of form F_7, are deductively invalid.

When hypotheses pass tests, we find ourselves in a very similar situation to that of inductive generalization. The test results do not guarantee that the hypothesis is true, but the larger the number of cases and the more varied they are, the higher is our rational confidence in the hypothesis. Moreover, as in the inductive case, a single failure spells doom. One observational consequence that is not borne out shows us that the hypothesis is wrong. However strikingly successful Holmes's hypothesis about Moriarty may have been, we must abandon it if it implies an effect we find to be absent. Suppose that it follows from the hypothesis that there should be a size 12A footprint in the flowerbed beneath the kitchen window. Then, for all the success with the grandfather clock, the missing goblet and the hallway rug, the absence of that footprint defeats Holmes's hypothesis.

At this stage we ought to acknowledge a point that may have bothered readers. Observational consequences of a single hypothesis are hard to come by. Indeed, it should have been clear that our discussion of Holmes's hypothesis about Moriarty is extremely fanciful. *By itself,* that hypothesis does not imply any such results about observation as those that we have ascribed to it. To make predictions about clocks, clay, and curios we have to appeal (tacitly) to

all sorts of other premises, unspoken *auxiliary assumptions*. When our predictions go awry we can always lay the blame on one of these auxiliary assumptions. Saving the central hypothesis, we choose to reject some other statement that is used in deriving from it the observational result that has proved faulty.

What this means is that the simple argument form F_8, while deductively valid, does not often provide us with a realistic account of what goes on in abortive tests. The following form of argument is much more widely applicable:

$$F_{10} \quad \frac{\text{If H and } (A_1 \text{ and } A_2 \text{ and } \ldots \text{ and } A_n) \text{ then O}}{\text{Not O}}$$
$$\text{Not H or not } (A_1 \text{ and } A_2 \text{ and } \ldots \text{ and } A_n)$$

F_{10}, like F_8, is deductively valid. However, it lacks the bite of F_8, for it leaves open the possibility that, given uncomfortable observational findings, we may lay the blame on some auxiliary assumption (i.e. A_1 or A_2 or $\ldots$ or A_n).

In the abstract, it may be hard to understand how this could ever work, or how the rejection of auxiliary assumptions could ever be justified. So we shall conclude our discussion of hypothesis testing by describing a classic case. In 1543, Nicolaus Copernicus published an astronomical treatise, claiming that the earth revolves annually about the sun. Orthodox astronomers pointed out that, if Copernicus were right, then, at different times of the year, we should observe the fixed stars from different angles. (Compare: As you run around a running track, the objects you see are seen at different angles from different points of the track.) Yet we do not observe any change in the angle at which we see the fixed stars. So Copernicus is instantly refuted! However, the alleged refutation is too quick. As Galileo (and other Copernicans) pointed out, the prediction that the fixed stars should be seen at different angles at different times of the year does not follow from the claim that the earth revolves annually about the sun. One must also assume that the stars are relatively close, for if they are very distant, the shifts in angle will not be big enough for us to detect. Thus Galileo rejected an auxiliary assumption, and maintained that the universe is much bigger than his predecessors had supposed. He was vindicated in the nineteenth century, when minute differences in the angles at which the fixed stars appear were finally detected.

Inference to Best Explanation

Another common and indispensable type of non-deductive inference should be familiar to readers of both scientific essays and detective stories. Sherlock Holmes uses this type of reasoning in his first encounter with Dr. Watson in *A Study in Scarlet*:

> "I *knew* you came from Afghanistan. From long habit the train of thoughts ran so swiftly through my mind that I arrived at the conclusion without being conscious of intermediate steps. There were such steps, however. The train of reasoning ran, 'Here is a gentleman of a medical type, but with the air of a military

man. Clearly an army doctor, then. He has just come from the tropics, for his face is dark, and that is not the natural tint of his skin, for his wrists are fair. He has undergone hardship and sickness, as his haggard face says clearly. His left arm has been injured. He holds it in a stiff and unnatural manner. Where in the tropics could an English army doctor have seen much hardship and got his arm wounded? Clearly in Afghanistan.' The whole train of thought did not occupy a second. I then remarked that you came from Afghanistan, and you were astonished."

It is no help to students of reasoning that Sir Arthur Conan Doyle consistently misdescribes Holmes's reasoning as "deduction." Holmes's argument is obviously invalid. Even though Watson has a deep tan and a wounded arm, it is still entirely possible that he has never been in Afghanistan. He could have obtained the tan in Florida and the wound in a knife fight in Soho. Still, Holmes's argument does provide considerable suport for his claim that Watson had been in Afghanistan. This is the way Holmes's reasoning (here and in most other places) actually works. He lists a number of facts: the military bearing, the medical bag, the tan, the wounded arm. Then he uses those facts to infer a conclusion, *on the grounds that the claim made by the conclusion would explain all the facts presented.* In this case, if Watson is, in fact, a military doctor who has just returned from active service in Afghanistan, that would explain why he has a medical bag, a tan, and so forth. The correct, if clumsy, name for this type of reasoning is *argument by inference to the best explanation.* Argument (16) about the dining room window and the baseball is also an argument by inference to the best explanation. If the baseball was hit through the window, that would explain why the window was broken, why there is a baseball in the middle of the room and why there is a baseball bat out in the yard.

Inference to best explanation is related to hypothesis testing. In hypothesis testing, a hypothesis is supported when observations which can be deduced from that hypothesis are borne out by observation. In inference to best explanation, the relation between the conclusion—the explanation—and the observed facts is looser. For example, the fact that Watson was in Afghanistan does not deductively imply that his face was tanned. (He could have worn a large hat to protect his face from the sun.) Still, the conclusion, that he was in Afghanistan, makes it likely that, other things being equal, he would be deeply tanned. So, in argument by inference to the best explanation, the premises support the conclusion because, if the conclusions were true, that would give us good reason to expect that the premises would be true, and the premises are true.

Inference to best explanation is a mainstay of scientific reasoning. A classic example is Alfred Wegener's defense of the hypothesis of continental drift (1915). One striking observation that led Wegener to endorse continental drift was the shape of the continents. If you look at a globe, you will be able to see a remarkable correlation between the shapes of South America and Africa: it looks as if you could move Africa next to South America and the two continents would fit together like pieces of a jigsaw puzzle. This observation, and various other considerations, led Wegener to hypothesize that all the continents had once been part of a supercontinent, "Pan-gaia," and had reached their present

locations by drifting apart. Wegener reasoned that the hypothesis of continental drift was the best explanation of the observed facts, and so the hypothesis was probably true. This case provides a useful illustration of how arguments by inference to the best explanation may be evaluated. Wegener's argument for continental drift was largely dismissed by the scientific community and for good reason. The complaint was that Wegener had not really explained anything, because he had not provided any explanation of how the continents could drift. This weakness in his case was disastrous. An argument by inference to best explanation is acceptable only if the conclusion actually offers an explanation for the observed data. Wegener's hypothesis was confirmed many years later by the theory of plate tectonics. This defense for Wegener's claim succeeded precisely because it offered an explanation for how the continents could move.

The case of continental drift also illustrates the difficulties—perhaps insuperable difficulties—of providing a complete and precise account of inference to best explanation on a par with the theory of deductive logic. On a superficial level, the criteria for evaluating inferences to best explanation are easy to state: the conclusion should explain the observed facts; the conclusion should provide a better explanation of those facts than any of its rivals. These criteria would permit the development of a rigorous science of inference to best explanation, however, only if we could develop a tight (and defensible) system of rules for evaluating explanations. While philosophers of science have made some suggestions on this topic, no such set of rules has ever been developed.

This same problem afflicts other types of non-deductive inference we have examined, induction and hypothesis testing. To have a real science of induction, we need to know, for example, what kinds of factors contribute to a genuine diversity in a sample population. A theory of hypothesis testing would require a precise account of when auxiliary assumptions are reasonable, as opposed to *ad hoc*, and many other canons of sound scientific practice as well. In general, a science of non-deductive inference would need, as a prerequisite to its full development, a precise and complete set of rules for good science, a complete philosophy of science. It is not clear that this ideal can ever be achieved. Nevertheless, we can appeal to our current understanding of good scientific practice in evaluating non-deductive arguments. Often, it will be fairly clear that an argument by inference to best explanation fails, because superior alternative explanations are available, or that an inductive generalization rests on a biased sample.

Argument Analysis

We have examined various types of inference. Now we will consider how this information may be used in analyzing reasoning. The basic task of argument analysis is to provide a clear formulation of the chain of argumentation presented in a piece of prose. It is important to realize that arguments do not come neatly packaged, with labels clearly identifying the premises and the conclusion. A critic needs to be careful and sympathetic. The best critic works

hard at finding the optimal version of the argumentation contained in a passage before evaluating it.

While it may seem surprising, the first step in evaluating a piece of reasoning is to find the conclusion. The conclusion may occur at the beginning, or at the end, or in the middle of the passage. Often the conclusion will not be stated at all! To find the conclusion, you need to ask yourself, What is the author trying to get us to believe? If you encounter difficulty in locating the conclusion, one technique is simply to examine each claim in the passage and ask, Is it a premise or a (sub-)conclusion? All of the claims will have to be assigned to one of three categories: premise, conclusion, or rhetorical fluff. Sometimes you can find the conclusion by elimination: If a claim cannot be regarded either as a premise or as a mere rhetorical flourish, then it must be some sort of conclusion. Of course, for some arguments, all the stated claims will be premises, as in (20).

> (20) The only legitimate reason to own a handgun is self-defense. But statistics show that a person who owns a handgun is six times more likely to injure himself or a member of his family than any potential attacker.

We include two further examples, one with the conclusion at the beginning (21), the other with the conclusion tucked into the middle of the passage (22).

> (21) Intelligence must be determined largely by genetic factors. For, how else could we explain the significant correlation between the scores of parents and children on IQ tests?

> (22) Although Edward Kennedy claimed that he withdrew from the 1984 presidential race for "personal reasons," many pundits claimed that Kennedy's reasons were actually political. The pollsters had told him that he could not win. However, there is a third possibility. Kennedy may have withdrawn for both sorts of reasons [C]. If Kennedy had run, it is inevitable that people would have raised questions about his moral character. And, while those questions would have hurt him politically, they would also have been painful for his family.

After locating the conclusion, the next step in analyzing an argument is to list the stated premises. To find the stated premises of an argument, you need to ask about the author's starting place. What claims is the author assuming, without argument? Once you have found the conclusion and found the stated premises (and eliminated any other apparent claims as rhetorical fluff), then you are ready to move to the most difficult stage in argument analysis. You need to trace a plausible route from the premises to the conclusion. This stage is difficult for two reasons. The first reason is that authors will very rarely tell you what kind of argument they are trying to make—deductive, inductive, or whatever. Sometimes, the authors themselves may not fully understand how

their arguments are supposed to work. However, it is absolutely critical for appraising an argument that you determine how the premises are supposed to support the conclusion. Consider argument (23), for example.

> (23) The spread of Legionnaire's disease in Hospital X was probably caused by the virus getting into the air cooling system. For that is the only hypothesis that can explain how the disease was dispersed so widely in the hospital.

If this argument is regarded as deductive, then it must be dismissed immediately as invalid. Whatever the pattern of the disease's spread through the hospital, it is still possible that the conclusion about the air cooling system may be false. This argument would also be a very poor inductive argument, since the conclusion that the fault lay with the air cooling system would be based on a single case, namely, the spread of the disease at this particular hospital. However, if we understand this argument correctly—as inference to best explanation—then it may be a perfectly good argument, depending on the details of the disease's spread and the difficulty of finding good alternative explanations.

Another reason why reconstructing an argument may be difficult is that most arguments make tacit assumptions in addition to those stated explicitly in the text. An example is argument (24).

> (24) The minimum drinking age should be raised. For statistics have shown that when the drinking age is lowered, traffic fatalities go up, and when the drinking age is raised, traffic fatalities go down.

The opening sentence in this passage states the conclusion. The next sentence offers two premises: when the drinking age is lowered, traffic fatalities go up; when the drinking age is raised, traffic fatalities go down. Our question is, How are these premises supposed to lead to that conclusion? The first point to realize is that the premises would provide no support at all for the conclusion unless we assume that high traffic fatalities are bad, and lower fatalities are better. Of course, even though these premises are unstated, they are completely uncontroversial, so the author may legitimately assume them. Indeed, an argument that took explicit account of such obvious assumptions would be both tedious and overly long. Even if we add these uncontroversial premises to the stated premises, however, we are still a long way from the conclusion. Some stronger tacit premise has to be added, like P_3 below.

> (24) P_1 When the drinking age is lowered, traffic fatalities go up.
> P_2 When the drinking age is raised, traffic fatalities go down.
> P_3 The number of lives saved by raising the drinking age fully justifies the loss of liberty imposed on young people.
> C Therefore, the minimum drinking age should be raised.

When P_3 is added, the argument becomes deductively valid. It is no longer possible to deny C while maintaining that traffic fatalities vary with the drinking age (P_1 and P_2) and that the number of lives saved justifies the restriction on liberty. However, P_3 is a fairly controversial assumption; some parties to this debate would want to deny it. This argument also illustrates how the two constraints on reconstructing an argument may conflict. A successful reconstruction must both trace a path from the premises to the conclusion that shows how the premises are supposed to support the conclusion, and fill out the reasoning by adding only *uncontroversial* unstated assumptions. In a case of uncompelling reasoning such as (24), it will be impossible to meet both constraints at once. For the only ways to move from the premises to the conclusion will involve the assumption of one or another controversial unstated assumption, showing that important matters have been swept under the rug.

To sum up: The last stage of reconstructing an argument—tracing a plausible route from the stated premises to the conclusion—is frequently the most difficult. Authors do not tell us what kinds of arguments they are making, nor (obviously) do they tell us their unstated assumptions. Often it will be necessary to try several alternative reconstructions before you are satisfied that you have found the argument buried in the prose. Besides adding needed unstated assumptions and deleting any unnecessary rhetorical flourishes, you will often have to clarify the meanings of key terms, as we noted above. Once you have reconstructed the argument, so that you know how it is supposed to work, then you can appraise its success or failure. This step employs the criteria for evaluating different types of inferences, some of which are presented above.

Evaluating reasoning is a complex task, because human language is rich and fluid, and because we are able to see a large number of subtle connections among the facts we confront. While the task is difficult, the alternative is unacceptable. For if we give up trying to understand reasoning, then we must either naively accept the arguments of others, as if we were children, or play the cynic, and forswear the possibility of learning from the insights of others.

I
ETHICS

MANY PEOPLE, when they hear the term "morality," think vaguely about Sunday-school prohibitions against sex. But morality is both more widely applicable and more interesting than this. We are, in effect, thinking morally whenever we wonder whether we should turn down the stereo to avoid disturbing the neighbors, or whether we should make a personally advantageous promise which we will have no way to keep. We make moral judgments about others whenever we say that a teacher's grading policy is unfair, or that a friend's shoplifting is all right because it "doesn't hurt anybody." We are, in a sense, even thinking morally when we say that it is wrong to judge the behavior of others, or that we need not consider anyone's interests but our own. Conceived as the question of how we ought to live, and how the world ought to be, the subject of morality is an inescapable part of everyone's life.

Although moral judgments are extremely common, their basis can seem mysterious. When we make them, we typically appear to be relying on more general principles or standards. For example, if I say that Smith acts wrongly when he beats his dog, I seem committed to saying that anyone else who was cruel to an animal in the same way would also act wrongly. But what reason do I have for saying this? Where do such principles or standards come from? Do they have any objective basis at all? As soon as we raise these questions, we move from an uncritical to a critical stance toward morality. We have started thinking philosophically about it.

Suppose someone were to say that moral principles have no absolute or objective basis. Although this contention is superficially clear, it may mean a number of very different things. One view that is sometimes associated with it is that even persons who seem to act morally are really only pursuing their own happiness or self-interest. If this is true, then the applicability of principles that sometimes require that we sacrifice our own interest will be thrown into doubt. The view that each person seeks only his own satisfaction is known as *psychological egoism*. It is discussed and criticized in the first reading by Joel Feinberg.

Even if we reject psychological egoism, as perhaps we should, we may still believe that moral judgments are "subjective" in a second sense. In particular, we may still believe that moral judgments merely record the attitudes of one's own culture or society, and are valid or binding only within that society. This popular view, that what is right for a given person is always relative to the attitudes of his society, is called *moral relativism*. Moral relativism is often thought to be supported by the fact that different societies follow widely differing moral codes. However, as Paul Taylor argues in reading 2, neither this "fact" nor its connection with moral relativism is as obvious as it first appears to be.

There is also a third way of understanding the claim that morality lacks an objective basis. When we believe that it is raining, or that snow is white, what we believe is either true or false. Very roughly, our belief is true if it corresponds to the appropriate fact in the world, and false if it does not. But can we say anything similar about moral beliefs—beliefs that murder is wrong, that we should treat people fairly, and the like? According to Gilbert Harman (reading 3), it is doubtful that a separate class of "moral facts" exists. The world does not appear to contain the fact that murder is wrong as it contains the fact the snow is white. Hence, if the objectivity of moral judgments requires that they correspond to moral facts, then the objectivity thesis is doubtful as well.

This sort of challenge to moral objectivity is serious and important. It is, however, not conclusive. To escape it, some have argued that moral objectivity does not require correspondence with moral facts. As an alternative, it is sometimes held that moral beliefs are made true not by moral facts, but rather by the nonmoral fact that God commands us to act in certain ways. If so, then calling an act right will simply be equivalent to saying that it is what God tells us to do. This view is called the Divine Command theory of ethics. If we accept it, we will obviously face the problem of deciding which of many conflicting scriptures and reports really do record God's will. But in addition, we will also face several more subtle difficulties first noticed by Plato. His discussion of them is reprinted as reading 45 in Part V, the section on Philosophy of Religion. Given these difficulties, we may find it preferable to defend the objectivity of ethics in a somewhat different way. Instead of searching for appropriate facts to which true moral judgments might correspond, we may accept John Rawls's suggestion that moral objectivity is best understood in terms of a rationally defensible procedure for arriving at moral principles, and for settling conflicts among them. In reading 4, Rawls sketches just such a "decision procedure for ethics."

Whether or not these questions of ultimate objectivity can be resolved, morality will continue to play a central role in our lives. Hence, the question of how we ought to act—of which moral principles to accept—defines a second important area of moral inquiry. Although many variants exist, all moral principles can be divided into two main types. According to one type, the acts that are right, and that we should perform, are those with certain valuable consequences. According to the other type, the rightness of an act depends not on the value of its consequences but rather on something else, such as the nature of the act itself or the intention of the agent. The first sort of principle is called *teleological* or *consequentialist* and the second *deontological*.

Because consequentialist principles hold that acts are right when they produce more valuable consequences than their alternatives, the content of such principles will obviously vary with what is said to have value. At first glance, many things seem to have value: health, prosperity, loving relationships, knowledge, beauty, and human excellence are only a few obvious examples. However, on closer inspection, the situation may seem less complicated than this; for the value of these things is often said to reside entirely in the fact that they make us happy, give us pleasure, or satisfy our desires or preferences. Moreover, if happiness or satisfaction are the only things that ultimately have value, then it may seem obvious that it is always better to produce more of them than less. If we accept these assumptions, and incorporate them into a single consequentialist principle, then what we get is "Always perform the act, of those available, that will bring more overall happiness, or less unhappiness, than any alternative." This principle is standardly known as the *principle of utility*. *Utilitarianism* is by far the best known and widely accepted version of consequentialism. It is developed from a variety of perspectives by John Stuart Mill in reading 5.

Although utilitarianism has great initial appeal, a closer examination reveals problems with it. If all that matters about an act is its consequences, then it does not matter how those consequences are achieved. In particular, it does not matter if they are brought about by betraying a trust, treating someone unfairly, or even taking someone's life. But surely any moral theory that is indifferent to treachery or murder has a lot of explaining to do. This and related difficulties are discussed by Norman Bowie and Robert Simon in reading 6. The utilitarian's answer to these problems is presented by R.M. Hare in reading 7. If you are convinced by Hare's response, you probably will find utilitarianism an attractive moral theory. If not, you may be drawn to the deontological alternative presented by Immanuel Kant in reading 8.

In sharp contrast to the utilitarian, Kant denies than an act's consequences can ever determine whether we morally ought to perform it. If a principle tells us only to act in a certain way to achieve a certain result—if, in Kant's terminology, it is a hypothetical imperative—then we will only be bound by it as long as we happen to want that result. By contrast, Kant argues that any genuine moral principle must apply no matter what we want. Its command must, in other words, be not hypothetical but categorical. Moreover, because such a categorical imperative must be independent of our desires, its appeal can only be that of reason itself. According to Kant, there is only one basic categorical

imperative, though it may be formulated in different ways. By applying it, we learn that honesty and other ways of acting are morally obligatory whatever their consequences.

In Kant's hands, these elements are forged into a moral theory of great persuasiveness and power. Many people accept some version of it. But there are also questions here. As Philippa Foot notes in reading 9, it is far from clear that we can be motivated to act by reason alone. It is not even entirely clear what this might mean. If this part of Kant's theory cannot be sustained, then we will have to fall back on desires, though perhaps desires of an especially deep and inescapable sort, as the motivation for acting morally. As many others have noted, Kant's claim that certain acts should be performed whatever their consequences is also questionable. Should we really keep a promise even when breaking it might save hundreds of lives? Thousands? Millions? Impressed by these sorts of questions, some have tried to produce a moral theory which combines both deontological and consequentialist elements. The most famous of these attempts, that of William David Ross, is excerpted here as reading 10.

Given what has been said, the philosophical approach to morality may seem quite abstract. However, what we must remember is that moral philosophy arises from the inescapable need to make choices which affect others, and is valuable precisely because it illuminates the rational basis for these choices. In their own way, both concluding selections remind us of this. As Aristotle notes in reading 11, a theoretical knowledge of morality is useful only if it is internalized and made part of our character. Thus, an essential aspect of moral philosophy must be the study of what makes someone a good person—the study of moral virtue. Moreover, as Peter Singer argues in reading 12, taking morality seriously may require far-reaching revisions of the ways we usually act. Although Singer's topic is the provision of aid to famine victims, many other examples could be produced as well. In both of these selections, the connection between moral philosophy and human reality is reaffirmed. Here, as elsewhere, philosophical thought may not only enrich our lives, but change them.

1

Psychological Egoism

JOEL FEINBERG

Joel Feinberg (b. 1926) is Professor of Philosophy at the University of Arizona. His publications include Doing and Deserving, Social Philosophy, *and other important books and articles in social and political philosophy.*

In this article, Feinberg examines psychological egoism—the view that we never want or pursue anything except our own happiness or self-interest. Although this view claims to explain why we act as we do, Feinberg points out that it rarely is supported by factual evidence. Instead, it exploits certain arguments that are seldom carefully examined. For example, psychological egoism is often thought to hold because each person is motivated by his own desires and no one else's. However, as Feinberg notes, the fact that my desires are my own implies nothing about what I desire. Thus, it does not imply that I desire only my own happiness or satisfaction. Again, psychological egoism may seem to draw support from the fact that we get pleasure from helping others (or feel pangs of conscience about not helping). Yet far from supporting psychological egoism, this fact actually tells against it. For why should we feel such pleasure, unless helping others satisfies a desire to help them—a desire that is emphatically not aimed only at our own happiness?

These examples do not exhaust the arguments considered by Feinberg. However, throughout his discussion, the main point is clear. When we consider the matter carefully, we find no good reason to accept psychological egoism. We are, therefore, free to accept the common view that people often act not to increase their own happiness, but simply to help others or to do the right thing.

The Theory

1. "Psychological egoism" is the name given to a theory widely held by ordinary men, and at one time almost universally accepted by political economists, philosophers, and psychologists, according to which all human actions when properly understood can be seen to be motivated by selfish desires. More precisely, psychological egoism is the doctrine that the only thing anyone is capable of desiring or pursuing ultimately (as an end in itself) is his *own* self-interest. No psychological egoist denies that men sometimes do desire things other than their own welfare—the happiness of other people, for example; but all psychological egoists insist that men are capable of desiring the happiness

of others only when they take it to be a *means* to their own happiness. In short, purely altruistic and benevolent actions and desires do not exist; but people sometimes appear to be acting unselfishly and disinterestedly when they take the interests of others to be means to the promotion of their own self-interest.

2. This theory is called *psychological* egoism to indicate that it is not a theory about what *ought* to be the case, but rather about what, as a matter of fact, *is* the case. That is, the theory claims to be a description of psychological facts, not a prescription of ethical ideals. It asserts, however, not merely that all men do as a contingent matter of fact "put their own interests first," but also that they are capable of nothing else, human nature being what it is. Universal selfishness is not just an accident or a coincidence on this view; rather, it is an unavoidable consequence of psychological laws.

The theory is to be distinguished from another doctrine, so-called "ethical egoism," according to which all men *ought* to pursue their own well-being. This doctrine, being a prescription of what *ought* to be the case, makes no claim to be a psychological theory of human motives; hence the word "ethical" appears in its name to distinguish it from *psychological* egoism.

3. There are a number of types of motives and desires which might reasonably be called "egoistic" or "selfish," and corresponding to each of them is a possible version of psychological egoism. Perhaps the most common version of the theory is that apparently held by Jeremy Bentham.[1] According to this version, all persons have only one ultimate motive in all their voluntary behavior and that motive is a selfish one; more specifically, it is one particular kind of selfish motive—namely, a desire for one's own *pleasure*. According to this version of the theory, "the only kind of ultimate desire is the desire to get or to prolong pleasant experiences, and to avoid or to cut short unpleasant experiences for oneself."[2] This form of psychological egoism is often given the cumbersome name—*psychological egoistic hedonism.*

Prima Facie Reasons in Support of the Theory

4. Psychological egoism has seemed plausible to many people for a variety of reasons, of which the following are typical:

    a. "Every action of mine is prompted by motives or desires or impulses which are *my* motives and not somebody else's. This fact might be expressed by saying that whenever I act I am always pursuing my own ends or trying to satisfy my own desires. And from this we might pass on to—'I am always pursuing something for myself or seeking my own satisfaction.'

---

[1] See his *Introduction to the Principles of Morals and Legislation* (1789), Chap. I, first paragraph: "Nature has placed mankind under the governance of two sovereign masters, *pain* and *pleasure*. It is for them alone to point out what we ought to do, as well as to determine what we shall do. . . . They govern us in all we do, in all we say, in all we think: every effort we can make to throw off our subjection will serve but to demonstrate and confirm it."

[2] C. D. Broad, *Ethics and the History of Philosophy* (New York: The Humanities Press, 1952), Essay 10—"Egoism as a Theory of Human Motives," p. 218. This essay is highly recommended.

Here is what seems like a proper description of a man acting selfishly, and if the description applies to all actions of all men, then it follows that all men in all their actions are selfish."[3]

b. It is a truism that when a person gets what he wants he characteristically feels pleasure. This has suggested to many people that what we really want in every case is our own pleasure, and that we pursue other things only as a means.

c. *Self-Deception.* Often we deceive ourselves into thinking that we desire something fine or noble when what we really want is to be thought well of by others or to be able to congratulate ourselves, or to be able to enjoy the pleasures of a good conscience. It is a well-known fact that people tend to conceal their true motives from themselves by camouflaging them with words like "virtue," "duty," etc. Since we are so often misled concerning both our own real motives and the real motives of others, is it not reasonable to suspect that we might *always* be deceived when we think motives disinterested and altruistic? . . .

d. *Moral education.* Morality, good manners, decency, and other virtues must be teachable. Psychological egoists often notice that moral education and the inculcation of manners usually utilize what Bentham calls the "sanctions of pleasure and pain." Children are made to acquire the civilizing virtues only by the method of enticing rewards and painful punishments. Much the same is true of the history of the race. People in general have been inclined to behave well only when it is made plain to them that there is "something in it for them." Is it not then highly probable that just such a mechanism of human motivation as Bentham describes must be presupposed by our methods of moral education?

Critique of Psychological Egoism: Confusions in the Arguments

5. *Non-Empirical Character of the Arguments.* If the arguments of the psychological egoist consisted for the most part of carefully acquired empirical evidence (well-documented reports of controlled experiments, surveys, interviews, laboratory data, and so on), then the critical philosopher would have no business carping at them. After all, since psychological egoism purports to be a scientific theory of human motives, it is the concern of the experimental psychologist, not the philosopher, to accept or reject it. But as a matter of fact, empirical evidence of the required sort is seldom presented in support of psychological egoism. Psychologists, on the whole, shy away from generalizations about human motives which are so sweeping and so vaguely formulated that they are virtually incapable of scientific testing. It is usually the "armchair scientist" who holds the theory of universal selfishness, and his usual arguments are either based simply on his "impressions" or else are largely of a non-

---

[3] Austin Duncan-Jones, *Butler's Moral Philosophy* (London: Penguin Books, 1952), p. 96. Duncan-Jones goes on to reject this argument. See p. 512f.

empirical sort. The latter are often shot full of a very subtle kind of logical confusion, and this makes their criticism a matter of special interest to the analytic philosopher.

6. The psychological egoist's first argument (see 4a) is a good example of logical confusion. It begins with a truism—namely, that all of my motives and desires are *my* motives and desires and not someone else's. (Who would deny this?) But from this simple tautology nothing whatever concerning the nature of my motives or the objective of my desires can possibly follow. The fallacy of this argument consists in its violation of the general logical rule that analytic statements (tautologies), * cannot entail synthetic (factual) ones.† That every voluntary act is prompted by the agent's own motives is a tautology; hence, it cannot be equivalent to "A person is always seeking something for himself" or "All of a person's motives are selfish," which are synthetic. What the egoist must prove is not merely:

(i) Every voluntary action is prompted by a motive of the agent's own.

but rather:

(ii) Every voluntary action is prompted by a motive of a quite particular kind, viz. a selfish one.

Statement (i) is obviously true, but it cannot all by itself give any logical support to statement (ii).

The source of the confusion in this argument is readily apparent. It is not the genesis of an action or the *origin* or its motives which makes it a "selfish" one, but rather the "purpose" of the act or the *objective* of its motives; *not where the motive comes from* (in voluntary actions it always comes from the agent) but *what it aims at* determines whether or not it is selfish. There is surely a valid distinction between voluntary behavior, in which the agent's action is motivated by purposes of his own, and *selfish* behavior in which the agent's motives are of one exclusive sort. The egoist's argument assimilates all voluntary action into the class of selfish action, by requiring, in effect, that an unselfish action be one which is not really motivated at all.

. . .

7. But if argument 4a fails to prove its point, argument 4b does no better. From the fact that all our successful actions (those in which we get what we were after) are accompanied or followed by pleasure it does not follow, as the egoist claims, that the *objective* of every action is to get pleasure for oneself. To begin with, the premise of the argument is not, strictly speaking, even true. Fulfillment of desire (simply getting what one was after) is no guarantee of satisfaction (pleasant feelings of gratification in the mind of the agent). Sometimes when we get what we want we *also* get, as a kind of extra dividend, a

---

* Traditionally, analytic statements have been taken to be statements that are true by virtue of the meanings of words, and hence convey no information about the world.

† Traditionally, statements that do convey information about the world.

warm, glowing feeling of contentment; but often, far too often, we get no dividend at all, or, even worse, the bitter taste of ashes. Indeed, it has been said that the characteristic psychological problem of our time is the *dissatisfaction* that attends the fulfillment of our very most powerful desires.

Even if we grant, however, for the sake of argument, that getting what one wants *usually* yields satisfaction, the egoist's conclusion does not follow. We can concede that we normally get pleasure (in the sense of satisfaction) when our desires are satisfied, *no matter what our desires are for*; but it does not follow from this roughly accurate generalization that the only thing we ever desire is our own satisfaction. Pleasure may well be the usual accompaniment of all actions in which the agent gets what he wants; but to infer from this that what the agent always wants is his own pleasure is like arguing, in William James's example,[4] that because an ocean liner constantly consumes coal on its trans-Atlantic passage that therefore the *purpose* of its voyage is to consume coal. The immediate inference from even constant accompaniment to purpose (or motive) is always a *non sequitur*.

Perhaps there is a sense of "satisfaction" (desire fulfillment) such that it is certainly and universally true that we get satisfaction whenever we get what we want. But satisfaction in this sense is simply the "coming into existence of that which is desired." Hence, to say that desire fulfillment always yields "satisfaction" in this sense is to say no more than that we always get what we want when we get what we want, which is to utter a tautology like "a rose is a rose." It can no more entail a synthetic truth in psychology (like the egoistic thesis) than "a rose is a rose" can entail significant information in botany.

8. *Disinterested Benevolence.* The fallacy in argument 4b then consists, as Garvin puts it, "in the supposition that the apparently unselfish desire to benefit others is transformed into a selfish one by the fact that we derive pleasure from carrying it out."[5] Not only is this argument fallacious; it also provides us with a suggestion of a counter-argument to show that its conclusion (psychological egoistic hedonism) is false. Not only is the presence of pleasure (satisfaction) as a by-product of an action no proof that the action was selfish; in some special cases it provides rather conclusive proof that the action was *unselfish*. For in those special cases the fact that we get pleasure from a particular action *presupposes that we desired something else*—something other than our own pleasure—as an end in itself and not merely as a means to our own pleasant state of mind.

This way of turning the egoistic hedonist's argument back on him can be illustrated by taking a typical egoist argument, one attributed (perhaps apocryphally) to Abraham Lincoln, and then examining it closely:

> Mr. Lincoln once remarked to a fellow-passenger on an old-time mud-coach that all men were prompted by selfishness in doing good. His fellow-passenger was antagonizing this position when they were passing over a corduroy bridge that

---

[4] *The Principles of Psychology,* (New York: Henry Holt, 1890), Vol II, p. 558.

[5] Lucius Garvin, *A Modern Introduction to Ethics* (Boston: Houghton Mifflin, 1953), p. 39.

spanned a slough. As they crossed this bridge they espied an old razor-backed sow on the bank making a terrible noise because her pigs had got into the slough and were in danger of drowning. As the old coach began to climb the hill, Mr. Lincoln called out, "Driver, can't you stop just a moment?" Then Mr. Lincoln jumped out, ran back and lifted the little pigs out of the mud and water and placed them on the bank. When he returned, his companion remarked: "Now Abe, where does selfishness come in on this little episode?" "Why, bless your soul Ed, that was the very essence of selfishness. I should have had no peace of mind all day had I gone on and left that suffering old sow worrying over those pigs. I did it to get peace of mind, don't you see?"[6]

If Lincoln had cared not a whit for the welfare of the little pigs and their "suffering" mother, but only for his own "peace of mind," it would be difficult to explain how he could have derived pleasure from helping them. The very fact that he did feel satisfaction as a result of helping the pigs presupposes that he had a preexisting desire for something other than his own happiness. Then when *that* desire was satisfied, Lincoln of course derived pleasure. The *object* of Lincoln's desire was not pleasure; rather pleasure was the *consequence* of his preexisting desire for something else. If Lincoln had been wholly indifferent to the plight of the little pigs as he claimed, how could he possibly have derived any pleasure from helping them? He could not have achieved peace of mind from rescuing the pigs, had he not a prior concern—on which his peace of mind depended—for the welfare of the pigs for its own sake.

In general, the psychological hedonist analyzes apparent benevolence into a desire for "benevolent pleasure." No doubt the benevolent man does get pleasure from his benevolence, but in most cases, this is only because he has previously desired the good of some person, or animal, or mankind at large. Where there is no such desire, benevolent conduct is not generally found to give pleasure to the agent.

9. *Malevolence.* Difficult cases for the psychological egoist include not only instances of disinterested benevolence, but also cases of "disinterested malevolence." Indeed, malice and hatred are generally no more "selfish" than benevolence. Both are motives likely to cause an agent to sacrifice his own interests—in the case of benevolence, in order to help someone else, in the case of malevolence in order to harm someone else. The selfish man is concerned ultimately only with his own pleasure, happiness, or power; the benevolent man is often equally concerned with the happiness of others; to the malevolent man, the *injury* of another is often an end in itself—an end to be pursued sometimes with no thought for his own interests. There is reason to think that men have as often sacrificed themselves to injure or kill others as to help or to save others, and with as much "heroism" in the one case as in the other. The unselfish nature of malevolence was first noticed by the Anglican Bishop and moral

---

[6] Quoted from the *Springfield* (Illinois) *Monitor*, by F. C. Sharp in his *Ethics* (New York: Appleton-Century, 1928), p. 75.

philosopher Joseph Butler (1692-1752), who regretted that men are no more selfish than they are.[7]

10. *Lack of Evidence for Universal Self-Deception.* The more cynical sort of psychological egoist who is impressed by the widespread phenomenon of self-deception (see 4c) cannot be so quickly disposed of, for he has committed no *logical* mistakes. We can only argue that the acknowledged frequency of self-deception is insufficient evidence for his universal generalization. His argument is not fallacious, but inconclusive.

No one but the agent himself can ever be certain what conscious motives really prompted his action, and where motives are disreputable, even the agent may not admit to himself the true nature of his desires. Thus, for every apparent case of altruistic behavior, the psychological egoist can argue, with some plausibility, that the true motivation *might* be selfish, appearance to the contrary. Philanthropic acts are really motivated by the desire to receive gratitude; acts of self-sacrifice, when truly understood, are seen to be motivated by the desire to feel self-esteem; and so on. We must concede to the egoist that all apparent altruism might be deceptive in this way; but such a sweeping generalization requires considerable empirical evidence, and such evidence is not presently available.

11. *The "Paradox of Hedonism" and Its Consequences for Education.* The psychological egoistic Hedonist (e.g., Jeremy Bentham) has the simplest possible theory of human motivation. According to this variety of egoistic theory, all human motives without exception can be reduced to one—namely, the desire for one's own pleasure. But this theory, despite its attractive simplicity, or perhaps because of it, involves one immediately in a paradox. Astute observers of human affairs from the time of the ancient Greeks have often noticed that pleasure, happiness, and satisfaction are states of mind which stand in a very peculiar relation to desire. An exclusive desire for happiness is the surest way to prevent happiness from coming into being. Happiness has a way of "sneaking up" on persons when they are preoccupied with other things; but when persons deliberately and single-mindedly set off in pursuit of happiness, it vanishes utterly from sight and cannot be captured. This is the famous "paradox of hedonism": the single-minded pursuit of happiness is necessarily self-defeating, for *the way to get happiness is to forget it;* then perhaps it will come to you. If you aim exclusively at pleasure itself, with no concern for the things that bring pleasure, then pleasure will never come. To derive satisfaction, one must ordinarily first desire something other than satisfaction, and then find the means to get what one desires.

To feel the full force of the paradox of hedonism the reader should conduct an experiment in his imagination. Imagine a person (let's call him "Jones") who is, first of all, devoid of intellectual curiosity. He has no desire to acquire

---

[7] See his *Fifteen Sermons on Human Nature Preached at the Rolls Chapel* (1726), especially the first and eleventh.

any kind of knowledge for its own sake, and thus is utterly indifferent to questions of science, mathematics, and philosophy. Imagine further that the beauties of nature leave Jones cold: he is unimpressed by the autumn foliage, the snow-capped mountains, and the rolling oceans. Long walks in the country on spring mornings and skiing forays in the winter are to him equally a bore. Moreover, let us suppose that Jones can find no appeal in art. Novels are dull, poetry a pain, paintings nonsense and music just noise. Suppose further that Jones has neither the participant's nor the spectator's passion for baseball, football, tennis, or any other sport. Swimming to him is a cruel aquatic form of calisthenics, the sun only a cause of sunburn. Dancing is coeducational idiocy, conversation a waste of time, the other sex an unappealing mystery. Politics is a fraud, religion mere superstition; and the misery of millions of underprivileged human beings is nothing to be concerned with or excited about. Suppose finally that Jones has no talent for any kind of handicraft, industry, or commerce, and that he does not regret that fact.

What then is Jones interested in? He must desire something. To be sure, he does. Jones has an overwhelming passion for, a complete preoccupation with, his own happiness. The one exclusive desire of his life is *to be happy*. It takes little imagination at this point to see that Jones's one desire is bound to be frustrated. People who—like Jones—most hotly pursue their own happiness are the least likely to find it. Happy people are those who successfully pursue such things as aesthetic or religious experience, self-expression, service to others, victory in competitions, knowledge, power, and so on. If none of these things in themselves and for their own sakes mean anything to a person, if they are valued at all then only as a means to one's own pleasant states of mind—then that pleasure can never come. The way to achieve happiness is to pursue something else.

Almost all people at one time or another in their lives feel pleasure. Some people (though perhaps not many) really do live lives which are on the whole happy. But if pleasure and happiness presuppose desires for something other than pleasure and happiness, then the existence of pleasure and happiness in the experience of some people proves that those people have strong desires for something other than their own happiness—egoistic hedonism to the contrary.

The implications of the "paradox of hedonism" for educational theory should be obvious. The parents least likely to raise a happy child are those who, even with the best intentions, train their child to seek happiness directly. How often have we heard parents say:

> I don't care if my child does not become an intellectual, or a football star, or a great artist. I just want him to be a plain average sort of person. Happiness does not require great ambitions and great frustrations; it's not worth it to suffer and become neurotic for the sake of science, art, or do-goodism. I just want my child to be happy.

This can be a dangerous mistake, for it is the child (and the adult for that matter) without "outer-directed" interests who is the most likely to be unhappy. The pure egoist would be the most wretched of persons.

The educator might well beware of "life adjustment" as the conscious goal of the educational process for similar reasons. "Life adjustment" can be achieved only as a by-product of other pursuits. A whole curriculum of "life adjustment courses" unsupplemented by courses designed to incite an interest in things other than life adjustment would be tragically self-defeating.

As for moral education, it is probably true that punishment and reward are indispensable means of inculcation. But if the child comes to believe that the *sole* reasons for being moral are that he will escape the pain of punishment thereby and/or that he will gain the pleasure of a good reputation, then what is to prevent him from doing the immoral thing whenever he is sure that he will not be found out? While punishment and reward then are important tools for the moral educator, they obviously have their limitations. Beware of the man who does the moral thing only out of fear of pain or love of pleasure. He is not likely to be wholly trustworthy. Moral education is truly successful when it produces persons who are willing to do the right thing *simply because it is right*, and not merely because it is popular or safe.

12. *Pleasure as Sensation.* One final argument against psychological hedonism should suffice to put that form of the egoistic psychology to rest once and for all. The egoistic hedonist claims that all desires can be reduced to the single desire for one's own *pleasure*. Now the word "pleasure" is ambiguous. On the one hand, it can stand for a certain indefinable, but very familiar and specific kind of sensation, or more accurately, a property of sensations; and it is generally, if not exclusively, associated with the senses. For example, certain taste sensations such as sweetness, thermal sensations of the sort derived from a hot bath or the feel of the August sun while one lies on a sandy beach, erotic sensations, olfactory sensations (say) of the fragrance of flowers or perfume, and tactual and kinesthetic sensations from a good massage, are all pleasant in this sense. Let us call this sense of "pleasure," which is the converse of "physical pain," pleasure₁.

On the other hand, the word "pleasure" is often used simply as a synonym for "satisfaction" (in the sense of gratification, not mere desire fulfillment). In this sense, the existence of pleasure presupposes the prior existence of desire. Knowledge, religious experience, aesthetic expression, and other so-called "spiritual activities" often give pleasure in this sense. In fact, as we have seen, we tend to get pleasure in this sense whenever we get what we desire, no matter what we desire. The masochist even derives pleasure (in the sense of "satisfaction") from his own physically painful sensations. Let us call the sense of "pleasure" which means "satisfaction"—pleasure₂.

Now we can evaluate the psychological hedonist's claim that the sole human motive is a desire for one's own pleasure, bearing in mind (as he often does not) the ambiguity of the word"pleasure." First, let us take the hedonist to be saying that it is the desire for pleasure₁ (pleasant sensation) which is the sole ultimate desire of all people and the sole desire capable of providing a motive for action. Now I have little doubt that all (or most) people desire their own pleasure, *sometimes*. But even this familiar kind of desire occurs, I think, rather rarely. When I am very hungry, I often desire to eat, or, more specifically, to

2

Ethical
Relativism

PAUL TAYLOR

*Paul Taylor (b. 1923) is Professor of Philosophy at Brooklyn College, City
University of New York. He is the author of* Normative Discourse, *and of
numerous articles on ethics.*

*In this selection, Taylor considers ethical relativism—the view that moral
rules or standards are somehow relative to the attitudes of one's society or
group. Although ethical relativism is accepted by many, those who accept it
are not always completely clear about what they mean. As Taylor notes, the
view may be taken to assert either that (1) different societies do, in fact,
accept different moral codes (descriptive relativism), that (2) each person
ought to do what is dictated by his society's code (normative ethical
relativism), or that (3) there is no standard of reasoning about morality that
is independent of the practices of particular societies (meta-ethical
relativism).*

*Why should we accept ethical relativism in any form? As Taylor suggests,
normative and meta-ethical relativism are often grounded in descriptive
relativism. That is, it is because different societies seem to disagree about
what is right or wrong, and about the standards for reasoning about such
matters, that many people simply equate what one ought to do, and the way
one ought to reason, with what one's society considers right or valid.
Moreover, descriptive relativism seems to be supported by the findings of
anthropologists and by our own observations of diverse attitudes and
customs. However, as Taylor notes, there are at least two problems here.
First, diversity of behavior does not necessarily show that different societies
disagree in their deepest moral convictions. They may, instead, be agreed on
fundamental principles (for example, that it is always best to maximize
happiness), but disagree about which practices will achieve this end. Second,
even if different societies do disagree about what is right or wrong, it
remains possible that some views are correct while others are in error.
Although different societies disagree about the causes of disease, we do not
say that all views about this are equally correct. If moral values should be
treated differently, this must be shown by some further argument.*

ARE MORAL VALUES ABSOLUTE, or are they relative? We may understand this question as asking: Are there any moral standards and rules of
conduct that are universal (applicable to all mankind) or are they all culture-
bound (applicable only to the members of a particular society or group)? Even

when the question is interpreted in this way, however, it still remains unclear. For those who answer the question by claiming that all moral values are relative or culture-bound may be expressing any one of three different ideas. They may, first, be making an empirical or factual assertion. Or secondly, they may be making a normative claim. And thirdly, they may be understood to be uttering a meta-ethical principle. The term "ethical relativism" has been used to refer to any or all of these three positions. In order to keep clear the differences between them, we shall use the following terminology. We shall call the first position "descriptive relativism," the second "normative ethical relativism," and the third "meta-ethical relativism." Let us consider each in turn.

Descriptive Relativism

Certain facts about the moral values of different societies and about the way an individual's values are dependent on those of his society have been taken as empirical evidence in support of the claim that all moral values are relative to the particular culture in which they are accepted. These facts are cited by the relativist as reasons for holding a general theory about moral norms, namely, that no such norms are universal. This theory is what we shall designate "descriptive relativism." It is a factual or empirical theory because it holds that, as a matter of historical and sociological fact, no moral standard or rule of conduct has been universally recognized to be the basis of moral obligation. According to the descriptive relativist there are no moral norms common to all cultures. Each society has its own view of what is morally right and wrong and these views vary from society to society because of the differences in their moral codes. Thus it is a mistake to think there are common norms that bind all mankind in one moral community.

Those who accept the position of descriptive relativism point to certain facts as supporting evidence for their theory. These facts may be conveniently summed up under the following headings:

(1) The facts of cultural variability
(2) Facts about the origin of moral beliefs and moral codes
(3) The fact of ethnocentrism

(1) The facts of cultural variability are now so familiar to everyone that they need hardly be enumerated in detail. We all know from reading anthropologists' studies of primitive cultures how extreme is the variation in the customs and taboos, the religions and moralities, the daily habits and the general outlook on life to be found in the cultures of different peoples. But we need not go beyond our own culture to recognize the facts of variability. Historians of Western civilization have long pointed out the great differences in the beliefs and values of people living in different periods. Great differences have also been discovered among the various socio-economic classes existing within the social structure at any one time. Finally, our own contemporary world reveals a tremendous variety of ways of living. No one who dwells in a modern city can escape the impact of this spectrum of different views on work and play, on

family life and education, on what constitutes personal happiness, and on what is right and wrong.

(2) When we add to these facts of cultural and historical variability the recent psychological findings about how the individual's values reflect those of his own social group and his own time, we may begin to question the universal validity of our own values. For it is now a well-established fact that no moral values or beliefs are inborn. All our moral attitudes and judgments are learned from the social environment. Even our deepest convictions about justice and the rights of man are originally nothing but the "introjected" or "internalized" views of our culture, transmitted to us through our parents and teachers. Our very conscience itself is formed by the internalizing of the sanctions used by our society to support its moral norms. When we were told in childhood what we ought and ought not to do, and when our parents expressed their approval and disapproval of us for what we did, we were being taught the standards and rules of conduct accepted in our society. The result of this learning process (sometimes called "acculturation") was to ingrain in us a set of attitudes about our own conduct, so that even when our parents were no longer around to guide us or to blame us, we would guide or blame ourselves by thinking, "This is what I ought to do"; "That would be wrong to do"; and so on. If we then did something we believed was wrong we would feel guilty about it, whether or not anyone caught us at it or punished us for it.

It is this unconscious process of internalizing the norms of one's society through early childhood training that explains the origin of an individual's moral values. If we go beyond this and ask about the origin of society's values, we find a long and gradual development of traditions and customs which have given stability to the society's way of life and whose obscure beginnings lie in ritual magic, taboos, tribal ceremonies, and practices of religious worship. Whether we are dealing with the formation of an individual's conscience or the development of a society's moral code, then, the origin of a set of values seems to have little or nothing to do with rational, controlled thought. Neither individuals nor societies originally acquire their moral beliefs by means of logical reasoning or through the use of an objective method for gaining knowledge.

(3) Finally, the descriptive relativist points out another fact about men and their moralities that must be acknowledged. This is the fact that most men are ethnocentric (group centered). They think not only that there is but one true morality for all mankind, but that the one true morality is their own. They are convinced that the moral code under which they grew up and which formed their deepest feelings about right and wrong—namely, the moral code of their own society—is the only code for anyone to live by. Indeed, they often refuse even to entertain the possibility that their own values might be false or that another society's code might be more correct, more enlightened, or more advanced than their own. Thus ethnocentrism often leads to intolerance and dogmatism. It causes men to be extremely narrow-minded in their ethical outlook, afraid to admit any doubt about a moral issue, and unable to take a detached, objective stance regarding their own moral beliefs. Being absolutely certain that their beliefs are true, they can think only that those who disagree with them are in

total error and ignorance on moral matters. Their attitude is: We are advanced, they are backward. We are civilized, they are savages.

It is but a short step from dogmatism to intolerance. Intolerance is simply dogmatism in action. Because the moral values of people directly affect their conduct, those who have divergent moral convictions will often come into active conflict with one another in the area of practical life. Each will believe he alone has the true morality and the other is living in the darkness of sin. Each will see the other as practising moral abominations. Each will then try to force the other to accept the truth, or at least will not allow the other to live by his own values. The self-righteous person will not tolerate the presence of "shocking" acts which he views with outraged indignation. Thus it comes about that no differences of opinion on moral matters will be permitted within a society. The ethnocentric society will tend to be a closed society, as far as moral belief and practice are concerned.

The argument for descriptive relativism, then, may be summarized as follows. Since every culture varies with respect to its moral rules and standards, and since each individual's moral beliefs—including his inner conviction of their absolute truth—have been learned within the framework of his own culture's moral code, it follows that there are no universal moral norms. If a person believes there are such norms, this is to be explained by his ethnocentrism, which leads him to project his own culture's norms upon everyone else and to consider those who disagree with him either as innocent but "morally blind" people or as sinners who do not want to face the truth about their own evil ways.

In order to assess the soundness of this argument it is necessary to make a distinction between (a) specific moral standards and rules, and (b) ultimate moral principles. Both (a) and (b) can be called "norms," and it is because the descriptive relativist often overlooks this distinction that his argument is open to doubt. A specific moral standard (such as personal courage or trustworthiness) functions as a criterion for judging whether and to what degree a person's character is morally good or bad. A specific rule of conduct (such as "Help others in time of need" or "Do not tell lies for one's own advantage") is a prescription of how people ought or ought not to act. It functions as a criterion for judging whether an action is right or wrong. In contrast with specific standards and rules, an ultimate moral principle is a universal proposition or statement about the conditions that must hold if a standard or rule is to be used as a criterion for judging *any* person or action. Such a principle will be of the form: Standard S or rule R applies to a person or action if and only if condition C is fulfilled. An example of an ultimate moral principle is that of utility. . . . The principle of utility may be expressed thus: A standard or rule applies to a person or action if and only if the use of the standard or rule in the actual guidance of people's conduct will result in an increase in everyone's happiness or a decrease in everyone's unhappiness.

Now it is perfectly possible for an ultimate moral principle to be consistent with a variety of specific standards and rules as found in the moral codes of different societies. For if we take into account the traditions of a culture, the

beliefs about reality and the attitudes toward life that are part of each culture's world-outlook, and if we also take into account the physical or geographical setting of each culture, we will find that a standard or rule which increases people's happiness in one culture will not increase, but rather decrease, people's happiness in another. In one society, for example, letting elderly people die when they can no longer contribute to economic production will be necessary for the survival of everyone else. But another society may have an abundant economy that can easily support people in their old age. Thus the principle of utility would require that in the first society the rule "Do not keep a person alive when he can no longer produce" be part of its moral code, and in the second society it would require a contrary rule. In this case the very same kind of action that is wrong in one society will be right in another. Yet there is a single principle that makes an action of that kind wrong (in one set of circumstances) and another action of that kind right (in a different set of circumstances). In other words, the reason why one action is wrong and the other right is based on one and the same principle, namely utility.

Having in mind this distinction between specific standards and rules on the one hand and ultimate moral principles on the other, what can we say about the argument for descriptive relativism given above? It will immediately be seen that the facts pointed out by the relativist as evidence in support of his theory do not show that ultimate moral principles are relative or culture-bound. They show only that specific standards and rules are relative or culture-bound. The fact that different societies accept different norms of good and bad, right and wrong, is a fact about the standards and rules that make up the various moral codes of those societies. Such a fact does not provide evidence that there is no single ultimate principle which, explicitly or implicitly, every society appeals to as the final justifying ground for its moral code. For if there were such a common ultimate principle, the actual variation in moral codes could be explained in terms of the different world-outlooks, traditions, and physical circumstances of the different societies.

Similarly, facts about ethnocentrism and the causal dependence of an individual's moral beliefs upon his society's moral code do not count as evidence against the view that there is a universal ultimate principle which everyone would refer to in giving a final justification for his society's standards and rules, if he were challenged to do so. Whether there is such a principle and if there is, what sort of conditions it specifies for the validity of specific standards and rules, are questions still to be explored. . . . But the facts cited by the descriptive relativist leave these questions open. We may accept those facts and still be consistent in affirming a single universal ultimate moral principle.

Normative Ethical Relativism

The statement, "What is right in one society may be wrong in another," is a popular way of explaining what is meant by the "relativity of morals." It is usually contrasted with "ethical absolutism," taken as the view that "right and wrong do not vary from society to society." These statements are ambiguous,

however, and it is important for us as moral philosophers to be mindful of their ambiguity. For they may be understood either as factual claims or as normative claims, and it makes a great deal of difference which way they are understood. (They may also be taken as meta-ethical claims, but we shall postpone this way of considering them until later.)

When it is said that what is right in one society may be wrong in another, this may be understood to mean that what is believed to be right in one society is believed to be wrong in another. And when it is said that moral right and wrong norms are adopted by different societies, so that an act which fulfills the norms of one society may violate the norms of another. If this is what is meant, then we are here being told merely of the cultural variability of specific standards and rules, which we have already considered in connection with descriptive relativism.

But the statement, "What is right in one society may be wrong in another," may be interpreted in quite a different way. It may be taken as a normative claim rather than as a factual assertion. In that case it is understood to mean that moral norms are to be considered valid only within the society which has adopted them as part of its way of life. Such norms are not to be considered valid outside that society. The conclusion is then drawn that it is not legitimate to judge people in other societies by applying these norms to their conduct. This is the view we shall designate "normative ethical relativism." In order to be perfectly clear about what it claims, we shall examine two ways in which it can be stated, one focusing our attention upon moral judgments, the other on moral norms.

With regard to moral judgements, normative ethical relativism holds that two *apparently* contradictory statements can both be true. The argument runs as follows. Consider the two statements:

(1) It is wrong for unmarried women to have their faces unveiled in front of strangers.
(2) It is not wrong for . . . (as above).

Here it seems as if there is a flat contradiction between two moral judgments, so that if one is true the other must be false. But the normative ethical relativist holds that they are both true, because the statements as given in (1) and (2) are incomplete. They should read as follows:

(3) It is wrong for unmarried women *who are members of society S* to have their faces unveiled in front of strangers.
(4) It is not wrong for unmarried women *outside of society S* to have their faces unveiled in front of strangers.

Statements (3) and (4) are not contradictories. To assert one is not to deny the other. The normative ethical relativist simply translates all moral judgments of the form "Doing act X is right" into statements of the form "Doing X is right when the agent is a member of society S." The latter statement can then be seen to be consistent with statements of the form "Doing X is wrong when the agent is not a member of society S."

41

The normative ethical relativist's view of moral norms accounts for the foregoing theory of moral judgments. A moral norm, we have seen, is either a standard used in a judgment of good and bad character or a rule used in a judgment of right and wrong conduct. Thus a person is judged to be good in so far as he fulfills the standard and an action is judged to be right or wrong according to whether it conforms to or violates the rule. Now when a normative ethical relativist says that moral norms vary from society to society, he does not intend merely to assert the fact that different societies have adopted different norms. He is going beyond descriptive relativism and is making a normative claim. He is denying any universal validity to moral norms. He is saying that a moral standard or rule is applicable only to those who are members of the particular society which has adopted the standard or rule as part of its moral code. He therefore thinks it is illegitimate to judge the character or conduct of those outside the society by such a standard or rule. Anyone who use the norms of one society as the basis for judging the character or conduct of persons in another society is consequently in error.

It is not that a normative ethical relativist necessarily believes in tolerance of other people's norms and their right to live by their norms. He would hold a relativist position even about tolerance itself. A society whose code included a rule of tolerance would be right in tolerating others, while a society that denied tolerance would be right (relatively to its own norm of intolerance) in prohibiting others from living by different norms. The normative ethical relativist would simply say that *we* should not judge the tolerant society to be any better than the intolerant one, for this would be applying our own norm of tolerance to those in other societies. Tolerance, like any other norm, is culture-bound. Anyone who claimed that every society has a *right* to live by its own norms, provided that it respects a similar right on the part of other societies, is a normative ethical absolutist, since he holds at least one norm to apply validly to all societies, namely, the right to practice a way of life without interference from others.

If the normative ethical relativist is challenged to prove his position, he may do either of two things. On the one hand he may try to argue that his position follows from, or is based on, the very same facts that are cited by the descriptive relativist as evidence for *his* position. Or, on the other hand, he may turn for support to meta-ethical considerations. Putting aside the second move for the moment, look more closely at the first.

The logical relation between the *facts* cited by the descriptive relativist and the *theory* of normative ethical relativism is of central concern. . . .

> [In the rest of this paragraph, Taylor
> considers an argument advanced by W. T.
> Stace.]

. . . The fact that societies differ about what is right and wrong does not mean that one society may not have more correct or enlightened moral beliefs than another. After all, just because two people disagree about whether a disease is

caused by bacteria or by evil spirits does not lead us to conclude that there is no correct or enlightened view about the cause of the disease. So it does not follow from the fact that two societies differ about whether genocide is right that there is no correct or enlightened view about this moral matter.

It should be noted that a similar argument can be used with regard to the second and third facts asserted by the descriptive relativist. No contradiction is involved in asserting that all moral beliefs come from the social environment and denying normative ethical relativism. For the fact that a belief is learned from one's society does not mean it is neither true nor false, or that, if it is true, its truth is "relative" to the society in which it was learned. All of our beliefs, empirical ones no less than moral ones, are learned from our society. We are not born with any innate beliefs about chemistry or physics, which we learn only in our schools. Yet this does not make us sceptical about the universal validity of these sciences. So the fact that our moral beliefs come from our society and are learned in our homes and schools has no bearing on whether they have any universal validity. The origin or cause of a person's *acquiring* a belief does not determine whether the *content* of the belief is true or false, or even whether there are good grounds for his accepting that content to be true or false.

The same kind of argument holds for the third fact of descriptive relativism, the fact of ethnocentrism. People who are ethnocentric *believe* that the one true moral code is the code of their own society. But this leaves open the question: Is their belief true or false? Even when two people of different cultures have opposite moral beliefs and yet are both ethnocentric, so that one thinks his moral norms are valid for everyone and the other thinks *his* are, this has no bearing on the question of whether either one of them is correct, or whether neither is correct. We must inquire independently into the possibility of establishing the universal validity of a set of moral norms, regardless of who might or might not believe these norms to be universally valid.

Meta-Ethical Relativism

It will be convenient to discuss two forms of meta-ethical relativism separately. We shall call these two forms "semantical relativism" and "methodological relativism." According to semantical relativism, the meanings of moral terms like 'good" and "right" vary from culture to culture. In one culture, saying that someone is a good man will be taken to mean that he is meek and humble and forgiving. In another culture the same statement will be taken to mean that the man is quick to avenge himself on others and is ruthless with his enemies. A similar variation exists in the meaning of the word "right." Thus in one society the statement "That act is right" might mean "That act must be done to uphold the honor of one's family." In another society it might mean "That act must be done if all the persons concerned are to be treated fairly and impartially." On the basis of considerations like these, semantical relativists argue that what a given word means in moral discourse depends on the culture in which the word is used. There is no one meaning of "good," "right," "duty,"

or "obligation." Whether this view can stand up to criticism depends on what analysis is given of the meaning of words and statements in moral language. . . .

The second form of meta-ethical relativism, methodological relativism, maintains that different cultures use different methods of reasoning to justify moral judgments. The conclusion drawn is that the same judgment may be justified in one culture but not in another. Each method provides its own criteria for determining whether a reason given in a moral argument is a good or valid reason. If such criteria vary from culture to culture it may be possible to establish the truth of a moral belief in one culture and to show the same belief to be false in another culture. Moral knowledge, being based on different methods of verification, would then be culturally relative. Unless there were some uniform, cross-cultural method for gaining moral knowledge or a uniform, cross-cultural set of rules of reasoning that could tell us whether a person in *any* culture is reasoning correctly, no claim could be made for the universal validity of moral norms. And the methodological relativist argues that there is no such uniform, cross-cultural method or set of rules of reasoning. Whether his argument is to be accepted is a question that must be considered in the light of those methods that have been proposed by moral philosophers as ways of obtaining genuine moral knowledge. . . .

It has been claimed that one serious implication of methodological relativism is ethical scepticism, or the complete denial of moral knowledge. The reasoning behind this claim is as follows. When the methodological relativist asserts that all moral knowledge is "relative" to a given culture, he is ruling out the very conditions that make it possible for there to be such a thing as genuine moral knowledge at all. For he is saying that, if we investigate the assumptions underlying the alleged universal methods adopted by different cultures, we find that in every case one method will define "valid" or "good" reasons in one way and another method will define them in another way. It follows that the question of which, if any, of these given methods really does lead to moral knowledge is *logically undecidable*. For in order to choose between any two methods, a neutral third method must be used—a method that would enable us to give reasons for accepting one method and rejecting the other. But any such third method will itself merely postulate its own criteria of "valid" reasons, and we would then have to justify our choice of *these* criteria. Justifying our choice of these criteria, however, would in turn require our giving reasons for our choice, and such reasons would presuppose still another method. Since we cannot go to infinity in methods for justifying other methods, we are left at some point with an arbitrary decision. But no claim to genuine moral knowledge can rest on an arbitrary decision, since a different decision might lead to opposite conclusions regarding a moral issue and each decision would be completely without justification. This is precisely the kind of situation that the word "knowledge" precludes, if that word is to be understood in its ordinary sense. Therefore genuine moral knowledge is impossible.

Now the reply made to this argument by moral philosophers is simply to construct, clearly and systematically, a method of moral reasoning whose logical principles can be shown to be those which are in fact presupposed by

anyone, in any culture, who wants to think rationally about moral matters. By considering how any reasonable being would carry on his thinking when he understood clearly the meaning of moral concepts and the function of moral judgments, the philosopher attempts to show that there is a valid way of determining whether any moral judgment is true or false and hence that there is a warranted method for obtaining genuine moral knowledge. . . .

Ethical Absolutism

Some consideration should here be given to the term "ethical absolutism," which is frequently used to refer to the opposite of ethical relativism, but which may also be used in other senses. Sometimes people will argue against ethical absolutism in one sense and think that they have thereby established the truth of ethical relativism, when in fact they have not. Let us see how this can happen.

When "ethical absolutism" is taken to mean the contradictory of ethical relativism it can be understood in three different ways, corresponding to the three kinds of relativism. Descriptive absolutism would be the view that there is one universal ultimate moral principle which, implicitly or explicitly, lies at the foundation of all the varying moral codes of different societies. We have seen how this position can be maintained in the face of the evidence of great variation among the specific standards and rules that constitute those moral codes. For different standards and rules can be derived from one ultimate principle when it is applied to the varying social and physical conditions under which the different ways of life of cultures are pursued.

Sometimes, however, when an ethical absolutist asserts that there is one true morality for all cultures, no matter how different may be their ways of life and their conditions of existence, he means something other than that all cultures do basically appeal to one ultimate principle. When the evidence of cultural variation is pointed out to this type of ethical absolutist, he will reply: "I was not asserting that there is one principle which all societies *consider to be* the ultimate foundation of morality. I was asserting that there is one principle that *is* the ultimate foundation of morality, whether all societies consider it to be so or not." As soon as his position is stated in this way, it is seen to be the denial of normative ethical relativism, not the denial of descriptive relativism. Let us therefore call this view "normative ethical absolutism." According to it there is an ultimate moral principle applicable to all mankind. This principle defines an ideal moral community of man based on a single "moral law" that applies to all men whether they recognize it or not. The people of a given culture might not acknowledge such an ultimate principle or law, but nevertheless it is binding upon them and is the source of their true rights and duties.

This view, of course, presupposes that there is a method of finding out what the ultimate "moral law" is and hence a method of finding out whether any given moral belief is true or false. The great task of the normative ethical absolutist is to tell us what this method is. But all he insists on, when confronted with the actual disagreements among people about what is right and wrong, is that these disagreements do not rule out the possibility of such a method. (This

is parallel to the position we would all take concerning a scientific or empirical belief. The fact that different cultures might hold different beliefs about the causes of a disease, for instance, does not lead us to say that there are no true beliefs about the real causes of the disease. We simply say that the beliefs of some cultures are true and those of others are false. And we can say this even about a disease whose causes are still unknown, although in that case we cannot specify which of the disagreeing beliefs are true and which are false.)

The foregoing account of normative ethical absolutism shows that it presupposes that there is a cross-cultural method by which moral beliefs can be verified, even if no philosopher has yet succeeded in discovering that method or in establishing its universal validity. Now the view that such a method can be discovered and can be shown to be universally valid may be called "methodological absolutism." It is the exact opposite of methodological relativism. It should be noted that if methodological absolutism is true, then not only methodological relativism but also normative ethical relativism would be false. For if we know a way of verifying moral beliefs or justifying moral norms, we can claim that there is a set of norms valid for all mankind, and this is the denial of normative ethical relativism. Hence the logical foundation for normative ethical absolutism lies in methodological absolutism, and the meta-ethical task of showing that there is a cross-cultural method for acquiring moral knowledge becomes the first problem for the ethical absolutist.

In sharp contrast with the foregoing meanings of "ethical absolutism," the term may also be used to designate a certain view concerning the *nature* of moral norms. According to this view, if a rule of conduct is a moral rule, it must have no exceptions. The moral rule "It is wrong to break a promise" is taken by the ethical absolutist to mean that it is always wrong to break a promise, no matter what the circumstances might be. It would follow that it is our duty to keep a promise, even though we might do great harm to someone by keeping it. In other words an ethical absolutist (in the present sense of "ethical absolutism") believes that the application of a moral rule to varying circumstances does not allow us to make legitimate exceptions to it. Whether any moral philosopher has actually held such a position is questionable, although it is sometimes claimed that Immanuel Kant was an ethical absolutist in this sense. . . .

What is important for us to understand at this point is that a normative ethical absolutist or a methodological absolutist, as defined earlier, may reject ethical absolutism in this latter sense. When the normative ethical absolutist says that there are moral norms applicable to all mankind, he does not mean that the application of these norms in varying circumstances must determine that one kind of act is always right (or that it is always wrong). One and the same norm can yield different results in the following way. Suppose the norm is expressed in the rule: Always do that act which will probably have better consequences than any alternative act open to your choice, where the standard of "better" is understood as "brings about more pleasure." Then in one situation a person might be following this rule by keeping his promise, while in a different situation he might be following this rule by breaking his promise. The

latter case is illustrated by the person's failing to meet a friend at a time he had promised to because he has stopped on the way to help someone who had just been injured in an accident. Thus one and the same norm allows us to say either of two things regarding the keeping of promises: "Sometimes keeping one's promise is right and sometimes it is wrong" or "Although as a general rule it is right to keep one's promise, this rule does have legitimate exceptions."

Now this variation in the rightness and wrongness of keeping promises does not involve the giving up of normative ethical absolutism. For the basis for such variation lies in one moral norm that holds "absolutely"in all cultures, namely, the rule that we ought always to do what will bring about the best consequences in every situation. In so far as he considers it a valid rule for all mankind to follow, the absolutist would maintain that this rule does not vary from culture to culture. He would say that a culture which did not accept this rule was mistaken in its moral beliefs. Nevertheless, he would assert that when this one unchanging rule is applied to varying circumstances, the same kind of act that is right in one situation might be wrong in another. The normative ethical relativist, on the other hand, claims that what makes an act right is the society's believing it to be right (or the society's adopting norms according to which it is right) and that what makes the same kind of act wrong in another society is *that* society's believing it to be wrong (or adopting norms according to which it is wrong). Thus no society can be mistaken in its moral beliefs. It is this position which the absolutist emphatically rejects.

In a similar manner, the methodological absolutist might well accept a method of reasoning that justifies the varying judgments about keeping and breaking promises we have considered. But the variation in moral judgments is grounded on the one unvarying method by which the given rule was established. And it is this method that the absolutist claims to be cross-cultural, so that any society that did not use the method would, for that reason, be incapable of attaining genuine moral knowledge.

There is an important conclusion to be drawn from these considerations. It is that ethical absolutism (when understood as the denial of ethical relativism) may be true while ethical absolutism (when understood as the idea that no exceptions are to be made to moral rules) may be false. One need not be an ethical relativist in any of the three senses we have discussed to reject the latter type of absolutism. It is possible for relativism in any of these senses to be false and for the latter type of absolutism to be false at the same time. Whether either or both are false is a matter for each reader to try to decide by his own philosophical reflection as he engages in the study of ethics.

3

Ethics and Observation

GILBERT HARMAN

*Gilbert Harman (b. 1938) is Professor of Philosophy at Princeton
University. In addition to his work in ethics, he has made major
contributions in the theory of knowledge. He is the author of* Thought,
The Nature of Morality, *and many articles.*

In this selection from The Nature of Morality, *Harman compares the
principles of ethics to those of science. He argues that while observation and
experiment can make it reasonable to accept or reject scientific principles,
the principles of ethics cannot be confirmed or tested in any similar way.
At first glance, his reason for saying this may appear to be simply that
observation can tell us what happens, but never whether what happens is
right or wrong. But this is not quite Harman's position. On his account, an
observation is any opinion that is formed as a direct result of perception
without conscious inference. Because a given perception (say of some
children setting fire to a cat) may directly cause us to believe that what is
happening is wrong, Harman believes that there can be moral observation.*

*If moral observations are possible, why can't they confirm moral
principles as laboratory observations confirm scientific principles? The
answer, according to Harman, lies in the explanatory role of what is
observed. When a physicist sees a vapor trail in a cloud chamber, and
directly forms the opinion that he is confronted with a proton, the best
explanation of his forming this opinion will include a reference to the fact of
his being confronted with a proton. By contrast, when a moralist sees a
child torturing a cat, and directly forms the opinion that the child's activity
is wrong, the best explanation of his forming this opinion will include no
reference to the moral fact that the child's activity is wrong. Instead, it will
include only references to the moralist's upbringing, conditioning, and so
on. Because moral facts are not needed to explain moral observations,
Harman concludes that these observations cannot confirm moral principles
as scientific observations can confirm scientific principles.*

The Basic Issue

CAN MORAL PRINCIPLES be tested and confirmed in the way scientific
principles can? Consider the principle that, if you are given a choice between
five people alive and one dead or five people dead and one alive, you should
always choose to have five people alive and one dead rather than the other way
round. We can easily imagine examples that appear to confirm this principle.

Here is one:

> You are a doctor in a hospital's emergency room when six accident victims are brought in. All six are in danger of dying but one is much worse off than the others. You can just barely save that person if you devote all of your resources to him and let the others die. Alternatively, you can save the other five if you are willing to ignore the most seriously injured person.

It would seem that in this case you, the doctor, would be right to save the five and let the other person die. So this example, taken by itself, confirms the principle under consideration. Next, consider the following case.

> You have five patients in the hospital who are dying, each in need of a separate organ. One needs a kidney, another a lung, a third a heart, and so forth. You can save all five if you take a single healthy person and remove his heart, lungs, kidneys, and so forth, to distribute to these five patients. Just such a healthy person is in room 306. He is in the hospital for routine tests. Having seen his test results, you know that he is perfectly healthy and of the right tissue compatibility. If you do nothing, he will survive without incident; the other patients will die, however. The other five patients can be saved only if the person in Room 306 is cut up and his organs distributed. In that case, there would be one dead but five saved.

The principle in question tells us that you should cut up the patient in Room 306. But in this case, surely you must not sacrifice this innocent bystander, even to save the five other patients. Here a moral principle has been tested and disconfirmed in what may seem to be a surprising way.

This, of course, was a "thought experiment." We did not really compare a hypothesis with the world. We compared an explicit principle with our feelings about certain imagined examples. In the same way, a physicist performs thought experiments in order to compare explicit hypotheses with his "sense" of what should happen in certain situations, a "sense" that he has acquired as a result of his long working familiarity with current theory. But scientific hypotheses can also be tested in real experiments, out in the world.

Can moral principles be tested in the same way, out in the world? You can observe someone do something, but can you ever perceive the rightness or wrongness of what he does? If you round a corner and see a group of young hoodlums pour gasoline on a cat and ignite it, you do not need to *conclude* that what they are doing is wrong; you do not need to figure anything out; you can *see* that it is wrong. But is your reaction due to the actual wrongness of what you see or is it simply a reflection of your moral "sense," a "sense" that you have acquired perhaps as a result of your moral upbringing?

Observation

The issue is complicated. There are no pure observations. Observations are always "theory laden." What you perceive depends to some extent on the theory you hold, consciously or unconsciously. You see some children pour

gasoline on a cat and ignite it. To really see that, you have to possess a great deal of knowledge, know about a considerable number of objects, know about people: that people pass through the life stages infant, baby, child, adolescent, adult. You must know what flesh and blood animals are, and in particular, cats. You must have some idea of life. You must know what gasoline is, what burning is, and much more. In one sense, what you "see" is a pattern of light on your retina, a shifting array of splotches, although, even that is theory, and you could never adequately describe what you see in that sense. In another sense, you see what you do because of the theories you hold. Change those theories and you would see something else, given the same pattern of light.

Similarly, if you hold a moral view, whether it is held consciously or unconsciously, you will be able to perceive rightness or wrongness, goodness or badness, justice or injustice. There is no difference in this respect between moral propositions and other theoretical propositions. If there is a difference, it must be found elsewhere.

Observation depends on theory because perception involves forming a belief as a fairly direct result of observing something; you can form a belief only if you understand the relevant concepts and a concept is what it is by virtue of its role in some theory or system of beliefs. To recognize a child as a child is to employ, consciously or unconsciously, a concept that is defined by its place in a framework of the stages of human life. Similarly, burning is an empty concept apart from its theoretical connections to the concepts of heat, destruction, smoke, and fire.

Moral concepts—Right and Wrong, Good and Bad, Justice and Injustice—also have a place in your theory or system of beliefs and are the concepts they are because of their context. If we say that observation has occurred whenever an opinion is a direct result of perception, we must allow that there is moral observation, because such an opinion can be a moral opinion as easily as any other sort. In this sense, observation may be used to confirm or disconfirm moral theories. The observational opinions that, in this sense, you find yourself with can be in either agreement or conflict with your consciously explicit moral principles. When they are in conflict, you must choose between your explicit theory and observation. In ethics, as in science, you sometimes opt for theory, and say that you made an error in observation or were biased or whatever, or you sometimes opt for observation, and modify your theory.

In other words, in both science and ethics, general principles are invoked to explain particular cases and, therefore, in both science and ethics, the general principles you accept can be tested by appealing to particular judgments that certain things are right or wrong, just or unjust, and so forth; and these judgments are analogous to direct perceptual judgments about facts.

Observational Evidence

Nevertheless, observation plays a role in science that it does not seem to play in ethics. The difference is that you need to make assumptions about certain physical facts to explain the occurrence of the observations that support a

scientific theory, but you do not seem to need to make assumptions about any moral facts to explain the occurrence of the so-called moral observations I have been talking about. In the moral case, it would seem that you need only make assumptions about the psychology or moral sensibility of the person making the moral observation. In the scientific case, theory is tested against the world.

The point is subtle but important. Consider a physicist making an observation to test a scientific theory. Seeing a vapor trail in a cloud chamber, he thinks, "There goes a proton." Let us suppose that this is an observation in the relevant sense, namely, an immediate judgment made in response to the situation without any conscious reasoning having taken place. Let us also suppose that his observation confirms his theory, a theory that helps give meaning to the very term "proton" as it occurs in his observational judgment. Such a confirmation rests on inferring an explanation. He can count his making the observation as confirming evidence for his theory only to the extent that it is reasonable to explain his making the observation by assuming that, not only is he in a certain psychological "set," given the theory he accepts and his beliefs about the experimental apparatus, but furthermore, there really was a proton going through the cloud chamber, causing the vapor trail, which he saw as a proton. (This is evidence for the theory to the extent that the theory can explain the proton's being there better than competing theories can.) But, if his having made that observation could have been equally well explained by his psychological set alone, without the need for any assumption about a proton, then the observation would not have been evidence for the existence of that proton and therefore would not have been evidence for the theory. His making the observation supports the theory only because, in order to explain his making the observation, it is reasonable to assume something about the world over and above the assumptions made about the observer's psychology. In particular, it is reasonable to assume that there was a proton going through the cloud chamber, causing the vapor trail.

Compare this case with one in which you make a moral judgment immediately and without conscious reasoning, say, that the children are wrong to set the cat on fire or that the doctor would be wrong to cut up one healthy patient to save five dying patients. In order to explain your making the first of these judgments, it would be reasonable to assume, perhaps, that the children really are pouring gasoline on a cat and you are seeing them do it. But, in neither case is there any obvious reason to assume anything about "moral facts," such as that it really is wrong to set the cat on fire or to cut up the patient in Room 306. Indeed, an assumption about moral facts would seem to be totally irrelevant to the explanation of your making the judgment you make. It would seem that all we need assume is that you have certain more or less well articulated moral principles that are reflected in the judgments you make, based on your moral sensibility. It seems to be completely irrelevant to our explanation whether your intuitive immediate judgment is true or false.

The observation of an event can provide observational evidence for or against a scientific theory in the sense that the truth of that observation can be relevant to a reasonable explanation of why that observation was made. A moral obser-

vation does not seem, in the same sense, to be observational evidence for or against any moral theory, since the truth or falsity of the moral observation seems to be completely irrelevant to any reasonable explanation of why that observation was made. The fact that an observation of an event was made at the time it was made is evidence not only about the observer but also about the physical facts. The fact that you made a particular moral observation when you did does not seem to be evidence about moral facts, only evidence about you and your moral sensibility. Facts about protons can affect what you observe, since a proton passing through the cloud chamber can cause a vapor trail that reflects light to your eye in a way that, given your scientific training and psychological set, leads you to judge that what you see is a proton. But there does not seem to be any way in which the actual rightness or wrongness of a given situation can have any effect on your perceptual apparatus. In this respect, ethics seems to differ from science.

In considering whether moral principles can help explain observations, it is therefore important to note an ambiguity in the word "observation." You see the children set the cat on fire and immediately think, "That's wrong." In one sense, your observation is that what the children are doing is wrong. In another sense, your observation is your thinking that thought. Moral [principles] might explain observations in the first sense but not in the second sense. Certain moral principles might help to explain why it was *wrong* of the children to set the cat on fire, but moral principles seem to be of no help in explaining *your thinking* that that is wrong. In the first sense of "observation," moral principles can be tested by observation—"That this act is wrong is evidence that causing unnecessary suffering is wrong." But in the second sense of "observation," moral principles cannot clearly be tested by observation, since they do not appear to help explain observations in this second sense of "observation." Moral principles do not seem to help explain your observing what you observe.

Of course, if you are already given the moral principle that it is wrong to cause unnecessary suffering, you can take your seeing the children setting the cat on fire as observational evidence that they are doing something wrong. Similarly, you can suppose that your seeing the vapor trail is observational evidence that a proton is going through the cloud chamber, if you are given the relevant physical theory. But there is an important apparent difference between the two cases. In the scientific case, your making that observation is itself evidence for the physical theory because the physical theory explains the proton, which explains the trail, which explains your observation. In the moral case, your making your observation does not seem to be evidence for the relevant moral principle because that principle does not seem to help explain your observation. The explanatory chain from principle to observation seems to be broken in morality. The moral principle may "explain" why it is wrong for the children to set the cat on fire. But the wrongness of that act does not appear to help explain the act, which you observe, itself. The explanatory chain appears to be broken in such a way that neither the moral principle nor the wrongness of the act can help explain why you observe what you observe.

A qualification may seem to be needed here. Perhaps the children perversely

set the cat on fire simply "because it is wrong." Here it may seem at first that the actual wrongness of the act does help explain why they do it and therefore indirectly helps explain why you observe what you observe just as a physical theory, by explaining why the proton is producing a vapor trail, indirectly helps explain why the observer observes what he observes. But on reflection we must agree that this is probably an illusion. What explains the children's act is not clearly the actual wrongness of the act but, rather, their belief that the act is wrong. The actual rightness or wrongness of their act seems to have nothing to do with why they do it.

Observational evidence plays a part in science it does not appear to play in ethics, because scientific principles can be justified ultimately by their role in explaining observations, in the second sense of observation—by their explanatory role. Apparently, moral principles cannot be justified in the same way. It appears to be true that there can be no explanatory chain between moral principles and particular observings in the way that there can be such a chain between scientific principles and particular observings. Conceived as an explanatory theory, morality, unlike science, seems to be cut off from observation.

Not that every legitimate scientific hypothesis is susceptible to direct observational testing. Certain hypotheses about "black holes" in space cannot be directly tested, for example, because no signal is emitted from within a black hole. The connection with observation in such a case is indirect. And there are many similar examples. Nevertheless, seen in the large, there is the apparent difference between science and ethics we have noted. The scientific realm is accessible to observation in a way the moral realm is not.

Ethics and Mathematics

Perhaps ethics is to be compared, not with physics, but with mathematics. Perhaps such a moral principle as "You ought to keep your promises" is confirmed or disconfirmed in the way (whatever it is) in which such a mathematical principle as "$5 + 7 = 12$" is. Observation does not seem to play the role in mathematics it plays in physics. We do not and cannot perceive numbers, for example, since we cannot be in causal contact with them. We do not even understand what it would be like to be in causal contact with the number 12, say. Relations among numbers cannot have any more of an effect on our perceptual apparatus than moral facts can.

Observation, however, *is* relevant to mathematics. In explaining the observations that support a physical theory, scientists typically appeal to mathematical principles. On the other hand, one never seems to need to appeal in this way to moral principles. Since an observation is evidence for what best explains it, and since mathematics often figures in the explanations of scientific observations, there is indirect obervational evidence for mathematics. There does not seem to be observational evidence, even indirectly, for basic moral principles. In explaining why certain observations have been made, we never seem to use purely moral assumptions. In this respect, then, ethics appears to differ not only from physics but also from mathematics.

· · ·

4

Outline of a Decision Procedure for Ethics

JOHN RAWLS

John Rawls (b. 1921) is Professor of Philosophy at Harvard University. He is among the leading moral and political theorists of the twentieth century. His book A Theory of Justice *is a contemporary classic.*

In this early paper, Rawls presents an alternative to the view that objectivity requires that moral judgments correspond to moral facts. According to Rawls, this fact-based model of moral judgment, taken for granted by Harman in reading 3, is inappropriate. In its place, Rawls argues that we should require only that correct moral principles be reasonable or justifiable. Moreover, justifiability should be understood as derivability through a rationally defensible procedure.

When moral objectivity is conceived in this way, the obvious challenge is to describe the procedure that confers justification upon moral principles. Rawls does this in a series of stages. First, he specifies certain features (a degree of intelligence, rationality, and so on) that make someone a competent judge. Next, he specifies certain features that make the judgments of competent judges worthy of acceptance, for example, the fact that the judge is uninfluenced by fear or the promise of gain, feels certain of his judgment, and so on. Finally, he suggests that there may well be moral principles that imply precisely the judgments that share these features. As an example, he cites the principle "a man shall not be morally condemned for the possession of characteristics which would not have been otherwise even if he had chosen." Taken together, such principles provide what Rawls calls an "explication" of the considered judgments of competent judges. If any moral principles are worthy of acceptance, and so are objectively justified, these are.

1.1 The question with which we shall be concerned can be stated as follows: Does there exist a reasonable decision procedure which is sufficiently strong, at least in some cases, to determine the manner in which competing interests should be adjudicated, and, in instances of conflict, one interest given preference over another; and, further, can the existence of this procedure, as well as its reasonableness, be established by rational methods of inquiry? In order to answer both parts of this question in the affirmative, it is necessary to describe a reasonable procedure and then to evidence that it satisfies certain criteria. This I attempt to do beginning at 2.1 below.

1.2 It should be noted that we are concerned here only with the existence of a reasonable method, and not with the problem of how to make it psychologically effective in the settling of disputes. How much allegiance the method is able to gain is irrelevant for our present purposes.

1.3 The original question has been framed the way it is because the objectivity or the subjectivity of moral knowledge turns, not on the question whether ideal value entities exist or whether moral judgments are caused by emotions or whether there is a variety of moral codes the world over, but simply on the question: does there exist a reasonable method for validating and invalidating given or proposed moral rules and those decisions made on the basis of them? For to say of scientific knowledge that it is objective is to say that the propositions expressed therein may be evidenced to be true by a reasonable and reliable method, that is, by the rules and procedures of what we may call "inductive logic";* and, similarly, to establish the objectivity of moral rules, and the decisions based upon them, we must exhibit the decision procedure, which can be shown to be both reasonable and reliable, at least in some cases, for deciding between moral rules and lines of conduct consequent to them.

2.1 For the present, we may think of ethics as being more analogous to the study of inductive logic than to any other established inquiry. Just as in inductive logic we are concerned with discovering reasonable criteria which, when we are given a proposition, or theory, together with the empirical evidence for it, will enable us to decide the extent to which we ought to consider it to be true so in ethics we are attempting to find reasonable principles which, when we are given a proposed line of conduct and the situation in which it is to be carried out and the relevant interests which it affects, will enable us to determine whether or not we ought to carry it out and hold it to be just and right.

2.2 There is no way of knowing ahead of time how to find and formulate these reasonable principles. Indeed, we cannot even be certain that they exist, and it is well known that there are no mechanical methods of discovery. In what follows, however, a method will be described, and it remains for the reader to judge for himself to what extent it is, or can be, successful.

2.3 First it is necessary to define a class of competent moral judges as follows: All those persons having to a certain requisite degree each of the following characteristics, which can, if desired, be made more determinate:

(i) A competent moral judge is expected to have a certain requisite degree of intelligence, which may be thought of as that ability which intelligence tests are designed to measure. The degree of this ability required should not be set too high, on the assumption that what we call "moral insight" is the possession of the normally intelligent man as well as of the more brilliant. Therefore I am inclined to say that a competent moral judge need not be more than normally intelligent.

(ii) A competent judge is required to know those things concerning the world

---

* What Rawls calls "inductive logic" is what we have referred to as "non-deductive logic" in our introduction.

about him and those consequences of frequently performed actions, which it is reasonable to expect the average intelligent man to know. Further, a competent judge is expected to know, in all cases whereupon he is called to express his opinion, the peculiar facts of those cases. It should be noted that the kind of knowledge here referred to is to be distinguished from sympathetic knowledge discussed below.

(iii) A competent judge is required to be a reasonable man as this characteristic is evidenced by his satisfying the following tests: First, a reasonable man shows a willingness, if not a desire, to use the criteria of inductive logic in order to determine what is proper for him to believe. Second, a reasonable man, whenever he is confronted with a moral question, shows a disposition to find reasons for and against the possible lines of conduct which are open to him. Third, a reasonable man exhibits a desire to consider questions with an open mind, and consequently, while he may already have an opinion on some issue, he is always willing to reconsider it in the light of further evidence and reasons which may be presented to him in discussion. Fourth, a reasonable man knows, or tries to know, his own emotional, intellectual, and moral predilections and makes a conscientious effort to take them into account in weighing the merits of any question. He is not unaware of the influences of prejudice and bias even in his most sincere efforts to annul them; nor is he fatalistic about their effect so that he succumbs to them as being those factors which he thinks must sooner or later determine his decision.

(iv) Finally, a competent judge is required to have a sympathetic knowledge of those human interests which, by conflicting in particular cases, give rise to the need to make a moral decision. The presence of this characteristic is evidenced by the following: First, by the person's direct knowledge of those interests gained by experiencing, in his own life, the goods they represent. The more interests which a person can appreciate in terms of his own direct experience, the greater the extent to which he satisfies this first test. Yet it is obvious that no man can know all interests directly, and therefore the second test is that, should a person not be directly acquainted with an interest, his competency as a judge is seen, in part, by his capacity to give that interest an appraisal by means of an imaginative experience of it. This test also requires of a competent judge that he must not consider his own *de facto* preferences as the necessarily valid measure of the actual worth of those interests which come before him, but that he be both able and anxious to determine, by imaginative appreciation, what those interests mean to persons who share them, and to consider them accordingly. Third, a competent judge is required to have the capacity and the desire to lay before himself in imagination all the interests in conflict, together with the relevant facts of the case, and to bestow upon the appraisal of each the same care which he would give to it if that interest were his own. He is required to determine what he would think to be just and unjust if each of the interests were as thoroughly his own as they are in fact those of other persons, and to render his judgment on the case as he feels his sense of justice requires after he has carefully framed in his mind the issues which are to be decided.

. . .

2.5 The next step in the development of our procedure is to define the class of considered moral judgments, the determining characteristics of which are as follows:

(i) It is required first that the judgment on a case be given under such conditions that the judge is immune from all of the reasonably foreseeable consequences of the judgment. For example, he will not be punished for deciding the case one way rather than another.

(ii) It is required that the conditions be such that the integrity of the judge can be maintained. So far as possible, the judge must not stand to gain in any immediate and personal way by his decision. These two tests are designed to exclude judgments wherein a person must weigh the merit of one of his own interests. The imposition of these conditions is justified on the grounds that fear and partiality are recognized obstructions in the determination of justice.

(iii) It is required that the case, on which the judgment is given, be one in which there is an actual conflict of interests. Thus, all judgments on hypothetical cases are excluded. In addition, it is preferable that the case be not especially difficult and be one that is likely to arise in ordinary life. These restrictions are desirable in order that the judgments in question be made in the effort to settle problems with which men are familiar and whereupon they have had an opportunity to reflect.

(iv) It is required that the judgment be one which has been preceded by a careful inquiry into the facts of the question at issue, and by a fair opportunity for all concerned to state their side of the case. This requirement is justified on the ground that it is only by chance that a just decision can be made without a knowledge of the relevant facts.

(v) It is required that the judgment be felt to be certain by the person making it. This characteristic may be called "certitude" and it is to be sharply distinguished from certainty, which is a logical relation between a proposition, or theory, and its evidence. This test is justified on the ground that it seems more profitable to study those judgments which are felt to be correct than those which seem to be wrong or confused even to those who make them.

(vi) It is required that the judgment be stable, that is, that there be evidence that at other times and at other places competent judges have rendered the same judgment on similar cases, understanding similar cases to be those in which the relevant facts and the competing interests are similar. The stability must hold, by and large, over the class of competent judges and over their judgments at different times. Thus, if on similar cases of a certain type, competent judges decided one way one day, and another the next, or if a third of them decided one way, a third the opposite way, while the remaining third said they did not know how to decide the cases, then none of these judgments would be stable judgments, and therefore none would be considered judgments. These restrictions are justified on the grounds that it seems unreasonable to have any confidence that a judgment is correct if competent persons disagree about it.

(vii) Finally, it is required that the judgment be intuitive with respect to ethical principles, that is, that it should not be determined by a conscious application of principles so far as this may be evidenced by introspection. By

the term "intuitive" I do not mean the same as that expressed by the terms "impulsive" and "instinctive." An intuitive judgment may be consequent to a thorough inquiry into the facts of the case, and it may follow a series of reflections on the possible effects of different decisions, and even the application of a common sense rule, e.g., promises ought to be kept. What is required is that the judgment not be determined by a systematic and conscious use of ethical principles. The reason for this restriction will be evident if one keeps in mind the aim of the present inquiry, namely, to describe a decision procedure whereby principles, by means of which we may justify specific moral decisions, may themselves be shown to be justifiable. Now part of this procedure will consist in showing that these principles are implicit in the considered judgments of competent judges. It is clear that if we allowed these judgments to be determined by a conscious and systematic application of these principles, then the method is threatened with circularity. We cannot test a principle honestly by means of judgments wherein it has been consciously and systematically used to determine the decision.

2.6 Up to this point I have defined, first, a class of competent judges and, second, a class of considered judgments. If competent judges are those persons most likely to make correct decisions, then we should take care to abstract those judgments of theirs which, from the conditions and circumstances under which they are made, are most likely to be correct. With the exception of certain requirements, which are needed to prevent circularity, the defining characteristics of considered judgments are such that they select those judgments most likely to be decided by the habits of thought and imagination deemed essential for a competent judge. One can say, then, that those judgments which are relevant for our present purposes are the considered judgments of competent judges as these are made from day to day on the moral issues which continually arise. No other judgments, for reasons previously stated, are of any concern.

3.1 The next step in the present method is as follows: once the class of considered judgments of competent judges has been selected, there remains to discover and formulate a satisfactory explication of the total range of these judgments. This process is understood as being a heuristic device which is likely to yield reasonable and justifiable principles.

3.2 The term "explication" is given meaning somewhat graphically as follows: Consider a group of competent judges making considered judgments in review of a set of cases which would be likely to arise in ordinary life. Then an explication of these judgments is defined to be a set of principles, such that, if any competent man were to apply them intelligently and consistently to the same cases under review, his judgments, made systematically nonintuitive by the explicit and conscious use of the principles, would be, nevertheless, identical, case by case, with the considered judgments of the group of competent judges . . .

4.3 In what follows we shall assume that a satisfactory and comprehensive explication of the considered judgments of competent judges is already known (note proviso under fourth test below). Now consider the question as to what reasons we can have for accepting these principles as justifiable.

The first reason for accepting them has already been touched upon: namely, since the principles explicate the considered judgments of competent judges, and since these judgments are more likely than any other judgments to represent the mature convictions of competent men as they have been worked out under the most favorable existing conditions, the invariant in what we call "moral insight," if it exists, is more likely to be approximated by the principles of a successful explication than by principles which a man might fashion out of his own head. Individual predilections will tend to be canceled out once the explication has included judgments of many persons made on a wide variety of cases. Thus the fact that the principles constitute a comprehensive explication of the considered judgments of competent judges is reason for accepting them. That this should be so is understandable if we reflect, to take the contrary case, how little confidence we would have in principles which should happen to explicate the judgments of men under strong emotional or physical duress, or of those mentally ill. Hence the type of judgments which make up the range of the explication is the first ground for accepting the principles thereof.

Secondly, the reasonableness of a principle is tested by seeing whether it shows a capacity to become accepted by competent moral judges after they have freely weighed its merits by criticism and open discussion, and after each has thought it over and compared it with his own considered judgments. It is hoped that some principles will exhibit a capacity to win free and willing allegiance and be able to implement a gradual convergence of uncoerced opinion.

Thirdly, the reasonableness of a principle is tested by seeing whether it can function in existing instances of conflicting opinion, and in new cases causing difficulty, to yield a result which, after criticism and discussion, seems to be acceptable to all, or nearly all, competent judges, and to conform to their intuitive notion of a reasonable decision. For example, the problem of punishment has been a troublesome moral issue for some time, and if a principle or set of principles should be formulated which evidenced a capacity to settle this problem to the satisfaction of all, or nearly all, competent judges, then this principle, or set of principles, would meet this test in one possible instance of its application. In general, a principle evidences its reasonableness by being able to resolve moral perplexities which existed at the time of its formulation and which will exist in the future. This test is somewhat analogous to a test which we impose upon an empirical theory: namely, its ability to foresee laws and facts hitherto unknown, and to explain facts and laws hitherto unexplainable.

Finally, the reasonableness of a principle is tested by seeing whether it shows a capacity to hold its own (that is, to continue to be felt reasonable), against a subclass of the considered judgments of competent judges, as this fact may be evidenced by our intuitive conviction that the considered judgments are incorrect rather than the principle, when we confront them with the principle. A principle satisfies this test when a subclass of considered judgments, rather than the principle, is felt to be mistaken when the principle fails to explicate it. For example, it often happens that competent persons, in judging the moral worth of character, blame others in conflict with the rule that a man shall not be morally condemned for the possession of characteristics which would not have

been otherwise even if he had so chosen. Frequently, however, when we point out that their judgments conflict with this rule, these persons, upon reflection, will decide that their judgments are incorrect, and acknowledge the principle. To the extent that principles exhibit this capacity to alter what we think to be our considered judgments in cases of conflict, they satisfy the fourth test. It is, of course, desirable, although not essential, that whenever a principle does successfully militate against what is taken to be a considered judgment, some convincing reason can be found to account for the anomaly. We should like to find that the once accepted intuitive conviction is actually caused by a mistaken belief as to a matter fact of which we were unaware or fostered by what is admittedly a narrow bias of some kind. The rationale behind this fourth test is that while the considered judgments of competent judges are the most likely repository of the working out of men's sense of right and wrong, a more likely one, for example, than that of any particular individual's judgments alone, they may, nevertheless, contain certain deviations, or confusions, which are best discovered by comparing the considered judgments with principles which pass the first three tests and seeing which of the two tends to be felt incorrect in the light of reflection. . . .

4.4 A principle is evidenced to be reasonable to the extent that it satisfies jointly all of the foregoing tests. In practice, however, we are wise if we expect less than this. We are not likely to find easily a comprehensive explication which convinces all competent judges, which resolves all existing difficulties, and which, should there be anomalies in the considered judgments themselves, always tends to overcome them. We should expect satisfactory explications of but delimited areas of the considered judgments. Ethics must, like any other discipline, work its way piece by piece.

. . .

6.4 The manner of describing the decision procedure here advocated may have led the reader to believe that it claims to be a way of discovering justifiable ethical principles. There are, however, no precisely describable methods of discovery, and certainly the finding of a successful explication satisfying the tests of 4.3 will require at least some ingenuity. Therefore it is best to view the exposition as a description of the procedure of justification stated in reverse. Thus if a man were asked to justify his decision on a case, he should proceed as follows: first, he should show that, given the circumstances and the interests in conflict, his decision is capable of being explicated by the principles of justice. Second, he should evidence that these principles satisfy the tests in 4.3. If asked to proceed further, he should remark on the nature of considered judgments and competent judges and urge that one could hardly be expected to prefer judgments made under emotional duress, or in ignorance of the facts by unintelligent or mentally sick persons, and so on. Finally, he should stress that such considerations arise, if the demands for justification are pushed far enough, in validating inductive criteria as well as in justifying ethical principles. Provided an explication exists satisfying the tests in 4.3, moral actions can be justified in a manner analogous to the way in which decisions to believe a proposition, or theory, are justified.

6.5 Two possible objections remain to be considered. First, it may be said that, even if the foregoing decision procedure could be carried out in a particular case, the decision in question still would not be justified. To this I should say that we ought to inquire whether the person making the objection is not expecting too much. Perhaps he expects a justification procedure to show him how the decision is deducible from a synthetic a priori proposition.* The answer to a person with such hopes is that they are logically impossible to satisfy and that all we should expect is that moral decisions and ethical principles are capable of the same sort of justification as decisions to believe and inductive criteria. Secondly, it may be said that a set of principles satisfying the tests of 4.3 does not exist. To this I should say that while it is obvious that moral codes and customs have varied in time, and change from place to place, yet when we think of a successful explication as representing the invariant in the considered judgments of competent judges, then the variation of codes and customs is not decisive against the existence of such an explication. Such a question cannot be decided by analysis or by talking about possibilities, but only by exhibiting explications which are capable of satisfying the tests which are properly applied to them.

---

* Traditionally, a proposition which is known independently of particular sense experiences, yet which conveys genuine information about the world.

5

Utilitarianism

JOHN STUART MILL

John Stuart Mill (1806–1873) was among the most important British thinkers of the nineteenth century. A philosopher in the Empiricist tradition,* he published works on logic, scientific method, and epistemology, as well as ethics and social and political philosophy. His books include A System of Logic, Utilitarianism, *and* On Liberty.

In this selection, Mill presents an extended defense of utilitarianism, the view that the ultimate principle of morality is "Strive to produce as much overall happiness as possible." Mill was taught this approach by his father James Mill, who in turn learned it from the philosopher and social reformer Jeremy Bentham. However, whereas Bentham made no distinction between types of pleasures, Mill believed that some forms of happiness are more worthwhile than others. He argues that the pleasures of a Socrates are more valuable than those we share with animals because anyone who was "competently acquainted" with both would invariably choose the former. Whether this is true, and if so exactly what it proves, are questions for further thought.

Whatever form of it we favor, utilitarianism offers many advantages. As Mill notes, it provides a ready-made answer to the question of what to do when obligations conflict. For example, suppose you have promised to meet someone for lunch, but on the way encounter someone else drowning in a lake. If no single moral principle dominates, then you will have no principled way of deciding between your conflicting obligations to provide aid and keep your promises. However, if you are a utilitarian, you will give priority to whichever act brings more overall happiness—in this case, rescuing the drowning person. Aside from resolving conflicts, Mill points out that the principle of utility also explains why we accept such moral principles as "help others" and "keep your promises" in the first place. Such principles, Mill argues, reflect the fact that keeping promises and other favored practices generally bring great social benefits. These principles serve as signposts; they reflect collective past experience as to what maximizes happiness.

Toward the end of this selection, Mill offers a famous argument for the principle of utility. He appears to argue that whatever is desired is desirable, that in the last analysis people desire happiness and nothing else, that happiness is therefore the only truly desirable thing, and so that it should be maximized. This argument offers a number of opportunities for careful reflection and analysis. In assessing it, you may find it helpful to recall Feinberg's discussion of psychological egoism in reading 1.

---

*Empiricism is the view that all knowledge is grounded in, and derived from, experience.

What Utilitarianism Is   . . .

THE CREED WHICH accepts as the foundation of morals "utility" or the "greatest happiness principle" holds that actions are right in proportion as they tend to promote happiness; wrong as they tend to produce the reverse of happiness. By happiness is intended pleasure and the absence of pain; by unhappiness, pain and the privation of pleasure. To give a clear view of the moral standard set up by the theory, much more requires to be said; in particular, what things it includes in the ideas of pain and pleasure, and to what extent this is left an open question. But these supplementary explanations do not affect the theory of life on which this theory of morality is grounded—namely, that pleasure and freedom from pain are the only things desirable as ends; and that all desirable things (which are as numerous in the utilitarian as in any other scheme) are desirable either for pleasure inherent in themselves or as means to the promotion of pleasure and the prevention of pain.

Now such a theory of life excites in many minds, and among them in some of the most estimable in feeling and purpose, inveterate dislike. To suppose that life has (as they express it) no higher end than pleasure—no better and nobler object of desire and pursuit—they designate as utterly mean and groveling, as a doctrine worthy only of swine, to whom the followers of Epicurus were, at a very early period, contemptuously likened; and modern holders of the doctrine are occasionally made the subject of equally polite comparisons by its German, French, and English assailants.

When thus attacked, the Epicureans have always answered that it is not they, but their accusers, who represent human nature in a degrading light, since the accusation supposes human beings to be capable of no pleasures except those of which swine are capable. If this supposition were true, the charge could not be gainsaid, but would then be no longer an imputation; for if the sources of pleasure were precisely the same to human beings and to swine, the rule of life which is good enough for the one would be good enough for the other. The comparison of the Epicurean life to that of beasts is felt as degrading, precisely because a beast's pleasures do not satisfy a human being's conceptions of happiness. Human beings have faculties more elevated than the animal appetites and, when once made conscious of them, do not regard anything as happiness which does not include their gratification. I do not indeed, consider the Epicureans to have been by any means faultless in drawing out their scheme of consequences from the utilitarian principle. To do this in any sufficient manner, many Stoic, as well as Christian, elements require to be included. But there is no known Epicurean theory of life which does not assign to the pleasures of the intellect, of the feelings and imagination, and of the moral sentiments a much higher value as pleasures than to those of mere sensation. It must be admitted, however, that utilitarian writers in general have placed the superiority of mental over bodily pleasures chiefly in the greater permanency, safety, uncostliness, etc., of the former—that is, in their circumstantial advantages rather than in their intrinsic nature. And on all these points utilitarians have fully proved their case; but they might have taken the other and, as it may be called,

higher ground with entire consistency. It is quite compatible with the principle of utility to recognize the fact that some kinds of pleasure are more desirable and more valuable than others. It would be absurd that, while in estimating all other things quality is considered as well as quantity, the estimation of pleasure should be supposed to depend on quantity alone.

If I am asked what I mean by difference of quality in pleasures, or what makes one pleasure more valuable than another, merely as a pleasure, except its being greater in amount, there is but one possible answer. Of two pleasures, if there be one to which all or almost all who have experience of both give a decided preference, irrespective of any feeling of moral obligation to prefer it, that is the more desirable pleasure. If one of the two is, by those who are competently acquainted with both, placed so far above the other that they prefer it, even though knowing it to be attended with a greater amount of discontent, and would not resign it for any quantity of the other pleasure which their nature is capable of, we are justified in ascribing to the preferred enjoyment a superiority in quality so far outweighing quantity as to render it, in comparison, of small account.

Now it is an unquestionable fact that those who are equally acquainted with and equally capable of appreciating and enjoying both do give a most marked preference to the manner of existence which employs their higher faculties. Few human creatures would consent to be changed into any of the lower animals for a promise of the fullest allowance of a beast's pleasures; no intelligent human being would consent to be a fool, no instructed person would be an ignoramus, no person of feeling and conscience would be selfish and base, even though they should be persuaded that the fool, the dunce, or the rascal is better satisfied with his lot than they are with theirs. They would not resign what they possess more than he for the most complete satisfaction of all the desires which they have in common with him. If they ever fancy they would, it is only in cases of unhappiness so extreme that to escape from it they would exchange their lot for almost any other, however undesirable in their own eyes. A being of higher faculties requires more to make him happy, is capable probably of more acute suffering, and certainly accessible to it at more points, than one of an inferior type; but in spite of these liabilities, he can never really wish to sink into what he feels to be a lower grade of existence. We may give what explanation we please of this unwillingness; we may attribute it to pride, a name which is given indiscriminately to some of the most and to some of the least estimable feelings of which mankind are capable; we may refer it to the love of liberty and personal independence, an appeal to which was with the Stoics one of the most effective means for the inculcation of it; to the love of power or to the love of excitement, both of which do really enter into and contribute to it; but its most appropriate appellation is a sense of dignity, which all human beings possess in one form or other, and in some, though by no means in exact, proportion to their higher faculties, and which is so essential a part of the happiness of those in whom it is strong that nothing which conflicts with it could be otherwise than momentarily an object of desire to them. Whoever supposes that this preference takes place at a sacrifice of happiness—that the

superior being, in anything like equal circumstances, is not happier than the inferior—confounds the two very different ideas of happiness and content. It is indisputable that the being whose capacities of enjoyment are low has the greatest chance of having them fully satisfied; and a highly endowed being will always feel that any happiness which he can look for, as the world is constituted, is imperfect. But he can learn to bear its imperfections, if they are at all bearable; and they will not make him envy the being who is indeed unconscious of the imperfections, but only because he feels not at all the good which those imperfections qualify. It is better to be a human being dissatisfied than a pig satisfied; better to be Socrates dissatisfied than a fool satisfied. And if the fool, or the pig, are of a different opinion, it is because they only know their own side of the question. The other party to the comparison knows both sides.

It may be objected that many who are capable of the higher pleasures occasionally, under the influence of temptation, postpone them to the lower. But this is quite compatible with a full appreciation of the intrinsic superiority of the higher. Men often, from infirmity of character, make their election for the nearer good, though they know it to be the less valuable; and this no less when the choice is between two bodily pleasures than when it is between bodily and mental. They pursue sensual indulgences to the injury of health, though perfectly aware that health is the greater good. It may be further objected that many who begin with youthful enthusiasm for everything noble, as they advance in years, sink into indolence and selfishness. But I do not believe that those who undergo this very common change voluntarily choose the lower description of pleasures in preference to the higher. I believe that, before they devote themselves exclusively to the one, they have already become incapable of the other. Capacity for the nobler feelings is in most natures a very tender plant, easily killed, not only by hostile influences, but by mere want of sustenance; and in the majority of young persons it speedily dies away if the occupations to which their position in life has devoted them, and the society into which it has thrown them, are not favorable to keeping that higher capacity in exercise. Men lose their high aspirations as they lose their intellectual tastes, because they have not time or opportunity for indulging them; and they addict themselves to inferior pleasures, not because they deliberately prefer them, but because they are either the only ones to which they have access or the only ones which they are any longer capable of enjoying. It may be questioned whether anyone who has remained equally susceptible to both classes of pleasures ever knowingly and calmly preferred the lower, though many, in all ages, have broken down in an ineffectual attempt to combine both.

From this verdict of the only competent judges, I apprehend there can be no appeal. On a question which is the best worth having of two pleasures, or which of two modes of existence is the most grateful to the feelings, apart from its moral attributes and from its consequences, the judgment of these who are qualified by knowledge of both, or, if they differ, that of the majority among them, must be admitted as final. And there needs be the less hesitation to accept this judgment respecting the quality of pleasures, since there is no other tribunal to be referred to even on the question of quantity. What means are there of

determining which is the acutest of two pains, or the intensest of two pleasurable sensations, except the general suffrage of those who are familiar with both? Neither pains nor pleasures are homogeneous, and pain is always heterogeneous with pleasure. What is there to decide whether a particular pleasure is worth purchasing at the cost of a particular pain, except the feelings and judgment of the experienced? When, therefore, those feelings and judgment declare the pleasures derived from the higher faculties to be preferable *in kind,* apart from the question of intensity, to those of which the animal nature, disjoined from the higher faculties, is susceptible, they are entitled on this subject to the same regard.

. . .

I must again repeat what the assailants of utilitarianism seldom have the justice to acknowledge, that the happiness which forms the utilitarian standard of what is right in conduct is not the agent's own happiness but that of all concerned. As between his own happiness and that of others, utilitarianism requires him to be as strictly impartial as a disinterested and benevolent spectator. In the golden rule of Jesus of Nazareth, we read the complete spirit of the ethics of utility. "To do as you would be done by," and "to love your neighbor as your self," constitute the ideal perfection of utilitarian morality. As the means of making the nearest approach to this ideal, utility would enjoin, first, that laws and social arrangements should place the happiness or (as, speaking practically, it may be called) the interest of every individual as nearly as possible in harmony with the interest of the whole; and, secondly, that education and opinion, which have so vast a power over human character, should so use that power as to establish in the mind of every individual an indissoluble association between his own happiness and the good of the whole, especially between his own happiness and the practice of such modes of conduct, negative and positive, as regard for the universal happiness prescribes; so that not only he may be unable to conceive the possibility of happiness to himself, consistently with conduct opposed to the general good, but also that a direct impulse to promote the general good may be in every individual one of the habitual motives of action, and the sentiments connected therewith may fill a large and prominent place in every human being's sentient existence. If the impugners of the utilitarian morality represented it to their own minds in this its true character, I know not what recommendation possessed by any other morality they could possibly affirm to be wanting to it; what more beautiful or more exalted developments of human nature any other ethical system can be supposed to foster, or what springs of action, not accessible to the utilitarian, such systems rely on for giving effect to their mandates.

The objectors to utilitarianism cannot always be charged with representing it in a discreditable light. On the contrary, those among among them who entertain anything like a just idea of its disinterested character sometimes find fault with its standard as being too high for humanity. They say it is exacting too much to require that people shall always act from the inducement of promoting the general interest of society. But this is to mistake the very meaning

of a standard of morals and confound the rule of action with the motive of it. It is the business of ethics to tell us what are our duties, or by what test we may know them; but no system of ethics requires that the sole motive of all we do shall be a feeling of duty; on the contrary, ninety-nine hundredths of all our actions are done from other motives, and rightly so done if the rule of duty does not condemn them. It is the more unjust to utilitarianism that this particular misapprehension should be made a ground of objection to it, inasmuch as utilitarian moralists have gone beyond almost all others in affirming that the motive has nothing to do with the morality of the action, though much with the worth of the agent. He who saves a fellow creature from drowning does what is morally right, whether his motive be duty or the hope of being paid for his trouble; he who betrays the friend that trusts him is guilty of a crime, even if his object be to serve another friend to whom he is under greater obligations. But to speak only of actions done from the motive or duty, and in direct obedience to principle: it is a misapprehension of the utilitarian mode of thought to conceive it as implying that people should fix their minds upon so wide a generality as the world, or society at large. The great majority of good actions are intended not for the benefit of the world, but for that of individuals, of which the good of the world is made up; and the thoughts of the most virtuous man need not on these occasions travel beyond the particular persons concerned, except so far as is necessary to assure himself that in benefiting them he is not violating the rights, that is, the legitimate and authorized expectations, of anyone else. The multiplication of happiness is, according to the utilitarian ethics, the object of virtue: the occasions on which any person (except one in a thousand) has it in his power to do this on an extended scale—in other words, to be a public benefactor—are but exceptional; and on these occasions alone is he called on to consider public utility; in every other case, private utility, the interest or happiness of some few persons, is all he has to attend to. Those alone the influence of whose actions extends to society in general need concern themselves habitually about so large an object. In the case of abstinences indeed— of things which people forbear to do from moral considerations, though the consequences in the particular case might be beneficial—it would be unworthy of an intelligent agent not to be consciously aware that the action is of a class which, if practiced generally, would be generally injurious, and that this is the ground of the obligation to abstain from it. The amount of regard for the public interest implied in this recognition is no greater than is demanded by every system of morals, for they all enjoin to abstain from whatever is manifestly pernicious to society.

. . .

Again, utility is often summarily stigmatized as an immoral doctrine by giving it the name of "expediency," and taking advantage of the popular use of that term to contrast it with principle. But the expedient, in the sense in which it is opposed to the right, generally means that which is expedient for the particular interest of the agent himself; as when a minister sacrifices the interests of his country to keep himself in place. When it means anything better than this, it

means that which is expedient for some immediate object, some temporary purpose, but which violates a rule whose observance is expedient in a much higher degree. The expedient, in this sense, instead of being the same thing with the useful, is a branch of the hurtful. Thus it would often be expedient, for the purpose of getting over some momentary embarassment, or attaining some object immediately useful to ourselves or others, to tell a lie. But inasmuch as the cultivation in ourselves of a sensitive feeling on the subject of veracity is one of the most useful, and the enfeeblement of that feeling one of the most hurtful, things to which our conduct can be instrumental; and inasmuch as any, even unintentional, deviation from truth does that much toward weakening the trustworthiness of human assertion, which is not only the principal support of all present social well-being, but the insufficiency of which does more than any one thing that can be named to keep back civilization, virtue, everything on which human happiness on the largest scale depends—we feel that the violation, for a present advantage, of a rule of such transcendent expediency is not expedient, and that he who, for the sake of convenience to himself or to some other individual, does what depends on him to deprive mankind of the good, and inflict upon them the evil, involved in the greater or less reliance which they can place in each other's words, acts the part of one of their worst enemies. Yet that even this rule, sacred as it is, admits of possible exceptions is acknowledged by all moralists; the chief of which is when the withholding of some fact (as of information from a malefactor, or of bad news from a person dangerously ill) would save an individual (especially an individual other than oneself) from great and unmerited evil, and when the withholding can only be effected by denial. But in order that the exception may not extend itself beyond the need, and may have the least possible effect in weakening reliance on veracity, it ought to be recognized and, if possible, its limits defined; and, if the principle of utility is good for anything, it must be good for weighing these conflicting utilities against one another and marking out the region within which one or the other preponderates.

Again, defenders of utility often find themselves called upon to reply to such objections as this—that there is not time, previous to action, for calculating and weighing the effects of any line of conduct on the general happiness. This is exactly as if anyone were to say that it is impossible to guide our conduct by Christianity because there is not time, on every occasion on which anything has to be done, to read through the Old and New Testaments. The answer to the objection is that there has been ample time, namely, the whole past duration of the human species. During all that time mankind have been learning by experience the tendencies of actions; on which experience all the prudence as well as all the morality of life are dependent. People talk as if the commencement of this course of experience had hitherto been put off, and as if, at the moment when some man feels tempted to meddle with the property or life of another, he had to begin considering for the first time whether murder and theft are injurious to human happiness. Even then I do not think that he would find the question very puzzling; but, at all events, the matter is now done to his hand. It is truly a whimsical supposition that, if mankind were agreed in

considering utility to be the test of morality, they would remain without any agreement as to what *is* useful, and would take no measures for having their notions on the subject taught to the young and enforced by law and opinion. There is no difficulty in proving any ethical standard whatever to work ill if we suppose universal idiocy to be conjoined with it; but on any hypothesis short of that, mankind must by this time have acquired positive beliefs as to the effects of some actions on their happiness; and the beliefs which have thus come down are the rules of morality for the multitude, and for the philosopher until he has succeeded in finding better. That philosophers might easily do this, even now, on many subjects; that the received code of ethics is by no means of divine right; and that mankind have still much to learn as to the effects of actions on the general happiness, I admit or rather earnestly maintain. The corollaries from the principle of utility, like the precepts of every practical art, admit of indefinite improvement, and, in a progressive state of the human mind, their improvement is perpetually going on. But to consider the rules of morality as improvable is one thing; to pass over the intermediate generalization entirely and endeavor to test each individual action directly by the first principle is another. It is a strange notion that the acknowledgment of a first principle is inconsistent with the admission of secondary ones. To inform a traveler respecting the place of his ultimate destination is not to forbid the use of landmarks and direction-posts on the way. The proposition that happiness is the end and aim of morality does not mean that no road ought to be laid down to that goal, or that persons going thither should not be advised to take one direction rather than another. Men really ought to leave off talking a kind of nonsense on this subject, which they would neither talk nor listen to on other matters of practical concernment. Nobody argues that the art of navigation is not founded on astronomy because sailors cannot wait to calculate the Nautical Almanac. Being rational creatures, they go to sea with it ready calculated; and all rational creatures go out upon the sea of life with their minds made up on the common questions of right and wrong, as well as on many of the far more difficult questions of wise and foolish. And this, as long as foresight is a human quality, it is to be presumed they will continue to do. Whatever we adopt as the fundamental principle of morality, we require subordinate principles to apply it by; the impossibility of doing without them, being common to all systems, can afford no argument against any one in particular; but gravely to argue as if no such secondary principles could be had, and as if mankind had remained till now, and always must remain, without drawing any general conclusions from the experience of human life is as high a pitch, I think, as absurdity has ever reached in philosophical controversy.

The remainder of the stock arguments against utilitarianism mostly consist in laying to its charge the common infirmities of human nature, and the general difficulties which embarrass conscientious persons in shaping their course through life. We are told that a utilitarian will be apt to make his own particular case an exception to moral rules, and, when under temptation, will see a utility in the breach of a rule, greater than he will see in its observance. But is utility the only creed which is able to furnish us with excuses for evil-doing and means

of cheating our own conscience? They are afforded in abundance by all doctrines which recognize as a fact in morals the existence of conflicting considerations, which all doctrines do that have been believed by sane persons. It is not the fault of any creed, but of the complicated nature of human affairs, that rules of conduct cannot be so framed as to require no exceptions, and that hardly any kind of action can safely be laid down as either always obligatory or always condemnable. There is no ethical creed which does not temper the rigidity of its laws by giving a certain latitude, under the moral responsibility of the agent, for accommodation to peculiarities of circumstances; and under every creed, at the opening thus made, self-deception and dishonest casuistry get in. There exists no moral system under which there do not arise unequivocal cases of conflicting obligation. These are the real difficulties, the knotty points both in the theory of ethics and in the conscientious guidance of personal conduct. They are overcome practically, with greater or with less success, according to the intellect and virtue of the individual; but it can hardly be pretended that anyone will be the less qualified for dealing with them, from possessing an ultimate standard to which conflicting rights and duties can be referred. If utility is the ultimate source of moral obligations, utility may be invoked to decide between them when their demands are incompatible. Though the application of the standard may be difficult, it is better than none at all; while in other systems, the moral laws all claiming independent authority, there is no common umpire entitled to interfere between them; their claims to precedence one over another rest on little better than sophistry, and, unless determined, as they generally are, by the unacknowledged influence of consideration of utility, afford a free scope for the action of personal desires and partialities. We must remember that only in these cases of conflict between secondary principles is it requisite that first principles should be appealed to. There is no case of moral obligation in which some secondary principle is not involved; and if only one, there can seldom be any real doubt which one it is, in the mind of any person by whom the principle itself is recognized.

. . .

Of What Sort of Proof the Principle of Utility Is Susceptible

It has already been remarked that questions of ultimate ends do not admit of proof, in the ordinary acceptation of the term. To be incapable of proof by reasoning is common to all first principles, to the first premises of our knowledge, as well as to those of our conduct. But the former, being matters of fact, may be the subject of a direct appeal to the faculties which judge of fact—namely, our senses and our internal consciousness. Can an appeal be made to the same faculties on questions of practical ends? Or by what other faculty is cognizance taken of them?

Questions about ends are, in other words, questions about what things are desirable. The utilitarian doctrine is that happiness is desirable, and the only thing desirable, as an end; all other things being only desirable as means to

that end. What ought to be required of this doctrine, what conditions is it requisite that the doctrine should fulfill—to make good its claim to be believed?

The only proof capable of being given that an object is visible is that people actually see it. The only proof that a sound is audible is that people hear it; and so of the other sources of our experience. In like manner, I apprehend, the sole evidence it is possible to produce that anything is desirable is that people do actually desire it. If the end which the utilitarian doctrine proposes to itself were not, in theory and in practice, acknowledged to be an end, nothing could ever convince any person that it was so. No reason can be given why the general happiness is desirable, except that each person, so far as he believes it to be attainable, desires his own happiness. This, however, being a fact, we have not only all the proof which the case admits of, but all which it is possible to require, that happiness is a good, that each person's happiness is a good to that person, and the general happiness, therefore, a good to the aggregate of all persons. Happiness has made out its title as *one* of the ends of conduct and, consequently, one of the criteria of morality.

But it has not, by this alone, proved itself to be the sole criterion. To do that, it would seem, by the same rule, necessary to show, not only that people desire happiness, but that they never desire anything else. Now it is palpable that they do desire things which, in common language, are decidedly distinguished from happiness. They desire, for example, virtue and the absence of vice no less really than pleasure and the absence of pain. The desire of virtue is not as universal, but it is as authentic a fact as the desire of happiness. And hence the opponents of the utilitarian standard deem that they have a right to infer that there are other ends of human action besides happiness, and that happiness is not the standard of approbation and disapprobation.

But does the utilitarian doctrine deny that people desire virtue, or maintain that virtue is not a thing to be desired? The very reverse. It maintains not only that virtue is to be desired, but that is is to be desired disinterestedly, for itself. Whatever may be the opinion of utilitarian moralists as to the original conditions by which virtue is made virtue, however they may believe (as they do) that actions and dispositions are only virtuous because they promote another end than virtue, yet this being granted, and it having been decided, from considerations of this description, what *is* virtuous, they not only place virtue at the very head of the things which are good as means to the ultimate end, but they also recognize as a psychological fact the possibility of its being, to the individual, a good in itself, without looking to any end beyond it; and hold that the mind is not in a right state, not in a state conformable to utility, not in the state most conducive to the general happiness, unless it does love virtue in this manner—as a thing desirable in itself, even although, in the individual instance, it should not produce those other desirable consequences which it tends to produce, and on account of which it is held to be virtue. This opinion is not, in the smallest degree, a departure from the happiness principle. The ingredients of happiness are very various, and each of them is desirable in itself, and not merely when considered as swelling an aggregate. The principle of

utility does not mean that any given pleasure, as music, for instance, or any given exemption from pain, as for example health, is to be looked upon as means to a collective something termed happiness, and to be desired on that account. They are desired and desirable in and for themselves; besides being means, they are a part of the end. Virtue, according to the utilitarian doctrine is not naturally and originally part of the end, but it is capable of becoming so; and in those who live it disinterestedly it has become so, and is desired and cherished, not as a means to happiness, but as a part of their happiness.

To illustrate this further, we may remember that virtue is not the only thing originally a means, and which if it were not a means to anything else would be and remain indifferent, but which by association with what it is a means to comes to be desired for itself, and that too with the utmost intensity. What, for example, shall we say of the love of money? There is nothing originally more desirable about money than about any heap of glittering pebbles. Its worth is solely that of the things which it will buy; the desires for other things than itself, which it is a means of gratifying. Yet the love of money is not only one of the strongest moving forces of human life, but money is, in many cases, desired in and for itself; the desire to possess it is often stronger than the desire to use it, and goes on increasing when all the desires which point to ends beyond it, to be compassed by it, are falling off. It may, then, be said truly that money is desired not for the sake of an end, but as part of the end. From being a means to happiness, it has come to be itself a principal ingredient of the individual's conception of happiness. The same may be said of the majority of the great objects of human life: power, for example, or fame, except that to each of these there is a certain amount of immediate pleasure annexed, which has at least the semblance of being naturally inherent in them—a thing which cannot be said of money. Still, however, the strongest natural attraction, both of power and of fame, is the immense aid they give to the attainment of our other wishes; and it is the strong association thus generated between them and all our objects of desire which gives to the direct desire of them the intensity it often assumes, so as in some characters to surpass in strength all other desires. In these cases the means have become a part of the end, and a more important part of it than any of the things which they are means to. What was once desired as an instrument for the attainment of happiness has come to be desired for its own sake. In being desired for its own sake it is, however, desired as *part* of happiness. The person is made, or thinks he would be made, happy by its mere possession; and is made unhappy by failure to obtain it. The desire of it is not a different thing from the desire of happiness any more than the love of music or the desire of health. They are included in happiness. They are some of the elements of which the desire of happiness is made up. Happiness is not an abstract idea but a concrete whole; and these are some of its parts. And the utilitarian standard sanctions and approves their being so. Life would be a poor thing, very ill provided with sources of happiness, if there were not this provision of nature by which things originally indifferent, but conducive to, or otherwise associated with, the satisfaction of our primitive desires, become in themselves sources of pleasure more valuable than the primitive pleasures, both in per-

manency, in the space of human existence that they are capable of covering, and even in intensity.

Virtue, according to the utilitarian conception, is a good of this description. There was no original desire of it, or motive to it, save its conduciveness to pleasure, and especially to protection from pain. But through the association thus formed it may be felt a good in itself, and desired as such with as great intensity as any other good; and with this difference between it and the love of money, of power, or of fame—that all of these may, and often do, render the individual noxious to the other members of the society to which he belongs, whereas there is nothing which makes him so much a blessing to them as the cultivation of the disinterested love of virtue. And consequently, the utilitarian standard, while it tolerates and approves those other acquired desires, up to the point beyond which they would be more injurious to the general happiness than promotive of it, enjoins and requires the cultivation of the love of virtue up to the greatest strength possible, as being above all things important to the general happiness.

It results from the preceding considerations that there is in reality nothing desired except happiness. Whatever is desired otherwise than as a means to some end beyond itself, and ultimately to happiness, is desired as itself a part of happiness, and is not desired for itself until it has become so. Those who desire virtue for its own sake desire it either because the consciousness of it is a pleasure, or because the consciousness of being without it is a pain, or for both reasons united; as in truth the pleasure and pain seldom exist separately, but almost always together—the same person feeling pleasure in the degree of virtue attained, and pain in not having attained more. If one of these gave him no pleasure, and the other no pain, he would not love or desire virtue, or would desire it only for the other benefits which it might produce to himself or to persons whom he cared for.

We have now, then, an answer to the question, of what sort of proof the principle of utility is susceptible. If the opinion which I have now stated is psychologically true—if human nature is so constituted as to desire nothing which is not either a part of happiness or a means of happiness—we can have no other proof, and we require no other, that these are the only things desirable. If so, happiness is the sole end of human action, and the promotion of it the test by which to judge of all human conduct; from whence it necessarily follows that it must be the criterion of morality, since a part is included in the whole.

And now to decide whether this is really so, whether mankind do desire nothing for itself but that which is a pleasure to them, or of which the absence is a pain, we have evidently arrived at a question of fact and experience, dependent, like all similar questions, upon evidence. It can only be determined by practiced self-consciousness and self-observation, assisted by observation of others. I believe that these sources of evidence, impartially consulted, will declare that desiring a thing and finding it pleasant, aversion to it and thinking of it as painful, are phenomena entirely inseparable or, rather, two parts of the same phenomenon—in strictness of language, two different modes of naming the same psychological fact; that to think of an object as desirable (unless for the

sake of its consequences) and to think of it as pleasant are one and the same thing; and that to desire anything except in proportion as the idea of it is pleasant is a physical and metaphysical impossibility.

So obvious does this appear to me that I expect it will hardly be disputed; and the objection made will be, not that desire can possibly be directed to anything ultimately except pleasure and exemption from pain, but that the will is a different thing from desire; that a person of confirmed virtue or any other person whose purposes are fixed carries out his purposes without any thought of the pleasure he has in contemplating them or expects to derive from their fulfillment, and persists in acting on them, even though these pleasures are much diminished by changes in his character or decay of his passive sensibilities, or are outweighed by the pains which the pursuit of the purposes may bring upon him. All this I fully admit and have stated it elsewhere as positively and emphatically as anyone. Will, the active phenomenon, is a different thing from desire, the state of passive sensibility, and, though originally an offshoot from it, may in time take root and detach itself from the parent stock, so much so that in the case of a habitual purpose, instead of willing the thing because we desire it, we often desire it only because we will it. This, however, is but an instance of that familiar fact, the power of habit, and is nowise confined to the case of virtuous actions. Many indifferent things which men originally did from a motive of some sort they continue to do from habit. Sometimes this is done unconsciously, the consciousness coming only after the action; at other times with conscious volition, but volition which has become habitual and is put in operation by the force of habit, in opposition perhaps to the deliberate preference, as often happens with those who have contracted habits of vicious or hurtful indulgence. Third and last comes the case in which the habitual act of will in the individual instance is not in contradiction to the general intention prevailing at other times, but in fulfillment of it, as in the case of the person of confirmed virtue and of all who pursue deliberately and consistently any determinate end. The distinction between will and desire thus understood is an authentic and highly important psychological fact; but the fact consists solely in this—that will, like all other parts of our constitution, is amenable to habit, and that we may will from habit what we no longer desire for itself, or desire only because we will it. It is not the less true that will, in the beginning, is entirely produced by desire, including in that term the repelling influence of pain as well as the attractive one of pleasure. Let us take into consideration no longer the person who has a confirmed will to do right, but him in whom that virtuous will is still feeble, conquerable by temptation, and not to be fully relied on; by what means can it be strengthened? How can the will to be virtuous, where it does not exist in sufficient force, be implanted or awakened? Only by making the person *desire* virtue—by making him think of it in a pleasurable light, or of its absence in a painful one. It is by associating the doing right with pleasure, or the wrong with pain, or by eliciting and impressing and bringing home to the person's experience the pleasure naturally involved in the one or the pain in the other, that it is possible to call forth that will to be virtuous which, when confirmed, acts without any thought of either pleasure or pain.

Will is the child of desire, and passes out of the dominion of its parent only to come under that of habit. That which is the result of habit affords no presumption of being intrinsically good; and there would be no reason for wishing that the purpose of virtue should become independent of pleasure and pain were it not that the influence of the pleasurable and painful associations which prompt to virtue is not sufficiently to be depended on for unerring constancy of action until it has acquired the support of habit. Both in feeling and in conduct, habit is the only thing which imparts certainty; and it is because of the importance to others of being able to rely absolutely on one's feelings and conduct, and to oneself of being able to rely on one's own, that the will to do right ought to be cultivated into this habitual independence. In other words, this state of the will is a means to good, not intrinsically a good; and does not contradict the doctrine that nothing is a good to human beings but in so far as it is either itself pleasurable or a means of attaining pleasure or averting pain.

But if this doctrine be true, the principle of utility is proved. Whether it is so or not must now be left to the consideration of the thoughtful reader.

6

Some Problems with Utilitarianism

NORMAN E. BOWIE and ROBERT L. SIMON

Norman Bowie (b. 1942) is Professor of Philosophy at the University of Delaware. Robert Simon (b. 1941) is Kenan Professor of Philosophy at Hamilton College. Both have written extensively on topics in social and political philosophy. This selection is from their book The Individual and the Political Order.

In this brief selection, Bowie and Simon discuss three important objections to utilitarianism. The first objection, dramatized by a story introduced by Bernard Williams, is that because utilitarianism considers only an act's consequences, it is insensitive to the ways in which bringing about those consequences may compromise an agent's integrity. The second objection, introduced in a quotation from John Rawls (see readings 4 and 18), is that in tolerating the unhappiness of one person to promote the greater happiness of another, utilitarianism mistakenly treats individuals as though they were merely parts of a single superperson. (For relevant discussion, see reading 40 by Derek Parfit.) The third objection, also introduced in a quotation from Rawls, is that because utilitarianism does not consider what *makes people happy, it assigns weight to the satisfaction of some desires, such as those of the racist, which we intuitively feel should have no weight.*

· · ·

PERHAPS THE PLACE to begin this aspect of the debate is with a hypothetical but very dramatic example described by Bernard Williams:

Jim finds himself in the central square of a small South American town. Tied up against the wall are a row of twenty Indians, most terrified, a few defiant, in front of them several armed men in uniform. A heavy man in a sweat-stained khaki shirt turns out to be the captain in charge and, after a good deal of questioning of Jim which establishes that he got there by accident while on a botanical expedition, explains that the Indians are a random group of the inhabitants who, after recent acts of protest against the government, are just about to be killed to remind other possible protestors of the advantages of not protesting. However, since Jim is an honoured visitor from another land, the captain is happy to offer him a guest's privilege of killing one of the Indians himself. If Jim accepts, then as a special mark of the occasion, the other Indians will be let off. Of course, if Jim refuses, then there is no special occasion, and Pedro here will do what he was about to do when Jim arrived, and kill them all. Jim, with some desperate rec-

ollection of schoolboy fiction, wonders whether if he got hold of a gun, he could hold the captain, Pedro and the rest of the soldiers to threat, but it is quite clear from the set-up that nothing of the kind is going to work: any attempt at that sort of thing will mean that all the Indians will be killed, and himself. The men against the wall, and the other villagers, understand the situation, and are obviously begging him to accept. What should he do?[1]

It would seem that on any utilitarian analysis—even on the complex versions of Brandt and Braybrooke, Jim ought to kill one Indian so that nineteen others would be saved. A utilitarian of any stripe should find Jim's question rather easy to answer. A nonutilitarian might find Jim's question very difficult to answer, however. What makes the question difficult for the nonutilitarian is that something other than future consequences should be considered. Jim must consider not only the number of dead Indians, but the fact that if he chooses one way he is a killer, whereas if he chooses another way he is not. If Jim kills an Indian, then Jim himself has killed. However, if Jim refuses to kill an Indian, than we cannot say that Jim has killed twenty Indians; perhaps we cannot even say that Jim caused the twenty Indians to be killed. What we think Williams is driving at is the fact that one's *position* in a situation makes a difference. There is an integrity of a position or role that cannot be captured under the utilitarian umbrella.

Jim does not have the same responsibility to the twenty Indians that Pedro would kill as Jim does to the one Indian he would kill. Of course, it may be that he should kill one to save twenty, but there are *complications* in that question that no utilitarian can understand.

The utilitarian's failure to consider the position or role one holds in the chain of consequences is symptomatic of a serious deficiency in the way utilitarians consider individuals. John Rawls—at one time an adherent of rule utilitarianism—puts the criticism this way:

He charges the individualist theory of utilitarianism with ignoring the distinctions that exist among persons. Since utilitarianism has traditionally been viewed as an individualist theory par excellence, how is it possible that it ignores personalities? Rawls says that utilitarianism extends to society the principle of choice for one man:

> It is customary to think of utilitarianism as individualistic, and certainly there are good reasons for this. The utilitarians were strong defenders of liberty and freedom of thought and they held that the good of society is constituted by the advantages enjoyed by individuals. Yet utilitarianism is not individualistic, at least when arrived at by the more natural course of reflection, in that, by conflating all systems of desires, it applies to the society the principle of choice for one

---

[1] Bernard Williams, "A Critique of Utilitarianism," in *Utilitarianism: For and Against* by J. J. C. Smart and Bernard Williams (New York: Cambridge University Press, 1973) pp. 98–99.

man. . . . There is no reason to suppose that the principles which should regulate an association of men is simply an extension of the principle of choice for one man.[2]

What Rawls seems to be saying is this. Under utilitarian theory, each person strives to maximize his net happiness with due account given to the intensity of his desires. So far, the utilitarian analysis is individualistic in the accepted sense. We then ask what policies a society should pursue. At this point, the utilitarian treats society as a single person. The satisfactions and frustrations of desires of the individuals in society are summed up, with the frustrations of some individuals canceling out the happiness of others. The policy that ought to be adopted is the one that maximizes net happiness. This answer looks at society as an individual who has balanced the gains and losses in order to achieve the greatest balance of happiness. Note the contrast in point of view, however. When Jones's desire for a third martini is denied because Jones wishes to avoid a headache tomorrow, both the desire frustrated and the desire fulfilled are desires of the same individual. However, when policy X, which leads to the greatest happiness on balance, cancels out the wants of Jones in favor of the wants of Smith, the analogy with a single individual is no longer legitimate. The frustration of Smith is not like the frustration of Jones's desire for a third martini.

. . .

Just as the utilitarians make no distinctions among persons they also make no distinctions among desires. Utilitarians make much of the fact that utilitarianism is committed to equality, since each person's desires are given consideration. The important question, however, is how much each person's desires should count. The only factor most utilitarians consider is intensity. Those with more intense desires are provided with proportionally more pleasure. However, this is hardly the only difference that should enter in. Consider a racist society, for example. On strictly utilitarian grounds, the intense desires of the racist majority would count more than the more passive desires of the oppressed. Surely that is unjust. Indeed, the reader might ask, "Should certain desires be counted at all?" For example, would it be unjust not to count the racist's hatred? Many would think not:

> In utilitarianism the satisfaction of any desire has some value in itself which must be taken into account in deciding what is right. In calculating the greatest balance of satisfaction it does not matter, except indirectly what the desires are for. We are to arrange institutions so as to obtain the greatest sum of satisfactions, we ask no questions about their source or quality but only how their satisfaction would affect the total of well-being. Social welfare depends directly and solely upon the levels of satisfaction or dissatisfaction of individuals. Thus, if men take

[2] John Rawls, *A Theory of Justice* (Cambridge, Massachusetts: Harvard University Press, 1971), pp. 28–29.

a certain pleasure in discriminating against one another, in subjecting others to a lesser liberty as a means of enhancing their self-respect, then the satisfaction of these desires must be weighed in our deliberations according to their intensity, or whatever, along with other desires.[3]

To conclude this discussion, one might ask what would motivate an individual to sacrifice his good for the public good even if those who gain are already better off. Traditionally the utilitarians have appealed to sympathy. However, to expect one to sacrifice further for those who are already better off is to place a heavy burden on sympathy indeed! Would not the less fortunate be extremely bitter at having to sacrifice even more for the benefit of the more fortunate? Rawls believes that sympathy cannot supply the complete motivation for utilitarian behavior on the part of individuals and that as a result a society with a utilitarian morality and political philosophy would be highly unstable.

. . .

[3] Ibid., pp. 30–31.

7
Utilitarianism and Non-Utilitarian Intuitions

R. M. HARE

R.M. Hare (b. 1919) is White's Professor of Moral Philosophy at Corpus Christi College, Oxford University. He has done important work both in moral theory and in the application of moral theory to practical problems. His major works include The Language of Morals, Freedom and Reason, *and* Moral Thinking.

In this selection, Hare defends utilitarianism against the charge that it sometimes licenses intuitively wrong acts such as theft and murder, and that it otherwise yields apparently unacceptable results. (Norman Bowie and Robert Simon present variants of this charge in reading 6.) Hare's response rests on a distinction between two levels of moral thought. When people are detached and at leisure, they function at what Hare calls the "critical level." Here the aim is to choose relatively simple principles of action that can guide us in our day-to-day activities. The proper way of selecting such principles is to ask which courses of action generally maximize happiness. By contrast, at the level of immediate action, or "intuitive level," we do not appeal to the principle of utility. Instead, we merely apply the principles previously chosen at the critical level.

Once the two levels are clearly distinguished, Hare argues that the intuitive objections to utilitarianism disappear. The intuitions that murder and theft are wrong merely reflect our commitment to principles chosen at the critical level for their utility—a commitment that has been reinforced by a system of moral conditioning, that was chosen itself for its social utility. Moreover, even in cases that are said to pose problems for the utilitarian— for example, cases in which a doctor can save two lives by killing one person and transplanting his organs—the consequences of acts such as killing are hard to predict. Because of this, we can best maximize utility by sticking with the prohibition against killing that was adopted at the critical level.

By distinguishing between the critical and intuitive levels, Hare elaborates and sharpens Mill's contention that received moral beliefs, though subject to revision, serve as signposts or guides to what maximizes happiness (reading 5). The success of Hare's approach is left for you to judge. One way of testing it is to apply it to Bernard Williams's story about Pedro and the Indians in reading 6; another is to compare it with John Rawls's very different approach to moral judgments or intuitions in reading 4.

8.1 The two remaining chapters of this part will be devoted to answering some objections commonly made against utilitarianism, which might also be, and have been, encountered by my own theory. Since nearly all these objections employ the same basic move, originating in the same misunderstanding, it may be helpful if I first explain the move and the answer to it in quite general terms. I shall do this in the form of some simple instructions to students, first on how to manufacture objections of this sort, and then on how to demolish them. I hope thereby to forewarn and forearm them against anybody who tries to waste too much of their time with such objections; the answer to them all is the same, and one exercise in dealing with them is enough.

Suppose then that you are in a disputation with a utilitarian. Your object should be to enlist the sympathies of your audience on your side by showing that the utilitarian is committed to views which nearly everybody finds counterintuitive. What you have to do, therefore, is to find some moral opinion which nearly everybody will agree with, and bring utilitarianism into conflict with it. It is not necessary to choose for this purpose an opinion that can be defended by argument; any widely held prejudice will do. I have heard this kind of objection based on premises like 'Surely any theory is absurd which makes cruelty to animals as wicked as the same degree of cruelty to humans;' and no doubt in earlier centuries 'blacks' and 'whites' would have done as well. But obviously it is better if the opinion is a defensible one; the objection will then seem even more plausible.

Having selected your favoured received opinion, you can then proceed to bring utilitarianism into conflict with it in the following way. You find some example, rather simply described, in which, on an obvious interpretation of utilitarianism (and nearly all the versions of it can be made susceptible to this treatment, except for some versions of rule-utilitarianism* which are highly implausible on other grounds) the utilitarian is committed to prescribing an act which almost everybody will agree is wrong. Give your case as much verisimilitude as you can. Professional opponents of utilitarianism are not always as careful as they should be about this. Sometimes they use extremely jejune examples, thinking the game to be a push-over, so that they need not take too much trouble with them. But it is better if the case is something which your audience can be got to believe really could happen. Thus you will seem to have established a knock-down counterinstance to the utilitarian theory; it will have been shown to require us to say some act is right when we all know it to be wrong.

8.2 Now suppose by contrast that you are on the opposite side in the disputation. . . .

. . . suppose that your opponent's case is the following: there are in a hospital two patients, one needing for survival a new heart and the other new

---

* A kind of utilitarianism which applies the principle of utility not to choices among acts, but rather to choices of general rules of conduct.

kidneys; a down-and-out who is known to nobody and who happens to have the same tissue-type as both the patients strays in out of the cold. Ought they not to kill him, give his heart and kidneys to the patients, and thus save two lives at the expense of one? The utilitarian is supposed to have to say that they ought; the audience is supposed to say that they ought not, because it would be murder. Let us suppose that your opponent manages to get the audience to treat murder as a descriptive, not a secondarily evaluative, word . . . , and thus to call the statement that it would be murder a purely factual one, which can be established prior to any judgement that it would be wrong. I have simplified the case a little from the way it has sometimes been presented in the literature . . . , because the complications will not affect the moves we shall be making.

On this example you have to mount a two-pronged attack. If we are to do intuitive thinking, the matter is fairly simple. It *is* murder, and *would* therefore be wrong. A utilitarian does not have to dissent from this verdict at the intuitive level. If he has been well brought up (and in particular if he has been brought up by a sound critical utilitarian thinker) he will have that intuition, and it is a very good thing, from the utilitarian point of view, that he will have it. For just think what would be the consequences of a moral education which contained no prohibition on murder!

Your opponent will now object that although on the utilitarian view it is a good thing for people to have these intuitions or feelings, it also follows from that view that they ought to overcome and act contrary to them in cases like this, in which, *ex hypothesi,** it is for the best to do so. Let us ask, then, whether the doctors in the hospital ought to do this if they are utilitarians. It will turn upon their estimate of the *probability* of hitting off the act which is for the best by so doing. The crucial words are, of course, '*ex hypothesi;*' for your opponent has constructed his example with the express purpose of making the murder the act which will have the best consequences. You must not allow him simply to *assume* that this is so; he has to convince the audience, not just that it really could be so in a real-life situation, but that it could be known to be so by the doctors with a high degree of probability. For utilitarianism, as a method of choosing the most rational action (the best bet for a utilitarian) in a moral dilemma of this sort, requires them to maximize the *expectation* of utility (i.e. preference-satisfaction); and since, if they get it wrong, the consequences will be pretty catastrophic, the doctors have to be very sure that they are not getting it wrong. There is perhaps no need to go into any technicalities of games-theory to establish this point, though a full account would need to contain a method of weighing combinations of probabilities with utilities against one another, by asking which combination one would prefer, after exposure to logic and the facts.

It is fairly obvious that this high degree of probability will not be forthcoming in many actual situations, if any at all. Have the doctors checked on the down-and-out's connexions or lack of them? (How? By consulting the police records, perhaps! But a colleague of my psychiatrist sister once wrote in his notes, about

---

* By hypothesis.

a dishevelled individual brought in off the streets very late at night by the police, 'Has delusion that he is a high-ranking civil servant,' and it turned out that he was in fact a *very* high-ranking civil servant.) Have they absolute confidence in the discretion and support of all the nurses, porters, mortuarists, etc., who will know what has happened? Add to this the extreme unlikelihood of there being no other way of saving these patients, if they can be saved at all, and it will be evident that your opponent is not going to get much help out of this example, once it is insisted that it has to be fleshed out and given verisimilitude.

But perhaps that was not his intention. Perhaps, that is to say, he all along intended the example to be a dummy. Is he not allowed, after a brief intro-duction of the example to give its general shape, to skip the details and simply *posit* that it is a case where murder would be for the best? The audience, which is probably prejudiced against utilitarians anyway, will have no difficulty in imagining that the details could be filled in in a way that would suit his case and damage yours. But you must not let him get away with this. If we are talking about intuitive thinking in a real-life sort of situation, the example needs to be a real-life sort of example.

. . .

Your opponent may say 'Are there not some cases occurring in real life, albeit rarely, in which murder is justified on utilitarian grounds?' To which you should reply that he has not produced any, but that if he really did find one, we should have to do some critical thinking on it because it would be clearly so unusual as to be beyond the range of our intuitions. If we then found that murder really was justified in that case, we still should not have shown that the rational moral agent would commit the murder; for he would be unlikely to have sufficient evidential grounds for saying that it was the right act. But, giving your opponent everything that he ask for, if he did actually have suffi-cient evidence (a very unlikely contingency), murder would *in that case* be justified; though even then the agent in question, if he had been well brought up, might not do it, because it would go so much against all his moral feelings, which in a good man are powerful. So, owing to being a good man, he might fail to do the right act. If he did bring himself to do it, it would haunt him for the rest of his life. But until your opponent produces actual cases, you should not let yourself be troubled overmuch with fictional ones. If the actual cases are produced, you will probably find that the critical discussion of them will leave you and the audience at one, provided that the discussion is serious.

8.3 We are now in a position to apply the same technique to some more genuine problems. Let us take first the objection commonly made to utilitar-ianism that it does not allow us to give any weight to the duties usually thought to exist towards particular persons, or to ties of affection and loyalty which bind us to them but not to mankind in general. . . . For example, it is usually held that we have special duties to our spouses and children, and ought to have greater affection and loyalty to them than to total strangers, and so seek their good more earnestly. Similar things are said about the relation between a doctor and his patient, or a teacher and his pupil. And similar things *used* to be universally, and are still quite widely, accepted about that between a citizen

and his country. I have heard the same argued about the loyalty of a worker to his union.

These last two instances might make us pause before proceeding on the assumption that all commonly upheld loyalties can be used as a stick to beat utilitarians with. They show how palpable, and how dubious, is the appeal to intuition when people say that utilitarianism treats everybody's preferences as of equal weight (e.g. those of my children and other people's children), and therefore has to be rejected as giving no weight to these feelings of special affection which we all think it a good thing to encourage. We have first to be sure that, in a particular example, it *is* a good thing to encourage these feelings. Even family loyalties provide examples of extremely various intuitions. In some countries it is considered wrong if someone who has obtained a position of power does not use it to advance the interests of the members of his family; in others this is called nepotism and thought corrupt. And even in Britain there is dispute about whether it is right for a well endowed father to try to get the best possible education for his children by sending them to expensive schools which others cannot afford.

This should warn us that even where intuitions are all in agreement, they should not be taken for granted; it needs to be established by critical thought which of them ought, in our present circumstances, to be fostered. Anybody who asks himself whether, and in what sense, he ought to bring up his children to be patriotic will see the force of this question. So let us proceed as before and ask our anti-utilitarian objector what level of thinking he is talking about, intuitive or critical. In order to make it easy for him, let us allow him to choose an example in which nearly everybody will agree that the loyalty in question is a good thing. A mother, say, has a new-born child and her maternal feelings make her provide for this child, but they do not, or not to anything like the same degree, impel her to provide for other people's children. Ought a utilitarian to condemn this partiality?

At the intuitive level we all think that the mother is to be praised, in all normal circumstances (barring a few extreme radical advocates of communes, and Plato). Given our two-level structure, there is nothing in this that a utilitarian need object to. *If* the intuition is one that ought to be inculcated (and this cannot be determined without critical thinking), the most likely way of doing the right thing in normal circumstances will be to follow the intuition. If this were not so, then the intuition would not be the one which ought to be inculcated. If we ascend to the critical level and ask why it ought to be, the answer is fairly obvious. If mothers had the propensity to care equally for all the children in the world, it is unlikely that children would be as well provided for even as they are. The dilution of the responsibility would weaken it out of existence. Our traditional upbringing has taken account of this. And evidently Evolution (if we may personify her) has had the same idea; there are, we are told, a great many of these particular loyalties and affections which are genetically transmitted, and have no doubt favoured the survival of the genes which transmit them. . . .

8.4 The general lines of the utilitarian answer to this objection should by now be clear. *In so far* as the intuitions are desirable ones, they can be defended on utilitarian grounds by critical thinking, as having a high acceptance-utility;* if they can be so defended, the best bet, even for an act-utilitarian, will be to cultivate them and follow them in all normal cases; if he cultivates them seriously, or has had them cultivated for him by those who brought him up, all the associated moral feelings will be present, but will provide no argument whatever against utilitarianism. Unlike intuitionism, it is actually able to *justify* the intuitions, where they can be justified.

Faced with this argument the anti-utilitarian will produce examples in which we would all have the intuitions, but in which, he asks us to suppose, the utilitarian would have to prescribe that we acted contrary to them. This would be because in the particular cases sufficient information is assumed to be available to show that the intuitively right act would not be for the best. To take a pasteboard example with which I was once confronted by Professor Bernard Williams on television: you are in an air crash and the aircraft catches fire, but you have managed to get out; in the burning plane are, among others, your son and a distinguished surgeon who could, if rescued, save many injured passengers' lives, to say nothing of those whose lives he would save in his subsequent career. You have time to rescue only one person.

It is hard to make Williams' example realistic. How do you know he is so distinguished a surgeon—perhaps he was only shooting a line when you struck up an acquaintance in the departure lounge? Has he got his tools with him, and can he do any more for the injured people than the first aid which the crew are trained to give (which probably prescribes keeping them warm and immobile and giving some common drugs which, we hope, they managed to extract from the aircraft)? How promising is your son's future (he can probably look forward to a greater span of it than the surgeon)? However, setting aside all these minor points, we find that you have a very strong feeling that you ought to rescue your son and let the surgeon burn. But what does this show?

It would take a very hardened intuitionist to think that it shows that to rescue your son is your undoubted duty. You almost certainly will rescue your son. But that is because you have (rightly from the critical utilitarian point of view) been brought up to attach dominant importance to these family loyalties. Of course no upbringing takes into account such rare cases as this (they are not what those who influenced you were preparing you for, nor would evolution be affected by them). To be in an air crash of any sort is, fortunately, a statistically very rare experience; to be in one in which one has the opportunity to rescue anybody is rarer still; to be in one in which one can rescue precisely one person and no more is hardly to be expected. So you come to this unhappy experience entirely unprepared for it. Your intuitions were simply not designed

---

* A principle's acceptance-utility is the amount of happiness that would result if most or all people followed it.

to cope with it. However, you do have the strong moral feelings and will probably act on them in the split second which is all you have in which to decide. And who is to blame you? Probably in a situation of complete uncertainty and panic it is the rational thing to do. The fraudulence of the example consists in suggesting that you can at one and the same time be in this emergency situation, and do the leisured critical thinking which would be necessary in order to justify you in going against your intuitions.

Undoubtedly critics of utilitarianism will go on trying to produce examples which are both fleshed out and reasonably likely to occur, and also support their argument. I am prepared to bet, however, that the nearer they get to realism and specificity, and the further from playing trains—a sport which has had such a fascination for them—the more likely the audience is, on reflection, to accept the utilitarian solution. I am thinking of their examples in which trolleys hurtling down the line out of control have to be shunted into various alternative groups of unfortunate people. I have myself, when helping to build a railway, seen trolleys run out of control, and therefore find the unrealism of the examples very obvious. The point is that one has no time to think what to do, and so relies on one's immediate intuitive reactions; but these give no guide to what critical thinking would prescribe if there were time for it. But, personal experience aside, I have done quite a lot of work on serious practical problems in medicine, war, politics, urban planning and the like, and have never come across any actual example in which this kind of anti-utilitarian argument was in the least convincing.

8

Morality and Rationality

IMMANUEL KANT

Any short list of the greatest philosophers in Western thought will include Immanuel Kant (1724–1804). Kant made major contributions to most of the central areas of philosophy: ethics, political philosophy, epistemology, metaphysics, philosophy of art, philosophy of mind, and philosophy of religion. His two most important works are The Critique of Pure Reason *(1781) and the* Foundations of the Metaphysics of Morals *(1785).*

The Foundations of the Metaphysics of Morals, *excerpted here, has had a profound influence on the development of ethical thought. Kant's theory is extremely difficult and the reader must be prepared to exert considerable intellectual effort to come to grips with this very important perspective on ethics. Because Kant's approach is superficially rather puzzling, we will provide a roadmap, pointing out some of the major landmarks of Kant's theory. We have also provided descriptive section titles for different parts of Kant's long argument.*

In a sense, the true starting place of Kant's essays are his reflections on the need for philosophy in ethical thinking (section D below). Kant believes that the ordinary person knows perfectly well which actions are right and which actions are wrong. (Below, we will see why Kant has such faith in the average person.) The role of philosophy is, therefore, not to tell people what is right or wrong, but to enable people to defend their ordinary moral views when attacked by a skeptic. Kant's work falls into two halves. First, he will try to provide an illuminating description of our ordinary moral views, and second, he will try to show how those common moral views may be defended.

Kant describes our common moral views in the two passages we have called "The Good Will" (section A) and "Acting from the Motive of Duty" (section B). His point in "The Good Will" is that when evaluating the moral worth of an action, we usually do not consider the consequences, but rather the intention with which the act was done. If the intention was good—if the agent had a good will—then the action is good. Kant expands upon this theme in the section on duty. He claims that we believe that an agent deserves moral praise for an action, not simply because he or she has in fact done the right thing, but because the agent was motivated by the intention to do the right thing. The agent was motivated by a sense of duty.

How do we figure out what our duties are? Kant believes that persons, unlike animals, are capable of formulating laws of conduct for themselves and of acting on those laws (section E). The fundamental law of conduct— the "moral law"—is that one should do an act only if one would will that anyone in similar circumstances do the same thing. That is, one should will

to do an act only if one would will that that type of behavior be a law of human conduct. Kant believes that it is a fundamental fact about human reason that whenever we think about doing a particular act, we always think about that act from a more general standpoint. We always ask, Should that be a universal law governing human action? This is why Kant believes that the ordinary person can always tell right from wrong, because, when considering an action, the ordinary person possessed of reason will always ask, Should it be a universal law of conduct that people do this action? Immorality arises when we flout the moral law. Even though we would not want a particular type of behavior to be the law, we selfishly make an exception in our own case and allow ourselves to engage in the behavior anyway.

In section G, Kant draws out a startling consequence of his theory of morality. According to that theory, persons themselves are the ultimate source of morality. Hence, Kant claims that all persons have ultimate and intrinsic worth. No "market value" can be placed on any individual person. This leads Kant to restate the moral law in a different way: We must always treat persons with respect and never as mere means to some goal. Finally, in section H, Kant tries to illuminate the moral law from yet another stand-point. He suggests that when acting we must always think of ourselves as belonging to a community of persons, each of whom creates the laws governing this realm by his or her own actions.

[A. The Good Will]

NOTHING IN THE WORLD—indeed nothing even beyond the world—can possibly be conceived which could be called good without qualification except a *good will*. Intelligence, wit, judgment, and the other talents of the mind, however they may be named, or courage, resoluteness, and perseverance as qualities of temperament, are doubtless in many respects good and desirable. But they can become extremely bad and harmful if the will, which is to make use of these gifts of nature and which in its special constitution is called character, is not good. It is the same with the gifts of fortune, Power, riches, honor, even health, general well-being, and the contentment with one's condition which is called happiness, make for pride and even arrogance if there is not a good will to correct their influence on the mind and on its principles of action so as to make it universally conformable to its end. It need hardly be mentioned that the sight of a being adorned with no feature of a pure and good will, yet enjoying uninterrupted prosperity, can never give pleasure to a rational impartial observer. Thus the good will seems to constitute the indispensable condition even of worthiness to be happy.

Some qualities seem to be conducive to this good will and can facilitate its action, but, in spite of that, they have no intrinsic unconditional worth. They rather presuppose a good will, which limits the high esteem which one otherwise rightly has for them and prevents their being held to be absolutely good. Moderation in emotions and passions, self-control, and calm deliberation not

only are good in many respects but even seem to constitute a part of the inner worth of the person. But however unconditionally they were esteemed by the ancients, they are far from being good without qualification. For without the principle of a good will they can become extremely bad, and the coolness of a villain makes him not only far more dangerous but also more directly abominable in our eyes than he would have seemed without it.

The good will is not good because of what it effects or accomplishes or because of its adequacy to achieve some proposed end; it is good only because of its willing, i.e., it is good of itself. And, regarded for itself, it is to be esteemed incomparably higher than anything which could be brought about by it in favor of any inclination or even of the sum total of all inclinations. Even if it should happen that, by a particularly unfortunate fate or by the niggardly provision of a stepmotherly nature, this will should be wholly lacking in power to accomplish its purpose, and if even the greatest effort should not avail it to achieve anything of its end, and if there remained only the good will (not as a mere wish but as the summoning of all the means in our power), it would sparkle like a jewel in its own right, as something that had its full worth in itself. Usefulness or fruitlessness can neither diminish nor augment this worth. Its usefulness would be only its setting, as it were, so as to enable us to handle it more conveniently in commerce or to attract the attention of those who are not yet connoisseurs, but not to recommend it to those who are experts or to determine its worth.

But there is something so strange in this idea of the absolute worth of the will alone, in which no account is taken of any use, that, notwithstanding the agreement even of common sense, the suspicion must arise that perhaps only high-flown fancy is its hidden basis, and that we may have misunderstood the purpose of nature in its appointment of reason as the ruler of our will. We shall therefore examine this idea from this point of view.

In the natural constitution of an organized being, i.e., one suitably adapted to life, we assume as an axiom that no organ will be found for any purpose which is not the fittest and best adapted to that purpose. Now if its preservation, its welfare—in a word, its happiness—were the real end of nature in a being having reason and will, then nature would have hit upon a very poor arrangement in appointing the reason of the creature to be the executor of this purpose. For all the actions which the creature has to perform with this intention, and the entire rule of its conduct, would be dictated much more exactly by instinct, and that end would be far more certainly attained by instinct than it ever could be by reason. And if, over and above this, reason should have been granted to the favored creature, it would have served only to let it contemplate the happy constitution of its nature, to admire it, to rejoice in it, and to be grateful for it to its beneficent cause. But reason would not have been given in order that the being should subject its faculty of desire to that weak and delusive guidance and to meddle with the purpose of nature. In a word, nature would have taken care that reason did not break forth into practical use nor have the presumption, with its weak insight, to think out for itself the plan of happiness and the means of attaining it. Nature would have taken over not only the choice of ends but

also that of the means, and with wise foresight she would have entrusted both to instinct alone.

And, in fact, we find that the more a cultivated reason deliberately devotes itself to the enjoyment of life and happiness, the more the man falls short of true contentment. From this fact there arises in many persons, if only they are candid enough to admit it, a certain degree of misology, hatred of reason. This is particularly the case with those who are most experienced in its use. After counting all the advantages which they draw—I will not say from the invention of the arts of common luxury—from the sciences (which in the end seem to them to be also a luxury of the understanding), they nevertheless find that they have actually brought more trouble on their shoulders instead of gaining in happiness; they finally envy, rather than despise, the common run of men who are better guided by mere natural instinct and who do not permit their reason much influence on their conduct. And we must at least admit that a morose attitude or ingratitude to the goodness with which the world is governed is by no means found always among those who temper or refute the boasting eulogies which are given of the advantages of happiness and contentment with which reason is supposed to supply us. Rather their judgment is based on the idea of another and far more worthy purpose of their existence for which, instead of happiness, their reason is properly intended, this purpose, therefore, being the supreme condition to which the private purposes of men must for the most part defer.

Reason is not, however, competent to guide the will safely with regard to its objects and the satisfaction of all our needs (which it in part multiplies), and to this end an innate instinct would have led with far more certainty. But reason is given to us as a practical faculty, i.e., one which is meant to have an influence on the will. As nature has elsewhere distributed capacities suitable to the functions they are to perform, reason's proper function must be to produce a will good in itself and not one good merely as a means, for to the former reason is absolutely essential. This will must indeed not be the sole and complete good but the highest good and the condition of all others, even of the desire for happiness. In this case it is entirely compatible with the wisdom of nature that the cultivation of reason, which is required for the former unconditional purpose, at least in this life restricts in many ways—indeed can reduce to less than nothing—the achievement of the latter conditional purpose, happiness. For one perceives that nature here does not proceed unsuitably to its purpose, because reason, which recognizes its highest practical vocation in the establishment of a good will, is capable only of a contentment of its own kind, i.e., one that springs from the attainment of a purpose which is determined by reason, even though this injures the ends of inclination.

We have, then, to develop the concept of a will which is to be esteemed as good of itself without regard to anything else. It dwells already in the natural sound understanding and does not need so much to be taught as only to be brought to light. In the estimation of the total worth of our actions it always takes first place and is the condition of everything else. In order to show this,

we shall take the concept of duty. It contains that of a good will, though with certain subjective restrictions and hindrances; but these are far from concealing it and making it unrecognizable, for they rather bring it out by contrast and make it shine forth all the brighter.

[B. Acting from the Motive of Duty]

I here omit all actions which are recognized as opposed to duty, even though they may useful in one respect or another, for with these the question does not arise at all as to whether they may be carried out *from* duty, since they conflict with it. I also pass over the actions which are really in accordance with duty and to which one has no direct inclination, rather executing them because impelled to do so by another inclination. For it is easily decided whether an action in accord with duty is performed from duty or for some selfish purpose. It is far more difficult to note this difference when the action is in accordance with duty and, in addition, the subject has a direct inclination to do it. For example, it is in fact in accordance with duty that a dealer should not overcharge an inexperienced customer, and wherever there is much business the prudent merchant does not do so, having a fixed price for everyone, so that a child may buy of him as cheaply as any other. Thus the customer is honestly served. But this is far from sufficient to justify the belief that the merchant has behaved in this way from duty and principles of honesty. His own advantage required this behavior; but it cannot be assumed that over and above that he had a direct inclination to the purchaser and that, out of love, as it were, he gave none an advantage in price over another. Therefore the action was done neither from duty nor from direct inclination but only for a selfish purpose.

On the other hand, it is a duty to preserve one's life, and moreover everyone has a direct inclination to do so. But for that reason the often anxious care which most men take of it has no intrinsic worth, and the maxim of doing so has no moral import. They preserve their lives according to duty, but not from duty. But if adversities and hopeless sorrow completely take away the relish for life, if an unfortunate man, strong in soul, is indignant rather than despondent or dejected over his fate and wishes for death, and yet preserves his life without loving it and from neither inclination nor fear but from duty—then his maxim has a moral import.

To be kind where one can is duty, and there are, moreover, many persons so sympathetically constituted that without any motive of vanity or selfishness they find an inner satisfaction in spreading joy, and rejoice in the contentment of others which they have made possible. But I say that, however dutiful and amiable it may be, that kind of action has no true moral worth. It is on a level with [actions arising from] other inclinations, such as the inclination to honor, which, if fortunately directed to what in fact accords with duty and is generally useful and thus honorable, deserve praise and encouragement but no esteem. For the maxim lacks the moral import of an action done not from inclination but from duty. But assume that the mind of that friend to mankind was clouded

by a sorrow of his own which extinguished all sympathy with the lot of others and that he still had the power to benefit others in distress, but that their need left him untouched because he was preoccupied with his own need. And now suppose him to tear himself, unsolicited by inclination, out of this dead insensibility and to perform this action only from duty and without any inclination— then for the first time his action has genuine moral worth. Furthermore, if nature has put little sympathy in the heart of a man, and if he, though an honest man, is by temperament cold and indifferent to the sufferings of others, perhaps because he is provided with special gifts of patience and fortitude and expects or even requires that others should have the same—and such a man would certainly not be the meanest product of nature—would not he find in himself a source from which to give himself a far higher worth than he could have got by having a good-natured temperament? This is unquestionably true even though nature did not make him philanthropic, for it is just here that the worth of the character is brought out, which is morally and incomparably the highest of all: he is beneficent not from inclination but from duty.

To secure one's own happiness is at least indirectly a duty, for discontent with one's condition under pressure from many cares and amid unsatisfied wants could easily become a great temptation to transgress duties. But without any view to duty all men have the strongest and deepest inclination to happiness, because in this idea all inclinations are summed up. But the precept of happiness is often so formulated that it definitely thwarts some inclinations, and men can make no definite and certain concept of the sum of satisfaction of all inclinations which goes under the name of happiness. It is not to be wondered at, therefore, that a single inclination, definite as to what it promises and as to the time at which it can be satisfied, can outweigh a fluctuating idea, and that, for example, a man with the gout can choose to enjoy what he likes and to suffer what he may, because according to his calculations at least on this occasion he has not sacrificed the enjoyment of the present moment to a perhaps groundless expectation of a happiness supposed to lie in health. But even in this case, if the universal inclination to happiness did not determine his will, and if health were not at least for him a necessary factor in these calculations, there yet would remain, as in all other cases, a law that he ought to promote his happiness, not from inclination but from duty. Only from this law would his conduct have true moral worth.

It is in this way, undoubtedly, that we should understand those passages of Scripture which command us to love our neighbor and even our enemy, for love as an inclination cannot be commanded. But beneficence from duty, when no inclination impels it and even when it is opposed by a natural and unconquerable aversion, is practical love, not pathological love; it resides in the will and not in the propensities of feeling, in principles of action and not in tender sympathy; and it alone can be commanded.

[Thus the first proposition of morality is that to have moral worth an action must be done from duty.] The second proposition is: An action performed from duty does not have its moral worth in the purpose which is to be achieved

through it but in the maxim by which it is determined. Its moral value, there-fore, does not depend on the realization of the object of the action but merely on the principle of volition by which the action is done, without any regard to the objects of the faculty of desire. From the preceding discussion it is clear that the purposes we may have for our actions and their effects as ends and incentives of the will cannot give the actions any unconditional and moral worth. Wherein, then, can this worth lie, if it is not in the will in relation to its hoped-for effect? It can lie nowhere else than in the principle of the will, irrespective of the ends which can be realized by such action. For the will stands, as it were, at the crossroads halfway between its a priori principle which is formal and its a posteriori incentive which is material. Since it must be deter-mined by something, if it is done from duty it must be determined by the formal principle of volition as such since every material principle has been withdrawn from it.

The third principle, as a consequence of the two preceding, I would express as follows: Duty is the necessity of an action executed from respect for law. I can certainly have an inclination to the object as an effect of the proposed action, but I can never have respect for it precisely because it is a mere effect and not an activity of a will. Similarly, I can have no respect for any inclination whatsoever, whether my own or that of another; in the former case I can at most approve of it and in the latter I can even love it, i.e., see it as favorable to my own advantage. But that which is connected with my will merely as ground and not as consequence, that which does not serve my inclination but overpowers it or at least excludes it from being considered in making a choice—in a word, law itself—can be an object of respect and thus a command. Now as an act from duty wholly excludes the influence of inclination and therewith every object of the will, nothing remains which can determine the will objec-tively except the law, and nothing subjectively except pure respect for this practical law. This subjective element is the maxim[1] that I ought to follow such a law even if it thwarts all my inclinations.

Thus the moral worth of an action does not lie in the effect which is expected from it or in any principle of action which has to borrow its motive from this expected effect. For all these effects (agreeableness of my own condition, indeed even the promotion of the happiness of others) could be brought about through other causes and would not require the will of a rational being, while the highest and unconditional good can be found only in such a will. Therefore, the pre-eminent good can consist only in the conception of the law in itself (which can be present only in a rational being) so far as this conception and not the hoped-for effect is the determining ground of the will. This pre-eminent good, which

---

[1] A maxim is the subjective principle of volition. The objective principle (i.e., that which would serve all rational beings also subjectively as a practical principle if reason had full power over the faculty of desire) is the practical law.

we call moral, is already present in the person who acts according to this conception, and we do not have to look for it first in the result.[2]

[C. The Moral Law]

But what kind of a law can that be, the conception of which must determine the will without reference to the expected result? Under this condition alone the will can be called absolutely good without qualification. Since I have robbed the will of all impulses which could come to it from obedience to any law, nothing remains to serve as a principle of the will except universal conformity of its action to law as such. That is, I should never act in such a way that I could not also will that my maxim should be a universal law. Mere conformity to law as such (without assuming any particular law applicable to certain actions) serves as the principle of the will, and it must serve as such a principle if duty is not to be a vain delusion and chimerical concept. The common reason of mankind in its practical judgments is in perfect agreement with this and has this principle constantly in view.

Let the question, for example, be: May I, when in distress, make a promise with the intention not to keep it? I easily distinguish the two meanings which the question can have, viz., whether it is prudent to make a false promise, or whether it conforms to my duty. Undoubtedly the former can often be the case, though I do see clearly that it is not sufficient merely to escape from the present difficulty by this expedient, but that I must consider whether inconveniences much greater than the present one may not later spring from this lie. Even with all my supposed cunning, the consequences cannot be so easily foreseen. Loss of credit might be far more disadvantageous than the misfortune I now seek to avoid, and it is hard to tell whether it might not be more prudent to act according to a universal maxim and to make it a habit not to promise anything without intending to fulfill it. But it is soon clear to me that such a maxim is based only on an apprehensive concern with consequences.

---

[2] It might be objected that I seek to take refuge in an obscure feeling behind the word "respect," instead of clearly resolving the question with a concept of reason. But though respect is a feeling, it is not one received through any [outer] influence but is self-wrought by a rational concept; thus it differs specifically from all feelings of the former kind which may be referred to inclination or fear. What I recognize directly as a law for myself I recognize with respect, which means merely the consciousness of the submission of my will to a law without the intervention of other influences on my mind. The direct determination of the will by the law and the consciousness of this determination is respect; thus respect can be regarded as the effect of the law on the subject and not as the cause of the law. Respect is properly the conception of a worth which thwarts my self-love. Thus it is regarded as an object neither of inclination nor of fear, though it has something analogous to both. The only object of respect is the law, and indeed only the law which we impose on ourselves and yet recognize as necessary in itself. As a law, we are subject to it without consulting self-love; as imposed on us by ourselves, it is a consequence of our will. In the former respect it is analogous to fear and in the latter to inclination. All respect for a person is only respect for the law (of rightousness, etc.) of which the person provides an example. Because we see the improvement of our talents as a duty, we think of a person of talents as the example of a law, as it were (the law that we should by practice become like him in his talents), and that constitutes our respect. All so-called moral interest consists solely in respect for the law.

To be truthful from duty, however, is an entirely different thing from being truthful out of fear of disadvantageous consequences, for in the former case the concept of the action itself contains a law for me, while in the latter I must first look about to see what results for me may be connected with it. For to deviate from the principle of duty is certainly bad, but to be unfaithful to my maxim of prudence can sometimes be very advantageous to me, though it is certainly safe to abide by it. The shortest but most infallible way to find the answer to the question as to whether a deceitful promise is consistent with duty is to ask myself: Would I be content that my maxim (of extricating myself from difficulty by a false promise) should hold as a universal law for myself as well as for others? And could I say to myself that everyone may make a false promise when he is in a difficulty from which he otherwise cannot escape? I immediately see that I could will the lie but not a universal law to lie. For with such a law there would be no promises at all, inasmuch as it would be futile to make a pretense of my intention in regard to future actions to those who would not believe this pretense or—if they overhastily did so—who would pay me back in my own coin.Thus my maxim would necessarily destroy itself as soon as it was made a universal law.

[D. Common Morality and the Need for Philosophy]

I do not, therefore, need any penetrating acuteness in order to discern what I have to do in order that my volition may be morally good. Inexperienced in the course of the world, incapable of being prepared for all its contingencies, I ask myself only: Can I will that my maxim become a universal law? If not, it must be rejected, not because of any disadvantage accruing to myself or even to others, but because it cannot enter as a principle into a possible universal legislation, and reason extorts from me an immediate respect for such legislation. I do not as yet discern on what it is grounded (a question the philosopher may investigate), but I at least understand that it is an estimation of the worth which far outweighs all the worth of whatever is recommended by the inclinations, and that the necessity of my actions from pure respect for the practical law constitutes duty. To duty every other motive must give place, because duty is the condition of a will good in itself, whose worth transcends everything.

Thus within the moral knowledge of common human reason we have attained its principle. To be sure, common human reason does not think of it abstractly in such a unversal form, but it always has it in view and uses it as the standard of its judgments. It would be easy to show how common human reason, with this compass, knows well how to distinguish what is good, what is bad, and what is consistent or inconsistent with duty. Without in the least teaching common reason anything new, we need only to draw its attention to its own principle, in the manner of Socrates, thus showing that neither science nor philosophy is needed in order to know what one has to do in order to be honest and good, and even wise and virtuous. We might have conjectured beforehand that the knowledge of what everyone is obliged to do and thus also to know would be within the reach of everyone, even the most ordinary man. Here we

cannot but admire the great advantages which the practical faculty of judgment has over the theoretical in ordinary human understanding. In the theoretical, if ordinary reason ventures to go beyond the laws of experience and perceptions of the senses, it falls into sheer inconceivabilities and self-contradictions, or at least into a chaos of uncertainty, obscurity, and instability. In the practical, on the other hand, the power of judgment first shows itself to advantage when common understanding excludes all sensuous incentives from practical laws. It then becomes even subtle, quibbling with its own conscience or with other claims to what should be called right, or wishing to determine correctly for its own instruction the worth of certain actions. But the most remarkable thing about ordinary reason in its practical concern is that it may have as much hope as any philosopher of hitting the mark. In fact, it is almost more certain to do so than the philosopher, because he has no principle which the common understanding lacks, while his judgment is easily confused by a mass of irrelevant considerations, so that it easily turns aside from the correct way. Would it not, therefore, be wiser in moral matters to acquiesce in the common rational judgment, or at most to call in philosophy in order to make the system of morals more complete and comprehensible and its rules more convenient for use (especially in disputation) than to steer the common understanding from its happy simplicity in practical matters and to lead it through philosophy into a new path of inquiry and instruction?

Innocence is indeed a glorious thing, but, on the other hand, it is very sad that it cannot well maintain itself, being easily led astray. For this reason, even wisdom—which consists more in acting than in knowing—needs science, not to learn from it but to secure admission and permanence to its precepts. Man feels in himself a powerful counterpoise against all commands of duty which reason presents to him as so deserving of respect; this counterpoise is his needs and inclinations, the complete satisfaction of which he sums up under the name of happiness. Now reason issues inexorable commands without promising anything to the inclinations. It disregards, as it were, and holds in contempt those claims which are so impetuous and yet so plausible, and which will not allow themselves to be abolished by any command. From this a natural dialectic arises, i.e., a propensity to argue against the stern laws of duty and their validity, or at least to place their purity and strictness in doubt and, where possible, to make them more accordant with our wishes and inclinations. This is equivalent to corrupting them in their very foundations and destroying their dignity—a thing which even common practical reason cannot ultimately call good.

In this way common human reason is impelled to go outside its sphere and to take a step into the field of practical philosophy. But it is forced to do so not by any speculative need, which never occurs to it so long as it is satisfied to remain merely healthy reason; rather, it is so impelled on practical grounds in order to obtain information and clear instruction respecting the source of its principle and the correct determination of this principle in its opposition to the maxims which are based on need and inclination. It seeks this information in order to escape from the perplexity of opposing claims and to avoid the danger of losing all genuine moral principles through the equivocation in which

it is easily involved. Thus, when practical common reason cultivates itself, a dialectic surreptitiously ensues which forces it to seek aid in philosophy, just as the same thing happens in the theoretical use of reason. In this case, as in the theoretical, it will find rest only in a thorough critical examination of our reason.

. . .

[E. Acting According to the Concept of Law]

In this study we do not advance merely from the common moral judgment (which here is very worthy of respect) to the philosophical, as this has already been done, but we advance by natural stages from a popular philosophy (which goes no further than it can grope by means of examples) to metaphysics (which is not held back by anything empirical and which, as it must measure out the entire scope of rational knowledge of this kind, reaches even Ideas, where examples fail us). In order to make this advance, we must follow and clearly present the practical faculty of reason from its universal rules of determination to the point where the concept of duty arises from it.

Everything in nature works according to laws. Only a rational being has the capacity of acting according to the conception of laws, i.e., according to principles. This capacity is will. Since reason is required for the derivation of actions from laws, will is nothing else than practical reason. If reason infallibly determines the will, the actions which such a being recognizes as objectively necessary are also subjectively necessary. That is, the will is a faculty of choosing only that which reason, independently of inclination, recognizes as practically necessary, i.e., as good. But if reason of itself does not sufficiently determine the will, and if the will is subjugated to subjective conditions (certain incentives) which do not always agree with objective conditions; in a word, if the will is not of itself in complete accord with reason (the actual case of men), then the actions which are recognized as objectively necessary are subjectively contingent, and the determination of such a will according to objective laws is constraint. That is, the relation of objective laws to a will which is not completely good is conceived as the determination of the will of a rational being by principles of reason to which this will is not by nature necessarily obedient.

The conception of an objective principle, so far as it constrains a will, is a command (of reason), and the formula of this command is called an *imperative*.

All imperatives are expressed by an "ought" and thereby indicate the relation of an objective law of reason to a will which is not in its subjective constitution necessarily determined by this law. This relation is that of constraint. Imperatives say that it would be good to do or to refrain from doing something, but they say it to a will which does not always do something simply because it is presented as a good thing to do. Practical good is what determines the will by means of the conception of reason and hence not by subjective causes but, rather, objectively, i.e., on grounds which are valid for every rational being as such. It is distinguished from the pleasant as that which has an influence on the will only by means of a sensation from merely subjective causes, which

hold only for the senses of this or that person and not as a principle of reason which holds for everyone.

A perfectly good will, therefore, would be equally subject to objective laws (of the good), but it could not be conceived as constrained by them to act in accord with them, because, according to its own subjective constitution, it can be determined to act only through the conception of the good. Thus no imperatives hold for the divine will or, more generally, for a holy will. The "ought" is here out of place, for the volition of itself is necessarily in unison with the law. Therefore imperatives are only formulas expressing the relation of objective laws of volition in general to the subjective imperfection of the will of this or that rational being, e.g., the human will.

All imperatives command either hypothetically or categorically. The former present the practical necessity of a possible action as a means to achieving something else which one desires (or which one may possibly desire). The categorical imperative would be one which presented an action as of itself objectively necessary, without regard to any other end.

Since every practical law presents a possible action as good and thus as necessary for a subject practically determinable by reason, all imperatives are formulas of the determination of action which is necessary by the principle of a will which is in any way good. If the action is good only as a means to something else, the imperative is hypothetical; but if it is thought of as good in itself, and hence as necessary in a will which of itself conforms to reason as the principle of this will, the imperative is categorical.

The imperative thus says what action possible to me would be good, and it presents the practical rule in relation to a will which does not forthwith perform an action simply because it is good, in part because the subject does not always know that the action is good and in part (when he does know it) because his maxims can still be opposed to the objective principles of practical reason.

The hypothetical imperative, therefore, says only that the action is good to some purpose, possible or actual. In the former case it is a problematical, in the latter an assertorical, practical principle. The categorical imperative, which declares the action to be of itself objectively necessary without making any reference to a purpose, i.e., without having any other end, holds as an apodictical (practical) principle.

. . .

[F. How is the Categorical Imperative Possible?]

In attacking this problem, we will first inquire whether the mere concept of a categorical imperative does not also furnish the formula containing the proposition which alone can be a categorical imperative. For even when we know the formula of the imperative, to learn how such an absolute law is possible will require difficult and special labors which we shall postpone to the last section.

If I think of a hypothetical imperative as such, I do not know what it will contain until the condition is stated [under which it is an imperative]. But if I

think of a categorical imperative, I know immediately what it contains. For since the imperative contains besides the law only the necessity that the maxim should accord with this law, while the law contains no condition to which it is restricted, there is nothing remaining in it except the universality of law as such to which the maxim of the action should conform; and in effect this conformity alone is represented as necessary by the imperative.

There is, therefore, only one categorical imperative. It is: Act only according to that maxim by which you can at the same time will that it should become a universal law.

Now if all imperatives of duty can be derived from this one imperative as a principle, we can at least show what we understand by the concept of duty and what it means, even though it remain undecided whether that which is called duty is an empty concept or not.

The universality of law according to which effects are produced constitutes what is properly called nature in the most general sense (as to form), i.e., the existence of things so far as it is determined by universal laws. [By analogy], then, the universal imperative of duty can be expressed as follows: Act as though the maxim of your action were by your will to become a universal law of nature.

We shall now enumerate some duties, adopting the usual division of them into duties to ourselves and to others and into perfect and imperfect duties.

1. A man who is reduced to despair by a series of evils feels a weariness with life but is still in possession of his reason sufficiently to ask whether it would not be contrary to his duty to himself to take his own life. Now he asks whether the maxim of his action could become a universal law of nature. His maxim, however, is: For love of myself, I make it my principle to shorten my life when by a longer duration it threatens more evil than satisfaction. But it is questionable whether this principle of self-love could become a universal law of nature. One immediately sees a contradiction in a system of nature whose law would be to destroy life by the feeling whose special office is to impel the improvement of life. In this case it would not exist as nature; hence that maxim cannot obtain as a law of nature, and thus it wholly contradicts the supreme principle of all duty.

2. Another man finds himself forced by need to borrow money. He well knows that he will not be able to repay it, but he also sees that nothing will be loaned him if he does not firmly promise to repay it at a certain time. He desires to make such a promise, but he has enough conscience to ask himself whether it is not improper and opposed to duty to relieve his distress in such a way. Now, assuming he does decide to do so, the maxim of his action would be as follows: When I believe myself to be in need of money, I will borrow money and promise to repay it, although I know I shall never do so. Now this principle of self-love or of his own benefit may very well be compatible with his whole future welfare, but the question is whether it is right. He changes the pretension of self-love into a universal law and then puts the question: How would it be if my maxim became a universal law? He immediately sees that it could never hold as a universal law of nature and be consistent with itself; rather it must

necessarily contradict itself. For the universality of a law which says that anyone who believes himself to be in need could promise what he pleased with the intention of not fulfilling it would make the promise itself and the end to be accomplished by it impossible; no one would believe what was promised to him but would only laugh at any such assertion as vain pretense.

3. A third finds in himself a talent which could, by means of some cultivation, make him in many respects a useful man. But he finds himself in comfortable circumstances and prefers indulgence in pleasure to troubling himself with broadening and improving his fortunate natural gifts. Now, however, let him ask whether his maxim of neglecting his gifts, besides agreeing with his propensity to idle amusement, agrees also with what is called duty. He sees that a system of nature could indeed exist in accordance with such a law, even though man (like the inhabitants of the South Sea Islands) should let his talents rust and resolve to devote his life merely to idleness, indulgence, and propagation—in a word, to pleasure. But he cannot possibly will that this should become a universal law of nature or that it should be implanted in us by a natural instinct. For, as a rational being, he necessarily wills that all his faculties should be developed, inasmuch as they are given to him for all sorts of possible purposes.

4. A fourth man, for whom things are going well, sees that others (whom he could help) have to struggle with great hardships, and he asks, "What concern of mine is it? Let each one be as happy as heaven wills, or as he can make himself; I will not take anything from him or even envy him; but to his welfare or to his assistance in time of need I have no desire to contribute." If such a way of thinking were a universal law of nature, certainly the human race could exist, and without doubt even better than in a state where everyone talks of sympathy and good will, or even exerts himself occasionally to practice them while, on the other hand, he cheats when he can and betrays or otherwise violates the rights of man. Now although it is possible that a universal law of nature according to that maxim could exist, it is nevertheless impossible to will that such a principle should hold everywhere as a law of nature. For a will which resolved this would conflict with itself, since instances can often arise in which he would need the love and sympathy of others, and in which he would have robbed himself, by such a law of nature springing from his own will, of all hope of the aid he desires.

The foregoing are a few of the many actual duties, or at least of duties we hold to be actual, whose derivation from the one stated principle is clear. We must be able to will that a maxim of our action become a universal law; this is the canon of the moral estimation of our action generally. Some actions are of such a nature that their maxim cannot even be *thought* as a universal law of nature without contradiction, far from it being possible that one could will that it should be such. In others this internal impossibility is not found, though it is still impossible to *will* that their maxim should be raised to the universality of a law of nature, because such a will would contradict itself. We easily see that the former maxim conflicts with the stricter or narrower (imprescriptible)

duty, the latter with broader (meritorious) duty. Thus all duties, so far as the kind of obligation (not the object of their action) is concerned, have been completely exhibited by these examples in their dependence on the one principle.

When we observe ourselves in any transgression of a duty, we find that we do not actually will that our maxim should become a universal law. That is impossible for us; rather, the contrary of this maxim should remain as a law generally, and we only take the liberty of making an exception to it for ourselves or for the sake of our inclination, and for this one occasion. Consequently, if we weighed everything from one and the same standpoint, namely, reason, we would come upon a contradiction in our own will, viz., that a certain principle is objectively necessary as a universal law and yet subjectively does not hold universally but rather admits exceptions. However, since we regard our action at one time from the point of view of a will wholly conformable to reason and then from that of a will affected by inclinations, there is actually no contradiction, but rather an opposition of inclination to the precept of reason (*antagonismus*). In this the universality of the principle (*universalitas*) is changed into mere generality (*generalitas*), whereby the practical principle of reason meets the maxim halfway. Although this cannot be justified in our own impartial judgment, it does show that we actually acknowledge the validity of the categorical imperative and allow ourselves (with all respect to it) only a few exceptions which seem to us to be unimportant and forced upon us.

We have thus at least established that if duty is a concept which is to have significance and actual legislation for our actions, it can be expressed only in categorical imperatives and not at all in hypothetical ones. For every application of it we have also clearly exhibited the content of the categorical imperative which must contain the principle of all duty (if there is such). This is itself very much. But we are not yet advanced far enough to prove a priori that that kind of imperative really exists, that there is a practical law which of itself commands absolutely and without any incentives, and that obedience to this law is duty.

[G. The Ultimate Worth of Persons]

[We must now inquire how such a categorical imperative is possible.]

With a view to attaining this, it is extremely important to remember that we must not let ourselves think that the reality of this principle can be derived from the particular constitution of human nature. For duty is practical unconditional necessity of action; it must, therefore, hold for all rational beings (to which alone an imperative can apply), and only for that reason can it be a law for all human wills. Whatever is derived from the particular natural situation of man as such, or from certain feelings and propensities, or even from a particular tendency of the human reason which might not hold necessarily for the will of every rational being (if such a tendency is possible), can give a maxim

them, nothing of absolute worth could be found, and if all worth is conditional and thus contingent, no supreme practical principle for reason could be found anywhere.

Thus if there is to be a supreme practical principle and a categorical imperative for the human will, it must be one that forms an objective principle of the will from the conception of that which is necessarily an end for everyone because it is an end in itself. Hence this objective principle can serve as a universal practical law. The ground of this principle is: rational nature exists as an end in itself. Man necessarily thinks of his own existence in this way; thus far it is a subjective principle of human actions. Also every other rational being thinks of his existence by means of the same rational ground which holds also for myself; thus it is at the same time an objective principle from which, as a supreme practical ground, it must be possible to derive all laws of the will. The practical imperative, therefore, is the following: Act so that you treat humanity, whether in your own person or in that of another, always as an end and never as a means only.

. . .

[H. Moral Agents as Law—Givers to Themselves]

If we now look back upon all previous attempts which have ever been undertaken to discover the principle of morality, it is not to be wondered at that they all had to fail. Man was seen to be bound to laws by his duty, but it was not seen that he is subject only to his own, yet universal, legislation, and that he is only bound to act in accordance with his own will, which is, however, designed by nature to be a will giving universal laws. For if one thought of him as subject only to a law (whatever it may be), this necessarily implied some interest as a stimulus or compulsion to obedience because the law did not arise from his will. Rather, his will was constrained by something else according to a law to act in a certain way. By this strictly necessary consequence, however, all the labor of finding a supreme ground for duty was irrevocably lost, and one never arrived at duty but only at the necessity of action from a certain interest. This might be his own interest or that of another, but in either case the imperative always had to be conditional and could not at all serve as a moral command. This principle I will call the principle of *autonomy* of the will in contrast to all other principles which I accordingly count under heteronomy.

The concept of each rational being as a being that must regard itself as giving universal law through all the maxims of its will, so that it may judge itself and its actions from this standpoint, leads to a very fruitful concept, namely, that of a *realm of ends*.

By "realm" I understand the systematic union of different rational beings through common laws. Because laws determine ends with regard to their universal validity, if we abstract from the personal difference of rational beings and thus from all content of their private ends, we can think of a whole of all ends in systematic connection, a whole of rational beings as ends in themselves

as well as of the particular ends which each may set for himself. This is a realm of ends, which is possible on the aforesaid principles. For all rational beings stand under the law that each of them should treat himself and all others never merely as means but in every case also as an end in himself. Thus there arises a systematic union of rational beings through common objective laws. This is a realm which may be called a realm of ends (certainly only an ideal), because what these laws have in view is just the relation of these beings to each other as ends and means.

A rational being belongs to the realm of ends as a member when he gives universal laws in it while also himself subject to these laws. He belongs to it as sovereign when he, as legislating, is subject to the will of no other. The rational being must regard himself always as legislative in a realm of ends possible through the freedom of the will, whether he belongs to it as member or as sovereign. He cannot maintain the latter position merely through the maxims of his will but only when he is a completely independent being without need and with power adequate to his will.

Morality, therefore, consists in the relation of every action to that legislation through which alone a realm of ends is possible. This legislation, however, must be found in every rational being. It must be able to arise from his will, whose principle then is to take no action according to any maxim which would be inconsistent with its being a universal law and thus to act only so that the will through its maxims could regard itself at the same time as universally lawgiving. If now the maxims do not by their nature already necessarily conform to this objective principle of rational beings as universally lawgiving, the necessity of acting according to that principle is called practical constraint, i.e., duty. Duty pertains not to the sovereign in the realm of ends, but rather to each member, and to each in the same degree.

The practical necessity of acting according to this principle, i.e., duty, does not rest at all on feelings, impulses, and inclinations; it rests merely on the relation of rational beings to one another, in which the will of a rational being must always be regarded as legislative, for otherwise it could not be thought of as an end in itself. Reason, therefore, relates every maxim of the will as giving universal laws to every other will and also to every action toward itself; it does so not for the sake of any other practical motive or future advantage but rather from the idea of the dignity of a rational being who obeys no law except that which he himself also gives.

In the realm of ends everything has either a *price* or a *dignity*. Whatever has a price can be replaced by something else as its equivalent; on the other hand, whatever is above all price, and therefore admits of no equivalent, has a dignity.

That which is related to general human inclinations and needs has a *market price*. That which, without presupposing any need, accords with a certain taste, i.e., with pleasure in the mere purposeless play of our faculties, has an *affective price*. But that which constituted the condition under which alone something can be an end in itself does not have mere relative worth, i.e., a price, but an intrinsic worth, i.e., *dignity*.

Now morality is the condition under which alone a rational being can be an end in itself, because only through it is it possible to be a legislative member in the realm of ends. Thus morality and humanity, so far as it is capable of morality, alone have dignity. Skill and diligence in work have a market value; wit, lively imagination, and humor have an affective price; but fidelity in promises and benevolence on principle (not from instinct) have intrinsic worth. Nature and likewise art contain nothing which could replace their lack, for their worth consists not in effects which flow from them, nor in advantage and utility which they procure; it consists only in intentions, i.e., maxims of the will which are ready to reveal themselves in this manner through actions even though success does not favor them. These actions need no recommendation from any subjective disposition or taste in order that they may be looked upon with immediate favor and satisfaction, nor do they have need of any immediate propensity or feeling directed to them. They exhibit the will which performs them as the object of an immediate respect, since nothing but reason is required in order to impose them on the will. The will is not to be cajoled into them, for this, in the case of duties, would be a contradiction. This esteem lets the worth of such a turn of mind be recognized as dignity and puts it infinitely beyond any price, with which it cannot in the least be brought into competition or comparison without, as it were, violating its holiness.

And what is it that justifies the morally good disposition or virtue in making such lofty claims? It is nothing less than the participation it affords the rational being in giving universal laws. He is thus fitted to be a member in a possible realm of ends to which his own nature already destined him. For, as an end in himself, he is destined to be legislative in the realm of ends, free from all laws of nature and obedient only to those which he himself gives. Accordingly, his maxims can belong to a universal legislation to which he is at the same time also subject. A thing has no worth other than that determined for it by the law. The legislation which determines all worth must therefore have a dignity, i.e., unconditional and incomparable worth. For the esteem which a rational being must have for it, only the word "respect" is a suitable expression. Autonomy is thus the basis of the dignity of both human nature and every rational nature.

The three aforementioned ways of presenting the principle of morality are fundamentally only so many formulas of the very same law, and each of them unites the others in itself.

. . .

9

Morality as a System of Hypothetical Imperatives

PHILIPPA FOOT

*Philippa Foot (b. 1920) is Professor of Philosophy at the University of
California at Los Angeles, and Senior Research Fellow at Somerville
College, Oxford. She has published influential articles on free will, the
problem of abortion, and other topics in moral philosophy.*

*In this essay, Foot takes issue with the central Kantian claim that morality
must be grounded in a categorical rather than in hypothetical imperatives.
Kant's position (see reading 8) is that any genuinely moral reason for acting
must operate independently of any desires or inclinations that an agent
merely happens to have. Foot disagrees. She acknowledges that it may make
sense to say that a person should do something that will not further his
desires, as when we say that even a person who cares nothing about
etiquette should, according to the rules, not eat peas with a knife. However,
Foot insists that the rules of etiquette provide no reason for acting unless
one wants to obey them, and that the rules of morality are precisely similar
in this regard. Contrary to Kantian theory, an amoral person can rationally
and consistently disregard moral rules.*

*If moral rules do not compel rational assent, then don't they lose all their
force and special status? According to Foot, they do not. Even if moral
considerations only provide reasons for acting when someone wants to act
morally, it hardly follows that the desire to act morally must be a shallow or
transient one. To the contrary, among those who have it, that desire is often
extremely deep and stable. If we reject psychological hedonism and other
forms of psychological egoism (reading 1), we will have to agree that such a
desire can lead people to make great sacrifices to achieve moral ends. This,
Foot argues, is all that any moralist needs or should ask.*

THERE ARE MANY DIFFICULTIES and obscurities in Kant's moral philosophy, and few contemporary moralists will try to defend it all. Many, for
instance, agree in rejecting Kant's derivation of duties from the mere form of
the law expressed in terms of a universally legislative will. Nevertheless, it is
generally supposed, even by those who would not dream of calling themselves
his followers, that Kant established one thing beyond doubt—namely, the necessity
of disinguishing moral judgements from hypothetical imperatives. That moral
judgements cannot be hypothetical imperatives has come to seem an unquestionable truth. It will be argued here that it is not.

In discussing so thoroughly Kantian a notion as that of the hypothetical imperative, one naturally begins by asking what Kant himself meant by a hypothetical imperative, and it may be useful to say a little about the idea of an imperative as this appears in Kant's works. In writing about imperatives Kant seems to be thinking at least as much of statements about what ought to be or should be done, as of injunctions expressed in the imperative mood. He even describes as an imperative the assertion that it would be 'good to do or refrain from doing something'[1] and explains that for a will that 'does not always do something simply because it is presented to it as a good thing to do' this has the force of a command of reason. We may therefore think of Kant's imperatives as statements to the effect that something ought to be done or that it would be good to do it.

The distinction between hypothetical imperatives and categorical imperatives, which plays so important a part in Kant's ethics, appears in characteristic form in the following passages from the *Foundations of the Metaphysics of Morals*:

> All imperatives command either hypothetically or categorically. The former present the practical necessity of a possible action as a means to achieving something else which one desires (or which one may possibly desire). The categorical imperative would be one which presented an action as of itself objectively necessary, without regard to any other end.[2]

> If the action is good only as a means to something else, the imperative is hypothetical; but if it is thought of as good in itself, and hence as necessary in a will which of itself conforms to reason as the principle of this will, the imperative is categorical.[3]

The hypothetical imperative, as Kant defines it, 'says only that the action is good to some purpose' and the purpose, he explains, may be possible or actual. Among imperatives related to actual purposes Kant mentions rules of prudence, since he believes that all men necessarily desire their own happiness. Without committing ourselves to this view it will be useful to follow Kant in classing together as 'hypothetical imperatives' those telling a man what he ought to do because (or if) he wants something and those telling him what he ought to do on grounds of self-interest. Common opinion agrees with Kant in insisting that a moral man must accept a rule of duty whatever his interests or desires.

Having given a rough description of the class of Kantian hypothetical imperatives it may be useful to point to the heterogeneity within it. Sometimes what a man should do depends on his passing inclination, as when he wants his coffee hot and should warm the jug. Sometimes it depends on some long-term

---

[1] *Foundations of the Metaphysics of Morals*, Sec. II, trans. by L. W. Beck.

[2] Ibid.

[3] Ibid.

project, when the feelings and inclinations of the moment are irrelevant. If one wants to be a respectable philosopher one should get up in the mornings and do some work, though just at that moment when one should do it the thought of being a respectable philosopher leaves one cold. It is true nevertheless to say of one, at that moment, that one wants to be a respectable philosopher, and this can be the foundation of a desire-dependent hypothetical imperative. The term 'desire' as used in the original account of the hypothetical imperative was meant as a grammatically convenient substitute for 'want', and was not meant to carry any implication of inclination rather than long-term aim or project. Even the word 'project', taken strictly, introduces undesirable restrictions. If someone is devoted to his family or his country or to any cause, there are certain things he wants, which may then be the basis of hypothetical imperatives, without either inclinations or projects being quite what is in question. Hypothetical imperatives should already be appearing as extremely diverse; a further important distinction is between those that concern an individual and those that concern a group. The desires on which a hypothetical imperative is dependent may be those of one man, or may be taken for granted as belonging to a number of people engaged in some common project or sharing common aims.

Is Kant right to say that moral judgements are categorical, not hypothetical, imperatives? It may seem that he is, for we find in our language two different uses of words such as 'should' and 'ought', apparently corresponding to Kant's hypothetical and categorical imperatives, and we find moral judgements on the 'categorical' side. Suppose, for instance, we have advised a traveller that he should take a certain train, believing him to be journeying to his home. If we find that he has decided to go elsewhere, we will most likely have to take back what we said: the 'should' will now be unsupported and in need of support. Similarly, we must be prepared to withdraw our statement about what he should do if we find that the right relation does not hold between the action and the end—that it is either no way of getting what he wants (or doing what he wants to do) or not the most eligible among possible means. The use of 'should' and 'ought' in moral contexts is, however, quite different. When we say that a man should do something and intend a moral judgement we do not have to back up what we say by considerations about his interests or his desires; if no such connexion can be found the 'should' need not be withdrawn. It follows that the agent cannot rebut an assertion about what, morally speaking, he should do by showing that the action is not ancillary to his interests or desires. Without such a connexion the 'should' does not stand unsupported and in need of support; the support that *it* requires is of another kind.

There is, then, one clear difference between moral judgements and the class of 'hypothetical imperatives' so far discussed. In the latter 'should' is 'used hypothetically', in the sense defined, and if Kant were merely drawing attention to this piece of linguistic usage his point would easily be proved. But obviously Kant meant more than this; in describing moral judgements as non-hypothetical—that is, categorical imperatives—he is ascribing to them a special dignity and necessity which this usage cannot give. Modern philosophers follow Kant

in talking, for example, about the 'unconditional requirement' expressed in moral judgements. These, they say, tell us what we have to do whatever our interests or desires, and by their inescapability they are distinguished from hypothetical imperatives.

The problem is to find proof for this further feature of moral judgements. If anyone fails to see the gap that has to be filled it will be useful to point out to him that we find 'should' used non-hypothetically in some non-moral statements to which no one attributes the special dignity and necessity conveyed by the description 'categorical imperative'. For instance, we find this non-hypothetical use of 'should' in sentences enunciating rules of etiquette, as, for example, that an invitation in the third person should be answered in the third person, where the rule does not *fail to apply* to someone who has his own good reasons for ignoring this piece of nonsense, or who simply does not care about what, from the point of view of etiquette, he should do. Similarly, there is a non-hypothetical use of 'should' in contexts where something like a club rule is in question. The club secretary who has told a member that he should not bring ladies into the smoking-room does not say, 'Sorry, I was mistaken' when informed that this member is resigning tomorrow and cares nothing about his reputation in the club. Lacking a connexion with the agent's desires or interests, this 'should' does not stand 'unsupported and in need of support'; it requires only the backing of the rule. The use of 'should' is therefore 'non-hypothetical' in the sense defined.

It follows that if a hypothetical use of 'should' gave a hypothetical imperative, and a non-hypothetical use of 'should' a categorical imperative, then 'should' statements based on rules of etiquette, or rules of a club would be categorical imperatives. Since this would not be accepted by defenders of the categorical imperative in ethics, who would insist that these other 'should' statements give hypothetical imperatives, they must be using this expression in some other sense. We must therefore ask what they mean when they say that 'You should answer . . . in the third person' is a hypothetical imperative. Very roughly the idea seems to be that one may reasonably ask why anyone should bother about what should (from the point of view of etiquette) be done, and that such considerations deserve no notice unless reason is shown. So although people give as their reason for doing something the fact that it is required by etiquette, we do not take this consideration as *in itself giving us reason to act*. Considerations of etiquette do not have any automatic reason-giving force, and a man might be right if he denied that he had reason to do 'what's done'.

This seems to take us to the heart of the matter, for, by contrast, it is supposed that moral considerations necessarily give reasons for acting to any man. The difficulty is, of course, to defend this proposition which is more often repeated than explained. Unless it is said, implausibly, that all 'should' or 'ought' statements give reasons for acting, which leaves the old problem of assigning a special categorical status to moral judgement, we must be told what it is that makes the moral 'should' relevantly different from the 'shoulds' appearing in

normative statements of other kinds.[4] Attempts have sometimes been made to show that some kind of irrationality is involved in ignoring the 'should' of morality: in saying 'Immoral—so what?' as one says 'Not *comme il faut**—so what?' But as far as I can see these have all rested on some illegitimate assumption, as, for instance, of thinking that the amoral man, who agrees that some piece of conduct is immoral but takes no notice of that, is inconsistently disregarding a rule of conduct that he has accepted; or again of thinking it inconsistent to desire that others will not do to one what one proposes to do to them. The fact is that the man who rejects morality because he sees no reason to obey its rules can be convicted of villainy but not of inconsistency. Nor will his action necessarily be irrational. Irrational actions are those in which a man in some way defeats his own purposes, doing what is calculated to be disadvantageous or to frustrate his ends. Immorality does not *necessarily* involve any such thing.

It is obvious that the normative character of moral judgement does not guarantee its reason-giving force. Moral judgements are normative,[†] but so are judgements of manners, statements of club rules, and many others. Why should the first provide reasons for acting as the others do not? In every case it is because there is a background of teaching that the non-hypothetical 'should' can be used. The behaviour is required, not simply recommended, but the question remains as to why we should do what we are required to do. It is true that moral rules are often enforced much more strictly than the rules of etiquette, and our reluctance to press the non-hypothetical 'should' of etiquette may be one reason why we think of the rules of etiquette as hypothetical imperatives. But are we then to say that there is nothing behind the idea that moral judgements are categorical imperatives but the relative stringency of our moral teaching? I believe that this may have more to do with the matter than the defenders of the categorical imperative would like to admit. For if we look at the kind of thing that is said in its defence we may find ourselves puzzled about what the words can even mean unless we connect them with the feelings

---

[4] To say that moral considerations are *called* reasons is blatantly to ignore the problem.

In the case of etiquette or club rules it is obvious that the non-hypothetical use of 'should' has resulted in the loss of the usual connexion between what one should do and what one has reason to do. Someone who objects that in the moral case a man cannot be justified in restricting his practical reasoning in this way, since every moral 'should' gives reasons for acting, must face the following dilemma. Either it is possible to create reasons for acting simply by putting together any silly rules and introducing a non-hypothetical 'should', or else the non-hypothetical 'should' does not necessarily imply reasons for acting. If it does not necessarily imply reasons for acting we may ask why it is supposed to do so in the case of morality. Why cannot the indifferent amoral man say that for him 'should$_m$' gives no reason for acting, treating 'should$_m$' as most of us treat 'should$_e$'? Those who insist that 'should$_m$' is categorical in this second 'reason-giving' sense do not seem to realise that they never prove this to be so. They sometimes say that moral considerations 'just do' give reasons for acting, without explaining why some devotee of etiquette could not say the same about the rules of etiquette.

* The proper way.

[†] Prescribing action with respect to a standard.

that this stringent teaching implants. People talk, for instance, about the 'binding force' of morality, but it is not clear what this means if not that we *feel* ourselves unable to escape. Indeed the 'inescapability' of moral requirements is often cited when they are being contrasted with hypothetical imperatives. No one, it is said, escapes the requirements of ethics by having or not having particular interests or desires. Taken in one way this only reiterates the contrast between the 'should' of morality and the hypothetical 'should', and once more places morality alongside of etiquette. Both are inescapable in that behaviour does not cease to offend against either morality or etiquette because the agent is indifferent to their purposes and to the disapproval he will incur by flouting them. But morality is supposed to be inescapable in some special way and this may turn out to be merely the reflection of the way morality is taught. Of course, we must try other ways of expressing the fugitive thought. It may be said, for instance, that moral judgements have a kind of necessity since they tell us what we 'must do' or 'have to do' whatever our interests and desires. The sense of this is, again, obscure. Sometimes when we use such expressions we are referring to physical or mental compulsion. (A man has to go along if he is pulled by strong men and he has to give in if tortured beyond endurance.) But it is only in the absence of such conditions that moral judgements apply. Another and more common sense of the words is found in sentences such as 'I caught a bad cold and had to stay in bed' where a penalty for acting otherwise is in the offing. The necessity of acting morally is not, however, supposed to depend on such penalties. Another range of examples, not necessarily having to do with penalties, is found where there is an unquestioned acceptance of some project or rôle, as when a nurse tells us that she has to make her rounds at a certain time, or we say that we have to run for a certain train. But these too are irrelevant in the present context, since the acceptance condition can always be revoked.

No doubt it will be suggested that it is in some other sense of the words 'have to' or 'must' that one has to or must do what morality demands. But why should one insist that there must be such a sense when it proves so difficult to say what it is? Suppose that what we take for a puzzling thought were really no thought at all but only the reflection of our *feelings* about morality? Perhaps it makes no sense to say that we 'have to' submit to the moral law, or that morality is 'inescapable' in some special way. For just as one may feel as if one is falling without believing that one is moving downward, so one may feel as if one has to do what is morally required without believing oneself to be under physical or psychological compulsion, or about to incur a penalty if one does not comply. No one thinks that if the word 'falling' is used in a statement reporting one's sensations it must be used in a special sense. But this kind of mistake may be involved in looking for the special sense in which one 'has to' do what morality demands. There is no difficulty about the idea that we feel we *have to* behave morally, and given the psychological conditions of the learning of moral behaviour it is natural that we should have such feelings. What we cannot do is quote them in support of the doctrine of the categorical imperative. It seems, then, that in so far as it is backed up by statements to the effect

that the moral law *is* inescapable, or that we *do* have to do what is morally required of us, it is uncertain whether the doctrine of the categorical imperative even makes sense.

The conclusion we should draw is that moral judgements have no better claim to be categorical imperatives than do statements about matters of etiquette. People may indeed follow either morality or etiquette without asking why they should do so, but equally well they may not. They may ask for reasons and may reasonably refuse to follow either if reasons are not to be found.

It will be said that this way of viewing moral considerations must be totally destructive of morality, because no one could ever act morally unless he accepted such considerations as in themselves sufficient reason for action. Actions that are truly moral must be done 'for their own sake', 'because they are right', and not for some ulterior purpose. This argument we must examine with care, for the doctrine of the categorical imperative has owed much to its persuasion.

Is there anything to be said for the thesis that a truly moral man acts 'out of respect for the moral law' or that he does what is morally right because it is morally right? That such propositions are not prima facie absurd depends on the fact that moral judgement concerns itself with a man's reasons for acting as well as with what he does. Law and etiquette require only that certain things are done or left undone, but no one is counted as charitable if he gives alms 'for the praise of men', and one who is honest only because it pays him to be honest does not have the virtue of honesty. This kind of consideration was crucial in shaping Kant's moral philosophy. He many times contrasts acting out of respect for the moral law with acting from an ulterior motive, and what is more from one that is self-interested. In the early *Lectures on Ethics* he gave the principle of truth-telling under a system of hypothetical imperatives as that of not lying *if it harms one to lie*. In the *Metaphysics of Morals* he says that ethics cannot start from the ends which a man may propose to himself, since these are all 'selfish'.[5] In the *Critique of Practical Reason* he argues explicitly that when acting not out of respect for moral law but 'on a material maxim' men do what they do for the sake of pleasure or happiness.

> All material practical principles are, as such, of one and the same kind and belong under the general principle of self love or one's own happiness.[6]

Kant, in fact, was a psychological hedonist* in respect of all actions except those done for the sake of the moral law, and this faulty theory of human nature was one of the things preventing him from seeing that moral virtue might be compatible with the rejection of the categorical imperative.

If we put this theory of human action aside, and allow as ends the things

---

[5] Pt. II, Introduction, sec. II.

[6] Immanuel Kant, *Critique of Practical Reason*, trans. L. W. Beck, p. 133.

* One who believes that actions are performed to gain pleasure or avoid pain. For discussion, see Joel Feinberg, "Psychological Egoism," reading 1.

that seem to be ends, the picture changes. It will surely be allowed that quite apart from thoughts of duty a man may care about the suffering of others, having a sense of identification with them, and wanting to help if he can. Of course he must want not the reputation of charity, nor even a gratifying rôle helping others, but, quite simply, their good. If this is what he does care about, then he will be attached to the end proper to the virtue of charity and a comparison with someone acting from an ulterior motive (even a respectable ulterior motive) is out of place. Nor will the conformity of his action to the rule of charity be merely contingent. Honest action may happen to further a man's career; charitable actions do not *happen* to further the good of others.

Can a man accepting only hypothetical imperatives possess other virtues besides that of charity? Could he be just or honest? This problem is more complex because there is no end related to such virtues as the good of others is related to charity. But what reason could there be for refusing to call a man a just man if he acted justly because he loved truth and liberty, and wanted every man to be treated with a certain respect? And why should the truly honest man not follow honesty for the sake of the good that honest dealing brings to men? Of course, the usual difficulties can be raised about the rare case in which no good is foreseen from an individual act of honesty. But it is not evident that a man's desires could not give him reason to act honestly even here. He wants to live openly and in good faith with his neighbours; it is not all the same to him to lie and conceal.

If one wants to know whether there could be a truly moral man who accepted moral principles as hypothetical rules of conduct, as many people accept rules of etiquette as hypothetical rules of conduct, one must consider the right kind of example. A man who demanded that morality should be brought under the heading of self-interest would not be a good candidate, nor would anyone who was ready to be charitable or honest only so long as he felt inclined. A cause such as justice makes strenuous demands, but this is not peculiar to morality, and men are prepared to toil to achieve many ends not endorsed by morality. That they are prepared to fight so hard for moral ends—for example, for liberty and justice— depends on the fact that these are the kinds of ends that arouse devotion. To sacrifice a great deal for the sake of etiquette one would need to be under the spell of the emphatic 'ought'. One could hardly be devoted to behaving *comme il faut*.

In spite of all that has been urged in favour of the hypothetical imperative in ethics, I am sure that many people will be unconvinced and will argue that one element essential to moral virtue is still missing. This missing feature is the recognition of a *duty* to adopt those ends which we have attributed to the moral man. We have said that he *does* care about others, and about causes such as liberty and justice; that it is on this account that he will accept a system of morality. But what if he never cared about such things, or what if he ceased to care? Is it not the case that he *ought* to care? This is exactly what Kant would say, for though at times he sounds as if he thought that morality is not concerned with ends, at others he insists that the adoption of ends such as the

happiness of others is itself dictated by morality.[7] How is this proposition to be regarded by one who rejects all talk about the binding force of the moral law? He will agree that a moral man has moral ends and cannot be indifferent to matters such as suffering and injustice. Further, he will recognise in the statement that one *ought* to care about these things a correct application of the non-hypothetical moral 'ought' by which society is apt to voice its demands. He will not, however, take the fact that he ought to have certain ends as in itself reason to adopt them. If he himself is a moral man then he cares about such things, but not 'because he ought'. If he is an amoral man he may deny that he has any reason to trouble his head over this or any other moral demand. Of course he may be mistaken, and his life as well as others' lives may be most sadly spoiled by his selfishness. But this is not what is urged by those who think they can close the matter by an emphatic use of 'ought'. My argument is that they are relying on an illusion, as if trying to give the moral 'ought' a magic force.[8]

This conclusion may, as I said, appear dangerous and subversive of morality. We are apt to panic at the thought that we ourselves, or other people, might stop caring about the things we do care about, and we feel that the categorical imperative gives us some control over the situation. But it is interesting that the people of Leningrad were not struck by the thought that only the *contingent* fact that other citizens shared their loyalty and devotion to the city stood between them and the Germans during the terrible years of the siege. Perhaps we should be less troubled than we are by fear of defection from the moral cause; perhaps we should even have less reason to fear it if people thought of themselves as volunteers banded together to fight for liberty and justice and against inhumanity and oppression. It is often felt, even if obscurely, that there is an element of deception in the official line about morality. And while some have been persuaded by talk about the authority of the moral law, others have turned away with a sense of distrust.

[7] See e.g., *The Metaphysics of Morals*, pt. II, sec. 30.

[8] See G. E. M. Anscombe, 'Modern Moral Philosophy', *Philosophy* (1958). My view is different from Miss Anscombe's, but I have learned from her.

10

What Makes
Right Acts Right?

W. D. ROSS

Sir William David Ross (1877–1971) was Provost of Oriel College, Oxford University. His book, The Right and the Good, *from which this selection is taken, is a major contribution to ethics. He also has published influential translations of, and commentaries upon, the works of Aristotle.*

Ross takes a position that incorporates elements of both utilitarianism and Kantianism. He rejects the utilitarian assumptions that happiness is the only good thing, and that our only obligation or duty is to maximize what is good. However, he agrees that our duties include the promotion of happiness (and other goods) as well as the performance of such acts as keeping our promises, promoting justice, and developing our talents. Because an act which satisfies one of these duties will often not satisfy another, Ross calls all such duties prima facie. *We have a* prima facie *duty to perform an act when the act "would be a duty proper if it were not at the same time of another kind which is morally significant." By contrast, our duty proper in a given situation is what we should do in that situation all things considered.*

How do we know what our prima facie *and all-things-considered duties are? According to Ross, we know that such acts as promise-keeping, gratitude, and the production of happiness are* prima facie *duties through a kind of direct apprehension. The fact that these features always count in an act's favor is simply self-evident. By contrast, what we should actually do in a given situation is not self-evident. To ascertain this, we must carefully weigh all the relevant factors. Our knowledge of our duty proper is always arrived at through the conscientious exercise of judgment.*

As many critics have pointed out, Ross's account tells us little about either what is learned through direct apprehension and judgment or what equips us to learn it. For relevant discussion, though it does not address Ross directly, see Gilbert Harman (reading 3), and John Rawls (reading 4). Yet even if we are dissatisfied with Ross's approach to moral knowledge, we may still find his views about what we should actually do attractive. Of all the theories represented here, Ross's claim that there are a number of irreducibly distinct sorts of moral obligations is probably the closest to what many thoughtful people come to believe after careful consideration of problematic cases.

THE REAL POINT at issue between hedonism and utilitarianism on the one hand and their opponents on the other is not whether 'right' means 'productive of so and so'; for it cannot with any plausibility be maintained that it does. The point at issue is that to which we now pass, viz. whether there is any general character which makes right acts right, and if so, what it is. Among the main historical attempts to state a single characteristic of all right actions which is the foundation of their rightness are those made by egoism and utilitarianism. But I do not propose to discuss these, not because the subject is unimportant, but because it has been dealt with so often and so well already, and because there has come to be so much agreement among moral philosophers that neither of these theories is satisfactory. A much more attractive theory has been put forward by Professor Moore: that what makes actions right is that they are productive of more *good* than could have been produced by any other action open to the agent.

This theory is in fact the culmination of all the attempts to base rightness on productivity of some sort of result. The first form this attempt takes is the attempt to base rightness on conduciveness to the advantage or pleasure of the agent. This theory comes to grief over the fact, which stares us in the face, that a great part of duty consists in an observance of the rights and a furtherance of the interests of others, whatever the cost to ourselves may be. Plato and others may be right in holding that a regard for the rights of others never in the long run involves a loss of happiness for the agent, that 'the just life profits a man'. But this, even if true, is irrelevant to the rightness of the act. As soon as a man does an action *because* he thinks he will promote his own interests thereby, he is acting not from a sense of its rightness but from self-interest.

To the egoistic theory hedonistic utilitarianism supplies a much-needed amendment. It points out correctly that the fact that a certain pleasure will be enjoyed by the agent is no reason why he *ought* to bring it into being rather than an equal or greater pleasure to be enjoyed by another, though, human nature being what it is, it makes it not unlikely that he *will* try to bring it into being. But hedonistic utilitarianism in its turn needs a correction. On reflection it seems clear that pleasure is not the only thing in life that we think good in itself, that for instance we think the possession of a good character, or an intelligent understanding of the world, as good or better. A great advance is made by the substitution of 'productive of the greatest good' for 'productive of the greatest pleasure'.

Not only is this theory more attractive than hedonistic utilitarianism, but its logical relation to that theory is such that the latter could not be true unless *it* were true, while it might be true though hedonistic utilitarianism were not. It is in fact one of the logical bases of hedonistic utilitarianism. For the view that what produces the maximum pleasure is right has for its bases the views (1) that what produces the maximum good is right, and (2) that pleasure is the only thing good in itself. If they were not assuming that what produces the maximum *good* is right, the utilitarians' attempt to show that pleasure is the only thing good in itself, which is in fact the point they take most pains to establish, would have been quite irrelevant to their attempt to prove that only

what produces the maximum *pleasure* is right. If, therefore, it can be shown that productivity of the maximum good is not what makes all right actions right, we shall *a fortiori** have refuted hedonistic utilitarianism.

When a plain man fulfils a promise because he thinks he ought to do so, it seems clear that he does so with no thought of its total consequences, still less with any opinion that these are likely to be the best possible. He thinks in fact much more of the past than of the future. What makes him think it right to act in a certain way is the fact that he has promised to do so—that and, usually, nothing more. That his act will produce the best possible consequences is not his reason for calling it right. What lends colour to the theory we are examining, then, is not the actions (which form probably a great majority of our actions) in which some such reflection as 'I have promised' is the only reason we give ourselves for thinking a certain action right, but the exceptional cases in which the consequences of fulfilling a promise (for instance) would be so disastrous to others that we judge it right not to do so. It must of course be admitted that such cases exist. If I have promised to meet a friend at a particular time for some trivial purpose, I should certainly think myself justified in breaking my engagement if by doing so I could prevent a serious accident or bring relief to the victims of one. And the supporters of the view we are examining hold that my thinking so is due to my thinking that I shall bring more good into existence by the one action than by the other. A different account may, however, be given of the matter, an account which will, I believe, show itself to be the true one. It may be said that besides the duty of fulfilling promises I have and recognize a duty of relieving distress, and that when I think it right to do the latter at the cost of not doing the former, it is not because I think I shall produce more good thereby but because I think it the duty which is in the circumstances more of a duty. This account surely corresponds much more closely with what we really think in such a situation. If, so far as I can see, I could bring equal amounts of good into being by fulfilling my promise and by helping some one to whom I had made no promise, I should not hesitate to regard the former as my duty. Yet on the view that what is right is right because it is productive of the most good I should not so regard it.

There are two theories, each in its way simple, that offer a solution of such cases of conscience. One is the view of Kant, that there are certain duties of perfect obligation, such as those of fulfilling promises, of paying debts, of telling the truth, which admit of no exception whatever in favour of duties of imperfect obligation, such as that of relieving distress. The other is the view of, for instance, Professor Moore and Dr. Rashdall, that there is only the duty of producing good, and that all 'conflicts of duties' should be resolved by asking 'by which action will most good be produced?' But it is more important that our theory fit the facts than that it be simple, and the account we have given above corresponds (it seems to me) better than either of the simpler theories

---

* *A fortiori* literally means "for even stronger reasons." Here it is used to mean that we will have done even more than is required.

with what we really think, viz. that normally promise-keeping, for example, should come before benevolence, but that when and only when the good to be produced by the benevolent act is very great and the promise comparatively trivial, the act of benevolence becomes our duty.

In fact the theory of 'ideal utilitarianism', if I may for brevity refer so to the theory of Professor Moore, seems to simplify unduly our relations to our fellows. It says, in effect, that the only morally significant relation in which my neighbours stand to me is that of being possible beneficiaries by my action. They do stand in this relation to me, and this relation is morally significant. But they may also stand to me in the relation of promisee to promiser, of creditor to debtor, of wife to husband, of child to parent, of friend to friend, of fellow countryman to fellow countryman, and the like; and each of these relations is the foundation of a *prima facie* duty, which is more or less incumbent on me according to the circumstances of the case. When I am in a situation, as perhaps I always am, in which more than one of these *prima facie* duties is incumbent on me, what I have to do is to study the situation as fully as I can until I form the considered opinion (it is never more) that in the circumstances one of them is more incumbent than any other; then I am bound to think that to do this *prima facie* duty is my duty *sans phrase* in the situation.

I suggest '*prima facie* duty' or 'conditional duty' as a brief way of referring to the characteristic (quite distinct from that of being a duty proper) which an act has, in virtue of being of a certain kind (e.g. the keeping of a promise), of being an act which would be a duty proper if it were not at the same time of another kind which is morally significant. Whether an act is a duty proper or actual duty depends on *all* the morally significant kinds it is an instance of. The phrase '*prima facie* duty' must be apologized for, since (1) it suggests that what we are speaking of is a certain kind of duty, whereas it is in fact not a duty, but something related in a special way to duty. Strictly speaking, we want not a phrase in which duty is qualified by an adjective, but a separate noun. (2) '*Prima' facie* suggests that one is speaking only of an appearance which a moral situation presents at first sight, and which may turn out to be illusory; whereas what I am speaking of is an objective fact involved in the nature of the situation, or more strictly in an element of its nature, though not, as duty proper does, arising from its *whole* nature. . . .

There is nothing arbitrary about these *prima facie* duties. Each rests on a definite circumstance which cannot seriously be held to be without moral significance. Of *prima facie* duties I suggest, without claiming completeness or finality for it, the following division.

(I) Some duties rest on previous acts of my own. These duties seem to include two kinds, (*a*) those resting on a promise or what may fairly be called an implicit promise, such as the implicit undertaking not to tell lies which seems to be implied in the act of entering into conversation (at any rate by civilized men), or of writing books that purport to be history and not fiction. These may be called the duties of fidelity. (*b*) Those resting on a previous wrongful act. These may be called the duties of reparation. (2) Some rest on previous acts of other men, i.e. services done by them to me. These may be loosely described as the

duties of gratitude. (3) Some rest on the fact or possibility of a distribution of pleasure or happiness (or of the means thereto) which is not in accordance with the merit of the persons concerned; in such cases there arises a duty to upset or prevent such a distribution. These are the duties of justice. (4) Some rest on the mere fact that there are other beings in the world whose condition we can make better in respect of virtue, or of intelligence, or of pleasure. These are the duties of beneficience. (5) Some rest on the fact that we can improve our own condition in respect of virtue or of intelligence. These are the duties of self-improvement. (6) I think that we should distinguish from (4) the duties that may be summed up under the title of 'not injuring others'. No doubt to injure others is incidentally to fail to do them good; but it seems to me clear that non-maleficence is apprehended as a duty distinct from that of beneficience, and as a duty of a more stringent character. . . . We should not in general consider it justifiable to kill one person in order to keep another alive, or to steal from one in order to give alms to another.

The essential defect of the 'ideal utilitarian' theory is that it ignores, or at least does not do full justice to, the highly personal character of duty. If the only duty is to produce the maximum of good, the question who is to have the good—whether it is myself, or my benefactor, or a person to whom I have made a promise to confer that good on him, or a mere fellow man to whom I stand in no such special relation—should make no difference to my having a duty to produce that good. But we are all in fact sure that it makes a vast difference.

. . .

If the objection be made, that this catalogue of the main types of duty is an unsystematic one resting on no logical principle, it may be replied, first, that it makes no claim to being ultimate. It is a *prima facie* classification of the duties which reflection on our moral convictions seems actually to reveal. And if these convictions are, as I would claim that they are, of the nature of knowledge, and if I have not misstated them, the list will be a list of authentic conditional duties, correct as far as it goes though not necessarily complete. The list of *goods* put forward by the rival theory is reached by exactly the same method— the only sound one in the circumstances—viz. that of direct reflection on what we really think. Loyalty to the facts is worth more than a symmetrical architectonic or a hastily reached simplicity. If further reflection discovers a perfect logical basis for this or for a better classification, so much the better.

It may, again, be objected that our theory that there are these various and often conflicting types of *prima facie* duty leaves us with no principle upon which to discern what is our actual duty in particular circumstances. But this objection is not one which the rival theory is in a position to bring forward. For when we have to choose between the production of two heterogeneous goods, say knowledge and pleasure, the 'ideal utilitarian' theory can only fall back on an opinion, for which no logical basis can be offered, that one of the goods is the greater; and this is no better than a similar opinion that one of two duties is the more urgent. And again, when we consider the infinite variety

of the effects of our actions in the way of pleasure, it must surely be admitted that the claim which *hedonism* sometimes makes, that it offers a readily applicable criterion of right conduct, is quite illusory.

I am unwilling, however, to content myself with an *argumentum ad hominem,* and I would contend that in principle there is no reason to anticipate that every act that is our duty is so for one and the same reason. Why should two sets of circumstances, or one set of circumstances, *not* possess different characteristics, any one of which makes a certain act our *prima facie* duty? When I ask what it is that makes me in certain cases sure that I have a *prima facie* duty to do so and so, I find that it lies in the fact that I have made a promise; when I ask the same question in another case, I find the answer lies in the fact that I have done a wrong. And if on reflection I find (as I think I do) that neither of these reasons is reducible to the other, I must not on any *a priori* ground assume that such a reduction is possible.

. . .

The duty of justice is particularly complicated, and the word is used to cover things which are really very different—things such as the payment of debts, the reparation of injuries done by oneself to another, and the bringing about of a distribution of happiness between other people in proportion to merit. I use the word to denote only the last of these three. In the fifth chapter I shall try to show that besides the three (comparatively) simple goods, virtue, knowledge, and pleasure, there is a more complex good, not reducible to these, consisting in the proportionment of happiness to virtue. The bringing of this about is a duty which we owe to all men alike, though it may be reinforced by special responsibilities that we have undertaken to particular men. This, therefore, with beneficience and self-improvement, comes under the general principle that we should produce as much good as possible, though the good here involved is different in kind from any other.

But besides this general obligation, there are special obligations. These may arise, in the first place, incidentally, from acts which were not essentially meant to create such an obligation, but which nevertheless create it. From the nature of the case such acts may be of two kinds—the infliction of injuries on others, and the acceptance of benefits from them. It seems clear that these put us under a special obligation to other men, and that only these acts can do so incidentally. From these arise the twin duties of reparation and gratitude.

And finally there are special obligations arising from acts the very intention of which, when they were done, was to put us under such an obligation. The name for such acts is 'promises'; the name is wide enough if we are willing to include under it implicit promises, i.e. modes of behaviour in which without explicit verbal promise we intentionally create an expectation that we can be counted on to behave in a certain way in the interest of another person.

These seem to be, in principle, all the ways in which *prima facie* duties arise. In actual experience they are compounded together in highly complex ways. Thus, for example, the duty of obeying the laws of one's country arises partly (as Socrates contends in the *Crito*) from the duty of gratitude for the benefits

one has received from it; partly from the implicit promise to obey which seems to be involved in permanent residence in a country whose laws we know we are *expected* to obey, and still more clearly involved when we ourselves invoke the protection of its laws (this is the truth underlying the doctrine of the social contract); and partly (if we are fortunate in our country) from the fact that its laws are potent instruments for the general good.

Or again, the sense of a general obligation to bring about (so far as we can) a just apportionment of happiness to merit is often greatly reinforced by the fact that many of the existing injustices are due to a social and economic system which we have, not indeed created, but taken part in and assented to; the duty of justice is then reinforced by the duty of reparation.

It is necessary to say something by way of clearing up the relation between *prima facie* duties and the actual or absolute duty to do one particular act in particular circumstances. If, as almost all moralists except Kant are agreed, and as most plain men think, it is sometimes right to tell a lie or to break a promise, it must be maintained that there is a difference between *prima facie* duty and actual or absolute duty. When we think ourselves justified in breaking, and indeed morally obliged to break, a promise in order to relieve some one's distress, we do not for a moment cease to recognize a *prima facie* duty to keep our promise, and this leads us to feel, not indeed shame or repentance, but certainly compunction, for behaving as we do; we recognize, further, that it is our duty to make up somehow to the promisee for the breaking of the promise. We have to distinguish from the characteristic of being our duty that of tending to our duty. Any act that we do contains various elements in virtue of which it falls under various categories. In virtue of being the breaking of a promise, for instance, it tends to be wrong; in virtue of being an instance of relieving distress it tends to be right. . . .

Another instance of the same distinction may be found in the operation of natural laws. *Qua* subject to the force of gravitation towards some other body, each body tends to move in a particular direction with a particular velocity; but its actual movement depends on *all* the forces to which it is subject. It is only by recognizing this distinction that we can preserve the absoluteness of laws of nature, and only by recognizing a corresponding distinction that we can preserve the absoluteness of the general principles of morality. But an important difference between the two cases must be pointed out. When we say that in virtue of gravitation a body tends to move in a certain way, we are referring to a causal influence actually exercised on it by another body or other bodies. When we say that in virtue of being deliberately untrue a certain remark tends to be wrong, we are referring to no causal relation, to no relation that involves succession in time, but to such a relation as connects the various attributes of a mathematical figure. And if the word 'tendency' is thought to suggest too much a causal relation, it is better to talk of certain types of act as being *prima facie* right or wrong (or of different persons as having different and possibly conflicting claims upon us), than of their tending to be right or wrong.

Something should be said of the relation between our apprehension of the

prima facie rightness of certain types of act and our mental attitude towards particular acts. It is proper to use the word 'apprehension' in the former case and not in the latter. That an act, *qua* fulfilling a promise, or *qua* effecting a just distribution of good, or *qua* returning services rendered, or *qua* promoting the good of others, or *qua* promoting the virtue or insight of the agent, is *prima facie* right, is self-evident; not in the sense that it is evident from the beginning of our lives, or as soon as we attend to the proposition for the first time, but in the sense that when we have reached sufficient mental maturity and have given sufficient attention to the proposition it is evident without any need of proof, or of evidence beyond itself. It is self-evident just as a mathematical axiom, or the validity of a form of inference, is evident. The moral order expressed in these propositions is just as much part of the fundamental nature of the universe (and, we may add, of any possible universe in which there were moral agents at all) as is the spatial or numerical structure expressed in the axioms of geometry or arithmetic. In our confidence that these propositions are true there is involved the same trust in our reason that is involved in our confidence in mathematics; and we should have no justification for trusting it in the latter sphere and distrusting it in the former. In both cases we are dealing with propositons that cannot be proved, but that just as certainly need no proof.

. . .

Our judgements about our actual duty in concrete situations have none of the certainty that attaches to our recognition of the general principles of duty. A statement is certain, i.e. is an expression of knowledge, only in one or other of two cases: when it is either self-evident, or a valid conclusion from self-evident premises. And our judgements about our particular duties have neither of these characters. (I) They are not self-evident. Where a possible act is seen to have two characteristics, in virtue of one of which it is *prima facie* right, and in virtue of the other *prima facie* wrong, we are (I think) well aware that we are not certain whether we ought or ought not to do it; that whether we do it or not, we are taking a moral risk. We come in the long run, after consideration, to think one duty more pressing than the other, but we do not feel certain that it is so. And though we do not always recognize that a possible act has two such characteristics, and though there *may* be cases in which it has not, we are never certain that any particular possible act has not, and therefore never certain that it is right, nor certain that it is wrong. For, to go no further in the analysis, it is enough to point out that any particular act will in all probability in the course of time contribute to the bringing about of good or of evil for many human beings, and thus have a *prima facie* rightness or wrongness of which we know nothing. (2) Again, our judgements about our particular duties are not logical conclusions from self-evident premises. The only possible premises would be the general principles stating their *prima facie* rightness or wrongness *qua* having the different characteristics they do have; and even if we could (as we cannot) apprehend the extent to which an act will tend on the one hand, for example, to bring out advantages for our benefactors, and on the other hand to bring about disadvantages for fellow men who are not our

benefactors, there is no principle by which we can draw the conclusion that it is on the whole right or on the whole wrong. In this respect the judgement as to the rightness of a particular act is just like the judgement as to the beauty of a particular natural object or work of art. A poem is, for instance, in respect of certain qualities beautiful and in respect of certain others not beautiful; and our judgement as to the degree of beauty it possesses on the whole is never reached by logical reasoning from the apprehension of its particular beauties or particular defects. Both in this and in the moral case we have more or less probable opinions which are not logically justified conclusions from the general principles that are recognized as self-evident.

There is therefore much truth in the description of the right act as a fortunate act. If we cannot be certain that it is right, it is our good fortune if the act we do is the right act. This consideration does not, however, make the doing of our duty a mere matter of chance. There is a parallel here between the doing of duty and the doing of what will be to our personal advantage. We never *known* what act will in the long run be to our advantage. Yet it is certain that we are more likely in general to secure our advantage if we estimate to the best of our ability the probable tendencies of our actions in this respect, than if we act on caprice. And similarly we are more likely to do our duty if we reflect to the best of our ability on the *prima facie* rightness or wrongness of various possible acts in virtue of the characteristics we perceive them to have, than if we act without reflection. With this greater likelihood we must be content.

Many people would be inclined to say that the right act for me is not that whose general nature I have been describing, viz. that which if I were omniscient I should see to be my duty, but that which on all the evidence available to me I should think to be my duty. But suppose that from the state of partial knowledge in which I think act A to be my duty, I could pass to a state of perfect knowledge in which I saw act B to be my duty, should I not say 'act B was the right act for me to do'? I should no doubt add 'though I am not to be blamed for doing act A'. . . .

It might seem absurd to suggest that it could be right for any one to do an act which would produce consequences less good than those which would be produced by some other act in his power. Yet a little thought will convince us that this is not absurd. The type of case in which it is easiest to see that this is so is, perhaps, that in which one has made a promise. In such a case we all think that *prima facie* it is our duty to fulfil the promise irrespective of the precise goodness of the total consequences. And though we do not think it is necessarily our actual or absolute duty to do so, we are far from thinking that any, even the slightest, gain in the value of the total consequences will necessarily justify us in doing something else instead. Suppose, to simplify the case by abstraction, that the fulfilment of a promise to A would produce 1,000 units of good for him, but that by doing some other act I could produce 1,001 units of good for B, to whom I have made no promise, the other consequences of the two acts being of equal value; should we really think it self-evident that it was our duty to do the second act and not the first? I think not. We should, I fancy, hold that only a much greater disparity of value between the total con-

sequences would justify us in failing to discharge our *prima facie* duty to A. After all, a promise is a promise, and is not to be treated so lightly as the theory we are examining would imply. What, exactly, a promise is, is not so easy to determine, but we are surely agreed that it constitutes a serious moral limitation to our freedom of action. To produce the 1,001 units of goods for B rather than fulfil our promise to A would be to take, not perhaps our duty as philanthropists too seriously, but certainly our duty as makers of promises too lightly.

. . .

I conclude that the attributes 'right' and 'optimific'* are not identical, and that we do not know either by intuition, by deduction, or by induction that they coincide in their application, still less that the latter is the foundation of the former. It must be added, however, that if we are ever under no special obligation such as that of fidelity to a promisee or of gratitude to a benefactor, we ought to do what will produce most good; and that even when we are under a special obligation the tendency of acts to promote general good is one of the main factors in determining whether they are right.

In what has preceded, a good deal of use has been made of 'what we really think' about moral questions; a certain theory has been rejected because it does not agree with what we really think. It might be said that this is in principle wrong; that we should not be content to expound what our present moral consciousness tells us but should aim at a criticism of our existing moral consciousness in the light of theory. Now I do not doubt that the moral consciousness of men has in detail undergone a good deal of modification as regards the things we think right, at the hands of moral theory. But if we are told, for instance, that we should give up our view that there is a special obligatoriness attaching to the keeping of promises because it is self-evident that the only duty is to produce as much good as possible, we have to ask ourselves whether we really, when we reflect, *are* convinced that this is self-evident, and whether we really *can* get rid of our view that promise-keeping has a bindingness independent of productiveness of maximum good. In my own experience I find that I cannot, in spite of a very genuine attempt to do so; and I venture to think that most people will find the same, and that just because they cannot lose the sense of special obligation, they cannot accept as self-evident, or even as true, the theory which would require them to do so. In fact it seems, on reflection, self-evident that a promise, simply as such, is something that *prima facie* ought to be kept, and it does *not*, on reflection, seem self-evident that production of maximum good is the only thing that makes an act obligatory. And to ask us to give up at the bidding of a theory our actual apprehension of what is right and what is wrong seems like asking people to repudiate their actual experience of beauty, at the bidding of a theory which says 'only that which satisfies such and such conditions can be beautiful'. If what I have called our actual appre-

---

* Productive of the most possible good.

hension is (as I would maintain that it is) truly an apprehension, i.e. an instance of knowledge, the request is nothing less than absurd.

I would maintain, in fact, that what we are apt to describe as 'what we think' about moral questions contains a considerable amount that we do not think but know, and that this forms the standard by reference to which the truth of any moral theory has to be tested, instead of having itself to be tested by reference to any theory. I hope that I have in what precedes indicated what in my view these elements of knowledge are that are involved in our ordinary moral consciousness.

It would be a mistake to found a natural science on 'what we really think', i.e. on what reasonably thoughtful and well-educated people think about the subjects of the science before they have studied them scientifically. For such opinions are interpretations, and often misinterpretations, of sense-experience; and the man of science must appeal from these to sense-experience itself, which furnishes his real data. In ethics no such appeal is possible. We have no more direct way of access to the facts about rightness and goodness and about what things are right or good, than by thinking about them; the moral convictions of thoughtful and well-educated people are the data of ethics just as sense-perceptions are the data of a natural science. Just as some of the latter have to be rejected as illusory, so have some of the former; but as the latter are rejected only when they are in conflict with other more accurate sense-perceptions, the former are rejected only when they are in conflict with convictions which stand better the test of reflection. The existing body of moral convictions of the best people is the cumulative product of the moral reflection of many generations, which has developed an extremely delicate power of appreciation of moral distinctions; and this the theorist cannot afford to treat with anything other than the greatest respect. The verdicts of the moral consciousness of the best people are the foundation on which we must build; though he must first compare them with one another and eliminate any contradictions they may contain.

11

The Nature of
Moral Virtue

ARISTOTLE

*Aristotle (384–322 B.C.) was perhaps the most comprehensive thinker who
ever lived. Besides systematically exploring virtually every branch of what is
now thought of as philosophy, he did pioneering work in rhetoric, politics,
astronomy, physics, biology, and other areas. His work exercised a
profound influence on Western thought through the Middle Ages. The
selection included here is from his treatise on ethics, the* Nichomachean
Ethics.

*Many discussions of ethics attempt primarily to formulate and defend
principles of right conduct. Aristotle does not deny the importance of this—
indeed, he remarks that it is common ground "that when we act we should
do so according to the right principle"—but his discussion in this selection
has a different emphasis. He points out that even someone who does act on
a right principle may not do so from a settled disposition or character trait.
Thus, if we are interested in the deeper springs of right action, we must
ask not only which acts are right, but also how to inculcate the proper
dispositions to perform them. One possible answer is simply to teach
the correct principles or reasons for acting; but Aristotle objects that mere
theoretical knowledge of what is right makes us like invalids "who listen
carefully to all the doctor says but do not carry out a single one of his
orders." He proposes, instead, that we best learn virtue by actually
practicing it. If we continually act rightly, we will eventually acquire
the appropriate habits. Although Aristotle's view of moral education is
controversial (compare it, for example, with the view implicit in Kant's
discussion in reading 8), it continues to warrant and receive careful
consideration.*

*Aside from discussing the teaching of moral virtue, Aristotle also
addresses the proper content of such education. His view is that moral virtue
is in every case a mean between two extremes. The virtuous person is
neither rash nor cowardly but brave, neither obsequious nor surly but
friendly, and so on. Here, as elsewhere, Aristotle's emphasis differs from
that of more recent discussions—to see how much, compare his list of moral
virtues with the duties listed by W.D. Ross in reading 10. Whether
Aristotle's doctrine of the mean can be extended to provide a complete
account of virtue is left for you to decide.*

Chapter I

VIRTUE, then, is of two kinds, intellectual and moral. Of these the intellectual is in the main indebted to teaching for its production and growth, and this calls for time and experience. Moral goodness, on the other hand, is the child of habit, from which it has got its very name, ethics being derived from *ethos*, 'habit,' by a slight alteration in the quantity of the *e*. This is an indication that none of the moral virtues is implanted in us by nature, since nothing that nature creates can be taught by habit to change the direction of its development. For instance a stone, the natural tendency of which is to fall down, could never, however often you threw it up in the air, be trained to go in that direction. No more can you train fire to burn downwards. Nothing in fact, if the law of its being is to behave in one way, can be habituated to behave in another. The moral virtues, then, are produced in us neither *by* Nature nor *against* Nature. Nature, indeed, prepares in us the ground for their reception, but their complete formation is the product of habit.

Consider again these powers or faculties with which Nature endows us. We acquire the ability to use them before we do use them. The senses provide us with a good illustration of this truth. We have not acquired the sense of sight from repeated acts of seeing, or the sense of hearing from repeated acts of hearing. It is the other way round. We had these senses before we used them, we did not acquire them as a result of using them. But the moral virtues we do acquire by first exercising them. The same is true of the arts and crafts in general. The craftsman has to learn how to make things, but he learns in the process of making them. So men become builders by building, harp players by playing the harp. By a similar process we become just by performing just actions, temperate by performing temperate actions, brave by performing brave actions. Look at what happens in political societies—it confirms our view. We find legislators seeking to make good men of their fellows by making good behaviour habitual with them. That is the aim of every lawgiver, and when he is unable to carry it out effectively, he is a failure; nay, success or failure in this is what makes the difference between a good constitution and a bad.

Again, the creation and the destruction of any virtue are effected by identical cause and identical means; and this may be said, too, of every art. It is as a result of playing the harp that harpers become good or bad in their art. The same is true of builders and all other craftsmen. Men will become good builders as a result of building well, and bad builders as a result of building badly. Otherwise what would be the use of having anyone to teach a trade? Craftsmen would all be born either good or bad. Now this holds also of the virtues. It is in the course of our dealings with our fellow-men that we become just or unjust. It is our behaviour in a crisis and our habitual reactions to danger that make us brave or cowardly, as it may be. So with our desires and passions. Some men are made temperate and gentle, others profligate and passionate, the former by conducting themselves in one way, the latter by conducting themselves in another, in situations in which their feelings are involved. We may sum it all up in the generalization, 'Like activities produce like dispositions.' This

makes it our duty to see that our activities have the right character, since the differences of quality in them are repeated in the dispositions that follow in their train. So it is a matter of real importance whether our early education confirms us in one set of habits or another. It would be nearer the truth to say that it makes a very great difference indeed, in fact all the difference in the world.

Chapter II

Since the branch of philosophy on which we are at present engaged differs from the others in not being a subject of merely intellectual interest—I mean we are not concerned to know what goodness essentially is, but how we are to become good men, for this alone gives the study its practical value—we must apply our minds to the solution of the problems of conduct. For, as I remarked, it is our actions that determine our dispositions.

Now that when we act we should do so according to the right principle, is common ground and I propose to take it as a basis of discussion.[1] But we must begin with the admission that any theory of conduct must be content with an outline without much precision in details. We noted this when I said at the beginning of our discussion of this part of our subject that the measure of exactness of statement in any field of study must be determined by the nature of the matter studied. Now matters of conduct and considerations of what is to our advantage have no fixity about them any more than matters affecting our health. And if this be true of moral philosophy as a whole, it is still more true that the discussion of particular problems in ethics admits of no exactitude. For they do not fall under any science or professional tradition, but those who are following some line of conduct are forced in every collocation of circumstances to think out for themselves what is suited to these circumstances, just as doctors and navigators have to do in their different *métiers*. We can do no more than give our arguments, inexact as they necessarily are, such support as is available.

Let us begin with the following observation. It is in the nature of moral qualities that they can be destroyed by deficiency on the one hand and excess on the other. We can see this in the instances of bodily health and strength.[2] Physical strength is destroyed by too much and also by too little exercise. Similarly health is ruined by eating and drinking either too much or too little, while it is produced, increased and preserved by taking the right quantity of drink and victuals. Well, it is the same with temperance, courage, and the other virtues. The man who shuns and fears everything and can stand up to nothing

---

[1] There will be an opportunity later of considering what is meant by this formula, in particular what is meant by 'the right principle' and how, in its ethical aspect, it is related to the moral virtues.

[2] If we are to illustrate the material, it must be by concrete images.

becomes a coward. The man who is afraid of nothing at all, but marches up to every danger, becomes foolhardy. In the same way the man who indulges in every pleasure without refraining from a single one becomes incontinent. If, on the other hand, a man behaves like the Boor in comedy and turns his back on every pleasure, he will find his sensibilities becoming blunted. So also temperance and courage are destroyed both by excess and deficiency, and they are kept alive by observance of the mean.

Let us go back to our statement that the virtues are produced and fostered as a result, and by the agency, of actions of the same quality as effect their destruction. It is also true that after the virtues have been formed they find expression in actions of that kind. We may see this in a concrete instance—bodily strength. It results from taking plenty of nourishment and going in for hard training, and it is the strong man who is best fitted to cope with such conditions. So with the virtues. It is by refraining from pleasures that we become temperate, and it is when we have become temperate that we are most able to abstain from pleasures. Or take courage. It is by habituating ourselves to make light of alarming situations and to confront them that we become brave, and it is when we have become brave that we shall be most able to face an alarming situation.

Chapter III

We may use the pleasure (or pain) that accompanies the exercise of our dispositions as an index of how far they have established themselves. A man is temperate who abstaining from bodily pleasures finds this abstinence pleasant; if he finds it irksome, he is intemperate. Again, it is the man who encounters danger gladly, or at least without painful sensations, who is brave; the man who has these sensations is a coward. In a word, moral virtue has to do with pains and pleasures. There are a number of reasons for believing this. (1) Pleasure has a way of making us do what is disgraceful; pain deters us from doing what is right and fine. Hence the importance—I quote Plato—of having been brought up to find pleasure and pain in the right things. True education is just such a training. (2) The virtues operate with actions and emotions, each of which is accompanied by pleasure or pain. This is only another way of saying that virtue has to do with pleasures and pains. (3) Pain is used as an instrument of punishment. For in her remedies Nature works by opposites, and pain can be remedial. (4) When any disposition finds its complete expression it is, as we noted, in dealing with just those things by which it is its nature to be made better or worse, and which constitute the sphere of its operations. Now when men become bad it is under the influence of pleasures and pains when they seek the wrong ones among them, or seek them at the wrong time, or in the wrong manner, or in any of the wrong forms which such offences may take; and in seeking the wrong pleasures and pains they shun the right. This has led some thinkers to identify the moral virtues with conditions of the soul in which passion is eliminated or reduced to a minimum. But this is to make too absolute a statement—it needs to be qualified by adding that such a condition must be

attained 'in the right manner and at the right time' together with the other modifying circumstances.

So far, then, we have got this result. Moral goodness is a quality disposing us to act in the best way when we are dealing with pleasures and pains, while vice is one which leads us to act in the worst way when we deal with them.

The point may be brought out more clearly by some other considerations. There are three kinds of things that determine our choice in all our actions—the morally fine, the expedient, the pleasant; and three that we shun—the base, the harmful, the painful. Now in his dealings with all of these it is the good man who is most likely to go right, and the bad man who tends to go wrong, and that most notably in the matter of pleasure. The sensation of pleasure is felt by us in common with all animals, accompanying everything we choose, for even the fine and the expedient have a pleasurable effect upon us. (6) The capacity for experiencing pleasure has grown in us from infancy as part of our general development, and human life, being dyed in grain with it, receives therefrom a colour hard to scrape off. (7) Pleasure and pain are also the standards by which with greater or less strictness we regulate our considered actions. Since to feel pleasure and pain rightly or wrongly is an important factor in human behaviour, it follows that we are primarily concerned with these sensations. (8) Heraclitus says it is hard to fight against anger, but it is harder still to fight against pleasure. Yet to grapple with the harder has always been the business, as of art, so of goodness, success in a task being proportionate to its difficulty. This gives us another reason for believing that morality and statesmanship must concentrate on pleasures and pains, seeing it is the man who deals rightly with them who will be good, and the man who deals with them wrongly who will be bad.

Here, then, are our conclusions. (*a*) Virtue is concerned with pains and pleasures. (*b*) The actions which produce virtue are identical in character with those which increase it. (*c*) These actions differently performed destroy it. (*d*) The actions which produced it are identical with those in which it finds expression.

Chapter IV

A difficulty, however, may be raised as to what we mean when we say that we must perform just actions if we are to become just, and temperate actions if we are to be temperate. It may be argued that, if I do what is just and temperate, I am just and temperate already, exactly as, if I spell words or play music correctly, I must already be literate or musical. This I take to be a false analogy, even in the arts. It is possible to spell a word right by accident or because somebody tips you the answer. But you will be a scholar only if your spelling is done as a scholar does it, that is thanks to the scholarship in your own mind. Nor will the suggested analogy with the arts bear scrutiny. A work of art is good or bad in itself—let it possess a certain quality, and that is all we ask of it. But virtuous actions are not done in a virtuous—a just or temperate—way merely because *they* have the appropriate quality. The *doer* must be in a certain frame of mind when he does them. Three conditions are involved.

(1) The agent must act in full consciousness of what he is doing. (2) He must 'will' his action, and will it for its own sake. (3) The act must proceed from a fixed and unchangeable disposition. Now these requirements, if we except mere knowledge, are not counted among the necessary qualifications of an artist. For the acquisition of virtue, on the other hand, knowledge is of little or no value, but the other requirements are of immense, of sovran, importance, since it is the repeated performance of just and temperate actions, that produces virtue. Actions, to be sure, are *called* just and temperate when they are such as a just or temperate man would do. But the doer is just or temperate not because he does such things but when he does them in the way of just and temperate persons. It is therefore quite fair to say that a man becomes just by the performance of just, and temperate by the performance of temperate, actions; nor is there the smallest likelihood of a man's becoming good by any other course of conduct. It is not, however, a popular line to take, most men preferring theory to practice under the impression that arguing about morals proves them to be philosophers, and that in this way they will turn out to be fine characters. Herein they resemble invalids, who listen carefully to all the doctor says but do not carry out a single one of his orders. The bodies of such people will never respond to treatment—nor will the souls of such 'philosophers.'

Chapter V

We now come to the formal definition of virtue. Note first, however, that the human soul is conditioned in three ways. It may have (1) feelings, (2) capacities, (3) dispositions; so virtue must be one of these three. By 'feelings' I mean desire, anger, fear, daring, envy , gratification, friendliness, hatred, longing, jealousy, pity and in general all states of mind that are attended by pleasure or pain. By 'capacities' I mean those faculties in virtue of which we may be described as capable of the feelings in question—anger, for instance, or pain, or pity. By 'dispositions' I mean states of mind in virtue of which we are well or ill disposed in respect of the feelings concerned. We have, for instance, a bad disposition where angry feelings are concerned if we are disposed to become excessively or insufficiently angry, and a good disposition in this respect if we consistently feel the due amount of anger, which comes between these extremes. So with the other feelings.

Now, neither the virtues nor the vices are feelings. We are not spoken of as good or bad in respect of our feelings but of our virtues and vices. Neither are we praised or blamed for the way we feel. A man is not praised for being frightened or angry, nor is he blamed just for being angry; it is for being angry in a particular way. But we *are* praised and blamed for our virtues and vices. Again, feeling angry or frightened is something we can't help, but our virtues are in a manner expressions of our will; at any rate there is an element of will in their formation. Finally, we are said to be 'moved' when our feelings are affected, but when it is a question of moral goodness or badness we are not said to be 'moved' but to be 'disposed' in a particular way. A similar line of reasoning will prove that the virtues and vices are not capacities either. We are

not spoken of as good or bad, nor are we praised or blamed, merely because we are *capable* of feeling. Again, what capacities we have, we have by nature; but it is not nature that makes us good or bad. . . . So, if the virtues are neither feelings nor capacities, it remains that they must be dispositions. . . .

Chapter VI

It is not, however, enough to give this account of the *genus* of virtue—that it is a disposition; we must describe its *species*. Let us begin, then, with this proposition. Excellence of whatever kind affects that of which it is the excellence in two ways. (1) It produces a good state in it. (2) It enables it to perform its function well. Take eyesight. The goodness of your eye is not only that which makes your eye good, it is also that which makes it function well. Or take the case of a horse. The goodness of a horse makes him a good horse, but it also makes him good at running, carrying a rider and facing the enemy. Our proposition, then, seems to be true, and it enables us to say that virtue in a man will be the disposition which (*a*) makes him a good man, (*b*) enables him to perform his function well. We have already touched on this point, but more light will be thrown upon it if we consider what is the specific nature of virtue.

In anything continuous and divisible it is possible to take the half, or more than the half, or less than the half. Now these parts may be larger, smaller or equal either in relation to the thing divided or in relation to us. The equal part may be described as a mean between too much and too little. By the mean of the thing I understand a point equidistant from the extremes; and this is one and the same for everybody. Let me give an illustration. Ten, let us say, is 'many' and two is 'few' of something. We get the mean of the thing if we take six;[3] that is, six exceeds and is exceeded by an equal number. This is the rule which gives us the arithmetical mean. But such a method will not give us the mean in relation to ourselves. Let ten pounds of food be a large, and two pounds a small, allowance for an athlete, It does not follow that the trainer will prescribe six pounds. That might be a large or it might be a small allowance for the particular athlete who is to get it. It would be little for Milo but a lot for a man who has just begun his training.[4] It is the same in all walks of life. The man who knows his business avoids both too much and too little. It is the mean he seeks and adopts—not the mean of the thing but the relative mean.

Every form, then, of applied knowledge, when it performs its function well, looks to the mean and works to the standard set by that. It is because people feel this that they apply the *cliché*, 'You couldn't add anything to it or take anything from it' to an artistic masterpiece, the implication being that too much and too little alike destroy perfection, while the mean preserves it. Now if this be so, and if it be true, as we say, that good craftsmen work to the standard of the mean, then, since goodness like nature is more exact and of a higher

---

[3] $6 - 2 = 10 - 6$

[4] What applies to gymnastics applies also to running and wrestling.

character than any art, it follows that goodness is the quality that hits the mean. By 'goodness' I mean goodness of moral character, since it is moral goodness that deals with feelings and actions, and it is in them that we find excess, deficiency and a mean. It is possible, for example, to experience fear, boldness, desire, anger, pity, and pleasures and pains generally, too much or too little or to the right amount. If we feel them too much or too little, we are wrong. But to have these feelings at the right times on the right occasions towards the right people for the right motive and in the right way is to have them in the right measure, that is somewhere between the extremes; and this is what character-izes goodness. The same may be said of the mean and extremes in actions. Now it is in the field of actions and feelings that goodness operates; in them we find excess, deficiency and, between them, the mean, the first two being wrong, the mean right and praised as such.[5] Goodness, then, is a mean con-dition in the sense that it aims at and hits the mean.

Consider, too, that it is possible to go wrong in more ways than one. (In Pythagorean terminology evil is a form of the Unlimited, good of the Limited.) But there is only one way of being right. That is why going wrong is easy, and going right difficult; it is easy to miss the bull's eye and difficult to hit it. Here, then is another explanation of why the too much and the too little are connected with evil and the mean with good. As the poet says,

> Goodness is one, evil is multiform.

We may now define virtue as a disposition of the soul in which, when it has to choose among actions and feelings, it observes the mean relative to us, this being determined by such a rule or principle as would take shape in the mind of a man of sense or practical wisdom. We call it a mean condition as lying between two forms of badness, one being excess and the other deficiency; and also for this reason, that, whereas badness either falls short of or exceeds the right measure in feelings and actions, virtue discovers the mean and deliberately chooses it. Thus, looked at from the point of view of its essence as embodied in its definition, virtue no doubt is a mean; judged by the standard of what is right and best, it is an extreme.

But choice of a mean is not possible in every action or every feeling. The very names of some have an immediate connotation of evil. Such are malice, shamelessness, envy among feelings, and among actions adultery, theft, murder. All these and more like them have a bad name as being evil in themselves; it is not merely the excess or deficiency of them that we censure. In their case, then, it is impossible to act rightly; whatever we do is wrong. Nor do circumstances make any difference in the rightness or wrongness of them. When a man com-mits adultery there is no point in asking whether it is with the right woman or at the right time or in the right way, for to do anything like that is simply wrong. It would amount to claiming that there is a mean and excess and defect

---

[5] Being right or successful and being praised are both indicative of excellence.

in unjust or cowardly or intemperate actions. If such a thing were possible, we should find ourselves with a mean quantity of excess, a mean of deficiency, an excess of excess and a deficiency of deficiency. But just as in temperance and justice there can be no mean or excess or deficiency, because the mean in a sense *is* an extreme, so there can be no mean or excess or deficiency in those vicious actions—however done, they are wrong. Putting the matter into general language, we may say that there is no mean in the extremes, and no extreme in the mean, to be observed by anybody.

Chapter VII

But a generalization of this kind is not enough; we must show that our definition fits particular cases. When we are discussing actions particular statements come nearer the heart of the matter, though general statements cover a wider field. The reason is that human behaviour consists in the performance of particular acts, and our theories must be brought into harmony with them.

You see here a diagram of the virtues.* Let us take our particular instances from that.

In the section confined to the feelings inspired by danger you will observe that the mean state is 'courage.' Of those who go to extremes in one direction or the other the man who shows an excess of fearlessness has no name to describe him,[6] the man who exceeds in confidence or daring is called 'rash' or 'foolhardy,' the man who shows an excess of fear and a deficiency of confidence is called a 'coward.' In the pleasures and pains—though not all pleasures and pains, especially pains—the virtue which observes the mean is 'temperance,' the excess is the vice of 'intemperance.' Persons defective in the power to enjoy pleasures are a somewhat rare class, and so have not had a name assigned to them: suppose we call them 'unimpressionable.' Coming to the giving and acquiring of money, we find that the mean is 'liberality,' the excess 'prodigality,' the deficiency 'meanness.' But here we meet a complication. The prodigal man and the mean man exceed and fall short in opposite ways. The prodigal exceeds in giving and falls short in getting money, whereas the mean man exceeds in getting and falls short in giving it away. Of course this is but a summary account of the matter—a bare outline. But it meets our immediate requirements. Later on these types of character will be more accurately delineated.

But there are other dispositions which declare themselves in the way they deal with money. One is 'lordliness' or 'magnificence,' which differs from liberality in that the lordly man deals in large sums, the liberal man in small. Magnificence is the mean state here, the excess is 'bad taste' or 'vulgarity,' the defect is 'shabbiness.' These are not the same as the excess and defect on either side of liberality. How they differ is a point which will be discussed later. In

---

* Aristotle's diagram is omitted here.

[6] We shall often have to make similar admissions.

the matter of honour the mean is 'proper pride,' the excess 'vanity,' the defect 'poor-spiritedness.' And just as liberality differs, as I said, from magnificence in being concerned with small sums of money, so there is a state related to proper pride in the same way, being concerned with small honours, while pride is concerned with great. For it is possible to aspire to small honours in the right way, or to greater or less extent than is right. The man who has this aspiration to excess is called 'ambitious'; if he does not cherish it enough, he is 'unambitious'; but the man who has it to the right extent—that is, strikes the mean—has no special designation. This is true also of the corresponding dispositions with one exception, that of the ambitious man, which is called 'ambitiousness.' This will explain why each of the extreme characters stakes out a claim in the middle region. Indeed we ourselves call the character between the extremes sometimes 'ambitious' and sometimes 'unambitious.' That is proved by our sometimes praising a man for being ambitious and sometimes for being unambitious. The reason will appear later. In the meantime let us continue our discussion of the remaining virtues and vices, following the method already laid down.

Let us next take anger. Here too we find excess, deficiency and the mean. Hardly one of the states of mind involved has a special name; but, since we call the man who attains the mean in this sphere 'gentle,' we may call his disposition 'gentleness.' Of the extremes the man who is angry overmuch may be called 'irascible,' and his vice 'irascibility'; while the man who reacts too feebly to anger may be called 'poor-spirited' and his disposition 'poor-spiritedness.'

There are, in addition to those we have named, three other modes of observing the mean which in some ways resemble and in other ways differ from one another. They are all concerned with what we do and say in social intercourse, but they differ in this respect, that one is concerned with truthfulness in such intercourse, the other two with the agreeable, one of these two with the agreeable in amusement, the other with the agreeable element in every relation of life. About these two, then, we must say a word, in order that we may more fully convince ourselves that in all things the mean is to be commended, while the extremes are neither commendable nor right but reprehensible. I am afraid most of these too are nameless; but, as in the other cases, we must try to coin names for them in the interests of clearness and to make it easy to follow the argument. Well then, as regards veracity, the character who aims at the mean may be called 'truthful' and what he aims at 'truthfulness.' Pretending, when it goes too far, is 'boastfulness' and the man who shows it is a 'boaster' or 'braggart.' If it takes the form of understatement, the pretence is called 'irony' and the man who shows it 'ironical.' In agreeableness in social amusement the man who hits the mean is 'witty' and what characterizes him is 'wittiness.' The excess is 'buffoonery' and the man who exhibits that is a 'buffoon.' The opposite of the buffoon is the 'boor' and his characteristic is 'boorishness.' In the other sphere of the agreeable—the general business of life—the person who is agreeable in the right way is 'friendly' and his disposition 'friendliness.' The man who makes himself too agreeable, supposing him to have no ulterior object, is 'obsequious'; if he has such an object, he is a 'flatterer.' The man who

is deficient in this quality and takes every opportunity of making himself disagreeable may be called 'peevish' or 'sulky' or 'surly.'

Even when feelings and emotional states are involved one notes that mean conditions exist. And here also, it would be agreed, we may find one man observing the mean and another going beyond it. For instance the 'shamefaced' man, who is put out of countenance by anything. Or a man may fall short here of the due mean. Thus anyone who is deficient in a sense of shame, or has none at all, is called 'shameless.' The man who avoids both extremes is 'modest,' and him we praise. For, while modesty is not a form of goodness, it is praised; it and the modest man. Then there is 'righteous indignation.' This is felt by anyone who strikes the mean between 'envy' and 'malice,' by which last word I mean a pleased feeling at the misfortunes of other people. These are emotions concerned with the pains and pleasures we feel at the fortunes of our neighbours. The man who feels righteous indignation is pained by undeserved good fortune; but the envious man goes beyond that and is pained at anybody's success. The malicious man, on the other hand, is so far from being pained by the misfortunes of another that he is actually tickled by them.

However, a fitting opportunity of discussing these matters will present itself in another place. And after that we shall treat of justice. In that connexion we shall have to distinguish between the various kinds of justice—for the word is used in more senses than one—and show in what way each of them is a mean. . . .

Chapter VIII

Thus there are three dispositions, two of them taking a vicious form (one in the direction of excess, the other of defect) and one a good form, namely the observance of the mean. They are all opposed to one another, though not all in the same way. The extreme states are opposed both to the mean and one another, and the mean is opposed to both extremes. For just as the equal is greater compared with the less, and less compared with the greater, so the mean states (whether in feelings or actions) are in excess if compared with the deficient, and deficient if compared with the excessive, states. Thus a brave man appears rash when set beside a coward, and cowardly when set beside a rash man; a temperate man appears intemperate beside a man of dull sensibilities, and dull if contrasted with an intemperate man. This is the reason why each extreme character tries to push the mean nearer the other. The coward calls the brave man rash, the rash man calls him a coward. And so in the other cases. But, while all the dispositions are opposed to one another in this way, the greatest degree of opposition is that which is found between the two extremes. For they are separated by a greater interval from one another than from the mean, as the great is more widely removed from the small, and the small from the great, than either from the equal. It may be added that sometimes an extreme bears a certain resemblance to a mean. For example, rashness resembles courage, and prodigality resembles liberality. But between the extremes there is always the maximum dissimilarity. Now opposites are by definition things as far removed as possible from one another. Hence the farther apart

things are, the more opposite they will be. Sometimes it is the deficiency, in other instances it is the excess, that is more directly opposed to the mean. Thus cowardice, a deficiency, is more opposed to courage than is rashness, an excess. And it is not insensibility, the deficiency, that is more opposed to temperance but intemperance, the excess. This arises from one or other of two causes. One lies in the nature of the thing itself and may be explained as follows. When one extreme is nearer to the mean and resembles it more, it is not that extreme but the other which we tend to oppose to the mean. For instance, since rashness is held to be nearer and liker to courage than is cowardice, it is cowardice which we tend to oppose to courage on the principle that the extremes which are remoter from the mean strike us as more opposite to it. The other cause lies in ourselves. It is the things to which we are naturally inclined that appear to us more opposed to the mean. For example, we have a natural inclination to pleasure, which makes us prove to fall into intemperance. Accordingly we tend to describe as opposite to the mean those things towards which we have an instinctive inclination. For this reason intemperance, the excess, is more opposed to temperance than is insensibility to pleasure, the deficiency.

Chapter IX

I have said enough to show that moral excellence is a mean, and I have shown in what sense it is so. It is, namely, a mean between two forms of badness, one of excess and the other of defect, and is so described because it aims at hitting the mean point in feelings and in actions. This makes virtue hard of achievement, because finding the middle point is never easy. It is not everybody, for instance, who can find the centre of a circle—that calls for a geometrician. Thus, too, it is easy to fly into a passion—anybody can do that— but to be angry with the right person and to the right extent and at the right time and with the right object and in the right way—that is not easy, and it is not everyone who can do it. This is equally true of giving or spending money. Hence we infer that to do these things properly is rare, laudable and fine.

In view of this we shall find it useful when aiming at the mean to observe these rules. (1) *Keep away from that extreme which is the more opposed to the mean.* It is Calypso's advice:

'Swing round the ship clear of this surf and surge.'

For one of the extremes is always a more dangerous error than the other; and— since it is hard to hit the bull's-eye—we must take the next best course and choose the least of the evils. And it will be easiest for us to do this if we follow the rule I have suggested. (2) *Note the errors into which we personally are most liable to fall.* (Each of us has his natural bias in one direction or another.) We shall find out what ours are by noting what gives us pleasure and pain. After that we must drag ourselves in the opposite direction. For our best way of reaching the middle is by giving a wide berth to our darling sin. It is the method used by a carpenter when he is straightening a warped board. (3) *Always be*

particularly on your guard against pleasure and pleasant things. When Pleasure is at the bar the jury is not impartial. So it will be best for us if we feel towards her as the Trojan elders felt towards Helen, and regularly apply their words to her. If we are for packing her off, as they were with Helen, we shall be the less likely to go wrong.

To sum up. These are the rules by observation of which we have the best chance of hitting the mean. But of course difficulties spring up, especially when we are confronted with an exceptional case. For example, it is not easy to say precisely what is the right way to be angry and with whom and on what grounds and for how long. In fact we are inconsistent on this point, sometimes praising people who are deficient in the capacity for anger and calling them 'gentle,' sometimes praising the choleric and calling them 'stout fellows.' To be sure we are not hard on a man who goes off the straight path in the direction of too much or too little, if he goes off only a little way. We reserve our censure for the man who swerves widely from the course, because then we are bound to notice it. Yet it is not easy to find a formula by which we may determine how far and up to what point a man may go wrong before he incurs blame. But this difficulty of definition is inherent in every object of perception; such questions of degree are bound up with the circumstances of the individual case, where our only criterion *is* the perception.

So much, then, has become clear. In all our conduct it is the mean state that is to be praised. But one should lean sometimes in the direction of the more, sometimes in that of the less, because that is the readiest way of attaining to goodness and the mean.

12

Famine, Affluence, and Morality

PETER SINGER

Peter Singer (b. 1946) teaches philosophy at Monash University in Australia. He has written several books and many philosophical essays on social and political problems. His book, Animal Liberation, *was influential in bringing many people to rethink the way we ought to treat animals.*

In this selection Singer discusses the moral status of providing food to persons who are starving. Many people believe that while it is praiseworthy and charitable to help the destitute, the affluent have no moral obligation to do so. However, Singer challenges this way of distinguishing charity from obligation. His argument rests on the principle that "if it is in our power to prevent something bad from happening, without thereby sacrificing any thing of comparable moral importance, we ought, morally, to do it." If we accept this principle, Singer argues, then we ought to forego many of the luxuries we currently enjoy to prevent others from starving. The fact that the starving live in far-off lands, and that others could help them as easily as we could, are not good reasons for withholding aid.

The success of Singer's argument depends on the acceptability of his central principle. Although most utilitarians would accept it, many deon-tologists would not. On various deontological accounts, the obligation not to cause harm is more stringent or far-reaching, or leaves the agent less discretion in its application, than the obligation to take positive steps to prevent harm. Whether this distinction has a rational basis, or whether it is merely an excuse for non-action are questions left for further consideration.

As I WRITE THIS, in November 1971, people are dying in East Bengal from lack of food, shelter, and medical care. The suffering and death that are occurring there now are not inevitable, not unavoidable in any fatalistic sense of the term. Constant poverty, a cyclone, and a civil war have turned at least nine million people into destitute refugees; nevertheless, it is not beyond the capacity of the richer nations to give enough assistance to reduce any further suffering to very small proportions. The decisions and actions of human beings can prevent this kind of suffering. Unfortunately, human beings have not made the necessary decisions. At the individual level, people have, with very few exceptions, not responded to the situation in any significant way. Generally speaking, people have not given large sums to relief funds; they have not written to their parliamentary representatives demanding increased government assis-tance; they have not demonstrated in the streets, held symbolic fasts, or done

anything else directed toward providing the refugees with the means to satisfy their essential needs. At the government level, no government has given the sort of massive aid that would enable the refugees to survive for more than a few days. Britain, for instance, has given rather more than most countries. It has, to date, given £14,750,000. For comparative purposes, Britain's share of the nonrecoverable development costs of the Anglo-French Concorde project is already in excess of £275,000,000, and on present estimates will reach £440,000,000. The implication is that the British government values a supersonic transport more than thirty times as highly as it values the lives of the nine million refugees. Australia is another country which, on a per capita basis, is well up in the "aid to Bengal" table. Australia's aid, however, amounts to less than one-twelfth of the cost of Sydney's new opera house. The total amount given, from all sources, now stands at about £65,000,000. The estimated cost of keeping the refugees alive for one year is £464,000,000. Most of the refugees have now been in the camps for more than six months. The World Bank has said that India needs a minimum of £300,000,000 in assistance from other countries before the end of the year. It seems obvious that assistance on this scale will not be forthcoming. India will be forced to choose between letting the refugees starve or diverting funds from her own development program, which will mean that more of her own people will starve in the future.[1]

These are the essential facts about the present situation in Bengal. So far as it concerns us here, there is nothing unique about this situation except its magnitude. The Bengal emergency is just the latest and most acute of a series of major emergencies in various parts of the world, arising both from natural and from man-made causes. There are also many parts of the world in which people die from malnutrition and lack of food independent of any special emergency. I take Bengal as my example only because it is the present concern, and because the size of the problem has ensured that it has been given adequate publicity. Neither individuals nor governments can claim to be unaware of what is happening there.

What are the moral implications of a situation like this? In what follows, I shall argue that the way people in relatively affluent countries react to a situation like that in Bengal cannot be justified; indeed, the whole way we look at moral issues—our moral conceptual scheme—needs to be altered, and with it, the way of life that has come to be taken for granted in our society.

In arguing for this conclusion I will not, of course, claim to be morally neutral. I shall, however, try to argue for the moral position that I take, so that anyone who accepts certain assumptions, to be made explicit, will, I hope, accept my conclusion.

I begin with the assumption that suffering and death from lack of food, shelter, and medical care are bad. I think most people will agree about this,

---

[1] There was also a third possibility: that India would go to war to enable the refugees to return to their lands. Since I wrote this paper, India has taken this way out. The situation is no longer that described above, but this does not affect my argument, as the next paragraph indicates.

although one may reach the same view by different routes. I shall not argue for this view. People can hold all sorts of eccentric positions, and perhaps from some of them it would not follow that death by starvation is in itself bad. It is difficult, perhaps impossible, to refute such positions, and so for brevity I will henceforth take this assumption as accepted. Those who disagree need read no further.

My next point is this: if it is in our power to prevent something bad from happening, without thereby sacrificing anything of comparable moral importance, we ought, morally, to do it. By "without sacrificing anything of comparable moral importance" I mean without causing anything else comparably bad to happen, or doing something that is wrong in itself, or failing to promote some moral good, comparable in significance to the bad thing that we can prevent. This principle seems almost as uncontroversial as the last one. It requires us only to prevent what is bad, and not to promote what is good, and it requires this of us only when we can do it without sacrificing anything that is, from the moral point of view, comparably important. I could even, as far as the application of my argument to the Bengal emergency is concerned, qualify the point so as to make it: if it is in our power to prevent something very bad from happening, without thereby sacrificing anything morally significant, we ought, morally, to do it. An application of this principle would be as follows: if I am walking past a shallow pond and see a child drowning in it, I ought to wade in and pull the child out. This will mean getting my clothes muddy, but this is insignificant, while the death of the child would presumably be a very bad thing.

The uncontroversial appearance of the principle just stated is deceptive. If it were acted upon, even in its qualified form, our lives, our society, and our world would be fundamentally changed. For the principle takes, firstly, no account of proximity or distance. It makes no moral difference whether the person I can help is a neighbor's child ten yards from me or a Bengali whose name I shall never know, ten thousand miles away. Secondly, the principle makes no distinction between cases in which I am the only person who could possibly do anything and cases in which I am just one among millions in the same position.

I do not think I need to say much in defense of the refusal to take proximity and distance into account. The fact that a person is physically near to us, so that we have personal contact with him, may make it more likely that we *shall* assist him, but this does not show that we *ought* to help him rather than another who happens to be further away. If we accept any principle of impartiality, universalizability, equality, or whatever, we cannot discriminate against someone merely because he is far away from us (or we are far away from him). Admittedly, it is possible that we are in a better position to judge what needs to be done to help a person near to us than one far away, and perhaps also to provide the assistance we judge to be necessary. If this were the case, it would be a reason for helping those near to us first. This may once have been a justification for being more concerned with the poor in one's own town than with famine victims in India. Unfortunately for those who like to keep their

moral responsibilities limited, instant communication and swift transportation have changed the situation. From the moral point of view, the development of the world into a "global village" has made an important, though still unrecognized, difference to our moral situation. Expert observers and supervisors, sent out by famine relief organizations or permanently stationed in famine-prone areas, can direct our aid to a refugee in Bengal almost as effectively as we could get it to someone in our own block. There would seem, therefore, to be no possible justification for discriminating on geographical grounds.

There may be a greater need to defend the second implication of my principle—that the fact that there are millions of other people in the same position, in respect to the Bengali refugees, as I am, does not make the situation significantly different from a situation in which I am the only person who can prevent something very bad from occurring. Again, of course, I admit that there is a psychological difference between the cases; one feels less guilty about doing nothing if one can point to others, similarly placed, who have also done nothing. Yet this can make no real difference to our moral obligations.[2] Should I consider that I am less obliged to pull the drowning child out of the pond if on looking around I see other people, no further away than I am, who have also noticed the child but are doing nothing? One has only to ask this question to see the absurdity of the view that numbers lessen obligation. It is a view that is an ideal excuse for inactivity; unfortunately most of the major evils—poverty, overpopulation, pollution—are problems in which everyone is almost equally involved.

The view that numbers do make a difference can be made plausible if stated in this way: if everyone in circumstances like mine gave £5 to the Bengal Relief Fund, there would be enough to provide food, shelter, and medical care for the refugees; there is no reason why I should give more than anyone else in the same circumstances as I am; therefore I have no obligation to give more than £5. Each premise in this argument is true, and the argument looks sound. It may convince us, unless we notice that it is based on a hypothetical premise, although the conclusion is not stated hypothetically. The argument would be sound if the conclusion were: if everyone in circumstances like mine were to give £5, I would have no obligation to give more than £5. If the conclusion were so stated, however, it would be obvious that the argument has no bearing on a situation in which it is not the case that everyone else gives £5. This, of course, is the actual situation. It is more or less certain that not everyone in circumstances like mine will give £5. So there will not be enough to provide the needed food, shelter, and medical care. Therefore by giving more than £5 I will prevent more suffering than I would if I gave just £5.

---

[2] In view of the special sense philosophers, often give to the term, I should say that I use "obligation" simply as the abstract noun derived from "ought," so that "I have an obligation to" means no more, and no less, than "I ought to." This usage is in accordance with the definition of "ought" given by the *Shorter Oxford English Dictionary:* "the general verb to express duty or obligation." I do not think any issue of substance hangs on the way the term is used; sentences in which I use "obligation" could all be rewritten, although somewhat clumsily, as sentences in which a clause containing "ought" replaces the term "obligation."

It might be thought that this argument has an absurd consequence. Since the situation appears to be that very few people are likely to give substantial amounts, it follows that I and everyone else in similar circumstances ought to give as much as possible, that is, at least up to the point at which by giving more one would begin to cause serious suffering for oneself and one's dependents—perhaps even beyond this point to the point of marginal utility, at which by giving more one would cause oneself and one's dependents as much suffering as one would prevent in Bengal. If everyone does this, however, there will be more than can be used for the benefit of the refugees, and some of the sacrifice will have been unnecessary. Thus, if everyone does what he ought to do, the result will not be as good as it would be if everyone did a little less than he ought to do, or if only some do all that they ought to do.

The paradox here arises only if we assume that the actions in question—sending money to the relief funds—are performed more or less simultaneously, and are also unexpected. For if it is to be expected that everyone is going to contribute something, then clearly each is not obliged to give as much as he would have been obliged to had others not been giving too. And if everyone is not acting more or less simutaneously, then those giving later will know how much more is needed, and will have no obligation to give more than is necessary to reach this amount. To say this is not to deny the principle that people in the same circumstances have the same obligations, but to point out that the fact that others have given, or may be expected to give, is a relevant circumstance: those giving after it has become known that many others are giving and those giving before are not in the same circumstances. So the seemingly absurd consequence of the principle I have put forward can occur only if people are in error about the actual circumstances—that is, if they think they are giving when others are not, but in fact they are giving when others are. The result of everyone doing what he really ought to do cannot be worse than the result of everyone doing less than he ought to do, although the result of everyone doing what he reasonably believes he ought to do could be.

If my argument so far has been sound, neither our distance from a preventable evil nor the number of other people who, in respect to that evil, are in the same situation as we are, lessens our obligation to mitigate or prevent that evil. I shall therefore take as established the principle I asserted earlier. As I have already said, I need to assert it only in its qualified form: if it is in our power to prevent something very bad from happening, without thereby sacrificing anything else morally significant, we ought, morally, to do it.

The outcome of this argument is that our traditional moral categories are upset. The traditional distinction between duty and charity cannot be drawn, or at least, not in the place we normally draw it. Giving money to the Bengal Relief Fund is regarded as an act of charity in our society. The bodies which collect money are known as "charities." These organizations see themselves in this way—if you send them a check, you will be thanked for your "generosity." Because giving money is regarded as an act of charity, it is not thought that there is anything wrong with not giving. The charitable man may be praised,

but the man who is not charitable is not condemned. People do not feel in any way ashamed or guilty about spending money on new clothes or a new car instead of giving it to famine relief. (Indeed, the alternative does not occur to them.) This way of looking at the matter cannot be justified. When we buy new clothes not to keep ourselves warm but to look "well-dressed" we are not providing for any important need. We would not be sacrificing anything significant if we were to continue to wear our old clothes, and give the money to famine relief. By doing so, we would be preventing another person from starving. It follows from what I have said earlier that we ought to give money away, rather than spend it on clothes which we do not need to keep us warm. To do so is not charitable, or generous. Nor is it the kind of act which philosophers and theologians have called "supererogatory"—an act which it would be good to do, but not wrong not to do. On the contrary, we ought to give the money away, and it is wrong not to do so.

I am not maintaining that there are no acts which are charitable, or that there are no acts which it would be good to do but not wrong not to do. It may be possible to redraw the distinction between duty and charity in some other place. All I am arguing here is that the present way of drawing the distinction, which makes it an act of charity for a man living at the level of affluence which most people in the "developed nations" enjoy to give money to save someone else from starvation, cannot be supported. It is beyond the scope of my argument to consider whether the distinction should be redrawn or abolished altogether. There would be many other possible ways of drawing the distinction—for instance, one might decide that it is good to make other people as happy as possible but not wrong not to do so.

Despite the limited nature of the revision in our moral conceptual scheme which I am proposing, the revision would, given the extent of both affluence and famine in the world today, have radical implications. These implications may lead to further objections, distinct from those I have already considered. I shall discuss two of these.

One objection to the position I have taken might be simply that it is too drastic a revision of our moral scheme. People do not ordinarily judge in the way I have suggested they should. Most people reserve their moral condemnation for those who violate some moral norm, such as the norm against taking another person's property. They do not condemn those who indulge in luxury instead of giving to famine relief. But given that I did not set out to present a morally neutral description of the way people make moral judgments, the way people do in fact judge has nothing to do with the validity of my conclusion. My conclusion follows from the principle which I advanced earlier, and unless that principle is rejected, or the arguments shown to be unsound, I think the conclusion must stand, however strange it appears.

It might, nevertheless, be interesting to consider why our society, and most other societies, do judge differently from the way I have suggested they should. In a well-known article, J. O. Urmson suggests that the imperatives of duty, which tell us what we must do, as distinct from what it would be good to do

but not wrong not to do, function so as to prohibit behavior that is intolerable if men are to live together in society.[3] This may explain the origin and continued existence of the present division between acts of duty and acts of charity. Moral attitudes are shaped by the needs of society, and no doubt society needs people who will observe the rules that makes social existence tolerable. From the point of view of a particular society, it is essential to prevent violations of norms against killing, stealing, and so on. It is quite inessential, however, to help people outside one's own society.

If this is an explanation of our common distinction between duty and supererogation, however, it is not a justification of it. The moral point of view requires us to look beyond the interests of our own society. Previously, as I have already mentioned, this may hardly have been feasible, but it is quite feasible now. From the moral point of view, the prevention of the starvation of millions of people outside our society must be considered at least as pressing as the upholding of property norms within our society.

It has been argued by some writers, among them Sidgwick and Urmson, that we need to have a basic moral code which is not too far beyond the capacities of the ordinary man, for otherwise there will be a general breakdown of compliance with the moral code. Crudely stated, this argument suggests that if we tell people that they ought to refrain from murder and give everything they do not really need to famine relief, they will do neither, whereas if we tell them that they ought to refrain from murder and that it is good to give to famine relief but not wrong not to do so, they will at least refrain from murder. The issue here is: Where should we draw the line between conduct that is required and conduct that is good although not required, so as to get the best possible result? This would seem to be an empirical question, although a very difficult one. One objection to the Sidgwick-Urmson line of argument is that it takes insufficient account of the effect that moral standards can have on the decisions we make. Given a society in which a wealthy man who gives five percent of his income to famine-relief is regarded as most generous, it is not surprising that a proposal that we all ought to give away half our incomes will be thought to be absurdly unrealistic. In a society which held that no man should have more than enough while others have less than they need, such a proposal might seem narrowminded. What it is possible for a man to do and what he is likely to do are both, I think, very greatly influenced by what people around him are doing and expecting him to do. In any case, the possibility that by spreading the idea that we ought to be doing very much more than we are to relieve famine we shall bring about a general breakdown of moral behavior seems remote. If the stakes are an end to widespread starvation, it is worth the risk. Finally, it should be emphasized that these considerations are relevant only to

---

[3] J. O. Urmson, "Saints and Heroes," in *Essays in Moral Philosophy,* ed. Abraham I. Melden (Seattle and London, 1958), p. 214. For a related but significantly different view see also Henry Sidgwick, *The Methods of Ethics,* 7th edn. (London, 1907), pp. 220–221, 492–493.

the issue of what we should require from others, and not to what we ourselves ought to do.

The second objection to my attack on the present distinction between duty and charity is one which has from time to time been made against utilitarianism. It follows from some forms of utilitarian theory that we all ought, morally, to be working full time to increase the balance of happiness over misery. The position I have taken here would not lead to this conclusion in all circumstances, for if there were no bad occurrences that we could prevent without sacrificing something of comparable moral importance, my argument would have no application. Given the present conditions in many parts of the world, however, it does follow from my argument that we ought, morally, to be working full time to relieve great suffering of the sort that occurs as a result of famine or other disasters. Of course, mitigating circumstances can be adduced—for instance, that if we wear ourselves out through overwork, we shall be less effective than we would otherwise have been. Nevertheless, when all considerations of this sort have been taken into account, the conclusion remains: we ought to be preventing as much suffering as we can without sacrificing something else of comparable moral importance. This conclusion is one which we may be reluctant to face. I cannot see, though, why it should be regarded as a criticism of the position for which I have argued, rather than a criticism of our ordinary standards of behavior. Since most people are self-interested to some degree, very few of us are likely to do everything that we ought to do. It would, however, hardly be honest to take this as evidence that it is not the case that we ought to do it.

It may still be thought that my conclusions are so wildly out of line with what everyone else thinks and has always thought that there must be something wrong with the argument somewhere. In order to show that my conclusions, while certainly contrary to contemporary Western moral standards, would not have seemed so extraordinary at other times and in other places, I would like to quote a passage from a writer not normally thought of as a way-out radical, Thomas Aquinas.

> Now, according to the natural order instituted by devine providence, material goods are provided for the satisfaction of human needs. Therefore the division and appropriation of property, which proceeds from human law, must not hinder the satisfaction of man's necessity from such goods. Equally, whatever a man has in superabundance is owed, of natural right, to the poor for their sustenance. So Ambrosius says, and it is also to be found in the *Decretum Gratiani:* "The bread which you withhold belongs to the hungry; the clothing you shut away, to the naked; and the money you bury in the earth is the redemption and freedom of the penniless."[4]

---

[4] *Summa Theologica,* II–II, Question 66, Article 7, in *Aquinas, Selected Political Writings,* ed. A. P. d'Entreves, trans. J. G. Dawson (Oxford, 1948), p. 171.

I now want to consider a number of points, more practical than philosoph-ical, which are relevant to the application of the moral conclusion we have reached. These points challenge not the idea that we ought to be doing all we can to prevent starvation, but the idea that giving away a great deal of money is the best means to this end.

It is sometimes said that overseas aid should be a government responsibility, and that therefore one ought not to give to privately run charities. Giving privately, it is said, allows the government and the noncontributing members of society to escape their responsibilities.

This argument seems to assume that the more people there are who give to privately organized famine relief funds, the less likely it is that the government will take over full responsibility for such aid. This assumption is unsupported, and does not strike me as at all plausible. The opposite view—that if no one gives voluntarily, a government will assume that its citizens are uninterested in famine relief and would not wish to be forced into giving aid—seems more plausible. In any case, unless there were a definite probability that by refusing to give one would be helping to bring about massive government assistance, people who do refuse to make voluntary contributions are refusing to prevent a certain amount of suffering without being able to point to any tangible ben-eficial consequence of their refusal. So the onus of showing how their refusal will bring about government action is on those who refuse to give.

I do not, of course, want to dispute the contention that governments of affluent nations should be giving many times the amount of genuine, no-strings-attached aid that they are giving now. I agree, too, that giving privately is not enough, and that we ought to be campaigning actively for entirely new stan-dards for both public and private contributions to famine relief. Indeed, I would sympathize with someone who thought that campaigning, was more important than giving oneself, although I doubt whether preaching what one does not practice would be very effective. Unfortunately, for many people the idea that "it's the governments's responsibility" is a reason for not giving which does not appear to entail any political action either.

Another, more serious reason for not giving to famine relief funds is that until there is effective population control, relieving famine merely postpones starvation. If we save the Bengal refugees now, others, perhaps the children of these refugees, will face starvation in a few years' time. In support of this, one may cite the now well-known facts about the population explosion and the relatively limited scope for expanded production.

This point, like the previous one, is an argument against relieving suffering that is happening now, because of a belief about what might happen in the future; it is unlike the previous point in that very good evidence can be adduced in support of this belief about the future. I will not go into the evidence here. I accept that the earth cannot support indefinitely a population rising at the present rate. This certainly poses a problem for anyone who thinks it important to prevent famine. Again, however, one could accept the argument without drawing the conclusion that it absolves one from any obligation to do anything to prevent famine. The conclusion that should be drawn is that the best means

of preventing famine, in the long run, is population control. It would then follow from the position reached earlier that one ought to be doing all one can to promote population control (unless one held that all forms of population control were wrong in themselves, or would have significantly bad consequences). Since there are organizations working specifically for population control, one would then support them rather than more orthodox methods of preventing famine.

A third point raised by the conclusion reached earlier relates to the question of just how much we all ought to be giving away. One possibility, which has already been mentioned, is that we ought to give until we reach the level of marginal utility—that is, the level at which, by giving more, I would cause as much suffering to myself or my dependents as I would relieve by my gift. This would mean, of course, that one would reduce oneself to very near the material circumstances of a Bengali refugee. It will be recalled that earlier I put forward both a strong and a moderate version of the principle of preventing bad occurrences. The strong version, which required us to prevent bad things from happening unless in doing so we would be sacrificing something of comparable moral significance, does seem to require reducing ourselves to the level of marginal utility. I should also say that the strong version seems to me to be the correct one. I proposed the more moderate version—that we should prevent bad occurrences unless, to do so, we had to sacrifice something morally significant—only in order to show that even on this surely undeniable principle a great change is our way of life is required. On the more moderate principle, it may not follow that we ought to reduce ourselves to the level of marginal utility, for one might hold that to reduce oneself and one's family to this level is to cause something significantly bad to happen. Whether this is so I shall not discuss, since, as I have said, I can see no good reason for holding the moderate version of the principle rather than the strong version. Even if we accepted the principle only in its moderate form, however, it should be clear that we would have to give away enough to ensure that the consumer society, dependent as it is on people spending on trivia rather than giving to famine relief, would slow down and perhaps disappear entirely. There are several reasons why this would be desirable in itself. The value and necessity of economic growth are now being questioned not only by conservationists, but by economists as well.[5] There is no doubt, too, that the consumer society has had a distorting effect on the goals and purposes of its members. Yet looking at the matter purely from the point of view of overseas aid, there must be a limit to the extent to which we should deliberately slow down our economy; for it might be the case that if we gave away, say, forty percent of our Gross National Product, we would slow down the economy so much that in absolute terms we would be giving less than if we gave twenty-five percent of the much larger GNP that we would have if we limited our contribution to this smaller percentage.

[5] See, for instance, John Kenneth Galbraith, *The New Industrial State* (Boston, 1967); and E. J. Mishan, *The Costs of Economic Growth* (London, 1967).

I mention this only as an indication of the sort of a factor that one would have to take into account in working out an ideal. Since Western societies generally consider one percent of the GNP an acceptable level for overseas aid, the matter is entirely academic. Nor does it affect the question of how much an individual should give in a society in which very few are giving substantial amounts.

It is sometimes said, though less often now that it used to be, that philosophers have no special role to play in public affairs, since most public issues depend primarily on an assessment of facts. On questions of fact, it is said, philosophers as such have no special expertise, and so it has been possible to engage in philosophy without committing oneself to any position on major public issues. No doubt there are some issues of social policy and foreign policy about which it can truly be said that a really expert assessment of the facts is required before taking sides or acting, but the issue of famine is surely not one of these. The facts about the existence of suffering are beyond dispute. Nor, I think, is it disputed that we can do something about it, either through orthodox methods of famine relief or through population control or both. This is therefore an issue on which philosophers are competent to take a position. The issue is one which faces everyone who has more money than he needs to support himself and his dependents, or who is in a position to take some sort of political action. These categories must include practically every teacher and student of philosophy in the universities of the Western world. If philosophy is to deal with matters that are relevant to both teachers and students, this is an issue that philosophers should discuss.

Discussion, though, is not enough. What is the point of relating philosophy to public (and personal) affairs if we do not take our conclusions seriously? In this instance, taking our conclusion seriously means acting upon it. The philosopher will not find it any easier than anyone else to alter his attitudes and way of life to the extent that, if I am right, is involved in doing everything that we ought to be doing. At the very least, though, one can make a start. The philosopher who does so will have to sacrifice some of the benefits of the consumer society, but he can find compensation in the satisfaction of a way of life in which theory and practice, if not yet in harmony, are at least coming together.

PART I   Suggestions For Further Reading

Aiken, William and LaFollette, Hugh, eds. *World Hunger and Moral Obligation* (Prentice-Hall, 1977)

Baier, Kurt. *The Moral Point of View* (Cornell University Press, 1958)

Bayles, Michael D., ed. *Contemporary Utilitarianism* (Anchor Books, 1968)

Fried, Charles. *Right and Wrong* (Harvard University Press, 1979)

Gauthier, David, ed. *Morality and Rational Self-Interest* (Prentice-Hall, 1970)

Hardie, W. F. *Aristotle's Ethical Theory,* Second Edition (Oxford University Press, 1981)

Hume, David. *An Enquiry Concerning the Principles of Morals* (Open Court, 1966)

Ladd, John, ed. *Ethical Relativism* (Wadsworth, 1973)

Mackie, J. L. *Ethics: Inventing Right and Wrong* (Penguin, 1977)

Moore, George E. *Ethics* (Oxford University Press, 1967)

Nagel, Thomas. *Mortal Questions,* essays 1–10 (Cambridge University Press, 1979)

Sidgwick, Henry. *Methods of Ethics,* 7th edition (Hackett Publishers, 1981)

Smart, J. J. C. and Williams, Bernard. *Utilitarianism: For and Against* (Cambridge University Press, 1973)

Stevenson, Charles L. *Ethics and Language* (AMS Press, Reprint of 1944 edition)

II

SOCIAL AND POLITICAL PHILOSOPHY

WE LIVE in society. This is a truism, but it is a profound one; for the question of how society should be ordered is among the least tractable of all philosophical problems.

The source of the difficulty is clear. Put simply, it is that people generally have enough of a common interest to require some form of cooperative arrangement, but divergent enough interests to make it extremely difficult for them to agree about what sort of cooperative arrangement to accept. More specifically, our interests coincide in the sense that by cooperatively pooling our efforts and talents, we can produce far more goods and services than any of us could produce independently. In addition, the self-restraint of each person promotes the security of all. However, our interests conflict in the sense that resources and opportunities are finite; one person's gain is often another's loss. In addition, one person's exercise of liberty often interferes with the liberty of another. Given this irregular pattern of conflicting and coinciding interests, the obvious task is to find some fair and mutually acceptable way of ordering the situation. How to do this is the central problem of social and political philosophy.

It is natural to suppose that any workable scheme for reconciling our competing interests will involve some centralized mechanism for making and enforcing decisions. Thus, the notion of a social ordering leads directly to the notion of government. In the abstract, most people would grant the need for some form of government. However, at the level of specifics, many questions arise. What function, exactly, does government serve? What is the best form of government?

153

What justifies a government in levying taxes, passing laws, and otherwise restricting our liberty? What are the limits of permissible interference with our liberty? And why, if at all, are we obligated to support our government when we seriously disagree with its policies? Taken together, these and related questions define the subfield of political philosophy.

As an introduction to this subject, we can do no better than to consider Plato's classic dialogue, the *Crito,* reprinted here as reading 13. This dialogue asks whether we should obey even those laws that we consider wrong. Plato's position is that we should, for at least two reasons: first, because in the past government has provided us with many benefits, and, second, because we have, in effect, agreed to obey. Although Plato's discussion is not lengthy, it sets the agenda for much further discussion. For consider the benefits that he attributes to government—our education, our upbringing, and "a share of all the good things at our disposal." In what sense, exactly, can the government, or its laws, be said to provide these things? To ask this question is really to ask what function, if any, government uniquely serves. Although answers vary, one popular view is that government's special contribution is not the benefits themselves, but rather the security that makes them possible. This view, that government is needed mainly to provide security, is argued with elegance and force by Thomas Hobbes in reading 14.

Hobbes's position is straightforward. He contends that the best way to see why we need a government is to imagine what life would be like without one. Given what people are like, Hobbes believes that the situation in such a "state of nature" would be tantamount to war. Because each person would constantly be trying to get what others have, and to prevent others from getting what he has, there would be constant insecurity and strife. Besides threatening our lives, this would occupy all our attention, and so would preclude the kind of long-range planning that makes prosperity possible. Moreover, agreements to end the "war of all against all" would have no force; for each party would realize that the others would break such agreements whenever it was advantageous. In view of this, the fundamental need is to remove the incentive to attack others and break their agreements. A strong government, with the power and will to punish, fulfills this function. By making peace advantageous, it indirectly makes possible all the other benefits of civilization.

Assuming that government provides this (and perhaps other) benefits, what follows about its legitimacy, and about our moral obligation to obey its laws? Plato contends, in part, that we are obligated to obey the law because we have agreed to do so. Moreover, Hobbes's talk of a covenant or compact suggests a similar conclusion. But is this conclusion warranted? Doubts are raised by the fact that there is no historical record of any such agreement or "social contract." However, as John Locke notes in reading 15, not all agreements are explicit. We may, in effect, tacitly agree to bear our share of the burden of a cooperative scheme merely by accepting its benefits. Alternatively, even if we have not agreed to participate, it can be argued that the benefits we receive make it only fair that we do so. Through some such argument, we may be able to establish the legitimacy of government and law despite the absence of any

express agreement. However, there are also problems here; some of these are brought out by Robert Nozick in reading 16.

Although many laws are widely accepted, others are not. Some well-intentioned laws, such as the 1920s prohibition against alcoholic beverages, are widely regarded as intolerably intrusive. Moreover, a similar criticism is leveled against many less formal efforts to regulate other people's lives. But what determines whether an attempt to curtail another's liberty is justified? What principle sets the limits of legitimate interference in people's lives? In his famous essay *On Liberty,* excerpted here as reading 17, John Stuart Mill proposes that such interference is justified only when a proposed act poses a substantial risk of harm to another. The prevention of harm to the agent himself, Mill argues, is never a sufficient reason to interfere. There is little doubt that Mill's "harm principle" is extremely appealing. However, before accepting it, you should ask whether Mill's distinction between actions which affect only the agent and those which also affect other people is as clear cut as it first seems to be.

Thus far, we have addressed mainly problems associated with government. But although these problems are important, they hardly exhaust the difficulties raised by the structuring of the social order. Equally important problems are raised by the economic system that government upholds—the system that determines the distribution of wealth, income, and related goods and opportunities. These goods and opportunities may be concentrated in few hands or in many. Their acquisition may be hereditary or non-hereditary. They may be distributed according to need, effort, contribution to others, or on some other basis. When we ask which of these possibilities to accept, we raise the problems of distributive justice. These problems are taken up by John Rawls in reading 18.

Although Rawls's theory of justice is complex and many-sided, its basic ideas can be put simply enough. He contends that the fairest way to distribute goods is through principles that everyone would accept. To achieve fairness, Rawls strives to eliminate the morally irrelevant features of different people's situations. For example, since no one has had any control over either his talents and abilities or the social circumstances into which he was born, Rawls argues that such factors should not be allowed to bias our choice of principles. To prevent such bias, Rawls asks us to imagine ourselves choosing basic principles in ignorance of our actual situation in life. When rational people are placed behind such a "veil of ignorance," Rawls argues that they will invariably choose that all persons should have maximal and equal amounts of liberty, and that economic goods should be distributed unequally only if this will benefit even the least advantaged. Since these principles would be chosen by everyone under fair conditions, they are the ones we should accept.

Robert Nozick disagrees. He argues in reading 19 that in treating all goods as unowned objects to be distributed fairly, we ignore the fact that most goods exist only because particular people have invested their own labor and ingenuity to create them. Once we realize this, we must acknowledge that past history plays a crucial role in determining who should have what. Specifically, we must

acknowledge that a thing is justly held if and only if its current holder either produced it from unowned objects, or was given it (perhaps in return for something else) by another productive person. This "entitlement theory of justice" is an elaboration of a theory originally introduced by John Locke in reading 15.

One striking feature of Nozick's account is its attempt to link the distribution of economic goods to the circumstances of their production. Such a link is also present in the very different account of Karl Marx and Friedrich Engels. The position of Marx and Engels, as set forth in reading 20(a), is that capitalism—the economic system in which workers sell labor power to others who own the factories, land, and tools—must inevitably reduce the workers to an ever-lower level of subsistence while capitalists grow ever richer. Under such a system, such principles as Nozick's are mere rationalizations which serve the interests of the ruling class. Indeed, Marx maintains in 20(b) that even to raise the question of distributive justice is to display the attitudes of a particular class. According to Marx and Engels, the current subordination and exploitation of workers by property owners will inevitably be replaced by a system in which workers rule. When it is, everyone will contribute in accordance with his ability, and will use only what he needs.

At first glance, this vision of social harmony may seem unrealistic. However, as Edward Nell and Onora O'Neill point out in reading 21, to dismiss it out of hand is to presume that such attitudes as acquisitiveness and aversion to labor are fixed and unchangeable. This view of human nature is at least debatable. Given sufficient alteration of human attitudes and behavior, the communist vision of society may indeed be workable.

In the writings of Rawls, Nozick, and Marx, we encounter able representatives of the liberal, conservative, and radical approaches to economic justice. Although much can be said for each approach, together the alternatives are clearly incompatible. Thus, each thinking person must somehow decide among them. To do this, we must resolve many complex questions about what is fair and what human nature permits. The difficulty of the task is matched only by its importance.

13

What Do We Owe to Our Country?

PLATO

> *Plato (427–347 B.C.), the eminent Athenian philosopher, wrote a series of dialogues which immortalized his teacher Socrates. The extent to which the historical Socrates espoused the views attributed to the character "Socrates" in Plato's dialogues is a matter of long-standing historical controversy, but not of major philosophical significance. Most important are the dialogues themselves, for in them Plato posed in striking form many of the issues and competing answers that have been at the center of philosophical study for more than two thousand years.*
>
> *In the* Crito, *we encounter Socrates shortly before his death. Socrates has just been convicted for corrupting the youth of Athens through his teachings. He has refused to leave the city, and so has been sentenced to die. His friend Crito is willing to help him escape; but Socrates insists that acting on principle is more important than prolonging life at any cost. The conversation then shifts to whether sound moral principles dictate escape from a decision which is legal but unjust.*
>
> *Socrates insists that he should not escape. No matter how much we are wronged, he argues, we must never do wrong in return. Moreover, to flee would be wrong, for it would injure the laws and constitution of Athens under which Socrates has been duly convicted. These laws provided the context in which he was born, raised, and educated; and for this, they are owed devotion and gratitude. Moreover, when Socrates became an adult, nobody forced him to remain in Athens. If he had found the laws unacceptable, he could have left. Since he did not, he was evidently willing to accept them. Having thus agreed to be bound by the laws, he would now be breaking a promise if he were to disobey.*
>
> *Like others, this dialogue can be read on different levels. Plato's arguments that we should work "within the system" are powerful if controversial contributions to substantive political philosophy. But at another level, the subject is not how to resolve political conflict, but simply how to live. By presenting Socrates as willing to die for his beliefs, and as unconcerned about the uninformed opinions of others, Plato presents an inspiring model of the examined and reasoned life.*

SOCRATES: Here already, Crito? Surely it is still early?
CRITO: Indeed it is.
SOCRATES: About what time?
CRITO: Just before dawn.

SOCRATES: I wonder that the warder paid any attention to you.

CRITO: He is used to me now, Socrates, because I come here so often; besides, he is under some small obligation to me.

SOCRATES: Have you only just come, or have you been here for long?

CRITO: Fairly long.

SOCRATES: Then why didn't you wake me at once, instead of sitting by my bed so quietly?

CRITO: I wouldn't dream of such a thing, Socrates. I only wish I were not so sleepless and depressed myself. I have been wondering at you, because I saw how comfortably you were sleeping; and I deliberately didn't wake you because I wanted you to go on being as comfortable as you could. I have often felt before in the course of my life how fortunate you are in your disposition, but I feel it more than ever now in your present misfortune when I see how easily and placidly you put up with it.

SOCRATES: Well, really, Crito, it would be hardly suitable for a man of my age to resent having to die.

CRITO: Other people just as old as you are get involved in these misfortunes, Socrates, but their age doesn't keep them from resenting it when they find themselves in your position.

SOCRATES: Quite true. But tell me, why have you come so early?

CRITO: Because I bring bad news, Socrates; not so bad from your point of view, I suppose, but it will be very hard to bear for me and your other friends, and I think that I shall find it hardest of all.

SOCRATES: Why, what is this news? Has the boat come in from Delos—the boat which ends my reprieve when it arrives?

CRITO: It hasn't actually come in yet, but I expect that it will be here to-day, judging from the report of some people who have just arrived from Sunium and left it there. It's quite clear from their account that it will be here to-day; and so by to-morrow, Socrates, you will have to—to end your life.

SOCRATES: Well, Crito, I hope that it may be for the best; if the gods will it so, so be it. All the same, I don't think it will arrive to-day.

CRITO: What makes you think that?

SOCRATES: I will try to explain. I think I am right in saying that I have to die on the day after the boat arrives?

CRITO: That's what the authorities say, at any rate.

SOCRATES: Then I don't think it will arrive on this day that is just beginning, but on the day after. I am going by a dream that I had in the night, only a little while ago. It looks as though you were right not to wake me up.

CRITO: Why, what was the dream about?

SOCRATES: I thought I saw a gloriously beautiful woman dressed in white robes, who came up to me and addressed me in these words: 'Socrates, To the pleasant land of Phthia on the third day thou shalt come.'

CRITO: Your dream makes no sense, Socrates.

SOCRATES: To my mind, Crito, it is perfectly clear.

CRITO: Too clear, apparently. But look here, Socrates, it is still not too late to take my advice and escape. Your death means a double calamity for me.

158

I shall not only lose a friend whom I can never possibly replace, but besides a great many people who don't know you and me very well will be sure to think that I let you down, because I could have saved you if I had been willing to spend the money; and what could be more contemptible than to get a name for thinking more of money than of your friends? Most people will never believe that it was you who refused to leave this place although we tried our hardest to persuade you.

SOCRATES: But my dear Crito, why should we pay so much attention to what 'most people' think? The really reasonable people, who have more claim to be considered, will believe that the facts are exactly as they are.

CRITO: You can see for yourself, Socrates, that one has to think of popular opinion as well. Your present position is quite enough to show that the capacity of ordinary people for causing trouble is not confined to petty annoyances, but has hardly any limits if you once get a bad name with them.

SOCRATES: I only wish that ordinary people *had* an unlimited capacity for doing harm; then they might have an unlimited power for doing good; which would be a splendid thing, if it were so. Actually they have neither. They cannot make a man wise or stupid; they simply act at random.

CRITO: Have it that way if you like; but tell me this, Socrates. I hope that you aren't worrying about the possible effects on me and the rest of your friends, and thinking that if you escape we shall have trouble with informers for having helped you to get away, and have to forfeit all our property or pay an enormous fine, or even incur some further punishment? If any idea like that is troubling you, you can dismiss it altogether. We are quite entitled to run that risk in saving you, and even worse, if necessary. Take my advice, and be reasonable.

SOCRATES: All that you say is very much in my mind, Crito, and a great deal more besides.

CRITO: Very well, then, don't let it distress you. I know some people who are willing to rescue you from here and get you out of the country for quite a moderate sum. And then surely you realize how cheap these informers are to buy off; we shan't need much money to settle them; and I think you've got enough of my money for yourself already. And then even supposing that in your anxiety for my safety you feel that you oughtn't to spend my money, there are these foreign gentlemen staying in Athens who are quite willing to spend theirs. One of them, Simmias of Thebes, has actually brought the money with him for this very purpose; and Cebes and a number of others are quite ready to do the same. So as I say, you mustn't let any fears on these grounds make you slacken your efforts to escape; and you mustn't feel any misgivings about what you said at your trial, that you wouldn't know what to do with yourself if you left this country. Wherever you go, there are plenty of places where you will find a welcome; and if you choose to go to Thessaly, I have friends there who will make much of you and give you complete protection, so that no one in Thessaly can interfere with you.

Besides, Socrates, I don't even feel that it is right for you to try to do what you are doing, throwing away your life when you might save it. You are

doing your best to treat yourself in exactly the same way as your enemies would, or rather did, when they wanted to ruin you. What is more, it seems to me that you are letting your sons down too. You have it in your power to finish their bringing up and education, and instead of that you are proposing to go off and desert them, and so far as you are concerned they will have to take their chance. And what sort of chance are they likely to get? The sort of thing that usually happens to orphans when they lose their parents. Either one ought not to have children at all, or one ought to see their upbringing and education through to the end. It strikes me that you are taking the line of least resistance, whereas you ought to make the choice of a good man and a brave one, considering that you profess to have made goodness your object all through life. Really, I am ashamed, both on your account and on ours your friends'; it will look as though we had played something like a coward's part all through this affair of yours. First there was the way you came into court when it was quite unnecessary—that was the first act; then there was the conduct of the defence—that was the second; and finally, to complete the farce, we get this situation, which makes it appear that we have let you slip out of our hands through some lack of courage and enterprise on our part, because we didn't save you, and you didn't save yourself, when it would have been quite possible and practicable, if we had been any use at all.

There, Socrates; if you aren't careful, besides the suffering there will be all this disgrace for you and us to bear. Come, make up your mind. Really it's too late for that now; you ought to have it made up already. There is no alternative; the whole thing must be carried through during this coming night. If we lose any more time, it can't be done, it will be too late. I appeal to you, Socrates, on every ground; take my advice and please don't be unreasonable!

SOCRATES: My dear Crito, I appreciate your warm feelings very much—that is, assuming that they have some justification; if not, the stronger they are, the harder they will be to deal with. Very well, then; we must consider whether we ought to follow your advice or not. You know that this is not a new idea of mine; it has always been my nature never to accept advice from any of my friends unless reflexion shows that it is the best course that reason offers. I cannot abandon the principles which I used to hold in the past simply because this accident has happened to me; they seem to me to be much as they were, and I respect and regard the same principles now as before. So unless we can find better principles on this occasion, you can be quite sure that I shall not agree with you; not even if the power of the people conjures up fresh hordes of bogies to terrify our childish minds, by subjecting us to chains and executions and confiscations of our property.

Well, then, how can we consider the question most reasonably? Suppose that we begin by reverting to this view which you hold about people's opinions. Was it always right to argue that some opinions should be taken seriously but not others? Or was it always wrong? Perhaps it was right before the question of my death arose, but now we can see clearly that it was a

mistaken persistence in a point of view which was really irresponsible nonsense. I should like very much to inquire into this problem, Crito, with your help, and to see whether the argument will appear in any different light to me now that I am in this position, or whether it will remain the same; and whether we shall dismiss it or accept it.

Serious thinkers, I believe, have always held some such view as the one which I mentioned just now: that some of the opinions which people entertain should be respected, and others should not. Now I ask you, Crito, don't you think that this is a sound principle?—You are safe from the prospect of dying to-morrow, in all human probability; and you are not likely to have your judgement upset by this impending calamity. Consider, then; don't you think that this is a sound enough principle, that one should not regard all the opinions that people hold, but only some and not others? What do you say? Isn't that a fair statement?

CRITO: Yes, it is.

SOCRATES: In other words, one should regard the good ones and not the bad?

CRITO: Yes.

SOCRATES: The opinions of the wise being good, and the opinions of the foolish bad?

CRITO: Naturally.

SOCRATES: To pass on, then: what do you think of the sort of illustration that I used to employ? When a man is in training, and taking it seriously, does he pay attention to all praise and criticism and opinion indiscriminately, or only when it comes from the one qualified person, the actual doctor or trainer?

CRITO: Only when it comes from the one qualified person.

SOCRATES: Then he should be afraid of the criticism and welcome the praise of the one qualified person, but not those of the general public.

CRITO: Obviously.

SOCRATES: So he ought to regulate his actions and exercises and eating and drinking by the judgement of his instructor, who has expert knowledge, rather than by the opinions of the rest of the public.

CRITO: Yes, that is so.

SOCRATES: Very well. Now if he disobeys the one man and disregards his opinion and commendations, and pays attention to the advice of the many who have no expert knowledge, surely he will suffer some bad effect?

CRITO: Certainly.

SOCRATES: And what is this bad effect? Where is it produced?—I mean, in what part of the disobedient person?

CRITO: His body, obviously; that is what suffers.

SOCRATES: Very good. Well now, tell me, Crito—we don't want to go through all the examples one by one—does this apply as a general rule, and above all to the sort of actions which we are trying to decide about: just and unjust, honourable and dishonourable, good and bad? Ought we to be guided and intimidated by the opinion of the many or by that of the one—assuming that there is someone with expert knowledge? Is it true that we ought to respect

and fear this person more than all the rest put together; and that if we do not follow his guidance we shall spoil and mutilate that part of us which, as we used to say, is improved by right conduct and destroyed by wrong? Or is this all nonsense?

CRITO: No, I think it is true, Socrates.

SOCRATES: Then consider the next step. There is a part of us which is improved by healthy actions and ruined by unhealthy ones. If we spoil it by taking the advice of nonexperts, will life be worth living when this part is once ruined? The part I mean is the body; do you accept this?

CRITO: Yes.

SOCRATES: Well, is life worth living with a body which is worn out and ruined in health?

CRITO: Certainly not.

SOCRATES: What about the part of us which is mutilated by wrong actions and benefited by right ones? Is life worth living with this part ruined? Or do we believe that this part of us, whatever it may be, in which right and wrong operate, is of less importance than the body?

CRITO: Certainly not.

SOCRATES: It is really more precious?

CRITO: Much more.

SOCRATES: In that case, my dear fellow, what we ought to consider is not so much what people in general will say about us but how we stand with the expert in right and wrong, the one authority, who represents the actual truth. So in the first place your proposition is not correct when you say that we should consider popular opinion in questions of what is right and honourable and good, or the opposite. Of course one might object 'All the same, the people have the power to put us to death.'

CRITO: No doubt about that! Quite true, Socrates; it is a possible objection.

SOCRATES: But so far as I can see, my dear fellow, the argument which we have just been through is quite unaffected by it. At the same time I should like you to consider whether we are still satisfied on this point: that the really important thing is not to live, but to live well.

CRITO: Why, yes.

SOCRATES: And that to live well means the same thing as to live honourably or rightly?

CRITO: Yes.

SOCRATES: Then in the light of this agreement we must consider whether or not it is right for me to try to get away without an official discharge. If it turns out to be right, we must make the attempt; if not, we must let it drop. As for the considerations you raise about expense and reputation and bringing up children, I am afraid, Crito, that they represent the reflexions of the ordinary public, who put people to death, and would bring them back to life if they could, with equal indifference to reason. Our real duty, I fancy, since the argument leads that way, is to consider one question only, the one which we raised just now: Shall we be acting rightly in paying money and showing gratitude to these people who are going to rescue me, and in escaping or

arranging the escape ourselves, or shall we really be acting wrongly in doing all this? If it becomes clear that such conduct is wrong, I cannot help thinking that the question whether we are sure to die, or to suffer any other ill effect for that matter, if we stand our ground and take no action, ought not to weigh with us at all in comparison with the risk of doing what is wrong.

CRITO: I agree with what you say, Socrates; but I wish you would consider what we ought to *do*.

SOCRATES: Let us look at it together, my dear fellow; and if you can challenge any of my arguments, do so and I will listen to you; but if you can't, be a good fellow and stop telling me over and over again that I ought to leave this place without official permission. I am very anxious to obtain your approval before I adopt the course which I have in mind; I don't want to act against your convictions. Now give your attention to the starting point of this inquiry—I hope that you will be satisfied with my way of stating it—and try to answer my questions to the best of your judgement.

CRITO: Well, I will try.

SOCRATES: Do we say that one must never willingly do wrong, or does it depend upon circumstances? Is it true, as we have often agreed before, that there is no sense in which wrongdoing is good or honourable? Or have we jettisoned all our former convictions in these last few days? Can you and I at our age, Crito, have spent all these years in serious discussions without realizing that we were no better than a pair of children? Surely the truth is just what we have always said. Whatever the popular view is, and whether the alternative is pleasanter than the present one or even harder to bear, the fact remains that to do wrong is in every sense bad and dishonourable for the person who does it. Is that our view, or not?

CRITO: Yes, it is.

SOCRATES: Then in no circumstances must one do wrong.

CRITO: No.

SOCRATES: In that case one must not even do wrong when one is wronged, which most people regard as the natural course.

CRITO: Apparently not.

SOCRATES: Tell me another thing, Crito: ought one to do injuries or not?

CRITO: Surely not, Socrates.

SOCRATES: And tell me: is it right to do an injury in retaliation, as most people believe, or not?

CRITO: No, never.

SOCRATES: Because, I suppose, there is no difference between injuring people and wronging them.

CRITO: Exactly.

SOCRATES: So one ought not to return a wrong or an injury to any person, whatever the provocation is. Now be careful, Crito, that in making these single admissions you do not end by admitting something contrary to your real beliefs. I know that there are and always will be few people who think like this; and consequently between those who do think so and those who do not there can be no agreement on principle; they must always feel con-

tempt when they observe one another's decisions. I want even you to consider very carefully whether you share my views and agree with me, and whether we can proceed with our discussion from the established hypothesis that it is never right to do a wrong or return a wrong or defend one's self against injury by retaliation; or whether you dissociate yourself from any share in this view as a basis for discussion. I have held it for a long time, and still hold it; but if you have formed any other opinion, say so and tell me what it is. If, on the other hand, you stand by what we have said, listen to my next point.

CRITO: Yes, I stand by it and agree with you. Go on.

SOCRATES: Well, here is my next point, or rather question. Ought one to fulfil all one's agreements, provided that they are right, or break them?

CRITO: One ought to fulfil them.

SOCRATES: Then consider the logical consequence. If we leave this place without first persuading the State to let us go, are we or are we not doing an injury, and doing it in a quarter where it is least justifiable? Are we or are we not abiding by our just agreements?

CRITO: I can't answer your question, Socrates; I am not clear in my mind.

SOCRATES: Look at it in this way. Suppose that while we were preparing to run away from here (or however one should describe it) the Laws and Constitution of Athens were to come and confront us and ask this question: 'Now, Socrates, what are you proposing to do? Can you deny that by this act which you are contemplating you intend, so far as you have the power, to destroy us, the Laws, and the whole State as well? Do you imagine that a city can continue to exist and not be turned upside down, if the legal judgements which are pronounced in it have no force but are nullified and destroyed by private persons?'—how shall we answer this question, Crito, and others of the same kind? There is much that could be said, especially by a professional advocate, to protest against the invalidation of this law which enacts that judgements once pronounced shall be binding. Shall we say 'Yes, I do intend to destroy the laws, because the State wronged me by passing a faulty judgement at my trial'? Is this to be our answer, or what?

CRITO: What you have just said, by all means, Socrates.

SOCRATES: Then what supposing the Laws say 'Was there provision for this in the agreement between you and us, Socrates? Or did you undertake to abide by whatever judgements the State pronounced?' If we expressed surprise at such language, they would probably say: 'Never mind our language, Socrates, but answer our questions; after all, you are accustomed to the method of question and answer. Come now, what charge do you bring against us and the State, that you are trying to destroy us? Did we not give you life in the first place? was it not through us that your father married your mother and begot you? Tell us, have you any complaint against those of us Laws that deal with marriage?' 'No, none', I should say. 'Well, have you any against the laws which deal with children's upbringing and education, such as you had yourself? Are you not grateful to those of us Laws which were instituted for this end, for requiring your father to give you a cultural and

physical education?' 'Yes', I should say. 'Very good. Then since you have been born and brought up and educated, can you deny, in the first place, that you were our child and servant, both you and your ancestors? And if this is so, do you imagine that what is right for us is equally right for you, and that whatever we try to do to you, you are justified in retaliating? You did not have equality of rights with your father, or your employer (supposing that you had had one), to enable you to retaliate; you were not allowed to answer back when you were scolded or to hit back when you were beaten, or to do a great many other things of the same kind. Do you expect to have such licence against your country and its laws that if we try to put you to death in the belief that it is right to do so, you on your part will try your hardest to destroy your country and us its Laws in return? and will you, the true devotee of goodness, claim that you are justified in doing so? Are you so wise as to have forgotten that compared with your mother and father and all the rest of your ancestors your country is something far more precious, more venerable, more sacred, and held in greater honour both among gods and among all reasonable men? Do you not realize that you are even more bound to respect and placate the anger of your country than your father's anger? that if you cannot persuade your country you must do whatever it orders, and patiently submit to any punishment that it imposes, whether it be flogging or imprisonment? And if it leads you out to war, to be wounded or killed, you must comply, and it is right that you should do so; you must not give way or retreat or abandon your position. Both in war and in the law-courts and everywhere else you must do whatever your city and your country commands, or else persuade it in accordance with universal justice; but violence is a sin even against your parents, and it is a far greater sin against your country.'—What shall we say to this, Crito?—that what the Laws say is true, or not?

CRITO: Yes, I think so.

SOCRATES: 'Consider, then, Socrates,' the Laws would probably continue, 'whether it is also true for us to say that what you are now trying to do to us is not right. Although we have brought you into the world and reared you and educated you, and given you and all your fellow-citizens a share in all the good things at our disposal, nevertheless by the very fact of granting our permission we openly proclaim this principle: that any Athenian, on attaining to manhood and seeing for himself the political organization of the state and us its Laws, is permitted, if he is not satisfied with us, to take his property and go away wherever he likes. If any of you chooses to go to one of our colonies, supposing that he should not be satisfied with us and the State, or to emigrate to any other country, not one of us Laws hinders or prevents him from going away wherever he likes, without any loss of property. On the other hand, if any one of you stands his ground when he can see how we administer justice and the rest of our public organization, we hold that by so doing he has in fact undertaken to do anything that we tell him; and we maintain that anyone who disobeys is guilty of doing wrong on three separate counts: first because we are his parents, and secondly

because we are his guardians; and thirdly because, after promising obedience, he is neither obeying us nor persuading us to change our decision if we are at fault in any way; and although all our orders are in the form of proposals, not of savage commands, and we give him the choice of either persuading us or doing what we say, he is actually doing neither. These are the charges, Socrates, to which we say that you will be liable if you do what you are contemplating; and you will not be the least culpable of your fellow-countrymen, but one of the most guilty.' If I said 'Why do you say that?' they would no doubt pounce upon me with perfect justice and point out that there are very few people in Athens who have entered into this agreement with them as explicitly as I have. They would say 'Socrates, we have substantial evidence that you are satisfied with us and with the State. You would not have been so exceptionally reluctant to cross the borders of your country if you had not been exceptionally attached to it. You have never left the city to attend a festival or for any other purpose, except on some military expedition; you have never travelled abroad as other people do, and you have never felt the impulse to acquaint yourself with another country or constitution; you have been content with us and with our city. You have definitely chosen us, and undertaken to observe us in all your activities as a citizen; and as the crowning proof that you are satisfied with our city, you have begotten children in it. Furthermore, even at the time of your trial you could have proposed the penalty of banishment, if you had chosen to do so; that is, you could have done then with the sanction of the State what you are now trying to do without it. But whereas at that time you made a noble show of indifference if you had to die, and in fact preferred death, as you said, to banishment, now you show no respect for your earlier professions, and no regard for us, the Laws, whom you are trying to destroy; you are behaving like the lowest type of menial, trying to run away in spite of the contracts and undertakings by which you agreed to live as a member of our State. Now first answer this question: Are we or are we not speaking the truth when we say that you have undertaken, in deed if not in word, to live your life as a citizen in obedience to us?' What are we to say to that, Crito? Are we not bound to admit it?

CRITO: We cannot help it, Socrates.

SOCRATES: 'It is a fact, then,' they would say, 'that you are breaking covenants and undertakings made with us, although you made them under no compulsion or misunderstanding, and were not compelled to decide in a limited time; you had seventy years in which you could have left the country, if you were not satisfied with us or felt that the agreements were unfair. You did not choose Sparta or Crete—your favourite models of good government—or any other Greek or foreign state; you could not have absented yourself from the city less if you had been lame or blind or decrepit in some other way. It is quite obvious that you stand by yourself above all other Athenians in your affection for this city and for us its Laws;—who would care for a city without laws? And now, after all this, are you not going to

stand by your agreement? Yes, you are, Socrates, if you will take our advice; and then you will at least escape being laughed at for leaving the city.

'We invite you to consider what good you will do to yourself or your friends if you commit this breach of faith and stain your conscience. It is fairly obvious that the risk of being banished and either losing their citizenship or having their property confiscated will extend to your friends as well. As for yourself, if you go to one of the neighbouring states, such as Thebes or Megara, which are both well governed, you will enter them as an enemy to their constitution, and all good patriots will eye you with suspicion as a destroyer of law and order. Incidentally you will confirm the opinion of the jurors who tried you that they gave a correct verdict; a destroyer of laws might very well be supposed to have a destructive influence upon young and foolish human beings. Do you intend, then, to avoid well governed states and the higher forms of human society? and if you do, will life be worth living? Or will you approach these people and have the impudence to converse with them? What arguments will you use, Socrates? The same which you used here, that goodness and integrity, institutions and laws, are the most precious possessions of mankind? Do you not think that Socrates and everything about him will appear in a disreputable light? You certainly ought to think so. But perhaps you will retire from this part of the world and go to Crito's friends in Thessaly? That is the home of indiscipline and laxity, and no doubt they would enjoy hearing the amusing story of how you managed to run away from prison by arraying yourself in some costume or putting on a shepherd's smock or some other conventional runaway's disguise, and altering your personal appearance. And will no one comment on the fact that an old man of your age, probably with only a short time left to live, should dare to cling so greedily to life, at the price of violating the most stringent laws? Perhaps not, if you avoid irritating anyone. Otherwise, Socrates, you will hear a good many humiliating comments. So you will live as the toady and slave of all the populace, literally "roystering in Thessaly", as though you had left this country for Thessaly to attend a banquet there; and where will your discussions about goodness and uprightness be then, we should like to know? But of course you want to live for your children's sake, so that you may be able to bring them up and educate them. Indeed! by first taking them off to Thessaly and making foreigners of them, so that they may have that additional enjoyment? Or if that is not your intention, supposing that they are brought up here with you still alive, will they be better cared for and educated without you, because of course your friends will look after them? Will they look after your children if you go away to Thessaly, and not if you go away to the next world? Surely if those who profess to be your friends are worth anything, you must believe that they would care for them.

'No, Socrates; be advised by us your guardians, and do not think more of your children or of your life or of anything else than you think of what is right; so that when you enter the next world you may have all this to plead in your defence before the authorities there. It seems clear that if you do this

thing, neither you nor any of your friends will be the better for it or be more upright or have a cleaner conscience here in this world, nor will it be better for you when you reach the next. As it is, you will leave this place, when you do, as the victim of a wrong done not by us, the Laws, but by your fellow-men. But if you leave in that dishonourable way, returning wrong for wrong and evil for evil, breaking your agreements and covenants with us, and injuring those whom you least ought to injure—yourself, your friends, your country, and us—then you will have to face our anger in your lifetime, and in that place beyond when the laws of the other world know that you have tried, so far as you could, to destroy even us their brothers, they will not receive you with a kindly welcome. Do not take Crito's advice, but follow ours.'

That, my dear friend Crito, I do assure you, is what I seem to hear them saying, just as a mystic seems to hear the strains of music; and the sound of their arguments rings so loudly in my head that I cannot hear the other side. I warn you that, as my opinion stands at present, it will be useless to urge a different view. However, if you think that you will do any good by it, say what you like.

CRITO: No, Socrates, I have nothing to say.

SOCRATES: Then give it up, Crito, and let us follow this course, since God points out the way.

14

Authority and Security

THOMAS HOBBES

Thomas Hobbes (1588–1679) made important contributions in metaphysics and psychology as well as political theory. The following selection is from his masterpiece Leviathan.

Hobbes argues that the need for government can be deduced from certain facts about human nature. According to Hobbes, each person is naturally inclined to do whatever will best advance his own interests. Left to themselves, people will fight to gain the possessions of others, to prevent others from getting an advantage over them, and to uphold their own prestige. Given these "causes of quarrel," life without government—what Hobbes calls a "state of nature"—would be "solitary, poor, nasty, brutish, and short." Only government, with its power to punish, can alter the behavior that is in each person's interest. If I know that attacking you will lead to a punishment that will outweigh anything I can gain, then I will not attack you for gain. If I know that you cannot gain by attacking me, then I will not attack you out of fear.

Given this logic, Hobbes believes that reason demands a sovereign, or government, that is stronger than any citizen or combination of citizens. Such a sovereign is brought into being through a transfer of each citizen's power, via a "covenant" or agreement, to a ruling person or group. This covenant, and the ensuing stability, make justice and morality possible for the first time. Moreover, the same reasoning that calls for the covenant also determines the rights and obligations that it establishes. Since the citizens' own interest has led them to make the sovereign absolute, they are not entitled to resist or depose him, or to complain that he has treated them unjustly. However, since the citizens have entered into the agreement to protect their own lives and persons, they cannot be obligated to obey any command that threatens their physical security.

Hobbes's argument is rigorous and elegant. Still, there are questions. How accurate, for example, is Hobbes's view of human nature, and what role does it really play in his argument? Must a government be absolute, in Hobbes's sense, to provide security? Are there other functions that government should serve besides providing security? To ask these questions is to look beyond Hobbes's theory of government. It is not, however, to deny that his theory is one of great originality and interest.

NATURE HATH MADE MEN so equal, in the faculties of the body, and mind; as that though there be found one man sometimes manifestly stronger in body, or of quicker mind than another; yet when all is reckoned together, the difference between man, and man, is not so considerable, as that one man

can thereupon claim to himself any benefit, to which another may not pretend, as well as he. For as to the strength of body, the weakest has strength enough to kill the strongest, either by secret machination, or by confederacy with others, that are in the same danger with himself.

And as to the faculties of the mind, setting aside the arts grounded upon words, and especially that skill of proceeding upon general, and infallible rules, called science; which very few have, and but in few things; as being not a native faculty, born with us; nor attained, as prudence, while we look after somewhat else, I find yet a greater equality amongst men, than that of strength. For prudence, is but experience; which equal time, equally bestows on all men, in those things they equally apply themselves unto. That which may perhaps make such equality incredible, is but a vain conceit of one's own wisdom, which almost all men think they have in a greater degree, than the vulgar; that is, than all men but themselves, and a few others, whom by fame, or for concurring with themselves, they approve. For such is the nature of men, that howsoever they may acknowledge many others to be more witty, or more eloquent, or more learned; yet they will hardly believe there be many so wise as themselves; for they see their own wit at hand, and other men's at a distance. But this proveth rather that men are in that point equal, than unequal. For there is not ordinarily a greater sign of the equal distribution of any thing, than that every man is contented with his share.

From this equality of ability, ariseth equality of hope in the attaining of our ends. And therefore if any two men desire the same thing, which nevertheless they cannot both enjoy, they become enemies; and in the way to their end, which is principally their own conservation, and sometimes their delectation only, endeavour to destroy, or subdue one another. And from hence it comes to pass, that where an invader hath no more to fear, than another man's single power; if one plant, sow, build, or possess a convenient seat, others may probably be expected to come prepared with forces united, to dispossess, and deprive him, not only of the fruit of his labour, but also of his life, or liberty. And the invader again is in the like danger of another. And from this diffidence of one another, there is no way for any man to secure himself, so reasonable, as anticipation; that is, by force, or wiles, to master the persons of all men he can, so long, till he see no other power great enough to endanger him: and this is no more than his own conservation requireth, and is generally allowed. Also because there be some, that taking pleasure in contemplating their own power in the acts of conquest, which they pursue farther than their security requires; if others, that otherwise would be glad to be at ease within modest bounds, should not by invasion increase their power, they would not be able, long time, by standing only on their defence, to subsist. And by consequence, such augmentation of dominion over men being necessary to a man's conservation, it ought to be allowed him.

Again, men have no pleasure, but on the contrary a great deal of grief, in keeping company, where there is no power able to over-awe them all. For every man looketh that his companion should value him, at the same rate he sets upon himself; and upon all signs of contempt, or undervaluing, naturally endeav-

ours, as far as he dares, (which amongst them that have no common power to keep them in quiet, is far enough to make them destroy each other), to extort a greater value from his contemners, by damage; and from others, by the example.

So that in the nature of man, we find three principal causes of quarrel. First, competition; secondly, diffidence; thirdly, glory.

The first, maketh men invade for gain; the second, for safety; and the third, for reputation. The first use violence, to make themselves masters of other men's persons, wives, children, and cattle; the second, to defend them; the third, for trifles, as a word, a smile, a different opinion, and any other sign of undervalue, either direct in their persons, or by reflection in their kindred, their friends, their nation, their profession, or their name.

Hereby it is manifest, that during the time men live without a common power to keep them all in awe, they are in that condition which is called war; and such a war, as is of every man, against every man. For WAR, consisteth not in battle only, or the act of fighting; but in a tract of time, wherein the will to contend by battle is sufficiently known: and therefore the notion of *time,* is to be considered in the nature of war; as it is in the nature of weather. For as the nature of foul weather, lieth not in a shower or two of rain; but in an inclination thereto of many days together: so the nature of war, consisteth not in actual fighting; but in the known disposition thereto, during all the time there is no assurance to the contrary. All other time is PEACE.

Whatsoever therefore is consequent to a time of war, where every man is enemy to every man; the same is consequent to the time, wherein men live without other security, than what their own strength, and their own invention shall furnish them withal. In such condition, there is no place for industry; because the fruit thereof is uncertain: and consequently no culture of the earth; no navigation, nor use of the commodities that may be imported by sea; no commodious building; no instruments of moving, and removing, such things as require much force; no knowledge of the face of the earth; no account of time; no arts; no letters; no society; and which is worst of all, continual fear, and danger of violent death; and the life of man, solitary, poor, nasty, brutish, and short.

It may seem strange to some man, that has not well weighed these things; that nature should thus dissociate, and render men apt to invade, and destroy one another: and he may therefore, not trusting to this inference, made from the passions, desire perhaps to have the same confirmed by experience. Let him therefore consider with himself, when taking a journey, he arms himself, and seeks to go well accompanied; when going to sleep, he locks his doors; when even in his house he locks his chests; and this when he knows there be laws, and public officers, armed, to revenge all injuries shall be done him; what opinion he has of his fellow subjects, when he rides armed; of his fellow citizens, when he locks his doors; and of his children, and servants, when he locks his chests. Does he not there as much accuse mankind by his actions, as I do by my words? But neither of us accuse man's nature in it. The desires, and other passions of man, are in themselves no sin. No more are the actions, that proceed

from those passions, till they know a law that forbids them: which till laws be made they cannot know: nor can any law be made, till they have agreed upon the person that shall make it.

It may peradventure be thought, there was never such a time, nor condition of war as this; and I believe it was never generally so, over all the world: but there are many places, where they live so now. For the savage people in many places of America, except the government of small families, the concord whereof dependeth on natural lust, have no government at all; and live at this day in that brutish manner, as I said before. Howsoever, it may be perceived what manner of life there would be, where there were no common power to fear, by the manner of life, which men that have formerly lived under a peaceful government, use to degenerate into, in a civil war.

But though there had never been any time, wherein particular men were in a condition of war one against another; yet in all times, kings, and persons of sovereign authority, because of their independency, are in continual jealousies, and in the state and posture of gladiators; having their weapons pointing, and their eyes fixed on one another; that is, their forts, garrisons, and guns upon the frontiers of their kingdoms; and continual spies upon their neighbours; which is a posture of war. But because they uphold thereby, the industry of their subjects; there does not follow from it, that misery, which accompanies the liberty of particular men.

To this war of every man, against every man, this also is consequent; that nothing can be unjust. The notions of right and wrong, justice and injustice have there no place. Where there is no common power, there is no law: where no law, no injustice. Force, and fraud, are in war the two cardinal virtues. Justice, and injustice are none of the faculties neither of the body, nor mind. If they were, they might be in a man that were alone in the world, as well as his senses, and passions. They are qualities, that relate to men in society, not in solitude. It is consequent also to the same condition, that there be no propriety, no dominion, no *mine* and *thine* distinct; but only that to be every man's, that he can get: and for so long, as he can keep it. And thus much for the ill condition, which man by mere nature is actually placed in; though with a possibility to come out of it, consisting partly in the passions, partly in his reason.

The passions that incline men to peace, are fear of death; desire of such things as are necessary to commodious living; and a hope by their industry to obtain them. And reason suggesteth convenient articles of peace, upon which men may be drawn to agreement. These articles, are they, which otherwise are called the Laws of Nature: whereof I shall speak more particularly, in the two following chapters.

. . .

THE RIGHT OF NATURE, which writers commonly call *jus naturale*, is the liberty each man hath, to use his own power, as he will himself, for the preservation of his own nature; that is to say, of his own life; and consequently, of doing any thing, which in his own judgment, and reason, he shall conceive to be the aptest means thereunto.

172

BY LIBERTY, is understood, according to the proper signification of the word, the absence of external impediments: which impediments, may oft take away part of a man's power to do what he would; but cannot hinder him from using the power left him, according as his judgment, and reason shall dictate to him.

A LAW OF NATURE, *lex naturalis,* is a precept or general rule, found out by reason, by which a man is forbidden to do that, which is destructive of his life, or taketh away the means of preserving the same; and to omit that, by which he thinketh it may be best preserved. For though they that speak of this subject, use to confound *jus,* and *lex, right* and *law:* yet they ought to be distinguished; because RIGHT, consisteth in liberty to do, or to forbear: whereas LAW, determineth, and bindeth, to one of them: so that law, and right, differ as much, as obligation, and liberty; which in one and the same matter are inconsistent.

And because the condition of man, as hath been declared in the precedent chapter, is a condition of war of every one against every one; in which case every one is governed by his own reason; and there is nothing he can make use of, that may not be a help unto him, in preserving his life against his enemies; it followeth, that in such a condition, every man has a right to every thing; even to one another's body. And therefore, as long as this natural right of every man to every thing endureth, there can be no security to any man, how strong or wise soever he be, of living out the time, which nature ordinarily alloweth men to live. And consequently it is a precept, or general rule of reason, *that every man, ought to endeavour peace, as far as he has hope of obtaining it; and when he cannot obtain it, that he may seek, and use, all helps, and advantages of war.* The first branch of which rule, containeth the first, and fundamental law of nature; which is, *to seek peace, and follow it.* The second, the sum of the right of nature; which is, *by all means we can, to defend ourselves.*

From this fundamental law of nature, by which men are commanded to endeavour peace, is derived this second law; *that a man be willing, when others are so too, as far-forth, as for peace, and defence of himself he shall think it necessary, to lay down this right to all things; and be contented with so much liberty against other men, as he would allow other men against himself.* For as long as every man holdeth this right, of doing any thing he liketh; so long are all men in the condition of war. But if other men will not lay down their right, as well as he; then there is no reason for any one, to divest himself of his: for that were to expose himself to prey, which no man is bound to, rather than to dispose himself to peace. This is that law of the Gospel; *whatsoever you require that others should do to you, that do ye to them.* And that law of all men, *quod tibi fieri non vis, alteri ne feceris.* *

. . .

Whensoever a man transferreth his right, or renounceth it; it is either in consideration of some right reciprocally transferred to himself; or for some other good he hopeth for thereby. For it is a voluntary act: and of the voluntary acts of every man, the object is some *good to himself.* And therefore there be

---

* Do not do to others what you do not want them to do to you.

some rights, which no man can be understood by any words, or other signs, to have abandoned, or transferred. As first a man cannot lay down the right of resisting them, that assault him by force, to take away his life; because he cannot be understood to aim thereby, at any good to himself. The same may be said of wounds, and chains, and imprisonment; both because there is no benefit consequent to such patience; as there is to the patience of suffering another to be wounded, or imprisoned: as also because a man cannot tell, when he seeth men proceed against him by violence, whether they intend his death or not. And lastly the motive, and end for which this renouncing, and transferring of right is introduced, is nothing else but the security of a man's person, in his life, and in the means of so preserving life, as not to be weary of it. And therefore if a man by words, or other signs, seem to despoil himself of the end, for which those signs were intended; he is not to be understood as if he meant it, or that it was his will; but that he was ignorant of how such words and actions were to be interpreted.

. . .

If a covenant be made, wherein neither of the parties perform presently, but trust one another; in the condition of mere nature, which is a condition of war of every man against every man, upon any reasonable suspicion, it is void: but if there be a common power set over them both, with right and force sufficient to compel performance, it is not void. For he that performeth first, has no assurance the other will perform after; because the bonds of words are too weak to bridle men's ambition, avarice, anger, and other passions, without the fear of some coercive power; which in the condition of mere nature, where all men are equal, and judges of the justness of their own fears, cannot possibly be supposed. And therefore he which performeth first, does but betray himself to his enemy; contrary to the right, he can never abandon, of defending his life, and means of living.

But in a civil estate, where there is a power set up to constrain those that would otherwise violate their faith, that fear is no more reasonable; and for that cause, he which by the covenant is to perform first, is obliged so to do.

The cause of fear, which maketh such a covenant invalid, must be always something arising after the covenant made; as some new fact, or other sign of the will not to perform: else it cannot make the covenant void. For that which could not hinder a man from promising, ought not to be admitted as a hindrance of performing.

. . .

A covenant not to defend myself from force, by force, is always void. For, as I have showed before, no man can transfer, or lay down his right to save himself from death, wounds, and imprisonment, the avoiding whereof is the only end of laying down any right; and therefore the promise of not resisting force, in no covenant transferreth any right; nor is obliging. For though a man may covenant thus, *unless I do so, or so, kill me;* he cannot covenant thus, *unless I do so, or so, I will not resist you, when you come to kill me.* For man by nature chooseth the lesser evil, which is danger of death in resisting; rather

than the greater, which is certain and present death in not resisting. And this is granted to be true by all men, in that they lead criminals to execution, and prison, with armed men, notwithstanding that such criminals have consented to the law, by which they are condemned.

. . .

From that law of nature, by which we are obliged to transfer to another, such rights, as being retained, hinder the peace of mankind, there followeth a third; which is this, *that men perform their covenants made:* without which, covenants are in vain, and but empty words; and the right of all men to all things remaining, we are still in the condition of war.

And in this law of nature, consisteth the fountain and original of JUSTICE. For where no covenant hath preceded, there hath no right been transferred, and every man has right to every thing; and consequently, no action can be unjust. But when a covenant is made, then to break it is *unjust:* and the definition of INJUSTICE, is no other than *the not performance of covenant.* And whatsoever is not unjust, is *just.*

But because covenants of mutual trust, where there is a fear of not performance on either part, as hath been said in the former chapter, are invalid; though the original of justice be the making of covenants; yet injustice actually there can be none, till the cause of such fear be taken away; which while men are in the natural condition of war, cannot be done. Therefore before the names of just, and unjust can have place, there must be some coercive power, to compel men equally to the performance of their covenants, by the terror of some punishment, greater than the benefit they expect by the breach of their covenant; and to make good that propriety, which by mutual contract men acquire, in recompense of the universal right they abandon: and such power there is none before the erection of a commonwealth. And this is also to be gathered out of the ordinary definition of justice in the Schools: for they say, that *justice is the constant will of giving to every man his own.* And therefore where there is no *own,* that is no propriety, there is no injustice; and where there is no coercive power erected, that is, where there is no commonwealth, there is no propriety; all men having right to all things: therefore where there is no commonwealth, there nothing is unjust. So that the nature of justice, consisteth in keeping of valid covenants: but the validity of covenants begins not but with the constitution of a civil power, sufficient to compel men to keep them: and then it is also that propriety begins.

. . .

A *commonwealth* is said to be *instituted,* when a *multitude* of men do agree, and *covenant, every one, with every one,* that to whatsoever *man,* or *assembly of men,* shall be given by the major part, the *right* to *present* the person of them all, that is to say, to be their *representative;* every one, as well he that *voted for it,* as he that *voted against it,* shall *authorize* all the actions and judgments, of that man, or assembly of men, in the same manner, as if they were his own, to the end, to live peaceably amongst themselves, and be protected against other men.

From this institution of a commonwealth are derived all the *rights,* and *faculties* of him, or them, on whom the sovereign power is conferred by the consent of the people assembled.

First, because they covenant, it is to be understood, they are not obliged by former covenant to any thing repugnant hereunto. And consequently they that have already instituted a commonwealth, being thereby bound by covenant, to own the actions, and judgments of one, cannot lawfully make a new covenant, amongst themselves, to be obedient to any other, in any thing whatsoever, without his permission. And therefore, they that are subjects to a monarch, cannot without his leave cast off monarchy, and return to the confusion of a disunited multitude; nor transfer their person from him that beareth it, to another man, or other assembly of men: for they are bound, every man to every man, to own, and be reputed author of all, that he that already is their sovereign, shall do, and judge fit to be done: so that any one man dissenting, all the rest should break their covenant made to that man, which is injustice: and they have also every man given the sovereignty to him that beareth their person; and therefore if they depose him, they take from him that which is his own, and so again it is injustice. Besides, if he that attempteth to depose his sovereign, be killed, or punished by him for such attempt, he is author of his own punishment, as being by the institution, author of all his sovereign shall do: and because it is injustice for a man to do any thing, for which he may be punished by his own authority, he is also upon that title, unjust. And whereas some men have pretended for their disobedience to their sovereign, a new covenant, made, not with men, but with God; this also is unjust: for there is no covenant with God, but by mediation of somebody that representeth God's person; which none doth but God's lieutenant, who hath the sovereignty under God. But this pretence of covenant with God, is so evident a lie, even in the pretenders' own consciences, that it is not only an act of an unjust, but also of a vile, and unmanly disposition.

Secondly, because the right of bearing the person of them all, is given to him they make sovereign, by covenant only of one to another, and not of him to any of them; there can happen no breach of covenant on the part of the sovereign; and consequently none of his subjects, by any pretence of forfeiture, can be freed from his subjection. That he which is made sovereign maketh no covenant with his subjects beforehand, is manifest; because either he must make it with the whole multitude, as one party to the covenant; or he must make a several covenant with every man. With the whole, as one party, it is impossible; because as yet they are not one person: and if he make so many several covenants as there be men, those covenants after he hath the sovereignty are void; because what act soever can be pretended by any one of them for breach thereof, is the act both of himself, and of all the rest, because done in the person, and by the right of every one of them in particular. Besides, if any one, or more of them, pretend a breach of the covenant made by the sovereign at his institution; and others, or one other of his subjects, or himself alone, pretend there was no such breach, there is in this case, no judge to decide the controversy; it returns therefore to the sword again; and every man recovereth the right of protecting

himself by his own strength, contrary to the design they had in the institution. It is therefore in vain to grant sovereignty by way of precedent covenant. The opinion that any monarch receiveth his power by covenant, this is to say, on condition, procedeth from want of understanding this easy truth, that covenants being but words and breath, have no force to oblige, contain, constrain, or protect any man, but what it has from the public sword; that is, from the untied hands of that man, or assembly of men that hath the sovereignty, and whose actions are avouched by them all, and performed by the strength of them all, in him united. But when an assembly of men is made sovereign; then no man imagineth any such covenant to have passed in the institution; for no man is so dull as to say, for example, the people of Rome made a covenant with the Romans, to hold the sovereignty on such or such conditions; which not performed, the Romans might lawfully depose the Roman people. That men see not the reason to be alike in a monarchy, and in a popular government, proceedeth from the ambition of some, that are kinder to the government of an assembly, whereof they may hope to participate, than of monarchy, which they despair to enjoy.

Thirdly, because the major part hath by consenting voices declared a sovereign; he that dissented must now consent with the rest; that is, be contented to avow all the actions he shall do, or else justly be destroyed by the rest. For if he voluntarily entered into the congregation of them that were assembled, he sufficiently declared thereby his will, and therefore tacitly covenanted, to stand to what the major part should ordain: and therefore if he refuse to stand thereto, or make protestation against any of their decrees, he does contrary to his covenant, and therefore unjustly. And whether he be of the congregation, or not; and whether his consent be asked, or not, he must either submit to their decrees, or be left in the condition of war he was in before; wherein he might without injustice be destroyed by any man whatsoever.

Fourthly, because every subject is by this institution author of all the actions, and judgments of the sovereign instituted; it follows, that whatsoever he doth, it can be no injury to any of his subjects; nor ought he to be by any of them accused of injustice. For he that doth anything by authority from another, doth therein no injury to him by whose authority he acteth: but by this institution of a commonwealth, every particular man is author of all the sovereign doth: and consequently he that complaineth of injury from his sovereign, complaineth of that whereof he himself is author; and therefore ought not to accuse any man but himself; no nor himself of injury; because to do injury to one's self, is impossible. It is true that they that have sovereign power may commit iniquity; but not injustice, or injury in the proper signification.

Fifthly, and consequently to that which was said last, no man that hath sovereign power can justly be put to death, or otherwise in any manner by his subjects punished. For seeing every subject is author of the actions of his sovereign; he punisheth another for the actions committed by himself.

. . .

And because the end of this institution, is the peace and defence of them all; and whosoever has right to the end, has right to the means; it belongeth of

right, to whatsoever man, or assembly that hath the sovereignty, to be judge both of the means of peace and defence, and also of the hindrances, and disturbances of the same; and to do whatsoever he shall think necessary to be done, both beforehand, for the preserving of peace and security, by prevention of discord at home, and hostility from abroad; and, when peace and security are lost, for the recovery of the same.

. . .

To come now to the particulars of the true liberty of a subject; that is to say, what are the things, which though commanded by the sovereign, he may nevertheless, without injustice, refuse to do; we are to consider, what rights we pass away, when we make a commonwealth; or, which is all one, what liberty we deny ourselves, by owning all the actions, without exception, of the man, or assembly we make our sovereign. For in the act of our *submission,* consisteth both our *obligation,* and our *liberty;* which must therefore be inferred by arguments taken from thence; there being no obligation on any man, which ariseth not from some act of his own; for all men equally, are by nature free. And because such arguments, must either be drawn from the express words, *I authorize all his actions,* or from the intention of him that submitteth himself to his power, which intention is to be understood by the end for which he so submitteth; the obligation, and liberty of the subject, is to be derived, either from those words, or others equivalent; or else from the end of the institution of sovereignty, namely, the peace of the subjects within themselves, and their defence against a common enemy.

First therefore, seeing sovereignty by institution, is by covenant of every one to every one; and sovereignty by acquisition, by covenants of the vanquished to the victor, or child to the parent; it is manifest, that every subject has liberty in all those things, the right whereof cannot by covenant be transferred. I have shewn before in the 14th chapter, that covenants, not to defend a man's own body, are void. Therefore, if the sovereign command a man, though justly condemned, to kill, wound, or main himself; or not to resist those that assault him, or to abstain from the use of food, air, medicine, or any other thing, without which he cannot live; yet hath that man the liberty to disobey.

If a man be interrogated by the sovereign, or his authority, concerning a crime done by himself, he is not bound, without assurance of pardon, to confess it; because no man, as I have shown in the same chapter, can be obliged by covenant to accuse himself.

Again, the consent of a subject to sovereign power, is contained in these words, *I authorize, or take upon me, all his actions;* in which there is no restriction at all, of his own former natural liberty: for by allowing him to *kill me,* I am not bound to kill myself when he commands me. It is one thing to say, *kill me, or my fellow, if you please;* another thing to say, *I will kill myself, or my fellow.* It followeth therefore that

No man is bound by these words themselves, either to kill himself, or any other man; and consequently, that the obligation a man may sometimes have,

upon the command of the sovereign to execute any dangerous, or dishonourable office, dependeth not on the words of our submission; but on the intention, which is to be understood by the end thereof. When therefore our refusal to obey, frustrates the end for which the sovereignty was ordained; then there is no liberty to refuse: otherwise there is.

Upon this ground, a man that is commanded as a soldier to fight against the enemy, though his sovereign have right enough to punish his refusal with death, may nevertheless in many cases refuse, without injustice; as when he substituteth a sufficient soldier in his place: for in this case he deserteth not the service of the commonwealth. And there is allowance to be made for natural timorousness; not only to women, of whom no such dangerous duty is expected, but also to men of feminine courage. When armies fight, there is on one side, or both, a running away; yet when they do it not out of treachery, but fear, they are not esteemed to do it unjustly, but dishonourably. For the same reason, to avoid battle, is not injustice, but cowardice. But he that enrolleth himself a soldier or taketh imprest money, taketh away the excuse of a timorous nature; and is obliged, not only to go to the battle, but also not to run from it, without his captain's leave. And when the defence of the commonwealth, requireth at once the help of all that are able to bear arms, every one is obliged; because otherwise the institution of the commonwealth, which they have not the purpose, or courage to preserve, was in vain.

To resist the sword of the commonwealth, in defence of another man, guilty, or innocent, no man hath liberty; because such liberty, takes away from the sovereign, the means of protecting us; and is therefore destructive of the very essence of government. But in case a great many men together, have already resisted the sovereign power unjustly, or committed some capital crime, for which every one of them expecteth death, whether have they not the liberty then to join together, and assist, and defend one another? Certainly they have: for they but defend their lives, which the guilty man may as well do, as the innocent. There was indeed injustice in the first breach of their duty; their bearing of arms subsequent to it, though it be to maintain what they have done, is no new unjust act. And if it be only to defend their persons, it is not unjust at all. But the offer of pardon taketh from them, to whom it is offered, the plea of self-defence, and maketh their perseverance in assisting, or defending the rest, unlawful.

As for other liberties, they depend on the silence of the law. In cases where the sovereign has prescribed no rule, there the subject hath the liberty to do, or forbear, according to his own discretion. And therefore such liberty is in some places more, and in some less; and in some times more, in other times less, according as they that have the sovereignty shall think most convenient. . . .

The obligation of subjects to the sovereign, is understood to last as long, and no longer, than the power lasteth, by which he is able to portect them. For the right men have by nature to protect themselves, when none else can protect them, can by no covenant be relinquished. The sovereignty is the soul of the

commonwealth; which once departed from the body, the members do no more receive their motion from it. The end of obedience is protection; which, wheresoever a man seeth it, either in his own, or in another's sword, nature applieth his obedience to it, and his endeavour to maintain it. And though sovereignty, in the intention of them that make it, be immortal; yet it is in its own nature, not only subject to violent death, by foreign war; but also through the ignorance, and passions of men, it hath in it, from the very institution, many seeds of a natural mortality, by intestine discord.

. . .

15

Limited Government as Defender of Property

JOHN LOCKE

John Locke (1632–1704) was a major British philosopher who made important contributions in two areas. His Essay Concerning Human Understanding *is a classic work of empiricism, the view that all knowledge is grounded in, and acquired through, the senses. His* Second Treatise of Government, *excerpted here, is a classic document of political philosophy. Many of its ideas are embodied in the United States Declaration of Independence.*

At least superficially, Locke's approach to government resembles that of Thomas Hobbes (reading 14). Like Hobbes, Locke believes that government serves to protect our lives and property, and arises through agreement of the governed. But these similarities conceal important differences. Unlike Hobbes, Locke believes that an absolute sovereign is neither needed to preserve peace nor defensible on any other grounds. Because an absolute sovereign could be as predatory as any other individual, but would be many times as powerful, he would actually pose more of a threat than the state of nature. What we need, instead of either, is a government of known and settled laws, capable of restricting even the activities of our rulers. Such a government is indeed grounded in our consent; but that consent is not unlimited. When a ruler abuses his power, and citizens lack effective redress, they may "appeal to heaven," and resort to force to set things right.

Given this approach, it is natural to wonder first, how we acquire property for government to protect, and second, how we have given our consent to be bound by government's laws. Locke gives important answers to both questions. To the first, Locke replies that everyone owns his body and labor, and that people acquire additional property by "mixing their labor" with unowned objects or trading their possessions for other things. To the second, he replies that our very enjoyment of the benefits of government is, in effect, a kind of tacit consent to obey its laws. Whether there is any real alternative to enjoying the benefits of government, and if not, whether enjoying them still amounts to any sort of consent, are questions to consider as you read the selection.

. . .

Of the State of Nature

4. To understand political power aright, and derive it from its original, we must consider what estate all men are naturally in, and that is, a state of perfect freedom to order their actions, and dispose of their possessions and persons as

they think fit, within the bounds of the law of Nature, without asking leave or depending upon the will of any other man.

A state also of equality, wherein all the power and jurisdiction is reciprocal, no one have more than another, there being nothing more evident than that creatures of the same species and rank, promiscuously born to all the same advantages of Nature, and the use of the same faculties, should also be equal one amongst another, without subordination or subjection, unless the lord and master of them all should, by any manifest declaration of his will, set one above another, and confer on him, by an evident and clear appointment, an undoubted right to dominion and sovereignty.

. . .

6. But though this be a state of liberty, yet it is not a state of license; though man in that state have an uncontrollable liberty to dispose of his person or possessions, yet he has not liberty to destroy himself, or so much as any creature in his possession, but where some nobler use than its bare preservation calls for it. The state of Nature has a law of Nature to govern it, which obliges everyone, and reason, which is that law, teaches all mankind who will but consult it, that being all equal and independent, no one ought to harm another in his life, health, liberty or possessions; for men being all the workmanship of one omnipotent and infinitely wise Maker; all the servants of one sovereign Master, sent into the world by His order and about His business; they are His property, whose workmanship they are made to last during His, not one another's pleasure. And, being furnished with like faculties, sharing all in one community of Nature, there cannot be supposed any such subordination among us that may authorize us to destroy one another, as if we were made for one another's uses, as the inferior ranks of creatures are for ours. Everyone as he is bound to preserve himself, and not to quit his station willfully, so by the like reason, when his own preservation comes not in competition, ought he as much as he can to preserve the rest of mankind, and not unless it be to do justice on an offender, take away or impair the life, or what tends to the preservation of the life, the liberty, health, limb, or goods of another.

7. And that all men may be restrained from invading others' rights, and from doing hurt to one another, and the law of Nature be observed, which willeth the peace and preservation of all mankind, the execution of the law of Nature is in that state put into every man's hands, whereby everyone has a right to punish the transgressors of that law to such a degree as may hinder its violation. For the law of Nature would, as all other laws that concern men in this world, be in vain if there were nobody that in the state of Nature had a power to execute that law, and thereby preserve the innocent and restrain offenders; and if anyone in the state of Nature may punish another for any evil he has done, everyone may do so. For in that state of perfect equality, where naturally there is no superiority or jurisdiction of one over another, what any may do in prosecution of that law, everyone must needs have a right to do.

8. And thus, in the state of Nature, one man comes by a power over another, but yet no absolute or arbitrary power to use a criminal, when he has got him in his hands, according to the passionate heats of boundless extravagancy of

his own will, but only to retribute to him so far as calm reason and conscience dictate, what is proportionate to his transgression, which is so much as may serve for reparation and restraint. For these two are the only reasons why one man may lawfully do harm to another, which is that we call punishment. In transgressing the law of Nature, the offender declares himself to live by another rule than that of reason and common equity, which is that measure God has set to the actions of men for their mutual security, and so he becomes dangerous to mankind; the tie which is to secure them from injury and violence being slighted and broken by him, which being a trespass against the whole species, and the peace and safety of it, provided for by the law of Nature, every man upon this score, by the right he hath to preserve mankind in general, may restrain, or where it is necessary, destroy things noxious to them, and so may bring such evil on anyone who hath transgressed that law, as may make him repent the doing of it, and thereby deter him, and, by his example, others from doing the like mischief. And in this case, and upon this ground, every man hath a right to punish the offender, and be executioner of the law of Nature.

. . .

10. Besides the crime which consists in violating the laws, and varying from the right rule of reason, whereby a man so far becomes degenerate, and declares himself to quit the principles of human nature and to be a noxious creature, there is commonly injury done, and some person or other, some other man, receives damage by his transgression; in which case, he who hath received any damage has (besides the right of punishment common to him, with other men) a particular right to seek reparation from him that hath done it. And any other person who finds it just may also join with him that is injured, and assist him in recovering from the offender so much as may make satisfaction for the harm he hath suffered.

. . .

13. To this strange doctrine—viz., That in the state of Nature everyone has the executive power to the law of Nature—I doubt not but it will be objected that it is unreasonable for men to be judges in their own cases, that self-love will make men partial to themselves and their friends; and, on the other side, ill-nature, passion, and revenge will carry them too far in punishing others, and hence nothing but confusion and disorder will follow, and that therefore God hath certainly appointed government to restrain the partiality and violence of men. I easily grant that civil government is the proper remedy for the inconveniences of the state of Nature, which must certainly be great where men may be judges in their own case, since it is easy to be imagined that he who was so unjust as to do his brother an injury will scarce be so just as to condemn himself for it. But I shall desire those who make this objection to remember that absolute monarchs are but men; and if government is to be the remedy of those evils which necessarily follow from men being judges in their own cases, and the state of Nature is therefore not to be endured, I desire to know what kind of government that is, and how much better it is than the state of Nature, where one man commanding a multitude has the liberty to be judge in his own case,

and may do to all his subjects whatever he pleases without the least question or control of those who execute his pleasure? and in whatsoever he doth, whether led by reason, mistake, or passion, must be submitted to? which men in the state of Nature are not bound to do one to another. And if he that judges, judges amiss in his own or any other case, he is answerable for it to the rest of mankind.

14. It is often asked as a mighty objection, where are, or ever were, there any men in such a state of Nature? To which it may suffice as an answer at present, that since all princes and rulers of "independent" governments all through the world are in a state of Nature, it is plain the world never was, nor never will be, without numbers of men in that state. I have named all govenors of "independent" communities, whether they are, or are not, in league with others; for it is not every compact that puts an end to the state of Nature between men, but only this one of agreeing together mutually to enter into one community, and make one body politic; other promises and compacts men may make one with another, and yet still be in the state of Nature. The promises and bargains for truck, etc., between the two men in Soldania, in or between a Swiss and an Indian, in the woods of America, are binding to them, though they are perfectly in a state of Nature in reference to one another for truth, and keeping of faith belongs to men as men, and not as members of society.

. . .

Of Property

. . .

25. God, who hath given the world to men in common, hath also given them reason to make use of it to the best advantage of life and convenience. The earth and all that is therein is given to men for the support and comfort of their being. And though all the fruits it naturally produces, and beasts it feeds, belong to mankind in common, as they are produced by the spontaneous hand of Nature, and nobody has originally a private dominion exclusive of the rest of mankind in any of them, as they are thus in their natural state, yet being given for the use of men, there must of necessity be a means to appropriate them some way or other before they can be of any use, or at all beneficial, to any particular men. The fruit or venison which nourishes the wild Indian, who knows no enclosure, and is still a tenant in common, must be his, and so his— i.e., a part of him, that another can no longer have any right to it before it can do him any good for the support of his life.

26. Though the earth and all inferior creatures be common to all men, yet every man has a "property" in his own "person." This nobody has any right to but himself. The "labor" of his body and the "work" of his hands, we may say, are properly his. Whatsoever, then, he removes out of the state that Nature hath provided and left it in, he hath mixed his labor with it, and joined to it something that is his own, and thereby makes it his property. It being by him removed from the common state Nature placed it in, it hath by this labor

something annexed to it that excludes the common right of other men. For this "labor" being the unquestionable property of the laborer, no man but he can have a right to what that is once joined to, at least where there is enough, and as good left in common for others.

27. He that is nourished by the acorns he picked up under an oak, or the apples he gathered from the trees in the wood, has certainly appropriated them to himself. Nobody can deny but the nourishment is his. I ask, then, when did they begin to be his? when he digested? or when he ate? or when he boiled? or when he brought them home? or when he picked them up? And it is plain, if the first gathering made them not his, nothing else could. . . .

30. It will, perhaps, be objected to this, that if gathering the acorns or other fruits of the earth, etc., makes a right to them, then anyone may engross as much as he will. To which I answer, Not so. The same law of Nature that does by this means give us property, does also bound that property too. "God has given us all things richly." Is the voice of reason confirmed by inspiration? But how far has He given it us "to enjoy"? As much as anyone can make use of to any advantage of life before it spoils, so much he may by his labor fix a property in. Whatever is beyond this is more than his share, and belongs to others. Nothing was made by God for man to spoil or destroy. And thus considering the plenty of natural provisions there was a long time in the world, and the few spenders, and to how small a part of that provision the industry of one man could extend itself and engross it to the prejudice of others, especially keeping within the bounds set by reason of what might serve for his use, there could be then little room for quarrels or contentions about property so established.

31. But the chief matter of property being now not the fruits of the earth and the beasts that subsist on it, but the earth itself, as that which takes in and carries with it all the rest, I think it is plain that property in that too is acquired as the former. As much land as a man tills, plants, improves, cultivates, and can use the product of, so much is his property. He by his labor does, as it were, enclose it from the common. . . .

32. Nor was this appropriation of any parcel of land, by improving it, any prejudice to any other man, since there was still enough and as good left, and more than the yet unprovided could use. So that, in effect, there was never the less left for others because of his enclosure for himself. For he that leaves as much as another can make use of does as good as take nothing at all. Nobody could think himself injured by the drinking of another man, though he took a good draught, who had a whole river of the same water left him to quench his thirst. And the case of land and water, where there is enough of both, is perfectly the same.

. . .

40. Nor is it so strange as, perhaps, before consideration, it may appear, that the property of labor should be able to overbalance the community of land, for it is labor indeed that puts the difference of value on everything; and let anyone consider what the difference is between an acre of land planted with tobacco or sugar, sown with wheat or barley, and an acre of the same land

lying in common without any husbandry upon it, and he will find that the improvement of labor makes the far greater part of the value. I think it will be but a very modest computation to say, that of the produts of the earth useful to the life of man, nine-tenths are the effects of labor. Nay, if we will rightly estimate things as they come to our use, and cast up the several expenses about them—what in them is purely owing to Nature and what to labor—we shall find that in most of them ninety-nine hundredths are wholly to be put on the account of labor.

. . .

46. The greatest part of things really useful to the life of man, and such as the necessity of subsisting made the first commoners of the world look after— as it doth the Americans now—are generally things of short duration, such as —if they are not consumed by use— will decay and perish of themselves. Gold, silver, and diamonds are things that fancy or agreement hath put the value on, more than real use and the necessary support of life. Now of those good things which Nature hath provided in common, everyone has a right (as has been said) to as much as he could use, and had a property in all he could effect with his labor; all that his industry could extend to, to alter from the state Nature had put it in, was his. He that gathered a hundred bushels of acorns or apples had thereby a property in them; they were his goods as soon as gathered. He was only to look that he used them before they spoiled, else he took more than his share, and robbed others. And, indeed, it was a foolish thing, as well as dishonest, to hoard up more than he could make use of. If he gave away a part to anybody else, so that it perished not uselessly in his possession, these he also made use of. And if he also bartered away plums that would have rotted in a week, for nuts that would last good for his eating a whole year, he did no injury; he wasted not the common stock; destroyed no part of the portion of good that belonged to others, so long as nothing perished uselessly in his hands. Again, if he would give his nuts for a piece of metal, pleased with its color, or exchange his sheep for shells, or wool for a sparkling pebble or a diamond, and keep those by him all his life, he invaded not the right of others; he might heap up as much of these durable things as he pleased; the exceeding of the bounds of his just property not lying in the largeness of his possession, but the perishing of anything uselessly in it.

47. And thus came in the use of money; some lasting thing that men might keep without spoiling, and that, by mutual consent, men would take in exchange for the truly useful but perishable supports of life.

48. And as different degrees of industry were apt to give men possessions in different proportions, so this invention of money gave them the opportunity to continue and enlarge them. For supposing an island, separate from all possible commerce with the rest of the world, wherein there were but a hundred families, but there were sheep, horses, and cows, with other useful animals, wholesome fruits, and land enough for corn for a hundred thousand times as many, but nothing in the island, either because of its commonness or perishableness, fit to supply the place of money. What reason could anyone have

there to enlarge his possessions beyond the use of his family, and a plentiful supply to its consumption, either in what their own industry produced, or they could barter for like perishable, useful commodities with others? Where there is not something both lasting and scarce, and so valuable to be hoarded up, there men will not be apt to enlarge their possessions of land, were it never so rich, never so free for them to take. For I ask, what would a man value ten thousand or a hundred thousand acres of excellent land, ready cultivated and well stocked, too, with cattle, in the middle of the inland parts of America, where he had no hopes of commerce with other parts of the world, to draw money to him by the sale of the product? It would not be worth the enclosing, and we should see him give up again to the wild common of Nature whatever was more than would supply the conveniences of life, to be had there for him and his family.

. . .

Of the Beginning of Political Societies

95. Men being, as has been said, by nature all free, equal, and independent, no one can be put out of this estate and subjected to the political power of another without his own consent, which is done by agreeing with other men, to join and unite into a community for their comfortable, safe, and peaceable living, one amongst another, in a secure enjoyment of their properties, and a greater security against any that are not of it. This any number of men may do, because it injures not the freedom of the rest; they are left, as they were, in the liberty of the state of Nature. When any number of men have so consented to make one community or government, they are thereby presently incorporated, and make one body politic, wherein the majority have a right to act and conclude the rest.

96. For, when any number of men have, by the consent of every individual, made a community, they have thereby made that community one body, with a power to act as one body, which is only by the will and determination of the majority. For that which acts any community, being only the consent of the individuals of it, and it being one body, must move one way, it is necessary the body should move that way wither the greater force carries it, which is the consent of the majority, or else it is impossible it should act or continue one body, one community, which the consent of every individual that united into it agreed that it should; and so everyone is bound by that consent to be concluded by the majority. And therefore we see that in assemblies empowered to act by positive laws where no number is set by that positive law which empowers them, the act of the majority passes for the act of the whole, and of course determines as having, by the law of Nature and reason, the power of the whole.

. . .

98. For if the consent of the majority shall not in reason be received as the act of the whole, and conclude every individual, nothing but the consent of

every individual can make anything to be the act of the whole, which, considering the infirmities of health and avocations of business, which in a number though much less than that of a commonwealth, will necessarily keep many away from the public assembly; and the variety of opinions and contrariety of interests which unavoidably happen in all collections of men, it is next impossible ever to be had. And, therefore, if coming into society be upon such terms, it will be only like Cato's coming into the theater, *tantum ut exiret.** Such a constitution as this would make the mighty leviathan of a shorter duration than the feeblest creatures, and not let it outlast the day it was born in, which cannot be supposed till we can think that rational creatures should desire and constitute societies only to be dissolved. For where the majority cannot conclude the rest, there they cannot act as one body, and consequently will be immediately dissolved again.

· · ·

119. Every man being, as has been showed, naturally free, and nothing being able to put him into subjection to any earthly power, but only his own consent, it is to be considered what shall be understood to be a sufficient declaration of a man's consent to make him subject to the laws of any government. There is a common distinction of an express and a tacit consent, which will concern our present case. Nobody doubts but an express consent of any man, entering into any society, makes him a perfect member of that society, a subject of that government. The difficulty is, what ought to be looked upon as a tacit consent, and how far it binds—i.e., how far anyone shall be looked on to have consented, and thereby submitted to any government, where he has made no expressions of it at all. And to this I say, that every man that hath any possession or enjoyment of any part of the dominions of any government doth hereby give his tacit consent, and is as far forth obliged to obedience to the laws of that government, during such enjoyment, as anyone under it, whether this his possession be of land to him and his heirs forever, or a lodging only for a week; or whether it be barely traveling freely on the highway; and, in effect, it reaches as far as the very being of anyone within the territories of that government.

· · ·

122. But submitting to the laws of any country, living quietly and enjoying privileges and protection under them, makes not a man a member of that society; it is only a local protection and homage due to and from all those who, not being in a state of war, come within the territories belonging to any government, to all parts whereof the force of its law extends. But this no more makes a man a member of that society, a perpetual subject of that commonwealth, than it would make a man a subject to another in whose family he found it convenient to abide for some time, though, whilst he continued in it, he were obliged to comply with the laws and submit to the government he found there. And thus we see that foreigners, by living all their lives under

---

* Merely to go out again.

another government, and enjoying the privileges and protection of it, though they are bound, even in conscience, to submit to its administration as far forth as any denizen, yet do not thereby come to be subjects or members of that commonwealth. Nothing can make any man so but his actually entering into it by positive engagement and express promise and compact. This is that which, I think, concerning the beginning of political societies, and that consent which makes anyone a member of any commonwealth.

Of the Ends of Political Society and Government

123. If man in the state of Nature be so free as has been said, if he be absolute lord of his own person and possessions, equal to the greatest and subject to nobody, why will he part with his freedom, this empire, and subject himself to the dominion and control of any other power? To which it is obvious to answer, that though in the state of Nature he has such a right, yet the enjoyment of it is very uncertain and constantly exposed to the invasion of others; for all being kings as much as he, every man his equal, and the greater part no strict observers of equity and justice, the enjoyment of the property he has in this state is very unsafe, very insecure. This makes him willing to quit this condition which, however free, is full of fears and continual dangers; and it is not without reason that he seeks out and is willing to join in society with others who are already united, or have a mind to unite for the mutual preservation of their lives, liberties and estates, which I call by the general name—property.

124. The great and chief end, therefore, of men uniting into commonwealths, and putting themselves under government, is the preservation of their property; to which in the state of Nature there are many things wanting.

Firstly, there wants an established, settled, known law, received and allowed by common consent to be the standard of right and wrong, and the common measure to decide all controversies between them. For though the law of Nature be plain and intelligible to all rational creatures, yet men, being biased by their interest, as well as ignorant for want of study of it, are not apt to allow of it as a law binding to them in the application of it to their particular cases.

125. Secondly, in the state of Nature there wants a known and indifferent judge, with authority to determine all differences according to the established law. For everyone in that state being both judge and executioner of the law of Nature, men being partial to themselves, passion and revenge is very apt to carry them too far, and with too much heat in their own cases, as well as negligence and unconcernedness, make them too remiss in other men's.

126. Thirdly, in the state of Nature there often wants power to back and support the sentence when right, and to give it due execution. They who by any injustice offended will seldom fail where they are able by force to make good their injustice. Such resistance many times makes the punishment dangerous, and frequently destructive to those who attempt it.

. . .

128. For in the state of Nature to omit the liberty he has of innocent delights, a man has two powers. The first is to do whatsover he thinks fit for the pres-

ervation of himself and others within the permission of the law of Nature; by which law, common to them all, he and all the rest of mankind are one community, make up one society distinct from all other creatures, and were it not for the corruption and viciousness of degenerate men, there would be no need of any other, no necessity that men should separate from this great and natural community, and associate into lesser combinations. The other power a man has in the state of Nature is the power to punish the crimes committed against that law. Both these he gives up when he joins in a private, if I may so call it, or particular political society, and incorporates into any commonwealth separate from the rest of mankind.

129. The first power—viz., of doing whatsoever he thought fit for the preservation of himself and the rest of mankind, he gives up to be regulated by laws made by the society, so far forth as the preservation of himself and the rest of that society shall require; which laws of the society in many things confine the liberty he had by the law of Nature.

130. Secondly, the power of punishing he wholly gives up, and engages his natural force, which he might before employ in the execution of the law of Nature, by his own single authority, as he thought fit, to assist the executive power of the society as the law thereof shall require. For being now in a new state, wherein he is to enjoy many conveniences from the labor, assistance, and society of others in the same community, as well as protection from its whole strength, he is to part also with as much of his natural liberty, in providing for himself, as the good, prosperity, and safety of the society shall require, which is not only necessary but just, since the other members of the society do the like.

. . .

Of the Extent of the Legislative Power

. . .

135. Though the legislative, whether placed in one or more, whether it be always in being or only by intervals, though it be the supreme power in every commonwealth, yet, first, it is not, nor can possibly be, absolutely arbitrary over the lives and fortunes of the people. For it being but the joint power of every member of the society given up to that person or assembly which is legislator, it can be no more than those persons had in a state of Nature before they entered into society, and gave it up to the community. For nobody can transfer to another more power than he has in himself, and nobody has an absolute arbitrary power over himself, or over any other, to destroy his own life, or take away the life or property of another. A man, as has been proved, cannot subject himself to the arbitrary power of another; and having, in the state of Nature, no arbitrary power over the life, liberty, or possession of another, but only so much as the law of Nature gave him for the preservation of himself and the rest of mankind, this is all he does, or can give up to the commonwealth, and by it to the legislative power, so that the legislative can

have no more than this. Their power in the utmost bounds of it is limited to the public good of the society. It is a power that has no other end but preservation, and therefore can never have a right to destroy, enslave, or designedly to impoverish the subjects; the obligations of the law of Nature cease not in society, but only in many cases are drawn closer, and have, by human laws, known penalties annexed to them to enforce their observation. Thus the law of Nature stands as an eternal rule to all men, legislators as well as others. The rules that they make for other men's actions must, as well as their own and other men's actions, be conformable to the law of Nature—i.e., to the will of God, of which that is a declaration, and the fundamental law of Nature being the preservation of mankind, no human sanction can be good or valid against it.

136. Secondly, the legislative or supreme authority cannot assume to itself a power to rule by extemporary arbitrary decrees, but is bound to dispense justice and decide the rights of the subject by promulgated standing laws, and known authorized judges. For the law of Nature being unwritten, and so nowhere to be found but in the minds of men, they who, through passion or interest, shall miscite or misapply it, cannot so easily be convinced of their mistake where there is no established judge; and so it serves not as it ought, to determine the rights and fence the properties of those that live under it, especially where everyone is judge, interpreter, and executioner of it too, and that in his own case; and he that has right on his side, having ordinarily but his own single strength, hath not force enough to defend himself from injuries or punish delinquents. . . .

137. Absolute arbitrary power, or governing without settled standing laws, can neither of them consist with the ends of society and government, which men would not quit the freedom of the state of Nature for, and tie themselves up under, were it not to preserve their lives, liberties, and fortunes, and by stated rules of right and property to secure their peace and quiet. It cannot be supposed that they should intend, had they a power so to do, to give anyone or more an absolute arbitrary power over their persons and estates, and put a force into the magistrate's hand to execute his unlimited will arbitrarily upon them; this were to put themselves into a worse condition than the state of Nature, wherein they had a liberty to defend their right against the injuries of others, and were upon equal terms of force to maintain it, whether invaded by a single man or many in combination. Whereas by supposing they have given up themselves to the absolute arbitrary power and will of a legislator, they have disarmed themselves, and armed him to make a prey of them when he pleases; he being in a much worse condition that is exposed to the arbitrary power of one man who has the command of a hundred thousand than he that is exposed to the arbitrary power of a hundred thousand single men, nobody being secure, that his will who has such a command is better than that of other men, though his force be a hundred thousand times stronger. And, therefore, what ever form the commonwealth is under, the ruling power ought to govern by declared and received laws, and not by extemporary dictates and undetermined resolutions, for then mankind will be in a far worse condition than in

the state of Nature if they shall have armed one or a few men with the joint power of a multitude, to force them to obey at pleasure the exorbitant and unlimited decrees of their sudden thoughts, or unrestrained, and till that moment, unknown wills, without having any measures set down which may guide and justify their actions. For all the power the government has, being only for the good of the society, as it ought not to be arbitrary and at pleasure, so it ought to be exercised by established and promulgated laws, that both the people may know their duty, and be safe and secure within the limits of the law, and the rulers, too, kept within their due bounds, and not be tempted by the power they have in their hands to employ it to purposes, and by such measures as they would not have known, and own not willingly.

138. Thirdly, the supreme power cannot take from any man any part of his property without his own consent. For the preservation of property being the end of government, and that for which men enter into society, it necessarily supposes and requires that the people should have property, without which they must be supposed to lose that by entering into society which was the end for which they entered into it; too gross an absurdity for any man to own. . . .

140. It is true governments cannot be supported without great charge, and it is fit everyone who enjoys his share of the protection should pay out of his estate his proportion for the maintenance of it. But still it must be with his own consent—i.e., the consent of the majority, giving it either by themselves or their representatives chosen by them; for if anyone shall claim a power to lay and levy taxes on the people by his own authority, and without such consent of the people, he thereby invades the fundamental law of property, and subverts the end of government. For what property have I in that which another may by right take when he pleases to himself?

141. Fourthly, the legislative cannot transfer the power of making laws to any other hands, for it being but a delegated power from the people, they who have it cannot pass it over to others. The people alone can appoint the form of the commonwealth, which is by constituting the legislative, and appointing in whose hands that shall be. And when the people have said, "We will submit, and be governed by laws made by such men, and in such forms," nobody else can say other men shall make laws for them; nor can they be bound by any laws but such as are enacted by those whom they have chosen and authorized to make laws for them.

. . .

Of the Dissolution of Government

. . .

222. The reason why men enter into society is the preservation of their property; and the end while they choose and authorize a legislative is that there may be laws made, and rules set, as guards and fences to the properties of all the society, to limit the power and moderate the dominion of every part and member of the society. For since it can never be supposed to be the will of the society that the legislative should have a power to destroy that which everyone

designs to secure by entering into society, and for which the people submitted themselves to legislators of their own making: whenever the legislators endeavor to take away and destroy the property of the people, or to reduce them to slavery under arbitrary power, they put themselves into a state of war with the people, who are thereupon absolved from any farther obedience, and are left to the common refuge which God hath provided for all men against force and violence. Whensoever, therefore, the legislative shall transgress this fundamental rule of society, and either by ambition, fear, folly, or corruption, endeavor to grasp themselves, or put into the hands of any other, an absolute power over the lives, liberties, and estates of the people, by this breach of trust they forfeit the power the people had put into their hands for quite contrary ends, and it devolves to the people, who have a right to resume their original liberty, and by the establishment of a new legislative (such as they shall think fit), provide for their own safety and security, which is the end for which they are in society.

· · ·

240. Here it is like the common question will be made: Who shall be judge whether the prince or legislative act contrary to their trust? This, perhaps, ill-affected and factious men may spread amongst the people, when the prince only makes use of his due prerogative. To this I reply, The people shall be judge; for who shall be judge whether his trustee or deputy acts well and according to the trust reposed in him, but he who deputes him and must, by having deputed him, have still a power to discard him when he fails in his trust? If this be reasonable in particular cases of private men, why should it be otherwise in that of the greatest moment, where the welfare of millions is concerned and also where the evil, if not prevented, is greater, and the redress very difficult, dear, and dangerous?

241. But, farther, this question, Who shall be judge? cannot mean that there is no judge at all. For where there is no judicature on earth to decide controversies amongst men, God in heaven is judge. He alone, it is true, is judge of the right. But every man is judge for himself, as in all other cases so in this, whether another hath put himself into a state of war with him, and whether he should appeal to the supreme Judge, as Jephtha did.

242. If a controversy arise betwixt a prince and some of the people in a matter where the law is silent or doubtful, and the thing be of great consequence, I should think the proper umpire in such a case should be the body of the people. For in such cases where the prince hath a trust reposed in him, and is dispensed from the common, ordinary rules of the law, there, if any men find themselves aggrieved, and think the prince acts contrary to, or beyond that trust, who so proper to judge as the body of the people (who at first lodged that trust in him) how far they meant it should extend? But if the prince, or whoever they be in the administration, decline that way of determination, the appeal then lies nowhere but to Heaven. Force between either persons who have no known superior on earth, or which permits no appeal to a judge on earth, being properly a state of war, wherein the appeal lies only to Heaven; and in that state the injured party must judge for himself when he will think fit to make use of that appeal and put himself upon it.

243. To conclude. The power that every individual gave the society when he entered into it can never revert to the individuals again, as long as the society lasts, but will always remain in the community; because without this there can be no community—no commonwealth, which is contrary to the original agreement; so also when the society hath placed the legislative in any assembly of men, to continue in them and their successors, with direction and authority for providing such successors, the legislative can never revert to the people whilst that government lasts; because, having provided a legislative with power to continue forever, they have given up their political power to the legislative, and cannot resume it. But if they have set limits to the duration of their legislative, and made this supreme power in any person or assembly only temporary; or else when, by the miscarriages of those in authority, it is forfeited; upon the forfeiture of their rulers, or at the determination of the time set, it reverts to the society, and the people have a right to act as supreme, and continue the legislative in themselves or place it in a new form, or new hands, as they think good.

16

"The Principle of Fairness"

ROBERT NOZICK

Robert Nozick (b. 1938) is Professor of Philosophy at Harvard University. His most recent book is Philosophical Explanations. *His earlier book,* Anarchy, State, and Utopia, *is an influential statement of one type of conservative position.*

Here Nozick tries to rebut an argument which, if successful, could be used to show that we are obligated to submit to a quite extensive government and system of laws. The argument states that society is, in effect, a cooperative arrangement within which many people restrain their liberty in ways that benefit everyone, and that fairness therefore requires that all others be subject to similar restraint. Although this argument resembles John Locke's appeal to tacit consent in reading 15, it differs by making no mention of any contract or agreement. Thus, it seems to avoid any difficulties which that notion raises. For what seems to be a compressed version of it, see Locke, paragraph 130.

Despite its promise, Nozick contends that this appeal to the "principle of fairness" fails. If merely benefitting from a cooperative scheme did obligate one to bear a share of the burden, then people could impose all sorts of unwanted obligations on others simply by providing them with unsought benefits. Through cleverly chosen examples, Nozick tries to convince us that this result is unacceptable. If one dislikes his conclusion, one must either acknowledge that new obligations do arise in his examples, or else show that the arrangements in the examples are importantly dissimilar to those of society as a whole.

A PRINCIPLE suggested by Herbert Hart, which (following John Rawls) we shall call the *principle of fairness,* would be of service here if it were adequate. This principle holds that when a number of persons engage in a just, mutually advantageous, cooperative venture according to rules and thus restrain their liberty in ways necessary to yield advantages for all, those who have submitted to these restrictions have a right to similar acquiescence on the part of those who have benefited from their submission.[1] Acceptance of benefits

---

[1] Herbert Hart, "Are There Any Natural Rights?" in *Philosophical Review,* 1955; John Rawls, *A Theory of Justice* (Cambridge, Massachusetts: Harvard University Press, 1971), Sect. 18. My statement of the principle stays close to Rawls'. . .

(even when this is not a giving of express or tacit undertaking to cooperate) is enough, according to this principle, to bind one. If one adds to the principle of fairness the claim that the others to whom the obligations are owed or their agents may *enforce* the obligations arising under this principle (including the obligation to limit one's actions), then groups of people in a state of nature who agree to a procedure to pick those to engage in certain acts will have legitimate rights to prohibit "free riders." Such a right may be crucial to the viability of such agreements. We should scrutinize such a powerful right very carefully, especially as it seems to make *unanimous* consent to coercive government in a state of nature *unnecessary!* . . .

The principle of fairness, as we stated it following Hart and Rawls, is objectionable and unacceptable. Suppose some of the people in your neighborhood (there are 364 other adults) have found a public address system and decide to institute a system of public entertainment. They post a list of names, one for each day, yours among them. On his assigned day (one can easily switch days) a person is to run the public address system, play records over it, give news bulletins, tell amusing stories he has heard, and so on. After 138 days on which each person has done his part, your day arrives. Are you obligated to take your turn? You *have* benefited from it, occasionally opening your window to listen, enjoying some music or chuckling at someone's funny story. The other people *have* put themselves out. But must you answer the call when it is your turn to do so? As it stands, surely not. Though you benefit from the arrangement, you may know all along that 364 days of entertainment supplied by others will not be worth your giving up *one* day. You would rather not have any of it and not give up a day than have it all and spend one of your days at it. Given these preferences, how can it be that you are required to participate when your scheduled time comes? It would be nice to have philosophy readings on the radio to which one could tune in at any time, perhaps late at night when tired. But it may not be nice enough for you to want to give up one whole day of your own as a reader on the program. Whatever you want, can others create an obligation for you to do so by going ahead and starting the program themselves? In this case you can choose to forgo the benefit by not turning on the radio; in other cases the benefits may be unavoidable. If each day a different person on your street sweeps the entire street, must you do so when your time comes? Even if you don't care that much about a clean street? Must you imagine dirt as you traverse the street, so as not to benefit as a free rider? Must you refrain from turning on the radio to hear the philosophy readings? Must you mow your front lawn as often as your neighbors mow theirs?

At the very least one wants to build into the principle of fairness the condition that the benefits to a person from the actions of the others are greater than the costs to him of doing his share. How are we to imagine this? Is the condition satisfied if you do enjoy the daily broadcasts over the PA system in your neighborhood but would prefer a day off hiking, rather than hearing these broadcasts all year? For you to be obligated to give up your day to broadcast mustn't it be true, at least, that there is nothing you could do with a day (with that day,

with the increment in any other day by shifting some activities to that day) which you would prefer to hearing broadcasts for the year? If the only way to get the broadcasts was to spend the day participating in the arrangement, in order for the condition that the benefits outweigh the costs to be satisfied, you would have to be willing to spend it on the broadcasts rather than to gain *any* other available thing.

If the principle of fairness were modified so as to contain this very strong condition, it still would be objectionable. The benefits might only barely be worth the costs to you of doing your share, yet others might benefit from *this* institution much more than you do; they all treasure listening to the public broadcasts. As the person least benefited by the practice, are you obligated to do an equal amount for it? Or perhaps you would prefer that all cooperated in *another* venture, limiting their conduct and making sacrifices for *it*. It is true, *given* that they are not following your plan (and thus limiting what other options are available to you), that the benefits of their venture *are* worth to you the costs of your cooperation. However, you do not wish to cooperate, as part of your plan to focus their attention on your alternative proposal which they have ignored or not given, in your view at least, its proper due. (You want them, for example, to read the Talmud on the radio instead of the philosophy they are reading.) By lending the institution (their institution) the support of your cooperating in it, you will only make it harder to change or alter.

On the face of it, enforcing the principle of fairness is objectionable. You may not decide to give me something, for example a book, and then grab money from me to pay for it, even if I have nothing better to spend the money on. You have, if anything, even less reason to demand payment if your activity that gives me the book also benefits you; suppose that your best way of getting exercise is by throwing books into people's houses, or that some other activity of yours thrusts books into people's houses as an unavoidable side effect. Nor are things changed if your inability to collect money or payments for the books which unavoidably spill over into others' houses makes it inadvisable or too expensive for you to carry on the activity with this side effect. One cannot, whatever one's purposes, just act so as to give people benefits and then demand (or seize) payment. Nor can a group of persons do this. If you may not charge and collect for benefits you bestow without prior agreement, you certainly may not do so for benefits whose bestowal costs you nothing, and most certainly people need not repay you for costless-to-provide benefits which yet *others* provided them. So the fact that we partially are "social products" in that we benefit from current patterns and forms created by the multitudinous actions of a long string of long-forgotten people, forms which include institutions, ways of doing things, and language (whose social nature may involve our current use depending upon Wittgensteinian matching of the speech of others), does not create in us a general floating debt which the current society can collect and use as it will.

Perhaps a modified principle of fairness can be stated which would be free from these and similar difficulties. What seems certain is that any such principle,

if possible, would be so complex and involuted that one could not combine it with a special principle legitimating *enforcement* within a state of nature of the obligations that have arisen under it. Hence, even if the principle could be formulated so that it was no longer open to objection, it would not serve to obviate the need for other persons' *consenting* to cooperate and limit their own activities.

17

On Liberty

JOHN STUART MILL

For biographical information about John Stuart Mill, see reading 5.

In this selection, Mill discusses the degree to which government and society may interfere in the lives of citizens. He argues that such interference is warranted only to prevent one person from harming another. Compelling someone to act for his own good, or to prevent him from harming himself, is never justified. According to Mill, this implies that people should be allowed to think and speak as they like, to choose their own way of living, and to choose their associates. Because Mill's principle draws the line at harm to others, it is often called the "harm principle."

Mill believes that all of morality rests on the principle of utility: "Strive to produce as much happiness as possible" (see reading 5). Thus, to be consistent, Mill must defend the harm principle by showing that following it will maximize happiness. At first glance, this defense seems upromising; for when we allow someone to live self-destructively, or to spread false beliefs, we appear to allow more unhappiness than we need to. But according to Mill, this is not so. For one thing, all of society benefits from tolerance. By tolerating unpopular beliefs, we either learn new truths or reach a deeper understanding of received opinion; by tolerating unorthodox activities, we observe the results of many "experiments of living." In addition, each of us reaps a personal benefit from the development and expression of his individuality.

Mill's discussion is deservedly regarded as a classic of liberal thought. However, for all its greatness, it is not without its difficulties. It is unclear that there is any real utility in tolerating such "experiments of living" as the use of hard drugs. In addition, many actions that apparently affect only the agent, such as homosexuality and the private use of pornography, do harm other people at least to the extent that just knowing about them gives offense to many. Whether these objections undermine Mill's defense of the harm principle, and if so, how the principle or Mill's arguments should be revised, are left for further thought.

Introductory

THE SUBJECT OF THIS ESSAY is not the so-called "liberty of the will," so unfortunately opposed to the misnamed doctrine of philosophical necessity; but civil, or social liberty: the nature and limits of the power which can be legitimately exercised by society over the individual. A question seldom stated, and hardly ever discussed in general terms, but which profoundly influences

the practical controversies of the age by its latent presence, and is likely soon to make itself recognized as the vital question of the future. It is so far from being new that, in a certain sense, it has divided mankind almost from the remotest ages; but in the stage of progress into which the more civilized portions of the species have now entered, it presents itself under new conditions and requires a different and more fundamental treatment.

The struggle between liberty and authority is the most conspicuous feature in the portions of history with which we are earliest familiar, particularly in that of Greece, Rome, and England. But in old times this contest was between subjects, or some classes of subjects, and the government. By liberty was meant protection against the tyranny of the political rulers. The rulers were conceived (except in some of the popular governments of Greece) as in a necessarily antagonistic position to the people whom they ruled. They consisted of a governing One, or a governing tribe or caste, who derived their authority from inheritance or conquest, who, at all events, did not hold it at the pleasure of the governed, and whose supremacy men did not venture, perhaps did not desire, to contest, whatever precautions might be taken against its oppressive exercise. Their power was regarded as necessary, but also as highly dangerous; as a weapon which they would attempt to use against their subjects, no less than against external enemies. To prevent the weaker members of the community from being preyed upon by innumerable vultures, it was needful that there should be an animal of prey stronger than the rest, commissioned to keep them down. But as the king of the vultures would be no less bent upon preying on the flock than any of the minor harpies, it was indispensable to be in a perpetual attitude of defense against his beak and claws. The aim, therefore, of patriots was to set limits to the power which the ruler should be suffered to exercise over the community; and this limitation was what they meant by liberty. It was attempted in two ways. First, by obtaining a recognition of certain immunities, called political liberties or rights, which it was to be regarded as a breach of duty in the ruler to infringe, and which if he did infringe, specific resistance or general rebellion was held to be justifiable. A second, and generally a later, expedient was the establishment of constitutional checks by which the consent of the community, or of a body of some sort, supposed to represent its interests, was made a necessary condition to some of the more important acts of the governing power. To the first of these modes of limitation, the ruling power, in most European countries, was compelled, more or less, to submit. It was not so with the second; and, to attain this, or, when already in some degree possessed, to attain it more completely, became everywhere the principal object of the lovers of liberty. And so long as mankind were content to combat one enemy by another, and to be ruled by a master on condition of being guaranteed more or less efficaciously against his tyranny, they did not carry their aspirations beyond this point.

A time, however, came, in the progress of human affairs, when men ceased to think it a necessity of nature that their governors should be an independent power opposed in interest to themselves. It appeared to them much better that the various magistrates of the state should be their tenants or delegates, revoc-

able at their pleasure. In that way alone, it seemed, could they have complete security that the powers of government would never be abused to their disadvantage. By degrees this new demand for elective and temporary rulers became the prominent object of the exertions of the popular party wherever any such party existed, and superseded, to a considerable extent, the previous efforts to limit the power of rulers. As the struggle proceeded for making the ruling power emanate from the periodical choice of the ruled, some persons began to think that too much importance had been attached to the limitation of the power itself. *That* (it might seem) was a resource against rulers whose interests were habitually opposed to those of the people. What was now wanted was that the rulers should be identified with the people, that their interest and will should be the interest and will of the nation. The nation did not need to be protected against its own will. There was no fear of its tyrannizing over itself. Let the rulers be effectually responsible to it, promptly removable by it, and it could afford to trust them with power of which it could itself dictate the use to be made. Their power was but the nation's own power, concentrated and in a form convenient for exercise. This mode of thought, or rather perhaps of feeling, was common among the last generation of European liberalism, in the Continental section of which it still apparently predominates. Those who admit any limit to what a government may do, except in the case of such governments as they think ought not to exist, stand out as brilliant exceptions among the political thinkers of the Continent. A similar tone of sentiment might by this time have been prevalent in our own country if the circumstances which for a time encouraged it had continued unaltered.

But, in political and philosophical theories as well as in persons, success discloses faults and infirmities which failure might have concealed from observation. The notion that the people have no need to limit their power over themselves might seem axiomatic, when popular government was a thing only dreamed about, or read of as having existed at some distant period of the past. Neither was that notion necessarily disturbed by such temporary aberrations as those of the French Revolution, the worst of which were the work of a usurping few, and which, in any case, belonged, not to the permanent working of popular institutions, but to a sudden and convulsive outbreak against monarchical and aristocratic despotism. In time, however, a democratic republic came to occupy a large portion of the earth's surface and made itself felt as one of the most powerful members of the community of nations; and elective and responsible government became subject to the observations and criticisms which wait upon a great existing fact. It was now perceived that such phrases as "self-government," and "the power of the people over themselves," do not express the true state of the case. The "people" who exercise the power are not always the same people with those over whom it is exercised; and the "self-government" spoken of is not the government of each by himself, but of each by all the rest. The will of the people, moreover, practically means the will of the most numerous or the most active *part* of the people—the majority, or those who succeed in making themselves accepted as the majority; the people, consequently, *may* desire to oppress a part of their number, and precautions

are as much needed against this as against any other abuse of power. The limitations, therefore, of the power of government over individuals loses none of its importance when the holders of power are regularly accountable to the community, that is, to the strongest party therein. This view of things, recommending itself equally to the intelligence of thinkers and to the inclination of those important classes in European society to whose real or supposed interests democracy is adverse, has had no difficulty in establishing itself; and in political speculations "the tyranny of the majority" is now generally included among the evils against which society requires to be on its guard.

Like other tyrannies, the tyranny of the majority was at first, and is still vulgarly, held in dread, chiefly as operating through the acts of the public authorities. But reflecting persons perceived that when society is itself the tyrant—society collectively over the separate individuals who compose it—its means of tyrannizing are not restricted to the acts which it may do by the hands of its political functionaries. Society can and does execute its own mandates; and if it issues wrong mandates instead of right, or any mandates at all in things with which it ought not to meddle, it practices a social tyranny more formidable than many kinds of political oppression, since, though not usually upheld by such extreme penalties, it leaves fewer means of escape, penetrating much more deeply into the details of life, and enslaving the soul itself. Protection, therefore, against the tyranny of the magistrate is not enough; there needs protection also against the tyranny of the prevailing opinion and feeling, against the tendency of society to impose, by other means than civil penalties, its own ideas and practices as rules of conduct on those who dissent from them; to fetter the development and, if possible, prevent the formation of any individuality not in harmony with its ways, and compel all characters to fashion themselves upon the model of its own. There is a limit to the legitimate interference of collective opinion with individual independence; and to find that limit, and maintain it against encroachment, is as indispensable to a good condition of human affairs as protection against political despotism.

But though this proposition is not likely to be contested in general terms, the practical question where to place the limit—how to make the fitting adjustment between individual independence and social control—is a subject on which nearly everything remains to be done. All that makes existence valuable to anyone depends on the enforcement of restraints upon the actions of other people. Some rules of conduct, therefore, must be imposed—by law in the first place, and by opinion on many things which are not fit subjects for the operation of law. What these rules should be is the principal question in human affairs. . . .

The object of this essay is to assert one very simple principle, as entitled to govern absolutely the dealings of society with the individual in the way of compulsion and control, whether the means used be physical force in the form of legal penalties or the moral coercion of public opinion. That principle is that the sole end for which mankind are warranted, individually or collectively, in interfering with the liberty of action of any of their number is self-protection. That the only purpose for which power can be rightfully exercised over any

member of a civilized community, against his will, is to prevent harm to others. His own good, either physical or moral, is not a sufficient warrant. He cannot rightfully be compelled to do or forbear because it will be better for him to do so, because it will make him happier, because, in the opinions of others, to do so would be wise or even right. These are good reasons for remonstrating with him, or reasoning with him, or persuading him, or entreating him, but not for compelling him or visiting him with any evil in case he do otherwise. To justify that, the conduct from which it is desired to deter him must be calculated to produce evil to someone else. The only part of the conduct of anyone for which he is amenable to society is that which concerns others. In the part which merely concerns himself, his independence is, of right, absolute. Over himself, over his own body and mind, the individual is sovereign.

It is, perhaps, hardly necessary to say that this doctrine is meant to apply only to human beings in the maturity of their faculties. We are not speaking of children or of young persons below the age which the law may fix as that of manhood or womanhood. Those who are still in a state to require being taken care of by others must be protected against their own actions as well as against external injury. For the same reason we may leave out of consideration those backward states of society in which the race itself may be considered as in its nonage. The early difficulties in the way of spontaneous progress are so great that there is seldom any choice of means for overcoming them; and a ruler full of the spirit of improvement is warranted in the use of any expedients that will attain an end perhaps otherwise unattainable. Despotism is a legitimate mode of government in dealing with barbarians, provided the end be their improvement and the means justified by actually effecting that end. Liberty, as a principle, has no application to any state of things anterior to the time when mankind have become capable of being improved by free and equal discussion. Until then, there is nothing for them but implicit obedience to an Akbar or a Charlemagne, if they are so fortunate as to find one. But as soon as mankind have attained the capacity of being guided to their own improvement by conviction or persuasion (a period long since reached in all nations with whom we need here concern ourselves), compulsion, either in the direct form or in that of pains and penalties for noncompliance, is no longer admissible as a means to their own good, and justifiable only for the security of others.

It is proper to state that I forego any advantage which could be derived to my argument from the idea of abstract right as a thing independent of utility. I regard utility as the ultimate appeal on all ethical questions; but it must be utility in the largest sense, grounded on the permanent interests of man as a progressive being. Those interests, I contend, authorize the subjection of individual spontaneity to external control only in respect to those actions of each which concern the interest of other people. If anyone does an act hurtful to others, there is a *prima facie* case for punishing him by law or, where legal penalties are not safely applicable, by general disapprobation. There are also many positive acts for the benefit of others which he may rightfully be compelled to perform, such as to give evidence in a court of justice, to bear his fair share in the common defense or in any other joint work necessary to the interest

of the society of which he enjoys the protection, and to perform certain acts of individual beneficence, such as saving a fellow creature's life or interposing to protect the defenseless against ill usage—things which whenever it is obviously a man's duty to do he may rightfully be made responsible to society for not doing. A person may cause evil to others not only by his actions but by his inaction, and in either case he is justly accountable to them for the injury. The latter case, it is true, requires a much more cautious exercise of compulsion than the former. To make anyone answerable for doing evil to others is the rule; to make him answerable for not preventing evil is, comparatively speaking, the exception. Yet there are many cases clear enough and grave enough to justify that exception. In all things which regard the external relations of the individual, he is *de jure* amenable to those whose interests are concerned, and, if need be, to society as their protector. There are often good reasons for not holding him to the responsibility; but these reasons must arise from the special expediencies of the case: either because it is a kind of case in which he is on the whole likely to act better when left to his own discretion than when controlled in any way in which society have it in their power to control him; or because the attempt to exercise control would produce other evils, greater than those which it would prevent. When such reasons as these preclude the enforcement of responsibility, the conscience of the agent himself should step into the vacant judgment seat and protect those interests of others which have no external protection; judging himself all the more rigidly, because the case does not admit of his being made accountable to the judgment of his fellow creatures.

But there is a sphere of action in which society, as distinguished from the individual, has, if any, only an indirect interest: comprehending all that portion of a person's life and conduct which affects only himself or, if it also affects others, only with their free, voluntary, and undeceived consent and participation. When I say only himself, I mean directly and in the first instance; for whatever affects himself may affect others through himself; and the objection which may be grounded on this contingency will receive consideration in the sequel. This, then, is the appropriate region of human liberty. It comprises, first, the inward domain of consciousness, demanding liberty of conscience in the most comprehensive sense, liberty of thought and feeling, absolute freedom of opinion and sentiment on all subjects, practical or speculative, scientific, moral, or theological. The liberty of expressing and publishing opinions may seem to fall under a different principle, since it belongs to that part of the conduct of an individual which concerns other people, but, being almost of as much importance as the liberty of thought itself and resting in great part on the same reasons, is practically inseparable from it. Secondly, the principle requires liberty of tastes and pursuits, of framing the plan of our life to suit our own character, of doing as we like, subject to such consequences as may follow, without impediment from our fellow creatures, so long as what we do does not harm them, even though they should think our conduct foolish, perverse, or wrong. Thirdly, from this liberty of each individual follows the liberty,

within the same limits, of combination among individuals; freedom to unite for any purpose not involving harm to others: the persons combining being supposed to be of full age and not forced or deceived.

. . .

Of the Liberty of Thought and Discussion

The time, it is to be hoped, is gone by when any defense would be necessary of the "liberty of the press" as one of the securities against corrupt or tyrannical government. No argument, we may suppose, can now be needed against permitting a legislature or an executive, not identified in interest with the people, to prescribe opinions to them and determine what doctrines or what arguments they shall be allowed to hear. This aspect of the question, besides, has been so often and so triumphantly enforced by preceding writers that it needs not be specially insisted on in this place. Though the law of England, on the subject of the press, is as servile to this day as it was in the time of the Tudors, there is little danger of its being actually put in force against political discussion except during some temporary panic when fear of insurrection drives ministers and judges from their propriety; and, speaking generally, it is not, in constitutional countries, to be apprehended that the government, whether completely responsible to the people or not, will often attempt to control the expression of opinion, except when in doing so it makes itself the organ of the general intolerance of the public. Let us suppose, therefore, that the government is entirely at one with the people, and never thinks of exerting any power of coercion unless in agreement with what it conceives to be their voice.

But I deny the right of the people to exercise such coercion, either by themselves or by their government. The power itself is illegitimate. The best government has no more title to it than the worst. It is as noxious, or more noxious, when exerted in accordance with public opinion than when in opposition to it. If all mankind minus one were of one opinion, mankind would be no more justified in silencing that one person than he, if he had the power, would be justified in silencing mankind. Were an opinion a personal possession of no value except to the owner, if to be obstructed in the enjoyment of it were simply a private injury, it would make some difference whether the injury was inflicted only on a few persons or on many. But the peculiar evil of silencing the expression of an opinion is that it is robbing the human race, posterity as well as the existing generation—those who dissent from the opinion, still more than those who hold it. If the opinion is right, they are deprived of the opportunity of exchanging error for truth; if wrong, they lose, what is almost as great a benefit, the clearer perception and livelier impression of truth produced by its collision with error.

It is necessary to consider separately these two hypotheses, each of which has a distinct branch of the argument corresponding to it. We can never be sure that the opinion we are endeavoring to stifle is a false opinion; and if we were sure, stifling it would be an evil still.

First, the opinion which it is attempted to suppress by authority may possibly be true. Those who desire to suppress it, of course, deny its truth; but they are not infallible. They have no authority to decide the question for all mankind and exclude every other person from the means of judging. To refuse a hearing to an opinion because they are sure that it is false is to assume that *their* certainty is the same thing as *absolute* certainty. All silencing of discussion is an assumption of infallibility. Its condemnation may be allowed to rest on this common argument, not the worse for being common.

Unfortunately for the good sense of mankind, the fact of their fallibility is far from carrying the weight in their practical judgment which is always allowed to it in theory; for while everyone well knows himself to be fallible, few think it necessary to take any precautions against their own fallibility, or admit the supposition that any opinion of which they feel very certain may be one of the examples of the error to which they acknowledge themselves to be liable. Absolute princes, or others who are accustomed to unlimited deference, usually feel this complete confidence in their own opinions on nearly all subjects. People more happily situated, who sometimes hear their opinions disputed and are not wholly unused to be set right when they are wrong, place the same unbounded reliance only on such of their opinions as are shared by all who surround them, or to whom they habitually defer; for in proportion to a man's want of confidence in his own solitary judgment does he usually repose, with implicit trust, on the infallibility of "the world" in general. And the world, to each individual, means the part of it with which he comes in contact: his party, his sect, his church, his class of society; the man may be called, by comparison, almost liberal and large-minded to whom it means anything so comprehensive as his own country or his own age. Nor is his faith in this collective authority at all shaken by his being aware that other ages, countries, sects, churches, classes, and parties have thought, and even now think, the exact reverse. He devolves upon his own world the responsibility of being in the right against the dissentient worlds of other people; and it never troubles him that mere accident has decided which of these numerous worlds is the object of his reliance, and that the same causes which make him a churchman in London would have made him a Buddhist or a Confucian in Peking. Yet it is as evident in itself, as any amount of argument can make it, that ages are no more infallible than individuals—every age having held many opinions which subsequent ages have deemed not only false but absurd; and it is as certain that many opinions, now general, will be rejected by future ages, as it is that many, once general, are rejected by the present.

The objection likely to be made to this argument would probably take some such form as the following. There is no greater assumption of infallibility in forbidding the propagation of error than in any other thing which is done by public authority on its own judgment and responsibility. Judgment is given to men that they may use it. Because it may be used erroneously, are men to be told that they ought not to use it at all? To prohibit what they think pernicious is not claiming exemption from error, but fulfilling the duty incumbent on them, although fallible, of acting on their conscientious conviction. If we were

never to act on our opinions, because those opinions may be wrong, we should leave all our interests uncared for, and all our duties unperformed. An objection which applies to all conduct can be no valid objection to any conduct in particular. It is the duty of governments, and of individuals, to form the truest opinions they can; to form them carefully, and never impose them upon others unless they are quite sure of being right. But when they are sure (such reasoners may say), it is not conscientiousness but cowardice to shrink from acting on their opinions and allow doctrines which they honestly think dangerous to the welfare of mankind, either in this life or in another, to be scattered abroad without restraint, because other people, in less enlightened times, have persecuted opinions now believed to be true. Let us take care, it may be said, not to make the same mistake; but governments and nations have made mistakes in other things which are not denied to be fit subjects for the exercise of authority: they have laid on bad taxes, made unjust wars. Ought we therefore to lay on no taxes and, under whatever provocation, make no wars? Men and governments must act to the best of their ability. There is no such thing as absolute certainty, but there is assurance sufficient for the purposes of human life. We may, and must, assume our opinion to be true for the guidance of our own conduct; and it is assuming no more when we forbid bad men to pervert society by the propagation of opinions which we regard as false and pernicious.

I answer, that it is assuming very much more. There is the greatest difference between presuming an opinion to be true because, with every opportunity for contesting it, it has not been refuted, and assuming its truth for the purpose of not permitting its refutation. Complete liberty of contradicting and disproving our opinion is the very condition which justifies us in assuming its truth for purposes of action; and on no other terms can a being with human faculties have any rational assurance of being right.

When we consider either the history of opinion or the ordinary conduct of human life, to what is it to be ascribed that the one and the other are no worse than they are? Not certainly to the inherent force of the human understanding, for on any matter not self-evident there are ninety-nine persons totally incapable of judging of it for one who is capable; and the capacity of the hundredth person is only comparative, for the majority of the eminent men of every past generation held many opinions now known to be erroneous, and did or approved numerous things which no one will now justify. Why is it, then, that there is on the whole a preponderance among mankind of rational opinions and rational conduct? If there really is this preponderance—which there must be unless human affairs are, and have always been, in an almost desperate state—it is owing to a quality of the human mind, the source of everything respectable in man either as an intellectual or as a moral being, namely, that his errors are corrigible. He is capable of rectifying his mistakes by discussion and experience. Not by experience alone. There must be discussion to show how experience is to be interpreted. Wrong opinions and practices gradually yield to fact and argument; but facts and arguments, to produce any effect on the mind, must be brought before it. Very few facts are able to tell their own story, without comments to bring out their meaning. The whole strength and value, then, of

human judgment depending on the one property, that it can be set right when it is wrong, reliance can be placed on it only when the means of setting it right are kept constantly at hand. In the case of any person whose judgment is really deserving of confidence, how has it become so? Because he has kept his mind open to criticism of his opinions and conduct. Because it has been his practice to listen to all that could be said against him; to profit by as much of it as was just, and to expound to himself, and upon occasion to others, the fallacy of what was fallacious. Because he has felt that the only way in which a human being can make some approach to knowing the whole of a subject is by hearing what can be said about it by persons of every variety of opinion, and studying all modes in which it can be looked at by every character of mind. No wise man ever acquired his wisdom in any mode but this; nor is it in the nature of human intellect to become wise in any other manner. The steady habit of correcting and completing his own opinion by collating it with those of others, so far from causing doubt and hesitation in carrying it into practice, is the only stable foundation for a just reliance on it; for, being cognizant of all that can, at least obviously, be said against him, and having taken up his position against all gainsayers—knowing that he has sought for objections and difficulties instead of avoiding them, and has shut out no light which can be thrown upon the subject from any quarter—he has a right to think his judgment better than that of any person, or any multitude, who have not gone through a similar process.

. . .

Let us now pass to the second division of the argument, and dismissing the supposition that any of the received opinions may be false, let us assume them to be true and examine into the worth of the manner in which they are likely to be held when their truth is not freely and openly canvassed. However unwillingly a person who has a strong opinion may admit the possibility that his opinion may be false, he ought to be moved by the consideration that, however true it may be, if it is not fully, frequently, and fearlessly discussed, it will be held as a dead dogma, not a living truth.

There is a class of persons (happily not quite so numerous as formerly) who think it enough if a person assents undoubtingly to what they think true, though he has no knowledge whatever of the grounds of the opinion and could not make a tenable defense of it against the most superficial objections. Such persons, if they can once get their creed taught from authority, naturally think that no good, and some harm, comes of its being allowed to be questioned. Where their influence prevails, they make it nearly impossible for the received opinion to be rejected wisely and considerately, though it may still be rejected rashly and ignorantly; for to shut out discussion entirely is seldom possible, and when it once gets in, beliefs not grounded on conviction are apt to give way before the slightest semblance of an argument. Waiving, however, this possibility—assuming that the true opinion abides in the mind, but abides as a prejudice, a belief independent of, and proof against, argument—this is not the way in which truth ought to be held by a rational being. This is not knowing the truth. Truth, thus held, is but one superstition the more, accidentally clinging to the words which enunciate a truth.

If the intellect and judgment of mankind ought to be cultivated, a thing which Protestants at least do not deny, on what can these faculties be more appropriately exercised by anyone than on the things which concern him so much that it is considered necessary for him to hold opinions on them? If the cultivation of the understanding consists in one thing more than in another, it is surely in learning the grounds of one's own opinions. Whatever people believe, on subjects on which it is of the first importance to believe rightly, they ought to be able to defend against at least the common objections. But, someone may say, "Let them be *taught* the grounds of their opinions. It does not follow that opinions must be merely parroted because they are never heard controverted. Persons who learn geometry do not simply commit the theorems to memory, but understand and learn likewise the demonstrations; and it would be absurd to say that they remain ignorant of the grounds of geometrical truths because they never hear anyone deny and attempt to disprove them." Undoubtedly; and such teaching suffices on a subject like mathematics, where there is nothing at all to be said on the wrong side of the question. The peculiarity of the evidence of mathematical truths is that all the argument is on one side. There are no objections, and no answers to objections. But on every subject on which difference of opinion is possible, the truth depends on a balance to be struck between two sets of conflicting reasons. Even in natural philosophy, there is always some other explanation possible of the same facts; some geocentric theory instead of heliocentric, some phlogiston instead of oxygen; and it has to be shown why that other theory cannot be the true one; and until this is shown, and until we know how it is shown, we do not understand the grounds of our opinion. But when we turn to subjects infinitely more complicated, to morals, religion, politics, social relations, and the business of life, three-fourths of the arguments for every disputed opinion consist in dispelling the appearances which favor some opinion different from it. The greatest orator, save one, of antiquity, has left it on record that he always studied his adversary's case with as great, if not still greater, intensity than even his own. What Cicero practiced as the means of forensic success requires to be imitated by all who study any subject in order to arrive at the truth. He who knows only his own side of the case knows little of that. His reasons may be good, and no one may have been able to refute them. But if he is equally unable to refute the reasons on the opposite side, if he does not so much as know what they are, he has no ground for preferring either opinion. The rational position for him would be suspension of judgment, and unless he contents himself with that, he is either led by authority or adopts, like the generality of the world, the side to which he feels most inclination. Nor is it enough that he should hear the arguments of adversaries from his own teachers, presented as they state them, and accompanied by what they offer as refutations. That is not the way to do justice to the arguments or bring them into real contact with his own mind. He must be able to hear them from persons who actually believe them, who defend them in earnest and do their very utmost for them. He must know them in their most plausible and persuasive form; he must feel the whole force of the difficulty which the true view of the subject has to encounter and dispose of, else he will

never really possess himself of the portion of truth which meets and removes that difficulty. Ninety-nine in a hundred of what are called educated men are in this condition, even of those who can argue fluently for their opinions. Their conclusion may be true, but it might be false for anything they know; they have never thrown themselves into the mental position of those who think differently from them, and considered what such persons may have to say; and, consequently, they do not, in any proper sense of the word, know the doctrine which they themselves profess. . . .

We have now recognized the necessity to the mental well-being of mankind (on which all their other well-being depends) of freedom of opinion, and freedom of the expression of opinion, on four distinct grounds, which we will now briefly recapitulate:

First, if any opinion is compelled to silence, that opinion may, for aught we can certainly know, be true. To deny this is to assume our own infallibility.

Secondly, though the silenced opinion be an error, it may, and very commonly does, contain a portion of truth; and since the general or prevailing opinion on any subject is rarely or never the whole truth, it is only by the collision of adverse opinions that the remainder of the truth has any chance of being supplied.

Thirdly, even if the received opinion be not only true, but the whole truth; unless it is suffered to be, and actually is, vigorously and earnestly contested, it will, by most of those who receive it, be held in the manner of a prejudice, with little comprehension or feeling of its rational grounds. And not only this, but, fourthly, the meaning of the doctrine itself will be in danger of being lost or enfeebled, and deprived of its vital effect on the character and conduct; the dogma becoming a mere formal profession, inefficacious for good, but cumbering the ground and preventing the growth of any real and heartfelt conviction from reason or personal experience.

. . .

Of Individuality, as One of the Elements of Well-being

Such being the reasons which make it imperative that human beings should be free to form opinions and to express their opinions without reserve; and such the baneful consequences to the intellectual, and through that to the moral nature of man, unless this liberty is either conceded or asserted in spite of prohibition; let us next examine whether the same reasons do not require that men should be free to act upon their opinions—to carry these out in their lives without hindrance, either physical or moral, from their fellow men, so long as it is at their own risk and peril. This last proviso is of course indispensable. No one pretends that actions should be as free as opinions. On the contrary, even opinions lose their immunity when the circumstances in which they are expressed are such as to constitute their expression a positive instigation to some mischievous act. An opinion that corn dealers are starvers of the poor, or that private property is robbery, ought to be unmolested when simply circulated through the press, but may justly incur punishment when delivered orally to an excited

mob assembled before the house of a corn dealer, or when handed about among the same mob in the form of a placard. Acts, of whatever kind, which without justifiable cause do harm to others may be, and in the more important cases absolutely require to be, controlled by the unfavorable sentiments, and, when needful, by the active interference of mankind. The liberty of the individual must be thus far limited; he must not make himself a nuisance to other people. But if he refrains from molesting others in what concerns them, and merely acts according to his own inclination and judgment in things which concern himself, the same reasons which show that opinion should be free prove also that he should be allowed, without molestation, to carry his opinions into practice at his own cost. That mankind are not infallible; that their truths, for the most part, are only half-truths; that unity of opinion, unless resulting from the fullest and freest comparison of opposite opinions, is not desirable, and diversity not an evil, but a good, until mankind are much more capable than at present of recognizing all sides of the truth, are principles applicable to men's modes of action not less than to their opinions. As it is useful that while mankind are imperfect there should be different opinions, so it is that there should be different experiments of living; that free scope should be given to varieties of character, short of injury to others; and that the worth of different modes of life should be proved practically, when anyone thinks fit to try them. It is desirable, in short, that in things which do not primarily concern others individuality should assert itself. Where not the person's own character but the traditions or customs of other people are the rule of conduct, there is wanting one of the principal ingredients of human happiness, and quite the chief ingredient of individual and social progress.

. . .

Having said that the individuality is the same thing with development, and that it is only the cultivation of individuality which produces, or can produce, well-developed human beings, I might here close the argument; for what more or better can be said of any condition of human affairs than that it brings human beings themselves nearer to the best thing they can be? Or what worse can be said of any obstruction to good than that it prevents this? Doubtless, however, these considerations will not suffice to convince those who most need convincing; and it is necessary further to show that these developed human beings are of some use to the undeveloped—to point out to those who do not desire liberty, and would not avail themselves of it, that they may be in some intelligible manner rewarded for allowing other people to make use of it without hindrance.

In the first place, then, I would suggest that they might possibly learn something from them. It will not be denied by anybody that originality is a valuable element in human affairs. There is always need of persons not only to discover new truths and point out when what were once truths are true no longer, but also to commence new practices and set the example of more enlightened conduct and better taste and sense in human life. This cannot well be gainsaid by anybody who does not believe that the world has already attained perfection in all its ways and practices. It is true that this benefit is not capable of being

rendered by everybody alike; there are but few persons, in comparison with the whole of mankind, whose experiments, if adopted by others, would be likely to be any improvement on established practice. But these few are the salt of the earth; without them, human life would become a stagnant pool. Not only is it they who introduce good things which did not before exist; it is they who keep the life in those which already exist. If there were nothing new to be done, would human intellect cease to be necessary? Would it be a reason why those who do the old things should forget why they are done, and do them like cattle, not like human beings? There is only too great a tendency in the best beliefs and practices to degenerate into the mechanical; and unless there were a succession of persons whose ever-recurring originality prevents the grounds of those beliefs and practices from becoming merely traditional, such dead matter would not resist the smallest shock from anything really alive, and there would be no reason why civilization should not die out, as in the Byzantine Empire. . . .

I have said that it is important to give the freest scope possible to uncustomary things, in order that it may in time appear which of these are fit to be converted into customs. But independence of action and disregard of custom are not solely deserving of encouragement for the chance they afford that better modes of action, and customs more worthy of general adoption, may be struck out; nor is it only persons of decided mental superiority who have a just claim to carry on their lives in their own way. There is no reason that all human existence should be constructed on some one or some small number of patterns. If a person possesses any tolerable amount of common sense and experience, his own mode of laying out his existence is the best, not because it is the best in itself, but because it is his own mode. Human beings are not like sheep; and even sheep are not undistinguishably alike. A man cannot get a coat or a pair of boots to fit him unless they are either made to his measure or he has a whole warehouseful to choose from; and is it easier to fit him with a life than with a coat, or are human beings more like one another in their whole physical and spiritual conformation than in the shape of their feet? If it were only that people have diversities of taste, that is reason enough for not attempting to shape them all after one model. But different persons also require different conditions for their spiritual development; and can no more exist healthily in the same moral than all the variety of plants can in the same physical, atmosphere and climate. The same things which are helps to one person toward the cultivation of his higher nature are hindrances to another. The same mode of life is a healthy excitement to one, keeping all his faculties of action and enjoyment in their best order, while to another it is a distracting burden which suspends or crushes all internal life. Such are the differences among human beings in their sources of pleasure, their susceptibilities of pain, and the operation on them of different physical and moral agencies that, unless there is a corresponding diversity in their modes of life, they neither obtain their fair share of happiness, nor grow up to the mental, moral, and aesthetic stature of which their nature is capable. . . .

18

A Theory of Justice

JOHN RAWLS

For biographical information about John Rawls, see reading 4.

In this selection from his book A Theory of Justice, *Rawls argues that social arrangements are just when they conform to principles arising out of certain choices. While Rawls's position falls within the social contract tradition (see readings 13, 14, and 15), it also departs from that tradition in important ways. Unlike some others, Rawls does not appeal to any agreement, even a tacit one, that anyone has actually made. Instead, he identifies the principles of justice as principles that would be chosen by persons who knew only the most general facts about the world. Such persons would recognize certain "primary goods," such as rights and liberties, powers and opportunities, wealth and income, and the social bases of self-respect, which it is rational to want whatever else one wants. However, they would know nothing about their own specific preferences; neither would they know anything about their own race, sex, degree of wealth, or natural abilities. Because of this, they would be unable to tailor any principles to their own advantage. Hence, whatever principles they chose to structure the social institution that determine their life prospects— such institutions as their society's political constitution and economic system—would automatically be just.*

What principles would such individuals choose? According to Rawls, they would treat rights to basic liberties differently from other primary goods. They would choose that "each person have a right to the most extensive basic liberty compatible with a similar liberty for others." However, they would choose to tolerate some social and economic inequalities provided that they (a) did not restrict equality of opportunity, and (b) raised the position of even the worst-off (for example, by providing the better-off with incentives that raised productivity, and so benefitted everyone). Of these requirements, maximizing equal liberty would take precedence over equal opportunity, which in turn would take precedence over raising the position of the worst off.

The Subject of Justice

MANY DIFFERENT KINDS of things are said to be just and unjust; not only laws, institutions, and social systems, but also particular actions of many kinds, including decisions, judgments, and imputations. We also call the attitudes and dispositions of persons, and persons themselves, just and unjust. Our topic, however, is that of social justice. For us the primary subject of justice is

the basic structure of society, or more exactly, the way in which the major social institutions distribute fundamental rights and duties and determine the division of advantages from social cooperation. By major institutions I understand the political constitution and the principal economic and social arrangements. Thus the legal protection of freedom of thought and liberty of conscience, competitive markets, private property in the means of production, and the monogamous family are examples of major social institutions. Taken together as one scheme, the major institutions define men's rights and duties and influence their life-prospects, what they can expect to be and how well they can hope to do. The basic structure is the primary subject of justice because its effects are so profound and present from the start. The intuitive notion here is that this structure contains various social positions and that men born into different positions have different expectations of life determined, in part, by the political system as well as by economic and social circumstances. In this way the institutions of society favor certain starting places over others. These are especially deep inequalities. Not only are they pervasive, but they affect men's initial chances in life; yet they cannot possibly be justified by an appeal to the notions of merit or desert. It is these inequalities, presumably inevitable in the basic structure of any society, to which the principles of social justice must in the first instance apply. These principles, then, regulate the choice of a political constitution and the main elements of the economic and social system. The justice of a social scheme depends essentially on how fundamental rights and duties are assigned and on the economic opportunities and social conditions in the various sectors of society.

. . .

The Main Idea of the Theory of Justice

My aim is to present a conception of justice which generalizes and carries to a higher level of abstraction the familiar theory of the social contract as found, say, in Locke, Rousseau, and Kant. In order to do this we are not to think of the original contract as one to enter a particular society or to set up a particular form of government. Rather, the guiding idea is that the principles of justice for the basic structure of society are the object of the original agreement. They are the principles that free and rational persons concerned to further their own interests would accept in an initial position of equality as defining the fundamental terms of their association. These principles are to regulate all further agreements; they specify the kinds of social cooperation that can be entered into and the forms of government that can be established. This way of regarding the principles of justice I shall call justice as fairness.

Thus we are to imagine that those who engage in social cooperation choose together, in one joint act, the principles which are to assign basic rights and duties and to determine the division of social benefits. Men are to decide in advance how they are to regulate their claims against one another and what is to be the foundation charter of their society. Just as each person must decide by rational reflection what constitutes his good, that is, the system of ends

which it is rational for him to pursue, so a group of persons must decide once and for all what is to count among them as just and unjust. The choice which rational men would make in this hypothetical situation of equal liberty, assuming for the present that this choice problem has a solution, determines the principles of justice.

In justice as fairness the original position of equality corresponds to the state of nature in the traditional theory of the social contract. This original position is not, of course, thought of as an actual historical state of affairs, much less as a primitive condition of culture. It is understood as a purely hypothetical situation characterized so as to lead to a certain conception of justice. Among the essential features of this situation is that no one knows his place in society, his class position or social status, nor does any one know his fortune in the distribution of natural assets and abilities, his intelligence, strength, and the like. I shall even assume that the parties do not know their conceptions of the good or their special psychological propensities. The principles of justice are chosen behind a veil of ignorance. This ensures that no one is advantaged or disadvantaged in the choice of principles by the outcome of natural chance or the contingency of social circumstances. Since all are similarly situated and no one is able to design principles to favor his particular condition, the principles of justice are the result of a fair agreement or bargain. For given the circumstances of the original position, the symmetry of everyone's relations to each other, this initial situation is fair between individuals as moral persons, that is, as rational beings with their own ends and capable, I shall assume, of a sense of justice. The original position is, one might say, the appropriate initial status quo, and thus the fundamental agreements reached in it are fair. This explains the propriety of the name "justice as fairness": it conveys the idea that the principles of justice are agreed to in an initial situation that is fair. The name does not mean that the concepts of justice and fairness are the same, any more than the phrase "poetry as metaphor" means that the concepts of poetry and metaphor are the same.

Justice as fairness begins, as I have said, with one of the most general of all choices which persons might make together, namely, with the choice of the first principles of a conception of justice which is to regulate all subsequent criticism and reform of institutions. Then, having chosen a conception of justice, we can suppose that they are to choose a constitution and a legislature to enact laws, and so on, all in accordance with the principles of justice initially agreed upon. Our social situation is just if it is such that by this sequence of hypothetical agreements we would have contracted into the general system of rules which defines it. Moreover, assuming that the original position does determine a set of principles (that is, that a particular conception of justice would be chosen), it will then be true that whenever social institutions satisfy these principles those engaged in them can say to one another that they are cooperating on terms to which they would agree if they were free and equal persons whose relations with respect to one another were fair. They could all view their arrangements as meeting the stipulations which they would acknowledge in an initial situation that embodies widely accepted and reasonable constraints on

the choice of principles. The general recognition of this fact would provide the basis for a public acceptance of the corresponding principles of justice. No society can, of course, be a scheme of cooperation which men enter voluntarily in a literal sense; each person finds himself placed at birth in some particular position in some particular society, and the nature of this position materially affects his life prospects. Yet a society satisfying the principles of justice as fairness comes as close as a society can to being a voluntary scheme, for it meets the principles which free and equal persons would assent to under circumstances that are fair. In this sense its members are autonomous and the obligations they recognize self-imposed.

One feature of justice as fairness is to think of the parties in the initial situation as rational and mutually disinterested. This does not mean that the parties are egoists, that is, individuals with only certain kinds of interests, say in wealth, prestige, and domination. But they are conceived as not taking an interest in one another's interests. They are to presume that even their spiritual aims may be opposed, in the way that the aims of those of different religions may be opposed. Moreover, the concept of rationality must be interpreted as far as possible in the narrow sense, standard in economic theory, of taking the most effective means to given ends. I shall modify this concept to some extent, as explained later, but one must try to avoid introducing into it any controversial ethical elements. The initial situation must be characterized by stipulations that are widely accepted.

In working out the conception of justice as fairness one main task clearly is to determine which principles of justice would be chosen in the original position. To do this we must describe this situation in some detail and formulate with care the problem of choice which it presents. These matters I shall take up in the immediately succeeding chapters. It may be observed, however, that once the principles of justice are thought of as arising from an original agreement in a situation of equality, it is an open question whether the principle of utility would be acknowledged. Offhand it hardly seems likely that persons who view themselves as equals, entitled to press their claims upon one another, would agree to a principle which may require lesser life prospects for some simply for the sake of a greater sum of advantages enjoyed by others. Since each desires to protect his interests, his capacity to advance his conception of the good, no one has a reason to acquiesce in an enduring loss for himself in order to bring about a greater net balance of satisfaction. In the absence of strong and lasting benevolent impulses, a rational man would not accept a basic structure merely because it maximized the algebraic sum of advantages irrespective of its permanent effects on his own basic rights and interests. Thus it seems that the principle of utility is incompatible with the conception of social cooperation among equals for mutual advantage. It appears to be inconsistent with the idea of reciprocity implicit in the notion of a well-ordered society. Or, at any rate, so I shall argue.

I shall maintain instead that the persons in the initial situation would choose two rather different principles: the first requires equality in the assignment of basic rights and duties, while the second holds that social and economic in-

equalities, for example inequalities of wealth and authority, are just only if they result in compensating benefits for everyone, and in particular for the least advantaged members of society. These principles rule out justifying institutions on the grounds that the hardships of some are offset by a greater good in the aggregate. It may be expedient but it is not just that some should have less in order that others may prosper. But there is no injustice in the greater benefits earned by a few provided that the situation of persons not so fortunate is thereby improved. The intuitive idea is that since everyone's well-being depends upon a scheme of cooperation without which no one could have a satisfactory life, the division of advantages should be such as to draw forth the willing cooperation of everyone taking part in it, including those less well situated. Yet this can be expected only if reasonable terms are proposed. The two principles mentioned seem to be a fair agreement on the basis of which those better endowed, or more fortunate in their social position, neither of which we can be said to deserve, could expect the willing cooperation of others when some workable scheme is a necessary condition of the welfare of all. Once we decide to look for a conception of justice that nullifies the accidents of natural endowment and the contingencies of social circumstance as counters in quest for political and economic advantage, we are led to these principles. They express the result of leaving aside those aspects of the social world that seem arbitrary from a moral point of view.

The problem of the choice of principles, however, is extremely difficult. I do not expect the answer I shall suggest to be convincing to everyone. It is, therefore, worth noting from the outset that justice as fairness, like other contract views, consists of two parts: (1) an interpretation of the initial situation and of the problem of choice posed there, and (2) a set of principles which, it is argued, would be agreed to. One may accept the first part of the theory (or some variant thereof), but not the other, and conversely. The concept of the initial contractual situation may seem reasonable although the particular principles proposed are rejected. To be sure, I want to maintain that the most appropriate conception of this situation does lead to principles of justice contrary to utilitarianism and perfectionism,* and therefore that the contract doctrine provides an alternative to these views. Still, one may dispute this contention even though one grants that the contractarian method is a useful way of studying ethical theories and of setting forth their underlying assumptions.

Justice as fairness is an example of what I have called a contract theory. Now there may be an objection to the term "contract" and related expressions, but I think it will serve reasonably well. Many words have misleading connotations which at first are likely to confuse. The terms "utility" and "utilitarianism" are surely no exception. They too have unfortunate suggestions which hostile critics have been willing to exploit; yet they are clear enough for those prepared to study utilitarian doctrine. The same should be true of the term "contract" applied to moral theories. As I have mentioned, to understand it

---

* The view that we should promote certain forms of human excellence or perfection.

one has to keep in mind that it implies a certain level of abstraction. In particular, the content of the relevant agreement is not to enter a given society or to adopt a given form of government, but to accept certain moral principles. Moreover, the undertakings referred to are purely hypothetical: a contract view holds that certain principles would be accepted in a well-defined initial situation.

The merit of the contract terminology is that it conveys the idea that principles of justice may be conceived as principles that would be chosen by rational persons, and that in this way conceptions of justice may be explained and justified. The theory of justice is a part, perhaps the most significant part, of the theory of rational choice. Furthermore, principles of justice deal with conflicting claims upon the advantages won by social cooperation; they apply to the relations among several persons or groups. The word "contract" suggests this plurality as well as the condition that the appropriate division of advantages must be in accordance with principles acceptable to all parties. The condition of publicity for principles of justice is also connoted by the contract phraseology. Thus, if these principles are the outcome of an agreement, citizens have a knowledge of the principles that others follow. It is characteristic of contract theories to stress the public nature of political principles. Finally there is the long tradition of the contract doctrine. Expressing the tie with this line of thought helps to define ideas and accords with natural piety. There are then several advantages in the use of the term "contract." With due precautions taken, it should not be misleading.

A final remark. Justice as fairness is not a complete contract theory. For it is clear that the contractarian idea can be extended to the choice of more or less an entire ethical system, that is, to a system including principles for all the virtues and not only for justice. Now for the most part I shall consider only principles of justice and others closely related to them; I make no attempt to discuss the virtues in a systematic way. Obviously if justice as fairness succeeds reasonably well, a next step would be to study the more general view suggested by the name "rightness as fairness." But even this wider theory fails to embrace all moral relationships, since it would seem to include only our relations with other persons and to leave out of account how we are to conduct ourselves toward animals and the rest of nature. I do not contend that the contract notion offers a way to approach these questions which are certainly of the first importance; and I shall have to put them aside. We must recognize the limited scope of justice as fairness and of the general type of view that it exemplifies. How far its conclusions must be revised once these other matters are understood cannot be decided in advance.

. . .

Two Principles of Justice

I shall now state in a provisional form the two principles of justice that I believe would be chosen in the original position. In this section I wish to make only the most general comments, and therefore the first formulation of these principles is tentative. As we go on I shall run through several formulations

and approximate step by step the final statement to be given much later. I believe that doing this allows the exposition to proceed in a natural way.

The first statement of the two principles reads as follows.

First: each person is to have an equal right to the most extensive basic liberty compatible with a similar liberty for others.

Second: social and economic inequalities are to be arranged so that they are both (a) reasonably expected to be to everyone's advantage, and (b) attached to positions and offices open to all. . . .

By way of general comment, these principles primarily apply, as I have said, to the basic structure of society. They are to govern the assignment of rights and duties and to regulate the distribution of social and economic advantages. As their formulation suggests, these principles presuppose that the social structure can be divided into two more or less distinct parts, the first principle applying to the one, the second to the other. They distinguish between those aspects of the social system that define and secure the equal liberties of citizenship and those that specify and establish social and economic inequalities. The basic liberties of citizens are, roughly speaking, political liberty (the right to vote and to be eligible for public office) together with freedom of speech and assembly; liberty of conscience and freedom of thought; freedom of the person along with the right to hold (personal) property; and freedom from arbitrary arrest and seizure as defined by the concept of the rule of law. These liberties are all required to be equal by the first principle, since citizens of a just society are to have the same basic rights.

The second principle applies, in the first approximation, to the distribution of income and wealth and to the design of organizations that make use of differences in authority and responsibility, or chains of command. While the distribution of wealth and income need not be equal, it must be to everyone's advantage, and at the same time, positions of authority and offices of command must be accessible to all. One applies the second principle by holding positions open, and then, subject to this constraint, arranges social and economic inequalities so that everyone benefits.

These principles are to be arranged in a serial order with the first principle prior to the second. This ordering means that a departure from the institutions of equal liberty required by the first principle cannot be justified by, or compensated for, by greater social and economic advantages. The distribution of wealth and income, and the hierarchies of authority, must be consistent with both the liberties of equal citizenship and equality of opportunity.

It is clear that these principles are rather specific in their content, and their acceptance rests on certain assumptions that I must eventually try to explain and justify. A theory of justice depends upon a theory of society in ways that will become evident as we proceed. For the present, it should be observed that the two principles (and this holds for all formulations) are a special case of a more general conception of justice that can be expressed as follows.

All social values—liberty and opportunity, income and wealth, and the bases of self-respect—are to be distributed equally unless an unequal distribution of any, or all, of these values is to everyone's advantage.

Injustice, then, is simply inequalities that are not to the benefit of all. Of course, this conception is extremely vague and requires interpretation.

As a first step, suppose that the basic structure of society distributes certain primary goods, that is, things that every rational man is presumed to want. These goods normally have a use whatever a person's rational plan of life. For simplicity, assume that the chief primary goods at the disposition of society are right and liberties, powers and opportunities, income and wealth. (Later on in Part Three the primary good of self-respect has a central place.) These are the social primary goods. Other primary goods such as health and vigor, intelligence and imagination, are natural goods; although their possession is influenced by the basic structure, they are not so directly under its control. Imagine, then, a hypothetical initial arrangement in which all the social primary goods are equally distributed: everyone has similar rights and duties, and income and wealth are evenly shared. This state of affairs provides a benchmark for judging improvements. If certain inequalities of wealth and organizational powers would make everyone better off than in this hypothetical starting situation, then they accord with the general conception.

Now it is possible, at least theoretically, that by giving up some of their fundamental liberties men are sufficiently compensated by the resulting social and economic gains. The general conception of justice imposes no restrictions on what sort of inequalities are permissible; it only requires that everyone's position be improved. We need not suppose anything so drastic as consenting to a condition of slavery. Imagine instead that men forego certain political rights when the economic returns are significant and their capacity to influence the course of policy by the exercise of these rights would be marginal in any case. It is this kind of exchange which the two principles as stated rule out; being arranged in serial order they do not permit exchanges between basic liberties and economic and social gains. The serial ordering of principles expresses an underlying preference among primary social goods. When this preference is rational so likewise is the choice of these principles in this order.

In developing justice as fairness I shall, for the most part, leave aside the general conception of justice and examine instead the special case of the two principles in serial order. The advantage of this procedure is that from the first the matter of priorities is recognized and an effort made to find principles to deal with it. One is led to attend throughout to the conditions under which the acknowledgement of the absolute weight of liberty with respect to social and economic advantages, as defined by the lexical order* of the two principles, would be reasonable. Offhand, this ranking appears extreme and too special a case to be of much interest; but there is more justification for it than would appear at first sight. Or at any rate, so I shall maintain. Furthermore, the distinction between fundamental rights and liberties and economic and social benefits marks a difference among primary social goods that one should try to

---

* Two principles are "lexically ordered" when we must satisfy the first principle before we can move on to the second.

exploit. It suggests an important division in the social system. Of course, the distinctions drawn and the ordering proposed are bound to be at best only approximations. There are surely circumstances in which they fail. But it is essential to depict clearly the main lines of a reasonable conception of justice; and under many conditions anyway, the two principles in serial order may serve well enough. When necessary we can fall back on the more general conception.

The fact that the two principles apply to institutions has certain consequences. Several points illustrate this. First of all, the rights and liberties referred to by these principles are those which are defined by the public rules of the basic structure. Whether men are free is determined by the rights and duties established by the major institutions of society. Liberty is a certain pattern of social forms. The first principle simply requires that certain sorts of rules, those defining basic liberties, apply to everyone equally and that they allow the most extensive liberty compatible with a like liberty for all. The only reason for circumscribing the rights defining liberty and making men's freedom less extensive than it might otherwise be is that these equal rights as institutionally defined would interfere with one another.

Another thing to bear in mind is that when principles mention persons, or require that everyone gain from an inequality, the reference is to representative persons holding the various social positions, or offices, or whatever, established by the basic structure. Thus in applying the second principle I assume that it is possible to assign an expectation of well-being to representative individuals holding these positions. This expectation indicates their life prospects as viewed from their social station. In general, the expectations of representative persons depend upon the distribution of rights and duties throughout the basic structure. When this changes, expectations change. I assume, then, that expectations are connected: by raising the prospects of the representative man in one position we presumably increase or decrease the prospects of representative men in other positions. Since it applies to institutional forms, the second principle (or rather the first part of it) refers to the expectations of representative individuals. As I shall discuss below, neither principle applies to distributions of particular goods to particular individuals who may be identified by their proper names. The situation where someone is considering how to allocate certain commodities to needy persons who are known to him is not within the scope of the principles. They are meant to regulate basic institutional arrangements. We must not assume that there is much similarity from the standpoint of justice between an administrative allotment of goods to specific persons and the appropriate design of society. Our common sense intuition for the former may be a poor guide to the latter.

Now the second principle insists that each person benefit from permissible inequalities in the basic structure. This means that it must be reasonable for each relevant representative man defined by this structure, when he views it as a going concern, to prefer his prospects with the inequality to his prospects without it. One is not allowed to justify differences in income or organizational powers on the ground that the disadvantages of those in one position are

outweighed by the greater advantages of those in another. Much less can infringements of liberty be counterbalanced in this way. Applied to the basic structure, the principle of utility would have us maximize the sum of expectations of representative men (weighted by the number of persons they represent, on the classical view); and this would permit us to compensate for the losses of some by the gains of others. Instead, the two principles require that everyone benefit from economic and social inequalities. . . .

Democratic Equality and the Difference Principle

. . .

To illustrate the difference principle, consider the distribution of income among social classes. Let us suppose that the various income groups correlate with representative individuals by reference to whose expectations we can judge the distribution. Now those starting out as members of the entrepreneurial class in property-owning democracy, say, have a better prospect than those who begin in the class of unskilled laborers. It seems likely that this will be true even when the social injustices which now exist are removed. What, then, can possibly justify this kind of initial inequality in life prospects? According to the difference principle, it is justifiable only if the difference in expectation is to the advantage of the representative man who is worse off, in this case the representative unskilled worker. The inequality in expectation is permissible only if lowering it would make the working class even more worse off. Supposedly, given the rider in the second principle concerning open positions, and the principle of liberty generally, the greater expectations allowed to entrepreneurs encourages them to do things which raise the long-term prospects of laboring class. Their better prospects act as incentives so that the economic process is more efficient, innovation proceeds at a faster pace, and so on. Eventually the resulting material benefits spread throughout the system and to the least advantaged. I shall not consider how far these things are true. The point is that something of this kind must be argued if these inequalities are to be just by the difference principle.

. . .

Fair Equality of Opportunity and Pure Procedural Justice

. . .

Now I have said that the basic structure is the primary subject of justice. This means, as we have seen, that the first distributive problem is the assignment of fundamental rights and duties and the regulation of social and economic inequalities and of the legitimate expectations founded on these. Of course, any ethical theory recognizes the importance of the basic structure as a subject of justice, but not all theories regard its importance in the same way. In justice as fairness society is interpreted as a cooperative venture for mutual advantage. The basic structure is a public system of rules defining a scheme of activities that leads men to act together so as to produce a greater sum of benefits and

assigns to each certain recognized claims to a share in the proceeds. What a person does depends upon what the public rules say he will be entitled to, and what a person is entitled to depends on what he does. The distribution which results is arrived at by honoring the claims determined by what persons undertake to do in the light of these legitimate expectations.

These considerations suggest the idea of treating the question of distributive shares as a matter of pure procedural justice. The intuitive idea is to design the social system so that the outcome is just whatever it happens to be, at least so long as it is within a certain range. The notion of pure procedural justice is best understood by a comparison with perfect and imperfect procedural justice. To illustrate the former, consider the simplest case of fair division. A number of men are to divide a cake: assuming that the fair division is an equal one, which procedure, if any, will give this outcome? Technicalities aside, the obvious solution is to have one man divide the cake and get the last piece, the others being allowed their pick before him. He will divide the cake equally, since in this way he assures for himself the largest share possible. This example illustrates the two characteristic features of perfect procedural justice. First, there is an independent criterion for what is a fair division, a criterion defined separately from and prior to the procedure which is to be followed. And second, it is possible to devise a procedure that is sure to give the desired outcome. Of course, certain assumptions are made here, such as that the man selected can divide the cake equally, wants as large a piece as he can get, and so on. But we can ignore these details. The essential thing is that there is an independent standard for deciding which outcome is just and a procedure guaranteed to lead to it. Pretty clearly, perfect procedural justice is rare, if not impossible, in cases of much practical interest.

Imperfect procedural justice is exemplified by a criminal trial. The desired outcome is that the defendant should be declared guilty if and only if he has committed the offense with which he is charged. The trial procedure is framed to search for and to establish the truth in this regard. But it seems impossible to design the legal rules so that they always lead to the correct result. The theory of trials examines which procedures and rules of evidence, and the like, are best calculated to advance this purpose consistent with the other ends of the law. Different arrangements for hearing cases may reasonably be expected in different circumstances to yield the right results, not always but at least most of the time. A trial, then, is an instance of imperfect procedural justice. Even though the law is carefully followed, and the proceedings fairly and properly conducted, it may reach the wrong outcome. An innocent man may be found guilty, a guilty man may be set free. In such cases we speak of a miscarriage of justice: the injustice springs from no human fault but from a fortuitous combination of circumstances which defeats the purpose of the legal rules. The characteristic mark of imperfect procedural justice is that while there is an independent criterion for the correct outcome, there is no feasible procedure which is sure to lead to it.

By contrast, pure procedural justice obtains when there is no independent criterion for the right result: instead there is a correct or fair procedure such

that the outcome is likewise correct or fair, whatever it is, provided that the procedure has been properly followed. This situation is illustrated by gambling. If a number of persons engage in a series of fair bets, the distribution of cash after the last bet is fair, or at least not unfair, whatever this distribution is. I assume here that fair bets are those having a zero expectation of gain, that the bets are made voluntarily, that no one cheats, and so on. The betting procedure is fair and freely entered into under conditions that are fair. Thus the background circumstances define a fair procedure. Now any distribution of cash summing to the initial stock held by all individuals could result from a series of fair bets. In this sense all of these particular distributions are equally fair. A distinctive feature of pure procedural justice is that the procedure for determining the just result must actually be carried out; for in these cases there is no independent criterion by reference to which a definite outcome can be known to be just. Clearly we cannot say that a particular state of affairs is just because it could have been reached by following a fair procedure. This would permit far too much and would lead to absurdly unjust consequences. It would allow one to say that almost any distribution of goods is just, or fair, since it could have come about as a result of fair gambles. What makes the final outcome of betting fair, or not unfair, is that it is the one which has arisen after a series of fair gambles. A fair procedure translates its fairness to the outcome only when it is actually carried out.

In order, therefore, to apply the notion of pure procedural justice to distributive shares it is necessary to set up and to administer impartially a just system of institutions. Only against the background of a just basic structure, including a just political constitution and a just arrangement of economic and social institutions, can one say that the requisite just procedure exists. In Part Two I shall describe in some detail a basic structure that has the necessary features. Its various institutions are explained and connected with the two principles of justice. The intuitive idea is familiar. Suppose that law and government act effectively to keep markets competitive, resources fully employed, property and wealth (especially if private ownership of the means of production is allowed) widely distributed by the appropriate forms of taxation, or whatever, and to guarantee a reasonable social minimum. Assume also that there is fair equality of opportunity underwritten by education for all; and that the other equal liberties are secured. Then it would appear that the resulting distribution of income and the pattern of expectations will tend to satisfy the difference principle. In this complex of institutions, which we think of as establishing social justice in the modern state, the advantages of the better situated improve the condition of the least favored. Or when they do not, they can be adjusted to do so, for example, by setting the social minimum at the appropriate level. As these institutions presently exist they are riddled with grave injustices. But there presumably are ways of running them compatible with their basic design and intention so that the difference principle is satisfied consistent with the demands of liberty and fair equality of opportunity. It is this fact which underlies our assurance that these arrangements can be made just.

. . .

The Tendency to Equality

· · ·

We see then that the difference principle represents, in effect, an agreement to regard the distribution of natural talents as a common asset and to share in the benefits of this distribution whatever it turns out to be. Those who have been favored by nature, whoever they are, may gain from their good fortune only on terms that improve the situation of those who have lost out. The naturally advantaged are not to gain merely because they are more gifted, but only to cover the costs of training and education and for using their endowments in ways that help the less fortunate as well. No one deserves his greater natural capacity nor merits a more favorable starting place in society. But it does not follow that one should eliminate these distinctions. There is another way to deal with them. The basic structure can be arranged so that these contingencies work for the good of the least fortunate. Thus we are led to the difference principle if we wish to set up the social system so that no one gains or loses from his arbitrary place in the distribution of natural assets or his initial position in society without giving or receiving compensating advantages in return.

In view of these remarks we may reject the contention that the injustice of institutions is always imperfect because the distribution of natural talents and the contingencies of social circumstance are unjust, and this injustice must inevitably carry over to human arrangements. Occasionally this reflection is offered as an excuse for ignoring injustice, as if the refusal to acquiesce in injustice is on a par with being unable to accept death. The natural distribution is neither just nor unjust; nor is it unjust that men are born into society at some particular position. These are simply natural facts. What is just and unjust is the way that institutions deal with these facts. Aristocratic and caste societies are unjust because they make these contingencies the ascriptive basis for belonging to more or less enclosed and privileged social classes. The basic structure of these societies incorporates the arbitrariness found in nature. But there is no necessity for men to resign themselves to these contingencies. The social system is not an unchangeable order beyond human control but a pattern of human action. In justice as fairness men agree to share one another's fate. In designing institutions they undertake to avail themselves of the accidents of nature and social circumstance only when doing so is for the common benefit. The two principles are a fair way of meeting the arbitrariness of fortune; and while no doubt imperfect in other ways, the institutions which satisfy these principles are just.

A further point is that the difference principle expresses a conception of reciprocity. It is a principle of mutual benefit. We have seen that, at least when chain connection holds, each representative man can accept the basic structure as designed to advance his interests. The social order can be justified to everyone, and in particular to those who are least favored; and in this sense it is egalitarian. But it seems necessary to consider in an intuitive way how the condition of mutual benefit is satisfied. Consider any two representative men A and B, and let B be the one who is less favored. Actually, since we are most

interested in the comparison with the least favored man, let us assume that B is this individual. Now B can accept A's being better off since A's advantages have been gained in ways that improve B's prospects. If A were not allowed his better position, B would be even worse off than he is. The difficulty is to show that A has no grounds for complaint. Perhaps he is required to have less than he might since his having more would result in some loss to B. Now what can be said to the more favored man? To begin with, it is clear that the well-being of each depends on a scheme of social cooperation without which no one could have a satisfactory life. Secondly, we can ask for the willing cooperation of everyone only if the terms of the scheme are reasonable. The difference principle, then, seems to be a fair basis on which those better endowed, or more fortunate in their social circumstances, could expect others to collaborate with them when some workable arrangement is a necessary condition of the good of all.

There is a natural inclination to object that those better situated deserve their greater advantages whether or not they are to the benefit of others. At this point it is necessary to be clear about the notion of desert. It is perfectly true that given a just system of cooperation as a scheme of public rules and the expectations set up by it, those who, with the prospect of improving their condition, have done what the system announces that it will reward are entitled to their advantages. In this sense the more fortunate have a claim to their better situation; their claims are legitimate expectations established by social institutions, and the community is obligated to meet them. But this sense of desert presupposes the existence of the cooperative scheme; it is irrelevant to the question whether in the first place the scheme is to be designed in accordance with the difference principle or some other criterion.

Perhaps some will think that the person with greater natural endowments deserves those assets and the superior character that made their development possible. Because he is more worthy in this sense, he deserves the greater advantages that he could achieve with them. This view, however, is surely incorrect. It seems to be one of the fixed points of our considered judgments that no one deserves his place in the distribution of native endowments, any more than one deserves one's initial starting place in society. The assertion that a man deserves the superior character that enables him to make the effort to cultivate his abilities is equally problematic; for his character depends in large part upon fortunate family and social circumstances for which he can claim no credit. The notion of desert seems not to apply to these cases. Thus the more advantaged representative man cannot say that he deserves and therefore has a right to a scheme of cooperation in which he is permitted to acquire benefits in ways that do not contribute to the welfare of others. There is no basis for his making this claim. From the standpoint of common sense, then, the difference principle appears to be acceptable both to the more advantaged and to the less advantaged individual. Of course, none of this is strictly speaking an argument for the principle, since in a contract theory arguments are made from the point of the original position. But these intuitive considerations help to clarify the nature of the principle and the sense in which it is egalitarian.

. . .

19

Distributive Justice

ROBERT NOZICK

For biographical information about Robert Nozick, see reading 16.

In this selection, Nozick argues that justice in the distribution of goods cannot be determined apart from what people have actually done. Goods do not simply spring into existence, but instead are produced through the efforts of particular individuals. Hence, any adequate theory of distributive justice must be historical as well. In particular, an object must be said to belong to someone if that person either (a) acquired it in some appropriate manner from the stock of unowned things, or (b) was voluntarily given it, perhaps in return for labor or something else, by another who owned it. Given the diversity of human talents and abilities, and given the widespread tendency to bequeath possessions to one's children, a set of holdings which satisfies this conception of justice is apt to be quite unequal. However, according to Nozick, this is inevitable if we are to respect people's rights. To make holdings equal (or to impose any other pattern upon them), we would have to prevent transactions that all parties want to make. This would violate people's rights to act freely.

Nozick's theory that we come to own things by acting upon unowned objects—his "entitlement theory of justice"—may seem unfair to those who are born too late. Past a certain point, most objects are already owned, and so those who do not inherit may seem to have few opportunities to acquire property. But in fact, the situation is more complicated than this. Following John Locke, who proposed a similar theory of the way in which property is acquired, (see reading 15), Nozick maintains that one may only appropriate an unowned object if one leaves behind "enough and as good" for others to use. Nozick calls this requirement the "Lockean Proviso". Because just appropriation cannot worsen the condition of others, there is a sense in which it cannot be unfair.

In view of this, the real question is whether, and if so when, the productive use of unowned objects does worsen the condition of others. In Nozick's view, this is rarely the case. As Locke noted, a farmer who cultivates a fallow patch of land greatly increases its output. He thus makes more food available, and so gives everyone new opportunities to make productive exchanges. Nozick applies similar reasoning to other elements of the free market system. He argues that because such a system greatly increases both the goods that are available and the opportunities to acquire them, it satisfies his "Lockean Proviso" on appropriation.

THE MINIMAL STATE is the most extensive state that can be justified. Any state more extensive violates people's rights. Yet many persons have put forth reasons purporting to justify a more extensive state. It is impossible within the compass of this book to examine all the reasons that have been put forth. Therefore, I shall focus upon those generally acknowledged to be most weighty and influential, to see precisely wherein they fail. In this chapter we consider the claim that a more extensive state is justified, because necessary (or the best instrument) to achieve distributive justice; in the next chapter we shall take up diverse other claims.

The term "distributive justice" is not a neutral one. Hearing the term "distribution," most people presume that some thing or mechanism uses some principle or criterion to give out a supply of things. Into this process of distributing shares some error may have crept. So it is an open question, at least, whether redistribution should take place; whether we should do again what has already been done once, though poorly. However, we are not in the position of children who have been given portions of pie by someone who now makes last minute adjustments to rectify careless cutting. There is no central distribution, no person or group entitled to control all the resources, jointly deciding how they are to be doled out. What each person gets, he gets from others who give to him in exchange for something, or as a gift. In a free society, diverse persons control different resources, and new holdings arise out of the voluntary exchanges and actions of persons. There is no more a distributing or distribution of shares than there is a distributing of mates in a society in which persons choose whom they shall marry. The total result is the product of many individual decisions which the different individuals involved are entitled to make. Some uses of the term "distribution," it is true, do not imply a previous distributing appropriately judged by some criterion (for example, "probability distribution"); nevertheless, despite the title of this chapter, it would be best to use a terminology that clearly is neutral. We shall speak of people's holdings; a principle of justice in holdings describes (part of) what justice tells us (requires) about holdings. I shall state first what I take to be the correct view about justice in holdings, and then turn to the discussion of alternate views.

SECTION I

The Entitlement Theory

The subject of justice in holdings consists of three major topics. The first is the *original acquisition of holdings,* the appropriation of unheld things. This includes the issues of how unheld things may come to be held, the process, or processes, by which unheld things may come to be held, the things that may come to be held by these processes, the extent of what comes to be held by a particular process, and so on. We shall refer to the complicated truth about this topic, which we shall not formulate here, as the principle of justice in acquisition. The second topic concerns the *transfer of holdings* from one person

to another. By what processes may a person transfer holdings to another? How may a person acquire a holding from another who holds it? Under this topic come general descriptions of voluntary exchange, and gift and (on the other hand) fraud, as well as reference to particular conventional details fixed upon in a given society. The complicated truth about this subject (with placeholders for conventional details) we shall call the principle of justice in transfer. (And we shall suppose it also includes principles governing how a person may divest himself of a holding, passing it into an unheld state.)

If the world were wholly just, the following inductive definition would exhaustively cover the subject of justice in holdings.

1. A person who acquires a holding in accordance with the principle of justice in acquisition is entitled to that holding.
2. A person who acquires a holding in accordance with the principle of justice in transfer, from someone else entitled to the holding, is entitled to the holding.
3. No one is entitled to a holding except by (repeated) applications of 1 and 2.

The complete principle of distributive justice would say simply that a distribution is just if everyone is entitled to the holdings they possess under the distribution.

A distribution is just if it arises from another just distribution by legitimate means. The legitimate means of moving from one distribution to another are specified by the principle of justice in transfer. The legitimate first "moves" are specified by the principle of justice in acquisition. Whatever arises from a just situation by just steps is itself just. The means of change specified by the principle of justice in transfer preserve justice. As correct rules of inference are truth-preserving, and any conclusion deduced via repeated application of such rules from only true premises is itself true, so the means of transition from one situation to another specified by the principle of justice in transfer are justice-preserving, and any situation actually arising from repeated transitions in accordance with the principle from a just situation is itself just. The parallel between justice-preserving transformations and truth-preserving transformations illuminates where it fails as well as where it holds. That a conclusion could have been deduced by truth-preserving means from premises that are true suffices to show its truth. That from a just situation a situation *could* have arisen via justice-preserving means does *not* suffice to show its justice. The fact that a thief's victims voluntarily *could* have presented him with gifts does not entitle the thief to his ill-gotten gains. Justice in holdings is historical; it depends upon what actually has happened. We shall return to this point later.

Not all actual situations are generated in accordance with the two principles of justice in holdings: the principle of justice in acquisition and the principle of justice in transfer. Some people steal from others, or defraud them, or enslave them, seizing their product and preventing them from living as they choose, or forcibly exclude others from competing in exchanges. None of these are permissible modes of transition from one situation to another. And some persons

acquire holdings by means not sanctioned by the principle of justice in acquisition. The existence of past injustice (previous violations of the first two principles of justice in holdings) raises the third major topic under justice in holdings: the rectification of injustice in holdings. If past injustice has shaped present holdings in various ways, some identifiable and some not, what now, if anything, ought to be done to rectify these injustices? What obligations do the performers of injustice have toward those whose position is worse than it would have been had the injustice not been done? Or, than it would have been had compensation been paid promptly? How, if at all, do things change if the beneficiaries and those made worse off are not the direct parties in the act of injustice, but, for example, their descendants? Is an injustice done to someone whose holding was itself based upon an unrectified injustice? How far back must one go in wiping clean the historical slate of injustices? What may victims of injustice permissibly do in order to rectify the injustices being done to them, including the many injustices done by persons acting through their government? I do not know of a thorough or theoretically sophisticated treatment of such issues. Idealizing greatly, let us suppose theoretical investigation will produce a principle of rectification. This principle uses historical information about previous situations and injustices done in them (as defined by the first two principles of justice and rights against interference), and information about the actual course of events that flowed from these injustices, until the present, and it yields a description (or descriptions) of holdings in the society. The principle of rectification presumably will make use of its best estimate of subjunctive information about what would have occurred (or a probability distribution over what might have occurred, using the expected value) if the injustice had not taken place. If the actual description of holdings turns out not to be one of the descriptions yielded by the principle, then one of the descriptions yielded must be realized.

The general outlines of the theory of justice in holdings are that the holdings of a person are just if he is entitled to them by the principles of justice in acquisition and transfer, or by the principle of rectification of injustice (as specified by the first two principles). If each person's holdings are just, then the total set (distribution) of holdings is just. To turn these general outlines into a specific theory we would have to specify the details of each of the three principles of justice in holdings: the principle of acquisition of holdings, the principle of transfer of holdings, and the principle of rectification of violations of the first two principles. I shall not attempt that task here. (Locke's principle of justice in acquisition is discussed below.)

·   ·   ·

How Liberty Upsets Patterns

It is not clear how those holding alternative conceptions of distributive justice can reject the entitlement conception of justice in holdings. For suppose a distribution favored by one of these non-entitlement conceptions is realized. Let us suppose it is your favorite one and let us call this distribution D_1; perhaps

everyone has an equal share, perhaps shares vary in accordance with some dimension you treasure. Now suppose that Wilt Chamberlain is greatly in demand by basketball teams, being a great gate attraction. (Also suppose contracts run only for a year, with players being free agents.) He signs the following sort of contract with a team: In each home game, twenty-five cents from the price of each ticket of admission goes to him. (We ignore the question of whether he is "gouging" the owners, letting them look out for themselves.) The season starts, and people cheerfully attend his team's games; they buy their tickets, each time dropping a separate twenty-five cents of their admission price into a special box with Chamberlain's name on it. They are excited about seeing him play; it is worth the total admission price to them. Let us suppose that in one season one million persons attend his home games, and Wilt Chamberlain winds up with \$250,000, a much larger sum than the average income and larger even than anyone else has. Is he entitled to this income? Is this new distribution D_2, unjust? If so, why? There is *no* question about whether each of the people was entitled to the control over the resources they held in D_1; because that was the distribution (your favorite) that (for the purposes of argument) we assumed was acceptable. Each of these persons *chose* to give twenty-five cents of their money to Chamberlain. They could have spent it on going to the movies, or on candy bars, or on copies of *Dissent* magazine, or of *Monthly Review*. But they all, at least one million of them, converged on giving it to Wilt Chamberlain in exchange for watching him play basketball. If D_1 was a just distribution, and people voluntarily moved from it to D_2, transferring parts of their shares they were given under D_1 (what was it for if not to do something with?), isn't D_2 also just? If the people were entitled to dispose of the resources to which they were entitled (under D_1), didn't this include their being entitled to give it to, or exchange it with, Wilt Chamberlain? Can anyone else complain on grounds of justice? Each other person already has his legitimate share under D_1. Under D_1, there is nothing that anyone has that anyone else has a claim of justice against. After someone transfers something to Wilt Chamberlain, third parties *still* have their legitimate shares; *their* shares are not changed. By what process could such a transfer among two persons give rise to a legitimate claim of distributive justice on a portion of what was transferred, by a third party who had no claim of justice on any holding of the others *before* the transfer? To cut off objections irrelevant here, we might imagine the exchanges occurring in a socialist society, after hours. After playing whatever basketball he does in his daily work, or doing whatever other daily work he does, Wilt Chamberlain decides to put in *overtime* to earn additional money. (First his work quota is set; he works time over that.) Or imagine it is a skilled juggler people like to see, who puts on shows after hours.

Why might someone work overtime in a society in which it is assumed their needs are satisfied? Perhaps because they care about things other than needs. I like to write in books that I read, and to have easy access to books for browsing at odd hours. It would be very pleasant and convenient to have the resources of Widener Library in my back yard. No society, I assume, will provide such resources close to each person who would like them as part of his regular

allotment (under D_1). Thus, persons either must do without some extra things that they want, or be allowed to do something extra to get some of these things. On what basis could the inequalities that would eventuate be forbidden? Notice also that small factories would spring up in a socialist society, unless forbidden. I melt down some of my personal possessions (under D_1) and build a machine out of the material. I offer you, and others, a philosophy lecture once a week in exchange for your cranking the handle on my machine, whose products I exchange for yet other things, and so on. (The raw materials used by the machine are given to me by others who possess them under D_1, in exchange for hearing lectures.) Each person might participate to gain things over and above their allotment under D_1. Some persons even might want to leave their job in socialist industry and work full time in this private sector. I shall say something more about these issues in the next chapter. Here I wish merely to note how private property even in means of production would occur in a socialist society that did not forbid people to use as they wished some of the resources they are given under the socialist distribution D_1. The socialist society would have to forbid capitalist acts between consenting adults.

The general point illustrated by the Wilt Chamberlain example and the example of the entrepreneur in a socialist society is that no end-state principle* or distributional patterned principle of justice† can be continuously realized without continuous interference with people's lives. Any favored pattern would be transformed into one unfavored by the principle, by people choosing to act in various ways; for example, by people exchanging goods and services with other people, or giving things to other people, things the transferrers are entitled to under the favored distributional pattern. To maintain a pattern one must either continually interfere to stop people from transferring resources as they wish to, or continually (or periodically) interfere to take from some persons resources that others for some reason chose to transfer to them. (But if some time limit is to be set on how long people may keep resources others voluntarily transfer to them, why let them keep these resources for *any* period of time? Why not have immediate confiscation?) It might be objected that all persons voluntarily will choose to refrain from actions which would upset the pattern. This presupposes unrealistically (1) that all will most want to maintain the pattern (are those who don't, to be "reeducated" or forced to undergo "self-criticism"?), (2) that each can gather enough information about his own actions and the ongoing activities of others to discover which of his actions will upset the pattern, and (3) that diverse and far-flung persons can coordinate their actions to dovetail into the pattern. Compare the manner in which the market is neutral

---

* According to Nozick, an "end-state principle" is one that tells us to distribute goods in a way that promotes a certain present or future structure of holdings. The principles that we should maximize utility or promote equality are end-state principles.

† For Nozick, "a patterned principle" is one that tells us to distribute goods in accordance with some natural feature or dimension of persons. The principles that we should distribute in accordance with need, or according to usefulness to society, or desert, are patterned principles.

among persons' desires, as it reflects and transmits widely scattered information via prices, and coordinates persons' activities.

It puts things perhaps a bit too strongly to say that every patterned (or end-state) principle is liable to be thwarted by the voluntary actions of the individual parties transferring some of their shares they receive under the principle. For perhaps some *very* weak patterns are not so thwarted. Any distributional pattern with any egalitarian component is overturnable by the voluntary actions of individual persons over time; as is every patterned condition with sufficient content so as actually to have been proposed as presenting the central core of distributive justice. Still, given the possibility that some weak conditions or patterns may not be unstable in this way, it would be better to formulate an explicit description of the kind of interesting and contentful patterns under discussion, and to prove a theorem about their instability. Since the weaker the patterning, the more likely it is that the entitlement system itself satisfies it, a plausible conjecture is that any patterning either is unstable or is satisfied by the entitlement system.

.   .   .

Redistribution and Property Rights

.   .   .

Taxation of earnings from labor is on a par with forced labor. Some persons find this claim obviously true: taking the earnings of n hours labor is like taking n hours from the person; it is like forcing the person to work n hours for another's purpose. Others find the claim absurd. But even these, *if* they object to forced labor, would oppose forcing unemployed hippies to work for the benefit of the needy. And they would also object to forcing each person to work five extra hours each week for the benefit of the needy. But a system that takes five hours' wages in taxes does not seem to them like one that forces someone to work five hours, since it offers the person forced a wider range of choice in activities than does taxation in kind with the particular labor specified. (But we can imagine a gradation of systems of forced labor, from one that specifies a particular activity, to one that gives a choice among two activities, to . . . ; and so on up.) Furthermore, people envisage a system with something like a proportional tax on everything above the amount necessary for basic needs. Some think this does not force someone to work extra hours, since there is no fixed number of extra hours he is forced to work, and since he can avoid the tax entirely by earning only enough to cover his basic needs. This is a very uncharacteristic view of forcing for those who *also* think people are forced to do something *whenever* the alternatives they face are considerably worse. However, *neither* view is correct. The fact that others intentionally intervene, in violation of a side constraint* against aggression, to threaten force to limit the

---

* According to Nozick, people's rights impose limits, or "side-constraints," upon the ways in which others may legitimately treat them.

233

alternatives, in this case to paying taxes or (presumably the worse alternative) bare subsistence, makes the taxation system one of forced labor and distinguishes it from other cases of limited choices which are not forcings.

The man who chooses to work longer to gain an income more than sufficient for his basic needs prefers some extra goods or services to the leisure and activities he could perform during the possible nonworking hours; whereas the man who chooses not to work the extra time prefers the leisure activities to the extra goods or services he could acquire by working more. Given this, if it would be illegitimate for a tax system to seize some of a man's leisure (forced labor) for the purpose of serving the needy, how can it be legitimate for a tax system to seize some of a man's goods for that purpose? Why should we treat the man whose happiness requires certain material goods or services differently from the man whose preferences and desires make such goods unnecessary for his happiness? Why should the man who prefers seeing a movie (and who has to earn money for a ticket) be open to the required call to aid the needy, while the person who prefers looking at a sunset (and hence need earn no extra money) is not? Indeed, isn't it surprising that redistributionists choose to ignore the man whose pleasures are so easily attainable without extra labor, while adding yet another burden to the poor unfortunate who must work for his pleasures? If anything, one would have expected the reverse. Why is the person with the nonmaterial or nonconsumption desire allowed to proceed unimpeded to his most favored feasible alternative, whereas the man whose pleasures or desires involve material things and who must work for extra money (thereby serving whomever considers his activities valuable enough to pay him) is constrained in what he can realize? . . .

Locke's Theory of Acquisition

Before we turn to consider other theories of justice in detail, we must introduce an additional bit of complexity into the structure of the entitlement theory. This is best approached by considering Locke's attempt to specify a principle of justice in acquisition. Locke views property rights in an unowned object as originating through someone's mixing his labor with it. This gives rise to many questions. What are the boundaries of what labor is mixed with? If a private astronaut clears a place on Mars, has he mixed his labor with (so that he comes to own) the whole planet, the whole uninhabited universe, or just a particular plot? Which plot does an act bring under ownership? The minimal (possibly disconnected) area such that an act decreases entropy in that area, and not elsewhere? Can virgin land (for the purposes of ecological investigation by high-flying airplane) come under ownership by a Lockean process? Building a fence around a territory presumably would make one the owner of only the fence (and the land immediately underneath it).

Why does mixing one's labor with something make one the owner of it? Perhaps because one owns one's labor, and so one comes to own a previously unowned thing that becomes permeated with what one owns. Ownership seeps over into the rest. But why isn't mixing what I own with what I don't own a

way of losing what I own rather than a way of gaining what I don't? If I own a can of tomato juice and spill it in the sea so that its molecules (made radioactive, so I can check this) mingle evenly throughout the sea, do I thereby come to own the sea, or have I foolishly dissipated my tomato juice? Perhaps the idea, instead, is that laboring on something improves it and makes it more valuable; and anyone is entitled to own a thing whose value he has created. (Reinforcing this, perhaps, is the view that laboring is unpleasant. If some people made things effortlessly, as the cartoon characters in *The Yellow Submarine* trail flowers in their wake, would they have lesser claim to their own products whose making didn't *cost* them anything?) Ignore the fact that laboring on something may make it less valuable (spraying pink enamel paint on a piece of driftwood that you have found). Why should one's entitlement extend to the whole object rather than just to the *added value* one's labor has produced? (Such reference to value might also serve to delimit the extent of ownership; for example, substitute "increases the value of" for "decreases entropy in" in the above entropy criterion.) No workable or coherent value-added property scheme has yet been devised, and any such scheme presumably would fall to objections (similar to those) that fell the theory of Henry George.

It will be implausible to view improving an object as giving full ownership to it, if the stock of unowned objects that might be improved is limited. For an object's coming under one person's ownership changes the situation of all others. Whereas previously they were at liberty (in Hohfeld's sense) to use the object, they now no longer are. This change in the situation of others (by removing their liberty to act on a previously unowned object) need not worsen their situation. If I appropriate a grain of sand from Coney Island, no one else may now do as they will with *that* grain of sand. But there are plenty of other grains of sand left for them to do the same with. Or if not grains of sand, then other things. Alternatively, the things I do with the grain of sand I appropriate might improve the position of others, counterbalancing their loss of the liberty to use that grain. The crucial point is whether appropriation of an unowned object worsens the situation of others.

. . .

Is the situation of persons who are unable to appropriate (there being no more accessible and useful unowned objects) worsened by a system allowing appropriation and permanent property? Here enter the various familiar social considerations favoring private property: it increases the social product by putting means of production in the hands of those who can use them most efficiently (profitably); experimentation is encouraged, because with separate persons controlling resources, there is no one person or small group whom someone with a new idea must convince to try it out; private property enables people to decide on the pattern and types of risks they wish to bear, leading to specialized types of risk bearing; private property protects future persons by leading some to hold back resources from current consumption for future markets; it provides alternate sources of employment for unpopular persons who don't have to convince any one person or small group to hire them, and so on.

These considerations enter a Lockean theory to support the claim that appropriation of private property satisfies the intent behind the "enough and as good left over" proviso, *not* as a utilitarian justification of property. They enter to rebut the claim that because the proviso is violated no natural right to private property can arise by a Lockean process. The difficulty in working such an argument to show that the proviso is satisfied is in fixing the appropriate base line for comparison. Lockean appropriation makes people no worse off than they would be *how?* This question of fixing the baseline needs more detailed investigation than we are able to give it here. It would be desirable to have an estimate of the general economic importance of original appropriation in order to see how much leeway there is for differing theories of appropriation and of the location of the baseline. Perhaps this importance can be measured by the percentage of all income that is based upon untransformed raw materials and given resources (rather than upon human actions), mainly rental income representing the unimproved value of land, and the price of raw material *in situ,* and by the percentage of current wealth which represents such income in the past.

We should note that it is not only persons favoring *private* property who need a theory of how property rights legitimately originate. Those believing in collective property, for example those believing that a group of persons living in an area jointly own the territory, or its mineral resources, also must provide a theory of how such property rights arise; they must show why the persons living there have rights to determine what is done with the land and resources there that persons living elsewhere don't have (with regard to the same land and resources).

The Proviso

Whether or not Locke's particular theory of appropriation can be spelled out so as to handle various difficulties, I assume that any adequate theory of justice in acquistion will contain a proviso similar to the weaker of the ones we have attributed to Locke. A process normally giving rise to a permanent bequeathable property right in a previously unowned thing will not do so if the position of others no longer at liberty to use the thing is thereby worsened. It is important to specify *this* particular mode of worsening the situation of others, for the proviso does not encompass other modes. It does not include the worsening due to more limited opportunities to appropriate ..., and it does not include how I "worsen" a seller's position if I appropriate materials to make some of what he is selling, and then enter into competition with him. Someone whose appropriation otherwise would violate the proviso still may appropriate provided he compensates the others so that their situation is not thereby worsened; unless he does compensate these others, his appropriation will violate the proviso of the principle of justice in acquisition and will be an illegitimate one. A theory of appropriation incorporating this Lockean proviso will handle correctly the cases (objections to the theory lacking the proviso) where someone appropriates the total supply of something necessary for life.

A theory which includes this proviso in its principle of justice in acquisition must also contain a more complex principle of justice in transfer. Some reflection of the proviso about appropriation constrains later actions. If my appropriating all of a certain substance violates the Lockean proviso, then so does my appropriating some and purchasing all the rest from others who obtained it without otherwise violating the Lockean proviso. If the proviso excludes someone's appropriating all the drinkable water in the world, it also excludes his purchasing it all. (More weakly, and messily, it may exclude his charging certain prices for some of his supply.) This proviso (almost?) never will come into effect; the more someone acquires of a scarce substance which others want, the higher the price of the rest will go, and the more difficult it will become for him to acquire it all. But still, we can imagine, at least, that something like this occurs: someone makes simultaneous secret bids to the separate owners of a substance, each of whom sells assuming he can easily purchase more from the other owners; or some natural catastrophe destroys all of the supply of something except that in one person's possession. The total supply could not be permissibly appropriated by one person at the beginning. His later acquisition of it all does not show that the original appropriation violated the proviso. . . . Rather, it is the combination of the original appropriation *plus* all the later transfers and actions that violates the Lockean proviso.

Each owner's title to his holding includes the historical shadow of the Lockean proviso on appropriation. This excludes his transferring it into an agglomeration that does violate the Lockean proviso and excludes his using it in a way, in coordination with others or independently of them, so as to violate the proviso by making the situation of others worse than their baseline situation. Once it is known that someone's ownership runs afoul of the Lockean proviso, there are stringent limits on what he may do with (what it is difficult any longer unreservedly to call) "his property." Thus a person may not appropriate the only water hole in a desert and charge what he will. Nor may he charge what he will if he possesses one, and unfortunately it happens that all the water holes in the desert dry up, except for his. This unfortunate circumstance, admittedly no fault of his, brings into operation the Lockean proviso and limits his property rights. Similarly, an owner's property right in the only island in an area does not allow him to order a castaway from a shipwreck off his island as a trespasser, for this would violate the Lockean proviso.

. . .

The fact that someone owns the total supply of something necessary for others to stay alive does *not* entail that his (or anyone's) appropriation of anything left some people (immediately or later) in a situation worse than the baseline one. A medical researcher who synthesizes a new substance that effectively treats a certain disease and who refuses to sell except on his terms does not worsen the situation of others by depriving them of whatever he has appropriated. The others easily can possess the same materials he appropriated; the researcher's appropriation or purchase of chemicals didn't make those chemicals scarce in a way so as to violate the Lockean proviso. Nor would someone

else's purchasing the total supply of the synthesized substance from the medical researcher. The fact that the medical researcher uses easily available chemicals to synthesize the drug no more violates the Lockean proviso than does the fact that the only surgeon able to perform a particular operation eats easily obtainable food in order to stay alive and to have the energy to work. This shows that the Lockean proviso is not an "end-state principle"; it focuses on a particular way that appropriative actions affect others, and not on the structure of the situation that results.

Intermediate between someone who takes all of the public supply and someone who makes the total supply out of easily obtainable substances is someone who appropriates the total supply of something in a way that does not deprive the others of it. For example, someone finds a new substance in an out-of-the-way place. He discovers that it effectively treats a certain disease and appropriates the total supply. He does not worsen the situation of others; if he did not stumble upon the substance no one else would have, and the others would remain without it. However, as time passes, the likelihood increases that others would have come across the substance; upon this fact might be based a limit to his property right in the substance so that others are not below their baseline position; for example, its bequest might be limited. The theme of someone worsening another's situation by depriving him of something he otherwise would possess may also illuminate the example of patents. An inventor's patent does not deprive others of an object which would not exist if not for the inventor. Yet patents would have this effect on others who independently invent the object. Therefore, these independent inventors, upon whom the burden of proving independent discovery may rest, should not be excluded from utilizing their own invention as they wish (including selling it to others). Furthermore, a known inventor drastically lessens the chances of actual independent invention. For persons who know of an invention usually will not try to reinvent it, and the notion of independent discovery here would be murky at best. Yet we may assume that in the absence of the original invention, sometime later someone else would have come up with it. This suggests placing a time limit on patents, as a rough rule of thumb to approximate how long it would have taken, in the absence of knowledge of the invention, for independent discovery.

I believe that the free operation of a market system will not actually run afoul of the Lockean proviso. . . .

20

Communism

(a) The Communist Manifesto

KARL MARX and FRIEDRICH ENGELS

Karl Marx (1818–1883), economist and social theorist, is the author of
Capital *and many other works. Born in Germany, Marx spent most of his
life in exile, first in France and then in England. His writings are the
theoretical basis of contemporary communism. Friedrich Engels (1820–
1895) was Marx's long-time friend and collaborator.*

*In the first selection (a), Marx and Engels present an overview of their
vision of history. In their view, the fundamental facts about any society are
those which concern its economic and productive arrangements. These facts
have largely, if not entirely, determined each society's religion, philosophy,
and legal system. Throughout the course of history, each set of economic
arrangements has contained within it the seeds of its own destruction. Thus,
the city-states of classical antiquity gave way to the hierarchical organization
of feudal society, and feudalism in turn gave way to the unbridled competition of capitalism. But capitalism, in which workers must sell their
labor for subsistence wages to owners of factories, land, and tools, also
contains an inner contradiction. It brings workers together even as it forces
them to compete; it fosters ever-increasing poverty in the midst of abundance; and it generates an ever more extreme cycle of prosperity and
depression. Eventually, this system too must burst its bounds. When it does,
the exploitation of workers by property owners, and the alienation of
workers from their labor and its product, will end.*

*In the second selection (b), Marx discusses the distribution of goods in a
communist society. Given his view that capitalists exploit workers (roughly,
by paying them less than the full value of their labor), one might expect
Marx to hold that a just society is one in which workers* do *receive the full
value of their labor. But in fact, Marx does not say this. He acknowledges
that some such conception of justice is inevitable "in the first phases of
communist society." However, one who insists on this sort of fair exchange
is not really liberated from the capitalist outlook. He still regards labor as
something to be sold. In the later stages of communism, once the division of
labor is abolished and "the springs of cooperative wealth flow more abundantly," work will be regarded not as a commodity, but as an end in itself.
At that point, each will contribute according to his ability and receive
according to his need, and the question of distributive justice will no longer
arise.*

Bourgeois and Proletarians

THE HISTORY of all hitherto existing society is the history of class struggles.

Freeman and slave, patrician and plebeian, lord and serf, guild-master and journeyman, in a word, oppressor and oppressed, stood in constant opposition to one another, carried on an uninterrupted, now hidden, now open fight, a fight that each time ended, either in a revolutionary re-constitution of society at large, or in the common ruin of the contending classes.

In the earlier epochs of history, we find almost everywhere a complicated arrangement of society into various orders, a manifold gradation of social rank. In ancient Rome we have patricians, knights, plebeians, slaves; in the Middle Ages, feudal lords, vassals, guild-masters, journeymen, apprentices, serfs; in almost all of these classes, again, subordinate gradations.

The modern bourgeois society that has sprouted from the ruins of feudal society has not done away with class antagonisms. It has but established new classes, new conditions of oppression, new forms of struggle in place of the old ones.

Our epoch, the epoch of the bourgeoisie, possesses, however, this distinctive feature: it has simplified the class antagonisms: Society as a whole is more and more splitting up into two great hostile camps, into two great classes directly facing each other: Bourgeoisie and Proletariat.

. . .

The bourgeoisie, wherever it has got the upper hand, has put an end to all feudal, patriarchal, idyllic relations. It has pitilessly torn asunder the motley feudal ties that bound man to his "natural superiors," and has left remaining no other nexus between man and man than naked self-interest, than callous "cash payment." It has drowned the most heavenly ecstasies of religious fervour, of chivalrous enthusiasm, of philistine sentimentalism, in the icy water of egotistical calculation. It has resolved personal worth into exchange value, and in place of the numberless indefeasible chartered freedoms, has set up that single, unconscionable freedom—Free Trade. In one word, for exploitation, veiled by religious and political illusions, it has substituted naked, shameless, direct, brutal exploitation.

. . .

The bourgeoisie has through its exploitation of the world-market given a cosmopolitan character to production and consumption in every country. To the great chagrin of Reactionists, it has drawn from under the feet of industry the national ground on which it stood. All old-established national industries have been destroyed or are daily being destroyed. They are dislodged by new industries, whose introduction becomes a life and death question for all civilised nations, by industries that no longer work up indigenous raw material, but raw material drawn from the remotest zones; industries whose products are consumed, not only at home, but in every quarter of the globe. In place of the old wants, satisfied by the productions of the country, we find new wants, requiring for their satisfaction the products of distant lands and climes. In place of the

240

old local and national seclusion and self-sufficiency, we have intercourse in every direction, universal inter-dependence of nations. And as in material, so also in intellectual production. The intellectual creations of individual nations become common property. National one-sidedness and narrow-mindedness become more and more impossible, and from the numerous national and local literatures, there arises a world literature.

. . .

The bourgeoisie has subjected the country to the rule of the towns. It has created enormous cities, has greatly increased the urban population as compared with the rural, and has thus rescued a considerable part of the population from the idiocy of rural life. Just as it has made the country dependent on the towns, so it has made barbarian and semi-barbarian countries dependent on the civilised ones, nations and peasants on nations of bourgeois, the East on the West.

. . .

The bourgeoisie, during its rule of scarce one hundred years, has created more massive and more colossal productive forces than have all preceding generations together. Subjection of Nature's forces to man, machinery, application of chemistry to industry and agriculture, steam-navigation, railways, electric telegraphs, clearing of whole continents for cultivation, canalisation of rivers, whole populations conjured out of the ground—what earlier century had even a presentiment that such productive forces slumbered in the lap of social labour?

We see then: the means of production and of exchange, on whose foundation the bourgeoisie built itself up, were generated in feudal society. At a certain stage in the development of these means of production and of exchange, the conditions under which feudal society produced and exchanged, the feudal organisation of agriculture and manufacturing industry, in one word, the feudal relations of property became no longer compatible with the already developed productive forces; they became so many fetters. They had to be burst asunder; they were burst asunder.

Into their place stepped free competition, accompanied by a social and political constitution adapted to it, and by the economical and political sway of the bourgeois class.

A similar movement is going on before our own eyes. Modern bourgeois society with its relations of production, of exchange and of property, a society that has conjured up such gigantic means of production and of exchange, is like the sorcerer, who is no longer able to control the powers of the nether world whom he has called up by his spells. For many a decade past the history of industry and commerce is but the history of the revolt of modern productive forces against modern conditions of production, against the property relations that are the conditions for the existence of the bourgeoisie and of its rule. It is enough to mention the commercial crises that by their periodical return put on

its trial, each time more threateningly, the existence of the entire bourgeois society. In these crises a great part not only of the existing products, but also of the previously created productive forces, are periodically destroyed. In these crises there breaks out an epidemic that, in all earlier epochs, would have seemed an absurdity—the epidemic of over-production. Society suddenly finds itself put back into a state of momentary barbarism; it appears as if a famine, a universal war of devastation had cut off the supply of every means of sub-sistence; industry and commerce seem to be destroyed; and why? Because there is too much civilisation, too much means of subsistence, too much industry, too much commerce. The productive forces at the disposal of society no longer tend to further the development of the conditions of bourgeois property; on the contrary, they have become too powerful for these conditions, by which they are fettered, and so soon as they overcome these fetters, they bring disorder into the whole of bourgeois society, endanger the existence of bourgeois prop-erty. The conditions of bourgeois society are too narrow to comprise the wealth created by them. And how does the bourgeoisie get over these crises? On the one hand by enforced destruction of a mass of productive forces; on the other, by the conquest of new markets, and by the more thorough exploitation of the old ones. That is to say, by paving the way for more extensive and more destructive crises, and by diminishing the means whereby crises are prevented.

The weapons with which the bourgeoisie felled feudalism to the ground are now turned against the bourgeoisie itself.

But not only has the bourgeoisie forged the weapons that bring death to itself; it has also called into existence the men who are to wield those weapons— the modern working class—the proletarians.

In proportion as the bourgeoisie, *i.e.*, capital, is developed, in the same pro-portion is the proletariat, the modern working class, developed—a class of labourers, who live only so long as they find work, and who find work only so long as their labour increases capital. These labourers, who must sell themselves piece-meal, are a commodity, like every other article of commerce, and are consequently exposed to all the vicissitudes of competition, to all the fluctua-tions of the market.

Owing to the extensive use of machinery and to division of labour, the work of the proletarians has lost all individual character, and consequently, all charm for the workman. He becomes an appendage of the machine, and it is only the most simple, most monotonous, and most easily acquired knack, that is required of him. Hence, the cost of production of a workman is restricted, almost entirely, to the means of subsistence that he requires for his maintenance, and for the propagation of his race. But the price of a commodity, and therefore also of labour, is equal to its cost of production. In proportion, therefore, as the repul-siveness of the work increases, the wage decreases. Nay more, in proportion as the use of machinery and division of labour increases, in the same proportion the burden of toil also increases, whether by prolongation of the working hours, by increase of the work exacted in a given time or by increased speed of the machinery, etc.

. . .

The lower strata of the middle class—the small tradespeople, shopkeepers, and retired tradesmen generally, the handicraftsmen and peasants—all these sink gradually into the proletariat, partly because their diminutive capital does not suffice for the scale on which Modern Industry is carried on, and is swamped in the competition with the large capitalists, partly because their specialised skill is rendered worthless by new methods of production. Thus the proletariat is recruited from all classes of the population.

. . .

All the preceding classes that got the upper hand, sought to fortify their already acquired status by subjecting society at large to their conditions of appropriation. The proletarians cannot become masters of the productive forces of society, except by abolishing their own previous mode of appropriation, and thereby also every other previous mode of appropriation. They have nothing of their own to secure and to fortify; their mission is to destroy all previous securities for, and insurances of, individual property.

All previous historical movements were movements of minorities, or in the interests of minorities. The proletarian movement is the self-conscious, independent movement of the immense majority, in the interests of the immense majority. The proletariat, the lowest stratum of our present society, cannot stir, cannot raise itself up, without the whole superincumbent strata of official society being sprung into the air.

. . .

Hitherto, every form of society has been based, as we have already seen, on the antagonism of oppressing and oppressed classes. But in order to oppress a class, certain conditions must be assured to it under which it can, at least, continue its slavish existence. The serf, in the period of serfdom, raised himself to membership in the commune, just as the petty bourgeois, under the yoke of feudal absolutism, managed to develop into a bourgeois. The modern labourer, on the contrary, instead of rising with the progress of industry, sinks deeper and deeper below the conditions of existence of his own class. He becomes a pauper, and pauperism develops more rapidly than population and wealth. And here it becomes evident, that the bourgeoisie is unfit any longer to be the ruling class in society, and to impose its conditions of existence upon society as an over-riding law. It is unfit to rule because it is incompetent to assure an existence to its slave within his slavery, because it cannot help letting him sink into such a state, that it has to feed him, instead of being fed by him. Society can no longer live under this bourgeoisie, in other words, its existence is no longer compatible with society.

The essential condition for the existence, and for the sway of the bourgeois class, is the formation and augmentation of capital; the condition for capital is wage-labour. Wage-labour rests exclusively on competition between the labourers. The advance of industry, whose involuntary promoter is the bourgeoisie, replaces the isolation of the labourers, due to competition, by their revolutionary combination, due to association. The development of Modern

Industry, therefore, cuts from under its feet the very foundation on which the bourgeoisie produces and appropriates products. What the bourgeoisie, therefore, produces, above all, is its own grave-diggers. Its fall and the victory of the proletariat are equally inevitable.

Proletarians and Communists

. . .

The Communists are distinguished from the other working-class parties by this only: (1) In the national struggles of the proletarians of the different countries, they point out and bring to the front the common interests of the entire proletariat, independently of all nationality. (2) In the various stages of development which the struggle of the working class against the bourgoisie has to pass through, they always and everywhere represent the interests of the movement as a whole.

The distinguishing feature of Communism is not the abolition of property generally, but the abolition of bourgeois property. But modern bourgeois private property is the final and most complete expression of the system of producing and appropriating products, that is based on class antagonisms, on the exploitation of the many by the few.

In this sense, the theory of the Communists may be summed up in the single sentence: Abolition of private property.

We Communists have been reproached with the desire of abolishing the right of personally acquiring property as the fruit of a man's own labour, which property is alleged to be the groundwork of all personal freedom, activity and independence.

Hard-won, self-acquired, self-earned property! Do you mean the property of the petty artisan and of the small peasant, a form of property that preceded the bourgeois form? There is no need to abolish that; the development of industry has to a great extent already destroyed it, and is still destroying it daily.

Or do you mean modern bourgeois private property?

But does wage-labour create any property for the labourer? Not a bit. It creates capital, *i.e.,* that kind of property which exploits wage-labour, and which cannot increase except upon condition of begetting a new supply of wage-labour for fresh exploitation. . . .

The average price of wage-labour is the minimum wage, *i.e.,* that quantum of the means of subsistence, which is absolutely requisite to keep the labourer in bare existence as a labourer. What, therefore, the wage-labourer appropriates by means of his labour, merely suffices to prolong and reproduce a bare existence. We by no means intend to abolish this personal appropriation of the products of labour, an appropriation that is made for the maintenance and reproduction of human life, and that leaves no surplus wherewith to command the labour of others. All that we want to do away with, is the miserable character of this appropriation, under which the labourer lives merely to increase

capital, and is allowed to live only in so far as the interest of the ruling class requires it.

In bourgeois society, living labour is but a means to increase accumulated labour. In Communist society, accumulated labour is but a means to widen, to enrich, to promote the existence of the labourer.

In bourgeois society, therefore, the past dominates the present; in Communist society, the present dominates the past. In bourgeois society capital is independent and has individuality, while the living person is dependent and has no individuality.

And the abolition of this state of things is called by the bourgeois, abolition of individuality and freedom! And rightly so. The abolition of bourgeois individuality, bourgeois independence, and bourgeois freedom is undoubtedly aimed at.

. . .

Communism deprives no man of the power to appropriate the products of society; all that it does is to deprive him of the power to subjugate the labour of others by means of such appropriation.

It has been objected that upon the abolition of private property all work will cease, and universal laziness will overtake us.

According to this, bourgeois society ought long ago to have gone to the dogs through sheer idleness; for those of its members who work, acquire nothing, and those who acquire anything, do not work. The whole of this objection is but another expression of the tautology: that there can no longer be any wage-labour when there is no longer any capital.

All objections urged against the Communistic mode of producing and appropriating material products, have, in the same way, been urged against the Communistic modes of producing and appropriating intellectual products. Just as, to the bourgeois, the disappearance of class property is the disappearance of production itself, so the disappearance of class culture is to him identical with the disappearance of all culture.

That culture, the loss of which he laments, is, for the enormous majority, a mere training to act as a machine.

But don't wrangle with us so long as you apply, to our intended abolition of bourgeois property, the standard of your bourgeois notions of freedom, culture, law, &c. Your very ideas are but the outgrowth of the conditions of your bourgeois production and bourgeois property, just as your jurisprudence is but the will of your class made into a law for all, a will, whose essential character and direction are determined by the economical conditions of existence of your class.

The selfish misconception that induces you to transform into eternal laws of nature and of reason, the social forms springing from your present mode of production and form of property—historical relations that rise and disappear in the progress of production—this misconception you share with every ruling class that has preceded you. What you see clearly in the case of ancient property,

what you admit in the case of feudal property, you are of course forbidden to admit in the case of your own bourgeois form of property.

Abolition of the family! Even the most radical flare up at this infamous proposal of the Communists.

On what foundation is the present family, the bourgeois family, based? On capital, on private gain. In its completely developed form this family exists only among the bourgeoisie. But this state of things finds its complement in the practical absence of the family among the proletarians, and in public prostitution.

The bourgeois family will vanish as a matter of course when its complement vanishes, and both will vanish with the vanishing of capital.

Do you charge us with wanting to stop the exploitation of children by their parents? To this crime we plead guilty.

But, you will say, we destroy the most hallowed of relations, when we replace home education by social.

And your education! Is not that also social, and determined by the social conditions under which you educate, by the intervention, direct or indirect, of society, by means of schools, &c.? The Communists have not invented the intervention of society in education; they do but seek to alter the character of that intervention, and to rescue education from the influence of the ruling class.

.   .   .

The Communists are further reproached with desiring to abolish countries and nationality.

The working men have no country. We cannot take from them what they have not got. Since the proletariat must first of all acquire political supremacy, must rise to be the leading class of the nation, must constitute itself *the* nation, it is, so far, itself national, though not in the bourgeois sense of the word.

.   .   .

In proportion as the exploitation of one individual by another is put an end to, the exploitation of one nation by another will also be put an end to. In proportion as the antagonism between classes within the nation vanishes, the hostility of one nation to another will come to an end.

The charges against Communism made from a religious, a philosophical, and, generally, from an ideological standpoint, are not deserving of serious examination.

Does it require deep intuition to comprehend that man's ideas, views and conceptions, in one word, man's consciousness, changes with every change in the conditions of his material existence, in his social relations and in his social life?

What else does the history of ideas prove, than that intellectual production changes its character in proportion as material production is changed? The ruling ideas of each age have ever been the ideas of its ruling class.

When people speak of ideas that revolutionise society, they do but express the fact, that within the old society, the elements of a new one have been

246

created, and that the dissolution of the old ideas keeps even pace with the dissolution of the old conditions of existence.

When the ancient world was in its last throes, the ancient religions were overcome by Christianity. When Christian ideas succumbed in the 18th century to rationalist ideas, feudal society fought its death battle with the then revolutionary bourgeoisie. The ideas of religious liberty and freedom of conscience merely gave expression to the sway of free competition within the domain of knowledge.

"Undoubtedly," it will be said, "religious, moral, philosophical and juridical ideas have been modified in the course of historical development. But religion, morality, philosophy, political science, and law, constantly survived this change."

"There are, besides, eternal truths, such as Freedom, Justice, etc., that are common to all states of society. But Communism abolishes eternal truths, it abolishes all religion, and all morality, instead of constituting them on a new basis; it therefore acts in contradiction to all past historical experience."

What does this accusation reduce itself to? The history of all past society has consisted in the development of class antagonisms, antagonisms that assumed different forms at different epochs.

But whatever form they may have taken, one fact is common to all past ages, *viz.,* the exploitation of one part of society by the other. No wonder, then, that the social consciousness of past ages, despite all the multiplicity and variety it displays, moves within certain common forms, or general ideas, which cannot completely vanish except with the total disappearance of class antagonisms.

The Communist revolution is the most radical rupture with traditional property relations; no wonder that its development involves the most radical rupture with traditional ideas.

But let us have done with the bourgeois objections to Communism.

We have seen above, that the first step in the revolution by the working class, is to raise the proletariat to the position of ruling class, to win the battle of democracy.

The proletariat will use its political supremacy to wrest, by degrees, all capital from the bourgeoisie, to centralise all instruments of production in the hands of the State, *i.e.,* of the proletariat organised as the ruling class; and to increase the total of productive forces as rapidly as possible.

Of course, in the beginning, this cannot be effected except by means of despotic inroads on the rights of property, and on the conditions of bourgeois production; by means of measures, therefore, which appear economically insufficient and untenable, but which, in the course of the movement, outstrip themselves, necessitate further inroads upon the old social order, and are unavoidable as a means of entirely revolutionising the mode of production.

These measures will of course be different in different countries.

Nevertheless in the most advanced countries, the following will be pretty generally applicable.

1. Abolition of property in land and application of all rents of land to public purposes.

2. A heavy progressive or graduated income tax.
3. Abolition of all right of inheritance.
4. Confiscation of the property of all emigrants and rebels.
5. Centralisation of credit in the hands of the State, by means of a national bank with State capital and an exclusive monopoly.
6. Centralisation of the means of communication and transport in the hands of the State.
7. Extension of factories and instruments of production owned by the State; the bringing into cultivation of waste-lands, and the improvement of the soil generally in accordance with a common plan.
8. Equal liability of all to labour. Establishment of industrial armies, especially for agriculture.
9. Combination of agriculture with manufacturing industries; gradual abolition of the distinction between town and country, by a more equable distribution of the population over the country.
10. Free education for all children in public schools. Abolition of children's factory labour in its present form. Combination of education with industrial production, &c., &c.

When, in the course of development, class distinctions have disappeared, and all production has been concentrated in the hands of a vast association of the whole nation, the public power will lose its political character. Political power, properly so called, is merely the organised power of one class for oppressing another. If the proletariat during its contest with the bourgeoisie is compelled, by the force of circumstances, to organise itself as a class, if, by means of a revolution, it makes itself the ruling class, and, as such, sweeps away by force the old conditions of production, then it will, along with these conditions, have swept away the conditions for the existence of class antagonisms and of classes generally, and will thereby have abolished its own supremacy as a class.

In place of the old bourgeois society, with its classes and class antagonisms, we shall have an association, in which the free development of each is the condition for the free development of all.

(b) Critique of the Gotha Program

KARL MARX

> [The first sentence of this selection is
> quoted from a program put forth to unify
> the German Social Democratic Party.
> Marx develops his own views concerning
> justice and the distribution of goods while
> criticizing this program.]

· · ·

3. "The emancipation of labour demands the promotion of the instruments of labour to the common property of society and the co-operative regulation of the total labour with a fair distribution of the proceeds of labour."

"Promotion of the instruments of labour to the common property" ought obviously to read their "conversion into the common property"; but this only in passing.

What are "proceeds of labour"? The product of labour or its value? And in the latter case, is it the total value of the product or only that part of the value which labour has newly added to the value of the means of production consumed?

"Proceeds of labour" is a loose notion which Lassalle has put in the place of definite economic conceptions.

What is "a fair distribution"?

Do not the bourgeois assert that the present-day distribution is "fair"? And is it not, in fact, the only "fair" distribution on the basis of the present-day mode of production? Are economic relations regulated by legal conceptions or do not, on the contrary, legal relations arise from economic ones? Have not also the socialist sectarians the most varied notions about "fair" distribution?

To understand what is implied in this connection by the phrase "fair distribution," we must take the first paragraph and this one together. The latter presupposes a society wherein "the instruments of labour are common property and the total labour is cooperatively regulated," and from the first paragraph we learn that "the proceeds of labour belong undiminished with equal right to all members of society."

"To all members of society"? To those who do not work as well? What remains then of the "undiminished proceeds of labour"? Only to those members of society who work? What remains then of the "equal right" of all members of society?

But "all members of society" and "equal right" are obviously mere phrases. The kernel consists in this, that in this communist society every worker must receive the "undiminished" Lassallean "proceeds of labour."

Let us take first of all the words "proceeds of labour" in the sense of the product of labour; then the co-operative proceeds of labour are the *total social product*.

From this must now be deducted:

First, cover for replacement of the means of production used up.

Secondly, additional portion for expansion of production.

Thirdly, reserve or insurance funds to provide against accidents, dislocations caused by natural calamities, etc.

These deductions from the "undiminished proceeds of labour" are an economic necessity and their magnitude is to be determined according to available means and forces, and partly by computation of probabilities, but they are in no way calculable by equity.

There remains the other part of the total product, intended to serve as means of consumption.

Before this is divided among the individuals, there has to be deducted again, from it:

First, the general costs of administration not belonging to production.

This part will, from the outset, be very considerably restricted in comparison

249

with present-day society and it diminishes in proportion as the new society develops.

Secondly, that which is intended for the common satisfaction of needs, such as schools, health services, etc.

From the outset this part grows considerably in comparison with present-day society and it grows in proportion as the new society develops.

Thirdly, funds for those unable to work, etc., in short, for what is included under so-called official poor relief today.

Only now do we come to the "distribution" which the programme, under Lassallean influence, alone has in view in its narrow fashion, namely, to that part of the means of consumption which is divided among the individual producers of the co-operative society.

The "undiminished proceeds of labour" have already unnoticeably become converted into the "diminished" proceeds, although what the producer is deprived of in his capacity as a private individual benefits him directly or indirectly in his capacity as a member of society.

Just as the phrase of the "undiminished proceeds of labour" has disappeared, so now does the phrase of the "proceeds of labour" disappear altogether.

Within the co-operative society based on common ownership of the means of production, the producers do not exchange their products; just as little does the labour employed on the products appear here *as the value* of these products, as a material quality possessed by them, since now, in contrast to capitalist society, individual labour no longer exists in an indirect fashion but directly as a component part of the total labour. The phrase "proceeds of labour," objectionable also today on account of its ambiguity, thus loses all meaning.

What we have to deal with here is a communist society, not as it has *developed* on its own foundations, but, on the contrary, just as it *emerges* from capitalist society; which is thus in every respect, economically, morally and intellectually, still stamped with the birth marks of the old society from whose womb it emerges. Accordingly, the individual producer receives back from society—after the deductions have been made—exactly what he gives to it. What he has given to it is his individual quantum of labour. For example, the social working day consists of the sum of the individual hours of work; the individual labour time of the individual producer is the part of the social working day contributed by him, his share in it. He receives a certificate from society that he has furnished such and such an amount of labour (after deducting his labour for the common funds), and with this certificate he draws from the social stock of means of consumption as much as costs the same amount of labour. The same amount of labour which he has given to society in one form he receives back in another.

Here obviously the same principle prevails as that which regulates the exchange of commodities, as far as this is exchange of equal values. Content and form are changed, because under the altered circumstances no one can give anything except his labour, and because, on the other hand, nothing can pass to the ownership of individuals except individual means of consumption. But, as far as the distribution of the latter among the individual producers is concerned,

the same principle prevails as in the exchange of commodity equivalents: a given amount of labour in one form is exchanged for an equal amount of labour in another form.

Hence, *equal right* here is still in principle—*bourgeois right,* although principle and practice are no longer at loggerheads, while the exchange of equivalents in commodity exchange only exists *on the average* and not in the individual case.

In spite of this advance, this *equal right* is still constantly stigmatised by a bourgeois limitation. The right of the producers is *proportional* to the labour they supply; the equality consists in the fact that measurement is made with an *equal standard,* labour.

But one man is superior to another physically or mentally and so supplies more labour in the same time, or can labour for a longer time; and labour, to serve as a measure, must be defined by its duration or intensity, otherwise it ceases to be a standard of measurement. This *equal* right is an unequal right for unequal labour. It recognises no class differences, because everyone is only a worker like everyone else; but it tacitly recognises unequal individual endowment and thus productive capacity as natural privileges. *It is, therefore, a right of inequality, in its content, like every right.* Right by its very nature can consist only in the application of an equal standard; but unequal individuals (and they would not be different individuals if they were not unequal) are measurable only by an equal standard in so far as they are brought under an equal point of view, are taken from one *definite* side only, for instance, in the present case, are regarded *only as workers* and nothing more is seen in them, everything else being ignored. Further, one worker is married, another not; one has more children than another, and so on and so forth. Thus, with an equal performance of labour, and hence an equal share in the social consumption fund, one will in fact receive more than another, one will be richer than another, and so on. To avoid all these defects, right instead of being equal would have to be unequal.

But these defects are inevitable in the first phase of communist society as it is when it has just emerged after prolonged birth pangs from capitalist society. Right can never be higher than the economic structure of society and its cultural development conditioned thereby.

In a higher phase of communist society, after the enslaving subordination of the individual to the division of labour, and therewith also the antithesis between mental and physical labour, has vanished; after labour has become not only a means of life but life's prime want; after the productive forces have also increased with the all-round development of the individual, and all the springs of co-operative wealth flow more abundantly—only then can the narrow horizon of bourgeois right be crossed in its entirety and society inscribe on its banner: From each according to his ability, to each according to his needs!

I have dealt more at length with the "undiminished proceeds of labour," on the one hand, and with "equal right" and "fair distribution," on the other, in order to show what a crime it is to attempt, on the one hand, to force on our Party again, as dogmas, ideas which in a certain period had some meaning but have now become obsolete verbal rubbish, while again perverting, on the other,

the realistic outlook, which it cost so much effort to instil into the Party but which has now taken root in it, by means of ideological nonsense about right and other trash so common among the democrats and French Socialists.

Quite apart from the analysis so far given, it was in general a mistake to make a fuss about so-called *distribution* and put the principal stress on it.

Any distribution whatever of the means of consumption is only a consequence of the distribution of the conditions of production themselves. The latter distribution, however, is a feature of the mode of production itself. The capitalist mode of production, for example, rests on the fact that the material conditions of production are in the hands of non-workers in the form of property in capital and land, while the masses are only owners of the personal condition of production, of labour power. If the elements of production are so distributed, then the present-day distribution of the means of consumption results automatically. If the material conditions of production are the co-operative property of the workers themselves, then there likewise results a distribution of the means of consumption different from the present one. Vulgar socialism (and from it in turn a section of the democracy) has taken over from the bourgeois economists the consideration and treatment of distribution as independent of the mode of production and hence the presentation of socialism as turning principally on distribution. After the real relation has long been made clear, why retrogress again?

. . .

21

On Justice
Under Socialism

EDWARD NELL and ONORA O'NEILL

Edward Nell (b. 1935) teaches economics at The New School for Social Research. He is coauthor of Rational Economic Man: A Philosophical Critique of Neo-Classical Economics. *Onora O'Neill (b. 1941) teaches philosophy at the University of Essex in England. She is the author of* Acting on Principle *and various articles in ethics and political philosophy.*

In this selection, Nell and O'Neill discuss some implications of Marx's principle: "From each according to his ability, to each according to his needs." As they note, this principle seems vulnerable to three objections: it says nothing about distributing goods when all needs cannot be met, it says nothing about distributing unneeded goods, and it does not explain what will motivate people to contribute according to their abilities. By contrast, the capitalist principle, "From each according to his choice, to each according to his contribution," does answer each question. Because of this, the latter may appear the more workable of the two.

Nell and O'Neill, however, disagree. They note, first, that Marx's principle is meant to apply only in the situation of abundance when the forces of production are highly developed. Hence, it will only encounter scarcity if there is insufficient or misdirected motivation to work. But motivation need not pose a difficulty. Once competition gives way to cooperation, and once tedious repetition is replaced by meaningful tasks, work will come to be valued for its own sake. The very act of producing will fill a need, and so no labor will be wasteful. Moreover, even products that do not fulfill biological needs will be needed to help workers "to perform their jobs as well as possible." To guarantee that all the necessary jobs are done, society will channel people's labor through intelligent planning and education. There may indeed be some unpleasant tasks that nobody wants to perform; but once these are reduced to a bare minimum, they can be divided up in some mutually acceptable way. In all, Nell and O'Neill conclude that Marx's principle is indeed workable.

"From each according to his ability, to each according to his need."

THE STIRRING SLOGAN that ends *The Critique of the Gotha Program* is generally taken as a capsule summary of the socialist approach to distributing the burdens and benefits of life. It can be seen as the statement of a noble ideal and yet be found wanting on three separate scores. First, there is no guarantee

that, even if all contribute according to their abilities, all needs can be met: the principle gives us no guidance for distributing goods when some needs must go unmet. Second, if all contribute according to their abilities, there may be a material surplus after all needs are met: again, the principle gives us no guidance for distributing such a surplus. Third, the principle incorporates no suggestion as to why each man would contribute according to his ability: no incentive structure is evident.

These apparent shortcomings can be compared with those of other principles a society might follow in distributing burdens and benefits. Let us call

1. "From each according to his ability to each according to his need," the *Socialist Principle of Justice*. Its Capitalist counterpart would be
2. From each according to his choice, given his assests, to each according to his contribution. We shall call this the *Laissez-Faire Principle*.

These two principles will require a good deal of interpretation, but at the outset we can say that in the Socialist Principle of Justice "abilities" and "needs" refer to persons, whereas the "choices" and "contributions" in the Laissez-Faire Principle refer also to the management of impersonal property, the given assets. It goes without saying that some of the "choices," particularly those of the propertyless, are normally made under considerable duress. As "choice" is the ideologically favored term, we shall retain it.

In a society where the Socialist Principle of Justice regulates distribution, the requirement is that everyone use such talents as have been developed in him (though this need not entail any allocation of workers to jobs), and the payment of workers is contingent not upon their contributions but upon their needs. In a laissez-faire society, where individuals may be endowed with more or less capital or with bare labor power, they choose in the light of these assets how and how much to work (they may be drop-outs or moonlighters), and/or how to invest their capital, and they are paid in proportion.

None of the three objections raised against the Socialist Principle of Justice holds for the Laissez-Faire Principle. Whatever the level of contribution individuals choose, their aggregate product can be distributed in proportion to the contribution—whether of capital or of labor—each individual chooses to make. The Laissez-Faire Principle is applicable under situations both of scarcity and of abundance, and it incorporates a theory of incentives: people choose their level of contribution in order to get a given level of material reward.

Principles 1 and 2 can be cross-fertilized, yielding two further principles:

3. From each according to his ability, to each according to his contribution.
4. From each according to his choice, to each according to his need.

Principle 3 could be called an *Incentive Socialist Principle* of distribution. Like the Socialist Principle of Justice, it pictures a society in which all are required to work in proportion to the talents that have been developed in them. Since unearned income is not available and rewards are hinged to contribution rather than need, all work is easily enforced in an economy based on the Incentive Socialist Principle. This principle, however, covers a considerable

range of systems. It holds for a Stalinist economy with an authoritarian job allocation. It also holds for a more liberal, market socialist economy in which there is a more or less free labor market, though without an option to drop out or live on unearned income, or the freedom to choose the level and type of qualification one is prepared to acquire. The Incentive Socialist Principle rewards workers according to their contribution: it is a principle of distribution in which an incentive system—reliance on material rewards—is explicit. Marx believed this principle would have to be followed in the early stages of socialism, in a society "still stamped with the birthmarks of the old society."

Under the Incentive Socialist Principle, each worker receives back the value of the amount of work he contributes to society in one form or another. According to Marx, this is a form of bourgeois right that "tacitly recognizes unequal individual endowments, and thus natural privileges in respect of productive capacity." So this principle holds for a still deficient society where the needs of particular workers, which depend on many things other than their productive capacity, may not be met. Although it may be less desirable than the Socialist Principle of Justice, the Incentive Socialist Principle clearly meets certain criteria the Socialist Principle of Justice cannot meet. It provides a principle of allocation that can be applied equally well to the various situations of scarcity, sufficiency, and abundance. Its material incentive structure explains how under market socialism, given a capital structure and a skill structure, workers will choose jobs and work hard at them—and also why under a Stalinist economy workers will work hard at jobs to which they have been allocated.

Under the Incentive Socialist Principle, workers—whether assigned to menial work or to specific jobs—respond to incentives of the same sort as do workers under the Laissez-Faire Principle. The difference is that, while the Laissez-Faire Principle leaves the measurement of the contribution of a worker to be determined by the level of wage he is offered, the Incentive Socialist Principle relies on a bureaucratically determined weighting that takes into account such factors as the difficulty, duration, qualification level, and risk involved in a given job.

There is another difference between societies living under the Laissez-Faire Principle and those following the Incentive Socialist Principle. Under the Laissez-Faire Principle, there is no central coordination of decisions, for assets are managed according to the choices of their owners. This gives rise to the well-known problems of instability and unemployment. Under the Incentive Socialist Principle, assets are managed by the central government; hence one would expect instability to be eliminated and full employment guaranteed. However, we do not regard this difference as a matter of principle on the same level with others we are discussing. Moreover, in practice some recognizable capitalist societies have managed to control fluctuations without undermining the Laissez-Faire Principle as the principle of distribution.

Let us call Principle 4 the *Utopian Principle of Justice*. It postulates a society without any requirement of contribution or material incentives, but with guaranteed minimal consumption. This principle suffers from the same defect as the Socialist Principle of Justice: it does not determine distributions of benefits under conditions either of scarcity or of abundance, and it suggests no incentive

structure to explain why enough should be contributed to its economy to make it possible to satisfy needs. Whether labor is contributed according to choice or according to ability, it is conceivable that the aggregate social product should be such that either some needs cannot be met or that, when all needs are met, a surplus remains that cannot be divided on the basis of needs.

On the surface, this Utopian Principle of Justice exudes the aroma of laissez-faire: though needs will not go unmet in utopia, contributions will be made for no more basic reason than individual whim. They are tied neither to the reliable effects of the incentive of material reward for oneself, nor to those of the noble ideal of filling the needs of others, nor to a conception of duty or self-sacrifice. Instead, contributions will come forth, if they do, according to the free and unconstrained choices of individual economic agents, on the basis of their given preferences. Preferences, however, are not "given"; they develop and change, are learned and unlearned, and follow fashions and fads. Whim, fancy, pleasure, desire, wish are all words suggesting this aspect of consumer choice. By tying the demand for products to needs and the supply of work to choice, the Utopian Principle of Justice ensures stability in the former but does not legislate against fluctuations and unpredictable variability in the latter.

So the Socialist Principle of Justice and the Utopian Principle of Justice suffer from a common defect. There is no reason to suppose these systems will operate at precisely the level at which aggregate output is sufficient to meet all needs without surplus. And since people do not need an income in money terms but rather an actual and quite precisely defined list of food, clothing, housing, etc. (bearing in mind the various alternatives that might be substituted), the *aggregate* measured in value terms could be right, yet the *composition* might still be unable to meet all the people's needs. People might choose or have the ability to do the right amount of work, but on the wrong projects. One could even imagine the economy growing from a situation of scarcity to one of abundance without ever passing through any point at which its aggregate output could be distributed to meet precisely the needs of its population.

So far, we have been considering not the justification or desirability of alternative principles of distribution, but their practicality. It appears that, in this respect, principles hinging reward on contribution rather than on need have a great advantage. They can both provide a general principle of distribution and indicate the pattern of incentives to which workers will respond.

It might be held that these advantages are restricted to the Incentive Socialist Principle in its various versions, since under the Laissez-Faire Principle there is some income—property income—which is not being paid in virtue of any contribution. This problem can be dealt with either, as we indicated above, by interpreting the notion of contribution to cover the contribution of one's assets to the capital market, or by restricting the scope of the Laissez-Faire Principle to cover workers only, or by interpreting the notion of property income so as to regard wages as a return to property, i.e., property in one's labor power. One can say that under capitalism part of the aggregate product is set aside for the owners of capital (and another part, as under market socialism, for government expenditure) and the remainder is distributed according to the Laissez-

Faire Principle. Or one may say that property income is paid in virtue of past contributions, whose reward was not consumed at the time it was earned but was stored. Apologists tend to favor interpretations that make the worker a sort of capitalist or the capitalist a sort of slow-consuming worker. Whichever line is taken, it is clear that the Laissez-Faire Principle—however undesirable we may find it—is a principle of distribution that can be of general use in two senses. Appropriately interpreted, it covers the distribution of earned and of unearned income, and it applies in situations both of scarcity and of abundance.

So we seen to have reached the paradoxical conclusion that the principle of distribution requiring that workers' needs be met is of no use in situations of need, since it does not assign priorities among needs, and that the principle demanding that each contribute according to his ability is unable to explain what incentives will lead him to do so. In this view, the Socialist Principle of Justice would have to be regarded as possibly noble but certainly unworkable.

But this view should not be accepted. Marx formulated the Socialist Principle of Justice on the basis of a conception of human abilities and needs that will yield some guidance to its interpretation. We shall now try to see whether the difficulties discussed above can be alleviated when we consider this principle in the light of Marxian theory.

Marx clearly thought that the Socialist Principle of Justice was peculiarly relevant to situations of abundance. In the last section we argued that, on the contrary, it was an adequate principle of distribution only when aggregate output exactly covered total needs. The source of this discrepancy lies in differing analyses of human needs.

By fulfillment of needs we understood at least a subsistence income. Needs are not met when a person lacks sufficient food, clothing, shelter, medical care, or socially necessary training/education. But beyond this biological and social minimum we can point to another set of needs, which men do not have qua men but acquire qua producers. Workers need not merely a biological and social minimum, but whatever other goods—be they holidays or contacts with others whose work bears on theirs or guaranteed leisure, which they need to perform their jobs as well as possible. So a principle of distribution according to needs will not be of use only to a subsistence-level economy. Very considerable goods over and above those necessary for biological subsistence can be distributed according to a principle of need.

But despite this extension of the concept of need the Socialist Principle of Justice still seems to face the three problems listed [earlier].

(1) What guarantees are there that even under abundance the *composition* of the output, with all contributing according to their abilities, will suffice to fill all needs? (There may still be scarcities of goods needed to fill either biological or job-related needs.)

(2) What principle can serve to distribute goods that are surplus both to biological and to job-related needs?

257

(3) What system of incentives explains why each will contribute to the full measure of his abilities, though he is not materially rewarded for increments of effort? Whether or not there is authoritative job allocation, job performance cannot be guaranteed.

Marx's solution to these problems does not seem too explicit. But much is suggested by the passage at the end of the *Critique of the Gotha Program* where he describes the higher phase of communist society as one in which "labor is no longer merely a means of life but has become life's principal need."

To most people it sounds almost comic to claim that labor could become life's principal need: it suggests a society of compulsive workers. Labor in the common view is intrinsically undesirable, but undertaken as a means to some further, typically material, end. For Marx this popular view would have been confirmation of his own view of the degree to which most labor under capitalism is alienating. He thought that under capitalism laborers experienced a threefold alienation: alienation from the *product* of their labor, which is for them merely a means to material reward; alienation from the *process* of labor, which is experienced as forced labor rather than as desirable activity; and alienation from *others,* since activities undertaken with others are undertaken as a means to achieving further ends, which are normally scarce and allocated competitively. Laborers cooperate in production but, under capitalism, compete for job and income, and the competition overrides the cooperation. Hence Marx claims (in the *Economic and Philosophical Manuscripts*) that "life itself appears only as a means to life." Though the horror of that situation is apparent in the very words, many people accept that labor should be only a means to life—whose real ends lie elsewhere; whether in religion, consumption, personal relations, or leisure.

Marx, on the other hand, held that labor could be more than a means; it could also be an end of life, for labor in itself—*the activity*—can, like other activities, be something for whose sake one does other things. We would be loath to think that activity itself should appear only as a means to life—on the contrary, life's worth for most people lies in the activities undertaken. Those we call labor do not differ intrinsically from the rest, only in relation to the system of production. In Marx's view a system was possible in which all activities undertaken would be nonalienating. Nobody would have to compete to engage in an activity he found unpleasant for the sake of a material reward. Instead, workers would cooperate in creative and fulfilling activities that provide occasions for the exercise of talents, for taking responsibilities, and that result in useful or beautiful products. In such a situation one can see why labor would be regarded as life's greatest need, rather than as its scourge. Nonalienated labor is humanly fulfilling activity.

In the course of switching from the conception of alienating labor to that of nonalienating labor, it might seem that we have moved into a realm for which principles of distribution may be irrelevant. What can the Socialist Principle of Justice tell us about the distribution of burdens and benefits in "the higher phase of communist society"?

In such a society each is to contribute according to his abilities. In the light of the discussion of nonalienated labor, it is clear that there is no problem of incentives. Each man works at what he wants to work at. He works because that is his need. (This is not a situation in which "moral incentives" have replaced material ones, for both moral and material incentives are based on alienating labor. The situation Marx envisages is one for which incentives of *all* sorts are irrelevant.)

Though this disposes of the problem of incentives under the Socialist Principle of Justice, it is much less clear whether this principle can work for a reasonable range of situations. Can it cope with both the situation of abundance and that of scarcity?

In the case of abundance, a surplus of goods over and above those needed is provided. But if all activities are need-fulfilling, then no work is done that does not fulfill some need. In a sense there is no surplus to be distributed, for nothing needless is being done. Nevertheless, there may be a surplus of material goods that are the by-product of need-fulfilling activity. In a society where everybody fulfills himself by painting pictures, there may be a vast surplus of pictures. If so, the Socialist Principle of Justice gives no indication of the right method for their distribution; they are not the goal for which the task was undertaken. Since they do not fulfill an objective need, the method for their distribution is not important. In this the higher phase of communist society is, as one might expect, the very antithesis of consumerism; rather than fabricate reasons for desiring and so acquiring what is not needed, it disregards anything that is not needed in decisions of distribution.

There, nevertheless, is a problem of distribution the Socialist Principle of Justice does not attempt to solve. Some of the products of need-fulfilling activity may be things other people either desire or detest. When need-fulfilling activity yields works of art or noisy block parties, its distribution cannot be disregarded. Not all planning problems can be solved by the Socialist Principle of Justice. We shall not discuss the merits of various principles that could serve to handle these cases, but shall only try to delimit the scope of the Socialist Principle of Justice.

This brings us to the problem of scarcity. Can the Socialist Principle of Justice explain why, when all contribute to the extent of their abilities, all needs can be met? Isn't it conceivable that everyone should find fulfillment in painting, but nobody find fulfillment in producing either biological necessities or the canvases, brushes, and paints everybody wants to use? Might not incentive payments be needed, even in this higher phase of communist society, to guarantee the production of subsistence goods and job-related necessities? In short, will not any viable system involve some alienating labor?

Marx at any rate guarantees that communism need not involve much alienating labor. He insists that the Socialist Principle of Justice is applicable only in a context of abundance. For only when man's needs can be met is it relevant to insist that they ought to be met. The Socialist Principle of Justice comes into its own only with the development of the forces of production. But, of course, higher productivity does not by itself guarantee the right composition of output.

Subsistence goods and job-related services and products might not be provided as the population fulfills itself in painting, poetry, and sculpture. Man cannot live by works of art alone.

This socialist version of the story of Midas should not alarm us too much. The possibility of starvation amidst abundant art works seemed plausible only because we abstracted it from other features of an abundant socialist society. Such a society is a planned society, and part of its planning concerns the ability structure of the population. Such a society would include people able to perform all tasks necessary to maintain a high level of material well-being.

Nevertheless, there may be certain essential tasks in such a society whose performance is not need-fulfilling for anybody. Their allocation presents another planning problem for which the Socialist Principle of Justice, by hypothesis, is not a solution. But the degree of coercion need not be very great. In a highly productive society the amount of labor expended on nonfulfilling tasks is a diminishing proportion of total labor time. Hence, given equitable allocation of this burden (and it is here that the planning decisions are really made), nobody would be prevented from engaging principally in need-fulfilling activities. In the limiting case of abundance, where automation of the production of material needs is complete, nobody would have to do any task he did not find intrinsically worthwhile. To the extent that this abundance is not reached, the Socialist Principle of Justice cannot be fully implemented.

However, the degree of coercion, experienced by those who are allocated to necessary but nonfulfilling chores, may be reducible if the planning procedure is of a certain sort. To the extent that people participate in planning and that they realize the necessity of the nonfulfilling chores in order for everyone to be able to do also what he finds need-fulfilling, they may find the performance of these chores less burdensome. As they want to achieve the ends, so—once they are informed—they cannot rationally resent the means, provided they perceive the distribution of chores as just.

The point can be taken a step further. Under the Socialist Principle of Justice, households do not put forth productive effort to be rewarded with an aliquot portion of time and means for self-fulfillment. It is precisely this market mentality from which we wish to escape. The miserable toil of society should be

> performed gratis for the benefit of society . . . performed not as a definite duty, not for the purpose of obtaining a right to certain products, not according to previously established and legally fixed quotas, but voluntary labor . . . performed because it has become a habit to work for the common good, and because of a conscious realization (that has become a habit) of the necessity of working for the common good. [V. I. Lenin, "From the Destruction of the Old Social System to the Creation of the New," April 11, 1920. From *Collected Works,* English trans., 40 vols. (London: Lawrence & Wishart, 1965), vol. 30, p. 517.]

Creative work should be done for its own sake, not for any reward. Drudgery should be done for the common good, not in order to be rewarded with oppor-

tunity and means for creative work. Of course, the better and more efficient the performance of drudgery, the more will be the opportunities for creative work. To realize this, however, is to understand the necessity of working for the common good, not to be animated by private material incentives. For the possibilities of creative work are opened by the simultaneous and parallel development of large numbers of people. To take the arts, poets need a public, authors readers, performers audiences, and all need (though few want) critics. One cannot sensibly wish, under the Socialist Principle of Justice, to be rewarded *privately* with opportunities and means for nonalienated work.

There is a question regarding the distribution of educational opportunities. Before men can contribute according to their abilities, their abilities must be developed. But in whom should society develop which abilities? If we regard education as consumption, then according to the Socialist Principle of Justice, each should receive it according to his need.

It is clear that all men require some early training to make them viable social beings; further, all men require certain general skills necessary for performing work. But we could hardly claim that some men need to be doctors or economists or lawyers, or need to receive any other specialized or expensive training. If, on the other hand, we regard education as production of those skills necessary for maintaining society and providing the possibility of fulfillment, then the Socialist Principle of Justice can determine a lower bound to the production of certain skills: so-and-so many farmers/doctors/mechanics must be produced to satisfy future subsistence and job-related needs. But the Socialist Principle of Justice cannot determine who shall get which of these educational opportunities. One traditional answer might be that each person should specialize at whatever he is relatively best suited to do. Yet this only makes sense in terms of tasks done as onerous means to desirable ends. Specialization on the basis of comparative advantage minimizes the effort in achieving given ends; but if work is itself fulfilling, it is not an "effort" that must be minimized.

In conditions of abundance, it is unlikely that anyone will be denied training they want and can absorb, though they may have to acquire skills they do not particularly want, since some onerous tasks may still have to be done. For even in conditions of abundance, it may be necessary to compel some or all to undertake certain unwanted training in the interests of the whole. But it is not necessary to supplement the Socialist Principle of Justice with an incentive scheme, whether material or moral. The principle already contains the Kantian maxim: develop your talents to the utmost, for only in this way can a person contribute to the limits of his ability. And if a society wills the end of self-fulfillment, it must will sufficient means. If the members of society take part in planning to maintain and expand the opportunities for everyone's nonalienated activity, they must understand the necessity of allocating the onerous tasks, and so the training for them.

Perhaps we can make our point clearer by looking briefly at Marx's schematic conception of the stages of modern history—feudalism, capitalism, socialism, communism—where each state is characterized by a higher productivity of

labor than the preceding stage. In feudalism, the principle of distribution would be:

5. From each according to his status, to each according to his status—the *Feudal Principle of Justice.*

There is no connexion between work and reward. There are no market incentives in the "ideal" feudal system. Peasants grow the stuff for their own subsistence and perform traditional labor services for their lord on domain land. He in turn provides protection and government in traditional fashion. Yet, though labor is not performed as a means to a distant or abstract end, as when it is done for money, it still is done for survival, not for its own sake, and those who do it are powerless to control their conditions of work or their own destinies. Man lives on the edge of famine and is subject to the vagaries of the weather and the dominion of tradition. Only a massive increase in productive powers frees him. But to engender this increase men must come to connect work directly with reward. This provides the incentive to labor, both to take those jobs most needed (moving from the farm to the factory) and to work sufficiently hard once on the job.

But more than work is needed; the surplus of output over that needed to maintain the work force (including managers) and replace and repair the means of production (machines, raw materials) must be put to productive use; it must be reinvested, not consumed. In capitalism, station at birth determines whether one works or owns capital; workers are rewarded for their contribution of work, capitalists for theirs of reinvestment. There is a stick as well as a carrot. Those worker who do not work, starve; those capitalists who fail to reinvest, fail to grow and will eventually be crushed by their larger rivals. Socialism rationalizes this by eliminating the two-class dichotomy and by making reinvestment a function of the institutions of the state, so that the capital structure of the society is the collective property of the citizenry, all of whom must work for reward. In this system the connexion between work and reward reaches its fullest development, and labor in one sense is most fully alienated. The transition to communism then breaks this link altogether.

The link between work and rewards serves a historical purpose, namely to encourage the development of the productive forces. But as the productive forces continue to develop, the demand for additional rewards will tend to decline, while the difficulty of stimulating still further growth in productivity may increase. This, at least, seems to be implied by the principles of conventional economics—diminishing marginal utility and diminishing marginal productivity. Even if one rejects most of the conventional wisdom of economics, a good case can be made for the diminishing efficacy of material incentives as prosperity increases. For as labor productivity rises, private consumption needs will be met, and the most urgent needs remaining will be those requiring *collective* consumption—and, indeed, some of these needs will be generated by the process of growth and technical progress. These last needs, if left unmet, may hinder further attempts to raise the productive power of labor. So the system of material incentives could in principle come to a point where the

weakened encourgements to extra productivity offered as private reward for contribution might be offset by the accumulated hindrances generated by the failures to meet collective needs and by the wastes involved in competition. At this point, it becomes appropriate to breakk the link between work and reward. Breaking the link, however, is not enough. Both the Socialist Principle of Justice and the Utopian Principle of Justice break the link between work and reward. But the Utopian Principle of Justice leaves the distinction between them. Work is a means, the products of work are the ends. Given a high productivity of labor, workers would in principle choose their occupations and work-leisure patterns, yet still producing enough to satisfy everyone's needs. This would be a society devoted to minimizing effort, a sort of high-technology Polynesia. Since it neither makes consumption dependent upon work nor regards work as other than a regrettable means to consumption, it fails to explain why sufficient work to supply basic needs should ever be done. The alienation of labor cannot be overcome by eliminating labor rather than alienation.

Breaking the link between work and reward, while leaving the distinction itself intact, may also lead to the loss of the productive powers of labor. For without reward, and when the object is to work as little as possible, why expend the effort to acquire highly complex skills? What is the motive to education, self-improvement, self-development? A high-technology Polynesia contains an inner contradiction.

By contrast, the Socialist Principle of Justice not only does not make reward depend upon work but denies that there is a distinction between the two. Because man needs fulfilling activity—work that he chooses and wants—men who get it contribute according to their ability.

Yet there still may remain routine and menial, unfulfilling jobs. But who wills the end wills the means. The society must plan to have such jobs done. No doubt, many will be mechanized or automated, but the remaining ones will form a burden that must be allocated.

The Socialist Principle of Justice cannot solve this problem of allocation. But everyone has some interest in getting uncoveted but essential work done. Hence it should not be difficult to find an acceptable supplementary principle of distribution for allocating these chores. For instance, the Principle of Comparative Advantage might be introduced to assign each the drudgery at which he is relatively best. There can be no quarrel with this so long as such alienating work is only a small fraction of a man's total activity, conferring no special status. It is only when alienating work takes up the bulk of one's waking hours, and determines status, that specialization inevitably entails some form of class structure.

The Socialist Principle of Justice cannot solve all allocation problems. But once one understands that it is based on a denial of a distinction between work, need, and reward, it is clear that it can solve an enormous range of such problems. In a highly productive society the only allocation problems the Socialist Principle of Justice cannot solve are the distribution of unmechanized and uncoveted chores and of the material by-products of creative endeavor.

PART II Suggestions For Further Reading

Benn, Stanley and Peters, R. S. *The Principles of Political Thought* (Free Press, 1959)

Cohen, Marshall, Nagel, Thomas, and Scanlon, Thomas, eds. *Marx, Justice, and History* (Princeton University Press, 1980)

Daniels, Norman, ed. *Reading Rawls* (Basic, 1975)

Dworkin, Ronald. *Taking Rights Seriously* (Harvard University Press, 1977)

Feinberg, Joel. *Social Philosophy* (Prentice-Hall, 1973)

Gauthier, David. *The Logic of Leviathan* (Oxford University Press, 1969)

Oakeshott, Michael. *Rationalism in Politics and Other Essays* (Methuen, Inc., 1981)

MacPherson, C. B. *The Political Theory of Possessive Individualism* (Oxford University Press, 1962)

Paul, Jeffery, ed. *Reading Nozick* (Rowman, 1981)

Rousseau, Jean-Jacques. *The Social Contract* (Hafner, 1954)

Simmons, A. John. *Moral Principles and Political Obligation* (Princeton University Press, 1979)

Reiss, Hans, ed. *Kant's Political Writings* (Cambridge University Press, 1970)

Rescher, Nicholas. *Distributive Justice* (Irvington, 1966)

Walzer, Michael. *Radical Principles* (Basic, 1980)

Wolff, Robert Paul. *In Defense of Anarchism* (Harper-Row, 1970)

III

THEORY OF
KNOWLEDGE

MANY YEARS AGO a famous scientist announced that he believed there to be intelligent life not only on earth, but elsewhere in the universe as well. Did he really know this statement to be true? Did he have adequate evidence for it? In order to answer these questions, we would, of course, have to look at the evidence upon which this statement was based. It seems, however, that even after examining the evidence, questions might arise as to whether anyone actually knows if there is intelligent life beyond earth. In order to answer these questions, we must begin to think about the theory of knowledge.

What is involved in knowing a statement to be true, and what is the extent of human knowledge? These are two of the central questions of epistemology, or the theory of knowledge. As we attempt to answer these questions, we will be led to address the wide range of concerns dealt with by the authors in this section.

Consider our first question: What is involved in knowing a statement to be true? Plato (reading 22) provides us with a plausible answer to this question; knowledge requires justified true belief. If I know a statement to be true, I must not only believe that statement to be true; it must in fact be true. In addition, I must have good reason to believe the statement true; that is, my belief must be justified.

This answer, while it seems to be correct as far as it goes, leads us to other questions. First, as Edmund Gettier shows in reading 23, knowledge seems to require more than justified true belief. Even if we could say what else knowledge

requires, however, there are still other questions to answer. Under what conditions is a person justified in believing a statement to be true? What makes some reasons for believing a statement good reasons and others bad reasons?

According to René Descartes (reading 24), we know a statement to be true just in case it is impossible for us to be mistaken about that statement. Thus our reasons for believing a statement true are good reasons just in case they leave no room for error. If Descartes is right about this, then there is an obvious way to go about answering our second question, the question about the extent of human knowledge. First, we must isolate a class of statements about which it is impossible to be wrong; Descartes, as well as subsequent writers, speaks of these statements as the foundation of knowledge. Second, we must construct arguments using statements from the foundation of knowledge as premises, and proceed by a series of steps about which it is also impossible to be wrong. Our knowledge extends as far as the conclusions of such arguments, and no further. It is well worth asking, if one accepts Descartes's conception of human knowledge, how far knowledge extends. The answer to this question is by no means obvious.

In John Locke (reading 25), we see quite a different approach to epistemological questions. ". . . how foolish and vain a thing it is . . . ," Locke insists, ". . . to expect demonstration and certainty in things not capable of it . . ." (IV, xi 10). It is clear, Locke argues, that it is possible to be mistaken in one's beliefs about the external world; our beliefs about physical objects fall short of Descartes's standard of absolute certainty. Nevertheless, our understanding of the physical world is a paradigm of knowledge, and if these beliefs fall short of absolute certainty this only shows that Descartes was mistaken to set the standards for knowledge so high. Accordingly, Locke examines our beliefs about the physical world in search of the features that make them reasonable, and the features that make it reasonable for us to regard them as knowledge. Our knowledge of the physical world, Locke argues, is based on experience. Locke attempts to explain how experience provides adequate ground for such knowledge.

The difference between Locke's approach and Descartes's should be of concern to all who care about knowledge. On the one hand, good common sense requires that we have at least some knowledge of the physical world. On the other hand, a theory of knowledge should be something more than a rubber stamp, certifying as genuine knowledge whatever beliefs we had before we began our theorizing. Many of the authors in this section attempt to set a standard for knowledge which steers between skepticism and dogmatism. They also try to explain what it is about such a standard that makes it worthy of the name "knowledge." All of the authors in this section give ample testimony to the difficulty of steering such a course.

The subject of special concern in the selection written by David Hume (reading 26) is our knowledge of the future. All of us believe that the future will, in relevant respects, be like the past. Moreover, such a belief seems clearly justified by the evidence of our senses. As Hume argues, however, any attempt to show

that we do indeed have reason to believe that the future will be like the past is doomed to circularity. In attempting to show that the future will resemble the past, we must assume the very conclusion we are trying to prove. If this is the best we can do in justifying our beliefs about the future, it is hard to see why we should claim that this is an area in which we might have knowledge. Nelson Goodman (reading 27) shows that the problem is even deeper than Hume imagined. Goodman suggests that the circularity involved in showing our beliefs about the future to be justified is much more subtle than Hume suggested, for it does not involve an argument in which one of the premises is identical to the conclusion. Goodman argues that the special kind of circularity involved allows for genuine justification. His view is a far cry from Descartes's project of setting knowledge on its proper foundation. According to Goodman, knowledge neither has nor needs such a foundation.

The attack on the suggestion that there is a foundation for knowledge is broadened in the selections by W. V. O. Quine and Michael Williams (readings 28, 29 and 30). Quine argues that all our beliefs are interdependent, that modification of any of our beliefs may ultimately affect any others. If Quine is correct, there is no Cartesian foundation for knowledge, no class of statements about which it is impossible to be wrong. Williams argues in particular against the suggestion that our knowledge of the physical world rests on a foundation of statements given to us through sensation. (This view is most clearly represented in reading 25 by John Locke.)

Many may wonder what remains in the concept of knowledge if the foundation of knowledge is rejected. It is important to remember that neither Quine nor Williams are skeptics. They do not seek to show that there is no such thing as knowledge, but rather that knowledge is very different than we might have thought. Not just any reconstruction of the concept of knowledge will do, of course. At the very least, we will want to know what it is about knowledge that makes it worthy of our pursuit.

Quine's positive views about knowledge are presented in his second selection, "The Nature of Natural Knowledge." Here Quine argues that the doubts that have led some philosophers to skepticism can be turned back through an understanding of the relevance of the theory of evolution to traditional epistemological questions. Very roughly, Quine suggests that the fact that our species has survived as long as it has constitutes strong evidence that our beliefs are at least roughly correct. Were our beliefs completely wrong, the species would have died out long ago. Alvin Goldman (reading 31) also champions this Darwinian approach in his attempt to explain the possibility of innate knowledge. It is interesting to compare the work of each of these authors with the selection from Friedrich Nietzsche (reading 32), in which a radically different slant is given to the role of evolution in belief acquisition. Read side by side, Quine, Goldman, and Nietzsche illustrate how the point and counterpoint of skepticism have progressed since Descartes.

The last two readings in this section by T. S. Kuhn and Philip Kitcher are concerned with the nature of scientific knowledge. Contemporary scientific

theorizing provides us with the clearest example of the achievement of human knowledge. Thus, if we wish to investigate what knowledge is and how it is acquired, we would do well to examine the development of scientific theory.

Kuhn (reading 33) is concerned with the topic of theory change: Why is it that scientists sometimes give up one theory and come to believe another? In particular, Kuhn is concerned with the extent to which the values of individual scientists affect the theories each accepts, and the extent to which theory choice proceeds on objective grounds. Kuhn denies that objective grounds are available for deciding between every pair of competing theories. He likens disputes between scientists to disputes in which the parties involved do not share a common language. Communication in this kind of situation is fraught with limitations. This, Kuhn claims, is an essential part of the development of science. Kitcher, too, is concerned with the reasons for which theories are rejected or accepted (reading 34). After he explains why scientific theories can never be properly said to be either proved or disproved, Kitcher develops an account of the hallmarks of good scientific theorizing.

In the face of all these controversies, the motivation for epistemological theorizing should not be lost. Descartes, perhaps, put the point best. At the opening of the *First Meditation* (reading 24), Descartes notes that he has in the past had many false beliefs; it would be surprising if many of his current beliefs were not false as well. Descartes attempts to discover what knowledge is in the hope that he might thereby better achieve it. We might all try to follow his example.

22

Knowledge as Justified True Belief

PLATO

For biographical information about Plato, see reading 13.

In this dialogue, Socrates and Theaetetus discuss the nature of knowledge. Theaetetus initially suggests knowledge is nothing more than true belief, but this analysis is quickly shown to be inadequate. It is then suggested that knowledge is true belief together with an account, or, what present day philosophers would refer to as true belief together with justification. The bulk of this selection examines this notion of having an account. Socrates argues that in order for one's account to be adequate for knowledge, it must not only be a correct account; it must be known to be correct. This makes the analysis of knowledge circular: one has knowledge just in case one has true belief together with an account that one knows to be correct. We explain what it is to know something in terms of the very concept we seek to explain. As Socrates and Theaetetus note, this is a highly unsatisfying result. Nevertheless, it is important to see that this result is not completely empty. We began by asking what knowledge is, and we have seen that in order to answer that question we must first find out what it is to have a proper account. In this way, Plato sets the stage for a further line of philosophical enquiry.

. . .

SOCRATES: To start all over again, then, what is one to say that knowledge is? For surely we are not going to give up yet.

THEAETETUS: Not unless you do so.

SOCRATES: Then tell me, what definition can we give with the least risk of contradicting ourselves?

THEAETETUS: The one we tried before, Socrates. I have nothing else to suggest.

SOCRATES: What was that?

THEAETETUS: That true belief is knowledge. Surely there can at least be no mistake in believing what is true and the consequences are always satisfactory.

SOCRATES: Try, and you will see, Theaetetus, as the man said when he was asked if the river was too deep to ford. So here, if we go forward on our search, we may stumble upon something that will reveal the thing we are looking for. We shall make nothing out, if we stay where we are.

THEAETETUS: True. Let us go forward and see.

SOCRATES: Well, we need not go far to see this much. You will find a whole profession to prove that true belief is not knowledge.

THEAETETUS: How so? What profession?

SOCRATES: The profession of those paragons of intellect known as orators and lawyers. There you have men who use their skill to produce conviction, not by instruction, but by making people believe whatever they want them to believe. You can hardly imagine teachers so clever as to be able, in the short time allowed by the clock, to instruct their hearers thoroughly in the true facts of a case of robbery or other violence which those hearers had not witnessed.

THEAETETUS: No, I cannot imagine that, but they can convince them.

SOCRATES: And by convincing you mean making them believe something.

THEAETETUS: Of course.

SOCRATES: And when a jury is rightly convinced of facts which can be known only by an eyewitness, then, judging by hearsay and accepting a true belief, they are judging without knowledge, although, if they find the right verdict, their conviction is correct?

THEAETETUS: Certainly.

SOCRATES: But if true belief and knowledge were the same thing, the best of jurymen could never have a correct belief without knowledge. It now appears that they must be different things.

THEAETETUS: Yes, Socrates, I have heard someone make the distinction. I had forgotten, but now it comes back to me. He said that true belief with the addition of an account (λόγος) was knowledge, while belief without an account was outside its range. Where no account could be given of a thing, it was not 'knowable'—that was the word he used—where it could, it was knowable.

SOCRATES: A good suggestion. But tell me how he distinguished these knowable things from the unknowable. It may turn out that what you were told tallies with something I have heard said.

THEAETETUS: I am not sure if I can recall that, but I think I should recognize it if I heard it stated.

SOCRATES: If you have had a dream, let me tell you mine in return. I seem to have heard some people say that what might be called the first elements of which we and all other things consist are such that no account can be given of them. Each of them just by itself can only be named; we cannot attribute to it anything further or say that it exists or does not exist, for we should at once be attaching to it existence or nonexistence, whereas we ought to add nothing if we are to express just it alone. We ought not even to add 'just' or 'it' or 'each' or 'alone' or 'this,' or any other of a host of such terms. These terms, running loose about the place, are attached to everything, and they are distinct from the things to which they are applied. If it were possible for an element to be expressed in any formula exclusively belonging to it, no other terms ought to enter into that expression. But in fact there is no formula in which any element can be expressed; it can only be named, for a name is all there is that belongs to it. But when we come to things composed of these elements, then, just as these things are complex, so the names are combined to make a description (λόγος), a description being precisely a combination

of names. Accordingly, elements are inexplicable and unknowable, but they can be perceived, while complexes ('syllables') are knowable and explicable, and you can have a true notion of them. So when a man gets hold of the true notion of something without an account, his mind does think truly of it, but he does not know it, for if one cannot give and receive an account of a thing, one has no knowledge of that thing. But when he has also got hold of an account, all this becomes possible to him and he is fully equipped with knowledge.

Does that version represent the dream as you heard it, or not?

THEAETETUS: Perfectly.

SOCRATES: So this dream finds favor and you hold that a true notion with the addition of an account is knowledge?

THEAETETUS: Precisely.

SOCRATES: Can it be, Theaetetus, that, all in a moment, we have found out today what so many wise men have grown old in seeking and have not found?

THEAETETUS: I, at any rate, am satisfied with our present statement, Socrates.

SOCRATES: Yes, the statement just in itself may well be satisfactory, for how can there ever be knowledge without an account and right belief? But there is one point in the theory as stated that does not find favor with me.

THEAETETUS: What is that?

SOCRATES: What might be considered its most ingenious feature. It says that the elements are unknowable, but whatever is complex ('syllables') can be known.

THEAETETUS: Is not that right?

SOCRATES: We must find out. We hold as a sort of hostage for the theory the illustration in terms of which it was stated.

THEAETETUS: Namely?

SOCRATES: Letters—the elements of writing—and syllables. That and nothing else was the prototype the author of this theory had in mind, don't you think?

THEAETETUS: Yes, it was.

SOCRATES: Let us take up that illustration, then, and put it to the question, or rather put the question to ourselves. Did we learn our letters on that principle or not? To begin with, is it true that an account can be given of syllables, but not of letters?

THEAETETUS: It may be so.

SOCRATES: I agree, decidedly. Suppose you are asked about the first syllable of 'Socrates.' Explain, Theaetetus, what is SO? How will you answer?

THEAETETUS: S and O.

SOCRATES: And you have there an account of the syllable?

THEAETETUS: Yes.

SOCRATES: Go on, then, give me a similar account of S.

THEAETETUS: But how can one state the elements of an element? The fact is, of course, Socrates, that S is one of the consonants, nothing but a noise, like a hissing of the tongue, while B not only has no articulate sound but is not even a noise, and the same is true of most of the letters. So they may well be

said to be inexplicable, when the clearest of them, the seven vowels themselves, have only a sound, and no sort of account can be given of them.

SOCRATES: So far, then, we have reached a right conclusion about knowledge.

THEAETETUS: Apparently.

SOCRATES: But now, have we been right in declaring that the letter cannot
be known, though the syllable can?

THEAETETUS: That seems all right.

SOCRATES: Take the syllable then. Do we mean by that both the two letters
or, if there are more than two, all the letters? Or do we mean a single entity
that comes into existence from the moment when they are put together?

THEAETETUS: I should say we mean all the letters.

SOCRATES: Then take the case of the two letters S and O. The two together
are the first syllable of my name. Anyone who knows that syllable knows
both the letters, doesn't he?

THEAETETUS: Naturally,

SOCRATES: So he knows the S and the O.

THEAETETUS: Yes.

SOCRATES: But has he, then, no knowledge of *each* letter, so that he knows
both without knowing either?

THEAETETUS: That is a monstrous absurdity, Socrates.

SOCRATES: And yet, if it is necessary to know each of two things before one
can know both, he simply must know the letters first, if he is ever to know
the syllable, and so our fine theory will vanish and leave us in the lurch.

THEAETETUS: With a startling suddenness.

SOCRATES: Yes, because we are not keeping a good watch upon it. Perhaps
we ought to have assumed that the syllable was not the letters but a single
entity that arises out of them with a unitary character of its own and different
from the letters.

THEAETETUS: By all means. Indeed, it may well be so rather than the other
way.

SOCRATES: Let us consider that. We ought not to abandon an imposing theory in this poor-spirited manner.

THEAETETUS: Certainly not.

SOCRATES: Suppose, then, it is as we say now. The syllable arises as a single
entity from any set of letters which can be combined, and that holds of every
complex, not only in the case of letters.

THEAETETUS: By all means.

SOCRATES: In that case, it must have no parts.

THEAETETUS: Why?

SOCRATES: Because, if a thing has parts, the whole thing must be the same
as all the parts. Or do you say that a whole likewise is a single entity that
arises out of the parts and is different from the aggregate of the parts?

THEAETETUS: Yes, I do.

SOCRATES: Then do you regard the sum (τὸ zso παν) as the same thing as
the whole, or are they different?

272

THEAETETUS: I am not at all clear, but you tell me to answer boldly, so I will take the risk of saying they are different.

SOCRATES: Your boldness, Theaetetus, is right; whether your answer is so, we shall have to consider.

THEAETETUS: Yes, certainly.

SOCRATES: Well, then, the whole will be different from the sum, according to our present view.

THEAETETUS: Yes.

SOCRATES: Well but now, is there any difference between the sum and all the things it includes? For instance, when we say, 'one, two, three, four, five, six,' or 'twice three' or 'three times two' or 'four and two' or 'three and two and one,' are we in all these cases expressing the same thing or different things?

THEAETETUS: The same.

SOCRATES: Just six, and nothing else?

THEAETETUS: Yes.

SOCRATES: In fact, in each form of expression we have expressed all the six.

THEAETETUS: Yes.

SOCRATES: But when we express them all, is there no sum that we express?

THEAETETUS: There must be.

SOCRATES: And is that sum anything else than 'six'?

THEAETETUS: No.

SOCRATES: Then, at any rate in the case of things that consist of a number, the words 'sum' and 'all the things' denote the same thing.

THEAETETUS: So it seems.

SOCRATES: Let us put our argument, then, in this way. The number of [square feet in] an acre, and the acre are the same thing, aren't they?

THEAETETUS: Yes.

SOCRATES: And so too with the number of [feet in] a mile?

THEAETETUS: Yes.

SOCRATES: And again with the number of [soldiers in] an army and the army, and so on, in all cases. The total number is the same as the total thing in each case.

THEAETETUS: Yes.

SOCRATES: But the number of [units in] any collection of things cannot be anything but *parts* of that collection?

THEAETETUS: No.

SOCRATES: Now, anything that has parts consists of parts.

THEAETETUS: Evidently.

SOCRATES: But all the parts, we have agreed, are the same as the sum, if the total number is to be the same as the total thing.

THEAETETUS: Yes.

SOCRATES: The whole, then, does not consist of parts, for if it were all the parts it would be a sum.

THEAETETUS: Apparently not.

SOCRATES: But can a part be a part of anything but its whole?

THEAETETUS: Yes, of the sum.

SOCRATES: You make a gallant fight of it, Theaetetus. But does not 'the sum' mean precisely something from which nothing is missing?

THEAETETUS: Necessarily.

SOCRATES: And is not a whole exactly the same thing—that from which nothing whatever is missing? Whereas, when something is removed, the thing becomes neither a whole nor a sum; it changes at the same moment from being both to being neither.

THEAETETUS: I think now that there is no difference between a sum and a whole.

SOCRATES: Well, we were saying, were we not, that when a thing has parts, the whole or sum will be the same thing as all the parts?

THEAETETUS: Certainly.

SOCRATES: To go back, then, to the point I was trying to make just now, if the syllable is not the same thing as the letters, does it not follow that it cannot have the letters as parts of itself; otherwise, being the same thing as the letters, it would be neither more nor less knowable than they are?

THEAETETUS: Yes.

SOCRATES: And it was to avoid that consequence that we supposed the syllable to be different from the letters.

THEAETETUS: Yes.

SOCRATES: Well, if the letters are not parts of the syllable, can you name any things, other than its letters, that are parts of a syllable?

THEAETETUS: Certainly not, Socrates. If I admitted that it had any parts, it would surely be absurd to set aside the letters and look for parts of any other kind.

SOCRATES: Then, on the present showing, a syllable will be a thing that is absolutely one and cannot be divided into parts of any sort?

THEAETETUS: Apparently.

SOCRATES: Do you remember then, my dear Theaetetus, our accepting a short while ago a statement that we thought satisfactory—that no account could be given of the primary things of which other things are composed, because each of them, taken just by itself, was incomposite, and that it was not correct to attribute even 'existence' to it, or to call it 'this,' on the ground that these words expressed different things that were extraneous to it, and this was the ground for making the primary thing inexplicable and unknowable?

THEAETETUS: I remember.

SOCRATES: Then is not exactly this, and nothing else, the ground of its being simple in nature and indivisible into parts? I can see no other.

THEAETETUS: Evidently there is no other.

SOCRATES: Then has not the syllable now turned out to be a thing of the same sort, if it has no parts and is a unitary thing?

THEAETETUS: Certainly.

SOCRATES: To conclude, then, if, on the one hand, the syllable is the same thing as a number of letters and is a whole with the letters as its parts, then

the letters must be neither more nor less knowable and explicable than syllables, since we made out that all the parts are the same thing as the whole.

THEAETETUS: True.

SOCRATES: But if, on the other hand, the syllable is a unity without parts, syllable and letter likewise are equally incapable of explanation and unknowable. The same reason will make them so.

THEAETETUS: I see no way out of that.

SOCRATES: If so, we must not accept this statement—that the syllable can be known and explained, the letter cannot.

THEAETETUS: No, not if we hold by our argument.

SOCRATES: And again, would not your own experience in learning your letters rather incline you to accept the opposite view?

THEAETETUS: What view do you mean?

SOCRATES: This—that all the time you were learning you were doing nothing else but trying to distinguish by sight or hearing each letter by itself, so as not to be confused by any arrangement of them in spoken or written words.

THEAETETUS: That is quite true.

SOCRATES: And in the music school the height of accomplishment lay precisely in being able to follow each several note and tell which string it belonged to, and notes, as everyone would agree, are the elements of music.

THEAETETUS: Precisely.

SOCRATES: Then, if we are to argue from our own experience of elements and complexes to other cases, we shall conclude that elements in general yield knowledge that is much clearer than knowledge of the complex and more effective for a complete grasp of anything we seek to know. If anyone tells us that the complex is by its nature knowable, while the element is unknowable, we shall suppose that, whether he intends it or not, he is playing with us.

THEAETETUS: Certainly.

SOCRATES: Indeed we might, I think, find other arguments to prove that point. But we must not allow them to distract our attention from the question before us, namely, what can really be meant by saying that an account added to true belief yields knowledge in its most perfect form.

THEAETETUS: Yes, we must see what that means.

SOCRATES: Well then, what is this term 'account' intended to convey to us? I think it must mean one of three things.

THEAETETUS: What are they?

SOCRATES: The first will be giving overt expression to one's thought by means of vocal sound with names and verbs, casting an image of one's notion on the stream that flows through the lips, like a reflection in a mirror or in water. Do you agree that expression of that sort is an 'account'?

THEAETETUS: I do. We certainly call that expressing ourselves in speech (λέγειν).

SOCRATES: On the other hand, that is a thing that anyone can do more or less readily. If a man is not born deaf or dumb, he can signify what he thinks on any subject. So in this sense anyone whatever who has a correct notion

evidently will have it 'with an account,' and there will be no place left anywhere for a correct notion apart from knowledge.

THEAETETUS: True.

SOCRATES: Then we must not be too ready to charge the author of the definition of knowledge now before us with talking nonsense. Perhaps that is not what he meant. He may have meant being able to reply to the question, what any given thing is, by enumerating its elements.

THEAETETUS: For example, Socrates?

SOCRATES: For example, Hesiod says about a wagon, 'In a wagon are a hundred pieces of wood.' I could not name them all; no more, I imagine, could you. If we were asked what a wagon is, we should be content if we could mention wheels, axle, body, rails, yoke.

THEAETETUS: Certainly.

SOCRATES: But I dare say he would think us just as ridiculous as if we replied to the question about your own name by telling the syllables. We might think and express ourselves correctly, but we should be absurd if we fancied ourselves to be grammarians and able to give such an account of the name Theaetetus as a grammarian would offer. He would say it is impossible to give a scientific account of anything, short of adding to your true notion a complete catalogue of the elements, as, I think, was said earlier.

THEAETETUS: Yes, it was.

SOCRATES: In the same way, he would say, we may have a correct notion of the wagon, but the man who can give a complete statement of its nature by going through those hundred parts has thereby added an account to his correct notion and, in place of mere belief, has arrived at a technical knowledge of the wagon's nature, by going through all the elements in the whole.

THEAETETUS: Don't you approve, Socrates?

SOCRATES: Tell me if you approve, my friend, and whether you accept the view that the complete enumeration of elements is an account of any given thing, whereas description in terms of syllables or of any larger unit still leaves it unaccounted for. Then we can look into the matter further.

THEAETETUS: Well, I do accept that.

SOCRATES: Do you think, then, that anyone has knowledge of whatever it may be, when he thinks that one and the same thing is a part sometimes of one thing, sometimes of a different thing, or again when he believes now one and now another thing to be part of one and the same thing?

THEAETETUS: Certainly not.

SOCRATES: Have you forgotten, then, that when you first began learning to read and write, that was what you and your school-fellows did?

THEAETETUS: Do you mean, when we thought that now one letter and now another was part of the same syllable, and when we put the same letter sometimes into the proper syllable, sometimes into another?

SOCRATES: That is what I mean.

THEAETETUS: Then I have certainly not forgotten, and I do not think that one has reached knowledge so long as one is in that condition.

SOCRATES: Well then, if at that stage you are writing 'Theaetetus' and you

think you ought to write T and H and E and do so, and again when you are
trying to write 'Theodorus,' you think you ought to write T and E and do
so, can we say that you know the first syllable of your two names?

THEAETETUS: No, we have just agreed that one has not knowledge so long
as one is in that condition.

SOCRATES: And there is no reason why a person should not be in the same
condition with respect to the second, third, and fourth syllables as well?

THEAETETUS: None whatever.

SOCRATES: Can we, then, say that whenever in writing 'Theaetetus' he puts
down all the letters in order, then he is in possession of the complete catalogue
of elements together with correct belief?

THEAETETUS: Obviously.

SOCRATES: Being still, as we agree, without knowledge, though his beliefs
are correct?

THEAETETUS: Yes.

SOCRATES: Although he possesses the 'account' in addition to right belief.
For when he wrote he was in possession of the catalogue of the elements,
which we agreed was the 'account.'

THEAETETUS: True.

SOCRATES: So, my friend, there is such a thing as right belief together with
an account, which is not yet entitled to be called knowledge.

THEAETETUS: I am afraid so.

SOCRATES: Then, apparently, our idea that we had found the perfectly true
definition of knowledge was no better than a golden dream. Or shall we not
condemn the theory yet? Perhaps the meaning to be given to 'account' is not
this, but the remaining one of the three, one of which we said must be
intended by anyone who defines knowledge as correct belief together with
an account.

THEAETETUS: A good reminder. There is still one meaning left. The first was
what might be called the image of thought in spoken sound, and the one we
have just discussed was going all through the elements to arrive at the whole.
What is the third?

SOCRATES: The meaning most people would give—being able to name some
mark by which the thing one is asked about differs from everything else.

THEAETETUS: Could you give me an example of such an account of a thing?

SOCRATES: Take the sun as an example. I dare say you will be satisfied with
the account of it as the brightest of the heavenly bodies that go round the
earth.

THEAETETUS: Certainly.

SOCRATES: Let me explain the point of this example. It is to illustrate what
we were just saying—that if you get hold of the difference distinguishing any
given thing from all others, then, so some people say, you will have an
'account' of it, whereas, so long as you fix upon something common to other
things, your account will embrace all the things that share it.

THEAETETUS: I understand. I agree that what you describe may fairly be
called an 'account.'

SOCRATES: And if, besides a right notion about a thing, whatever it may be, you also grasp its difference from all other things, you will have arrived at knowledge of what, till then, you had only a notion of.

THEAETETUS: We do say that, certainly.

SOCRATES: Really, Theaetetus, now I come to look at this statement at close quarters, it is like a scene painting. I cannot make it out at all, though, so long as I kept at a distance, there seemed to be some sense in it.

THEAETETUS: What do you mean? Why so?

SOCRATES: I will explain, if I can. Suppose I have a correct notion about you; if I add to that the account of you, then, we are to understand, I know you. Otherwise I have only a notion.

THEAETETUS: Yes.

SOCRATES: And 'account' means putting your differentness into words.

THEAETETUS: Yes.

SOCRATES: So, at the time when I had only a notion, my mind did not grasp any of the points in which you differ from others?

THEAETETUS: Apparently not.

SOCRATES: Then I must have had before my mind one of those common things which belong to another person as much as to you.

THEAETETUS: That follows.

SOCRATES: But look here! If that was so, how could I possibly be having a notion of you rather than of anyone else? Suppose I was thinking, Theaetetus is one who is a man and has a nose and eyes and a mouth and so forth, enumerating every part of the body. Will thinking in that way result in my thinking of Theaetetus rather than of Theodorus or, as they say, of the man in the street?

THEAETETUS: How should it?

SOCRATES: Well, now suppose I think not merely of a man with a nose and eyes, but of one with a snub nose and prominent eyes. Once more shall I be having a notion of you any more than of myself or anyone else of that description?

THEAETETUS: No.

SOCRATES: In fact, there will be no notion of Theaetetus in my mind, I suppose, until this particular snubness has stamped and registered within me a record distinct from all the other cases of snubness that I have seen, and so with every other part of you. Then, if I meet you tomorrow, that trait will revive my memory and give me a correct notion about you.

THEAETETUS: Quite true.

SOCRATES: If that is so, the correct notion of anything must itself include the differentness of that thing.

THEAETETUS: Evidently.

SOCRATES: Then what meaning is left for getting hold of an 'account' in addition to the correct notion? If, on the one hand, it means adding the notion of how a thing differs from other things, such an injunction is simply absurd.

THEAETETUS: How so?

SOCRATES: When we have a correct notion of the way in which certain things differ from other things, it tells us to add a correct notion of the way in which they differ from other things. On this showing, the most vicious of circles would be nothing to this injunction. It might better deserve to be called the sort of direction a blind man might give. To tell us to get hold of something we already have, in order to get to know something we are already thinking of, suggests a state of the most absolute darkness.

THEAETETUS: Whereas, if . . . ? The supposition you made just now implied that you would state some alternative. What was it?

SOCRATES: If the direction to add an 'account' means that we are to get to *know* the differentness, as opposed to merely having a notion of it, this most admirable of all definitions of knowledge will be a pretty business, because 'getting to know' means acquiring knowledge, doesn't it?

THEAETETUS: Yes.

SOCRATES: So, apparently, to the question, 'What is knowledge?' our definition will reply, 'Correct belief together with knowledge of a differentness,' for, according to it, 'adding an account' will come to that.

THEAETETUS: So it seems.

SOCRATES: Yes, and when we are inquiring after the nature of knowledge, nothing could be sillier than to say that it is correct belief together with a *knowledge* of differentness or of anything whatever.

So, Theaetetus, neither perception, nor true belief, nor the addition of an 'account' to true belief can be knowledge.

THEAETETUS: Apparently not.

SOCRATES: Are we in labor, then, with any further child, my friend, or have we brought to birth all we have to say about knowledge?

THEAETETUS: Indeed we have, and for my part I have already, thanks to you, given utterance to more than I had in me.

SOCRATES: All of which our midwife's skill pronounces to be mere wind eggs and not worth the rearing?

THEAETETUS: Undoubtedly.

SOCRATES: Then supposing you should ever henceforth try to conceive afresh, Theaetetus, if you succeed, your embryo thoughts will be the better as a consequence of today's scrutiny, and if you remain barren, you will be gentler and more agreeable to your companions, having the good sense not to fancy you know what you do not know. For that, and no more, is all that my art can effect; nor have I any of that knowledge possessed by all the great and admirable men of our own day or of the past. But this midwife's art is a gift from heaven; my mother had it for women, and I for young men of a generous spirit and for all in whom beauty dwells.

Now I must go to the portico of the King-Archon to meet the indictment which Meletus has drawn up against me. But tomorrow morning, Theodorus, let us meet here again.

23

Is Justified True Belief Knowledge?

EDMUND L. GETTIER

Edmund Gettier III (b. 1927) is Professor of Philosophy at the University of Massachusetts at Amherst.

We have seen in the previous selection by Plato that the analysis of knowledge as justified true belief is just the beginning of a proper understanding of knowledge, for the notion of justification—or having an account, as Plato put it—needs further explanation. In this selection, Gettier shows that the justified true belief analysis is deficient in another respect as well. Whatever account of justification is given, knowledge requires more than justified true belief. Gettier answers his title question by constructing several clear examples of justified true belief that are not knowledge.

VARIOUS ATTEMPTS HAVE BEEN MADE in recent years to state necessary and sufficient conditions* for someone's knowing a given proposition. The attempts have often been such that they can be stated in a form similar to the following:[1]

    (a) S knows that P   *IFF*   (i) P is true,
                                     (ii) S believes that P, and
                                     (iii) S is justified in believing that P.

For example, Chisholm has held that the following gives the necessary and sufficient conditions for knowledge:[2]

    (b) S knows that P   *IFF*   (i) S accepts P,
                                     (ii) S has adequate evidence for P, and
                                     (iii) P is true.

---

* A is a necessary condition for B just in case if B is true, A is true as well. A is a sufficient condition for B just in case if A is true, B is true. A is both necessary and sufficient for B just in case A is true if and only if B is true.

[1] Plato seems to be considering some such definition at *Theaetetus* 201, and perhaps accepting one at *Meno* 98.

[2] Roderick M. Chisholm, *Perceiving: A Philosophical Study*, Cornell University Press (Ithaca, New York, 1957), p. 16.

Ayer has stated the necessary and sufficient conditions for knowledge as follows:[3]

> (c) S knows that P *IFF* (i) P is true,
>   (ii) S is sure that P is true, and
>   (iii) S has the right to be sure that P is true.

I shall argue that (a) is false in that the conditions stated therein do not constitute a *sufficient* condition for the truth of the proposition that S knows that P. The same argument will show that (b) and (c) fail if 'has adequate evidence for' or 'has the right to be sure that' is substituted for 'is justified in believing that' throughout.

I shall begin by noting two points. First, in that sense of 'justified' in which S's being justified in believing P is a necessary condition of S's knowing that P, it is possible for a person to be justified in believing a proposition that is in fact false. Secondly, for any proposition P, if S is justified in believing P, and P entails Q, and S deduces Q from P and accepts Q as a result of this deduction, then S is justified in believing Q. Keeping these two points in mind, I shall now present two cases in which the conditions stated in (a) are true for some proposition, though it is at the same time false that the person in question knows that proposition.

Case I

Suppose that Smith and Jones have applied for a certain job. And suppose that Smith has strong evidence for the following conjunctive proposition:

> (d) Jones is the man who will get the job, and Jones has ten coins in his pocket.

Smith's evidence for (d) might be that the president of the company assured him that Jones would in the end be selected, and that he, Smith, had counted the coins in Jones's pocket ten minutes ago. Proposition (d) entails:

> (e) The man who will get the job has ten coins in his pocket.

Let us suppose that Smith sees the entailment from (d) to (e), and accepts (e) on the grounds of (d), for which he has strong evidence. In this case, Smith is clearly justified in believing that (e) is true.

But imagine, further, that unknown to Smith, he himself, not Jones, will get the job. And, also, unknown to Smith, he himself has ten coins in his pocket. Proposition (e) is then true, though proposition (d), from which Smith inferred (e), is false. In our example, then, all of the following are true: (*i*) (e) is true, (*ii*) Smith believes that (e) is true, and (*iii*) Smith is justified in believing that (e)

---

[3] A. J. Ayer, *The Problem of Knowledge*, Macmillan (London, 1956), p. 34

is true. But it is equally clear that Smith does not *know* that (e) is true; for (e) is true in virtue of the number of coins in Smith's pocket, while Smith does not know how many coins are in Smith's pocket, and bases his belief in (e) on a count of the coins in Jones's pocket, whom he falsely believes to be the man who will get the job.

Case II

Let us suppose that Smith has strong evidence for the following proposition:

(f) Jones owns a Ford.

Smith's evidence might be that Jones has at all times in the past within Smith's memory owned a car, and always a Ford, and that Jones has just offered Smith a ride while driving a Ford. Let us imagine, now, that Smith has another friend, Brown, of whose whereabouts he is totally ignorant. Smith selects three place names quite at random and constructs the following three propositions:

(g) Either Jones owns a Ford, or Brown is in Boston.
(h) Either Jones owns a Ford, or Brown is in Barcelona.
(i) Either Jones owns a Ford, or Brown is in Brest-Litovsk.

Each of these propositions is entailed by (f). Imagine that Smith realizes the entailment of each of these propositions he has constructed by (f), and proceeds to accept (g), (h), and (i) on the basis of (f). Smith has correctly inferred (g), (h), and (i) from a proposition for which he has strong evidence. Smith is therefore completely justified in believing each of these three propositions. Smith, of course, has no idea where Brown is.

But imagine now that two further conditions hold. First, Jones does *not* own a Ford, but is at present driving a rented car. And secondly, by the sheerest coincidence, and entirely unknown to Smith, the place mentioned in proposition (h) happens really to be the place where Brown is. If these two conditions hold, then Smith does *not* know that (h) is true, even though (*i*) (h) *is* true, (*ii*) Smith does believe that (h) is true, and (*iii*) Smith is justified in believing that (h) is true.

These two examples show that definition (a) does not state a *sufficient* condition for someone's knowing a given proposition. The same cases, with appropriate changes, will suffice to show that neither definition (b) nor definition (c) do so either.

24

Certain Knowledge

RENÉ DESCARTES

René Descartes (1596–1650) made major contributions to geometry, in addition to his work in philosophy. He is regarded as the founder of modern philosophy, and his approach to epistemological questions defined the field for centuries. Descartes's best-known works are the Meditations on First Philosophy *and the* Discourse on Method.

Descartes begins this selection from the Meditations *by noting that he has discovered that many of his current beliefs are mistaken. Descartes's situation, of course, is not unique. All of us have discovered at times that we had mistaken beliefs, thus we all probably have many mistaken beliefs right now. The question is, of course, what are we to do about this? Descartes suggests that first we suspend belief on all topics where there is room to doubt our current beliefs are true. Thus we will arrive at beliefs whose truth it is impossible to doubt. Having eliminated all beliefs that leave room for error, we may build upon this foundation of indubitable beliefs in a way that continues to insure immunity from doubt.*

This, in outline, is Descartes's project. In the First Meditation, *Descartes argues that we have some reason to doubt the truth of each of our beliefs about the physical world. We must therefore suspend belief in the existence of the physical world. In the* Second Meditation, *Descartes argues that there is one thing beyond doubt: his own existence. If Descartes's project is to be carried out, then it must be possible to derive all of our knowledge from beliefs that, like the belief each of us has in our own existence, are beyond doubt.*

FIRST MEDITATION

What can be called in Question

SOME YEARS AGO NOW I observed the multitude of errors that I had accepted as true in my earliest years, and the dubiousness of the whole superstructure I had since then reared on them; and the consequent need of making a clean sweep for once in my life, and beginning again from the very foundations, if I would establish some secure and lasting result in science. But the task appeared enormous, and I put it off till I should reach such a mature age that no increased aptitude for learning anything was likely to follow. Thus I delayed so long that

283

now it would be blameworthy to spend in deliberation what time I have left for action. Today is my chance; I have banished all care from mind, I have secured myself peace, I have retired by myself; at length I shall be at leisure to make a clean sweep, in all seriousness and with full freedom, of all my opinions.

To this end I shall not have to show they are all false, which very likely I could never manage; but reason already convinces me that I must withhold assent no less carefully from what is not plainly certain and indubitable than from what is obviously false; so the discovery of some reason for doubt as regards each opinion will justify the rejection of all. This will not mean going over each of them—an unending task; when the foundation is undermined, the superstructure will collapse of itself; so I will proceed at once to attack the very principles on which all my former beliefs rested.

What I have so far accepted as true *par excellence,* I have got either from the senses or by means of the senses. Now I have sometimes caught the senses deceiving me; and a wise man never entirely trusts those who have once cheated him.

'But although the senses may sometimes deceive us about some minute or remote objects, yet there are many other facts as to which doubt is plainly impossible, although these are gathered from the same source: e.g. that I am here, sitting by the fire, wearing a winter cloak, holding this paper in my hands, and so on. Again, these hands, and my whole body—how can their existence be denied? Unless indeed I likened myself to some lunatics, whose brains are so upset by persistent melancholy vapours that they firmly assert they are kings, when really they are miserably poor; or that they are clad in purple, when really they are naked; or that they have a head of pottery, or are pumpkins, or are made of glass; but then they are madmen, and I should appear no less mad if I took them as a precedent for my own case.'

A fine argument! As though I were not a man who habitually sleeps at night and has the same impressions (or even wilder ones) in sleep as these men do when awake! How often, in the still of the night, I have the familiar conviction that I am here, wearing a cloak, sitting by the fire—when really I am undressed and lying in bed! 'But now at any rate I am looking at this paper with wide-awake eyes; the head I am now shaking is not asleep; I put out this hand deliberately and consciously; nothing so distinct would happen to one asleep.' As if I did not recall having been deceived before by just such thoughts in sleep! When I think more carefully about this, I see so plainly that sleep and waking can never be distinguished by any certain signs, that I am bewildered; and this itself confirms the idea of my being asleep.

'Well, suppose I am dreaming, and these particulars, that I open my eyes, shake my head, put out my hand, are incorrect, suppose even that I have no such hand, no such body; at any rate it has to be admitted that the things that appear in sleep are like painted representations, which cannot have been formed except in the likeness of real objects. So at least these general kinds of things, eyes, head, hands, body, must be not imaginary but real objects. Painters themselves, even when they are striving to create sirens and satyrs with the most extraordinary forms, cannot give them wholly new natures, but only mix up

the limbs of different animals; or even if they did devise something so novel that nothing at all like it had ever been seen, something wholly fictitious and unreal, at least they must use real colours in its make-up. Similarly, even if these general kinds of things, eyes, head, hands and so on, could be imaginary, at least it must be admitted that some simple and more universal kinds of things are real, and are as it were the real colours out of which there are formed in our consciousness *(cogitatione)* all our pictures of real and unreal things. To this class there seem to belong: corporeal nature in general, and its extension; the shape of extended objects; quantity, or the size and number of these objects; place for them to exist in, and time for them to endure through; and so on.

'At this rate we might be justified in concluding that whereas physics, astronomy, medicine, and all other sciences depending on the consideration of composite objects, are doubtful; yet arithmetic, geometry, and so on, which treat only of the simplest and most general subject matter, and are indifferent whether it exists in nature or not, have an element of indubitable certainty. Whether I am awake or asleep, two and three add up to five, and a square has only four sides; and it seems impossible for such obvious truths to fall under a suspicion of being false.'

But there has been implanted in my mind the old opinion that there is a God who can do everything, and who made me such as I am. How do I know he has not brought it about that, while in fact there is no earth, no sky, no extended objects, no shape, no size, no place, yet all these things should appear to exist as they do now? Moreover, I judge that other men sometimes go wrong over what they think they know perfectly well; may not God likewise make me go wrong, whenever I add two and three, or count the sides of a square, or do any simpler thing that might be imagined? 'But perhaps it was not God's will to deceive me so; he is after all called supremely good.' But if it goes against his goodness to have so created me that I am always deceived, it seems no less foreign to it to allow me to be deceived sometimes; and this result cannot be asserted.

Perhaps some people would deny that there is a God powerful enough to do this, rather than believe everything else is uncertain. Let us not quarrel with them, and allow that all I have said about God is a fiction. But whether they ascribe my attaining my present condition to fate, or to chance, or to a continuous series of events, or to any other cause, delusion and error certainly seem to be imperfections, and so this ascription of less power to the source of my being will mean that I am more likely to be so imperfect that I always go wrong. I have no answer to these arguments; I am obliged in the end to admit that none of my former ideas are beyond legitimate doubt; and this, not from inconsideration or frivolity, but for strong and well-thought-out reasons. So I must carefully withhold assent from them just as if they were plainly false, if I want to find any certainty.

But it is not enough to have observed this; I must take care to bear it in mind. My ordinary opinions keep on coming back; and they take possession of my belief, on which they have a lien by long use and the right of custom, even against my will. I shall never get out of the habit of assenting to and trusting

285

them, so long as I have a view of them answering to their real nature; namely, that they are doubtful in a way, as has been shown, but are yet highly probable, and far more reasonably believed than denied. So I think it will be well to turn my will in the opposite direction; deceive myself, and pretend they are wholly false and imaginary; until in the end the influence of prejudice on either side is counterbalanced, and no bad habit can any longer deflect my judgment from a true perception of facts. For I am sure no danger or mistake can happen in the process, and I cannot be indulging my scepticism more than I ought; because I am now engaged, not in action, but only in thought.

I will suppose, then, not that there is a supremely good God, the source of truth; but that there is an evil spirit, who is supremely powerful and intelligent, and does his utmost to deceive me. I will suppose that sky, air, earth, colours, shapes, sounds and all external objects are mere delusive dreams, by means of which he lays snares for my credulity. I will consider myself as having no hands, no eyes, no flesh, no blood, no senses, but just having a false belief that I have all these things. I will remain firmly fixed in this meditation, and resolutely take care that, so far as in me lies, even if it is not in my power to know some truth, I may not assent to falsehood nor let myself be imposed upon by that deceiver, however powerful and intelligent he may be. But this plan is irksome, and sloth brings me back to ordinary life. I am like a prisoner who happens to enjoy an imaginary freedom during sleep, and then begins to suspect he is asleep; he is afraid to wake up, and connives at the agreeable illusion. So I willingly slip back into my old opinions, and dread waking up, in case peaceful rest should be followed by the toil of waking life, and I should henceforth have to live, not in the light, but amid the inextricable darkness of the problems I raised just now.

SECOND MEDITATION

The Nature of the Human Mind: it is better known than the Body

Yesterday's meditation plunged me into doubts of such gravity that I cannot forget them, and yet do not see how to resolve them. I am bewildered, as though I had suddenly fallen into a deep sea, and could neither plant my foot on the bottom nor swim up to the top. But I will make an effort, and try once more the same path as I entered upon yesterday; I will reject, that is, whatever admits of the least doubt, just as if I had found it was wholly false; and I will go on until I know something for certain—if it is only this, that there is nothing certain. Archimedes asked only for one fixed and immovable point so as to move the whole earth from its place; so I may have great hopes if I find even the least thing that is unshakably certain.

I suppose, therefore, that whatever things I see are illusions; I believe that none of the things my lying memory represents to have happened really did so; I have no senses; body, shape, extension, motion, place are chimeras. What then is true? Perhaps only this one thing, that nothing is certain.

How do I know, however, that there is not something different from all the things I have mentioned, as to which there is not the least occasion of doubt?—Is there a God (or whatever I call him) who gives me these very thoughts? But why, on the other hand, should I think so? Perhaps I myself may be the author of them.—Well, am *I*, at any rate, something?—'But I have already said I have no senses and no body—' At this point I stick; what follows from this? Am I so bound to a body and its senses that without them I cannot exist?—'But I have convinced myself that nothing in the world exists—no sky, no earth, no minds, no bodies; so am not I likewise non-existent?' But if I did convince myself of anything, I must have existed. 'But there is some deceiver, supremely powerful, supremely intelligent, who purposely always deceives me.' If he deceives me, then again I undoubtedly exist; let him deceive me as much as he may, he will never bring it about that, at the time of thinking *(quamdiu cogitabo)* that I am something, I am in fact nothing. Thus I have now weighed all considerations enough and more than enough; and must at length conclude that this proposition 'I am', 'I exist', whenever I utter it or conceive it in my mind, is necessarily true.

But I do not yet sufficiently understand what is this 'I' that necessarily exists. I must take care, then, that I do not rashly take something else for the 'I', and thus go wrong even in the knowledge that I am maintaining to be the most certain and evident of all. So I will consider afresh what I believe myself to be before I happened upon my present way of thinking; from this conception I will subtract whatever can be in the least shaken by the arguments adduced, so that what at last remains shall be precisely the unshakably certain element.

What, then, did I formerly think I was? A man. But what is a man? Shall I say 'a rational animal'? No; in that case I should have to go on to ask what an animal is and what 'rational' is, and so from a single question I should fall into several of greater difficulty; and I have not now the leisure to waste on such subtleties. I will rather consider what used to occur to me spontaneously and naturally whenever I was considering the question 'what am I?' First came the thought that I had a face, hands, arms—in fact the whole structure of limbs that is observable also in a corpse, and that I called 'the body'. Further, that I am nourished, that I move, that I have sensations *(sentire),* that I am conscious *(cogitare);* these acts I assigned to the soul. But as to the nature of this soul, either it did not attract my attention, or else I fancied something subtle like air or fire or aether mingled among the grosser parts of my body. As regards 'body' I had no doubt, and I thought I distinctly understood its nature; if I had tried to describe my conception, I might have given this explanation: 'By *body* I mean whatever is capable of being bounded by some shape, and comprehended by some place, and of occupying space in such a way that all other bodies are excluded; moreover of being perceived by touch, sight, hearing, taste, or smell; and further, of being moved in various ways, not of itself but by some other body that touches it.' For the power of self-movement, and the further powers of sensation and consciousness *(sentiendi, vel cogitandi),* I judged not to belong in any way to the essence of body *(naturam corporis);* indeed, I marvelled even that there were some bodies in which such faculties were found.

What am I to say now, when I am supposing that there is some all-powerful and (if it be lawful to say this) malignant deceiver, who has taken care to delude me about everything as much as he can? Can I, in the first place, say I have the least part of the characteristics that I said belonged to the essence of body? I concentrate, I think, I consider; nothing comes to mind; it would be wearisome and futile to repeat the reasons. Well, what of the properties I ascribed to the soul? Nutrition and locomotion? Since I have no body, these are mere delusions. Sensation? This cannot happen apart from a body; and in sleep I have seemed to have sensations that I have since realised never happened. Consciousness (cogitare)? At this point I come to the fact that there is consciousness (or experience: cogitatio); of this and this only I cannot be deprived. I am, I exist; that is certain. For how long? For as long as I am experiencing (cogito), maybe, if I wholly ceased from experiencing (ab omni cogitatione), I should at once wholly cease to be. For the present I am admitting only what is necessarily true; so 'I am' precisely taken refers only to a conscious being; that is a mind, a soul (animus), an intellect, a reason—words whose meaning I did not previously know. I am a real being, and really exist; but what sort of being? As I said, a conscious being (cogitans).

What now? I will use my imagination. I am not that set of limbs called the human body; I am not some rarefied gas infused into those limbs—air or fire or vapour or exhalation or whatever I may picture to myself; all these things I am supposing to be nonentities. But I still have the assertion 'nevertheless I am something'. 'But perhaps it is the case that these very things which I suppose to be nonentities, and which are not properly known to me, are yet in reality not different from the "I" of which I am aware?' I do not know, and will not dispute the point; I can judge only about the things I am aware of. I am aware of my own existence; I want to know what is this 'I' of which I am aware. Assuredly, the conception of this 'I', precisely as such, does not depend on things of whose existence I am not yet aware; nor, therefore, on what I feign in my imagination. And this very word 'feign' shows me my mistake; it would indeed be a fiction to *imagine* myself to be anything, for imagination consists in contemplating the likeness or picture of a body. Now I know for certain that I am, and that at the same time it is possible that all these images, and in general everything of the nature of body, are mere dreams. When I consider this, it seems as absurd to say 'I will use my imagination, so as to recognise more distinctly who I am', as though I were to say 'I am awake now, and discern some truth; but I do not yet see it clearly enough; so I will set about going to sleep, so that my dreams may give me a truer and clearer picture of the fact'. So I know that nothing I can comprehend by the help of imagination belongs to my conception of myself; the mind's attention must be carefully diverted from these things, so that she may discern her own nature as distinctly as possible.

What then am I? A conscious being (res cogitans). What is that? A being that doubts, understands, asserts, denies, is willing, is unwilling; further, that has sense and imagination. These are a good many properties—if only they all

belong to me. But how can they fail to? Am *I* not the very person who is now 'doubting' almost everything; who 'understands' something and 'asserts' this one thing to be true, and 'denies' other things; who 'is willing' to know more, and 'is unwilling' to be deceived; who 'imagines' many things, even involuntarily, and perceives many things coming as it were from the 'senses'? Even if I am all the while asleep; even if my creator does all he can to deceive me; how can any of these things be less of a fact than my existence? Is any of these something distinct from my consciousness *(cogitatione)?* Can any of them be called a separate thing from myself? It is so clear that it is I who doubt, understand, will, that I cannot think how to explain it more clearly. Further, it is I who imagine; for even if, as I supposed, no imagined object is real, yet the power of imagination really exists and goes to make up my experience *(cogitationis).* Finally, it is I who have sensations, or who perceive corporeal objects as it were by the senses. Thus, I am now seeing light, hearing a noise, feeling heat. These objects are unreal, for I am asleep; but at least I seem to see, to hear, to be warmed. This cannot be unreal; and this is what is properly called my sensation; further, sensation, precisely so regarded, is nothing but an act of consciousness *(cogitare).*

From these considerations I begin to be a little better acquainted with myself. But it still appears, and I cannot help thinking, that corporeal objects, whose images are formed in consciousness *(cogitatione),* and which the senses actually examine, are known far more distinctly than this 'I', this 'something I know not what', which does not fall under imagination. It is indeed surprising that I should comprehend more distinctly things that I can tell are doubtful, unknown, foreign to me, than what is real, what I am aware of—my very self. But I can see how it is; my mind takes pleasure in wandering, and is not yet willing to be restrained within the bounds of truth. So be it, then; just this once I will ride her on a loose rein, so that in good time I may pull her up and that thereafter she may more readily let me control her.

Consider the objects commonly thought to be the most distinctly known, the bodies we touch and see. I will take, not body in general, for these generic concepts *(perceptiones)* are often the more confused, but one particular body; say, this wax. It has just been extracted from the honeycomb; it has not completely lost the taste of the honey; it retains some of the smell of the flowers from which it was gathered; its colour, shape, size are manifest; it is hard, cold, and easily handled, and gives out a sound if you rap it with your knuckle; in fact it has all the properties that seem to be needed for our knowing a body with the utmost distinctness. But while I say this, the wax is put by the fire. It loses the remains of its flavour, the fragrance evaporates, the colour changes, the shape is lost, the size increases; it becomes fluid and hot, it can hardly be handled, and it will no longer give out a sound if you rap it. Is the same wax, then, still there? 'Of course it is; nobody denies it, nobody thinks otherwise.' Well, what was in this wax that was so distinctly known? Nothing that I got through the senses; for whatever fell under taste, smell, sight, touch, or hearing has now changed; yet the wax is still there.

'Perhaps what I distinctly knew was what I am now thinking of: namely, that the wax was not the sweetness, nor the fragrance of the flowers, nor the whiteness, nor the shape, nor the sound, but body; manifested to me previously in those aspects, and now in others.' But what exactly am I thus imagining? Let us consider; let us remove what is not proper to the wax and see what is left: simply, something extended, flexible, and changeable. But what is its being 'flexible' and 'changeable'? Does it consist in my imagining the wax to be capable of changing from a round shape to a square one and from that again to a triangular one? By no means; for I comprehend its potentiality for an infinity of such changes, but I cannot run through an infinite number of them in imagination; so I do not comprehend them by my imaginative power. What again is its being 'extended'? Is this likewise unknown? For extension grows greater when the wax melts, greater still when it boils, and greater still again with increase of heat; and I should mistake the nature of wax if I did not think this piece capable also of more changes, as regards extension, than my imagination has ever grasped. It remains then for me to admit that I know the nature even of this piece of wax not by imagination, but by purely mental perception. (I say this as regards a particular piece of wax; it is even clearer as regards wax in general.) What then is this wax, perceived only by the mind? It is the very same wax as I see, touch, and imagine—that whose existence I believed in originally. But it must be observed that perception of the wax is not sight, not touch, not imagination; nor was it ever so, though it formerly seemed to be; it is a purely mental contemplation *(inspectio);* which may be either imperfect or confused, as it originally was, or clear and distinct, as it now is, according to my degree of attention to what it consists in.

But it is surprising how prone my mind is to errors. Although I am considering these points within myself silently and without speaking, yet I stumble over words and am almost deceived by ordinary language. We say we see the wax itself, if it is there; not that we judge from its colour or shape that it is there. I might at once infer: I see the wax by ocular vision, not by merely mental contemplation. I chanced, however, to look out of the window, and see men walking in the street; now I say in ordinary language that I 'see' them, just as I 'see' the wax; but what can I 'see' besides hats and coats, which may cover automata? I judge that they are men; and similarly, the objects that I thought I saw with my eyes, I really comprehend only by my mental power of judgment.

It is disgraceful that a man seeking to know more than the mass of mankind should have sought occasions for doubt in popular modes of speech! Let us go on, and consider when I perceived the wax more perfectly and manifestly; was it when I first looked at it, and thought I was aware of it by my external senses, or at least by the so-called 'common' sense, i.e. the imaginative faculty? or is it rather now, after careful investigation of its nature and of the way that I am aware of it? It would be silly to doubt as to the matter; for what was there distinct in my original perception? Surely any animal could have one just as good. But when I distinguish the wax from its outward form, and as it were unclothe it and consider it in its naked self, I get something which, mistaken as my judgment may still be, I need a human mind to perceive.

What then am I to say about this mind, that is, about myself? (So far, I allow of no other element in myself except mind.) What is the 'I' that seems to perceive this wax so distinctly? Surely I am aware of myself not only much more truly and certainly, but also much more distinctly and manifestly. For if I judge that wax exists from the fact that I see this wax, it is much clearer that I myself exist because of this same fact that I see it. Possibly what I see is not wax; possibly I have no eyes to see anything; but it is just not possible, when I see or (I make no distinction here) I think I see *(cogitem me videre)*, that my conscious self *(ego ipse cogitans)* should not be something. Similarly, if I judge that wax exists from the fact that I touch this wax, the same result follows: I exist. If I judge this from the fact that I imagine it, or for some other reason, it is just the same. These observations about the wax apply to all external objects. Further, if the perception of the wax is more distinct when it has become known to me not merely by sight or by touch, but from a plurality of sources; how much more distinct than this must I admit my knowledge of myself to be! No considerations can help towards my perception of the wax or any other body, without at the same time all going towards establishing the nature of my mind. And the mind has such further resources within itself from which its self-knowledge may be made more distinct, that the information thus derived from the body appears negligible.

I have thus got back to where I wanted; I now know that even bodies are not really perceived by the senses or the imaginative faculty, but only by intellect; that they are perceived, not by being touched or seen, but by being understood; I thus clearly recognise that nothing is more easily or manifestly perceptible to me than my own mind. But because the habit of old opinion is not to be laid aside so quickly, I will stop here, so that by long meditation I may imprint this new knowledge deep in my memory.

25

Empiricism

JOHN LOCKE

For biographical information about John Locke, see reading 15.

In this selection from An Essay Concerning Human Understanding, *Locke argues that all our ideas can be traced to two sources: sensation and reflection on the operations of the mind. All our knowledge is thus derived from these two sources, and our knowledge of the physical world has its source in sensation alone. Locke makes clear that we cannot be absolutely certain of the existence of the external world; to use Descartes's terminology, its existence is not indubitable. Nevertheless, we clearly do have knowledge of the external world. For example, when I look at a table I come to know that there is a table in front of me. Moreover, it seems quite clear that this knowledge is based on my having a certain sort of sense experience. Locke's task is to explain how our sensations provide us with good reason for our beliefs about the world.*

Of Ideas in General and Their Original.

1. Every man being conscious to himself that he thinks; and that which his mind is applied about whilst thinking being the *ideas* that are there, it is past doubt that men have in their minds several ideas,—such as are those expressed by the words *whiteness, hardness, sweetness, thinking, motion, man, elephant, army, drunkenness,* and others: it is in the first place then to be inquired, *How he comes by them?*

I know it is a received doctrine, that men have native ideas, and original characters, stamped upon their minds in their very first being. This opinion I have at large examined already; and, I suppose what I have said in the foregoing Book will be much more easily admitted, when I have shown whence the understanding may get all the ideas it has; and by what ways and degrees they may come into the mind;—for which I shall appeal to every one's own observation and experience.

2. Let us then suppose the mind to be, as we say, white paper, void of all characters, without any ideas:—How comes it to be furnished? Whence comes it by that vast store which the busy and boundless fancy of man has painted on it with an almost endless variety? Whence has it all the *materials* of reason and knowledge? To this I answer, in one word, from EXPERIENCE. In that all our knowledge is founded; and from that it ultimately derives itself. Our observation employed either, about external sensible objects, or about the internal operations of our minds perceived and reflected on by ourselves, is that which

supplies our understandings with all the *materials* of thinking. These two are the fountains of knowledge, from whence all the ideas we have, or can naturally have, do spring.

3. First, our Senses, conversant about particular sensible objects, do convey into the mind several distinct perceptions of things, according to those various ways wherein those objects do affect them. And thus we come by those *ideas* we have of *yellow, white, heat, cold, soft, hard, bitter, sweet,* and all those which we call sensible qualities; which when I say the senses convey into the mind, I mean, they from external objects convey into the mind what produces there those perceptions. This great source of most of the ideas we have, depending wholly upon our senses, and derived by them to the understanding, I call SENSATION.

4. Secondly, the other fountain from which experience furnisheth the understanding with ideas is,—the perception of the operations of our own mind within us, as it is employed about the ideas it has got;—which operations, when the soul comes to reflect on and consider, do furnish the understanding with another set of ideas, which could not be had from things without. And such are *perception, thinking, doubting, believing, reasoning, knowing, willing,* and all the different actings of our own minds;—which we being conscious of, and observing in ourselves, do from these receive into our understandings as distinct ideas as we do from bodies affecting our senses. This source of ideas every man has wholly in himself; and though it be not sense, as having nothing to do with external objects, yet it is very like it, and might properly enough be called *internal sense.* But as I call the other Sensation, so I call this REFLECTION, the ideas it affords being such only as the mind gets by reflecting on its own operations within itself. By reflection then, in the following part of this discourse, I would be understood to mean, that notice which the mind takes of its own operations, and the manner of them, by reason whereof there come to be ideas of these operations in the understanding. These two, I say, viz. external material things, as the objects of SENSATION, and the operations of our own minds within, as the objects of REFLECTION, are to me the only originals from whence all our ideas take their beginnings. The term *operations* here I use in a large sense, as comprehending not barely the actions of the mind about its ideas, but some sort of passions arising sometimes from them, such as is the satisfaction or uneasiness arising from any thought.

5. The understanding seems to me not to have the least glimmering of any ideas which it doth not receive from one of these two. *External objects* furnish the mind with the ideas of sensible qualities, which are all those different perceptions they produce in us; and *the mind* furnishes the understanding with ideas of its own operations.

These, when we have taken a full survey of them, and their several modes, [combinations, and relations,] we shall find to contain all our whole stock of ideas; and that we have nothing in our minds which did not come in one of these two ways. Let any one examine his own thoughts, and thoroughly search into his understanding; and then let him tell me, whether all the original ideas he has there, are any other than of the objects of his senses, or of the operations

of his mind, considered as objects of his reflection. And how great a mass of knowledge soever he imagines to be lodged there, he will, upon taking a strict view, see that he has not any idea in his mind but what one of these two have imprinted;—though perhaps, with infinite variety compounded and enlarged by the understanding, as we shall see hereafter.

6. He that attentively considers the state of a child, at his first coming into the world, will have little reason to think him stored with plenty of ideas, that are to be the matter of his future knowledge. It is *by degrees* he comes to be furnished with them. And though the ideas of obvious and familiar qualities imprint themselves before the memory begins to keep a register of time or order, yet it is often so late before some unusual qualities come in the way, that there are few men that cannot recollect the beginning of their acquaintance with them. And if it were worth while, no doubt a child might be so ordered as to have but a very few, even of the ordinary ideas, till he were grown up to a man. But all that are born into the world, being surrounded with bodies that perpetually and diversely affect them, variety of ideas, whether care be taken of it or not, are imprinted on the minds of children. Light and colours are busy at hand everywhere, when the eye is but open; sounds and some tangible qualities fail not to solicit their proper senses, and force an entrance to the mind;—but yet, I think, it will be granted easily, that if a child were kept in a place where he never saw any other but black and white till he were a man, he would have no more ideas of scarlet or green, than he that from his childhood never tasted an oyster, or a pine-apple, has of those particular relishes.

7. Men then come to be furnished with fewer or more simple ideas from without, according as the objects they converse with afford greater or less variety; and from the operations of their minds within, according as they more or less reflect on them. For, though he that contemplates the operations of his mind, cannot but have plain and clear ideas of them; yet, unless he turn his thoughts that way, and considers them *attentively,* he will no more have clear and distinct ideas of all the operations of his mind, and all that may be observed therein, than he will have all the particular ideas of any landscape, or of the parts and motions of a clock, who will not turn his eyes to it, and with attention heed all the parts of it. The picture, or clock may be so placed, that they may come in his way every day; but yet he will have but a confused idea of all the parts they are made up of, till he applies himself with attention, to consider them each in particular.

8. And hence we see the reason why it is pretty late before most children get ideas of the operations of their own minds; and some have not any very clear or perfect ideas of the greatest part of them all their lives. Because, though they pass there continually, yet, like floating visions, they make not deep impressions enough to leave in their mind clear, distinct, lasting ideas, till the understanding turns inward upon itself, reflects on its own operations, and makes them the objects of its own contemplation. Children [when they come first into it, are surrounded with a world of new things, which, by a constant solicitation of their senses, draw the mind constantly to them; forward to take notice of new, and apt to be delighted with the variety of changing objects.

Thus the first years are usually employed and diverted in looking abroad. Men's business in them is to acquaint themselves with what is to be found without;] and so growing up in a constant attention to outward sensations, seldom make any considerable reflection on what passes within them, till they come to be of riper years; and some scarce ever at all.

9. To ask, at what *time* a man has first any ideas, is to ask, when he begins to perceive;—*having ideas*, and *perception* being the same thing. I know it is an opinion, that the soul always thinks, and that it has the actual perception of ideas in itself constantly, as long as it exists; and that actual thinking is as inseparable from the soul as actual extension is from the body; which if true, to inquire after the beginning of a man's ideas is the same as to inquire after the beginning of his soul. For, by this account, soul and its ideas, as body and its extension, will begin to exist both at the same time.

10. But whether the soul be supposed to exist antecedent to, or coeval with, or some time after the first rudiments of organization, or the beginnings of life in the body, I leave to be disputed by those who have better thought of that matter. I confess myself to have one of those dull souls, that doth not perceive itself always to contemplate ideas; nor can conceive it any more necessary for the soul always to think, than for the body always to move: the perception of ideas being (as I conceive) to the soul, what motion is to the body; not its essence, but one of its operations. And therefore, though thinking be supposed never so much the proper action of the soul, yet it is not necessary to suppose that it should be always thinking, always in action. That, perhaps, is the privilege of the infinite Author and Preserver of all things, who 'never slumbers nor sleeps'; but is not competent to any finite being, at least not to the soul of man. We know certainly, by experience, that we *sometimes* think; and thence draw this infallible consequence,—that there is something in us that has a power to think. But whether that substance *perpetually* thinks or no, we can be no further assured than experience informs us. For, to say that actual thinking is essential to the soul, and inseparable from it, is to beg what is in question, and not to prove it by reason;—which is necessary to be done, if it be not a self-evident proposition. But whether this, 'That the soul always thinks,' be a self-evident proposition, that everybody assents to at first hearing, I appeal to mankind. It is doubted whether I thought at all last night or no. The question being about a matter of fact, it is begging it to bring, as a proof for it, an hypothesis, which is the very thing in dispute: by which way one may prove anything, and it is but supposing that all watches, whilst the balance beats, think, and it is sufficiently proved, and past doubt, that my watch thought all last night. But he that would not deceive himself, ought to build his hypothesis on matter of fact, and make it out by sensible experience, and not presume on matter of fact, because of his hypothesis, that is, because he supposes it to be so; which way of proving amounts to this, that I must necessarily think all last night, because another supposes I always think, though I myself cannot perceive that I always do so.

But men in love with their opinions may not only suppose what is in question, but allege wrong matter of fact. How else could any one make it an inference

of mine, that a thing is not, because we are not sensible of it in our sleep? I do not say there is no *soul* in a man, because he is not sensible of it in his sleep; but I do say, he cannot *think* at any time, waking or sleeping, without being sensible of it. Our being sensible of it is not necessary to anything but to our thoughts; and to them it is; and to them it always will be necessary, till we can think without being conscious of it.

11. I grant that the soul, in a waking man, is never without thought, because it is the condition of being awake. But whether sleeping without dreaming be not an affection of the whole man, mind as well as body, may be worth a waking man's consideration; it being hard to conceive that anything should think and not be conscious of it. If the soul doth think in a sleeping man without being conscious of it, I ask whether, during such thinking, it has any pleasure or pain, or be capable of happiness or misery? I am sure the man is not; no more than the bed or earth he lies on. For to be happy or miserable without being conscious of it, seems to me utterly inconsistent and impossible. Or if it be possible that the *soul* can, whilst the body is sleeping, have its thinking, enjoyments, and concerns, its pleasures or pain, apart, which the *man* is not conscious of nor partakes in,—it is certain that Socrates asleep and Socrates awake is not the same person; but his soul when he sleeps, and Socrates the man, consisting of body and soul, when he is waking, are two persons: since waking Socrates has no knowledge of, or concernment for that happiness or misery of his soul, which it enjoys alone by itself whilst he sleeps, without perceiving anything of it; no more than he has for the happiness or misery of a man in the Indies, whom he knows not. For, if we take wholly away all consciousness of our actions and sensations, especially of pleasure and pain, and the concernment that accompanies it, it will be hard to know wherein to place personal identity.

12. The soul, during sound sleep, thinks, say these men. Whilst it thinks and perceives, it is capable certainly of those of delight or trouble, as well as any other perceptions; and *it* must necessarily be *conscious* of its own perceptions. But it has all this apart: the sleeping *man*, it is plain, is conscious of nothing of all this. Let us suppose, then, the soul of Castor, while he is sleeping, retired from his body; which is no impossible supposition for the men I have here to do with, who so liberally allow life, without a thinking soul, to all other animals. These men cannot then judge it impossible, or a contradiction, that the body should live without the soul; nor that the soul should subsist and think, or have perception, even perception of happiness or misery, without the body. Let us then, I say, suppose the soul of Castor separated during his sleep from his body, to think apart. Let us suppose, too, that it chooses for its scene of thinking the body of another man, v. g. Pollux, who is sleeping without a soul. For, if Castor's soul can think, whilst Castor is asleep, what Castor is never conscious of, it is no matter what *place* it chooses to think in. We have here, then, the bodies of two men with only one soul between them, which we will suppose to sleep and wake by turns; and the soul still thinking in the waking man, whereof the sleeping man is never conscious, has never the least perception. I ask, then, whether Castor and Pollux, thus with only one soul between

them, which thinks and perceives in one what the other is never conscious of, nor is concerned for, are not two as distinct *persons* as Castor and Hercules, or as Socrates and Plato were? And whether one of them might not be very happy, and the other very miserable? Just by the same reason, they make the soul and the man two persons, who make the soul think apart what the man is not conscious of. For, I suppose nobody will make identity of persons to consist in the soul's being united to the very same numerical particles of matter. For if that be necessary to identity, it will be impossible, in that constant flux of the particles of our bodies, that any man should be the same person two days, or two moments, together.

13. Thus, methinks, every drowsy nod shakes their doctrine, who teach that the soul is always thinking. Those, at least, who do at any time *sleep without dreaming,* can never be convinced that their thoughts are sometimes for four hours busy without their knowing of it; and if they are taken in the very act, waked in the middle of that sleeping contemplation, can give no manner of account of it.

14. It will perhaps be said,—That the soul thinks even in the soundest sleep, but the *memory* retains it not. That the soul in a sleeping man should be this moment busy a thinking, and the next moment in a waking man not remember nor be able to recollect one jot of all those thoughts, is very hard to be conceived, and would need some better proof than bare assertion to make it be believed. For who can without any more ado, but being barely told so, imagine that the greatest part of men do, during all their lives, for several hours every day, think of something, which if they were asked, even in the middle of these thoughts, they could remember nothing at all of? Most men, I think, pass a great part of their sleep without dreaming. I once knew a man that was bred a scholar, and had no bad memory, who told me he had never dreamed in his life, till he had that fever he was then newly recovered of, which was about the five or six and twentieth year of his age. I suppose the world affords more such instances: at least every one's acquaintance will furnish him with examples enough of such as pass most of their nights without dreaming.

15. To think often, and never to retain it so much as one moment, is a very useless sort of thinking; and the soul, in such a state of thinking, does very little, if at all, excel that of a looking-glass, which constantly receives variety of images, or ideas, but retains none; they disappear and vanish, and there remain no footsteps of them; the looking-glass is never the better for such ideas, nor the soul for such thoughts. Perhaps it will be said, that in a waking *man* the materials of the body are employed, and made use of, in thinking; and that the memory of thoughts is retained by the impressions that are made on the brain, and the traces there left after such thinking; but that in the thinking of the *soul,* which is not perceived in a sleeping man, there the soul thinks apart, and making no use of the organs of the body, leaves no impressions on it, and consequently no memory of such thoughts. Not to mention again the absurdity of two distinct persons, which follows from this supposition, I answer, further,—That whatever ideas the mind can receive and contemplate without the help of the body, it is reasonable to conclude it can retain without the help of

the body too; or else the soul, or any separate spirit, will have but little advantage by thinking. If it has no memory of its own thoughts; if it cannot lay them up for its own use, and be able to recall them upon occasion; if it cannot reflect upon what is past, and make use of its former experiences, reasonings, and contemplations, to what purpose does it think? They who make the soul a thinking thing, at this rate, will not make it a much more noble being than those do whom they condemn, for allowing it to be nothing but the subtilist parts of matter. Characters drawn on dust, that the first breath of wind effaces; or impressions made on a heap of atoms, or animal spirits, are altogether as useful, and render the subject as noble, as the thoughts of a soul that perish in thinking; that, once out of sight, are gone for ever, and leave no memory of themselves behind them. Nature never makes excellent things for mean or no uses: and it is hardly to be conceived that our infinitely wise Creator should make so admirable a faculty as the power of thinking, that faculty which comes nearest the excellency of his own incomprehensible being, to be so idly and uselessly employed, at least a fourth part of its time here, as to think constantly, without remembering any of those thoughts, without doing any good to itself or others, or being any way useful to any other part of the creation. If we will examine it, we shall not find, I suppose, the motion of dull and senseless matter, any where in the universe, made so little use of and so wholly thrown away.

16. It is true, we have sometimes instances of perception whilst we are asleep, and retain the memory of those thoughts: but how extravagant and incoherent for the most part they are; how little conformable to the perfection and order of a rational being, those who are acquainted with dreams need not be told. This I would willingly be satisfied in,—whether the soul, when it thinks thus apart, and as it were separate from the body, acts less rationally than when conjointly with it, or no. If its separate thoughts be less rational, then these men must say, that the soul owes the perfection of rational thinking to the body: if it does not, it is a wonder that our dreams should be, for the most part, so frivolous and irrational; and that the soul should retain none of its more rational soliloquies and meditations.

17. Those who so confidently tell us that the soul always actually thinks, I would they would also tell us, what those ideas are that are in the soul of a child, before or just at the union with the body, before it hath received any by sensation. The dreams of sleeping men are, as I take it, all made up of the waking man's ideas; though for the most part oddly put together. It is strange, if the soul has ideas of its own that it derived not from sensation or reflection, (as it must have, if it thought before it received any impressions from the body,) that it should never, in its private thinking, (so private, that the man himself perceives it not,) retain any of them the very moment it wakes out of them, and then make the man glad with new discoveries. Who can find it reason that the soul should, in its retirement during sleep, have so many hours' thoughts, and yet never light on any of those ideas it borrowed not from sensation or reflection; or at least preserve the memory of none but such, which, being occasioned from the body, must needs be less natural to a spirit? It is strange the soul should never once in a man's whole life recall over any of its pure

native thoughts, and those ideas it had before it borrowed anything from the body; never bring into the waking man's view any other ideas but what have a tang of the cask, and manifestly derive their original from that union. If it always thinks, and so had ideas before it was united, or before it received any from the body, it is not to be supposed but that during sleep it recollects its native ideas; and during that retirement from communicating with the body, whilst it thinks by itself, the ideas it is busied about should be, sometimes at least, those more natural and congenial ones which it had in itself, underived from the body, or its own operations about them: which, since the waking man never remembers, we must from this hypothesis conclude either that the soul remembers something that the man does not; or else that memory belongs only to such ideas as are derived from the body, or the mind's operations about them.

18. I would be glad also to learn from these men who so confidently pronounce that the human soul, or, which is all one, that a man always thinks, how they come to know it; nay, how they come to know that they themselves think, when they themselves do not perceive it. This, I am afraid, is to be sure without proofs, and to know without perceiving. It is, I suspect, a confused notion, taken up to serve an hypothesis; and none of those clear truths, that either their own evidence forces us to admit, or common experience makes it impudence to deny. For the most that can be said of it is, that it is possible the soul may always think, but not always retain it in memory. And I say, it is as possible that the soul may not always think; and much more probable that it should sometimes not think, than that it should often think, and that a long while together, and not be conscious to itself, the next moment after, that it had thought.

19. To suppose the soul to think, and the man not to perceive it, is, as has been said, to make two persons in one man. And if one considers well these men's way of speaking, one should be led into a suspicion that they do so. For they who tell us that the *soul* always thinks, do never, that I remember, say that a *man* always thinks. Can the soul think, and not the man? Or a man think, and not be conscious of it? This, perhaps, would be suspected of jargon in others. If they say the man thinks always, but is not always conscious of it, they may as well say his body is extended without having parts. For it is altogether as intelligible to say that a body is extended without parts, as that anything thinks without being conscious of it, or perceiving that it does so. They who talk thus may, with as much reason, if it be necessary to their hypothesis, say that a man is always hungry, but that he does not always feel it; whereas hunger consists in that very sensation, as thinking consists in being conscious that one thinks. If they say that a man is always conscious to himself of thinking, I ask, How they know it? Consciousness is the perception of what passes in a man's own mind. Can another man perceive that I am conscious of anything, when I perceive it not myself? No man's knowledge here can go beyond his experience. Wake a man out of a sound sleep, and ask him what he was that moment thinking of. If he himself be conscious of nothing he then thought on, he must be a notable diviner of thoughts that can assure him that

he was thinking. May he not, with more reason, assure him he was not asleep? This is something beyond philosophy; and it cannot be less than revelation, that discovers to another thoughts in my mind, when I can find none there myself. And they must needs have a penetrating sight who can certainly see that I think, when I cannot perceive it myself, and when I declare that I do not; and yet can see that dogs or elephants do not think, when they give all the demonstration of it imaginable, except only telling us that they do so. This some may suspect to be a step beyond the Rosicrucians; it seeming easier to make one's self invisible to others, than to make another's thoughts visible to me, which are not visible to himself. But it is but defining the soul to be 'a substance that always thinks,' and the business is done. If such definition be of any authority, I know not what it can serve for but to make many men suspect that they have no souls at all; since they find a good part of their lives pass away without thinking. For no definitions that I know, no suppositions of any sect, are of force enough to destroy constant experience; and perhaps it is the affectation of knowing beyond what we perceive, that makes so much useless dispute and noise in the world.

20. I see no reason, therefore, to believe that the soul thinks before the senses have furnished it with ideas to think on; and as those are increased and retained, so it comes by exercise, to improve its faculty of thinking in the several parts of it; as well as, afterwards, by compounding those ideas, and reflecting on its own operations, it increases its stock, as well as facility in remembering, imagining, reasoning, and other modes of thinking.

21. He that will suffer himself to be informed by observation and experience, and not make his own hypothesis the rule of nature, will find few signs of a soul accustomed to much thinking in a new-born child, and much fewer of any reasoning at all. And yet it is hard to imagine that the rational soul should think so much, and not reason at all. And he that will consider that infants newly come into the world spend the greatest part of their time in sleep, and are seldom awake but when either hunger calls for the teat, or some pain (the most importunate of all sensations), or some other violent impression on the body, forces the mind to perceive and attend to it;—he, I say, who considers this, will perhaps find reason to imagine that a *foetus* in the mother's womb differs not much from the state of a vegetable, but passes the greatest part of its time without perception or thought; doing very little but sleep in a place where it needs not seek for food, and is surrounded with liquor, always equally soft, and near of the same temper; where the eyes have no light, and the ears so shut up are not very susceptible of sounds; and where there is little or no variety, or change of objects, to move the senses.

22. Follow a child from its birth, and observe the alterations that time makes, and you shall find, as the mind by the senses comes more and more to be furnished with ideas, it comes to be more and more awake; thinks more, the more it has matter to think on. After some time it begins to know the objects which, being most familiar with it, have made lasting impressions. Thus it comes by degrees to know the persons it daily converses with, and distinguishes them from strangers; which are instances and effects of its coming to retain

and distinguish the ideas the senses convey to it. And so we may observe how the mind, *by degrees,* improves in these; and *advances* to the exercise of those other faculties of enlarging, compounding, and abstracting its ideas, and of reasoning about them, and reflecting upon all these; of which I shall have occasion to speak more hereafter.

23. If it shall be demanded then, *when* a man *begins* to have any ideas, I think the true answer is,—*when he first has any sensation.* For, since there appear not to be any ideas in the mind before the senses have conveyed any in, I conceive that ideas in the understanding are coeval with *sensation; which is such an impression or motion made in some part of the body, as [produces some perception] in the understanding.* It is about these impressions made on our senses by outward objects that the mind seems *first* to employ itself, in such operations as we call perception, remembering, consideration, reasoning, &c.

24. In time the mind comes to reflect on its own operations about the ideas got by sensation, and thereby stores itself with a new set of ideas, which I call ideas of reflection. These are the impressions that are made on our senses by outward objects that are extrinsical to the mind; and its own operations, proceeding from powers intrinsical and proper to itself, which, when reflected on by itself, become also objects of its contemplation—are, as I have said, the original of all knowledge. Thus the first capacity of human intellect is,—that the mind is fitted to receive the impressions made on it; either through the senses by outward objects, or by its own operations when it reflects on them. This is the first step a man makes towards the discovery of anything, and the groundwork whereon to build all those notions which ever he shall have naturally in this world. All those sublime thoughts which tower above the clouds, and reach as high as heaven itself, take their rise and footing here: in all that great extent wherein the mind wanders, in those remote speculations it may seem to be elevated with, it stirs not one jot beyond those ideas which *sense* or *reflection* have offered for its contemplation.

25. In this part the understanding is merely passive; and whether or no it will have these beginnings, and as it were materials of knowledge, is not in its own power. For the objects of our senses do, many of them, obtrude their particular ideas upon our minds whether we will or not; and the operations of our minds will not let us be without, at least, some obscure notions of them. No man can be wholly ignorant of what he does when he thinks. These simple ideas, when offered to the mind, the understanding can no more refuse to have, nor alter when they are imprinted, nor blot them out and make new ones itself, than a mirror can refuse, alter, or obliterate the images or ideas which the objects set before it do therein produce. As the bodies that surround us do diversely affect our organs, the mind is forced to receive the impressions; and cannot avoid the perception of those ideas that are annexed to them.

. . .

Of Our Knowledge of the Existence of Other Things

1. The knowledge of our own being we have by intuition. The existence of a God, reason clearly makes known to us, as has been shown.

The knowledge of the existence of *any other thing* we can have only by *sensation:* for there being no necessary connexion of real existence with any *idea* a man hath in his memory; nor of any other existence but that of God with the existence of any particular man: no particular man can know the existence of any other being, but only when, by actual operating upon him, it makes itself perceived by him. For, the having the idea of anything in our mind, no more proves the existence of that thing, than the picture of a man evidences his being in the world, or the visions of a dream make thereby a true history.

2. It is therefore the *actual receiving* of ideas from without that gives us notice of the existence of other things, and makes us know, that something doth exist at that time without us, which causes that idea in us; though perhaps we neither know nor consider how it does it. For it takes not from the certainty of our senses, and the ideas we receive by them, that we know not the manner wherein they are produced: v. g. whilst I write this, I have, by the paper affecting my eyes, that idea produced in my mind, which, whatever object causes, I call *white;* by which I know that that quality or accident (i. e. whose appearance before my eyes always causes that idea) doth really exist, and hath a being without me. And of this, the greatest assurance I can possibly have, and to which my faculties can attain, is the testimony of my eyes, which are the proper and sole judges of this thing; whose testimony I have reason to rely on as so certain, that I can no more doubt, whilst I write this, that I see white and black, and that something really exists that causes that sensation in me, than that I write or move my hand; which is a certainty as great as human nature is capable of, concerning the existence of anything, but a man's self alone, and of God.

3. The notice we have by our senses of the existing of things without us, though it be not altogether so certain as our intuitive knowledge, or the deductions of our reason employed about the clear abstract ideas of our own minds; yet it is an assurance that deserves the name of *knowledge.* If we persuade ourselves that our faculties act and inform us right concerning the existence of those objects that affect them, it cannot pass for an ill-grounded confidence: for I think nobody can, in earnest, be so sceptical as to be uncertain of the existence of those things which he sees and feels. At least, he that can doubt so far, (whatever he may have with his own thoughts,) will never have any controversy with me; since he can never be sure I say anything contrary to his own opinion. As to myself, I think God has given me assurance enough of the existence of things without me: since, by their different application, I can produce in myself both pleasure and pain, which is one great concernment of my present state. This is certain: the confidence that our faculties do not herein deceive us, is the greatest assurance we are capable of concerning the existence of material beings. For we cannot act anything but by our faculties; nor talk of knowledge itself, but by the help of those faculties which are fitted to apprehend even what knowledge is.

But besides the assurance we have from our senses themselves, that they do not err in the information they give us of the existence of things without us, when they are affected by them, we are further confirmed in this assurance by other concurrent reasons:—

4. I. It is plain those perceptions are produced in us by exterior causes affecting our senses: because those that want the *organs* of any sense, never can have the ideas belonging to that sense produced in their minds. This is too evident to be doubted: and therefore we cannot but be assured that they come in by the organs of that sense, and no other way. The organs themselves, it is plain, do not produce them: for then the eyes of a man in the dark would produce colours, and his nose smell roses in the winter: but we see nobody gets the relish of a pineapple, till he goes to the Indies, where it is, and tastes it.

5. II. Because sometimes I find that *I cannot avoid the having those ideas produced in my mind*. For though, when my eyes are shut, or windows fast, I can at pleasure recal to my mind the ideas of light, or the sun, which former sensations had lodged in my memory; so I can at pleasure lay by *that* idea, and take into my view that of the smell of a rose, or taste of sugar. But, if I turn my eyes at noon towards the sun, I cannot avoid the ideas which the light or sun then produces in me. So that there is a manifest difference between the ideas laid up in my memory, (over which, if they were there only, I should have constantly the same power to dispose of them, and lay them by at pleasure,) and those which force themselves upon me, and I cannot avoid having. And therefore it must needs be some exterior cause, and the brisk acting of some objects without me, whose efficacy I cannot resist, that produces those ideas in my mind, whether I will or no. Besides, there is nobody who doth not perceive the difference in himself between contemplating the sun, as he hath the idea of it in his memory, and actually looking upon it: of which two, his perception is so distinct, that few of his ideas are more distinguishable one from another. And therefore he hath certain knowledge that they are not *both* memory, or the actions of his mind, and fancies only within him; but that actual seeing hath a cause without.

6. III. Add to this, that many of those ideas are *produced in us with pain,* which afterwards we remember without the least offence. Thus, the pain of heat or cold, when the idea of it is revived in our minds, gives us no disturbance; which, when felt, was very troublesome; and is again, when actually repeated: which is occasioned by the disorder the external object causes in our bodies when applied to them: and we remember the pains of hunger, thirst, or the headache, without any pain at all; which would either never disturb us, or else constantly do it, as often as we thought of it, were there nothing more but ideas floating in our minds, and appearances entertaining our fancies, without the real existence of things affecting us from abroad. The same may be said of *pleasure,* accompanying several actual sensations. And though mathematical demonstration depends not upon sense, yet the examining them by diagrams gives great credit to the evidence of our sight, and seems to give it a certainty approaching to that of demonstration itself. For, it would be very strange, that a man should allow it for an undeniable truth, that two angles of a figure, which he measures by lines and angles of a diagram, should be bigger one than the other, and yet doubt of the existence of those lines and angles, which by looking on he makes use of to measure that by.

7. IV. Our *senses* in many cases *bear witness to the truth of each other's report,* concerning the existence of sensible things without us. He that *sees* a fire, may, if he doubt whether it be anything more than a bare fancy, *feel* it too; and be convinced, by putting his hand in it. Which certainly could never be put into such exquisite pain by a bare idea or phantom, unless that the pain be a fancy too: which yet he cannot, when the burn is well, by raising the idea of it, bring upon himself again.

Thus I see, whilst I write this, I can change the appearance of the paper; and by designing the letters, tell *beforehand* what new idea it shall exhibit the very next moment, by barely drawing my pen over it: which will neither appear (let me fancy as much as I will) if my hands stand still; or though I move my pen, if my eyes be shut: nor, when those characters are once made on the paper, can I choose afterwards but see them as they are; that is, have the ideas of such letters as I have made. Whence it is manifest, that they are not barely the sport and play of my own imagination, when I find that the characters that were made at the pleasure of my own thoughts, do not obey them; nor yet cease to be, whenever I shall fancy it, but continue to affect my senses constantly and regularly, according to the figures I made them. To which if we will add, that the sight of those shall, from another man, draw such sounds as I beforehand design they shall stand for, there will be little reason left to doubt that those words I write do really exist without me, when they cause a long series of regular sounds to affect my ears, which could not be the effect of my imagination, nor could my memory retain them in that order.

8. But yet, if after all this any one will be so sceptical as to distrust his senses, and to affirm that all we see and hear, feel and taste, think and do, during our whole being, is but the series and deluding appearances of a long dream, whereof there is no reality; and therefore will question the existence of all things, or our knowledge of anything: I must desire him to consider, that, if all be a dream, then he doth but dream that he makes the question, and so it is not much matter that a waking man should answer him. But yet, if he pleases, he may dream that I make him this answer, That the certainty of things existing in *rerum natura** when we have the testimony of our senses for it is not only as great as our frame can attain to, but as our condition needs. For, our faculties being suited not to the full extent of being, nor to a perfect, clear, comprehensive knowledge of things free from all doubt and scruple; but to the preservation of us, in whom they are; and accommodated to the use of life: they serve to our purpose well enough, if they will but give us certain notice of those things, which are convenient or inconvenient to us. For he that sees a candle burning, and hath experimented the force of its flame by putting his finger in it, will little doubt that this is something existing without him, which does him harm, and puts him to great pain: which is assurance enough, when no man requires greater certainty to govern his actions by than what is as certain as his actions themselves. And if our dreamer pleases to try whether the glowing heat of a

---

* The nature of things.

glass furnace be barely a wandering imagination in a drowsy man's fancy, by putting his hand into it, he may perhaps be wakened into a certainty greater than he could wish, that it is something more than bare imagination. So that this evidence is as great as we can desire, being as certain to us as our pleasure or pain, i.e. happiness or misery; beyond which we have no concernment, either of knowing or being. Such an assurance of the existence of things without us is sufficient to direct us in the attaining the good and avoiding the evil which is caused by them, which is the important concernment we have of being made acquainted with them.

9. In fine, then, when our senses do actually convey into our understandings any idea, we cannot but be satisfied that there doth something *at that time* really exist without us, which doth affect our senses, and by them give notice of itself to our apprehensive faculties, and actually produce that idea which we then perceive: and we cannot so far distrust their testimony, as to doubt that such *collections* of simple ideas as we have observed by our senses to be united together, do really exist together. But this knowledge extends as far as the present testimony of our senses, employed about particular objects that do then affect them, and no further. For if I saw such a collection of simple ideas as is wont to be called *man,* existing together one minute since, and am now alone, I cannot be certain that the same man exists now, since there is no *necessary connexion* of his existence a minute since with his existence now: by a thousand ways he may cease to be, since I had the testimony of my senses for his existence. And if I cannot be certain that the man I saw last to-day is now in being, I can less be certain that he is so who hath been longer removed from my senses, and I have not seen since yesterday, or since the last year: and much less can I be certain of the existence of men that I never saw. And, therefore, though it be highly probable that millions of men do now exist, yet, whilst I am alone, writing this, I have not that certainty of it which we strictly call knowledge; though the great likelihood of it puts me past doubt, and it be reasonable for me to do several things upon the confidence that there are men (and men also of my acquaintance, with whom I have to do) now in the world: but this is but probability, not knowledge.

10. Whereby yet we may observe how foolish and vain a thing it is for a man of a narrow knowledge, who having reason given him to judge of the different evidence and probability of things, and to be swayed accordingly; how vain, I say, it is to expect demonstration and certainty in things not capable of it; and refuse assent to very rational propositions, and act contrary to very plain and clear truths, because they cannot be made out so evident, as to surmount every the least (I will not say reason, but) pretence of doubting. He that, in the ordinary affairs of life, would admit of nothing but direct plain demonstration, would be sure of nothing in this world, but of perishing quickly. The wholesomeness of his meat or drink would not give him reason to venture on it: and I would fain know what it is he could do upon such grounds as are capable of no doubt, no objection.

. . .

26

The Problem of Induction

DAVID HUME

David Hume of Scotland (1711–1776), wrote extremely important works in the theory of knowledge, ethics, social philosophy, and the philosophy of religion. He was also a historian of note. His Treatise of Human Nature was published when he was twenty-eight.

How do we gain our knowledge about matters of fact? Hume claims that all such knowledge depends on knowledge of causal relations. How, then, do we gain knowledge of causal relations? It is impossible to know that one thing causes another, Hume argues, without having prior knowledge of matters of fact. This presents us with a very short circle: it is impossible to know any matter of fact without first having knowledge of causal relations, but impossible to have any knowledge of causal relations without first having knowledge of matters of fact. A skeptical conclusion seems inevitable: it is impossible to have knowledge of either.

Having presented us with this skeptical puzzle, Hume attempts to provide what he calls a "skeptical solution." This consists of nothing more than a psychological account of the manner in which beliefs are acquired. Hume argues that the conclusions we reach based on experience are not the product of proper reasoning, but merely a product of habit.

Skeptical Doubts Concerning the Operations of the Understanding

PART I

ALL THE OBJECTS OF HUMAN REASON or inquiry may naturally be divided into two kinds, to wit, "Relations of Ideas," and "Matters of Fact." Of the first kind are the sciences of Geometry, Algebra, and Arithmetic, and, in short, every affirmation which is either intuitively or demonstratively certain. *That the square of the hypotenuse is equal to the square of the two sides* is a proposition which expresses a relation between these figures. *That three times five is equal to the half of thirty* expresses a relation between these nunbers. Propositions of this kind are discoverable by the mere operation of thought, without dependence on what is anywhere existent in the universe. Though there never were a circle of triangle in nature, the truths demonstrated by Euclid would forever retain their certainty and evidence.

Matters of fact, which are the second objects of human reason, are not ascertained in the same manner, nor is our evidence of their truth, however great, of a like nature with the foregoing. The contrary of every matter of fact is still possible, because it can never imply a contradiction and is conceived by the mind with the same facility and distinctness as if ever so conformable to

reality. *That the sun will not rise tomorrow* is no less intelligible a proposition and implies no more contradiction than the affirmation *that it will rise*. We should in vain, therefore, attempt to demonstrate its falsehood. Were it demonstratively false, it would imply a contradiction and could never be distinctly conceived by the mind.

It may, therefore, be a subject worthy of curiosity to inquire what is the nature of that evidence which assures us of any real existence and matter of fact beyond the present testimony of our senses or the records of our memory. This part of philosophy, it is observable, had been little cultivated either by the ancients or moderns; and, therefore, our doubts and errors in the prosecution of so important an inquiry may be the more excusable while we march through such difficult paths without any guide or direction. They may even prove useful by exciting curiosity and destroying that implicit faith and security which is the bane of all reasoning and free inquiry. The discovery of defects in the common philosophy, if any such there be, will not, I presume, be a discouragement, but rather an incitement, as is usual, to attempt something more full and satisfactory than has yet been proposed to the public.

All reasonings concerning matter of fact seem to be founded on the relation of *cause* and *effect*. By means of that relation alone we can go beyond the evidence of our memory and senses. If you were to ask a man why he believes any matter of fact which is absent, for instance, that his friend is in the country or in France, he would give you a reason, and this reason would be some other fact: as a letter received from him or the knowledge of his former resolutions and promises. A man finding a watch or any other machine in a desert island would conclude that there had once been men in that island. All our reasonings concerning fact are of the same nature. And here it is constantly supposed that there is a connection between the present fact and that which is inferred from it. Were there nothing to bind them together, the inference would be entirely precarious. The hearing of an articulate voice and rational discourse in the dark assures us of the presence of some person. Why? Because these are the effects of the human make and fabric, and closely connected with it. If we anatomize all the other reasonings of this nature, we shall find that they are founded on the relation of cause and effect, and that this relation is either near or remote, direct or collateral. Heat and light are collateral effects of fire, and the one effect may justly be inferred from the other.

If we would satisfy ourselves, therefore, concerning the nature of that evidence which assures us of matters of fact, we must inquire how we arrive at the knowledge of cause and effect.

I shall venture to affirm, as a general proposition which admits of no exception, that the knowledge of this relation is not, in any instance, attained by reasonings *a priori*,* but arises entirely from experience, when we find that any particular objects are constantly conjoined with each other. Let an object be presented to a man of ever so strong natural reason and abilities—if that object be entirely new to him, he will not be able, by the most accurate exam-

---

* Independent of particular experience.

ination of its sensible qualities, to discover any of its causes or effects. Adam, though his rational faculties be supposed, at the very first, entirely perfect, could not have inferred from the fluidity and transparency of water that it would suffocate him, or from the light and warmth of fire that it would consume him. No object ever discovers, by the qualities which appear to the senses, either the causes which produced it or the effects which will arise from it; nor can our reason, unassisted by experience, ever draw any inference concerning real existence and matter of fact.

This proposition, *that causes and effects are discoverable, not by reason, but by experience,* will readily be admitted with regard to such objects as we remember to have once been altogether unknown to us, since we must be conscious of the utter inability which we then lay under of foretelling what would arise from them. Present two smooth pieces of marble to a man who has no tincture of natural philosophy; he will never discover that they will adhere together in such a manner as to require great force to separate them in a direct line, while they make so small a resistance to a lateral pressure. Such events as bear little analogy to the common course of nature are also readily confessed to be known only by experience, nor does any man imagine that the explosion of gunpowder or the attraction of a loadstone could ever be discovered by arguments *a priori.* In like manner, when an effect is supposed to depend upon an intricate machinery or secret structure of parts, we make no difficulty in attributing all our knowledge of it to experience. Who will assert that he can give the ultimate reason why milk or bread is proper nourishment for a man, not for a lion or tiger?

But the same truth may not appear at first sight to have the same evidence with regard to events which have become familiar to us from our first appearance in the world, which bear a close analogy to the whole course of nature, and which are supposed to depend on the simple qualities of objects without any secret structure of parts. We are apt to imagine that we could discover these effects by the mere operation of our reason without experience. We fancy that, were we brought on a sudden into this world, we could at first have inferred that one billiard ball would communicate motion to another upon impulse, and that we needed not to have waited for the event in order to pronounce with certainty concerning it. Such is the influence of custom that where it is strongest it not only covers our natural ignorance but even conceals itself, and seems not to take place, merely because it is found in the highest degree.

But to convince us that all the laws of nature and all the operations of bodies without exception are known only by experience, the following reflections may perhaps suffice. Were any object presented to us, and were we required to pronounce concerning the effect which will result from it without consulting past observation, after what manner, I beseech you, must the mind proceed in this operation? It must invent or imagine some event which it ascribes to the object as its effect; and it is plain that this invention must be entirely arbitrary. The mind can never possibly find the effect in the supposed cause by the most accurate scrutiny and examination. For the effect is totally different from the cause, and consequently can never be discovered in it. Motion in the second

billiard ball is a quite distinct event from motion in the first, nor is there anything in the one to suggest the smallest hint of the other. A stone or piece of metal raised into the air and left without any support immediately falls. But to consider the matter *a priori,* is there anything we discover in this situation which can beget the idea of a downward rather than an upward or any other motion in the stone or metal?

And as the first imagination or invention of a particular effect in all natural operations is arbitrary where we consult not experience, so must we also esteem the supposed tie or connection between the cause and effect which binds them together and renders it impossible that any other effect could result from the operation of that cause. When I see, for instance, a billiard ball moving in a straight line toward another, even suppose motion in the second ball should by accident be suggested to me as the result of their contact or impulse, may I not conceive that a hundred different events might as well follow from that cause? May not both these balls remain at absolute rest? May not the first ball return in a straight line or leap off from the second in any line or direction? All these suppositions are consistent and conceivable. Why, then, should we give the preference to one which is no more consistent or conceivable than the rest? All our reasonings *a priori* will never be able to show us any foundation for this preference.

In a word, then, every effect is a distinct event from its cause. It could not, therefore, be discovered in the cause, and the first invention or conception of it, *a priori,* must be entirely arbitrary. And even after it is suggested, the conjunction of it with the cause must appear equally arbitrary, since there are always many other effects which, to reason, must seem fully as consistent and natural. In vain, therefore, should we pretend to determine any single event or infer any cause or effect without the assistance of observation and experience.

Hence we may discover the reason why no philosopher who is rational and modest has ever pretended to assign the ultimate cause of any natural operation, or to show distinctly the action of that power which produces any single effect in the universe. It is confessed that the utmost effort of human reason is to reduce the principles productive of natural phenomena to a greater simplicity, and to resolve the many particular effects into a few general causes, by means of reasonings from analogy, experience, and observation. But as to the causes of these general causes, we should in vain attempt their discovery, nor shall we ever be able to satisfy ourselves by any particular explication of them. These ultimate springs and principles are totally shut up from human curiosity and inquiry. Elasticity, gravity, cohesion of parts, communication of motion by impulse—these are probably the ultimate causes and principles which we shall ever discover in nature; and we may esteem ourselves sufficiently happy if, by accurate inquiry and reasoning, we can trace up the particular phenomena to, or near to, these general principles. The most perfect philosophy of the natural kind only staves off our ignorance a little longer, as perhaps the most perfect philosophy of the moral or metaphysical kind serves only to discover larger portions of it. Thus the observation of human blindness and weakness is the result of all philosophy, and meets us, at every turn, in spite of our endeavors to elude or avoid it.

Nor is geometry, when taken into the assistance of natural philosophy, ever able to remedy this defect or lead us into the knowledge of ultimate causes by all that accuracy of reasoning for which it is so justly celebrated. Every part of mixed mathematics proceeds upon the supposition that certain laws are established by nature in her operations, and abstract reasonings are employed either to assist experience in the discovery of these laws or to determine their influence in particular instances where it depends upon any precise degree of distance and quantity. Thus it is a law of motion, discovered by experience, that the moment or force of any body in motion is in the compound ratio or proportion of its solid contents and its velocity, and, consequently, that a small force may remove the greatest obstacle or raise the greatest weight if by any contrivance or machinery we can increase the velocity of that force so as to make it an overmatch for its antagonist. Geometry assists us in the application of this law by giving us the just dimensions of all the parts and figures which can enter into any species of machine, but still the discovery of the law itself is owing merely to experience; and all the abstract reasonings in the world could never lead us one step toward the knowledge of it. When we reason *a priori* and consider merely any object or cause as it appears to the mind, independent of all observation, it never could suggest to us the notion of any distinct object, such as its effect, much less show us the inseparable and inviolable connection between them. A man must be very sagacious who could discover by reasoning that crystal is the effect of heat, and ice of cold, without being previously acquainted with the operation of these qualities.

PART II

But we have not yet attained any tolerable satisfaction with regard to the question first proposed. Each solution still gives rise to a new question as difficult as the foregoing and leads us on to further inquiries. When it is asked, *What is the nature of all our reasonings concerning matter of fact?* the proper answer seems to be, That they are founded on the relation of cause and effect. When again it is asked, *What is the foundation of all our reasonings and conclusions concerning that relation?* it may be replied in one word, *experience*. But if we still carry on our sifting humor and ask, *What is the foundation of all conclusions from experience?* this implies a new question which may be of more difficult solution and explication. Philosophers that give themselves airs of superior wisdom and sufficiency have a hard task when they encounter persons of inquisitive dispositions, who push them from every corner to which they retreat, and who are sure at last to bring them to some dangerous dilemma. The best expedient to prevent this confusion is to be modest in our pretensions and even to discover the difficulty ourselves before it is objected to us. By this means we may make a kind of merit of our very ignorance.

I shall content myself in this section with an easy task and shall pretend only to give a negative answer to the question here proposed. I say, then, that even after we have experience of the operations of cause and effect, our conclusions

from that experience are *not* founded on reasoning or any process of the understanding. This answer we must endeavor both to explain and to defend.

It must certainly be allowed that nature has kept us at a great distance from all her secrets and has afforded us only the knowledge of a few superficial qualities of objects, while she conceals from us those powers and principles on which the influence of these objects entirely depends. Our senses inform us of the color, weight, and consistency of bread, but neither sense nor reason can ever inform us of those qualities which fit it for the nourishment and support of the human body. Sight or feeling conveys an idea of the actual motion of bodies, but as to that wonderful force or power which would carry on a moving body forever in a continued change of place, and which bodies never lose but by communicating it to others, of this we cannot form the most distant conception. But notwithstanding this ignorance of natural powers and principles, we always presume when we see like sensible qualities that they have like secret powers, and expect that effects similar to those which we have experienced will follow from them. If a body of like color and consistency with that bread which we have formerly eaten be presented to us, we make no scruple of repeating the experiment and foresee with certainty like nourishment and support. Now this is a process of the mind or thought of which I would willingly know the foundation. It is allowed on all hands that there is no known connection between the sensible qualities and the secret powers, and, consequently, that the mind is not led to form such a conclusion concerning their constant and regular conjunction by anything which it knows of their nature. As to past *experience*, it can be allowed to give *direct* and *certain* information of those precise objects only, and that precise period of time which fell under its cognizance: But why this experience should be extended to future times and to other objects which, for aught we know, may be only in appearance similar, this is the main question on which I would insist. The bread which I formerly ate nourished me; that is, a body of such sensible qualities was, at that time, endued with such secret powers. But does it follow that other bread must also nourish me at another time, and that like sensible qualities must always be attended with like secret powers? The consequence seems nowise necessary. At least, it must be acknowledged that there is here a consequence drawn by the mind that there is a certain step taken, a process of thought, and an inference which wants to be explained. These two propositions are far from being the same: *I have found that such an object has always been attended with such an effect,* and *I foresee that other objects which are in appearance similar will be attended with similar effects.* I shall allow, if you please, that the one proposition may justly be inferred from the other: I know, in fact, that it always is inferred. But if you insist that the inference is made by a chain of reasoning, I desire you to produce that reasoning. The connection between these propositions is not intuitive. There is required a medium which may enable the mind to draw such an inference, if indeed it be drawn by reasoning and argument. What that medium is I must confess passes my comprehension; and it is incumbent on those to produce it who assert that it really exists and is the original of all our conclusions concerning matter of fact.

This negative argument must certainly, in process of time, become altogether convincing if many penetrating and able philosophers shall turn their inquiries this way, and no one be ever able to discover any connecting proposition or intermediate step which supports the understanding in this conclusion. But as the question is yet new, every reader may not trust so far to his own penetration as to conclude, because an argument escapes his inquiry, that therefore it does not really exist. For this reason it may be requisite to venture upon a more difficult task, and, enumerating all the branches of human knowledge, endeavor to show that none of them can afford such an argument.

All reasonings may be divided into two kinds, namely, demonstrative reasoning, or that concerning relations of ideas, and moral reasoning, or that concerning matter of fact and existence. That there are no demonstrative arguments in the case seems evident, since it implies no contradiction that the course of nature may change and that an object, seemingly like those which we have experienced, may be attended with different or contrary effects. May I not clearly and distinctly conceive that a body, falling from the clouds and which in all other respects resembles snow, has yet the taste of salt or feeling of fire? Is there any more intelligible proposition than to affirm that all the trees will flourish in December and January, and will decay in May and June? Now, whatever is intelligible and can be distinctly conceived implies no contradiction and can never be proved false by any demonstrative argument or abstract reasoning *a priori*.

If we be, therefore, engaged by arguments to put trust in past experience and make it the standard of our future judgment, these arguments must be probable only, or such as regard matter of fact and real existence, according to the division above mentioned. But that there is no argument of this kind must appear if our explication of that species of reasoning be admitted as solid and satisfactory. We have said that all arguments concerning existence are founded on the relation of cause and effect, that our knowledge of that relation is derived entirely from experience, and that all our experimental conclusions proceed upon the supposition that the future will be conformable to the past. To endeavor, therefore, the proof of this last supposition by probable arguments, or arguments regarding existence, must be evidently going in a circle and taking that for granted which is the very point in question.

In reality, all arguments from experience are founded on the similarity which we discover among natural objects, and by which we are induced to expect effects similar to those which we have found to follow from such objects. And though none but a fool or madman will ever pretend to dispute the authority of experience or to reject that great guide of human life, it may surely be allowed a philosopher to have so much curiosity at least as to examine the principle of human nature which gives this mighty authority to experience and makes us draw advantage from that similarity which nature has placed among different objects. From causes which appear similar, we expect similar effects. This is the sum of all our experimental conclusions. Now it seems evident that, if this conclusion were formed by reason, it would be as perfect at first, and upon one instance, as after ever so long a course of experience; but the case is far otherwise. Nothing so like as eggs, yet no one, on account of this appearing

similarity, expects the same taste and relish in all of them. It is only after a long course of uniform experiments in any kind that we attain a firm reliance and security with regard to a particular event. Now, where is that process of reasoning which, from one instance, draws a conclusion so different from that which it infers from a hundred instances that are nowise different from that single one? This question I propose as much for the sake of information as with an intention of raising difficulties. I cannot find, I cannot imagine any such reasoning. But I keep my mind still open to instruction if anyone will vouchsafe to bestow it on me.

Should it be said that, from a number of uniform experiments, we *infer* a connection between the sensible qualities and the secret powers, this, I must confess, seems the same difficulty, couched in different terms. The question still occurs, On what process of argument is this *inference* founded? Where is the medium, the interposing ideas which join propositions so very wide of each other? It is confessed that the color, consistency, and other sensible qualities of bread appear not of themselves to have any connection with the secret powers of nourishment and support; for otherwise we could infer these secret powers from the first appearance of these sensible qualities without the aid of experience, contrary to the sentiment of all philosophers, and contrary to plain matter of fact. Here, then, is our natural state of ignorance with regard to the powers and influence of all objects. How is this remedied by experience? It only shows us a number of uniform effects resulting from certain objects, and teaches us that those particular objects, at that particular time, were endowed with such powers and forces. When a new object endowed with similar sensible qualities is produced, we expect similar powers and forces, and look for a like effect. From a body of like color and consistency with bread, we expect like nourishment and support. But this surely is a step or progress of the mind which wants to be explained. When a man says, *I have found, in all past instances, such sensible qualities, conjoined with such secret powers,* and when he says, *similar sensible qualities will always be conjoined with similar secret powers,* he is not guilty of a tautology, nor are these propositions in any respect the same. You say that the one proposition is an inference from the other; but you must confess that the inference is not intuitive, neither is it demonstrative. Of what nature is it then? To say it is experimental is begging the question. For all inferences from experience suppose, as their foundation, that the future will resemble the past and that similar powers will be conjoined with similar sensible qualities. If there be any suspicion that the course of nature may change, and that the past may be no rule for the future, all experience becomes useless and can give rise to no inference or conclusion. It is impossible, therefore, that any arguments from experience can prove this resemblance of the past to the future, since all these arguments are founded on the supposition of that resemblance. Let the course of things be allowed hitherto ever so regular, that alone, without some new argument or inference, proves not that for the future it will continue so. In vain do you pretend to have learned the nature of bodies from your past experience. Their secret nature, and consequently all their effects and influence, may change without any change in their sensible qualities. This happens sometimes, and with regard to some objects. Why may it not happen

always, and with regard to all objects? What logic, what process of argument secures you against this supposition? My practice, you say, refutes my doubts. But you mistake the purport of my question. As an agent, I am quite satisfied in the point; but as a philosopher who has some share of curiosity, I will not say skepticism, I want to learn the foundation of this inference. No reading, no inquiry has yet been able to remove my difficulty or give me satisfaction in a matter of such importance. Can I do better than propose the difficulty to the public, even though, perhaps, I have small hopes of obtaining a solution? We shall at least, by this means, be sensible of our ignorance, if we do not augment our knowledge.

I must confess that a man is guilty of unpardonable arrogance who concludes, because an argument has escaped his own investigation, that therefore it does not really exist. I must also confess that, though all the learned, for several ages, should have employed themselves in fruitless search upon any subject, it may still, perhaps, be rash to conclude positively that the subject must therefore pass all human comprehension. Even though we examine all the sources of our knowledge and conclude them unfit for such a subject, there may still remain a suspicion that the enumeration is not complete or the examination not accurate. But with regard to the present subject, there are some considerations which seem to remove all this accusation of arrogance or suspicion of mistake.

It is certain that the most ignorant and stupid peasants, nay infants, nay even brute beasts, improve by experience and learn the qualities of natural objects by observing the effects which result from them. When a child has felt the sensation of pain from touching the flame of a candle, he will be careful not to put his hand near any candle, but will expect a similar effect from a cause which is similar in its sensible qualities and appearance. If you assert, therefore, that the understanding of the child is led into this conclusion by any process of argument or ratiocination, I may justly require you to produce that argument, nor have you any pretense to refuse so equitable a demand. You cannot say that the argument is abstruse and may possibly escape your inquiry, since you confess that it is obvious to the capacity of a mere infant. If you hesitate, therefore, a moment or if, after reflection, you produce an intricate or profound argument, you, in a manner, give up the question and confess that it is not reasoning which engages us to suppose the past resembling the future, and to expect similar effects from causes which are to appearance similar. This is the proposition which I intended to enforce in the present section. If I be right, I pretend not to have made any mighty discovery. And if I be wrong, I must acknowledge myself to be indeed a very backward scholar, since I cannot now discover an argument which, it seems, was perfectly familiar to me long before I was out of my cradle.

Skeptical Solution of These Doubts

PART I

THE PASSION FOR PHILOSOPHY, like that for religion, seems liable to this inconvenience, that though it aims at the correction of our manners and extir-

pation of our vices, it may only serve, by imprudent management, to foster a predominant inclination and push the mind with more determined resolution toward that side which already *draws* too much by the bias and propensity of the natural temper. It is certain that, while we aspire to the magnanimous firmness of the philosophic sage and endeavor to confine our pleasures altogether within our own minds, we may, at last, render our philosophy, like that of Epictetus and other Stoics, only a more refinded system of selfishness, and reason ourselves out of all virtue as well as social enjoyment. While we study with attention the vanity of human life and turn all our thoughts toward the empty and transitory nature of riches and honors, we are, perhaps, all the while flattering our natural indolence which, hating the bustle of the world and drudgery of business, seeks a pretense of reason to give itself a full and uncontrolled indulgence. There is, however, one species of philosophy which seems little liable to this inconvenience, and that because it strikes in with no disorderly passion of the human mind, nor can mingle itself with any natural affection or propensity; and that is the Academic or Skeptical philosophy. The Academics always talk of doubt and suspense of judgment, of danger in hasty determinations, of confining to very narrow bounds the inquiries of the understanding, and of renouncing all speculations which lie not within the limits of common life and practice. Nothing, therefore, can be more contrary than such a philosophy to the supine indolence of the mind, its rash arrogance, its lofty pretensions, and its superstitious credulity. Every passion is mortified by it, except the love of truth; and that passion never is nor can be carried to too high a degree. It is surprising, therefore, that this philosophy, which in almost every instance must be harmless and innocent, should be the subject of so much groundless reproach and obloquy. But, perhaps, the very circumstance which renders it so innocent is what chiefly exposes it to the public hatred and resentment. By flattering no irregular passion, it gains few partisans. By opposing so many vices and follies, it raises to itself abundance of enemies who stigmatize it as libertine, profane, and irreligious.

Nor need we fear that this philosophy, while it endeavors to limit our inquiries to common life, should ever undermine the reasonings of common life and carry its doubts so far as to destroy all action as well as speculation. Nature will always maintain her rights and prevail in the end over any abstract reasoning whatsoever. Though we should conclude, for instance, as in the foregoing section, that in all reasonings from experience there is a step taken by the mind which is not supported by any argument or process of the understanding, there is no danger that these reasonings, on which almost all knowledge depends, will ever be affected by such a discovery. If the mind be not engaged by argument to make this step, it must be induced by some other principle of equal weight and authority; and that principle will preserve its influence as long as human nature remains the same. What that principle is may well be worth the pains of inquiry.

Suppose a person, though endowed with the strongest faculties of reason and reflection, to be brought on a sudden into this world; he would, indeed, immediately observe a continual succession of objects and one event following

another, but he would not be able to discover anything further. He would not at first, by any reasoning, be able to reach the idea of cause and effect, since the particular powers by which all natural operations are performed never appear to the senses; nor is it reasonable to conclude, merely because one event in one instance precedes another, that therefore the one is the cause, the other the effect. The conjunction may be arbitrary and casual. There may be no reason to infer the existence of one from the appearance of the other: and, in a word, such a person without more experience could never employ his conjecture or reasoning concerning any matter of fact or be assured of anything beyond what was immediately present to his memory or senses.

Suppose again that he has acquired more experience and has lived so long in the world as to have observed similar objects or events to be constantly conjoined together—what is the consequence of this experience? He immediately infers the existence of one object from the appearance of the other, yet he has not, by all his experience, acquired any idea or knowledge of the secret power by which the one object produces the other, nor is it by any process of reasoning he is engaged to draw this inference; but still he finds himself determined to draw it, and though he should be convinced that his understanding has no part in the operation, he would nevertheless continue in the same course of thinking. There is some other principle which determines him to form such a conclusion.

This principle is *custom* or *habit*. For wherever the repetition of any particular act or operation produces a propensity to renew the same act or operation without being impelled by any reasoning or process of the understanding, we always say that this propensity is the effect of *custom*. By employing that word we pretend not to have given the ultimate reason of such a propensity. We only point out a principle of human nature which is universally acknowledged, and which is well known by its effects. Perhaps we can push our inquiries no further or pretend to give the cause of this cause, but must rest contented with it as the ultimate principle which we can assign of all our conclusions from experience. It is sufficient satisfaction that we can go so far without repining at the narrowness of our faculties, because they will carry us no further. And it is certain we here advance a very intelligible proposition at least, if not a true one, when we assert that after the constant conjunction of two objects, heat and flame, for instance, weight and solidity, we are determined by custom alone to expect the one from the appearance of the other. This hypothesis seems even the only one which explains the difficulty why we draw from a thousand instances an inference which we are not able to draw from one instance that is in no respect different from them. Reason is incapable of any such variation. The conclusions which it draws from considering one circle are the same which it would form upon surveying all the circles in the universe. But no man, having seen only one body move after being impelled by another, could infer that every other body will move after a like impulse. All inferences from experience, therefore, are effects of custom, not of reasoning.

Custom, then, is the great guide of human life. It is that principle alone which renders our experience useful to us and makes us expect, for the future, a similar

train of events with those which have appeared in the past. Without the influence of custom we should be entirely ignorant of every matter of fact beyond what is immediately present to the memory and senses. We should never know how to adjust means to ends or to employ our natural powers in the production of any effect. There would be an end at once of all action as well as of the chief part of speculation.

But here it may be proper to remark that though our conclusions from experience carry us beyond our memory and senses and assure us of matters of fact which happened in the most distant places and most remote ages, yet some fact must always be present to the senses or memory from which we may first proceed in drawing these conclusions. A man who should find in a desert country the remains of pompous buildings would conclude that the country had, in ancient times, been cultivated by civilized inhabitants; but did nothing of this nature occur to him, he could never form such an inference. We learn the events of former ages from history, but then we must peruse the volume in which this instruction is contained, and thence carry up our inferences from one testimony to another, till we arrive at the eyewitnesses and spectators of these distant events. In a word, if we proceed not upon some fact present to the memory or senses, our reasonings would be merely hypothetical; and however the particular links might be connected with each other, the whole chain of inferences would have nothing to support it, nor could we ever, by its means, arrive at the knowledge of any real existence. If I ask why you believe any particular matter of fact which you relate, you must tell me some reason; and this reason will be some other fact connected with it. But as you cannot proceed after this manner *in infinitum,** you must at last terminate in some fact which is present to your memory or senses or must allow that your belief is entirely without foundation.

What, then, is the conclusion of the whole matter? A simple one, though, it must be confessed, pretty remote from the common theories of philosophy. All belief of matter of fact or real existence is derived merely from some object present to the memory or senses and a customary conjunction between that and some other object; or, in other words, having found, in many instances, that any two kinds of objects, flame and heat, snow and cold, have always been conjoined together: if flame or snow be presented anew to the senses, the mind is carried by custom to expect heat or cold, and to *believe* that such a quality does exist and will discover itself upon a nearer approach. This belief is the necessary result of placing the mind in such circumstances. It is an operation of the soul, when we are so situated, as unavoidable as to feel the passion of love, when we receive benefits; or hatred, when we meet with injuries. All these operations are a species of natural instincts, which no reasoning or process of the thought and understanding is able either to produce or to prevent.

. . .

* To infinity.

27

The New Riddle of Induction

NELSON GOODMAN

Nelson Goodman (b. 1906) is Emeritus Professor of Philosophy at Harvard University. In addition to Fact, Fiction and Forecast, *from which this selection is drawn, he is the author of* The Structure of Appearance, Languages of Art, Problems and Projects, *and* Ways of Worldmaking.

Goodman argues that the problem Hume raised in the previous selection (reading 26) can be solved, or rather, as Goodman puts it, dissolved. Goodman focuses on the justification of induction. How do we, in practice, go about justifying our inductive inferences? There are two factors, according to Goodman, that we seek to balance. First, there is our inductive practice: we have a tendency to make certain sorts of inferences. For example, on seeing a large number of white swans, and no swans of any other color, we are inclined to believe all swans are white. Second, we have beliefs about which inferences are good ones. For example, inferences drawn from large samples are better than those drawn from smaller samples. Our practice does not always accord with our beliefs about proper inference, and when this happens, some modification is needed. We must modify our practice to accord with our beliefs, or modify our beliefs to accord with our practice. While this procedure involves a certain sort of circularity, it does not involve the sort of circularity claimed by David Hume. The question remains as to whether the circularity involved in Goodman's justification is a vicious one. Goodman argues that it is not.

1. The Old Problem of Induction

AT THE CLOSE of the preceding lecture, I said that today I should examine how matters stand with respect to the problem of induction. In a word, I think they stand ill. But the real difficulties that confront us today are not the traditional ones. What is commonly thought of as the Problem of Induction has been solved, or dissolved; and we face new problems that are not as yet very widely understood. To approach them, I shall have to run as quickly as possible over some very familiar ground.

The problem of the validity of judgments about future or unknown cases arises, as Hume pointed out, because such judgments are neither reports of experience nor logical consequences of it. Predictions, of course, pertain to what has not yet been observed. And they cannot be logically inferred from what has been observed; for what *has* happened imposes no logical restrictions

318

on what *will* happen. Although Hume's dictum that there are no necessary connections of matters of fact has been challenged at times, it has withstood all attacks. Indeed, I should be inclined not merely to agree that there are no necessary connections of matters of fact, but to ask whether there are any necessary connections at all[1]—but that is another story.

Hume's answer to the question how predictions are related to past experience is refreshingly non-cosmic. When an event of one kind frequently follows upon an event of another kind in experience, a habit is formed that leads the mind, when confronted with a new event of the first kind, to pass to the idea of an event of the second kind. The idea of necessary connection arises from the felt impulse of the mind in making this transition.

Now if we strip this account of all extraneous features, the central point is that to the question "Why one prediction rather than another?", Hume answers that the elect prediction is one that accords with a past regularity, because this regularity has established a habit. Thus among alternative statements about a future moment, one statement is distinguished by its consonance with habit and thus with regularities observed in the past. Prediction according to any other alternative is errant.

How satisfactory is this answer? The heaviest criticism has taken the right-eous position that Hume's account at best pertains only to the source of pre-dictions, not their legitimacy; that he sets forth the circumstances under which we make given predictions—and in this sense explains why we make them—but leaves untouched the question of our license for making them. To trace origins, runs the old complaint, is not to establish validity: the real question is not why a prediction is in fact made but how it can be justified. Since this seems to point to the awkward conclusion that the greatest of modern philosophers completely missed the point of his own problem, the idea has developed that he did not really take his solution very seriously, but regarded the main problem as unsolved and perhaps as insoluble. Thus we come to speak of 'Hume's problem' as though he propounded it as a question without answer.

All this seems to me quite wrong. I think Hume grasped the central question and considered his answer to be passably effective. And I think his answer is reasonable and relevant, even if it is not entirely satisfactory, I shall explain presently. At the moment, I merely want to record a protest against the prev-alent notion that the problem of justifying induction, when it is so sharply dissociated from the problem of describing how induction takes place, can fairly be called Hume's problem.

I suppose that the problem of justifying induction has called forth as much fruitless discussion as has any half-way respectable problem of modern philos-

---

[1] Although this remark is merely an aside, perhaps I should explain for the sake of some unusually sheltered reader that the notion of a necessary connection of ideas, or of an absolutely analytic statement, is no longer sacrosanct. Some, like Quine and White, have forthrightly attacked the notion; others, like myself, have simply discarded it; and still others have begun to feel acutely uncomfortable about it.

ophy. The typical writer begins by insisting that some way of justifying predictions must be found; proceeds to argue that for this purpose we need some resounding universal law of the Uniformity of Nature, and then inquires how this universal principle itself can be justified. At this point, if he is tired, he concludes that the principle must be accepted as an indispensable assumption; or if he is energetic and ingenious, he goes on to devise some subtle justification for it. Such an invention, however, seldom satisfies anyone else; and the easier course of accepting an unsubstantiated and even dubious assumption much more sweeping than any actual predictions we make seems an odd and expensive way of justifying them.

2. Dissolution of the Old Problem

Understandably, then, more critical thinkers have suspected that there might be something awry with the problem we are trying to solve. Come to think of it, what precisely would constitute the justification we seek? If the problem is to explain how we know that certain predictions will turn out to be correct, the sufficient answer is that we don't know any such thing. If the problem is to *find* some way of distinguishing antecedently between true and false predictions, we are asking for prevision rather than for philosophical explanation. Nor does it help matters much to say that we are merely trying to show that or why certain predictions are *probable*. Often it is said that while we cannot tell in advance whether a prediction concerning a given throw of a die is true, we can decide whether the prediction is a probable one. But if this means determining how the prediction is related to actual frequency distributions of future throws of the die, surely there is no way of knowing or proving this in advance. On the other hand, if the judgment that the prediction is probable has nothing to do with subsequent occurrences, then the question remains in what sense a probable prediction is any better justified than an improbable one.

Now obviously the genuine problem cannot be one of attaining unattainable knowledge or of accounting for knowledge that we do not in fact have. A better understanding of our problem can be gained by looking for a moment at what is involved in justifying non-inductive inferences. How do we justify a *deduction*? Plainly, by showing that it conforms to the general rules of deductive inference. An argument that so conforms is justified or valid, even if its conclusion happens to be false. An argument that violates a rule is fallacious even if its conclusion happens to be true. To justify a deductive conclusion therefore requires no knowledge of the facts it pertains to. Moreover, when a deductive argument has been shown to conform to the rules of logical inference, we usually consider it justified without going on to ask what justifies the rules. Analogously, the basic task in justifying an inductive inference is to show that it conforms to the general rules of *in*duction. Once we have recognized this, we have gone a long way towards clarifying our problem.

Yet, of course, the rules themselves must eventually be justified. The validity of a deduction depends not upon conformity to any purely arbitrary rules we

may contrive, but upon conformity to valid rules. When we speak of *the* rules of inference we mean the valid rules—or better, *some* valid rules, since there may be alternative sets of equally valid rules. But how is the validity of rules to be determined? Here again we encounter philosophers who insist that these rules follow from some self-evident axiom, and others who try to show that the rules are grounded in the very nature of the human mind. I think the answer lies much nearer the surface. Principles of deductive inference are justified by their conformity with accepted deductive practice. Their validity depends upon accordance with the particular deductive inferences we actually make and sanction. If a rule yields inacceptable inferences, we drop it as invalid. Justification of general rules thus derives from judgments rejecting or accepting particular deductive inferences.

This looks flagrantly circular. I have said that deductive inferences are justified by their conformity to valid general rules, and that general rules are justified by their conformity to valid inferences. But this circle is a virtuous one. The point is that rules and particular inferences alike are justified by being brought into agreement with each other. *A rule is amended if it yields an inference we are unwilling to accept; an inference is rejected if it violates a rule we are unwilling to amend.* The process of justification is the delicate one of making mutual adjustments between rules and accepted inferences; and in the agreement achieved lies the only justification needed for either.

All this applies equally well to induction. An inductive inference, too, is justified by conformity to general rules, and a general rule by conformity to accepted inductive inferences. Predictions are justified if they conform to valid canons of induction; and the canons are valid if they accurately codify accepted inductive practice.

A result of such analysis is that we can stop plaguing ourselves with certain spurious questions about induction. We no longer demand an explanation for guarantees that we do not have, or seek keys to knowledge that we cannot obtain. It dawns upon us that the traditional smug insistence upon a hard-and-fast line between justifying induction and describing ordinary inductive practice distorts the problem. And we owe belated apologies to Hume. For in dealing with the question how normally accepted inductive judgments are made, he was in fact dealing with the question of inductive validity.[2] The validity of a

---

[2] A hasty reader might suppose that my insistence here upon identifying the problem of justification with a problem of description is out of keeping with my parenthetical insistence in the preceding lecture that the goal of philosophy is something quite different from the mere description of ordinary or scientific procedure. Let me repeat that the point urged there was that the organization of the explanatory account need not reflect the manner or order in which predicates are adopted in practice. It surely must describe practice, however, in the sense that the extensions of predicates as explicated must conform in certain ways to the extensions of the same predicates as applied in practice. Hume's account is a description in just this sense. For it is an attempt to set forth the circumstances under which those inductive judgments are made that are normally accepted as valid; and to do that is to state necessary and sufficient conditions for, and thus to define, valid induction. What I am maintaining above is that the problem of justifying induction is not something over and above the problem of describing or defining valid induction.

prediction consisted for him in its arising from habit, and thus in its exemplifying some past regularity. His answer was incomplete and perhaps not entirely correct; but it was not beside the point. The problem of induction is not a problem of demonstration but a problem of defining the difference between valid and invalid predictions.

This clears the air but leaves a lot to be done. As principles of *de*ductive inference, we have the familiar and highly developed laws of logic; but there are available no such precisely stated and well-recognized principles of inductive inference. Mill's canons hardly rank with Aristotle's rules of the syllogism, let alone with *Principia Mathematica*. Elaborate and valuable treatises on probability usually leave certain fundamental questions untouched. Only in very recent years has there been any explicit and systematic work upon what I call the constructive task of confirmation theory.

. . .

4. The New Riddle of Induction

Confirmation of a hypothesis by an instance depends rather heavily upon features of the hypothesis other than its syntactical form. That a given piece of copper conducts electricity increases the credibility of statements asserting that other pieces of copper conduct electricity, and thus confirms the hypothesis that all copper conducts electricity. But the fact that a given man now in this room is a third son does not increase the credibility of statements asserting that other men now in this room are third sons, and so does not confirm the hypothesis that all men now in this room are third sons. Yet in both cases our hypothesis is a generalization of the evidence statement. The difference is that in the former case the hypothesis is a *lawlike* statement; while in the latter case, the hypothesis is a merely contingent or accidental generality. Only a statement that is *lawlike*—regardless of its truth or falsity or its scientific importance—is capable of receiving confirmation from an instance of it; accidental statements are not. Plainly, then, we must look for a way of distinguishing lawlike from accidental statements.

So long as what seems to be needed is merely a way of excluding a few odd and unwanted cases that are inadvertently admitted by our definition of confirmation, the problem may not seem very hard or very pressing. We fully expect that minor defects will be found in our definition and that the necessary refinements will have to be worked out patiently one after another. But some further examples will show that our present difficulty is of a much graver kind.

Suppose that all emeralds examined before a certain time *t* are green. At time *t*, then, our observations support the hypothesis that all emeralds are green; and this is in accord with our definition of confirmation. Our evidence statements assert that emerald *a* is green, that emerald *b* is green, and so on; and each confirms the general hypothesis that all emeralds are green. So far, so good.

Now let me introduce another predicate less familiar than "green". It is the predicate "grue" and it applies to all things examined before *t* just in case they

are green but to other things just in case they are blue. Then at time *t* we have, for each evidence statement asserting that a given emerald is green, a parallel evidence statement asserting that that emerald is grue. And the statements that emerald *a* is grue, that emerald *b* is grue, and so on, will each confirm the general hypothesis that all emeralds are grue. Thus according to our definition, the prediction that all emeralds subsequently examined will be green and the prediction that all will be grue are alike confirmed by evidence statements describing the same observations. But if an emerald subsequently examined is grue, it is blue and hence not green. Thus although we are well aware which of the two incompatible predictions is genuinely confirmed, they are equally well confirmed according to our present definition. Moreover, it is clear that if we simply choose an appropriate predicate, then on the basis of these same observations we shall have equal confirmation, by our definition, for any prediction whatever about other emeralds—or indeed about anything else.[3] As in our earlier example, only the predictions subsumed under lawlike hypothesis are genuinely confirmed; but we have no criterion as yet for determining lawlikeness. And now we see that without some such criterion, our definition not merely includes a few unwanted cases, but is so completely ineffectual that it virtually excludes nothing. We are left once again with the intolerable result that anything confirms anything. This difficulty cannot be set aside as an annoying detail to be taken care of in due course. It has to be met before our definition will work at all.

Nevertheless, the difficulty is often slighted because on the surface there seem to be easy ways of dealing with it. Sometimes, for example, the problem is thought to be much like the paradox of the ravens. We are here again, it is pointed out, making tacit and illegitimate use of information outside the stated evidence: the information, for example, that different samples of one material are usually alike in conductivity, and the information that different men in a lecture audience are usually not alike in the number of their older brothers. But while it is true that such information is being smuggled in, this does not by itself settle the matter as it settles the matter of the ravens. There the point was that when the smuggled information is forthrightly declared, its effect upon the confirmation of the hypothesis in question is immediately and properly registered by the definition we are using. On the other hand, if to our initial evidence we add statements concerning the conductivity of pieces of other materials or concerning the number of older brothers of members of other lecture audiences, this will not in the least affect the confirmation, according to our definition, of the hypothesis concerning copper or of that concerning this lecture audience. Since our definition is insensitive to the bearing upon

---

[3] For instance, we shall have equal confirmation, by our present definition, for the prediction that roses subsequently examined will be blue. Let "emerose" apply just to emeralds examined before time *t*, and to roses examined later. Then all emeroses so far examined are grue, and this confirms the hypothesis that all emeroses are grue and hence the prediction that roses subsequently examined will be blue. The problem raised by such antecedents has been little noticed, but is no easier to meet than that raised by similarly perverse consequents.

hypotheses of evidence so related to them, even when the evidence is fully declared, the difficulty about accidental hypotheses cannot be explained away on the ground that such evidence is being surreptitiously taken into account.

A more promising suggestion is to explain the matter in terms of the effect of this other evidence not directly upon the hypothesis in question but *in*directly through other hypotheses that *are* confirmed, according to our definition, by such evidence. Our information about other materials does by our definition confirm such hypotheses as that all pieces of iron conduct electricity, that no pieces of rubber do, and so on; and these hypotheses, the explanation runs, impart to the hypothesis that all pieces of copper conduct electricity (and also to the hypothesis that none do) the character of lawlikeness—that is, amenability to confirmation by direct positive instances when found. On the other hand, our information about other lecture audiences *dis*confirms many hypotheses to the effect that all the men in one audience are third sons, or that none are; and this strips any character of lawlikeness from the hypothesis that all (or the hypothesis that none) of the men in *this* audience are third sons. But clearly if this course is to be followed, the circumstances under which hypotheses are thus related to one another will have to be precisely articulated.

The problem, then, is to define the relevant way in which such hypotheses must be alike. Evidence for the hypothesis that all iron conducts electricity enhances the lawlikeness of the hypothesis that all zirconium conducts electricity, but does not similarly affect the hypothesis that all the objects on my desk conduct electricity. Wherein lies the difference? The first two hypotheses fall under the broader hypothesis—call it *"H"*—that every class of things of the same material is uniform in conductivity; the first and third fall only under some such hypothesis as—call it *"K"*—that every class of things that are either all of the same material or all on a desk is uniform in conductivity. Clearly the important difference here is that evidence for a statement affirming that one of the classes covered by *H* has the property in question increases the credibility of any statement affirming that another such class has this property; while nothing of the sort holds true with respect to *K*. But this is only to say that *H* is lawlike and *K* is not. We are faced anew with the very problem we are trying to solve: the problem of distinguishing between lawlike and accidental hypotheses.

The most popular way of attacking the problem takes its cue from the fact that accidental hypotheses seem typically to involve some spatial or temporal restriction, or reference to some particular individual. They seem to concern the people in some particular room, or the objects on some particular person's desk; while lawlike hypotheses characteristically concern all ravens or all pieces of copper whatsoever. Complete generality is thus very often supposed to be a sufficient condition of lawlikeness; but to define this complete generality is by no means easy. Merely to require that the hypothesis contain no term naming, describing, or indicating a particular thing or location will obviously not be enough. The troublesome hypothesis that all emeralds are grue contains no such term; and where such a term does occur, as in hypotheses about men in *this room*, it can be suppressed in favor of some predicate (short or long, new or old) that contains no such term but applies only to exactly the same things.

One might think, then, of excluding not only hypotheses that actually contain terms for specific individuals but also all hypotheses that are equivalent to others that do contain such terms. But, as we have just seen, to exclude only hypotheses of which *all* equivalents contain such terms is to exclude nothing. On the other hand, to exclude all hypotheses that have *some* equivalent containing such a term is to exclude everything; for even the hypothesis

All grass is green

has as an equivalent

All grass in London or elsewhere is green.

The next step, therefore, has been to consider ruling out predicates of certain kinds. A syntactically universal hypothesis is lawlike, the proposal runs, if its predicates are 'purely qualitative' or 'non-positional'. This will obviously accomplish nothing if a purely qualitative predicate is then conceived either as one that is equivalent to some expression free of terms for specific individuals, or as one that is equivalent to no expression that contains such a term; for this only raises again the difficulties just pointed out. The claim appears to be rather that at least in the case of a simple enough predicate we can readily determine by direct inspection of its meaning whether or not it is purely qualitative. But even aside from obscurities in the notion of 'the meaning' of a predicate, this claim seems to me wrong. I simply do not know how to tell whether a predicate is qualitative or positional, except perhaps by completely begging the question at issue and asking whether the predicate is 'well-behaved'—that is, whether simple syntactically universal hypotheses applying it are lawlike.

This statement will not go unprotested. "Consider", it will be argued, "the predicates 'blue' and 'green' and the predicate 'grue' introduced earlier, and also the predicate 'bleen' that applies to emeralds examined before time t just in case they are blue and to other emeralds just in case they are green. Surely it is clear", the argument runs, "that the first two are purely qualitative and the second two are not; for the meaning of each of the latter two plainly involves reference to a specific temporal position." To this I reply that indeed I do recognize the first two as well-behaved predicates admissible in lawlike hypotheses, and the second two as ill-behaved predicates. But the argument that the former but not the latter are purely qualitative seems to me quite unsound. True enough, if we start with "blue" and "green", then "grue" and "bleen" will be explained in terms of "blue" and "green" and a temporal term. But equally truly, if we start with "grue" and "bleen", then "blue" and "green" will be explained in terms of "grue" and "bleen" and a temporal term; "green", for example, applies to emeralds examined before time t just in case they are grue, and to other emeralds just in case they are bleen. Thus qualitativeness is an entirely relative matter and does not by itself establish any dichotomy of predicates. This relativity seems to be completely overlooked by those who contend that the qualitative character of a predicate is a criterion for its good behavior.

Of course, one may ask why we need worry about such unfamiliar predicates as "grue" or about accidental hypotheses in general, since we are unlikely to use them in making predictions. If our definition works for such hypotheses as are normally employed, isn't that all we need? In a sense, yes; but only in the sense that we need no definition, no theory of induction, and no philosophy of knowledge at all. We get along well enough without them in daily life and in scientific research. But if we seek a theory at all, we cannot excuse gross anomalies resulting from a proposed theory by pleading that we can avoid them in practice. The odd cases we have been considering are clinically pure cases that, though seldom encountered in practice, nevertheless display to best advantage the symptoms of a widespread and destructive malady.

We have so far neither any answer nor any promising clue to an answer to the question what distinguishes lawlike or confirmable hypotheses from accidental or non-confirmable ones; and what may at first have seemed a minor technical difficulty has taken on the stature of a major obstacle to the development of a satisfactory theory of confirmation. It is this problem that I call the new riddle of induction.

28

The Interdependence of Beliefs

W.V.O. QUINE

W. V. O. Quine (b. 1908) is Edgar Pierce Professor Emeritus at Harvard University. His work in logic, metaphysics, epistemology, philosophy of science, and philosophy of language has changed the course of philosophy in the twentieth century. His books include Word and Object, From a Logical Point of View *and* Ontological Relativity and Other Essays.

Descartes argued that all our knowledge is based on an indubitable foundation. Locke and Hume tried to show how our knowledge of the external world is based on a foundation of sense experience. In this brief selection from his seminal paper, "Two Dogmas of Empiricism," Quine argues that knowledge has no foundation of any kind. All our beliefs are interdependent, Quine argues, thus even beliefs about one's present sense experience are dependent on others. Knowledge has no foundation, but consists instead of a web of belief, a system of interdependent beliefs any of which may be revised in light of changes elsewhere in the system.

· · ·

THE TOTALITY OF our so-called knowledge or beliefs, from the most casual matters of geography and history to the profoundest laws of atomic physics or even of pure mathematics and logic, is a man-made fabric which impinges on experience only along the edges. Or, to change the figure, total science is like a field of force whose boundary conditions are experience. A conflict with experience at the periphery occasions readjustments in the interior of the field. Truth values have to be redistributed over some of our statements. Reëvaluation of some statements* entails reëvaluation of others, because of their logical interconnections—the logical laws being in turn simply certain further statements of the system, certain further elements of the field. Having reëvaluated one statement we must reëvaluate some others, which may be statements logically connected with the first or may be the statements of logical connections themselves. But the total field is so underdetermined by its boundary conditions, experience, that there is much latitude of choice as to what statements to reëvaluate in the light of any single contrary experience. No particular experiences are linked with any particular statements in the interior of the field, except indirectly through considerations of equilibrium affecting the field as a whole.

---

* That is, we must re-evaluate which statements are true and which are false.

327

If this view is right, it is misleading to speak of the empirical content of an individual statement—especially if it is a statement at all remote from the experiential periphery of the field. Furthermore it becomes folly to seek a boundary between synthetic statements, which hold contingently on experience, and analytic statements, which hold come what may. Any statement can be held true come what may, if we make drastic enough adjustments elsewhere in the system. Even a statement very close to the periphery can be held true in the face of recalcitrant experience by pleading hallucination or by amending certain statements of the kind called logical laws. Conversely, by the same token, no statement is immune to revision. Revision even of the logical law of the excluded middle* has been proposed as a means of simplifying quantum mechanics; and what difference is there in principle between such a shift and the shift whereby Kepler superseded Ptolemy, or Einstein Newton, or Darwin Aristotle?

For vividness I have been speaking in terms of varying distances from a sensory periphery. Let me try now to clarify this notion without metaphor. Certain statements, though *about* physical objects and not sense experience, seem peculiarly germane to sense experience—and in a selective way: some statements to some experiences, others to others. Such statements, especially germane to particular experiences, I picture as near the periphery. But in this relation of "germaneness" I envisage nothing more than a loose association reflecting the relative likelihood, in practice, of our choosing one statement rather than another for revision in the event of recalcitrant experience. For example, we can imagine recalcitrant experiences to which we would surely be inclined to accommodate our system by reëvaluating just the statement that there are brick houses on Elm Street, together with related statements on the same topic. We can imagine other recalcitrant experiences to which we would be inclined to accommodate our system by reëvaluating just the statement that there are no centaurs, along with kindred statements. A recalcitrant experience can, I have urged, be accommodated by any of various alternative reëvaluations in various alternative quarters of the total system; but, in the cases which we are now imagining, our natural tendency to disturb the total system as little as possible would lead us to focus our revisions upon these specific statements concerning brick houses or centaurs. These statements are felt, therefore, to have a sharper empirical reference than highly theoretical statements of physics or logic or ontology.† The latter statements may be thought of as relatively centrally located within the total network, meaning merely that little preferential connection with any particular sense data obtrudes itself.

As an empiricist I continue to think of the conceptual scheme of science as a tool, ultimately, for predicting future experience in the light of past experience. Physical objects are conceptually imported into the situation as convenient intermediaries—not by definition in terms of experience, but simply as irreducible posits comparable, epistemologically, to the gods of Homer. For

---

* The law that every statement is either true or false.

† Statements of ontology are statements about what exists.

my part I do, qua lay physicist, believe in physical objects and not in Homer's gods; and I consider it a scientific error to believe otherwise. But in point of epistemological footing the physical objects and the gods differ only in degree and not in kind. Both sorts of entities enter our conception only as cultural posits. The myth of physical objects is epistemologically superior to most in that it has proved more efficacious than other myths as a device for working a manageable structure into the flux of experience.

Positing does not stop with macroscopic physical objects. Objects at the atomic level are posited to make the laws of macroscopic objects, and ultimately the laws of experience, simpler and more manageable; and we need not expect or demand full definition of atomic and subatomic entities in terms of macroscopic ones, any more than definition of macroscopic things in terms of sense data. Science is a continuation of common sense, and it continues the common-sense expedient of swelling ontology to simplify theory.

Physical objects, small and large, are not the only posits. Forces are another example; and indeed we are told nowadays that the boundary between energy and matter is obsolete. Moreover, the abstract entities which are the substance of mathematics—ultimately classes and classes of classes and so on up—are another posit in the same spirit. Epistemologically these are myths on the same footing with physical objects and gods, neither better or worse except for differences in the degree to which they expedite our dealings with sense experiences.

The over-all algebra of rational and irrational numbers is underdetermined by the algebra of rational numbers, but is smoother and more convenient; and it includes the algebra of rational numbers as a jagged or gerrymandered part. Total science, mathematical and natural and human, is similarly but more extremely underdetermined by experience. The edge of the system must be kept squared with experience; the rest, with all its elaborate myths or fictions, has as its objective the simplicity of laws.

Ontological questions, under this view, are on a par with questions of natural science. Consider the question whether to countenance classes as entities. This, as I have argued elsewhere, is the question whether to quantify with respect to variables which take classes as values. Now Carnap has maintained that this is a question not of matters of fact but of choosing a convenient language form, a convenient conceptual scheme or framework for science. With this I agree, but only on the proviso that the same be conceded regarding scientific hypotheses generally. Carnap has recognized that he is able to preserve a double standard for ontological questions and scientific hypotheses only by assuming an absolute distinction between the analytic and the synthetic; and I need not say again that this is a distinction which I reject.

The issue over there being classes seems more a question of convenient conceptual scheme; the issue over there being centaurs, or brick houses on Elm Street, seems more a question of fact. But I have been urging that this difference is only one of degree, and that it turns upon our vaguely pragmatic inclination to adjust one strand of the fabric of science rather than another in accommodating some particular recalcitrant experience. Conservatism figures in such choices, and so does the quest for simplicity.

Carnap, Lewis, and others take a pragmatic stand on the question of choosing between language forms, scientific frameworks; but their pragmatism leaves off at the imagined boundary between the analytic and the synthetic. In repudiating such a boundary I espouse a more thorough pragmatism. Each man is given a scientific heritage plus a continuing barrage of sensory stimulation; and the considerations which guide him in warping his scientific heritage to fit his continuing sensory promptings are, where rational, pragmatic.

29

The Nature of
Natural Knowledge

W.V.O. QUINE

For biographical information about W. V. O. Quine, see reading 28.

In this selection, Quine argues that the challenge of skepticism has been misunderstood, and that this misunderstanding has led philosophers to approach the central questions of epistemology in a misguided manner. Descartes (reading 24) responded to skepticism by suspending belief wherever doubt was possible; knowledge was to be found by building on an indubitable foundation. This approach, claims Quine, misunderstands the source of the skeptic's concern. Skepticism is fueled by the discoveries of science. It is through science itself that we discover not only the falsity of our former beliefs, but our limitations as seekers of knowledge. This, in turn, may make us wonder whether knowledge is possible at all. Although science is the source of our skepticism, it is not inappropriate to show how scientific results themselves give us reason to believe our beliefs are, for the most part, true. Thus, we need not search for a foundation of indubitable beliefs in order to respond to the skeptic; we need only see whether science has at its disposal an answer to the very problem it raised.

Quine argues that the theory of evolution provides us with just such an answer: were our beliefs massively false, the species could not have survived. Our very existence is thus testimony to the truth of our beliefs.

DOUBT HAS OFT BEEN SAID to be the mother of philosophy. This has a true ring for those of us who look upon philosophy primarily as the theory of knowledge. For the theory of knowledge has its origin in doubt, in scepticism. Doubt is what prompts us to try to develop a theory of knowledge. Furthermore, doubt is also the first step to take in developing a theory of knowledge, if we adopt the line of Descartes.

But this is only half of a curious interplay between doubt and knowledge. Doubt prompts the theory of knowledge, yes; but knowledge, also, was what prompted the doubt. Scepticism is an offshoot of science. The basis for scepticism is the awareness of illusion, the discovery that we must not always believe our eyes. Scepticism battens on mirages, on seemingly bent sticks in water, on rainbows, after-images, double images, dreams. But in what sense are these illusions? In the sense that they seem to be material objects which they in fact are not. Illusions are illusions only relative to a prior acceptance of genuine bodies with which to contrast them. In a world of immediate sense data with

no bodies posited and no questions asked, a distinction between reality and illusion would have no place. The positing of bodies is already rudimentary physical science; and it is only after that stage that the sceptic's invidious distinctions can make sense. Bodies have to be posited before there can be a motive, however tenuous, for acquiescing in a non-committal world of the immediate given.

Rudimentary physical science, that is, common sense about bodies, is thus needed as a springboard for scepticism. It contributes the needed notion of a distinction between reality and illusion, and that is not all. It also discerns regularities of bodily behaviour which are indispensable to that distinction. The sceptic's example of the seemingly bent stick owes its force to our knowledge that sticks do not bend by immersion; and his examples of mirages, after-images, dreams, and the rest are similarly parasitic upon positive science, however primitive.

I am not accusing the sceptic of begging the question. He is quite within his rights in assuming science in order to refute science; this, if carried out, would be a straightforward argument by *reductio ad absurdum.* * I am only making the point that sceptical doubts are scientific doubts.

Epistemologists have coped with their sceptical doubts by trying to reconstruct our knowledge of the external world from sensations. A characteristic effort was Berkeley's theory of vision, in which he sought our clues for a third dimension, depth, in our two-dimensional visual field. The very posing of this epistemological problem depends in a striking way upon acceptations of physical science. The goal of the construction, namely the depth dimension, is of course deliberately taken from the science of the external world; but what particularly wants noticing is that also the accepted basis of the construction, the two-dimensional visual field, was itself dictated by the science of the external world as well. The light that informs us of the external world impinges on the two-dimensional surface of the eye, and it was Berkeley's awareness of this that set his problem.

Epistemology is best looked upon, then, as an enterprise within natural science. Cartesian doubt is not the way to begin. Retaining our present beliefs about nature, we can still ask how we can have arrived at them. Science tells us that our only source of information about the external world is through the impact of light rays and molecules upon our sensory surfaces. Stimulated in these ways, we somehow evolve an elaborate and useful science. How do we do this, and why does the resulting science work so well? These are genuine questions, and no feigning of doubt is needed to appreciate them. They are scientific questions about a species of primates, and they are open to investigation in natural science, the very science whose acquisition is being investigated.

The utility of science, from a practical point of view, lies in fulfilled expectation: true prediction. This is true not only of sophisticated science, but of its primitive progenitor as well; and it may be good strategy on our part to think

---

* Reduction to absurdity.

first of the most primitive case. This case is simple induction. It is the expectation, when some past event recurs, that the sequel of that past event will recur too. People are prone to this, and so are other animals.

It may be felt that I am unduly intellectualizing the dumb animals in attributing expectation and induction to them. Still the net resultant behaviour of dumb animals is much on a par with our own, at the level of simple induction. In a dog's experience, a clatter of pans in the kitchen has been followed by something to eat. So now, hearing the clatter again, he goes to the kitchen in expectation of dinner. His going to the kitchen is our evidence of his expectation, if we care to speak of expectation. Or we can skip this intervening variable, as Skinner calls it, and speak merely of reinforced response, conditioned reflex, habit formation.

When we talk easily of repetition of events, repetition of stimuli, we cover over a certain significant factor. It is the *similarity* factor. It can be brought into the open by speaking of events rather as unique, dated, unrepeated particulars, and then speaking of similarities between them. Each of the noisy episodes of the pans is a distinct event, however similar, and so is each of the ensuing dinners. What we can say of the dog in those terms is that he hears something similar to the old clatter and proceeds to expect something similar to the old dinner. Or, if we want to eliminate the intervening variable, we can still say this: when the dog hears something similar to the old clatter and, going to the kitchen, gets something similar to the old dinner, he is reinforced in his disposition to go to the kitchen after each further event similar to the old clatter.

What is significant about this similarity factor is its subjectivity. Is similarity the mere sharing of many attributes? But any two things share countless attributes—or anyway any two objects share membership in countless classes. The similarity that matters, in the clatter of the pans, is similarity for the dog. Again I seem to appeal to the dog's mental life, but again I can eliminate this intervening variable. We can analyse similarity, for the dog, in terms of his dispositions to behaviour: his patterns of habit formation. His habit of going to the kitchen after a clatter of pans is itself our basis for saying that the clatter events are similar for the dog, and that the dinner events are similar for the dog. It is by experimental reinforcement and extinction along these lines that we can assess similarities for the dog, determining whether event a is more similar to b than to c for him. Meanwhile his mental life is as may be.

Now our question 'Why is science so successful?' makes some rudimentary sense already at this level, as applied to the dog. For the dog's habit formation, his primitive induction, involved extrapolation along similarity lines: episodes similar to the old clattering episode engendered expectation of episodes similar to the old dinner episode. And now the crux of the problem is the subjectivity of similarity. Why should nature, however lawful, match up at all with the dog's subjective similarity ratings? Here, at its most primitive, is the question 'Why is science so successful?'

We are taking this as a scientific question, remember, open to investigation by natural science itself. Why should the dog's implicit similarity ratings tend to fit world trends, in such a way as to favour the dog's implicit expectations?

An answer is offered by Darwin's theory of natural selection. Individuals whose similarity groupings conduce largely to true expectations have a good chance of finding food and avoiding predators, and so a good chance of living to reproduce their kind.

What I have said of the dog holds equally of us, at least in our pursuit of the rudimentary science of common sense. We predict in the light of observed uniformities, and these are uniformities by our subjective similarity standards. These standards are innate ones, overlaid and modified by experience; and natural selection has endowed us, like the dog, with a head start in the way of helpful, innate similarity standards.

I am not appealing to Darwinian biology to justify induction. This would be circular, since biological knowledge depends on induction. Rather I am granting the efficacy of induction, and then observing that Darwinian biology, if true, helps explain why induction is as efficacious as it is.

We must notice, still, a further limitation. Natural selection may be expected only to have encouraged similarity standards conducive to rough and ready anticipations of experience in a state of nature. Such standards are not necessarily conducive to deep science. Colour is a case in point. Colour dominates our scene; similarity in colour is similarity at its most conspicuous. Yet, as J. J. C. Smart points out, colour plays little role in natural science. Things can be alike in colour even though one of them is reflecting green light of uniform wave length while the other is reflecting mixed waves of yellow and blue. Properties that are most germane to sophisticated science are camouflaged by colour more than revealed by it. Over-sensitivity to colour may have been all to the good when we were bent on quickly distinguishing predator from prey or good plants from bad. But true science cuts through all this and sorts things out differently, leaving colour largely irrelevant.

Colour is not the only such case. Taxonomy is rich in examples to show that visual resemblance is a poor index of kinship. Natural selection has even abetted the deception; thus some owls have grown to resemble cats, for their own good, and others resemble monkeys. Natural selection works both to improve a creature's similarity standards and to help him abuse his enemies' similarity standards.

For all their fallibility, our innate similarity standards are indispensable to science as an entering wedge. They continue to be indispensable, moreover, even as science advances. For the advance of science depends on continued observation, continued checking of predictions. And there, at the observational level, the unsophisticated similarity standards of common sense remain in force.

An individual's innate similarity standards undergo some revision, of course, even at the common-sense level, indeed even at the sub-human level, through learning. An animal may learn to tell a cat from an owl. The ability to learn is itself a product of natural selection, with evident survival value. An animal's innate similarity standards are a rudimentary instrument for prediction, and then learning is a progressive refinement of that instrument, making for more dependable prediction. In man, and most conspicuously in recent centuries, this refinement has consisted in the development of a vast and bewildering

growth of conceptual or linguistic apparatus, the whole of natural science. Biologically, still, it is like the animal's learning about cats and owls; it is a learned improvement over simple induction by innate similarity standards. It makes for more and better prediction.

Science revises our similarity standards, we saw; thus we discount colour, for some purposes, and we liken whales to cows rather than to fish. But this is not the sole or principal way in which science fosters prediction. Mere improvement of similarity standards would increase our success at simple induction, but this is the least of it. Science departs from simple induction. Science is a ponderous linguistic structure, fabricated of theoretical terms linked by fabricated hypotheses, and keyed to observable events here and there. Indirectly, via this labyrinthine superstructure, the scientist predicts future observations on the basis of past ones; and he may revise the superstructure when the predictions fail. It is no longer simple induction. It is the hypothetico-deductive method. But, like the animal's simple induction over innate similarities, it is still a biological device for anticipating experience. It owes its elements still to natural selection—notably, the similarity standards that continue to operate at the observational level. The biological survival value of the resulting scientific structure, however, is as may be. Traits that were developed by natural selection have been known to prove lethal, through over-development and remote effects or changing environment. In any event, and for whatever good it may do us, the hypothetico-deductive method is delivering knowledge hand over fist. It is facilitating prediction.

I said that science is a linguistic structure that is keyed to observation at some points. Some sentences are keyed directly to observation: the observation sentences. Let us examine this connection. First I must explain what I mean by an observation sentence. One distinctive trait of such a sentence is that its truth value varies with the circumstances prevailing at the time of the utterance. It is a sentence like 'This is red' or 'It is raining', which is true on one occasion and false on another; unlike 'Sugar is sweet', whose truth value endures regardless of occasion of utterance. In a word, observation sentences are occasion sentences, not standing sentences.

But their being occasion sentences is not the only distinctive trait of observation sentences. Not only must the truth value of an observation sentence depend on the circumstances of its utterance; it must depend on intersubjectively observable circumstances. Certainly the fisherman's sentence 'I just felt a nibble' is true or false depending on the circumstances of its utterance; but the relevant circumstances are privy to the speaker rather than being out in the open for all present witnesses to share. The sentence 'I just felt a nibble' is an occasion sentence but not an observation sentence, in my sense of the term.

An observation sentence, then, is an occasion sentence whose occasion is intersubjectively observable. But this is still not enough. After all, the sentence 'There goes John's old tutor' meets these requirements; it is an occasion sentence, and all present witnesses can see the old tutor plodding by. But the sentence fails of a third requirement: the witnesses must in general be able to appreciate that the observation which they are sharing is one that verifies the

sentence. They must have been in a position, equally with the speaker, to have assented to the sentence on their own in the circumstances. They are in that position in the case of 'This is red' and 'It is raining' and 'There goes an old man', but not in the case of 'There goes John's old tutor.'

Such, then, is an observation sentence: it is an occasion sentence whose occasion is not only intersubjectively observable but is generally adequate, moreover, to elicit assent to the sentence from any present witness conversant with the language. It is not a report of private sense data; typically, rather, it contains references to physical objects.

These sentences, I say, are keyed directly to observation. But how *keyed,* now—what is the nature of the connection? It is a case of conditioned response. It is not quite the simplest kind; we do not say 'red' or 'This is red' whenever we see something red. But we do assent if asked. Mastery of the term 'red' is acquisition of the habit of assenting when the term is queried in the presence of red, and only in the presence of red.

At the primitive level, an observation sentence is apt to take the form of a single word, thus 'ball', or 'red'. What makes it easy to learn is the intersubjective observability of the relevant circumstances at the time of utterance. The parent can verify that the child is seeing red at the time, and so can reward the child's assent to the query. Also the child can verify that the parent is seeing red when the parent assents to such a query.

In this habit formation the child is in effect determining, by induction, the range of situations in which the adult will assent to the query 'red', or approve the child's utterance of 'red'. He is extrapolating along similarity lines; this red episode is similar to that red episode by his lights. His success depends, therefore, on substantial agreement between his similarity standards and those of the adult. Happily the agreement holds; and no wonder, since our similarity standards are a matter partly of natural selection and partly of subsequent experience in a shared environment. If substantial agreement in similarity standards were not there, this first step in language acquisition would be blocked.

We have been seeing that observation sentences are the starting-points in the learning of language. Also, they are the starting-points and the check points of scientific theory. They serve both purposes for one and the same reason: the intersubjective observability of the relevant circumstances at the time of utterance. It is this, intersubjective observability at the time, that enables the child to learn when to assent to the observation sentence. And it is this also, intersubjective observability at the time, that qualifies observation sentences as check points for scientific theory. Observation sentences state the evidence, to which all witnesses must accede.

I had characterized science as a linguistic structure that is keyed to observation at some points. Now we have seen how it is keyed to observation: some of the sentences, the observation sentences, are conditioned to observable events in combination with a routine of query and assent. There is the beginning, here, of a partnership between the theory of language learning and the theory of scientific evidence. It is clear, when you think about it, that this partnership must continue. For when a child learns his language from his elders, what has

he to go on? He can learn observation sentences by consideration of their observable circumstances, as we saw. But how can he learn the rest of the language, including the theoretical sentences of science? Somehow he learns to carry his observation terms over into theoretical contexts, variously embedded. Somehow he learns to connect his observation sentences with standing sentences, sentences whose truth values do not depend on the occasion of utterance. It is only by such moves, however ill understood, that anyone masters the non-observational part of his mother tongue. He can learn the observational part in firm and well-understood ways, and then he must build out somehow, imitating what he hears and linking it tenuously and conjecturally to what he knows, until by dint of trial and social correction he achieves fluent dialogue with his community. This discourse depends, for whatever empirical content it has, on its devious and tenuous connections with the observation sentences; and those are the same connections, nearly enough, through which one has achieved one's fluent part in that discourse. The channels by which, having learned observation sentences, we acquire theoretical language, are the very channels by which observation lends evidence to scientific theory. It all stands to reason; for language is man-made and the locutions of scientific theory have no meaning but what they acquired by our learning to use them.

We see, then, a strategy for investigating the relation of evidential support, between observation and scientific theory. We can adopt a genetic approach, studying how theoretical language is learned. For the evidential relation is virtually enacted, it would seem, in the learning. This genetic strategy is attractive because the learning of language goes on in the world and is open to scientific study. It is a strategy for the scientific study of scientific method and evidence. We have here a good reason to regard the theory of language as vital to the theory of knowledge.

When we try to understand the relation between scientific theory and the observation sentences, we are brought up short by the break between occasion sentences and standing sentences; for observation sentences are of the one kind while theoretical sentences are of the other. The scientific system cannot digest occasion sentences; their substance must first be converted into standing sentences. The observation sentence 'Rain' or 'It is raining' will not do; we must put the information into a standing sentence: 'Rain at Heathrow 1600 G. M. T. 23 February 1974.' This report is ready for filing in the archives of science. It still reports an observation, but it is a standing report rather than an occasion sentence. How do we get from the passing observation of rain to the standing report?

This can be explained by a cluster of observations and observation sentences, having to do with other matters besides the rain. Thus take the term 'Heathrow'. Proper names of persons, buildings, and localities are best treated as observation terms, on a par with 'red' and 'rain'. All such terms can be learned by ostension, repeated sufficiently to suggest the intended scope and limits of application. 'Here is Heathrow,' then, is an observation sentence on a par with 'It is raining'; and their conjunction, 'Raining at Heathrow,' is an observation sentence as well. It is an occasion sentence still, of course, and not a standing

report of observation. But now the two further needed ingredients, hour and date, can be added as pointer readings: 'The clock reads 1600' and 'The calendar reads 23 February 1974' are further observation sentences. Taking the conjunction of all four, we still have an observation sentence: 'Rain at Heathrow with clock at 1600 and calendar at 23 February 1974.' But it is an observation sentence with this curious trait: it gives lasting information, dependent no longer on the vicissitudes of tense or of indicator words like 'here' and 'now'. It is suitable for filing.

True, the clock and calendar may have been wrong. As an observation sentence our report must be viewed as stating the temporal readings and not the temporal facts. The question of the temporal facts belongs to scientific theory, somewhat above the observational level. Theoretical repercussions of this and other observations could eventually even prompt a modest scientific hypothesis to the effect that the clock or the calendar had been wrong.

I think this example serves pretty well as a paradigm case, to show how we can get from the occasion sentences of observation to the standing reports of observation that are needed for scientific theory. But this connection is by no means the only connection between observation sentences and standing sentences. Thus consider the universal categorical, 'A dog is an animal.' This is a standing sentence, but it is not, like the example of rain at Heathrow, a standing report of observation. Let us resume our genetic strategy: how might a child have mastered such a universal categorical?

I shall venture one hypothesis, hoping that it may be improved upon. The child has learned to assent to the observation term 'a dog' when it is queried in the conspicuous presence of dogs, and he has learned to assent to 'an animal' likewise when it is queried in the conspicuous presence of dogs (though not only dogs). Because of his close association of the word 'dog' with dogs, the mere sound of the word 'dog' disposes him to respond to the subsequent query 'an animal' as he would have done if a dog had been there; so he assents when he hears 'a dog' followed by the query, 'an animal?'. Being rewarded for so doing, he ever after assents to the query 'A dog is an animal?' In the same way he learns a few other examples of the universal categorical. Next he rises to a mastery of the universal categorical construction 'An S is a P' in general: he learns to apply it to new cases on his own. This important step of abstraction can perhaps be explained in parallel fashion to the early learning of observation sentences, namely, by simple induction along similarity lines; but the similarity now is a language-dependent similarity.

Much the same account can be offered for the learning of the seemingly simpler construction, mere predication: 'Fido is a dog,' 'Sugar is sweet.'

The child has now made creditable progress from observation sentences towards theoretical language, by mastering predication and the universal categorical construction. Another important step will be mastery of the relative clause; and I think I can give a convincing hypothesis of how this comes about. What is conspicuous about the relative clause is its role in predication. Thus take a relative clause, 'something that chases its tail', and predicate it of Dinah: 'Dinah is something that chases its tail.' This is equivalent to the simple sentence

'Dinah chases its tail' (or 'her tail'). When we predicate the relative clause, the effect is the same as substituting the subject of the predication for the pronoun of the relative clause. Now my suggestion regarding the learning of the relative clause is that the child learns this substitution transformation. He discovers that the adult is prepared to assent to a predication of a relative clause in just the circumstances where he is prepared to assent to the simpler sentence obtained by the substitution.

This explains how the child could learn relative clauses in one standard position: predicative position. He learns how to eliminate them, in that position, by the substitution transformation—and how to introduce them into that position by the converse transformation, superstition. But then, having learned this much, he is struck by an analogy between relative clauses and ordinary simple predicates or general terms; for these also appear in predicative position. So, pursuing the analogy, he presses relative clauses into other positions where general terms have been appearing—notably into the universal categorical construction. Or, if the child does not press this analogy on his own, he is at any rate well prepared to grasp adult usage and follow it in the light of the analogy. In this way the relative clause gets into the universal categorical construction, from which it cannot be eliminated by the substitution transformation. It is there to stay.

We can easily imagine how the child might learn the truth functions—negation, conjunction, alternation. Take conjunction: the child notices, by degrees, that the adult affirms 'p and q' in only those circumstances where he is disposed, if queried, to assent to 'p' and also to 'q'.

We have now seen, in outline and crude conjecture, how one might start at the observational edge of language and work one's way into the discursive interior where scientific theory can begin to be expressed. Predication is at hand, and the universal categorical, the relative clause, and the truth functions. Once this stage is reached, it is easy to see that the whole strength of logical quantification is available. I shall not pause over the details of this, except to remark that the pronouns of relative clauses take on the role of the bound variable of quantification. By further conjectures in the same spirit, some of them more convincing and some less, we can outline the learner's further progress, to where he is bandying abstract terms and quantifying over properties, numbers, functions, and hypothetical physical particles and forces. This progress is not a continous derivation, which, followed backward, would enable us to reduce scientific theory to sheer observation. It is a progress rather by short leaps of analogy. One such was the pressing of relative clauses into universal categoricals, where they cease to be eliminable. There are further such psychological speculations that I could report, but time does not allow.

Such speculations would gain, certainly, from experimental investigation of the child's actual learning of language. Experimental findings already available in the literature could perhaps be used to sustain or correct these conjectures at points, and further empirical investigations could be devised. But a speculative approach of the present sort seems required to begin with, in order to isolate just the factual questions that bear on our purposes. For our objective

here is still philosophical—a better understanding of the relations between evidence and scientific theory. Moreover, the way to this objective requires consideration of linguistics and logic along with psychology. This is why the speculative phase has to precede, for the most part, the formulation of relevant questions to be posed to the experimental psychologist.

In any event the present speculations, however inaccurate, are presumably true to the general nature of language acquisition. And already they help us to understand how the logical links are forged that connect theoretical sentences with the reports of observation. We learn the grammatical construction '*p* and *q*' by learning, among other things, to assent to the compound only in circumstances where we are disposed to assent to each component. Thus it is that the logical law of inference which leads from '*p* and *q*' to '*p*' is built into our habits by the very learning of 'and'. Similarly for the other laws of conjunction, and correspondingly for the laws of alternation and other truth functions. Correspondingly, again, for laws of quantification. The law of inference that leads from '(x)Fx' to 'Fa'* should be traceable back, through the derivation of quantification that I have passed over, until it is found finally to hinge upon the substitution transformation by which we learn to use the relative clause. Thus, in general, the acquisition of our basic logical habits is to be accounted for in our acquisition of grammatical constructions.

Related remarks hold true of inferential habits that exceed pure logic. We learn when to assent to 'dog', and to 'animal', only by becoming disposed to assent to 'animal' in all circumstances where we will assent to 'dog'. Connections more accidental and causal in aspect can also come about through the learning of words; thus a child may have begun to learn the term 'good' in application to chocolate.

I characterized science as a linguistic structure that is keyed to observation here and there. I said also that it is an instrument for predicting observations on the basis of earlier observations. It is keyed to observations, earlier and later, forming a labyrinthine connection between them; and it is through this labyrinth that the prediction takes place. A powerful improvement, this, over simple induction from past observations to future ones; powerful and costly. I have now sketched the nature of the connection between the observations and the labyrinthine interior of scientific theory. I have sketched it in terms of the learning of language. This seemed reasonable, since the scientist himself can make no sense of the language of scientific theory beyond what goes into his learning of it. The paths of language learning, which lead from observation sentences to theoretical sentences, are the only connection there is between observation and theory. This has been a sketch, but a fuller understanding may be sought along the same line: by a more painstaking investigation of how we learn theoretical language.

---

*'(x)Fx': Everything has a certain property, the property F. 'Fa': A particular object, a, has the property F.

One important point that already stands forth, regarding the relation of theory to observation, is the vast freedom that the form of the theory must enjoy, relative even to all possible observation. Theory is empirically underdetermined. Surely even if we had an observational oracle, capable of assigning a truth value to every standing observational report expressible in our language, still this would not suffice to adjudicate between a host of possible physical theories, each of them completely in accord with the oracle. This seems clear in view of the tenuousness of the connections that we have noted between observation sentences and theoretical ones. At the level of observation sentences, even the general form of the eventual theoretical language remained indeterminate, to say nothing of the ontology. The observation sentences were associated, as wholes, with the stimulatory situations that warranted assent to them; but there was in this no hint of what aspects of the stimulatory situations to single out somehow as objects, if indeed any. The question of ontology simply makes no sense until we get to something recognizable as quantification, or perhaps as a relative clause, with pronouns as potential variables. At the level of observation sentences there was no foreseeing even that the superimposed theoretical language would contain anything recognizable as quantification or relative clauses. The steps by which the child was seen to progress from observational language to relative clauses and categoricals and quantification had the arbitrary character of historical accident and cultural heritage; there was no hint of inevitability.

It was a tremendous achievement, on the part of our long-term culture and our latter-day scientists, to develop a theory that leads from observation to predicted observation as successfully as ours. It is a near miracle. If our theory were in full conformity with the observational oracle that we just now imagined, which surely it is not, that would be yet a nearer miracle. But if, even granted that nearer miracle, our theory were not still just one of many equally perfect possible theories to the same observational effect, that would be too miraculous to make sense.

But it must be said that the issue of under-determination proves slippery when we try to grasp it more firmly. If two theories conform to the same totality of possible observations, in what sense are they two? Perhaps they are both stated in English, and they are alike, word for word, except that one of them calls molecules electrons and electrons molecules. Literally the two theories are in contradiction, saying incompatible things about so-called molecules. But of course we would not want to count this case; we would call it terminological. Or again, following Poincaré, suppose the two theories are alike except that one of them assumes an infinite space while the other has a finite space in which bodies shrink in proportion to their distance from centre. Even here we want to say that the difference is rather terminological than real; and our reason is that we see how to bring the theories into agreement by translation: by reconstruing the English of one of the theories.

At this point it may be protested that after all there can never be two complete theories agreeing on the total output of the observational oracle. It may be

protested that since such theories would be empirically equivalent, would have the same empirical meaning, their difference is purely verbal. For surely there is no meaning but empirical meaning, and theories with the same meaning must be seen as translations one of the other. This argument simply rules out, by definition, the doctrine that physical theory is under-determined by all possible observation.

The best reaction at this point is to back away from terminology and sort things out on their merits. Where the significant difference comes is perhaps where we no longer see how to state rules of translation that would bring the two empirically equivalent theories together. Terminology aside, what wants recognizing is that a physical theory of radically different form from ours, with nothing even recognizably similar to our quantification or objective reference, might still be empirically equivalent to ours, in the sense of predicting the same episodes of sensory bombardment on the strength of the same past episodes. Once this is recognized, the scientific achievement of our culture becomes in a way more impressive than ever. For, in the midst of all this formless freedom for variation, our science has developed in such a way as to maintain always a manageably narrow spectrum of visible alternatives among which to choose when need arises to revise a theory. It is this narrowing of sights, or tunnel vision, that has made for the continuity of science, through the vicissitudes of refutation and correction. And it is this also that has fostered the illusion of there being only one solution to the riddle of the universe.

30
Innate Knowledge

ALVIN I. GOLDMAN

Alvin Goldman (b. 1938) is Professor of Philosophy at the University of Arizona. He is the author of A Theory of Human Action, *as well as many articles on epistemology.*

Like W. V. O. Quine (reading 29), Goldman favors an evolutionary approach to epistemology. In this essay he tries to show how we might make sense of the idea of innate knowledge. Goldman begins by offering a causal theory of knowledge: a person knows a statement to be true just in case that person's belief is appropriately connected with the fact that makes the belief true. Thus, I know there is a table in front of me just in case my belief that there is a table in front of me was caused by there being a table in front of me. This account of knowledge does not require the knower be able to justify his belief, and Goldman offers a number of reasons why a proper account of knowledge should not require justification.

In light of this account, Goldman explains how there might be an evolutionary advantage to having certain beliefs "built in." Such beliefs, were they caused in an appropriate way, would constitute innate knowledge.

IF THERE WERE TRUE INNATE BELIEFS, would there also be innate *knowledge?* Much of the controversy over innate ideas, both historical and contemporary, has focused on two questions: (1) whether allegedly innate cognitive elements are supposed to be actual concepts or beliefs, or merely latent capacities to acquire concepts or beliefs under appropriate stimulus conditions; and (2) whether such cognitive elements, occurrent or dispositional, really are innate. But let us set these traditional problems aside. Assume, for the sake of argument, that an organism is born with certain beliefs, and that these beliefs are true. A further epistemological problem then arises: Do these true beliefs constitute *knowledge?* This question has been raised recently by W. D. Hart, Thomas Nagel, and R. Edgely. The existence of innate cognitive elements, even true ones, it is pointed out, does not ensure the existence of innate knowledge. Whether or not innate beliefs may be counted as knowledge depends on what

---

[1] W. D. Hart, "Innate Ideas and A Priori Knowledge," in Stephen P. Stich, ed., *Innate Ideas* (Berkeley: University of California Press, 1975); Thomas Nagel, in "Linguistics and Epistemology," in Sidney Hook, ed., *Language and Philosophy* (New York: New York University Press, 1969); and R. Edgely, in "Innate Ideas," *Knowledge and Necessity,* Royal Institute of Philosophy Lectures, vol. 3 (London: Macmillan, 1970).

knowledge is; in particular, it depends on what further conditions must be satisfied by an item of true belief in order for it to be an item of knowledge.

According to the traditional analysis of knowing, S knows that p if and only if (i) S believes that p, (ii) p is true, and (iii) S is justified in believing that p. Edmund Gettier has shown that (i), (ii), and (iii) are not jointly sufficient for "S knows that p," and most writers now maintain that condition (iii) must be strengthened. On the other hand, most epistemologists continue to maintain that (iii) is at least a *necessary* condition of knowledge, and if so, then it may be argued that the mere possession of innate true belief gives one no title to knowledge. For how does innateness provide a *justification* for one's belief?

This argument, however, depends on the assumption that justification is at least a necessary condition of knowing, and I find this assumption dubious. I do not deny, of course, that *many* of the propositions one knows satisfy the justification condition. But I think that there are *some* propositions one knows which one cannot be said to be justified in believing. If this is correct, then the fact that innateness does not confer justification does not preclude the possibility of innate knowledge.

Rejection of the justification condition, however, is only part of the job of vindicating innate knowledge. It must certainly be acknowledged that true belief per se is not knowledge. If innate true beliefs are to be items of knowledge, there must be some further condition or conditions that they satisfy. But what would such further conditions be? If we reject justification as an additional requirement for knowledge, what should be substituted in its place? And if we can find such a substitute, can it be shown that innate true beliefs can satisfy this substitute condition?

In a previous paper, entitled "A Causal Theory of Knowing,"[2] I argued that a necessary and sufficient condition of "S knows that p," at least where p is a contingent proposition, is that there be an appropriate *causal* connection between the fact that p and S's belief that p. Without reviewing the causal theory in detail, we can quickly see the plausibility of a causal requirement by examining three cases.

1. Suppose that holography has been so perfected that when a hologram of a vase is placed at a distance of, say, ten feet from a person, it looks to him exactly as if there were a vase, say, fifteen feet in front of him. Now suppose that there actually is a vase fifteen feet in front of S, but that S's view of the vase is blocked by a holographic photograph of another vase. Since the hologram makes it *appear* as if there is a vase in front of him, however, S forms the belief that there is one in front of him, S is clearly justified in believing that there is a vase in front of him—at any rate, he is *as* justified in believing this as he is on many other occasions when we would credit him with knowledge.

---

[2] "A Causal Theory of Knowing," *The Journal of Philosophy*, LXIV, 12 (June 22, 1967), 357–372; reprinted in Michael Roth and Leon Galis, eds., *Knowing* (New York: Random House, 1970).

Moreover, his belief is true. In this case, however, we would not be willing to say that S *knows* that there is a vase in front of him. The reason for this concerns the causal process by which S's belief is formed. There simply is no causal connection here between the fact that there is a vase in front of him and S's belief that there is a vase in front of him. Certainly there is no *appropriate* causal connection between this fact and S's belief.

2. S witnesses the occurrence of x at time t_1, but at time t_2 S has an accident that obliterates his memory of this occurrence. At time t_3 S's friend Brown, who is unaware that S witnessed x or even that x actually occurred, hypnotizes S into seeming to remember, and into believing, that he witnessed the occurrence of x. At time t_3 S does not *know* that x occurred. But the reason why he cannot be said to know this fact has nothing to do with his justification for believing it. In the case imagined S has the same memory-impressions, and the same evidence, as he would if he had genuinely remembered the occurrence of x. (Assume that S has no evidence about his accident or about his hypnosis.) So if in the case of genuine memory S would be justified in believing that x occurred, then he is also justified in the present case. The correct explanation of why S does not *know* that x occurred has nothing to do with his justification, but rather with the causal process that results in his believing, at t_3, that x occurred. The reason why S cannot be credited with *knowledge* is that there is no appropriate causal connection linking the fact that x occurred with S's belief of this fact. In a genuine case of memory there is an appropriate causal connection, but in the example described here such a causal connection is lacking.[3]

3. S perceives that there is solidified lava in various parts of the countryside. On the basis of this belief S concludes that a nearby mountain erupted many centuries ago. Suppose, however, that although the mountain did erupt centuries ago, the lava that S sees was not spewed forth, as S assumes it was, by that mountain. Rather, what happened was this. A century after the eruption a man came along and removed all the lava. Another century later another man, not knowing that there had ever been any lava in the vicinity, decided to make it look as if there had been a volcano, and therefore put lava in the appropriate places. In this case, S does not *know* that the mountain erupted. He may have good evidence for this, but he does not *know* it. And the reason for his lack of knowledge clearly has something to do with the nature of the causal process that resulted in his belief. In this case, indeed, there is no causal connection at all between the fact that the mountain erupted and his belief that the mountain erupted.

The above three cases are intended to provide an intuitive rationale—though, of course, not a complete defense—for a causal account of knowing. But these cases do not disprove the contention that justification is a necessary condition

---

[3] Cases of this sort are discussed by Max Deutscher and C. B. Martin, in "Remembering," *The Philosophical Review*, Vol. LXXV (1966).

of knowing. Against this contention I wish to adduce two different cases (many similar ones could be added).[4]

1. A professional chicken-sexer looks at a chick and forms the true belief that it is male. The chicken-sexer is unaware of the process by which he tells the sex of the chick, but, as always, he is correct in his judgment. Although the chicken-sexer is ignorant of *how* he tells the sex of the chick, most of us would say that he *knows* it is male.

2. Jones has a rheumatic condition that is affected by atmospheric pressure, so that whenever rain is in the offing he suffers pains in his joints. Jones does not *notice* the correlation between his aches and the onset of rain, but whenever it is going to rain (and only then) his joints start to ache, and whenever his joints start to ache this produces in Jones the belief that it is going to rain. Here too we would say, I think, that Jones *knows* that it is going to rain on each of these occasions.[5]

In both of these cases a person *knows* a certain proposition without being *justified* in believing it. Under the usual interpretation, S is "justified in believing a proposition p only if either (a) p is self-warranting or self-justifying for S, or (b) there are some other propositions S knows which are good reasons or good grounds for believing that p. In neither of these cases is p a self- warranting or self-justifying proposition. But, equally, in neither of these cases are there any propositions known by S which constitute good reasons or good grounds for believing that p. In particular, there are no propositions S could cite which would justify his belief that p. If asked to justify the belief that it is going to rain, the rheumatic could only say that he "feels" or "intuits" that it is going to rain. These responses would hardly constitute an adequate justification for the belief in question. A man who has no training whatever in chickensexing, for example, might also genuinely say that a chick "looks" like a male to him. But this would not incline us to say that he is *justified* in believing that it is a male. A similar point can be made in the rain-predicting case.

Perhaps we have not done justice to the nature of the justification of the chicken-sexer and of the rain-predictor. It might be argued that each man's justification does not depend simply on the proposition that he has an "intuition" about the proposition he believes, but on this proposition *conjoined* with the proposition that his intuitions on these matters have generally been right in the past. For example, the chicken-sexer's justification is not merely that the chick "looks" like a male to him. His justification consists in the conjunction of this proposition with the proposition (which he knows) that, generally, when a chick "looks" like a male to him it turns out actually to *be* a male.

But this defense is inadequate. Suppose that we falsely persuade the chicken-

---

[4] Another example used to make the same point is given by Peter Unger, in "Experience and Factual Knowledge," *The Journal of Philosophy*, LXIV, 5 (March 16, 1967), 152–173. I find Unger's example of the crystal-ball-gazing gypsy a bit too fanciful to be convincing, however.

[5] This example is due to Ronald de Sousa, "Knowing, Consistent Belief, and Self-consciousness," *The Journal of Philosophy*, LXVII, 3 (February 12, 1970), 66–73.

sexer that his chicken-sexing performance in the recent past has been very bad, that his intuitions have been turning out wrong of late. If he is persuaded by this story, the chicken-sexer is no longer justified in relying on his intuition. He can no longer appeal to the premise that his intuition is generally a reliable guide, for he himself no longer believes (or knows) this premise. Nevertheless, if the chicken-sexer actually does make correct judgments about each chick, and in fact shows no loss in his ability to form correct beliefs simply by looking at the chick, then we would be forced to admit to ourselves that he really does know the sex of the chicks. Despite the fact that he (no longer) has *justification* for these judgments, he must be credited with *knowledge*. An analogous argument can be developed for the rain-predictor case.

Why, then, are we inclined to credit knowledge to the chicken-sexer and the rain-predictor? The answer, I suggest, is given by the causal theory of knowing. In each of these cases there is a certain kind of causal connection between the fact that p and S's belief that p. In each case there is a certain kind of causal process that produces in S a true belief. In the chicken-sexing case the fact that the chick is male causes S to believe that it is male. And in the rain-predicting case the fact that it will rain and S's belief that it will rain are causally connected in virtue of sharing a *common* cause, viz., the drop in atmospheric pressure.[6] To be sure, the causal theory of knowing does not say that *any* causal connection between the fact that p and S's belief that p yields knowledge; the theory requires that the causal connection be an "appropriate" one. But in order for a particular causal connection to be appropriate, it is sufficient, I think, that it be an instance of a kind of process which *generally* leads to true beliefs of the sort in question. Now in our two cases this requirement is satisfied. In the case of the chicken-sexer there is a certain kind of causal process that always results in his having a true belief about the sex of the chick examined. And in the case of the rheumatic, there is a kind of causal process that always leads to true beliefs about the onset of rain. In other words, both the chicken-sexer and the rain-predictor *have reliable techniques* for forming beliefs about their respective subject matters, even though neither has any idea what his technique *is,* and even though neither may *know* that his technique is perfectly reliable.

It might be argued that whenever a person has a reliable "technique" for telling when it will rain, or for telling the sex of a chick, etc., then he is "justified" in holding beliefs that are formed by the use of this technique. Of course, it is open to us to interpret the phrase "S is justified in believing that p" in this way. But two comments would be in order. First, it should be noted that this is not the usual epistemological interpretation of the phrase. Secondly, under this interpretation the justification requirement may well turn out to be virtually equivalent to the causal requirement I have been defending. And if this is so,

---

[6] According to my causal theory of knowing, the causal connection between the fact that p and S's belief that p can either be one in which the fact that p *causes* (or is one of the causal ancestors of) S's belief that p or one in which the fact that p and S's belief that p have a *common* cause. For details see "A Causal Theory of Knowing," *op. cit.*

then it is not clear that the justification requirement stands in the way of the possibility of innate knowledge.

It is time to turn to the problem of innate knowledge. Granting the correctness of the causal theory of knowing, how could it be argued that an innate belief can be an item of knowledge? In order for an innate belief to qualify as an item of knowledge, it must be causally related in an appropriate way to the fact to which it corresponds. But what might such a causal connection be like? What sort of causal process might this be? The answer, I suggest, is *evolutionary adaptation*. Suppose there is a general fact p about the environment of a certain animal species, or about the relationship between members of the species and their environment. This fact p, let us suppose, has great survival value for the members of the species. In particular, recognition or apprehension of this fact by a member of the species is a crucial factor in ensuring its survival. Under these conditions, it would not be surprising if, by a process of natural selection, the members of this species eventually come to be born with the belief that p. If this does occur, then there is a causal connection between the fact that p and the belief that p which is innately present in each individual of this species. Moreover, it seems reasonable to say that the causal connection is an "appropriate" one, for the process of natural selection is presumably a kind of process that will generally produce *true* beliefs, if it produces beliefs at all. According to our causal theory of knowing, therefore, we could say of each member of this species not merely that it innately *believes* that p, but that it innately *knows* that p.

A detailed example would be helpful at this juncture. Let us take an example not from the species *Homo sapiens* but from another animal species. A problem with any such example is that it is usually difficult to decide when members of such species are to be credited with *beliefs*. But let us be generous on this point. Consider Eckhard H. Hess's description of the common tick, in the context of his discussion of innate behavioral mechanisms.[7]

> Instinctive behavior, in particular, is evoked in response to only a few of the stimuli in an animal's environment; these stimuli are called *sign stimuli,* or *releasers* of the behaviors which they elicit.
>
> An example of these facts is to be found in the behavior of the common tick, which was described in detail by von Uexküll (1909). The tick does not respond to the sight of a host, but when an odor of butyric acid from a mammal strikes the tick's sensory receptors, the tick drops from the twig to the host, finds a spot on the skin which is about 37° centigrade, and begins to drink blood. Only a few stimuli elicit the tick's behavior, this behavior being without doubt innate.
>
> But the simplicity of releasers can sometimes lead animals into grave situations. For instance, a patient tick climbs up a slippery twig to waylay its prey, a nice, juicy mammal. When it has reached the end of the twig, it is above a rock on which a fat, perspiring man has been sitting. The rock therefore emanates the

---

[7] "Ethology: An Approach Toward the Complete Analysis of Behavior," in Roger Brown et al., *New Directions in Psychology* (New York: Holt, Rinehart and Winston, 1962), p. 179.

typical odor of butyric acid, and is just the right temperature. So the tick jumps, and lands on the rock—whereupon, in trying to suck from the rock, it breaks its proboscis.

It seems plausible to ascribe at least two beliefs to our tick. First, it believes that there is a good place to suck blood just below the twig on which it has been sitting. Second, it believes that, in general, a certain odor (of butyric acid) and a certain temperature (about 37° centigrade) are signs of a good place to suck blood. The first of these two beliefs is neither innate nor a piece of knowledge. It is not innate inasmuch as it is formed as the result of certain current stimuli that the tick experiences. It is not knowledge because, in the case described, it is false. The second belief, however, has good claim to being both innate and an item of knowledge. According to Hess's assessment of the evidence, the tick has an *innate* propensity to suck blood at spots from which the odor of butyric acid emanates and which are about 37° centigrade. If this behavioral propensity justifies us in ascribing a *belief* to the tick, then we must surely say that this belief is innate. Moreover, there is good reason to say that this innate belief of the tick is an item of knowledge. First, it is clearly a *true* belief. It is true that, in general, the odor of butyric acid and a temperature of about 37° centigrade *are* signs of a good spot (for a tick) to suck blood. Second, it is very probable that there is a causal connection, indeed, an *appropriate* causal connection, between the tick's belief and the *fact* that such spots are good for sucking blood. In particular, it is probable that the innate propensity of the tick to suck blood under these stimulus conditions is attributable to a process of natural selection based on the fact that such spots *are* good for sucking blood. The causal theory of knowing, therefore, would vindicate the claim that the tick not only has innate true belief, but that it has innate knowledge.

Analogous cases pertaining to human beings are less easy to find. Although empirical evidence clearly shows that certain kinds of behavioral responses and perceptual preferences are innate,[8] these facts do not readily support ascriptions of "beliefs" or "cognitions." But let us suppose, as seems plausible,[9] that babies also have innate propensities to interpret various facial or vocal expressions in specific ways, e.g., to interpret smiling as a sign of affection. Here it seems reasonable to say that the organism has an innate *belief* (or disposition to believe) that smiling is a sign of affection, and clearly (judging by independent criteria of affection) this belief is true. The question then arises whether this true belief can be classified as *knowledge*. As before, the causal theory of knowing enables us to vindicate such a claim. If there is an innate propensity to

[8] See William Kessen, "Sucking and Looking: Two Organized Congenital Patterns of Behavior in the Human Newborn," and Robert L. Fantz, "Visual Perception and Experience in Early Infancy: A Look at the Hidden Side of Behavior Development," both in H. W. Stevenson, E. H. Hess, and H. L. Rheingold, eds., *Early Behavior, Comparative and Developmental Approaches* (New York: John Wiley, 1967).

[9] See I. Eibl-Eibesfeldt, "Concepts of Ethology and Their Significance in the Study of Human Behavior," ibid., especially pp. 142–143.

interpret smiling as a signal of affection, it is quite probable that the genesis of this propensity is attributable to a process of natural selection which is based on the fact that smiling *is* a signal of affection. Thus, there may well obtain an "appropriate" sort of causal connection between the innate belief and the fact to which it corresponds. If so, an ascription of "knowledge" would be sanctioned by the causal theory.

Needless to say, it is not the purpose of this paper to argue for the actual existence of innate knowledge, nor to speculate about its extent; such theses could only be fully defended by appeal to detailed empirical investigation, most of which still remains to be done. The point of the present discussion is simply to defend the possibility of innate knowledge against epistemological attack, i.e., against the claim that the concept of knowing precludes the possibility of innate knowledge. What I have tried to show is that the possibility of innate knowledge is fully compatible with an adequate analysis of the concept of knowing.

31
The Appeal to the Given

MICHAEL WILLIAMS

Michael Williams (b. 1947) is Associate Professor of Philosophy at the University of Maryland. He is the author of Groundless Belief, *from which this selection is taken.*

In this selection, Williams attacks the view that our knowledge rests on a foundation given through perception (see readings 26 and 27). He begins by presenting what he calls the two components view, a view which serves to motivate the foundational picture. According to this view, sensation provides us with data that are simply given to us, and we add to the given a layer of interpretation. When I look at a chair, for example, I am presented with a certain experience; I then interpret this experience as being the experience of a chair. My experience thus serves as a basis for my interpretation. My knowledge of the world is founded on such experience, experience that, when it is given to me, arrives free of any interpretation.

Attractive as this view is, Williams agrees that it is fundamentally flawed. The following dilemma is presented: Either the content of experience can be expressed or it cannot be expressed. To say our experience has built into it a content which can be expressed is to say it has a built-in interpretation; this is precisely what the two components view denies. To say the opposite— that our experience does not have a content which can be expressed—is to deny that experience serves as an adequate basis for interpretation. But, if the content of experience cannot be expressed, how can it serve as the foundation of knowledge? Williams thus denies that it is possible to make sense of the view that our knowledge rests on a foundation given in experience.

1. Introductory Remarks

PHENOMENALISM, BROADLY SPEAKING, is *the* empiricist theory of perceptual knowledge. Classical phenomenalism is the theory that physical objects are logical constructions out of sense-data. In a more explicitly linguistic guise, it is the theory that the content of any statement about physical objects can be expressed by some complex statement about sense-data. The classical theory has few adherents, if any, these days.[1] Reference to sense-data has been replaced

---

[1] A possible exception is Jonathan Bennett. See his *Locke, Berkeley, Hume: Central Themes* (Oxford: Clarendon Press, 1971).

by talk about how one is appeared to, and the idea that sufficiently complex statements about perceptual experience might *entail* statements about how things are in the physical world has given way to the idea that the connexion is *criteriological.** But these modifications do not touch the basic idea behind phenomenalism which is that there are epistemologically basic beliefs which are in some way perceptual beliefs and which serve as a foundation—or at least as a partial foundation—for our beliefs about the physical world.

The foundational role of perceptual beliefs was something we found to be presupposed by Ayer's formulation of the sceptical argument and by the various responses to it. Even Ayer's version of direct realism† accepts the idea of there being a foundation for knowledge, though the foundations stand at a higher level than they do for, say, the sense-datum theory.

According to the usage I am proposing, any theory which assigns a foundational role to perceptual beliefs of one kind or another deserves to be called 'phenomenalistic'. By this standard, even some forms of direct realism could be taken to be phenomenalist in spirit. I am aware that this marks a departure from normal usage. I adopt it because I want to emphasize the important continuities of thought which exist between various theories often taken to be implacable opponents.

For the time being, I shall leave the notion of a foundational role in relative obscurity. I do this because I think that it can best be understood by following through the arguments for the existence of foundations rather than through an attempt to present an encapsulating definition. But before turning to this task, I want to investigate some of the complexities to be found in the traditional sense-datum theory, and this will involve coming to grips with the idea that there is a given element in experience. An examination of some of these older ideas should stand us in good stead for the more general discussion of phenomenalism to come later since, as I shall argue, modern expressions of phenomenalist thought often turn out to be not-so-new variations on the old themes.

2. The Two Components in Knowledge

The expression 'the given' owes much of its philosophical currency to C. I. Lewis's influential book *Mind and the World Order*,[2] and to H. H. Price's *Perception*.[3] The idea that there is a given element in experience reflects one side of a distinction which Lewis regarded as 'one of the oldest and most universal of philosophical insights'. He put the point like this:

---

* To say that the connection between A and B is criteriological is to say that it is part of the very meaning of B that A is evidence for the truth of B.

† The view that we perceive physical objects directly, and not by way of something else, e.g. a mental image.

[2] C. I. Lewis, *Mind and the World Order* (New York: Dover, 1956; originally published by Scribners, New York, 1929).

[3] H. H. Price, *Perception* (London: Methuen, reprinted 1964).

> There are in our cognitive experience, two elements, the immediate data such as those of sense, which are presented or given to the mind, and a form, construction, or interpretation, which represents the activity of thought.[4]

I shall call the view that Lewis is alluding to 'the two components view'. He is surely right that epistemological theories embodying a distinction along the above lines have had a long run of philosophical popularity. The two components of knowledge are the sensuously given and the pure concept. The distinction drawn by Lewis is clearly related to the distinction between analytic truths—propositions which are true in virtue of meaning and hence a priori—and synthetic truths, which are dependent on matters of fact. As Lewis puts it, '... the concept gives rise to the a priori; all a priori truth is definitive, or explicative of concepts.'[5]

What are the philosophical reasons for continuing to recognize a distinction like this? Lewis thought that there was no question that such a distinction had to be recognized. To deny that there was a distinction between the given and its interpretation would be to turn one's back on obvious and fundamental characteristics of experience. Thus he argued:

> If there be no datum given to the mind, then knowledge must be altogether contentless and arbitrary; there would be nothing which it must be true to. And if there be no interpretation which the mind imposes, then thought is rendered superfluous, the possibility of error becomes inexplicable, and the distinction of true and false is in danger of becoming meaningless.[6]

It is not difficult to see what Lewis is getting at. Our knowledge of the physical world must have a foundation in perception or observation. It cannot all be a matter of theorizing or of inference: there must be some data on the basis of which to theorize or make inferences, if the result of such activity is not to be 'contentless and arbitrary'. This basic knowledge is certain because absolutely non-inferential: thus we have a permanent data-base of observational knowledge against which less guarded claims can be evaluated. That empirical knowledge as we understand it goes beyond what is given, and hence involves thought or inference, is shown by the fact that we allow for the possibility of error. If thought never ventured beyond what is given, error would never arise. And we find a similar view in Price's book. If we are to have inferential knowledge, he argues, we must ultimately be able to appeal to some data which are 'data simpliciter', otherwise there would be a vicious regress.[7]

What we have here are not 'obvious characteristics' of experience, but rather a highly compressed philosophical argument, one which I shall discuss in some

---

[4] Lewis, op. cit., p. 38.

[5] Ibid., p. 37.

[6] Ibid., p. 39.

[7] Price, op. cit., p. 4. But see the whole of chapter 1.

353

detail in chapter three. For the time being, I wish to concentrate more on the question of what the distinction between the sensuously given and its interpretation is supposed to be.

Since the apprehension of the given element is supposed to provide the ultimate check upon empirical knowledge, it must itself be some form of primitive knowledge or awareness. But when we recall the sharp distinction drawn between the pure concept and the sensuously given, a problem arises. The pure concept and the sensuously given are thought by Lewis to be mutually independent— 'neither limits the other'—but this makes it look as if the mind has to be able to grasp the given without conceptual mediation. In other words, the knowledge which is involved in the grasping of the sensuously given, since it is independent of conceptual interpretation by the mind, must be non-propositional or, to put the point more pejoratively, ineffable. But if it is ineffable, it cannot provide us with a check upon anything, let alone the entire edifice of empirical knowledge.

To illustrate the problem, we may consider for a moment the idealist attack on the notion of givenness. The doctrine of the given has acquired an association with empiricism. This is reflected by the fact that attacks on the notion of givenness have tended to concentrate, as I shall do, on empiricist versions of the theory. It is not uncommon to find the positions taken by those who would call in question the two components view described as idealist positions. I think that this is a mistake. Furthermore, it can be an important mistake in that it can lead one to think that one is rejecting the whole idea of givenness when one is only rejecting a particular empiricist version.

Lewis clearly believed that any adequate epistemological theory must start from the distinction between the given and its interpretation. Thus, although idealists have often seemed to be attacking givenness at large, Lewis argued, correctly in my judgment, that they never really meant to say that *nothing* is given. What they were opposed to were certain ways of characterizing the given element in experience.

The seeming hostility shown by idealists towards talk of givenness springs from their taking the distinction between the active and passive faculties of the mind even more seriously than many of their philosophical opponents. If thought is equated with activity and the apprehension of the sensuously given with passive receptivity, we cannot consistently treat the kind of awareness involved in apprehending the contents of the given as being nevertheless a kind of thinking—i.e. a form of propositional knowledge. This is the point underlying Bradley's insistence that all cognition is judgment and that what many philosophers have taken to be data could not really be data because awareness of them already involves conceptualization. It is a point which idealists have been fond of using against empiricists and is, for example, brought up again and again by Green in his polemic against Locke and Hume.[8] But although Bradley insists,

---

[8] T.H. Green, the introduction to his edition of Hume's works. Reprinted as *Thomas Hill Green's Hume and Locke* (New York: Apollo, 1968).

in the interests of consistency, that whatever is given can be nothing *for the intellect,* he does not dismiss the notion of givenness altogether. Rather, he is led to characterize the given as a kind of undifferentiated immediate experience in which the distinction between subject and object has not yet emerged. According to Bradley, the given is 'experienced altogether as a coexisting mass, not perceived as parted and joined even by relations of coexistence'.[9] However, in spite of the ineffable character of immediate experience, the content of which we know only as 'this', he holds that 'all our knowledge, in the first place, arises from the "this". It is the one source of our experience, and every element of the world must submit to pass through it.'[10]

Bradley's position is apt to strike one as merely ridiculous. But it is ridiculous just because his conception of immediate experience respects rigidly the distinction between the sensuously given and the element of thought or interpretation which he sees must be involved in anything that could be called cognition. Bradley's position must be taken as a reductio ad absurdum of the concept of givenness precisely because it throws into sharp relief a dilemma which ultimately confronts any consistent 'two elements in knowledge' view. The dilemma is this: that in so far as the content of immediate experience can be expressed, the sort of awareness we have in our apprehension of the given is just another type of perceptual judgment and hence no longer contact with anything which is *merely given.* But if the content of immediate experience turns out to be ineffable or non-propositional, then the appeal to the given loses any appearance of fulfilling an explanatory role in the theory of knowledge: specifically, it cannot explicate the idea that knowledge rests on a perceptual foundation. This, it seems to me, is why, after we have learned that we are aware in immediate experience only of 'a coexisting mass', the insistence that this kind of awareness is the source of all our experience and that 'every element of the world must submit to pass through it' strikes us as extraordinarily futile.

---

[9] F. H. Bradley, *Appearance and Reality* (Oxford: Clarendon Press, paperback edition 1969), p. 198.

[10] Ibid., p. 198.

32

The Utility of Truth*

FRIEDRICH NIETZSCHE

The dark and cryptic writings of German philosopher Friedrich Nietzsche (1844–1900) have had a wide impact on twentieth-century intellectual movements. Besides his work in epistemology, Nietzsche wrote an important book on aesthetics, The Birth of Tragedy, *and a number of books attacking Christian morality.*

Unlike most philosophers, Nietzsche does not present his views in the form of extended arguments, but in a series of aphorisms—terse and often witty pronouncements. This style gives the mistaken impression that Nietzsche never argues for his claims, but merely asserts them. If Nietzsche's aphorisms on a particular topic are read together, however, various lines of argument begin to emerge. The passages presented below contain a number of Nietzsche's most important pronouncements on truth and knowledge. Nietzsche thinks of our epistemological enterprises—our attempt to secure knowledge—as an integrated part of our general struggle for existence and for power. Thus he opposes the idea that we are ever detached and objective knowers seeking the truth for its own sake. Nietzsche's wide-ranging reflections include speculations about why we value truth, when we accept something as true, and even the origins of consciousness. With all these topics, Nietzsche attempts to show how apparently abstract issues in the theory of knowledge can be explained in terms of our basic needs for survival and for mastery of our surroundings.

THE DIFFERENT LANGUAGES placed side by side show that with words truth or adequate expression matters little: for otherwise there would not be so many languages.

(TL p. 178)†

---

* Nietzsche's widely scattered remarks on truth were originally collected by Richard Schacht for his book *Nietzsche* (Routledge and Kegan Paul: Arguments of the Philosophers Series, 1982). We are extremely grateful to Professor Schacht for his kind permission to excerpt from his collection. For a fuller presentation of Nietzsche's views on truth, see chapter 2 of Schacht's book.

† After each aphorism, we indicate the source by an abbreviation. TL refers to "On Truth and Lie in an Extra-Moral Sense."

What therefore is truth? A mobile army of metaphors, metonymies,* anthropomorphisms: in short a sum of human relations which became poetically and rhetorically intensified, metamorphosed, adorned, and after long usage seem to a nation fixed, canonic and binding; truths are illusions of which one has forgotten that they *are* illusions; worn-out metaphors which have become powerless to affect the senses. . . .

(TL p. 180)

Man builds "with the. . .delicate material of ideas, which he must first manufacture within himself. He is very much to be admired here—but not on account of his impulse for truth, his bent for pure cognition of things. If somebody hides a thing behind a bush, seeks it again and finds it in the self-same place, then there is not much to boast of, respecting this seeking and finding; thus, however, matters stand with the seeking and finding of 'truth' within the realm of reason. If I make the definition of the mammal and then declare after inspecting a camel, 'Behold a mammal,' then no doubt a truth is brought to light thereby, but it is of very limited value, I mean it is anthropocentric through and through, and does not contain one single point which is 'true-in-itself,' real and universally valid, apart from man. The seeker after such truths seeks at the bottom only the metamorphosis of the world in man, he strives for an understanding of the world as a human-like thing, and by his battling gains at best the feeling of an assimilation. . . . Such a seeker contemplates the whole world as related to man, as the infinitely protracted echo of an original sound: man; as the multiplied copy of one arch-type: man. His procedure is to apply man as the measure of all things, whereby he starts from the error of believing that he has these things immediately before him as pure objects. He therefore forgets that the original metaphors of perception *are* metaphors, and takes them for the things themselves."

(TL p. 183)

As we say, it is *language* which has worked originally at the construction of ideas; in later times it is *science*. Just as the bee works at the same time at the cells and fills them with honey, thus science works irresistibly at that great columbarium† of ideas, the cemetary of perceptions, builds ever newer and higher storeys; supports, purifies, renews the old cells, and endeavours above all to fill that gigantic framework and to arrange within it the whole of the empirical world, i.e., the anthropocentric world.

(TL p. 187)

---

* Metonymies are figures of speech where the name of one object is used to refer to another object to which it is related or of which it is a part, for example, "crown" for "king."

† A columbarium is a vault or other structure with recesses in the walls to receive the ashes of the dead.

Only as creators!—This has given me the greatest trouble and still does: to realize that what things *are called* is incomparably more important than what they are. The reputation, name, and appearance, the usual measure and weight of a thing, what it counts for—originally almost always wrong and arbitrary, thrown over things like a dress and altogether foreign to their nature and even to their skin—all this grows from generation unto generation, merely because people believe in it, until it gradually grows to be part of the thing and turns into its very body. What at first was appearance becomes in the end, almost invariably, the essence and is effective as such. How foolish it would be to suppose that one only needs to point out this origin and this misty shroud of delusion in order to *destroy* the world that counts for real, so-called *"reality."* We can destroy only as creators—But let us not forget this either; it is enough to create new names and estimations and probabilities in order to create in the long run new "things."

(GS 58)*

Origin of knowledge.—Over immense periods of time the intellect produced nothing but errors. A few of these proved to be useful and helped to preserve the species: those who hit upon or inherited these had better luck in their struggle for themselves and their progeny. Such erroneous articles of faith, which were continually inherited, until they became almost part of the basic endowment of the species, include the following: that there are enduring things; that there are equal things; that there are things, substances, bodies; that a thing is what it appears to be; that our will is free; that what is good for me is also good in itself. It was only very late that such propositions were denied and doubted; it was only very late that truth emerged—as the weakest form of knowledge. It seemed that one was unable to live with it: our organism was prepared for the opposite; all its higher functions, sense perception and every kind of sensation worked with those basic errors which had been incorporated since time immemorial. Indeed, even in the realm of knowledge these propositions became the norms according to which "true" and "untrue" were determined—down to the most remote regions of logic.

Thus the *strength* of knowledge does not depend on its degree of truth but on its age, on the degree to which it has been incorporated, on its character as a condition of life. Where life and knowledge seemed to be at odds there was never any real fight, but denial and doubt were simply considered madness. Those exceptional thinkers, like the Eleatics, who nevertheless posited and clung to the opposites of the natural errors, believed that it was possible to *live* in accordance with these opposites: they invented the sage as the man who was unchangeable and impersonal, the man of the universality of intuition who was One and All at the same time, with a special capacity for his inverted knowl-

---

* GS abbreviates *The Gay Science.* Nietzsche numbered the aphorisms in this volume.

edge: they had the faith that their knowledge was also the principle of *life*. But in order to claim all of this, they had to *deceive* themselves about their own state: they had to attribute to themselves, fictitiously, impersonality and changeless duration; they had to misapprehend the nature of the knower; they had to deny the role of the impulses in knowledge; and quite generally they had to conceive of reason as a completely free and spontaneous activity. They shut their eyes to the fact that they, too, had arrived at their propositions through opposition to common sense, or owing to a desire for tranquility, for sole possession, or for dominion. The subtler development of honesty and skepticism eventually made these people, too, impossible; their ways of living and judging were seen to be also dependent upon the primeval impulses and basic errors of all sentient existence.

This subtler honesty and skepticism came into being wherever two contradictory sentences appeared to be *applicable* to life because *both* were compatible with the basic errors, and it was therefore possible to argue about the higher or lower degree of *utility* for life; also wherever new propositions, though not useful for life, were also evidently not harmful to life: in such cases there was room for the expression of an intellectual play impulse, and honesty and skepticism were innocent and happy like all play. Gradually, the human brain became full of such judgments and convictions, and a ferment, struggle, and lust for power developed in this tangle. Not only utility and delight but every kind of impulse took sides in this fight about "truths." The intellectual fight became an occupation, an attraction, a profession, a duty, something dignified—and eventually knowledge and the striving for the true found their place as a need among other needs. Henceforth not only faith and conviction but also scrutiny, denial, mistrust, and contradiction became a *power*; all "evil" instincts were subordinated to knowledge, employed in her service, and acquired the splendor of what is permitted, honored, and useful—and eventually even the eye and innocence of the *good*.

Thus knowledge became a piece of life itself, and hence a continually growing power—until eventually knowledge collided with those primeval basic errors: two lives, two power, both in the same human being. A thinker is now that being in whom the impulse for truth and those life-preserving errors clash for their first fight, after the impulse for truth has proved to be also a life-preserving power. Compared to the significance of this fight, everything else is a matter of indifference: the ultimate question about the conditions of life has been posed here, and we confront the first attempt to answer this question by experiment. To what extent can truth endure incorporation?

(GS 110)

Origin of the logical.—How did logic come into existence in man's head? Certainly out of illogic, whose realm originally must have been immense. Innumerable beings who made inferences in a way different from ours perished: for all that, their ways might have been truer. Those, for example, who did not

know how to find often enough what is "equal" as regards both nourishment and hostile animals—those, in other words, who subsumed things too slowly and cautiously—were favored with a lesser probability of survival than those who guessed immediately upon encountering similar instances that they must be equal. The dominant tendency, however, to treat as equal what is merely similar—an illogical tendency, for nothing is really equal—is what first created any basis for logic.

In order that the concept of substance could originate—which is indispensable for logic although in the strictest sense nothing real corresponds to it—it was likewise necessary that for a long time one did not see nor perceive the changes in things. The beings that did not see so precisely had an advantage over those that saw everything "in flux." At bottom, every high degree of caution in making inferences and every skeptical tendency constitute a great danger for life. No living beings would have survived if the opposite tendency—to affirm rather than suspend judgement, to err and *make up* things rather than wait, to assent rather than negate, to pass judgement rather than be just—had not been bred to the point where it became extraordinarily strong.

The course of logical ideas and inferences in our brain today corresponds to a process and a struggle among impulses that are, taken singly, very illogical and unjust. We generally experience only the result of this struggle because this primeval mechanism now runs its course so quickly and is so well concealed.

(GS 111)

Cause and effect.—"Explanation" is what we call it, but it is "description" that distinguishes us from older stages of knowledge and science. Our descriptions are better—we do not explain any more than our predecessors. We have uncovered a manifold one-after-another where the naive man and inquirer of older cultures saw only two seperate things. "Cause" and "effect" is what one says; but we have merely perfected the image of becoming without reaching beyond the image or behind it. In every case the series of "causes" confronts us much more completely, and we infer: first, this and that has to precede in order that this or that may then follow—but this does not involve any *comprehension*. In every chemical process, for example, quality appears as a "miracle," as ever; also, every locomotion; nobody has "explained" a push. But how could we possibly explain anything? We operate only with things that do not exist: lines, planes, bodies, atoms, divisible time spans, divisible spaces. How should explanations be at all possible when we first turn everything into an *image*, our image!

It will do to consider science as an attempt to humanize things as faithfully as possible; as we describe things and their one-after-another, we learn how to describe ourselves more and more precisely. Cause and effect: such a duality probably never exists; in truth we are confronted by a continuum out of which we isolate a couple of pieces, just as we perceive motion only as isolated points and then infer it without ever actually seeing it. The suddenness with which many effects stand out misleads us; actually, it is sudden only for us. In this

moment of suddenness there is an infinite number of processes that elude us. An intellect that could see cause and effect as a continuum and a flux and not, as we do, in terms of an arbitrary division and dismemberment, would repudiate the concept of cause and effect and deny all conditionality.

(GS 112)

Life no argument.—We have arranged for ourselves a world in which we can live—by positing bodies, lines, planes, causes and effects, motion and rest, form and content; without these articles of faith nobody now could endure life. But that does not prove them. Life is no argument. The conditions of life might include error.

(GS 121)

*Ultimate skepsis.**—What are man's truths ultimately? Merely his *irrefutable* errors.

(GS 265)

How we, too, are still pious.—In science convictions have no rights of citizenship, as one says with good reason. Only when they decide to descend to the modesty of hypotheses, of a provisional experimental point of view, of a regulative fiction, they may be granted admission and even a certain value in the realm of knowledge—though always with the restriction that they remain under police supervision, under the police of mistrust.—But does this not mean, if you consider it more precisely, that a conviction may obtain admission to science only when it *ceases* to be a conviction? Would it not be the first step in the discipline of the scientific spirit that one would not permit oneself any more convictions?

Probably this is so; only we still have to ask: *To make it possible for this discipline to begin,* must there not be some prior conviction—even one that is so commanding and unconditional that it sacrifices all other convictions to itself? We see that science also rests on a faith; there simply is no science "without presuppositions." The question whether *truth* is needed must not only have been affirmed in advance, but affirmed to such a degree that the principle, the faith, the conviction finds expression: "*Nothing* is needed *more* than truth, and in relation to it everything else has only second-rate value.

This unconditional will to truth—what is it? Is it the will *not to allow oneself to be deceived*? Or is it the will *not to deceive*? For the will to truth could be interpreted in the second way, too—if only the special case "I do not want to deceive myself" is subsumed under the generalization "I do not want to deceive." But why not deceive? But why not allow oneself to be deceived?

Note that the reasons for the former principle belong to an altogether dif-

* *Skepsis* is a Greek word meaning "skepticism."

ferent realm from those for the second. One does not want to allow oneself to be deceived because one assumes that it is harmful, dangerous, calamitous to be deceived. In this sense, science would be a long-range prudence, a caution, a utility; but one could object in all fairness: How is that? Is wanting not to allow oneself to be deceived really less harmful, less dangerous, less calamitous? What do you know in advance of the character of existence to be able to decide whether the greater advantage is on the side of the unconditionally mistrustful or of the unconditionally trusting? But if both should be required much trust *as well as* much mistrust, from where would science then be permitted to take its unconditional faith or conviction on which it rests, that truth is more important than any other thing, including every other conviction? Precisely this conviction could never have come into being if both truth and untruth constantly proved to be useful, which is the case. Thus—the faith in science, which after all exists undeniably, cannot owe its origin to such a calculus of utility; it must have originated *in spite of* the fact that the disutility and dangerousness of "the will to truth," of "truth at any price" is proved to it constantly. "At any price": how well we understand these words once we have offered and slaughtered one faith after another on this altar!

Consequently, "will to truth" does *not* mean "I will not allow myself to be deceived" but—there is no alternative—"I will not deceive, not even myself"; *and with that we stand on moral ground.* For you only have to ask yourself carefully, "Why do you not want to deceive?" especially if it should seem— and it does seem!—as if life aimed at semblance, meaning error, deception, simulation, delusion, self-delusion, and when the great sweep of life has actually always shown itself to be on the side of the most unscrupulous *polytropoi.** Charitably interpreted, such a resolve might perhaps be a quixotism,[†] a minor slightly mad enthusiasm; but it might also be something more serious, namely, a principle that is hostile to life and destructive.—"Will to truth"—that might be a concealed will to death.

Thus the question "Why science?" leads back to the moral problem: *Why have morality at all* when life, nature, and history are "not moral"? No doubt, those who are truthful in that audacious and ultimate sense that is presupposed by the faith in science *thus affirm another world* than the world of life, nature, and history: and insofar as they affirm this "other world"—look, must they not by the same token negate its counterpart, this world, *our* world?—But you will have gathered what I am driving at, namely, that it is still a *metaphysical faith* upon which our faith in science rests—that even we seekers after knowledge today, we godless anti-metaphysicians still take our fire, too, from the flame lit by a faith that is thousands of years old, that Christian faith which was also the faith of Plato, that God is the truth, that truth is divine.—But what if this should become more and more incredible, if nothing should prove

---

* *Polytropoi* is a learned borrowing from the Greek meaning a "multiplicity of meanings."

† A "quixotism" is a quixotic, that is, a highly romantic or impractical idea.

to be divine any more unless it were error, blindness, the life—if God himself should prove to be our most enduring lie?—

(GS 344)

Now, if you are willing to listen to my answer and the perhaps extravagant surmise that it involves, it seems to me as if the subtlety and strength of consciousness always were proportionate to a man's (or animal's) *capacity for communication*, and as if this capacity in turn were proportionate to the *need for communication*. But this last point is not to be understood as if the individual human being who happens to be a master in communicating and making understandable his needs must also be most dependent on others in his needs. But it does seem to me as if it were that way when we consider whole races and chains of generations: Where need and distress have forced men for a long time to communicate and to understand each other quickly and subtly, the ultimate result is an excess of this strength and art of communication—as it were, a capacity that has gradually been accumulated and now waits for an heir who might squander it. (Those who are called artists are these heirs; so are orators, preachers, writers—all of them people who always come at the end of a long chain, "late born" every one of them in the best sense of that word and, as I have said, by their nature squanderers.)

Supposing that this observation is correct, I may now proceed to the surmise that *consciousness has developed only under the pressure of the need for communication*; that from the start it was needed and useful only between human beings (particularly between those who commanded and those who obeyed); and that it also developed only in proportion to the degree of this utility. Consciousness is really only a net of communication between human beings; it is only as such that it had to develop; a solitary human being who lived like a beast of prey would not have needed it. That our actions, thoughts, feelings, and movements enter our own consciousness—at least a part of them—that is the result of a "must" that for a terribly long time lorded it over man. As the most endangered animal, he *needed* help and protection, he needed his peers, he had to learn to express his distress and to make himself understood; and for all of this he needed "consciousness" first of all, he needed to "know" himself what distressed him, he needed to know how he felt, he needed to "know" what he thought. For, to say it once more: Man, like every living being, thinks continually without knowing it; the thinking that rises to *consciousness* is only the smallest part of all this—the most superficial and worst part—for only this conscious thinking *takes the form of words, which is to say signs of communication,* and the fact uncovers the origin of consciousness.

In brief, the development of language and the development of consciousness (*not* of reason but merely of the way reason enters consciousness) go hand in hand. Add to this that not only language serves as a bridge between human beings but also a mien, a pressure, a gesture. The emergence of our sense

impressions into our own consciousness, the ability to fix them and, as it were, exhibit them externally, increased proportionately with the need to communicate them to *others* by means of signs. The human being inventing signs is at the same time the human being who becomes ever more keenly conscious of himself. It was only as a social animal that man acquired self-consciousness—which he is still in the process of doing, more and more.

My idea is, as you see, that consciousness does not really belong to man's individual existence but rather to his social or herd nature; that, as follows from this, it has developed subtlety only insofar as this is required by social or herd utility. Consequently given the best will in the world to understand ourselves as individually as possible, "to know ourselves," each of us will always succeed in becoming conscious only of what is not individual but "average." Our thoughts themselves are continually governed by the character of consciousness—by the "genius of the species" that commands it—and translated back into the perspective of the herd. Fundamentally, all our actions are altogether incomparably personal, unique, and infinitely individual; there is no doubt of that. But as soon as we translate them into consciousness *they no longer seem to be.*

This is the essence of phenomenalism and perspectivism as I understand them: Owing to the nature of *animal consciousness*, the world of which we can become conscious is only a surface-and sign-world, a world that is made common and meaner; whatever becomes conscious *becomes* by the same token shallow, thin, relatively stupid, general, sign, herd signal; all becoming conscious involves a great and thorough corruption, falsification, reduction to superficialities, and generalization. Ultimately, the growth of consciousness becomes a danger; and anyone who lives among the most conscious Europeans even knows that it is a disease.

You will guess that it is not the opposition of subject and object that concerns me here: This distinction I leave to the epistemologists who have become entangled in the snares of grammar (the metaphysics of the people). It is even less the opposition of "thing-in-itself" and appearance; for we do not "know" nearly enough to be entitled to any such distinction. We simply lack any organ for knowledge, for "truth": we "know" (or believe or imagine) just as much as may be *useful* in the interests of the human herd, the species; and even what is here called "utility" is ultimately also a mere belief, something imaginary, and perhaps precisely that most calamitous stupidity of which we shall perish some day.

(GS 354)

What is it that the common people take for knowledge? What do they want when they want "knowledge"? Nothing more than this: Something strange is to be reduced to something *familiar*. And we philosophers—have we really meant *more* than this when we have spoken of knowledge? What is familiar means what we are used to so that we no longer marvel at it, our everyday,

some rule in which we are stuck, anything at all in which we feel at home. Look, isn't our need for knowledge precisely this need for the familiar, the will to uncover under everything strange, unusual, and questionable something that no longer disturbs us? Is it not the *instinct of fear* that bids us to know? And is the jubilation of those who attain knowledge not the jubilation over the restoration of a sense of security?

Behind all logic and its seeming sovereignty of movement . . . there stand valuations or, more clearly, physiological demands for the preservation of a certain type of life.

(BGE 3) *

And we are fundamentally inclined to claim . . . that without accepting the fictions of logic, without measuring reality against the purely invented world of the unconditional and self-identical, without a constant falsification of the world by means of numbers, man could not live—that renouncing false judgements would mean renouncing life and a denial of life.

(BGE 4)

There are still harmless self-observers who believe that there are 'immediate certainties'; for example, 'I think,' or as the superstition of Schopenhauer put it, 'I will'; as though knowledge here got hold of its object purely and nakedly as 'the thing in itself,' without any falsification on the part of either the subject or the object. But that 'immediate certainty,' as well as 'absolute knowledge' and the 'thing in itself,' involve a *contradiction in adjecto*.† I shall repeat a hundred times; we really ought to free ourselves from the seduction of words!

Let the people suppose that knowledge means knowing things entirely; the philosopher must say to himself: When I analyze the process that is expressed in the sentence, 'I think,' I find a whole series of daring assertions that would be difficult, perhaps impossible, to prove; for example, that it is *I* who think, that there must necessarily be something that thinks, that thinking is an activity and operation on the part of a being who is thought of as a cause, that there is an 'ego,' and, finally, that it is already determined what is to be designated by thinking—that I *know* what thinking is. . . . In short, the assertion 'I think' assumes that I *compare* my state at the present moment with other states of myself which I know, in order to determine what it is; on account of this retrospective connection with further 'knowledge,' it has, at any rate, no immediate certainty for me.

In place of the 'immediate certainty' in which the people may believe in the case at hand, the philosopher thus finds a series of metaphysical questions

---

* BGE abbreviates *Beyond Good and Evil*. Nietzsche numbered the aphorisms in this volume.

† A *contradiction in adjecto* occurs when an adjective predicates a property of an object that the object cannot have, for example, a circular square.

365

presented to him. . . . Whoever ventures to answer these metaphysical questions at once by an appeal to a sort of *intuitive* perception . . . will encounter a smile and two question marks from a philosopher nowadays.

(BGE 16)

But precisely because we seek knowledge, let us not be ungrateful to such resolute reversals of accustomed perspectives and valuations which the spirit has, with apparent mischievousness and futility, raged against itself for so long: to see differently in this way for once, to *want* to see differently, is no small discipline and preparation of the intellect for its future 'objectivity'—the latter understood not as 'contemplation without interest' (which is a nonsensical absurdity), but as the ability to *control* one's Pro and Con and to dispose of them, so that one knows how to employ a *variety* of perspectives and affective interpretations in the service of knowledge.

Henceforth, my dear philosophers, let us be on guard against the dangerous old conceptual fiction that posited a 'pure, will-less, painless, timeless knowing subject'; let us guard against the snares of such contradictory concepts as 'pure reason,' 'absolute spirituality,' 'knowledge in itself': these always demand that we should think of an eye that is completely unthinkable, an eye turned in no particular direction, in which the active and interpreting forces, through which alone seeing becomes seeing *something*, are supposed to be lacking; these always demand of the eye an absurdity and a nonsense. There is *only* a perspective seeing, *only* a perspective 'knowing'; and the *more* affects we allow to speak about one thing, the *more* eyes, different eyes, we can use to observe one thing, the more complete will our 'concept' of this thing, our 'objectivity,' more complete will our 'concept' of this thing our 'objectivity,' be.

(GM III: 12) *

Philosophers . . . have trusted in concepts as completely as they have mistrusted the senses: they have not stopped to consider that concepts and words are our inheritance from ages in which thinking was very modest and unclear. . . .

Hitherto one has generally trusted one's concepts as if they were a wonderful dowry from some sort of wonderland: but they are, after all, the inheritance from our most remote, most foolish as well as most intelligent ancestors. This piety toward what we find in us is perhaps part of the moral element in knowledge. What is needed above all is an absolute skepticism toward all inherited concepts. . . .

(WP 409) †

How is truth proved? By the feeling of enhanced power—by utility—by indispensability—in short, by advantages (namely, presuppositions concerning

---

* GM III refers to Part III of the *Geneology of Morals*. Here again the aphorisms are numbered.

† WP abbreviates *The Will to Power*, a collection of Nietzsche's notes which were published after his death. The numbers are from Walter Kaufmann's translation.

what truth *ought* to be like for us to recognize it). But that is a prejudice: a sign that truth is not involved at all—

(WP 455)

The presupposition that things are, at bottom, ordered so morally that human reason must be justified—is an ingenuous presupposition and a piece of naivete, the after-effect of belief in God's veracity. . . .

(WP 471)

The intellect cannot criticize itself, simply because . . . in order to criticize the intellect we should have to be a higher being with 'absolute knowledge.' This presupposes that, distinct from every perspective kind of outlook or sensual-spiritual appropriation, something exists, an 'in-itself.'—But the psychologic derivation of the belief in things forbids us to speak of 'things-in-themselves.'

(WP 473)

There exists neither 'spirit,' nor reason, nor thinking, nor consciousness, nor soul, nor will, nor truth: all are fictions that are of no use. There is no question of 'subject and object,' but of a particular species of animal that can prosper only through a certain *relative rightness;* above all, regularity of its perceptions (so that it can accumulate experience)—

Knowledge works as a tool of power. Hence it is plain that it increases with every increase of power.

The meaning of 'knowledge': here, as in the case of 'good' or 'beautiful,' the concept is to be regarded in a strict and narrow anthropocentric and biological sense. In order for a particular species to maintain itself and increase its power, its conception of reality must comprehend enough of the calculable and constant for it to base a scheme of behavior on it. The utility of preservation—not some abstract-theoretical need not to be deceived—stands as the motive behind the development of the organs of knowledge—they develop in such a way that their observations suffice for our preservation. In other words . . .: a species grasps a certain amount of reality in order to become master of it, in order to press it into service.

(WP 480)

Against positivism, which halts at phenomena—'There are only *facts*'—I would say: No, facts is precisely what there is not, only interpretations. We cannot establish any fact 'in itself': perhaps it is folly to want to do such a thing.

(WP 481)

'Everything is subjective,' you say; but even this is interpretation. The 'subject' is not something given, it is something added and invented and projected behind what there is.—Finally, is it necessary to posit an interpreter behind the interpretation? Even this is invention, hypothesis. . . .

It is our needs that interpret the world; our drives and their For and Against.

(WP 481)

In so far as the word 'knowledge' has any meaning, the world is knowable; but it is *interpretable* otherwise, it has no meaning behind it, but countless meanings.—'Perspectivism'

(WP 481)

'There is thinking: therefore there is something that thinks': this is the upshot of all Descartes' argumentation. But that means positing as 'true *a priori*' our belief in the concept of substance—that when there is thought there has to be something 'that thinks' is simply a formulation of our grammatical custom that adds a doer to every deed. In short, this is not merely the substantiation of a fact but a logical-metaphysical postulate—Along the lines followed by Descartes one does not come upon something absolutely certain but only upon the fact of a very strong belief.

(WP 484)

Truth is the kind of error without which a certain species of life could not live. The value for *life* is ultimately decisive.

(WP 493)

It is improbable that our 'knowledge' should extend further than is strictly necessary for the preservation of life. Morphology shows us how the senses and the nerves, as well as the brain, develop in proportion to the difficulty of finding nourishment.

(WP 494)

Our perceptions, as we understand them: i.e., the sum of all those perceptions the becoming-conscious of which was useful and essential to us and to the entire organic process—therefore not all perceptions in general . . . ; this means: we have senses only for a selection of perceptions—those with which we have to concern ourselves in order to preserve ourselves. *Consciousness is present only to the extent that consciousness is* useful. It cannot be doubted that *all sense perceptions are permeated with value judgements* (useful and harmful—consequently, pleasant or unpleasant).

(WP 505)

First *images*—to explain how images arise in the spirit. Then *words*, applied to images. Finally *concepts*, possible only when there are words—the collecting together of many images in something nonvisible but audible (word). The tiny amount of emotion to which the 'word' gives rise, as we contemplate similar images for which *one* word exists—this weak emotion is the common element,

the basis of the concept. That weak sensations are regarded as alike, sensed as being the same, is the fundamental fact.

(WP 506)

Not 'to know' but to schematize—to impose upon chaos as much regularity and form as our practical needs require.

In the formation of reason, logic, the categories, it was *need* that was authoritative: the need, not to 'know,' but to subsume, to schematize, for the purpose of intelligibility and calculation—(The development of reason is adjustment, invention, with the aim of making similar, equal—the same process that every sense impression goes through!) No pre-existing 'idea' was here at work, but the utilitarian fact that only when we see things coarsely and made equal do they become calculable and usable to us—Finality in reason is an effect, not a cause: life miscarries with any other kinds of reason, to which there is a continual impulse—it becomes difficult to survey—too unequal—

The categories are 'truths' only in the sense that they are conditions of life for us: as Euclidean space is a conditional 'truth.' (Between ourselves: since no one would maintain that there is any necessity for men to exist, reason, as well as Euclidean space, is a mere idiosyncrasy of a certain species of animal, and one among many—)

The subjective compulsion not to contradict here is a biological compulsion: the instinct for the utility of inferring as we do infer is part of us, we almost *are* this instinct—But what naivete to extract from this a proof that we are there with in possession of a 'truth in itself'!—Not being able to contradict is proof of an incapacity, not of 'truth.'

(WP 515)

We believe in reason: this, however, is the philosophy of gray *concepts*. Language depends on the most naive prejudices.

Now we read disharmonies and problems into things because we think *only* in the form of language—and thus believe in the 'eternal truth' of 'reason' (e.g., subject, attribute, etc.)

We cease to think when we refuse to do so under the constraint of language; we barely reach the doubt that sees this limitation as a limitation.

Rational thought is interpretation according to a scheme that we cannot throw off.

(WP 522)

"No matter how strongly a thing may be believed, strength of belief is no criterion of truth." But what is truth? Perhaps a kind of belief that has become a condition of life: In that case, to be sure, strength could be a criterion; e.g., in regard to causality.

(WP 532)

The criterion of truth resides in the enhancement of the feeling of power.

(WP 534)

'Truth': this, according to my way of thinking, does not necessarily denote the antithesis of error, but in the most fundamental cases only the posture of various errors in relation to one another. Perhaps one is older, more profound than another, even ineradicable, in so far as an organic entity of our species could not live without it; while other errors do not tyranize over us in this way as conditions of life, but on the contrary when compared with such 'tyrants' can be set aside and 'refuted.'

An assumption that is irrefutable—why should it for that reason be 'true'? This proposition may perhaps outrage logicians, who posit *their* limitations as the limitations of things: but I long ago declared war on this optimism of logicians.

(WP 535)

33

Objectivity, Value Judgments, and Theory Choice

THOMAS S. KUHN

Thomas Kuhn (b. 1922) is Professor of Philosophy at the Massachusetts Institute of Technology. Kuhn's work on the history and philosophy of science, and especially his Structure of Scientific Revolutions, *has been tremendously influential. He is also the author of* The Copernican Revolution *and* The Essential Tension, *from which this selection is taken.*

Many philosophers of science have argued that, at the very least, a theory must be compatible with available evidence if it is to be worthy of our belief. In this selection, Kuhn argues that there is always some tension between theory and evidence. There are no theories, according to Kuhn, that are wholly compatible with the available evidence. If this is so, is it ever reasonable to believe a theory to be true? If so, what reasons can there be for favoring one theory over another if neither is compatible with the evidence? In this essay, Kuhn addresses the second of these two questions. He argues that scientists betray a commitment to certain values in favoring one theory over another, and that these values are not dictated by the available evidence. Kuhn discusses the implications of his view for the objectivity of science.

IN THE PENULTIMATE CHAPTER of a controversial book first published fifteen years ago, I considered the ways scientists are brought to abandon one time honored theory or paradigm in favor of another. Such decision problems, I wrote, "cannot be resolved by proof." To discuss their mechanism is, therefore, to talk "about techniques of persuasion, or about argument and counterargument in a situation in which there can be no proof." Under these circumstances, I continued, "lifelong resistance [to a new theory] . . . is not a violation of scientific standards. . . . Though the historian can always find men—Priestley, for instance—who were unreasonable to resist for as long as they did, he will not find a point at which resistance becomes illogical or unscientific."[1] Statements of that sort obviously raise the question of why, in the absence of

---

[1] *The Structure of Scientific Revolutions,* 2d ed. (Chicago, 1970), pp. 148, 151–52, 159. All the passages from which these fragments are taken appeared in the same form in the first edition, published in 1962.

binding criteria for scientific choice, both the number of solved scientific problems and the precision of individual problem solutions should increase so markedly with the passage of time. Confronting that issue, I sketched in my closing chapter a number of characteristics that scientists share by virtue of the training which licenses their membership in one or another community of specialists. In the absence of criteria able to dictate the choice of each individual, I argued, we do well to trust the collective judgment of scientists trained in this way. "What better criterion could there be," I asked rhetorically, "than the decision of the scientific group?"[2]

A number of philosophers have greeted remarks like these in a way that continues to surprise me. My views, it is said, make of theory choice "a matter for mob psychology."[3] Kuhn believes, I am told, that "the decision of a scientific group to adopt a new paradigm cannot be based on good reasons of any kind, factual or otherwise."[4] The debates surrounding such choices must, my critics claim, be for me "mere persuasive displays without deliberative substance."[5] Reports of this sort manifest total misunderstanding, and I have occasionally said as much in papers directed primarily to other ends. But those passing protestations have had negligible effect, and the misunderstandings continue to be important. I conclude that it is past time for me to describe, at greater length and with greater precision, what has been on my mind when I have uttered statements like the ones with which I just began. If I have been reluctant to do so in the past, that is largely because I have preferred to devote attention to areas in which my views diverge more sharply from those currently received than they do with respect to theory choice.

What, I ask to begin with, are the characteristics of a good scientific theory? Among a number of quite usual answers I select five, not because they are exhaustive, but because they are individually important and collectively sufficiently varied to indicate what is at stake. First, a theory should be accurate: within its domain, that is, consequences deducible from a theory should be in demonstrated agreement with the results of existing experiments and observations. Second, a theory should be consistent, not only internally or with itself, but also with other currently accepted theories applicable to related aspects of nature. Third, it should have broad scope: in particular, a theory's consequences should extend far beyond the particular observations, laws, or subtheories it was initially designed to explain. Fourth, and closely related, it should be simple, bringing order to phenomena that in its absence would be

---

[2] Ibid., p. 170.

[3] Imre Lakatos, "Falsification and the Methodology of Scientific Research Programmes," in I. Lakatos and A. Musgrave, eds., *Criticism and the Growth of Knowledge* (Cambridge, 1970), pp. 91–195. The quoted phrase, which appears on p. 178, is italicized in the original.

[4] Dudley Shapere, "Meaning and Scientific Change," in R. G. Colodny, ed., *Mind and Cosmos: Essays in Contemporary Science and Philosophy,* University of Pittsburgh Series in the Philosophy of Science, vol. 3 (Pittsburgh, 1966), pp. 41–85. The quotation will be found on p. 67.

[5] Israel Scheffler, *Science and Subjectivity* (Indianapolis, 1967), p. 81.

individually isolated and, as a set, confused. Fifth—a somewhat less standard item, but one of special importance to actual scientific decisions—a theory should be fruitful of new research findings: it should, that is, disclose new phenomena or previously unnoted relationships among those already known.[6] These five characteristics—accuracy, consistency, scope, simplicity, and fruitfulness—are all standard criteria for evaluating the adequacy of a theory. If they had not been, I would have devoted far more space to them in my book, for I agree entirely with the traditional view that they play a vital role when scientists must choose between an established theory and an upstart competitor. Together with others of much the same sort, they provide *the* shared basis for theory choice.

Nevertheless, two sorts of difficulties are regularly encountered by the men who must use these criteria in choosing, say, between Ptolemy's astronomical theory and Copernicus's, between the oxygen and phlogiston theories of combustion, or between Newtonian mechanics and the quantum theory. Individually the criteria are imprecise: individuals may legitimately differ about their application to concrete cases. In addition, when deployed together, they repeatedly prove to conflict with one another; accuracy may, for example, dictate the choice of one theory, scope the choice of its competitor. Since these difficulties, especially the first, are also relatively familiar, I shall devote little time to their elaboration. Though my argument does demand that I illustrate them briefly, my views will begin to depart from those long current only after I have done so.

Begin with accuracy, which for present purposes I take to include not only quantitative agreement but qualitative as well. Ultimately it proves the most nearly decisive of all the criteria, partly because it is less equivocal than the others but especially because predictive and explanatory powers, which depend on it, are characteristics that scientists are particularly unwilling to give up. Unfortunately, however, theories cannot always be discriminated in terms of accuracy. Copernicus's system, for example, was not more accurate than Ptolemy's until drastically revised by Kepler more than sixty years after Copernicus's death. If Kepler or someone else had not found other reasons to choose heliocentric astronomy, those improvements in accuracy would never have been made, and Copernicus's work might have been forgotten. More typically, of course, accuracy does permit discriminations, but not the sort that lead regularly to unequivocal choice. The oxygen theory, for example, was universally acknowledged to account for observed weight relations in chemical reactions, something the phlogiston theory had previously scarcely attempted to do. But the phlogiston theory, unlike its rival, could account for the metals' being much more alike than the ores from which they were formed. One theory

---

[6] The last criterion, fruitfulness, deserves more emphasis than it has yet received. A scientist choosing between two theories ordinarily knows that his decision will have a bearing on his subsequent research career. Of course he is especially attracted by a theory that promises the concrete successes for which scientists are ordinarily rewarded.

thus matched experience better in one area, the other in another. To choose between them on the basis of accuracy, a scientist would need to decide the area in which accuracy was more significant. About that matter chemists could and did differ without violating any of the criteria outlined above, or any others yet to be suggested.

However important it may be, therefore, accuracy by itself is seldom or never a sufficient criterion for theory choice. Other criteria must function as well, but they do not eliminate problems. To illustrate I select just two—consistency and simplicity—asking how they functioned in the choice between the heliocentric and geocentric systems. As astronomical theories both Ptolemy's and Copernicus's were internally consistent, but their relation to related theories in other fields was very different. The stationary central earth was an essential ingredient of received physical theory, a tight-knit body of doctrine which explained, among other things, how stones fall, how water pumps function, and why the clouds move slowly across the skies. Heliocentric astronomy, which required the earth's motion, was inconsistent with the existing scientific explanation of these and other terrestrial phenomena. The consistency criterion, by itself, therefore, spoke unequivocally for the geocentric tradition.

Simplicity, however, favored Copernicus, but only when evaluated in a quite special way. If, on the one hand, the two systems were compared in terms of the actual computational labor required to predict the position of a planet at a particular time, then they proved substantially equivalent. Such computations were what astronomers did, and Copernicus's system offered them no labor-saving techniques; in that sense it was not simpler than Ptolemy's. If, on the other hand, one asked about the amount of mathematical apparatus required to explain, not the detailed quantitative motions of the planets, but merely their gross qualitative features—limited elongation, retrograde motion, and the like—then, as every schoolchild knows, Copernicus required only one circle per planet, Ptolemy two. In that sense the Copernican theory was the simpler, a fact vitally important to the choices made by both Kepler and Galileo and thus essential to the ultimate triumph of Copernicanism. But that sense of simplicity was not the only one available, nor even the one most natural to professional astronomers, men whose task was the actual computation of planetary position.

Because time is short and I have multiplied examples elsewhere, I shall here simply assert that these difficulties in applying standard criteria of choice are typical and that they arise no less forcefully in twentieth-century situations than in the earlier and better-known examples I have just sketched. When scientists must choose between competing theories, two men fully committed to the same list of criteria for choice may nevertheless reach different conclusions. Perhaps they interpret simplicity differently or have different convictions about the range of fields within which the consistency criterion must be met. Or perhaps they agree about these matters but differ about the relative weights to be accorded to these or to other criteria when several are deployed together. With respect to divergences of this sort, no set of choice criteria yet proposed is of any use. One can explain, as the historian characteristically does, why particular men made particular choices at particular times. But for that purpose

one must go beyond the list of shared criteria to characteristics of the individuals who make the choice. One must, that is, deal with characteristics which vary from one scientist to another without thereby in the least jeopardizing their adherence to the canons that make science scientific. Though such canons do exist and should be discoverable (doubtless the criteria of choice with which I began are among them), they are not by themselves sufficient to determine the decisions of individual scientists. For that purpose the shared canons must be fleshed out in ways that differ from one individual to another.

Some of the differences I have in mind result from the individual's previous experience as a scientist. In what part of the field was he at work when confronted by the need to choose? How long had he worked there; how successful had he been; and how much of his work depended on concepts and techniques challenged by the new theory? Other factors relevant to choice lie outside the sciences. Kepler's early election of Copernicanism was due in part to his immersion in the Neoplatonic and Hermetic movements of his day; German Romanticism predisposed those it affected toward both recognition and acceptance of energy conservation; nineteenth-century British social thought had a similar influence on the availability and acceptability of Darwin's concept of the struggle for existence. Still other significant differences are functions of personality. Some scientists place more premium than others on originality and are correspondingly more willing to take risks; some scientists prefer comprehensive, unified theories to precise and detailed problem solutions of apparently narrower scope. Differentiating factors like these are described by my critics as subjective and are contrasted with the shared or objective criteria from which I began. Though I shall later question that use of terms, let me for the moment accept it. My point is, then, that every individual choice between competing theories depends on a mixture of objective and subjective factors, or of shared and individual criteria. Since the latter have not ordinarily figured in the philosophy of science, my emphasis upon them has made my belief in the former hard for my critics to see.

What I have said so far is primarily simply descriptive of what goes on in the sciences at times of theory choice. As description, furthermore, it has not been challenged by my critics, who reject instead my claim that these facts of scientific life have philosophic import. Taking up that issue, I shall begin to isolate some, though I think not vast, differences of opinion. Let me begin by asking how philosophers of science can for so long have neglected the subjective elements which, they freely grant, enter regularly into the actual theory choices made by individual scientists? Why have these elements seemed to them an index only of human weakness, not at all of the nature of scientific knowledge?

One answer to that question is, of course, that few philosophers, if any, have claimed to possess either a complete or an entirely well-articulated list of criteria. For some time, therefore, they could reasonably expect that further research would eliminate residual imperfections and produce an algorithm able to dictate rational, unanimous choice. Pending that achievement, scientists would have no alternative but to supply subjectively what the best current list of objective criteria still lacked. That some of them might still do so even with a

375

perfected list at hand would then be an index only of the inevitable imperfection of human nature.

That sort of answer may still prove to be correct, but I think no philosopher still expects that it will. The search for algorithmic decision procedures has continued for some time and produced both powerful and illuminating results. But those results all presuppose that individual criteria of choice can be unambiguously stated and also that, if more than one proves relevant, an appropriate weight function is at hand for their joint application. Unfortunately, where the choice at issue is between scientific theories, little progress has been made toward the first of these desiderata and none toward the second. Most philosophers of science would, therefore, I think, now regard the sort of algorithm which has traditionally been sought as a not quite attainable ideal. I entirely agree and shall henceforth take that much for granted.

Even an ideal, however, if it is to remain credible, requires some demonstrated relevance to the situations in which it is supposed to apply. Claiming that such demonstration requires no recourse to subjective factors, my critics seem to appeal, implicitly or explicitly, to the well-known distinction between the contexts of discovery and of justification. They concede, that is, that the subjective factors I invoke play a significant role in the discovery or invention of new theories, but they also insist that that inevitably intuitive process lies outside of the bounds of philosophy of science and is irrelevant to the question of scientific objectivity. Objectivity enters science, they continue, through the processes by which theories are tested, justified, or judged. Those processes do not, or at least need not, involve subjective factors at all. They can be governed by a set of (objective) criteria shared by the entire group competent to judge.

I have already argued that that position does not fit observations of scientific life and shall now assume that that much has been conceded. What is now at issue is a different point: whether or not this invocation of the distinction between contexts of discovery and of justification provides even a plausible and useful idealization. I think it does not and can best make my point by suggesting first a likely source of its apparent cogency. I suspect that my critics have been misled by science pedagogy or what I have elsewhere called textbook science. In science teaching, theories are presented together with exemplary applications, and those applications may be viewed as evidence. But that is not their primary pedagogic function (science students are distressingly willing to receive the word from professors and texts). Doubtless *some* of them were *part* of the evidence at the time actual decisions were being made, but they represent only a fraction of the considerations relevant to the decision process. The context of pedagogy differs almost as much from the context of justification as it does from that of discovery.

Full documentation of that point would require longer argument than is appropriate here, but two aspects of the way in which philosophers ordinarily demonstrate the relevance of choice criteria are worth noting. Like the science textbooks on which they are often modelled, books and articles on the philosophy of science refer again and again to the famous crucial experiments: Foucault's pendulum, which demonstrates the motion of the earth; Cavendish's

demonstration of gravitational attraction; or Fizeau's measurement of the relative speed of sound in water and air. These experiments are paradigms of good reason for scientific choice; they illustrate the most effective of all the sorts of argument which could be available to a scientist uncertain which of two theories to follow; they are vehicles for the transmission of criteria of choice. But they also have another characteristic in common. By the time they were performed no scientist still needed to be convinced of the validity of the theory their outcome is now used to demonstrate. Those decisions had long since been made on the basis of significantly more equivocal evidence. The exemplary crucial experiments to which philosophers again and again refer would have been historically relevant to theory choice only if they had yielded unexpected results. Their use as illustrations provides needed economy to science pedagogy, but they scarcely illuminate the character of the choices that scientists are called upon to make.

Standard philosophical illustrations of scientific choice have another troublesome characteristic. The only arguments discussed are, as I have previously indicated, the ones favorable to the theory that, in fact, ultimately triumphed. Oxygen, we read, could explain weight relations, phlogiston could not; but nothing is said about the phlogiston theory's power or about the oxygen theory's limitations. Comparisons of Ptolemy's theory with Copernicus's proceed in the same way. Perhaps these examples should not be given since they contrast a developed theory with one still in its infancy. But philosophers regularly use them nonetheless. If the only result of their doing so were to simplify the decision situation, one could not object. Even historians do not claim to deal with the full factual complexity of the situations they describe. But these simplifications emasculate by making choice totally unproblematic. They eliminate, that is, one essential element of the decision situations that scientists must resolve if their field is to move ahead. In those situations there are always at least some good reasons for each possible choice. Considerations relevant to the context of discovery are then relevant to justification as well; scientists who share the concerns and sensibilities of the individual who discovers a new theory are ipso facto likely to appear disproportionately frequently among that theory's first supporters. That is why it has been difficult to construct algorithms for theory choice, and also why such difficulties have seemed so thoroughly worth resolving. Choices that present problems are the ones philosophers of science need to understand. Philosophically interesting decision procedures must function where, in their absence, the decision might still be in doubt.

That much I have said before, if only briefly. Recently, however, I have recognized another, subtler source for the apparent plausibility of my critics' position. To present it, I shall briefly describe a hypothetical dialogue with one of them. Both of us agree that each scientist chooses between competing theories by deploying some Bayesian algorithm which permits him to compute a value for $p(T,E)$, i.e., for the probability of a theory T on the evidence E available both to him and to the other members of his professional group at a particular period of time. "Evidence," furthermore, we both interpret broadly to include such considerations as simplicity and fruitfulness. My critic asserts,

however, that there is only one such value of p, that corresponding to objective choice, and he believes that all rational members of the group must arrive at it. I assert, on the other hand, for reasons previously given, that the factors he calls objective are insufficient to determine in full any algorithm at all. For the sake of the discussion I have conceded that each individual has an algorithm and that all their algorithms have much in common. Nevertheless, I continue to hold that the algorithms of individuals are all ultimately different by virtue of the subjective considerations with which each must complete the objective criteria before any computations can be done. If my hypothetical critic is liberal, he may now grant that these subjective differences do play a role in determining the hypothetical algorithm on which each individual relies during the early stages of the competition between rival theories. But he is also likely to claim that, as evidence increases with the passage of time, the algorithms of different individuals converge to the algorithm of objective choice with which his presentation began. For him the increasing unanimity of individual choices is evidence for their increasing objectivity and thus for the elimination of subjective elements from the decision process.

So much for the dialogue, which I have, of course, contrived to disclose the non sequitur underlying an apparently plausible position. What converges as the evidence changes over time need only be the values of p that individuals compute from their individual algorithms. Conceivably those algorithms themselves also become more alike with time, but the ultimate unanimity of theory choice provides no evidence whatsoever that they do so. If subjective factors are required to account for the decisions that initially divide the profession, they may still be present later when the profession agrees. Though I shall not here argue the point, consideration of the occasions on which a scientific community divides suggests that they actually do so.

My argument has so far been directed to two points. It first provided evidence that the choices scientists make between competing theories depend not only on shared criteria—those my critics call objective—but also on idiosyncratic factors dependent on individual biography and personality. The latter are, in my critics' vocabulary, subjective, and the second part of my argument has attempted to bar some likely ways of denying their philosophic import. Let me now shift to a more positive approach, returning briefly to the list of shared criteria—accuracy, simplicity, and the like—with which I began. The considerable effectiveness of such criteria does not, I now wish to suggest, depend on their being sufficiently articulated to dictate the choice of each individual who subscribes to them. Indeed, if they were articulated to that extent, a behavior mechanism fundamental to scientific advance would cease to function. What the tradition sees as eliminable imperfections in its rules of choice I take to be in part responses to the essential nature of science.

As so often, I begin with the obvious. Criteria that influence decisions without specifying what those decisions must be are familiar in many aspects of human life. Ordinarily, however, they are called, not criteria or rules, but maxims, norms, or values. Consider maxims first. The individual who invokes them when choice is urgent usually finds them frustratingly vague and often also in

conflict one with another. Contrast "He who hesitates is lost" with "Look before you leap," or compare "Many hands make light work" with "Too many cooks spoil the broth." Individually maxims dictate different choices, collectively none at all. Yet no one suggests that supplying children with contradictory tags like these is irrelevant to their education. Opposing maxims alter the nature of the decision to be made, highlight the essential issues it presents, and point to those remaining aspects of the decision for which each individual must take responsibility himself. Once invoked, maxims like these alter the nature of the decision process and can thus change its outcome.

Values and norms provide even clearer examples of effective guidance in the presence of conflict and equivocation. Improving the quality of life is a value, and a car in every garage once followed from it as a norm. But quality of life has other aspects, and the old norm has become problematic. Or again, freedom of speech is a value, but so is preservation of life and property. In application, the two often conflict, so that judicial soul-searching, which still continues, has been required to prohibit such behavior as inciting to riot or shouting fire in a crowded theater. Difficulties like these are an appropriate source for frustration, but they rarely result in charges that values have no function or in calls for their abandonment. That response is barred to most of us by an acute consciousness that there are societies with other values and that these value differences result in other ways of life, other decisions about what may and what may not be done.

I am suggesting, of course, that the criteria of choice with which I began function not as rules, which determine choice, but as values, which influence it. Two men deeply committed to the same values may nevertheless, in particular situations, make different choices as, in fact, they do. But that difference in outcome ought not to suggest that the values scientists share are less than critically important either to their decisions or to the development of the enterprise in which they participate. Values like accuracy, consistency, and scope may prove ambiguous in application, both individually and collectively; they may, that is, be an insufficient basis for a *shared* algorithm of choice. But they do specify a great deal: what each scientist must consider in reaching a decision, what he may and may not consider relevant, and what he can legitimately be required to report as the basis for the choice he has made. Change the list, for example by adding social utility as a criterion, and some particular choices will be different, more like those one expects from an engineer. Subtract accuracy of fit to nature from the list, and the enterprise that results may not resemble science at all, but perhaps philosophy instead. Different creative disciplines are characterized, among other things, by different sets of shared values. If philosophy and engineering lie too close to the sciences, think of literature or the plastic arts. Milton's failure to set *Paradise Lost* in a Copernican universe does not indicate that he agreed with Ptolemy but that he had things other than science to do.

Recognizing that criteria of choice can function as values when incomplete as rules has, I think, a number of striking advantages. First, as I have already argued at length, it accounts in detail for aspects of scientific behavior which

the tradition has seen as anomalous or even irrational. More important, it allows the standard criteria to function fully in the earliest stages of theory choice, the period when they are most needed but when, on the traditional view, they function badly or not at all. Copernicus was responding to them during the years required to convert heliocentric astronomy from a global conceptual scheme to mathematical machinery for predicting planetary position. Such predictions were what astronomers valued; in their absence, Copernicus would scarcely have been heard, something which had happened to the idea of a moving earth before. That his own version convinced very few is less important than his acknowledgment of the basis on which judgments would have to be reached if heliocentricism were to survive. Though idiosyncrasy must be invoked to explain why Kepler and Galileo were early converts to Copernicus's system, the gaps filled by their efforts to perfect it were specified by shared values alone.

That point has a corollary which may be more important still. Most newly suggested theories do not survive. Usually the difficulties that evoked them are accounted for by more traditional means. Even when this does not occur, much work, both theoretical and experimental, is ordinarily required before the new theory can display sufficient accuracy and scope to generate widespread conviction. In short, before the group accepts it, a new theory has been tested over time by the research of a number of men, some working within it, others within its traditional rival. Such a mode of development, however, *requires* a decision process which permits rational men to disagree, and such disagreement would be barred by the shared algorithm which philosophers have generally sought. If it were at hand, all conforming scientists would make the same decision at the same time. With standards for acceptance set too low, they would move from one attractive global viewpoint to another, never giving traditional theory an opportunity to supply equivalent attractions. With standards set higher, no one satisfying the criterion of rationality would be inclined to try out the new theory, to articulate it in ways which showed its fruitfulness or displayed its accuracy and scope. I doubt that science would survive the change. What from one viewpoint may seem the looseness and imperfection of choice criteria conceived as rules may, when the same criteria are seen as values, appear an indispensable means of spreading the risk which the introduction or support of novelty always entails.

Even those who have followed me this far will want to know how a value-based enterprise of the sort I have described can develop as a science does, repeatedly producing powerful new techniques for prediction and control. To that question, unfortunately, I have no answer at all, but that is only another way of saying that I make no claim to have solved the problem of induction. If science did progress by virtue of some shared and binding algorithm of choice, I would be equally at a loss to explain its success. The lacuna is one I feel acutely, but its presence does not differentiate my position from the tradition.

It is, after all, no accident that my list of the values guiding scientific choice is, as nearly as makes any difference, identical with the tradition's list of rules dictating choice. Given any concrete situation to which the philosopher's rules

could be applied, my values would function like his rules, producing the same choice. Any justification of induction, any explanation of why the rules worked, would apply equally to my values. Now consider a situation in which choice by shared rules proves impossible, not because the rules are wrong but because they are, as rules, intrinsically incomplete. Individuals must then still choose and be guided by the rules (now values) when they do so. For that purpose, however, each must first flesh out the rules, and each will do so in a somewhat different way even though the decision dictated by the variously completed rules may prove unanimous. If I now assume, in addition, that the group is large enough so that individual differences distribute on some normal curve, then any argument that justifies the philosopher's choice by rule should be immediately adaptable to my choice by value. A group too small, or a distribution excessively skewed by external historical pressures, would, of course, prevent the argument's transfer.[7] But those are just the circumstances under which scientific progress is itself problematic. The transfer is not then to be expected.

I shall be glad if these references to a normal distribution of individual differences and to the problem of induction make my position appear very close to more traditional views. With respect to theory choice, I have never thought my departures large and have been correspondingly startled by such charges as "mob psychology," quoted at the start. It is worth noting, however, that the positions are not quite identical, and for that purpose an analogy may be helpful. Many properties of liquids and gases can be accounted for on the kinetic theory by supposing that all molecules travel at the same speed. Among such properties are the regularities known as Boyle's and Charles's law. Other characteristics, most obviously evaporation, cannot be explained in so simple a way. To deal with them one must assume that molecular speeds differ, that they are distributed at random, governed by the laws of chance. What I have been suggesting here is that theory choice, too, can be explained only in part by a theory which attributes the same properties to all the scientists who must do the choosing. Essential aspects of the process generally known as verification will be understood only by recourse to the features with respect to which men may differ while still remaining scientists. The tradition takes it for granted that such features are vital to the process of discovery, which it at once and

[7] If the group is small, it is more likely that random fluctuations will result in its members' sharing an atypical set of values and therefore making choices different from those that would be made by a larger and more representative group. External environment—intellectual, ideological, or economic—must systematically affect the value system of much larger groups, and the consequences can include difficulties in introducing the scientific enterprise to societies with inimical values or perhaps even the end of that enterprise within societies where it had once flourished. In this area, however, great caution is required. Changes in the environment where science is practiced can also have fruitful effects on research. Historians often resort, for example, to differences between national environments to explain why particular innovations were initiated and at first disproportionately pursued in particular countries, e.g., Darwinism in Britain, energy conservation in Germany. At present we know substantially nothing about the minimum requisites of the social milieux within which a sciencelike enterprise might flourish.

for that reason rules out of philosophical bounds. That they may have significant functions also in the philosophically central problem of justifying theory choice is what philosophers of science have to date categorically denied.

What remains to be said can be grouped in a somewhat miscellaneous epilogue. For the sake of clarity and to avoid writing a book, I have throughout this paper utilized some traditional concepts and locutions about the viability of which I have elsewhere expressed serious doubts. For those who know the work in which I have done so, I close by indicating three aspects of what I have said which would better represent my views if cast in other terms, simultaneously indicating the main directions in which such recasting should proceed. The areas I have in mind are: value invariance, subjectivity, and partial communication. If my views of scientific development are novel—a matter about which there is legitimate room for doubt—it is in areas such as these, rather than theory choice, that my main departures from tradition should be sought.

Throughout this paper I have implicitly assumed that, whatever their initial source, the criteria or values deployed in theory choice are fixed once and for all, unaffected by their participation in transitions from one theory to another. Roughly speaking, but only very roughly, I take that to be the case. If the list of relevant values is kept short (I have mentioned five, not all independent) and if their specification is left vague, then such values as accuracy, scope, and fruitfulness are permanent attributes of science. But little knowledge of history is required to suggest that both the application of these values and, more obviously, the relative weights attached to them have varied markedly with time and also with the field of application. Furthermore, many of these variations in value have been associated with particular changes in scientific theory. Though the experience of scientists provides no philosophical justification for the values they deploy (such justification would solve the problem of induction), those values are in part learned from that experience, and they evolve with it.

The whole subject needs more study (historians have usually taken scientific values, though not scientific methods, for granted), but a few remarks will illustrate the sort of variations I have in mind. Accuracy, as a value, has with time increasingly denoted quantitative or numerical agreement, sometimes at the expense of qualitative. Before early modern times, however, accuracy in that sense was a criterion only for astronomy, the science of the celestial region. Elsewhere it was neither expected nor sought. During the seventeenth century, however, the criterion of numerical agreement was extended to mechanics, during the late eighteenth and early nineteenth centuries to chemistry and such other subjects as electricity and heat, and in this century to many parts of biology. Or think of utility, an item of value not on my initial list. It too has figured significantly in scientific development, but far more strongly and steadily for chemists than for, say, mathematicians and physicists. Or consider scope. It is still an important scientific value, but important scientific advances have repeatedly been achieved at its expense, and the weight attributed to it at times of choice has diminished correspondingly.

What may seem particularly troublesome about changes like these is, of course, that they ordinarily occur in the aftermath of a theory change. One of

the objections to Lavoisier's new chemistry was the roadblocks with which it confronted the achievement of what had previously been one of chemistry's traditional goals: the explanation of qualities, such as color and texture, as well as of their changes. With the acceptance of Lavoisier's theory such explanations ceased for some time to be a value for chemists; the ability to explain qualitative variation was no longer a criterion relevant to the evaluation of chemical theory. Clearly, if such value changes had occurred as rapidly or been as complete as the theory changes to which they related, then theory choice would be value choice, and neither could provide justification for the other. But, historically, value change is ordinarily a belated and largely unconscious concomitant of theory choice, and the former's magnitude is regularly smaller than the latter's. For the functions I have here ascribed to values, such relative stability provides a sufficient basis. The existence of a feedback loop through which theory change affects the values which led to that change does not make the decision process circular in any damaging sense.

About a second respect in which my resort to tradition may be misleading, I must be far more tentative. It demands the skills of an ordinary language philosopher, which I do not possess. Still, no very acute ear for language is required to generate discomfort with the ways in which the terms "objectivity" and, more especially, "subjectivity" have functioned in this paper. Let me briefly suggest the respects in which I believe language has gone astray. "Subjective" is a term with several established uses: in one of these it is opposed to "objective," in another to "judgmental." When my critics describe the idiosyncratic features to which I appeal as subjective, they resort, erroneously I think, to the second of these senses. When they complain that I deprive science of objectivity, they conflate that second sense of subjective with the first.

A standard application of the term "subjective" is to matters of taste, and my critics appear to suppose that that is what I have made of theory choice. But they are missing a distinction standard since Kant when they do so. Like sensation reports, which are also subjective in the sense now at issue, matters of taste are undiscussable. Suppose that, leaving a movie theater with a friend after seeing a western, I exclaim: "How I liked that terrible potboiler!" My friend, if he disliked the film, may tell me I have low tastes, a matter about which, in these circumstances, I would readily agree. But, short of saying that I lied, he cannot disagree with my report that I liked the film or try to persuade me that what I said about my reaction was wrong. What is discussable in my remark is not my characterization of my internal state, my exemplification of taste, but rather my *judgment* that the film was a potboiler. Should my friend disagree on that point, we may argue most of the night, each comparing the film with good or great ones we have seen, each revealing, implicitly or explicitly, something about how he *judges* cinematic merit, about his aesthetic. Though one of us may, before retiring, have persuaded the other, he need not have done so to demonstrate that our difference is one of judgment, not taste.

Evaluations or choices of theory have, I think, exactly this character. Not that scientists never say merely, I like such and such a theory, or I do not. After 1926 Einstein said little more than that about his opposition to the quantum

theory. But scientists may always be asked to explain their choices, to exhibit the bases for their judgments. Such judgments are eminently discussable, and the man who refuses to discuss his own cannot expect to be taken seriously. Though there are, very occasionally, leaders of scientific taste, their existence tends to prove the rule. Einstein was one of the few, and his increasing isolation from the scientific community in later life shows how very limited a role taste alone can play in theory choice. Bohr, unlike Einstein, did discuss the bases for his judgment, and he carried the day. If my critics introduce the term "subjective" in a sense that opposes it to judgmental—thus suggesting that I make theory choice undiscussable, a matter of taste—they have seriously mistaken my position.

Turn now to the sense in which "subjectivity" is opposed to "objectivity," and note first that it raises issues quite separate from those just discussed. Whether my taste is low or refined, my report that I liked the film is objective unless I have lied. To my judgment that the film was a potboiler, however, the objective-subjective distinction does not apply at all, at least not obviously and directly. When my critics say I deprive theory choice of objectivity, they must, therefore, have recourse to some very different sense of subjective, presumably the one in which bias and personal likes or dislikes function instead of, or in the face of, the actual facts. But that sense of subjective does not fit the process I have been describing any better than the first. Where factors dependent on individual biography or personality must be introduced to make values applicable, no standards of factuality or actuality are being set aside. Conceivably my discussion of theory choice indicates some limitations of objectivity, but not by isolating elements properly called subjective. Nor am I even quite content with the notion that what I have been displaying are limitations. Objectivity ought to be analyzable in terms of criteria like accuracy and consistency. If these criteria do not supply all the guidance that we have customarily expected of them, then it may be the meaning rather than the limits of objectivity that my argument shows.

Turn, in conclusion, to a third respect, or set of respects, in which this paper needs to be recast. I have assumed throughout that the discussions surrounding theory choice are unproblematic, that the facts appealed to in such discussions are independent of theory, and that the discussions' outcome is appropriately called a choice. Elsewhere I have challenged all three of these assumptions, arguing that communication between proponents of different theories is inevitably partial, that what each takes to be facts depends in part on the theory he espouses, and that an individual's transfer of allegiance from theory to theory is often better described as conversion than as choice. Though all these theses are problematic as well as controversial, my commitment to them is undiminished. I shall not now defend them, but must at least attempt to indicate how what I have said here can be adjusted to conform with these more central aspects of my view of scientific development.

For that purpose I resort to an analogy I have developed in other places. Proponents of different theories are, I have claimed, like native speakers of different languages. Communication between them goes on by translation, and

it raises all translation's familiar difficulties. That analogy is, of course, incomplete, for the vocabulary of the two theories may be identical, and most words function in the same ways in both. But some words in the basic as well as in the theoretical vocabularies of the two theories—words like "star" and "planet," "mixture" and "compound," or "force" and "matter"—do function differently. Those differences are unexpected and will be discovered and localized, if at all, only by repeated experience of communication breakdown. Without pursuing the matter further, I simply assert the existence of significant limits to what the proponents of different theories can communicate to one another. The same limits make it difficult or, more likely, impossible for an individual to hold both theories in mind together and compare them point by point with each other and with nature. That sort of comparison is, however, the process on which the appropriateness of any word like "choice" depends.

Nevertheless, despite the incompleteness of their communication, proponents of different theories can exhibit to each other, not always easily, the concrete technical results achievable by those who practice within each theory. Little or no translation is required to apply at least some value criteria to those results. (Accuracy and fruitfulness are most immediately applicable, perhaps followed by scope. Consistency and simplicity are far more problematic.) However incomprehensible the new theory may be to the proponents of tradition, the exhibit of impressive concrete results will persuade at least a few of them that they must discover how such results are achieved. For that purpose they must learn to translate, perhaps by treating already published papers as a Rosetta stone or, often more effective, by visiting the innovator, talking with him, watching him and his students at work. Those exposures may not result in the adoption of the theory; some advocates of the tradition may return home and attempt to adjust the old theory to produce equivalent results. But others, if the new theory is to survive, will find that at some point in the language-learning process they have ceased to translate and begun instead to speak the language like a native. No process quite like choice has occurred, but they are practicing the new theory nonetheless. Furthermore, the factors that have led them to risk the conversion they have undergone are just the ones this paper has underscored in discussing a somewhat different process, one which, following the philosophical tradition, it has labelled theory choice.

34

Believing Where
We Cannot Prove

PHILIP KITCHER

Philip Kitcher (b. 1947) is Professor of Philosophy at the University of Minnesota. He is the author of The Nature of Mathematical Knowledge *and* Abusing Science: The Case Against Creationism, *from which this selection is taken.*

Kitcher begins this selection by arguing that we can neither conclusively prove scientific theories to be true nor can we conclusively prove such theories to be false. Is it reasonable to believe one scientific theory rather than another if proof is impossible? Kitcher argues that it is, and presents three hallmarks of successful scientific theorizing. A scientific hypothesis is typically introduced to explain a certain set of facts. Kitcher argues that it must be possible to test such hypotheses independently of the facts they are designed to explain. Second, successful hypotheses allow us to unify a body of facts and problem-solving strategies previously seen as disparate. Finally, successful hypotheses serve to develop new areas of inquiry. Although Kitcher's criteria do not allow us to conclusively prove any theory to be true, they do, Kitcher argues, give us good reason to believe one theory rather than another.

Opening Moves

SIMPLE DISTINCTIONS come all too easily. Frequently we open the way for later puzzlement by restricting the options we take to be available. So, for example, in contrasting science and religion, we often operate with a simple pair of categories. On one side there is science, proof, and certainty; on the other, religion, conjecture, and faith.

The opening lines of Tennyson's *In Memoriam* offer an eloquent statement of the contrast:

> Strong Son of God, immortal love,
> Whom we, that have not seen Thy face,
> By faith, and faith alone, embrace,
> Believing where we cannot prove.

A principal theme of Tennyson's great poem is his struggle to maintain faith in the face of what seems to be powerful scientific evidence. Tennyson had read a popular work by Robert Chambers, *Vestiges of the Natural History of Cre-*

ation, and he was greatly troubled by the account of the course of life on earth that the book contains. *In Memoriam* reveals a man trying to believe where he cannot prove, a man haunted by the thought that the proofs may be against him.

Like Tennyson, contemporary Creationists accept the traditional contrast between science and religion. But where Tennyson agonized, they attack. While they are less eloquent, they are supremely confident of their own solution. They open their onslaught on evolutionary theory by denying that it is a science. In *The Troubled Waters of Evolution,* Henry Morris characterizes evolutionary theory as maintaining that large amounts of time are required for evolution to produce "new kinds." As a result, we should not expect to see such "new kinds" emerging. Morris comments, "Creationists in turn insist that this belief is not scientific evidence but only a statement of faith. The evolutionist seems to be saying, Of course, we cannot really *prove* evolution, since this requires ages of time, and so, therefore, you should accept it as a proved fact of science! Creationists regard this as an odd type of logic, which would be entirely unacceptable in any other field of science."[1] David Watson makes a similar point in comparing Darwin with Galileo: "So here is the difference between Darwin and Galileo: Galileo set a demonstrable *fact* against a few words of Bible poetry which the Church at that time had understood in an obviously naive way; Darwin set an unprovable *theory* against eleven chapters of straightforward history which cannot be reinterpreted in any satisfactory way."[2]

The idea that evolution is conjecture, faith, or "philosophy" pervades Creationist writings. . . . It is absolutely crucial to their case for equal time for "scientific" Creationism.

. . .

In their attempt to show that evolution is not science, Creationists receive help from the least likely sources. Great scientists sometimes claim that certain facts about the past evolution of organisms are "demonstrated" or "indubitable". . . . But Creationists also can (and do) quote scientists who characterize evolution as "dogma" and contend that there is no conclusive proof of evolutionary theory. . . . Evolution is not part of science because, as evolutionary biologists themselves concede, science demands proof, and, as other biologists point out, proof of evolution is not forthcoming.

The rest of the Creationist argument flows easily. We educate our children in evolutionary theory, as if it were a proven fact. We subscribe officially, in our school system, to one faith—an atheistic, materialistic faith—ignoring rival beliefs. Antireligious educators deform the minds of children, warping them to accept as gospel a doctrine that has no more scientific support than the true

---

[1] H. M. Morris, *The Troubled Waters of Evolution,* San Diego: Creation-Life Publishers, 1974, p. 16.

[2] D. C. C. Watson, *The Great Brain Robbery,* Chicago: Moody Press, 1976, p. 46.

Gospel. The very least that should be done is to allow for both alternatives to be presented.

We should reject the Creationists' gambit. Eminent scientists notwithstanding, science is not a body of demonstrated truths. Virtually all of science is an exercise in believing where we cannot prove. Yet, scientific conclusions are not embraced by faith alone. Tennyson's dichotomy was too simple.

Inconclusive Evidence

Sometimes we seem to have conclusive reasons for accepting a statement as true. It is hard to doubt that $2 + 2 = 4$. If, unlike Lord Kelvin's ideal mathematician, we do not find it obvious that

$$\int_{-\infty}^{+\infty} e^{-x^2} dx = \sqrt{\pi},$$

at least the elementary parts of mathematics appear to command our agreement. The direct evidence of our senses seems equally compelling. If I see the pen with which I am writing, holding it firmly in my unclouded view, how can I doubt that it exists? The talented mathematician who has proved a theorem and the keen-eyed witness of an episode furnish our ideals of certainty in knowledge. What they tell us can be engraved in stone, for there is no cause for worry that it will need to be modified.

Yet, in another mood, one that seems "deeper" or more "philosophical," skeptical doubts begin to creep in. Is there really anything of which we are so certain that later evidence could not give us reason to change our minds? Even when we think about mathematical proof, can we not imagine that new discoveries may cast doubt on the cogency of our reasoning? (The history of mathematics reveals that sometimes what seems for all the world like a proof may have a false conclusion.) Is it not possible that the most careful observer may have missed something? Or that the witness brought preconceptions to the observation that subtly biased what was reported? Are we not *always* fallible?

I am mildly sympathetic to the skeptic's worries. Complete certainty is best seen as an ideal toward which we strive and that is rarely, if ever, attained. Conclusive evidence always eludes us. Yet even if we ignore skeptical complaints and imagine that we are sometimes lucky enough to have conclusive reasons for accepting a claim as true, we should not include scientific reasoning among our paradigms of proof. Fallibility is the hallmark of science.

This point should not be so surprising. The trouble is that we frequently forget it in discussing contemporary science. When we turn to the history of science, however, our fallibility stares us in the face. The history of the natural sciences is strewn with the corpses of intricately organized theories, each of which had, in its day, considerable evidence in its favor. When we look at the confident defenders of those theories we should see anticipations of ourselves. The eighteenth-century scientists who believed that heat is a "subtle fluid," the

atomic theorists who maintained that water molecules are compounded out of one atom of hydrogen and one of oxygen, the biochemists who identified protein as the genetic material, and the geologists who thought that continents cannot move were neither unintelligent nor ill informed. Given the evidence available to them, they were eminently reasonable in drawing their conclusions. History proved them wrong. It did not show that they were unjustified.

Why is science fallible? Scientific investigation aims to disclose the general principles that govern the workings of the universe. These principles are not intended merely to summarize what some select groups of humans have witnessed. Natural science is not just natural history. It is vastly more ambitious. Science offers us laws that are supposed to hold universally, and it advances claims about things that are beyond our power to observe. The nuclear physicist who sets down the law governing a particular type of radioactive decay is attempting to state a truth that holds throughout the entire cosmos and also to describe the behavior of things that we cannot even see. Yet, of necessity, the physicist's ultimate evidence is highly restricted. Like the rest of us, scientists are confined to a relatively small region of space and time and equipped with limited and imperfect senses.

How is science possible at all? How are we able to have any confidence about the distant regions of the cosmos and the invisible realm that lies behind the surfaces of ordinary things? The answer is complicated. Natural science follows intricate and ingenious procedures for fathoming the secrets of the universe. Scientists devise ways of obtaining especially revealing evidence. They single out some of the things we are able to see as crucial clues to the way that nature works. These clues are used to answer questions that cannot be addressed by direct observation. Scientific theories, even those that are most respected and most successful, rest on indirect arguments from the observational evidence. New discoveries can always call those arguments into question, showing scientists that the observed data should be understood in a different way, that they have misread their evidence.

But scientists often forget the fallibility of their enterprise. This is not just absent mindedness or wishful thinking. During the heyday of a scientific theory, so much evidence may support the theory, so many observational clues may seem to attest to its truth, that the idea that it could be overthrown appears ludicrous. In addition, the theory may provide ways of identifying quickly what is inaccessible to our unaided senses. Electron microscopes and cloud chambers are obvious examples of those extensions of our perceptual system that theories can inspire. Trained biochemists will talk quite naturally of seeing large molecules, and it is easy to overlook the fact that they are presupposing a massive body of theory in describing what they "see." If that theory were to be amended, even in subtle ways, then the descriptions of the "observed characteristics" of large molecules might have to be given up. Nor should we pride ourselves that the enormous successes of contemporary science secure us against future amendments. No theory in the history of science enjoyed a more spectacular career than Newton's mechanics. Yet Newton's ideas had to give way to Einstein's.

When practicing scientists are reminded of these straightforward points, they frequently adopt what the philosopher George Berkeley called a "forlorn skepticism." From the idea of science as certain and infallible, they jump to a cynical description of their endeavors. Science is sometimes held to be a game played with arbitrary rules, an irrational acceptance of dogma, an enterprise based ultimately on faith. Once we have appreciated the fallibility of natural science and recognized its sources, we can move beyond the simple opposition of proof and faith. Between these extremes lies the vast field of cases in which we believe something on the basis of good—even excellent—but inconclusive evidence.

If we want to emphasize the fact that what scientists believe today may have to be revised in the light of observations made tomorrow, then we can describe all our science as "theory." But the description should not confuse us. To concede that evolutionary biology is a theory is not to suppose that there are alternatives to it that are equally worthy of a place in our curriculum. All theories are revisable, but not all theories are equal. Even though our present evidence does not *prove* that evolutionary biology—or quantum physics, or plate tectonics, or any other theory—is true, evolutionary biologists will maintain that the present evidence is overwhelmingly in favor of their theory and overwhelmingly against its supposed rivals. Their enthusiastic assertions that evolution is a proven fact can be charitably understood as claims that the (admittedly inconclusive) evidence we have for evolutionary theory is as good as we ever obtain for any theory in any field of science.

Hence the Creationist try for a quick Fools' Mate can easily be avoided. Creationists attempt to draw a line between evolutionary biology and the rest of science by remarking that large-scale evolution cannot be observed. This tactic fails. Large-scale evolution is no more inaccessible to observation than nuclear reactions or the molecular composition of water. For the Creationists to succeed in divorcing evolutionary biology from the rest of science, they need to argue that evolutionary theory is less well supported by the evidence than are theories in, for example, physics and chemistry. It will come as no surprise to learn that they try to do this. To assess the merits of their arguments we need a deeper understanding of the logic of inconclusive justification. We shall begin with a simple and popular idea: Scientific theories earn our acceptance by making successful predictions.

Predictive Success

Imagine that somebody puts forward a new theory about the origins of hay fever. The theory makes a number of startling predictions concerning connections that we would not have thought worth investigating. For example, it tells us that people who develop hay fever invariably secrete a particular substance in certain fatty tissues and that anyone who eats rhubarb as a child never develops hay fever. The theory predicts things that initially appear fantastic. Suppose that we check up on these predictions and find that they are borne out by clinical tests. Would we not begin to believe—and believe reasonably—that the theory was *at least* on the right track?

This example illustrates a pattern of reasoning that is familiar in the history of science. Theories win support by producing claims about what can be observed, claims that would not have seemed plausible prior to the advancement of the theory, but that are in fact found to be true when we make the appropriate observations. A classic (real) example is Pascal's confirmation of Torricelli's hypothesis that we live at the bottom of an ocean of air that presses down upon us. Pascal reasoned that if Torricelli's hypothesis were true, then air pressure should decrease at higher altitudes (because at higher altitudes we are closer to the "surface" of the atmosphere, so that the length of the column of air that presses down is shorter). Accordingly, he sent his brother-in-law to the top of a mountain to make some barometric measurements. Pascal's clever working out of the observational predictions of Torricelli's theory led to a dramatic predictive success for the theory.

The idea of predictive success has encouraged a popular picture of science. (We shall see later that this picture, while popular, is not terribly accurate.) Philosophers sometimes regard a theory as a collection of claims or statements. Some of these statements offer generalizations about the features of particular, recondite things (genes, atoms, gravitational force, quasars, and the like). These statements are used to infer statements whose truth or falsity can be decided by observation. (This appears to be just what Pascal did.) Statements belonging to this second group are called the *observational consequences* of the theory. Theories are supported when we find that their observational consequences (those that we have checked) are true. The credentials of a theory are damaged if we discover that some of its observational consequences are false.

We can make the idea more precise by being clearer about the inferences involved. Those who talk of inferring observational predictions from our theories think that we can *deduce* from the statements of the theory, and from those statements alone, some predictions whose accuracy we can check by direct observation. Deductive inference is well understood. The fundamental idea of deductive inference is this: We say that a statement S is a valid deductive consequence of a group of statements if and only if it is *impossible* that all the statements in the group should be true and that S should be false; alternatively, S is a valid deductive consequence (or, more simply, a valid consequence) of a group of statements if and only if it would be self-contradictory to assert all the statements in the group and to deny S.

It will be helpful to make the idea of valid consequence more familiar with some examples. Consider the statements "All lovers of baseball dislike George Steinbrenner" and "George Steinbrenner loves baseball." The statement "George Steinbrenner dislikes himself" is a deductively valid consequence of these two statements. For it is impossible that the first two should be true and the third false. However, in claiming that this is a case of deductively valid consequence, we do not commit ourselves to maintaining that *any* of the statements is true. (Perhaps there are some ardent baseball fans who admire Steinbrenner. Perhaps Steinbrenner himself has no time for the game.) What deductive validity means is that the truth of the first two statements would guarantee the truth of the third; that is, *if* the first two *were* true, then the third would have to be true.

Another example will help rule out other misunderstandings. Here are two statements: "Shortly after noon on January 1, 1982, in the Oval Office, a jelly bean was released from rest more than two feet above any surface"; "Shortly after noon on January 1, 1982, in the Oval Office, a jelly bean fell." Is the second statement a deductively valid consequence of the first? You might think that it is, on the grounds that it would have been impossible for the unfortunate object to have been released and not to have fallen. In one sense this is correct, but that is not the sense of impossibility that deductive logicians have in mind. Strictly speaking, it is not *impossible* for the jellybean to have been released without falling; we can imagine, for example, that the law of gravity might suddenly cease to operate. We do not *contradict* ourselves when we assert that the jellybean was released but deny that it fell; we simply refuse to accept the law of gravity (or some other relevant physical fact).

Thus, S is a deductively valid consequence of a group of statements if and only if there is *absolutely no possibility* that all the statements in the group should be true and S should be false. This conception allows us to state the popular view of theory and prediction more precisely. Theories are collections of statements. The observational consequences of a theory are statements that have to be true if the statements belonging to the theory are all true. These observational consequences also have to be statements whose truth or falsity can be ascertained by direct observation.

My initial discussion of predictive success presented the rough idea that, when we find the observational consequences of a theory to be true, our findings bring credit to the theory. Conversely, discovery that some observational consequences of a theory are false was viewed as damaging. We can now make the second point much more precise. Any theory that has a false observational consequence must contain some false statement (or statements). For if all the statements in the theory were true, then, according to the standard definitions of *deductive validity* and *observational consequence,* any observational consequence would also have to be true. Hence, if a theory is found to have a false observational consequence, we must conclude that one or more statements of the theory is false.

This means that theories can be conclusively falsified, through the discovery that they have false observational consequences. Some philosophers, most notably Sir Karl Popper,[3] have taken this point to have enormous significance for our understanding of science. According to Popper, the essence of a scientific theory is that it should be *falsifiable.* That is, if the theory is false, then it must be possible to show that it is false. Now, if a theory has utterly no observational consequences, it would be extraordinarily difficult to unmask that theory as false. So, to be a genuine scientific theory, a group of statements must have observational consequences. It is important to realize that Popper is not suggesting that every good theory must be false. The difference between being

---

[3] *The Logic of Scientific Discovery,* London: Hutchinson, 1959, and *Conjectures and Refutations,* New York: Harper, 1963.

falsifiable and being false is like the difference between being vulnerable and actually being hurt. A good scientific theory should not be false. Rather, it must have observational consequences that could reveal the theory as mistaken if the experiments give the wrong results.

While these ideas about theory testing may seem strange in their formal attire, they emerge quite frequently in discussions of science. They also find their way into the creation-evolution debate.

Predictive Failure

From the beginning, evolutionary theory has been charged with just about every possible type of predictive failure. Critics of the theory have argued that (a) the theory makes no predictions (it is unfalsifiable and so fails Popper's criterion for science), (b) the theory makes false predictions (it is falsified), (c) the theory does not make the kinds of predictions it ought to make (the observations and experiments that evolutionary theorists undertake have no bearing on the theory). Many critics, including several Creationists, . . . manage to advance all these objections in the same work. This is somewhat surprising, since points (a) and (b) are, of course, mutually contradictory.

The first objection is vitally important to the Creationist cause. Their opponents frequently insist that Creationism fails the crucial test for a scientific theory. The hypothesis that all kinds of organisms were separately fashioned by some "originator" is unfalsifiable.[4] Creationists retort that they can play the same game equally well. *Any* hypothesis about the origins of life, including that advanced by evolutionary theory, is not subject to falsification. Hence we cannot justify a decision to teach evolutionary theory and not to teach Creationism by appealing to the Popperian criterion for genuine science.

The allegation that evolutionary theory fails to make any predictions is a completely predictable episode in any Creationist discussion of evolution. Often the point is made by appeal to the authority of Popper. Here are two sample passages:

> The outstanding philosopher of science, Karl Popper, though himself an evolutionist, pointed out cogently that evolution, no less than creation, is untestable and thus unprovable.[5]

Thus, for a theory to qualify as a scientific theory, it must be supported by events, processes or properties which can be observed, and the theory must be useful in predicting the outcome of future natural phenomena or laboratory experiments. An additional limitation usually imposed is that the theory must be capable of falsification. That is, it must be possible to conceive some experiment, the failure of which would disprove the theory.

---

[4] S. J. Gould, "Evolution as Fact and Theory", *Discover*, 2, 34–37.

[5] *The Troubled Waters of Evolution*, p. 80.

It is on the basis of such criteria that most evolutionists insist that creation be refused consideration as a possible explanation for origins. Creation has not been witnessed by human observers, it cannot be tested experimentally, and as a theory it is nonfalsifiable.

The general theory of evolution also fails to meet all three of these criteria, however.[6]

. . .

These passages, and many others draw on the picture of science sketched above. It is not clear that the Creationists really understand the philosophical views that they attempt to apply. Gish presents the most articulate discussion of the falsifiability criterion. Yet he muddles the issue by describing falsifiability as an "additional limitation" beyond predictive power. (The previous section shows that theories that make predictions are automatically falsifiable.) Nevertheless, the Creationist challenge is a serious one, and, if it could not be met, evolutionary theory would be in trouble.

Creationists buttress their charge of unfalsifiability with further objections. They are aware that biologists frequently look as though they are engaged in observations and experiments. Creationists would allow that researchers in biology sometimes make discoveries. What they deny is that the discoveries support evolutionary theory. They claim that laboratory manipulations fail to teach us about evolution in nature: "Even if modern scientists should ever actually achieve the artificial creation of life from non-life, or of higher kinds from lower kinds, in the laboratory, this would not *prove* in any way that such changes did, or even could, take place in the past by random natural processes."[7] The standards of evidence to be applied to evolutionary biology have suddenly been raised. In this area of inquiry, it is not sufficient that a theory yield observational consequences whose truth or falsity can be decided in the laboratory. Creationists demand special kinds of predictions, and will dismiss as irrelevant any laboratory evidence that evolutionary theorists produce. [In this way, they try to defend point (c).]

Oddly enough, however, the most popular supplement to the charge that evolutionary theory is unfalsifiable is a determined effort to falsify it [point (b)]. Creationists cannot resist arguing that the theory is actually falsified. Some of them Morris and Gish, for example, recognize the tension between the two objections. They try to paper over the problem by claiming that evolutionary theory and the Creationist account are both "models." Each "model" would "naturally" incline us to expect certain observational results. A favorite Creationist ploy is to draw up tables in which these "predictions" are compared. When we look at the tables we find that the evolutionary expectations are confounded. By contrast, the Creationist "model" leads us to anticipate fea-

---

[6] D. T. Gish, *Evolution? The Fossils Say No!*, San Diego: Creation-Life Publishers, 1979, p. 13.

[7] H. M. Morris, *Scientific Creationism* (general edition) San Diego: Creation-Life Publishers, 1974, p. 6.

tures of the world that are actually there. Faced with such adverse results, the benighted evolutionary biologist is portrayed as struggling to "explain away" the findings by whatever means he can invent.

. . .

As Morris triumphantly concludes, "The data must be *explained* by the evolutionist, but they are *predicted* by the creationist".[8]

The careful reader ought to be puzzled. If Morris really thinks that evolutionary theory has been falsified, why does he not say so? Of course, he would have to admit that the theory is falsifiable. Seemingly, however, a staunch Creationist should be delighted to abandon a relatively abstruse point about unfalsifiability in favor of a clear-cut refutation. The truth of the matter is that the alleged refutations fail. No evolutionary theorist will grant that (for example) the theory predicts that the fossil record should show "innumerable transitions." Instead, paleontologists will point out that we can deduce conclusions about what we should find in the rocks only if we make assumptions about the fossilization process. Morris makes highly dubious assumptions, hails them as "natural," and then announces that the "natural predictions" of the theory have been defeated.

. . .

To make a serious assessment of these broad Creationist charges, we must begin by asking some basic methodological questions. We cannot decide whether evolutionary biologists are guilty of trying to save their theory by using ad hoc assumptions (new and implausible claims dreamed up for the sole purpose of protecting some cherished ideas) unless we have some way of deciding when a proposal is ad hoc. Similarly, we cannot make a reasoned response to the charge that laboratory experiments are irrelevant, or to the fundamental objection that evolutionary theory is unfalsifiable, unless we have a firmer grasp of the relation between theory and evidence.

Naive Falsificationism

The time has come to tell a dreadful secret. While the picture of scientific testing sketched above continues to be influential among scientists, it has been shown to be seriously incorrect. (To give my profession its due, historians and philosophers of science have been trying to let this particular cat out of the bag for at least thirty years. . . . Important work in the history of science has made it increasingly clear that no major scientific theory has ever exemplified the relation between theory and evidence that the traditional model presents.

What is wrong with the old picture? Answer: Either it debars most of what we take to be science from counting as science or it allows virtually anything

---

[8] *Scientific Creationism*, p. 13.

to count. On the traditional view of "theory," textbook cases of scientific theories turn out to be unfalsifiable. Suppose we identify Newtonian mechanics with Newton's three laws of motion plus the law of gravitation. What observational consequences can we deduce from these four statements? You might think that we could deduce that if, as the (undoubtedly apocryphal) story alleges, an apple became detached from a branch above where Newton was sitting, the apple would have fallen on his head. But this does not follow at all. To see why not, it is only necessary to recognize that the failure of this alleged prediction would not force us to deny any of the four statements of the theory. All we need do is assume that some other forces were at work that overcame the force of gravity and caused the apple to depart from its usual trajectory. So, given this simple way of applying Popper's criterion, Newtonian mechanics would be unfalsifiable. The same would go for any other scientific theory. Hence none of what we normally take to be science would count as science. (I might note that Popper is aware of this problem and has suggestions of his own as to how it should be overcome. However, what concerns me here are the *applications* of Popper's ideas, that are made by Creationists, as well as by scientists in their professional debates.)

The example of the last paragraph suggests an obvious remedy. Instead of thinking about theories in the simple way just illustrated, we might take them to be far more elaborate. Newton's laws (the three laws of motion and the law of gravitation) are *embedded* in Newtonian mechanics. They form the core of the theory, but do not constitute the whole of it. Newtonian mechanics also contains supplementary assumptions, telling us, for example, that for certain special systems the effects of forces other than gravity are negligible. This more elaborate collection of statements *does* have observational consequences and *is* falsifiable.

But the remedy fails. Imagine that we attempt to expose some self-styled spiritual teacher as an overpaid fraud. We try to point out that the teacher's central message—"Quietness is wholeness in the center of stillness"—is unfalsifiable. The teacher cheerfully admits that, taken by itself, this profound doctrine yields no observational consequences. He then points out that, by themselves, the central statements of scientific theories are also incapable of generating observational consequences. Alas, if all that is demanded is that a doctrine be embedded in a group of statements with observational consequences, our imagined guru will easily slither off the hook. He replies, "You have forgotten that my doctrine has many other claims. For example, I believe that if quietness is wholeness in the center of stillness, then flowers bloom in the spring, bees gather pollen, and blinkered defenders of so-called science raise futile objections to the world's spiritual benefactors. You will see that these three predictions are borne out by experience. Of course, there are countless others. Perhaps when you see how my central message yields so much evident truth, you will recognize the wealth of evidence behind my claim. Quietness is wholeness in the center of stillness."

More formally, the trouble is that *any* statement can be coupled with other statements to produce observational consequences. Given any doctrine *D*, and

any statement O that records the result of an observation, we can enable D to "predict" O by adding the extra assumption, "If D, then O." (In the example, D is "Quietness is wholeness in the center of stillness"; examples of O would be statements describing the blooming of particular flowers in the spring, the pollen gathering of specific bees, and so forth.)

The falsifiability criterion adopted from Popper—which I shall call the *naive falsificationist* criterion—is hopelessly flawed. It runs aground on a fundamental fact about the relation between theory and prediction: On their own, individual scientific laws, or the small groups of laws that are often identified as theories, do not have observational consequences. This crucial point about theories was first understood by the great historian and philosopher of science Pierre Duhem. Duhem saw clearly that individual scientific claims do not, and cannot, confront the evidence one by one. Rather, in his picturesque phrase, "Hypotheses are tested in bundles." Besides ruling out the possibility of testing an individual scientific theory (read, small group of laws), Duhem's insight has another startling consequence. We can only test relatively large bundles of claims. What this means is that when our experiments go awry we are not logically compelled to select any particular claim as the culprit. We can always save a cherished hypothesis from refutation by rejecting (however implausibly) one of the other members of the bundle. Of course, this is exactly what I did in the illustration of Newton and the apple above. Faced with disappointing results, I suggested that we could abandon the (tacit) additional claim that no large forces besides gravity were operating on the apple.

Creationists wheel out the ancient warhorse of naive falsificationism so that they can bolster their charge that evolutionary theory is not a science. The (very) brief course in deductive logic plus the whirlwind tour through naive falsificationism and its pitfalls enable us to see what is at the bottom of this seemingly important criticism. Creationists can appeal to naive falsificationism to show that evolution is not a science. But, given the traditional picture of theory and evidence I have sketched, one can appeal to naive falsificationism to show that *any* science is not a science. So, as with the charge that evolutionary change is unobservable, Creationists have again failed to find some "fault" of evolution not shared with every other science. (And, as we shall see, Creationists like some sciences, especially thermodynamics.) Consistent application of naive falsificationism can show that anybody's favorite science (whether it be quantum physics, molecular biology, or whatever) is not science. Of course, what this shows is that the naive falsificationist criterion is a very poor test of genuine science. To be fair, this point can cut both ways. Scientists who charge that "scientific" Creationism is unfalsifiable are not insulting the theory as much as they think.

Successful Science

Despite the inadequacies of naive falsificationism, there is surely something right in the idea that a science can succeed only if it can fail. An invulnerable "science" would not be science at all. To achieve a more adequate understand-

ing of how a science can succeed and how it runs the risk of failure, let us look at one of the most successful sciences and at a famous episode in its development.

Newtonian celestial mechanics is one of the star turns in the history of science. Among its numerous achievements were convincing explanations of the orbits of most of the known planets. Newton and his successors viewed the solar system as a collection of bodies subject only to gravitational interactions; they used the law of gravitation and the laws of motion to compute the orbits. (Bodies whose effects were negligible in any particular case would be disregarded. For example, the gravitational attraction due to Mercury would not be considered in working out the orbit of Saturn.) The results usually tallied beautifully with astronomical observations. But one case proved difficult. The outermost known planet, Uranus, stubbornly followed an orbit that diverged from the best computations. By the early nineteenth century it was clear that something was wrong. Either astronomers erred in treating the solar system as a Newtonian gravitational system or there was some particular difficulty in applying the general method to Uranus.

Perhaps the most naive of falsificationists would have recommended that the central claim of Newtonian mechanics—the claim that the solar system is a Newtonian gravitational system—be abandoned. But there was obviously a more sensible strategy. Astronomers faced one problematical planet, and they asked themselves what made Uranus so difficult. Two of them, John Adams and Urbain Leverrier, came up with an answer. They proposed (independently) that there was a hitherto unobserved planet beyond Uranus. They computed the orbit of the postulated planet and demonstrated that the anomalies of the motion of Uranus could be explained if a planet followed this path. There was a straightforward way to test their proposal. Astronomers began to look for the new planet. Within a few years, the planet—Neptune—was found.

I will extract several morals from this success story. The first concerns an issue we originally encountered in Morris's "table of natural predictions:" What is the proper use of auxiliary hypotheses? Adams and Leverrier saved the central claim of Newtonian celestial mechanics by offering an auxiliary hypothesis. They maintained that there were more things in the heavens than had been dreamed of in previous natural philosophy. The anomalies in the orbit of Uranus could be explained on the assumption of an extra planet. Adams and Leverrier worked out the exact orbit of that planet so that they could provide a detailed account of the perturbations—and so that they could tell their fellow astronomers where to look for Neptune. Thus, their auxiliary hypothesis was *independently testable*. The evidence for Neptune's existence was not just the anomalous motion of Uranus. The hypothesis could be checked independently of any assumptions about Uranus or about the correctness of Newtonian celestial mechanics—by making telescopic observations.

Since hypotheses are always tested in bundles, this method of checking presupposed other assumptions, in particular, the optical principles that justify the use of telescopes. The crucial point is that, while hypotheses are always tested in bundles, they can be tested in *different* bundles. An auxiliary hypoth-

esis ought to be testable independently of the particular problem it is introduced to solve, independently of the theory it is designed to save.

While it is obvious in retrospect—indeed it was obvious at the time—that the problem with Uranus should not be construed as "falsifying" celestial mechanics, it is worth asking explicitly why scientists should have clung to Newton's theory in the face of this difficulty. The answer is not just that nothing succeeds like success, and that Newton's theory had been strikingly successful in calculating the orbits of the other planets. The crucial point concerns the way in which Newton's successes had been achieved. Newton was no opportunist, using one batch of assumptions to cope with Mercury, and then moving on to new devices to handle Venus. Celestial mechanics was a remarkably *unified* theory. It solved problems by invoking the same pattern of reasoning, or *problem-solving strategy,* again and again: From a specification of the positions of the bodies under study, use the law of gravitation to calculate the forces acting; from a statement of the forces acting, use the laws of dynamics to compute the equations of motion; solve the equations of motion to obtain the motions of the bodies. This single pattern of reasoning was applied in case after case to yield conclusions that were independently found to be correct.

At a higher level, celestial mechanics was itself contained in a broader theory. Newtonian physics, as a whole, was remarkably unified. It offered a strategy for solving a diverse collection of problems. Faced with *any* question about motion, the Newtonian suggestion was the same: Find the forces acting, from the forces and the laws of dynamics work out the equations of motion, and solve the equations of motion. The method was employed in a broad range of cases. The revolutions of planets, the motions of projectiles, tidal cycles and pendulum oscillations—all fell to the same problem-solving strategy.

We can draw a second moral. A science should be *unified.* A thriving science is not a gerrymandered patchwork but a coherent whole. Good theories consist of just one problem-solving strategy, or a small family of problem-solving strategies, that can be applied to a wide range of problems. The theory succeeds as it is able to encompass more and more problem areas. Failure looms when the basic problem-solving strategy (or strategies) can resolve almost none of the problems in its intended domain without the "aid" of untestable auxiliary hypotheses.

Despite the vast successes of his theory, Newton hoped for more. He envisaged a time when scientists would recognize other force laws, akin to the law of gravitation, so that other branches of physics could model themselves after celestial mechanics. In addition, he suggested that many physical questions that are not ostensibly about motion—questions about heat and about chemical combination, for example—could be reduced to problems of motion. *Principia,* Newton's masterpiece, not only offered a theory; it also advertised a program:

> I wish we could derive the rest of the phenomena of Nature by the same kind of reasoning from mechanical principles, for I am induced by many reasons to suspect that they may all depend upon certain forces by which the particles of bodies,

by some causes hitherto unknown, are either mutually impelled towards one another, and cohere in regular figures, or are repelled and recede from one another. These forces being unknown, philosophers have hitherto attempted the search of Nature in vain; but I hope the principles here laid down will afford some light either to this or some truer method of philosophy.[9]

Newton's message was clear. His own work only began the task of applying an immensely fruitful, unifying idea.

Newton's successors were moved, quite justifiably, to extend the theory he had offered. They attempted to show how Newton's main problem-solving strategy could be applied to a broader range of physical phenomena. During the eighteenth and nineteenth centuries, the search for understanding of the forces of nature was carried into hydrodynamics, optics, chemistry, and the studies of heat, elasticity, electricity, and magnetism. Not all of these endeavors were equally successful. Nevertheless, Newton's directive fostered the rise of some important new sciences.

The final moral I want to draw from this brief look at Newtonian physics concerns *fecundity*. A great scientific theory, like Newton's, opens up new areas of research. Celestial mechanics led to the discovery of a previously unknown planet. Newtonian physics as a whole led to the development of previously unknown sciences. Because a theory presents a new way of looking at the world, it can lead us to ask new questions, and so to embark on new and fruitful lines of inquiry. Of the many flaws with the earlier picture of theories as sets of statements, none is more important than the misleading presentation of sciences as static and insular. Typically, a flourishing science is incomplete. At any time, it raises more questions than it can currently answer. But incompleteness is no vice. On the contrary, incompleteness is the mother of fecundity. Unresolved problems present challenges that enable a theory to flower in unanticipated ways. They also make the theory hostage to future developments. A good theory should be productive; it should raise new questions and presume that those questions can be answered without giving up its problem-solving strategies.

I have highlighted three characteristics of successful science. *Independent testability* is achieved when it is possible to test auxiliary hypotheses independently of the particular cases for which they are introduced. *Unification* is the result of applying a small family of problem-solving strategies to a broad class of cases. *Fecundity* grows out of incompleteness when a theory opens up new and profitable lines of investigation. Given these marks of successful science, it is easy to see how sciences can fall short, and how some doctrines can do so badly that they fail to count as science at all. A scientific theory begins to wither if some of its auxiliary assumptions can be saved from refutation only by rendering them untestable; or if its problem-solving strategies become a hodge-

---

[9] I. Newton (1687), Motte-Cajori trans., *The Mathematical Principles of Natural Philosophy,* Berkeley: University of California Press, 1960, xviii.

podge, a collection of unrelated methods, each designed for a separate recalcitrant case; or if the promise of the theory just fizzles, the few questions it raises leading only to dead ends.

When does a doctrine fail to be a science? If a doctrine fails sufficiently abjectly as a science, then it fails to be a science. Where bad science becomes egregious enough, pseudoscience begins. The example of Newtonian physics shows us how to replace the simple (and incorrect) naive falsificationist criterion with a battery of tests. Do the doctrine's problem-solving strategies encounter recurrent difficulties in a significant range of cases? Are the problem-solving strategies an opportunistic collection of unmotivated and unrelated methods? Does the doctrine have too cozy a relationship with auxiliary hypotheses, applying its strategies with claims that can be "tested" only in their applications? Does the doctrine refuse to follow up on unresolved problems, airily dismissing them as "exceptional cases"? Does the doctrine restrict the domain of its methods, forswearing excursions into new areas of investigation where embarrassing questions might arise? If all, or many, of these tests are positive, then the doctrine is not a poor scientific theory. It is not a scientific theory at all.

The account of successful science that I have given not only enables us to replace the naive falsificationist criterion with something better. It also provides a deeper understanding of how theories are justified. Predictive success is one important way in which a theory can win our acceptance. But it is not the only way. In general, theories earn their laurels by solving problems—providing answers that can be independently recognized as correct—and by their fruitfulness. Making a prediction is answering a special kind of question. The astronomers who used celestial mechanics to predict the motion of Mars were answering the question of where Mars would be found. Yet, very frequently, our questions do not concern *what* occurs, but *why* it occurs. We already know that something happens and we want an explanation. Science offers us explanations by setting the phenomena within a unified framework. Using a widely applicable problem-solving strategy, together with independently confirmed auxiliary hypotheses, scientists show that what happened was to be expected. It was known before Newton that the orbits of the planets are approximately elliptical. One of the great achievements of Newton's celestial mechanics was to apply its problem-solving strategy to deduce that the orbit of any planet will be approximately elliptical, thereby explaining the shape of the orbits. In general, science is at least as concerned with reducing the number of unexplained phenomena as it is with generating correct predictions.

The most global Creationist attack on evolutionary theory is the claim that evolution is not a science. If this claim were correct, then the dispute about what to teach in high school science classes would be over. In earlier parts of this chapter, we saw how Creationists were able to launch their broad criticisms. If one accepts the idea that science requires proof, or if one adopts the naive falsificationist criterion, then the theory of evolution—and every other scientific theory—will turn out not to be a part of science. So Creationist standards for science imply that there is no science to be taught.

However, we have seen that Creationist standards rest on a very poor understanding of science. In light of a clearer picture of the scientific enterprise, I have provided a more realistic group of tests for good science, bad science, and pseudoscience.

PART III   Suggestions For Further Reading

Armstrong, David M. *Belief, Truth and Knowledge,* (Cambridge University Press, 1973)

Ayer, A.J. *Language, Truth and Logic,* (Dover, 1936)

Chisholm, R.M. *Perceiving,* (Cornell University Press, 1957)

Goldman, Alvin. "What is Justified Belief?" in G. Pappas, ed., *Justification and Knowledge,* (Kluwer Boston, 1980)

Harman, Gilbert. *Thought,* (Princeton University Press, 1973)

Hempel, Carl. *Philosophy of Natural Science,* (Prentice-Hall, 1966)

Lehrer, Keith. *Knowledge,* (Oxford University Press, 1979)

Nozick, Robert. *Philosophical Explanations,* Chapter 3, (Harvard University Press, 1981)

Pitcher, George. *A Theory of Perception,* (Routledge & Kegan, 1977)

Popper, Karl R. *The Logic of Scientific Discovery,* (Harper & Row, 1959)

Quine, W. V. O. and Ullian, J. S. *The Web of Belief,* (Random House, 1978)

Russell, Bertrand. *The Problems of Philosophy,* (Oxford University Press, 1959)

IV

METAPHYSICS

IN RECENT YEARS, a number of writers have advocated the view that there really are no such things as "mental illnesses." Their claim is that "paranoia" or "schizophrenia," for example, are not names of diseases, because there are no such diseases. Rather, these terms are derogatory labels that society applies to individuals whose behavior deviates from the social norm. In opposition, psychiatrists and psychologists maintain that things like paranoia and schizophrenia really are diseases. While neither side is probably aware of it, this debate turns on a metaphysical question: What must be the case for it to be true that a particular disease exists? In general, metaphysics is concerned with questions about the nature of reality. What kinds of things exist? Are there some features that are pervasive throughout the universe? (For example, are all events in the universe caused?) What is the nature of space and time? How did the universe begin? Could the universe be different from the way that it actually is? (For example, could a universe exist even though it contained no matter?)

Some metaphysical questions have received such sustained and exhaustive discussion that they have spawned sub-branches of the discipline. The philosophy of religion grew out of one basic metaphysical question: Did God create the universe? Metaphysical concerns about the nature of the mind led to the development of philosophy of mind. Since discussions of metaphysics tend to cluster around particular problems, we have organized this section into three parts. The first concerns questions about necessity, possibility and essences.

The second takes up the question of what makes someone the same person through time. The third division deals with the issue of free will. These three problem areas, plus the readings in philosophy of religion and philosophy of mind, should provide a sense of the range of metaphysical problems and the variety of approaches taken by metaphysicians.

A. Necessity, Possibility, and Essence

People often wonder about what might have been. Had Lincoln survived, would Southerners have been treated so badly after the Civil War? Such speculations assume that particular events, which did not take place, might have taken place. The idea is that even though these things did not happen, the course of history could have been different. At first glance, it seems possible that the bullet might have missed Lincoln, or that John Wilkes Booth might have changed his mind on the way to the theater, or that Lincoln might have been too ill to go out that evening. Other speculations seem to take us beyond the realm of possibility. If a friend asks, "I wonder what my life would have been like if my mother had never met my father?" one is inclined to reply: "If your mother had not met your father, then *you* would not have existed at all, so there is no point in asking how your life might have been different."

These two examples suggest that some non-actual events are nonetheless possible, while other non-actual events could never occur. In opposition to this view, Gottfried Leibniz argues that every non-actual event is also not possible (reading 36). Leibniz believes that our conviction that non-actual events are possible is a function of our ignorance. For example, when we say that Caesar might not have crossed the Rubicon, what we really mean is that, from the limited facts available to us, it seems that matters could have gone either way— he might have crossed or failed to cross. Leibniz argues that, if we knew all the relevant facts and had greater cognitive capacities, then we would see that Caesar's crossing of the Rubicon was, in fact, inevitable.

By contrast, Saul Kripke argues in reading 37 that some non-actual things may be regarded as possible and others as impossible. Kripke's focus is more on objects than events. He considers how an object might be different, yet still be the same object with different properties, rather than a different object. Drawing on a lengthy philosophical tradition, Kripke makes a distinction between an object's essential properties and its inessential or contingent properties. For example, Kripke maintains that it is possible that Elizabeth II not be Queen of England. That is, that very woman could exist and not have the property of being Queen. Being a queen is one of Elizabeth's contingent properties. On the other hand, Elizabeth II would not exist at all if she were not the daughter of George VI and Queen Elizabeth (the Queen Mother). Like the rest of us, being the child of two particular individuals is an essential property of Elizabeth.

The distinction between an object's essential and contingent properties is also discussed by John Locke in reading 35. However, Locke's focus is different. Locke's question is: when are our classifications merely conventional, and when are our classifications natural? That is, when does a term by which we classify

things succeed in mirroring the divisions in nature? When do our terms name *natural kinds?* Locke answers this question by appealing to the notion of an essence. A term names a natural kind if all the objects classed together by that term share the same essential properties.

B. Personal Identity

If you meet a friend whom you have not seen for a number of years, you immediately recognize that individual as the same person whom you knew before. Considerable philosophical debate has centered around the question: what makes someone the same person through time? It seems clear that your friend could have changed quite a bit and still be the same person. The friend might now have gray hair, be quite a bit taller, have changed political affiliations, or have undergone numerous other alterations and still be identically the same person whom you knew at an earlier time. The metaphysical question is: what must be preserved if an individual is to remain the same person through time?

One obvious candidate for an answer is bodily continuity. Our bodies constantly produce new cells and shed old cells. So, the suggestion would be that the person before you is your old friend because the cells in the body before you are descendants of cells in the body of the person whom you knew before. In his classic discussion of personal identity (reading 38), John Locke argues against this view. Locke believes that personal identity is retained through memory. Your friend would still be the same person because he or she has memories of earlier parts of his or her life, including, presumably, the time of your earlier acquaintance. Contemporary philosopher Bernard Williams disagrees (reading 39). He argues that while continuity of memory and continuity of character seem very important to our personal identity, using mental criteria can yield paradoxical results in different cases. Locke's original discussion of personal identity was prompted by the reflection that our moral assessments of individuals depend directly on our views about their personal identity. We praise or blame, reward or punish people for their own past deeds. In reading 40, Derek Parfit examines how our moral attitudes towards people might vary, depending on how we resolve the question of personal identity.

C. Free Will and Determinism

Like the issue of personal identity, the issue of free will and determinism raises a rather fundamental question about human beings. In our scientific and everyday reasoning, we assume that every event has a cause. If you go to a dentist with a toothache, for example, you are hardly prepared to accept a diagnosis that this toothache is not, in fact, caused by anything. Similarly, if a car mechanic told you that the mysterious noise in your engine was one of those uncaused noises, you would not accept this explanation. You would probably change mechanics. Thus, it seems that we have a rather deeply rooted belief in the thesis of determinism: every event has some (known or unknown)

cause. On the other hand, we also seem to believe that at least some human actions are done freely. In our moral practice, we do not hold people responsible for events beyond their control, for example, being a certain height. But we do hold people responsible for actions that they freely undertake, such as lying or stealing. The problem of determinism arises because it also seems reasonable to believe that if human actions are caused, then they are not free. So, for example, if Willie Sutton's bank robberies were caused by his desire for money, and if his desire for money was caused by, say, particular circumstances of his childhood, then it does not seem entirely clear that he was free to rob banks—or not to rob them.

The problem of free will and determinism can be captured in three claims:

    I.   All events are caused.
    II. Some human actions are free.
    III. If a human action is caused, then it is not free.

These claims confront us with a metaphysical quandary. On its own, each claim seems reasonable. Yet, the claims are inconsistent: it is impossible for all three to be true together. Metaphysicians have exactly three possible lines of solution to the problem of determinism and free will. Libertarians like Jean-Paul Sartre, deny claim I, the thesis of universal causation (reading 42). Others adopt the solution defended by B. F. Skinner in reading 41, *determinism* (sometimes called "hard determinism"), and deny that human beings are free (claim II). Finally, R. E. Hobart (reading 43) and Gerald Dworkin (reading 44) suggest that claim III be rejected. Their view, *compatibilism,* maintains it is perfectly possible for human actions to be caused and still be free. Throughout Western intellectual history, the specter of determinism—the claim that human beings never exercise free will—has risen again and again. These selections should provide the reader with some intellectual resources for understanding this important and potentially very disturbing issue.

35

Real and Nominal Essence

JOHN LOCKE

For biographical information about John Locke, see reading 15.

In these excerpts from An Essay Concerning Human Understanding, *Locke poses a fundamental question about language. On the one hand, our languages seem to be conventional. We might have called red things "black" and black things "red," for example. Seemingly, we could change our practice tomorrow, and actually switch these labels. As Humpty Dumpty observes in* Through the Looking Glass, *words are our invention; we can use them to mean anything we choose. Yet, on the other hand, Humpty Dumpty's position seems too extreme (for reasons well understood by Lewis Carroll, who was a logician as well as a story writer). The problem is that there would be no point in having a term that we would use as a label for such motley collections as: the Statue of Liberty, old chewing gum wrappers, and orange-colored cats.*

Locke presents a theory of language which tries to do justice to these competing observations: the apparent conventionality of language and the need for using words to refer to natural collections. Locke argues that the words used to divide things into kinds—"sortal terms"—must have a nominal essence. A nominal essence is a kind of definition that lists the superficial features an object must have to be classed under that sortal term. For example, the nominal essence of "gold" would be something like: a yellow, malleable, fusible metal that dissolves in aqua regia. *Locke believes that all sortal terms have nominal essences, and that that is how a language user is able to use these words. By contrast, only some sortal terms have a real essence associated with them. A sortal term has an associated real essence only if the objects classed together according to the term's nominal essence all share the same inner constitution. For instance, the real essence of gold is a particular atomic structure. But the term "desk" has no real essence, for desks can have a great variety of inner structures.*

Of General Terms.

1. All things that exist being particulars, it may perhaps be thought reasonable that words, which ought to be conformed to things, should be so too,—I mean in their signification: but yet we find quite the contrary. The far greatest part of words that make all languages are general terms: which has not been the effect of neglect or chance, but of reason and necessity.

2. First, It is impossible that every particular thing should have a distinct peculiar name. For, the signification and use of words depending on that connexion which the mind makes between its ideas and the sounds it uses as signs of them, it is necessary, in the application of names to things, that the mind should have distinct ideas of the things, and retain also the particular name that belongs to every one, with its peculiar appropriation to that idea. But it is beyond the power of human capacity to frame and retain distinct ideas of all the particular things we meet with: every bird and beast men saw; every tree and plant that affected the senses, could not find a place in the most capacious understanding. If it be looked on as an instance of a prodigious memory, that some generals have been able to call every soldier in their army by his proper name, we may easily find a reason why men have never attempted to give names to each sheep in their flock, or crow that flies over their heads; much less to call every leaf of plants, or grain of sand that came in their way, by a peculiar name.

3. Secondly, If it were possible, it would yet be useless; because it would not serve to the chief end of language. Men would in vain heap up names of particular things, that would not serve them to communicate their thoughts. Men learn names, and use them in talk with others, only that they may be understood: which is then only done when, by use or consent, the sound I make by the organs of speech, excites in another man's mind who hears it, the idea I apply it to in mine, when I speak it. This cannot be done by names applied to particular things; whereof I alone having the ideas in my mind, the names of them could not be significant or intelligible to another, who was not acquainted with all those very particular things which had fallen under my notice.

4. Thirdly, But yet, granting this also feasible, (which I think is not,) yet a distinct name for every particular thing would not be of any great use for the improvement of knowledge: which, though founded in particular things, enlarges itself by general views; to which things reduced into sorts, under general names, are properly subservient. These, with the names belonging to them, come within some compass, and do not multiply every moment, beyond what either the mind can contain, or use requires. And therefore, in these, men have for the most part stopped: but yet not so as to hinder themselves from distinguishing particular things by appropriated names, where convenience demands it. And therefore in their own species, which they have most to do with, and wherein they have often occasion to mention particular persons, they make use of proper names; and there distinct individuals have distinct denominations.

5. Besides persons, countries also, cities, rivers, mountains, and other the like distinctions of place have usually found peculiar names, and that for the same reason; they being such as men have often an occasion to mark particularly, and, as it were, set before others in their discourses with them. And I doubt not but, if we had reason to mention particular horses as often as we have to mention particular men, we should have proper names for the one, as familiar as for the other, and Bucephalus would be a word as much in use as Alexander. And therefore we see that, amongst jockeys, horses have their proper names to be known and distinguished by, as commonly as their servants: because,

amongst them, there is often occasion to mention this or that particular horse when he is out of sight.

6. The next thing to be considered is,—How general words come to be made. For, since all things that exist are only particulars, how come we by general terms; or where find we those general natures they are supposed to stand for? Words become general by being made the signs of general ideas: and ideas become general, by separating from them the circumstances of time and place, and any other ideas that may determine them to this or that particular existence. By this way of abstraction they are made capable of representing more individuals than one; each of which having in it a conformity to that abstract idea, is (as we call it) of that sort.

7. But, to deduce this a little more distinctly, it will not perhaps be amiss to trace our notions and names from their beginning, and observe by what degrees we proceed, and by what steps we enlarge our ideas from our first infancy. There is nothing more evident, than that the ideas of the persons children converse with (to instance in them alone) are, like the persons themselves, only particular. The ideas of the nurse and the mother are well framed in their minds; and, like pictures of them there, represent only those individuals. The names they first gave to them are confined to these individuals; and the names of *nurse* and *mamma,* the child uses, determine themselves to those persons. Afterwards, when time and a larger acquaintance have made them observe that there are a great many other things in the world, that in some common agreements of shape, and several other qualities, resemble their father and mother, and those persons they have been used to, they frame an idea, which they find those many particulars do partake in; and to that they give, with others, the name *man,* for example. And thus they come to have a general name, and a general idea. Wherein they make nothing new; but only leave out of the complex idea they had of Peter and James, Mary and Jane, that which is peculiar to each, and retain only what is common to them all.

8. By the same way that they come by the general name and idea of *man,* they easily advance to more general names and notions. For, observing that several things that differ from their idea of man, and cannot therefore be comprehended under that name, have yet certain qualities wherein they agree with man, by retaining only those qualities, and uniting them into one idea, they have again another and more general idea; to which having given a name they make a term of a more comprehensive extension: which new idea is made, not by any new addition, but only as before, by leaving out the shape, and some other properties signified by the name man, and retaining only a body, with life, sense, and spontaneous motion, comprehended under the name animal.

9. That this is the way whereby men first formed general ideas, and general names to them, I think is so evident, that there needs no other proof of it but the considering of a man's self, or others, and the ordinary proceedings of their minds in knowledge. And he that thinks *general natures* or *notions* are anything else but such abstract and partial ideas of more complex ones, taken at first from particular existences, will, I fear, be at a loss where to find them. For let any one effect, and then tell me, wherein does his idea of *man* differ from that

of *Peter* and *Paul,* or his idea of *horse* from that of *Bucephalus,* but in the leaving out something that is peculiar to each individual, and retaining so much of those particular complex ideas of several particular existences as they are found to agree in? Of the complex ideas signified by the names *man* and *horse,* leaving out but those particulars wherein they differ, and retaining only those wherein they agree, and of those making a new distinct complex idea, and giving the name *animal* to it, one has a more general term, that comprehends with man several other creatures. Leave out of the idea of *animal,* sense and spontaneous motion, and the remaining complex idea, made up of the remaining simple ones of body, life, and nourishment, becomes a more general one, under the more comprehensive term, *vivens.* And, not to dwell longer upon this particular, so evident in itself; by the same way the mind proceeds to *body, substance,* and at last to *being, thing,* and such universal terms, which stand for any of our ideas whatsoever. To conclude: this whole mystery of genera and species, which make such a noise in the schools, and are with justice so little regarded out of them, is nothing else but *abstract ideas,* more or less comprehensive, with names annexed to them. In all which this is constant and unvariable, That every more general term stands for such an idea, and is but a part of any of those contained under it.

10. This may show us the reason why, in the defining of words, which is nothing but declaring their signification, we make use of the *genus,* or next general word that comprehends it. Which is not out of necessity, but only to save the labour of enumerating the several simple ideas which the next general word or *genus* stands for; or, perhaps, sometimes the shame of not being able to do it. But though defining by *genus* and *differentia* (I crave leave to use these terms of art, though originally Latin, since they most properly suit those notions they are applied to), I say, though defining by the *genus* be the shortest way, yet I think it may be doubted whether it be the best. This I am sure, it is not the only, and so not absolutely necessary. For, definition being nothing but making another understand by words what idea the term defined stands for, a definition is best made by enumerating those simple ideas that are combined in the signification of the term defined: and if, instead of such an enumeration, men have accustomed themselves to use the next general term, it has not been out of necessity, or for greater clearness, but for quickness and dispatch sake. For I think that, to one who desired to know what idea the word *man* stood for; if it should be said, that man was a solid extended substance, having life, sense, spontaneous motion, and the faculty of reasoning, I doubt not but the meaning of the term man would be as well understood, and the idea it stands for be at least as clearly made known, as when it is defined to be a rational animal: which, by the several definitions of *animal, vivens,* and *corpus,* resolves itself into those enumerated ideas. I have, in explaining the term *man,* followed here the ordinary definition of the schools; which, though perhaps not the most exact, yet serves well enough to my present purpose. And one may, in this instance, see what gave occasion to the rule, that a definition must consist of *genus* and *differentia;* and it suffices to show us the little necessity there is of such a rule, or advantage in the strict observing of it. For, definitions, as has

been said, being only the explaining of one word by several others, so that the meaning or idea it stands for may be certainly known; languages are not always so made according to the rules of logic, that every term can have its signification exactly and clearly expressed by two others. Experience sufficiently satisfies us to the contrary; or else those who have made this rule have done ill, that they have given us so few definitions conformable to it. But of definitions more in the next chapter.

11. To return to general words: it is plain, by what has been said, that *general* and *universal* belong not to the real existence of things; but are the inventions and creatures of the understanding, made by it for its own use, and concern only signs, whether words or ideas. Words are general, as has been said, when used for signs of general ideas, and so are applicable indifferently to many particular things; and ideas are general when they are set up as the representatives of many particular things: but universality belongs not to things themselves, which are all of them particular in their existence, even those words and ideas which in their signification are general. When therefore we quit particulars, the generals that rest are only creatures of our own making; their general nature being nothing but the capacity they are put into, by the understanding, of signifying or representing many particulars. For the signification they have is nothing but a relation that, by the mind of man, is added to them.

12. The next thing therefore to be considered is, What kind of signification it is that general words have. For, as it is evident that they do not signify barely one particular thing; for then they would not be general terms, but proper names, so, on the other side, it is as evident they do not signify a plurality; for *man* and *men* would then signify the same; and the distinction of numbers (as the grammarians call them) would be superfluous and useless. That then which general words signify is a *sort* of things; and each of them does that, by being a sign of an abstract idea in the mind; to which idea, as things existing are found to agree, so they come to be ranked under that name, or, which is all one, be of that sort. Whereby it is evident that the *essences* of the sorts, or, if the Latin word pleases better, *species* of things, are nothing else but these abstract ideas. For the having the essence of any species, being that which makes anything to be of that species; and the conformity to the idea to which the name is annexed being that which gives a right to that name; the having the essence, and the having that conformity, must needs be the same thing: since to be of any species, and to have a right to the name of that species, is all one. As, for example, to be a *man,* or of the *species* man, and to have right to the *name* man, is the same thing. Again, to be a man, or of the species man, and have the *essence* of a man, is the same thing. Now, since nothing can be a man, or have a right to the name man, but what has a conformity to the abstract idea the name man stands for, nor anything be a man, or have a right to the species man, but what has the essence of that species; it follows, that the abstract idea for which the name stands, and the essence of the species, is one and the same. From whence it is easy to observe, that the essences of the sorts of things, and, consequently, the sorting of things, is the workmanship of the understanding that abstracts and makes those general ideas.

13. I would not here be thought to forget, much less to deny, that Nature, in the production of things, makes several of them alike: there is nothing more obvious, especially in the races of animals, and all things propagated by seed. But yet I think we may say, *the sorting of them under names is the workmanship of the understanding, taking occasion, from the similitude it observes amongst them, to make abstract general ideas,* and set them up in the mind, with names annexed to them, as patterns or forms, (for, in that sense, the word *form* has a very proper signification,) to which as particular things existing are found to agree, so they come to be of that species, have that denomination, or are put into that *classis*. For when we say this is a man, that a horse; this justice, that cruelty; this a watch, that a jack; what do we else but rank things under different specific names, as agreeing to those abstract ideas, of which we have made those names the signs? And what are the essences of those species set out and marked by names, but those abstract ideas in the mind; which are, as it were, the bonds between particular things that exist, and the names they are to be ranked under? And when general names have any connexion with particular beings, these abstract ideas are the medium that unites them: so that the essences of species, as distinguished and denominated by us, neither are nor can be anything but those precise abstract ideas we have in our minds. And therefore the supposed real essences of substances, if different from our abstract ideas, cannot be the essences of the species *we* rank things into. For two species may be one, as rationally as two different essences be the essence of one species: and I demand what are the alterations [which] may, or may not be made in a *horse* or *lead*, without making either of them to be of another species? In determining the species of things by *our* abstract ideas, this is easy to resolve: but if any one will regulate himself herein by supposed *real* essences, he will, I suppose, be at a loss: and he will never be able to know when anything precisely ceases to be of the species of a *horse* or *lead*.

14. Nor will any one wonder that I say these essences, or abstract ideas (which are the measures of name, and the boundaries of species) are the workmanship of the understanding, who considers that at least the complex ones are often, in several men, different collections of simple ideas; and therefore that is *covetousness* to one man, which is not so to another. Nay, even in substances, where their abstract ideas seem to be taken from the things themselves, they are not constantly the same; no, not in that species which is most familiar to us, and with which we have the most intimate acquaintance: it having been more than once doubted, whether the *fœtus* born of a woman where a *man*, even so far as that it hath been debated, whether it were or were not to be nourished and baptized: which could not be, if the abstract idea or essence to which the name man belonged were of nature's making; and were not the uncertain and various collection of simple ideas, which the understanding put together, and then, abstracting it, affixed a name to it. So that, in truth, every distinct abstract idea is a distinct essence; and the names that stand for such distinct ideas are the names of things essentially different. Thus a circle is as essentially different from an oval as a sheep from a goat; and rain is as essentially different from snow as water from earth: that abstract idea which

is the essence of one being impossible to be communicated to the other. And thus any two abstract ideas, that in any part vary one from another, with two distinct names annexed to them, constitute two distinct sorts, or, if you please, *species,* as essentially different as any two of the most remote or opposite in the world.

15. But since the essences of things are thought by some (and not without reason) to be wholly unknown, it may not be amiss to consider the several significations of the word *essence.*

First, Essence may be taken for the very being of anything, whereby it is what it is. And thus the real internal, but generally (in substances) unknown constitution of things, whereon their discoverable qualities depend, may be called their essence. This is the proper original signification of the word, as is evident from the formation of it; *essentia,* in its primary notation, signifying properly, being. And in this sense it is still used, when we speak of the essence of *particular* things, without giving them any name.

Secondly, The learning and disputes of the schools having been much busied about *genus* and *species,* the word *essence* has almost lost its primary signification: and, instead of the real constitution of things, has been almost wholly applied to the artificial constitution of *genus* and *species.* It is true, there is ordinarily supposed a real constitution of the sorts of things; and it is past doubt there must be some real constitution, on which any collection of simple ideas co-existing must depend. But, it being evident that things are ranked under names into sorts or species, only as they agree to certain abstract ideas, to which we have annexed those names, the essence of each *genus,* or sort, comes to be nothing but that abstract idea which the general, or sortal (if I may have leave so to call it from sort, as I do general from genus,) name stands for. And this we shall find to be that which the word essence imports in its most familiar use.

These two sorts of essences, I suppose, may not unfitly be termed, the one the *real,* the other *nominal essence.*

16. Between the *nominal essence* and the *name* there is so near a connexion, that the name of any sort of things cannot be attributed to any particular being but what has this essence, whereby it answers that abstract idea whereof that name is the sign.

17. Concerning the *real essences* of corporeal substances (to mention these only) there are, if I mistake not, two opinions. The one is of those who, using the word essence for they know not what, suppose a certain number of those essences, according to which all natural things are made, and wherein they do exactly every one of them partake, and so become of this or that species. The other and more rational opinion is of those who look on all natural things to have a real, but unknown, constitution of their insensible parts; from which flow those sensible qualities which serve us to distinguish them one from another, according as we have occasion to rank them into sorts, under common denominations. The former of these opinions, which supposes these essences as a certain number of forms or moulds, wherein all natural things that exist are cast, and do equally partake, has, I imagine, very much perplexed the knowl-

edge of natural things. The frequent productions of monsters, in all the species of animals, and of changelings, and other strange issues of human birth, carry with them difficulties, not possible to consist with this hypothesis; since it is as impossible that two things partaking exactly of the same real essence should have different properties, as that two figures partaking of the same real essence of a circle should have different properties. But were there no other reason against it, yet the supposition of essences that cannot be known; and the making of them, nevertheless, to be that which distinguishes the species of things, is so wholly useless and unserviceable to any part of our knowledge, that that alone were sufficient to make us lay it by, and content ourselves with such essences of the sorts or species of things as come within the reach of our knowledge: which, when seriously considered, will be found, as I have said, to be nothing else but, those *abstract* complex ideas to which we have annexed distinct general names.

18. Essences being thus distinguished into nominal and real, we may further observe, that, in the species of simple ideas and modes, they are always the same; but in substances always quite different. Thus, a figure including a space between three lines, is the real as well as nominal essence of a triangle; it being not only the abstract idea to which the general name is annexed, but the very *essentia* or being of the thing itself; that foundation from which all its properties flow, and to which they are all inseparably annexed. But it is far otherwise concerning that parcel of matter which makes the ring on my finger; wherein these two essences are apparently different. For, it is the real constitution of its insensible parts, on which depend all those properties of colour, weight, fusibility, fixedness, &c., which are to be found in it; which constitution we know not, and so, having no particular idea of, having no name that is the sign of it. But yet it is its colour, weight, fusibility, fixedness, &c., which makes it to be gold, or gives it a right to that name, which is therefore its nominal essence. Since nothing can be called gold but what has a conformity of qualities to that abstract complex idea to which that name is annexed. But this distinction of essences, belonging particularly to substances, we shall, when we come to consider their names, have an occasion to treat of more fully.

19. That such abstract ideas, with names to them, as we have been speaking of are essences, may further appear by what we are told concerning essences, viz. that they are all ingenerable and incorruptible. Which cannot be true of the real constitutions of things, which begin and perish with them. All things that exist, besides their Author, are all liable to change; especially those things we are acquainted with, and have ranked into bands under distinct names or ensigns. Thus, that which was grass to-day is to-morrow the flesh of a sheep; and, within a few days after, becomes part of a man: in all which and the like changes, it is evident their real essence—i.e. that constitution whereon the properties of these several things depended—is destroyed, and perishes with them. But essences being taken for ideas established in the mind, with names annexed to them, they are supposed to remain steadily the same, whatever mutations the particular substances are liable to. For, whatever becomes of *Alexander* and *Bucephalus,* the ideas to which *man* and *horse* are annexed, are

supposed nevertheless to remain the same; and so the essences of those species are preserved whole and undestroyed, whatever changes happen to any or all of the individuals of those species. By this means the essence of a species rests safe and entire, without the existence of so much as one individual of that kind. For, were there now no circle existing anywhere in the world, (as perhaps that figure exists not anywhere exactly marked out,) yet the idea annexed to that name would not cease to be what it is; nor cease to be as a pattern to determine which of the particular figures we meet with have or have not a right to the *name* circle, and so to show which of them, by having that essence, was of that species. And though there neither were nor had been in nature such a beast as an *unicorn,* or such a fish as a *mermaid;* yet, supposing those names to stand for complex abstract ideas that contained no inconsistency in them, the essence of a mermaid is as intelligible as that of a man; and the idea of an unicorn as certain, steady, and permanent as that of a horse. From what has been said, it is evident, that the doctrine of the immutability of essences proves them to be only abstract ideas; and is founded on the relation established between them and certain sounds as signs of them; and will always be true, as long as the same name can have the same signification.

20. To conclude. This is that which in short I would say, viz. that all the great business of *genera* and *species,* and their *essences,* amounts to no more but this:— That men making abstract ideas, and settling them in their minds with names annexed to them, do thereby enable themselves to consider things, and discourse of them, as it were in bundles, for the easier and readier improvement and communication of their knowledge, which would advance but slowly were their words and thoughts confined only to particulars.

Of Universal Propositions: Their Truth and Certainty.

1. Though the examining and judging of ideas by themselves, their names being quite laid aside, be the best and surest way to clear and distinct knowledge: yet, through the prevailing custom of using sounds for ideas, I think it is very seldom practised. Every one may observe how common it is for names to be made use of, instead of the ideas themselves, even when men think and reason within their own breasts; especially if the ideas be very complex, and made up of a great collection of simple ones. This makes the consideration of *words* and *propositions* so necessary a part of the Treatise of Knowledge, that it is very hard to speak intelligibly of the one, without explaining the other.

2. All the knowledge we have, being only of particular or general truths, it is evident that whatever may be done in the former of these, the latter, which is that which with reason is most sought after, can never be well made known, and is very seldom apprehended, but as conceived and expressed in words. It is not, therefore, out of our way, in the examination of our knowledge, to inquire into the truth and certainty of universal propositions.

3. But that we may not be misled in this case by that which is the danger everywhere, I mean by the doubtfulness of terms, it is fit to observe that certainty is twofold: *certainty of truth* and *certainty of knowledge.* Certainty of

truth is, when words are so put together in propositions as exactly to express the agreement or disagreement of the ideas they stand for, as really it is. Certainty of knowledge is to perceive the agreement or disagreement of ideas, as expressed in any proposition. This we usually call knowing, or being certain of the truth of any proposition.

4. Now, because we cannot be certain of the truth of any general proposition, unless we know the precise bounds and extent of the species its terms stand for, it is necessary we should know the essence of each species, which is that which constitutes and bounds it.

This, in all simple ideas and modes, is not hard to do. For in these the real and nominal essence being the same, or, which is all one, the abstract idea which the general term stands for being the sole essence and boundary that is or can be supposed of the species, there can be no doubt how far the species extends, or what things are comprehended under each term; which, it is evident, are all that have an exact conformity with the idea it stands for, and no other.

But in substances, wherein a real essence, distinct from the nominal, is supposed to constitute, determine, and bound the species, the extent of the general word is very uncertain; because, not knowing this real essence, we cannot know what is, or what is not of that species; and, consequently, what may or may not with certainty be affirmed of it. And thus, speaking of a *man,* or *gold,* or any other species of natural substances, as supposed constituted by a precise and real essence which nature regularly imparts to every individual of that kind, whereby it is made to be of that species, we cannot be certain of the truth of any affirmation or negation made of it. For man or gold, taken in this sense, and used for species of things constituted by real essences, different from the complex idea in the mind of the speaker, stand for we know not what; and the extent of these species, with such boundaries, are so unknown and undetermined, that it is impossible with any certainty to affirm, that all men are rational, or that all gold is yellow. But where the nominal essence is kept to, as the boundary of each species, and men extend the application of any general term no further than to the particular things in which the complex idea it stands for is to be found, there they are in no danger to mistake the bounds of each species, nor can be in doubt, on this account, whether any proposition be true or not. I have chosen to explain this uncertainty of propositions in this scholastic way, and have made use of the terms of *essences,* and *species,* on purpose to show the absurdity and inconvenience there is to think of them as of any other sort of realities, than barely abstract ideas with names to them. To suppose that the species of things are anything but the sorting of them under general names, according as they agree to several abstract ideas of which we make those names the signs, is to confound truth, and introduce uncertainty into all general propositions that can be made about them. Though therefore these things might, to people not possessed with scholastic learning, be treated of in a better and clearer way; yet those wrong notions of essences or species having got root in most people's minds who have received any tincture from the learning which has prevailed in this part of the world, are to be discovered and

removed, to make way for that use of words which should convey certainty with it.

5. The names of substances, then, whenever made to stand for species which are supposed to be constituted by real essences which we know not, are not capable to convey certainty to the understanding. Of the truth of general propositions made up of such terms we cannot be sure. [The reason whereof is plain: for how can we be sure that this or that quality is in gold, when we know not what is or is not gold? Since in this way of speaking, nothing is gold but what partakes of an essence, which we, not knowing, cannot know where it is or is not, and so cannot be sure that any parcel of matter in the world is or is not in this sense gold; being incurably ignorant whether *it* has or has not that which makes anything to be called gold; i.e. that real essence of gold whereof we have no idea at all. This being as impossible for us to know as it is for a blind man to tell in what flower the colour of a pansy is or is not to be found, whilst he has no idea of the colour of a pansy at all. Or if we could (which is impossible) certainly know where a real essence, which we know not, is, v.g. in what parcels of matter the real essence of gold is, yet could we not be sure that this or that quality could with truth be affirmed of gold; since it is impossible for us to know that this or that quality or idea has a necessary connexion with a real essence of which we have no idea at all, whatever species that supposed real essence may be imagined to constitute.]

6. On the other side, the names of substances, when made use of as they should be, for the ideas men have in their minds, though they carry a clear and determinate signification with them, will not yet serve us to make many universal propositions of whose truth we can be certain. Not because in this use of them we are uncertain what things are signified by them, but because the complex ideas they stand for are such combinations of simple ones as carry not with them any discoverable connexion or repugnancy, but with a very few other ideas.

7. The complex ideas that our names of the species of substances properly stand for, are collections of such qualities as have been observed to co-exist in an unknown substratum, which we call substance; but what other qualities necessarily co-exist with such combinations, we cannot certainly know, unless we can discover their natural dependence; which, in their primary qualities, we can go but a very little way in; and in all their secondary qualities* we can discover no connexion at all: for the reasons mentioned, chap. iii. Viz. I. Because we know not the real constitutions of substances, on which each secondary quality particularly depends. 2. Did we know that, it would serve us only for experimental (not universal) knowledge; and reach with certainty no further than that bare instance: because our understandings can discover no conceiv-

---

* Locke distinguishes between an object's *primary* and its *secondary* qualities. For Locke, the primary qualities, like size and shape, are really properties of the object. Secondary qualities, like color and taste, are not properties of objects, but qualities in the mind of the perceiver.

able connexion between any secondary quality and any modification whatsoever of any of the primary ones. And therefore there are very few general
propositions to be made concerning substances, which can carry with them
undoubted certainty.

8. 'All gold is fixed,' is a proposition whose truth we cannot be certain of,
how universally soever it be believed. For if, according to the useless imagination of the Schools, any one supposes the term gold to stand for a species of
things set out by nature, by a real essence belonging to it, it is evident he knows
not what particular substances are of that species; and so cannot with certainty
affirm anything universally of gold. But if he makes gold stand for a species
determined by its nominal essence, let the nominal essence, for example, be the
complex idea of a body of a certain yellow colour, malleable, fusible, and
heavier than any other known;—in this proper use of the word gold, there is
no difficulty to know what is or is not gold. But yet no other quality can with
certainty be universally affirmed or denied of gold, but what hath a *discoverable*
connexion or inconsistency with that nominal essence. Fixedness, for example,
having no necessary connexion that we can discover, with the colour, weight,
or any other simple idea of our complex one, or with the whole combination
together; it is impossible that we should certainly know the truth of this proposition, that all gold is fixed.

9. As there is no discoverable connexion between fixedness and the colour,
weight, and other simple ideas of that nominal essence of gold; so, if we make
our complex idea of gold, a body yellow, fusible, ductile, weighty, and fixed,
we shall be at the same uncertainty concerning solubility in *aqua regia,* and for
the same reason. Since we can never, from consideration of the ideas themselves, with certainty affirm or deny of a body whose complex idea is made up
of yellow, very weighty, ductile, fusible, and fixed, that it is soluble in *aqua
regia:* and so on of the rest of its qualities. I would gladly meet with one general
affirmation concerning any quality of gold, that any one can certainly know is
true. It will, no doubt, be presently objected, Is not this an universal proposition, *All gold is malleable?* To which I answer, It is a very certain proposition,
if malleableness be a part of the complex idea the word gold stands for. But
then here is nothing affirmed of gold, but that that sound stands for an idea in
which malleableness is contained: and such a sort of truth and certainty as this
it is, to say a centaur is four-footed. But if malleableness make not a part of
the specific essence the name of gold stands for, it is plain, *all gold is malleable,*
is not a certain proposition. Because, let the complex idea of gold be made up
of whichsoever of its other qualities you please, malleableness will not appear
to depend on that complex idea, nor follow from any simple one contained in
it: the connexion that malleableness has (if it has any) with those other qualities
being only by the intervention of the real constitution of its insensible parts;
which, since we know not, it is impossible we should perceive that connexion,
unless we could discover that which ties them together.

10. The more, indeed, of these co-existing qualities we unite into one complex idea, under one name, the more precise and determinate we make the
signification of that word; but never yet make it thereby more capable of

universal certainty, *in respect of other qualities not contained in our complex idea:* since we perceive not their connexion or dependence on one another; being ignorant both of that real constitution in which they are all founded, and also how they flow from it. For the chief part of our knowledge concerning substances is not, as in other things, barely of the relation of two ideas that may exist separately; but is of the necessary connexion and co-existence of several distinct ideas in the same subject, or of their repugnancy so to co-exist. Could we begin at the other end, and discover what it was wherein that colour consisted, what made a body lighter or heavier, what texture of parts made it malleable, fusible, and fixed, and fit to be dissolved in this sort of liquor, and not in another;—if, I say, we had such an idea as this of bodies, and could perceive wherein all sensible qualities originally consist, and how they are produced; we might frame such abstract ideas of them as would furnish us with matter of more general knowledge, and enable us to make universal propositions, that should carry general truth and certainty with them. But whilst our complex ideas of the sorts of substances are so remote from that internal real constitution on which their sensible qualities depend, and are made up of nothing but an imperfect collection of those apparent qualities our senses can discover, there can be few general propositions concerning substances of whose real truth we can be certainly assured; since there are but few simple ideas of whose connexion and necessary co-existence we can have certain and undoubted knowledge. I imagine, amongst all the secondary qualities of substances, and the powers relating to them, there cannot any two be named, whose necessary co-existence, or repugnance to co-exist, can certainly be known; unless in those of the same sense, which necessarily exclude one another, as I have elsewhere showed. No one, I think, by the colour that is in any body, can certainly know what smell, taste, sound, or tangible qualities it has, nor what alterations it is capable to make or receive on or from other bodies. The same may be said of the sound of taste, &c. Our specific names of substances standing for any collections of such ideas, it is not to be wondered that we can with them make very few general propositions of undoubted real certainty. But yet so far as any complex idea of any sort of substances contains in it any simple idea, whose *necessary* co-existence with any other *may* be discovered, so far universal propositions may with certainty be made concerning it: v.g. could any one discover a necessary connexion between malleableness and the colour or weight of gold, or any other part of the complex idea signified by that name, he might make a certain universal proposition concerning gold in this respect; and the real truth of this proposition, that *all gold is malleable,* would be as certain as of this, *the three angles of all right-lined triangles are all equal to two right ones.*

36

On Possibility
and Necessity

GOTTFRIED WILHELM LEIBNIZ

Gottfried Wilhelm Leibniz (1646–1716) was a mathematician, a diplomat, and a historian, as well as a philosopher. With his many activities, Leibniz never produced a sustained and systematic presentation of his views. His theories are known as much through letters as through treatises intended for publication.

Leibniz is an important figure in Metaphysics, but his writings are quite cryptic and rather difficult to read. Because of the difficulty of this selection, we are providing a more extensive introduction. While we aim to offer a standard presentation of Leibniz's views, the reader should be advised that any substantive introduction must be interpretive to some degree.

We tend to think that the course of history could have been other than what it was: battles which were won might have been lost, a statesman might have made a different decision, a great leader might have died in infancy. In opposition to this view, Leibniz argues that every non-actual event is also not possible. Leibniz's argument rests on the assumption that every event is determined by preceding events (see also readings 41, 43, and 44). Thus, if we consider a situation in which a particular event does not take place, then we must eliminate not merely the event, but also various events which preceded it and led to its occurrence. By the same token, we must eliminate events preceding those preceding events and so on back through time to the beginning of the Universe! Leibniz believes that, in a sense, every event that actually happens is contingent (non-necessary), because in the original act of Creation God had a free choice about what sort of world He would create. However, Leibniz believes that once the Universe was under way, everything was determined, and thus necessary. It is impossible that things which did not happen could have happened, and it is inevitable that things which do happen actually occur.

Although Leibniz believes everything that will be must be, he does not believe we are capable of predicting the future. We can know the truth of some claims about the future, for example, "all future triangles will have three sides." Such truths, which Leibniz calls "absolutely necessary," can be known simply because we know the meanings of the terms involved. As Leibniz realizes, all that the claim "all future triangles will have three sides" really asserts is, "if there are any triangles in the future, then they will have three sides." We know this to be true, because it is part of the meaning of "triangle" that triangles have three sides. By contrast, we could never know the truth of "Caesar will cross the Rubicon" in advance of the event, because we do not know a definition of "Caesar" from which this follows. However, God, Who has a perfect understanding of all His Creatures, could

infer this from His perfect definition of "Caesar." Finally, we can never know in advance the truth of any claim about an actual future object. Even though we know the definition of a "triangle," and even if we knew the definition of "Caesar," we could never know the truth of "Caesar will exist" or "there will be a triangle in the year 2000" in advance of the event. Although the truth (or falsity) of these claims was determined at the moment of Creation, we lack the intellectual resources to deduce the claims from the initial state of the Universe—even if we knew what the initial state was.

A TRUE AFFIRMATION is one, the predicate of which is present in the subject. Thus in every true affirmative proposition, necessary or contingent, universal or singular, the concept of the predicate is in some way contained in the concept of the subject, so that he who perfectly understood each concept as GOD understands it, would by that very fact perceive that the predicate is present in the subject. Hence it follows that all the knowledge of propositions which is in GOD, whether it be of simple understanding about the essences of things, or of vision about the existences of things, or mediate knowledge about conditioned existences, results immediately from the perfect intellection of each term, which can be subject or predicate of any proposition; or that the *a priori* knowledge of complex things springs from the understanding of those that are incomplex.

An absolutely necessary proposition is one which can be resolved into identical propositions, or the opposite of which implies a contradiction. Let me show this by an example in numbers. I shall call binary every number which can be exactly divided by two, and ternary or quaternary—every one that can be exactly divided by three or four, and so on. For we understand every number to be resolved into those which exactly divide it. I say therefore that this proposition: that a duodenary number* is quaternary, is absolutely necessary, since it can be resolved into identical propositions in the following way. A duodenary number is binary-senary (by definition); senary is binary ternary (by definition). Therefore a duodenary number is binary binary ternary. Further binary binary is quaternary (by definition). Therefore a duodenary number is quaternary ternary. Therefore a duodenary number is quaternary. Q.E.D. But even if other definitions had been given, it could always have been shown that it comes to the same thing. Therefore I call this necessity metaphysical or geometrical. What lacks such necessity, I call contingent; but what implies a contradiction, or that the opposite of which is necessary, is called *impossible*. Other things are called *possible*. In contingent truth, even though the predicate is really present in the subject, nevertheless by whatever resolution you please of either term, indefinitely continued, you will never arrive at demonstration of identity.

---

* A duodenary number is a number evenly divisible by 12. Leibniz is trying to show in this passage that the claim, "every number evenly divisible by 12 is evenly divisible by 4" is true by definition, and so, absolutely necessary.

And it is for GOD alone, comprehending the infinite all at once, to perceive how one is present in the other, and to understand a priori the perfect reason of contingency, which in creatures is furnished *(a posteriori)* by experience. . . . And so I consider that I have unfolded something secret, which has long perplexed even myself—while I did not understand how the predicate could be in the subject, and yet the proposition not be necessary. But the knowledge of things geometrical and the analysis of infinities kindled this light for me, so that I understood that concepts too are resoluble to infinity.

Hence we now learn that propositions which pertain to the essences and those which pertain to the existences of things are different. Essential surely are those which can be demonstrated from the resolution of terms, that is, which are necessary, or virtually identical, and the opposite of which, moreover, is impossible or virtually contradictory. And these are the eternal truths. They did not obtain only while the world existed, but they would also obtain if GOD had created a world with a different plan. But from these, existential or contingent truths differ entirely. Their truth is understood a priori by the infinite mind alone, and they cannot be demonstrated by any resolution. They are of the sort that are true at a certain time, and they do not only express what pertains to the possibility of things, but also what actually does exist, or would exist contingently if certain things were supposed. For example, take the proposition, I am now living, the sun is shining. For suppose I say that the sun is shining in our hemisphere at this hour, because up to now its motion has been such that, granted its continuation, this certainly follows. Even then (not to mention the non-necessary obligation of its continuing) that its motion even before this was so much and of this kind is similarly a contingent truth, for which again the reason should be inquired—nor could it be fully produced except from the perfect knowledge of all parts of the universe. This, however, exceeds all created powers. For there is no portion of matter, which is not actually subdivided into other parts; hence the parts of any body whatsoever are actually infinite. Thus neither the sun nor any other body can be perfectly known by a creature. Much less can we arrive at the end of the analysis if we search for the mover causing the motion of any body whatsoever and again for the mover of this; for we shall always arrive at smaller bodies without end. But GOD is not in need of that transition from one contingent to another earlier or simpler contingent,—a transition which can never have an end (as also one contingent is in fact not the cause of another, even though it may seem so to us). But he perceives in any individual substance from its very concept the truth of all its accidents, calling in nothing extrinsic, since any one at all involves in its way all the others and the whole universe. Hence into all propositions into which existence and time enter, by that very fact the whole series of things enters, nor can the now or here be understood except in relation to other things. For this reason such propositions do not allow of a demonstration or terminable resolution by which their truth might appear. And the same holds of all accidents of individual created substances. Indeed even though someone were able to know the whole series of the universe, he still could not state the reason of it, except by having undertaken the comparison of it with all other

possible universes. From this it is clear why a demonstration of no contingent proposition can be found, however far the resolution of concepts be continued.

It must not be thought, however, that only singular propositions are contingent, for there are (and can be inferred by induction) some propositions true for the most part; and there are also propositions almost always true at least naturally, so that an exception is ascribed to a miracle. Indeed, I think there are certain propositions most universally true in this series of things, and certainly never to be violated even by miracle, not that they could not be violated by GOD, but that when he himself chose this series of things, by that very fact he decided to observe them (as the specific properties of this very series chosen). And through these propositions set up once for all by the force of the divine decree, it is possible to state the reason for other universal propositions and also for many contingent propositions which can be observed in this universe. For from the first essential laws of the series, true without exception, which contain the whole aim of GOD in choosing the universe, and even include miracles as well, subaltern laws of nature can be derived, which have only physical necessity, and which are not modified except by miracle, by reason of an intuition of some more powerful final cause. And from these finally are inferred others the universality of which is still less; and GOD can also reveal to creatures this kind of demonstration of intermediate universals from one another, a part of which makes up physical science. But one could never by any analysis come to the most universal laws nor to the perfect reasons for individual things; for this knowledge is necessarily appropriate only to GOD. Nor indeed should it disturb anyone, that I have said there are certain laws essential to this series of things, since we have nevertheless said above that these very laws are not necessary and essential, but contingent and existential. For since the fact that the series itself exists is contingent, and depends on a free decree of GOD, its laws too, considered absolutely, will be contingent; hypothetically, however, if the series is supposed, they are necessary and so far essential.

37

Metaphysical Necessity

SAUL A. KRIPKE

Saul A. Kripke (b. 1940) is McCosh Professor of Philosophy at Princeton University. An influential contemporary philosopher, Kripke has made major contributions to logic, the philosophy of language, and metaphysics. His Naming and Necessity *is a contemporary classic.*

In this essay, Kripke tries to chart the relations between two important philosophical concepts: apriority *and* necessity. *His central thesis is that these two concepts are distinct. "Apriority" is a concept that belongs to the theory of knowledge, because it is concerned with the way in which something is known. Traditionally, philosophers have argued that certain claims could be known* a priori—*roughly, in the absence of any sensory evidence. On the other hand, Kripke believes that claims about necessity fall within the province of metaphysics. To say that a certain state of affairs is "necessary" is to make a claim about the way the world is. For example, Kripke claims it is a necessary truth that gold has the atomic number 79. This means the world could not have contained gold that did not have the atomic number 79, for anything that did not have this atomic number would not be gold. However, as Kripke argues, if we assume that this is a necessary truth, it does not follow that we could come to know this truth* a priori. *In fact, atomic numbers are determined through standard empirical means. Thus, Kripke tries to show the traditional philosophical view that a claim is necessary if and only if it can be known* a priori *is mistaken.*

BEFORE I GO ANY FURTHER into this problem, I want to talk* about another distinction which will be important in the methodology of these talks. Philosophers have talked (and, of course, there has been considerable controversy in recent years over the meaningfulness of these notions) [about] various categories of truth, which are called *'a priori', 'analytic', 'necessary'*†—*and sometimes even 'certain' is thrown into this batch. The terms are often used as if whether* there are things answering to these concepts is an interesting question, but we might as well regard them all as meaning the same things. Now,

---

* This essay is from a transcript of a series of lectures which Kripke gave at Princeton University in 1970, so the wording is occasionally quite informal.

† *A priori* and "necessary" are technical philosophical terms. We do not include traditional interpretations in these notes, because one of Kripke's aims is to offer his own interpretations of these terms.

everyone remembers Kant (a bit) as making a distinction between 'a priori' and 'analytic'. So maybe this distinction is still made. In contemporary discussion very few people, if any, distinguish between the concepts of statements being *a priori* and their being necessary. At any rate I shall *not* use the terms 'a priori' and 'necessary' interchangeably here.

Consider what the traditional characterizations of such terms as 'a priori' and 'necessary' are. First the notion of a prioricity is a concept of epistemology. I guess the traditional characterization from Kant goes something like: *a priori* truths are those which can be known independently of any experience. This introduces another problem before we get off the ground, because there's another modality* in the characterization of 'a priori', namely, it is supposed to be something which *can* be known independently of any experience. That means that in some sense it's *possible* (whether we do or do not in fact know it independently of any experience) to know this independently of any experience. And possible for whom? For God? For the Martians? Or just for people with minds like ours? To make this all clear might [involve] a host of problems all of its own about what sort of possibility is in question here. It might be best therefore, instead of using the phrase 'a priori truth', to the extent that one uses it at all, to stick to the question of whether a particular person or knower knows something *a priori* or believes it true on the basis of *a priori* evidence.

I won't go further too much into the problems that might arise with the notion of a prioricity here. I will say that some philosophers somehow change the modality in this characterization from *can* to *must*. They think that if something belongs to the realm of *a priori* knowledge, it couldn't possibly be known empirically. This is just a mistake. Something may belong in the realm of such statements that *can* be known *a priori* but still may be known by particular people on the basis of experience. To give a really common sense example: anyone who has worked with a computing machine knows that the computing machine may give an answer to whether such and such a number is prime. No one has calculated or proved that the number is prime; but the machine has given the answer: this number is prime. We, then, if we believe that the number is prime, believe it on the basis of our knowledge of the laws of physics, the construction of the machine, and so on. We therefore do not believe this on the basis of purely *a priori* evidence. We believe it (if anything is *a posteriori* at all) on the basis of *a posteriori* evidence. Nevertheless, maybe this could be known *a priori* by someone who made the requisite calculations. So 'can be known *a priori*' doesn't mean 'must be known *a priori*'.

The second concept which is in question is that of necessity. Sometimes this is used in an epistemological way and might then just mean *a priori*. And of course, sometimes it is used in a physical way when people distinguish between physical and logical necessity. But what I am concerned with here is a notion

---

* A modal expression is one which includes a reference to possibility or necessity. Kripke is pointing out that the standard definition of *a priori*, namely, "something which *can* be known independently of any experience," includes a reference to possibility through the word "can."

which is not a notion of epistemology but of metaphysics, in some (I hope) nonpejorative sense. We ask whether something might have been true, or might have been false. Well, if something is false, it's obviously not necessarily true. If it is true, might it have been otherwise? Is it possible that, in this respect, the world should have been different from the way it is? If the answer is 'no', then this fact about the world is a necessary one. If the answer is 'yes', then this fact about the world is a contingent one. This in and of itself has nothing to do with anyone's knowledge of anything. It's certainly a philosophical thesis, and not a matter of obvious definitional equivalence, either that everything *a priori* is necessary or that everything necessary is *a priori*. Both concepts may be vague. That may be another problem. But at any rate they are dealing with two different domains, two different areas, the epistemological and the metaphysical. Consider, say, Fermat's last theorem—or the Goldbach conjecture. The Goldbach conjecture says that an even number greater than 2 must be the sum of two prime numbers. If this is true, it is presumably necessary, and, if it is false, presumably necessarily false. We are taking the classical view of mathematics here and assume that in mathematical reality it is either true or false.

If the Goldbach conjecture is false, then there is an even number, n, greater than 2, such that for no primes p_1 and p_2, both $< n$, does $n = p_1 + p_2$. This fact about n, if true, is verifiable by direct computation, and thus is necessary if the results of arithmetical computations are necessary. On the other hand, if the conjecture is true, then every even number exceeding 2 is the sum of two primes. Could it then be the case that, although in fact every such even number is the sum of two primes, there might have been such an even number which was not the sum of two primes? What would that mean? Such a number would have to be one of 4, 6, 8, 10, . . .; and, by hypothesis, since we are assuming Goldbach's conjecture to be true, each of these can be shown, again by direct computation, to be the sum of two primes. Goldbach's conjecture, then, cannot be contingently true or false; whatever truth-value it has belongs to it by necessity.

But what we can say, of course, is that right now, as far as we know, the question can come out either way. So, in the absence of a mathematical proof deciding this question, none of us has any *a priori* knowledge about this question in either direction. We don't know whether Goldbach's conjecture is true or false. So right now we certainly don't know anything *a priori* about it.

Perhaps it will be alleged that we *can* in principle know *a priori* whether it is true. Well, maybe we can. Of course an infinite mind which can search through all the numbers can or could. But I don't know whether a finite mind can or could. Maybe there just is no mathematical proof whatsoever which decides the conjecture. At any rate this might or might not be the case. Maybe there is a mathematical proof deciding this question; maybe every mathematical question is decidable by an intuitive proof or disproof. Hilbert thought so; others have thought not; still others have thought the question unintelligible unless the notion of intuitive proof is replaced by that of formal proof in a single system. Certainly no one formal system decides all mathematical questions, as we know from Gödel. At any rate, and this is the important thing, the question is not trivial; even though someone said that it's necessary, if true at

all, that every even number is the sum of two primes, it doesn't follow that anyone knows anything *a priori* about it. It doesn't even seem to me to follow without some further philosophical argument (it is an interesting philosophical question) that anyone *could* know anything *a priori* about it. The 'could', as I said, involves some other modality. We mean that even if no one, perhaps even in the future, knows or will know *a priori* whether Goldbach's conjecture is right, in principle there is a way, which *could* have been used, of answering the question *a priori*. This assertion is not trivial.

The terms 'necessary' and *'a priori'*, then, as applied to statements, are *not* obvious synonyms. There may be a philosophical argument connecting them, perhaps even identifying them; but an argument is required, not simply the observation that the two terms are clearly interchangeable. (I will argue below that in fact they are not even coextensive—that necessary *a posteriori* truths, and probably contingent *a priori* truths, both exist.)

I think people have thought that these two things must mean the same for these reasons:

First, if something not only happens to be true in the actual world but is also true in all possible worlds, then, of course, just by running through all the possible worlds in our heads, we ought to be able with enough effort to see, if a statement is necessary, that it is necessary, and thus know it *a priori*. But really this is not so obviously feasible at all.

Second, I guess it's thought that, conversely, if something is known *a priori* it must be necessary, because it was known without looking at the world. If it depended on some contingent feature of the actual world, how could you know it without looking? Maybe the actual world is one of the possible worlds in which it would have been false. This depends on the thesis that there can't be a way of knowing about the actual world without looking that wouldn't be a way of knowing the same thing about every possible world. This involves problems of epistemology and the nature of knowledge; and of course it is very vague as stated. But it is not really *trivial* either. More important than any particular example of something which is alleged to be necessary and not *a priori* or *a priori* and not necessary, is to see that the notions are different, that it's not trivial to argue on the basis of something's being something which maybe we can only know *a posteriori*, that it's not a necessary truth. It's not trivial, just because something is known in some sense *a priori*, that what is known is a necessary truth.

. . .

I want to mention at this point that other considerations about *de re* modality,* about an object having essential properties, can only be regarded correctly, in my view, if we recognize the distinction between a prioricity and necessity. One might very well discover essence empirically.

_____

* *De re* literally means "about the thing." A *de re* modality concerns a necessary or a possible feature of some *thing itself,* as opposed to some necessity (or possibility) involving our statements about the thing.

There are some examples of alleged essential properties in an article by Timothy Sprigge.

> The internalist [which means the believer that there are some essential properties] says that the Queen must have been born of royal blood. [He means that *this person* must have been of royal blood.] The anti-essentialist says there would be no contradiction in a news bulletin asserting that it had been established that the Queen was not in fact the child of her supposed parents, but had been secretly adopted by them, and therefore the proposition that she is of royal blood is synthetic. . .
>
> For a time [the anti-essentialist] is winning. Yet there comes a time when his claims appear a trifle too far fetched. The internalist suggests that we cannot imagine that particular we call the Queen having the property of at no stage in her existence being human. If the anti-internalist admits this, admits that it is logically inconceivable that the Queen should have had the property of, say, always being a swan, then he admits that she has at least one internal property. If on the other hand he says that it's only a contingent fact that the Queen has ever been human, he says what it is hard to accept. Can we really consider it as conceivable that she should never have been human?[1]

'At no stage in her existence' and 'always' are justifications Sprigge presumably introduces to allow such possibilities as her right now being changed into a swan—by a wicked witch, I guess. (Or a benign witch.)

One confusion I find in this discussion is that in the first case Sprigge talks about whether there would be any contradiction in supposing that we had an *announcement* that the Queen was born of parents different from the ones she actually had. And in that there is no contradiction. Similarly, though, there is no contradiction in an *announcement* that the Queen, this thing we thought to be a woman, was in fact an angel in human form, or an automaton cleverly constructed by the royal family, who did not want the succession to pass to that bastard so-and-so, or something. Neither of these announcements represent things that we couldn't possibly *discover,* either. What is the question we are asking when we ask whether it's necessary, concerning this woman, that she should either have been of royal blood or have been human? Royal blood is a little complicated, because in order for it to be necessary for her to have been of royal blood it has to be necessary that this particular family line at some time attained to royal power; but the latter fact seems to be contingent. Therefore I suppose it *is* contingent that her blood should ever have been royal.

Let's try and refine the question a little bit. The question really should be, let's say, could the Queen—could this woman herself—have been born of different parents from the parents from whom she actually came? Could she, let's say, have been the daughter instead of Mr. and Mrs. Truman? There would be no contradiction, of course, in an announcement that (I hope the ages do not make this impossible), fantastic as it may sound, she was indeed the daughter

---

[1] "Internal and External Properties", *Mind* 71 (April, 1962), pp. 202–03.

of Mr. and Mrs. Truman. I suppose there might even be no contradiction in the discovery that—it seems very suspicious anyway that on either hypothesis she has a sister called Margaret—that these two Margarets were one and the same person flying back and forth in a clever way. At any rate we can imagine discovering all of these things.

But let us suppose that such a discovery is not in fact the case. Let's suppose that the Queen really did come from these parents. Not to go into too many complications here about what a parent is, let's suppose that the parents are the people whose body tissues are sources of the biological sperm and egg. So you get rid of such recherché possibilities as transplants of the sperm from the father, or the egg from the mother, into other bodies, so that in one sense other people might have been her parents. If that happened, in another sense her parents were still the original king and queen. But other than that, can we imagine a situation in which it would have happened that this very woman came out of Mr. and Mrs. Truman? They might have had a child resembling her in many properties. Perhaps in some possible world Mr. and Mrs. Truman even had a child who actually became the Queen of England and was even passed off as the child of other parents. This still would not be a situation in which *this very woman* whom we call 'Elizabeth II' was the child of Mr. and Mrs. Truman, or so it seems to me. It would be a situation in which there was some other woman who had many of the properties that are in fact true of Elizabeth. Now, one question is, in this possible world, was Elizabeth herself ever born? Let's suppose she wasn't ever born. It would then be a situation in which, though Truman and his wife have a child with many of the properties of Elizabeth, Elizabeth herself didn't exist at all. One can only become convinced of this by reflection on how you would describe this situation. (That, I suppose, means in many cases that you won't become convinced of this, at least not at the moment. But it is something of which I personally have been convinced.)

How could a person originating from different parents, from a totally different sperm and egg, be *this very woman?* One can imagine, *given* the woman, that various things in her life could have changed: that she should have become a pauper; that her royal blood should have been unknown, and so on. One is given, let's say, a previous history of the world up to a certain time, and from that time it diverges considerably from the actual course. This seems to be possible. And so it's possible that even though she were born of these parents she never became queen. Even though she were born of these parents, like Mark Twain's character she was switched off with another girl. But what is harder to imagine is her being born of different parents. It seems to me that anything coming from a different origin would not be this object.

In the case of this table,[2] we may not know what block of wood the table came from. Now could *this table* have been made from a completely *different* block of wood, or even of water cleverly hardened into ice—water taken from

---

[2] Of course I was pointing to a wooden table in the room.

the Thames River? We could conceivably discover that, contrary to what we now think, this table is indeed made of ice from the river. But let us suppose that it is not. Then, though we can imagine making a table out of another block of wood or even from ice, identical in appearance with this one, and though we could have put it in this very position in the room, it seems to me that this is *not* to imagine *this* table as made of wood or ice, but rather it is to imagine another table, *resembling* this one in all external details, made of another block of wood, or even of ice.

These are only examples of essential properties. I won't dwell on them further because I want to go on to the more general case, which I mentioned in the last lecture, of some identities between terms for substances, and also the properties of substances and of natural kinds. Philosophers have, as I've said, been very interested in statements expressing theoretical identifications; among them, that light is a stream of photons, that water is H_2O, that lightning is an electrical discharge, that gold is the element with the atomic number 79.

To get clear about the status of these statements we must first maybe have some thoughts about the status of such substances as gold. What's gold? I don't know if this is an example which has particularly interested philosophers. Its interest in financial circles is diminishing because of increased stability of currencies. Even so gold has interested many people. Here is what Immanuel Kant says about gold. (He was a wealthy speculator who kept his possessions under his bed.) Kant is introducing the distinction between analytic and synthetic judgements, and he says: 'All analytic judgements depend wholly on the law of contradiction, and are in their nature *a priori* cognitions, whether the concepts that supply them with matter be empirical or not. For the predicate of an affirmative analytic judgement is already contained in the concept of the subject, of which it cannot be denied without contradiction. . . . For this very reason all analytic judgements are *a priori* even when the concepts are empirical, as, for example, "Gold is a yellow metal"; for to know this I require no experience beyond my concept of gold as a yellow metal. It is, in fact, the very concept, and I need only analyze it without looking beyond it.'[3] I should have looked at the German. 'It is in fact the very concept' sounds as if Kant is saying here that 'gold' just *means* 'yellow metal'. If he says that, then it's especially strange, so let's suppose that that is not what he's saying. At least Kant thinks it's a *part* of the concept that gold is to be a yellow metal. He thinks we know this *a priori*, and that we could not possibly discover this to be empirically false.

Is Kant right about this? First, what I would have wanted to do would have been to discuss the part about gold being a metal. This, however, is complicated because first, I don't know too much chemistry. Investigating this a few days ago in just a couple of references, I found in a more phenomenological account

---

[3] *Prolegonena to Any Future Metaphysics,* Preamble Section 2. b. (Prussian Academy edition, p. 267).

of metals the statement that it's very difficult to say what a metal is. (It talks about malleability, ductility, and the like, but none of these exactly work.) On the other hand, something about the periodic table gave a description of elements as metals in terms of their valency properties. This may make some people think right away that there are really two concepts of metal operating here, a phenomenological one and a scientific one which then replaces it. This I reject, but since the move will tempt many, and can be refuted only after I develop my own views, it will not be suitable to use 'Gold is a metal' as an example to introduce these views.

But let's consider something easier—the question of the yellowness of gold. Could we discover that gold was not in fact yellow? Suppose an optical illusion were prevalent, due to peculiar properties of the atmosphere in South Africa and Russia and certain other areas where gold mines are common. Suppose there were an optical illusion which made the substance appear to be yellow; but, in fact, once the peculiar properties of the atmosphere were removed, we would see that it is actually blue. Maybe a demon even corrupted the vision of all those entering the gold mines (obviously their *souls* were already corrupt), and thus made them believe that this substance was yellow, though it is not. Would there on this basis be an announcement in the newspapers: 'It has turned out that there is no gold. Gold does not exist. What we took to be gold is not in fact gold.'? Just imagine the world financial crisis under these conditions! Here we have an undreamt of source of shakiness in the monetary system.

It seems to me that there would be no such announcement. On the contrary, what would be announced would be that though it appeared that gold was yellow, in fact gold has turned out not to be yellow, but blue. The reason is, I think, that we use 'gold' as a term for a certain *kind* of thing. Others have discovered this kind of thing and we have heard of it. We thus as part of a community of speakers have a certain connection between ourselves and a certain kind of thing. The kind of thing is *thought* to have certain identifying marks. Some of these marks may not really be true of gold. We might discover that we are wrong about them. Further, there might be a substance which has all the identifying marks we commonly attributed to gold and used to identify it in the first place, but which is not the same kind of thing, which is not the same substance. We would say of such a thing that though it has all the appearances we initially used to identify gold, it is not gold. Such a thing is, for example, as we well know, iron pyrites or fool's gold. This is not another kind of gold. It's a completely different thing which to the uninitiated person looks just like the substance which we discovered and called gold. We can say this not because we have changed the *meaning* of the term gold, and thrown in some other criteria which distinguished gold from pyrites. It seems to me that that's not true. On the contrary, we *discovered* that certain properties were true of gold in addition to the initial identifying marks by which we identified it. These properties, then, being characteristic of gold and not true of iron pyrites, show that the fool's gold is not in fact gold.

431

We should look at this in another example. It says somewhere in here:[4] 'I say "The word 'tiger' has meaning in English". . . . If I am then asked "What is a tiger?" I might reply "A tiger is a large carnivorous quadrupedal feline, tawny yellow in color with blackish transverse stripes and white belly," (derived from the entry under "tiger" in the *Shorter Oxford English Dictionary*.)' And now suppose someone says 'You have just said what the word "tiger" means in English.' And Ziff asks, 'Is that so?' and he says, correctly, 'I think not.' His example is, 'Suppose in a jungle clearing one says "look, a three-legged tiger!": must one be confused? The phrase "a three-legged tiger" is not a *contradictio in adjecto*.* But if "tiger" in English meant, among other things, either quadruped or quadrupedal, the phrase "a three-legged tiger" could only be a *contradictio in adjecto*.' So, his example shows that if it is part of the concept of tiger that a tiger has four legs, there couldn't be a three-legged tiger. This is the sort of case which many philosophers tend to explain as a 'cluster concept'. Is it even a contradiction to suppose that we should discover that tigers *never* have four legs? Suppose the explorers who attributed these properties to tigers were deceived by an optical illusion, and that the animals they saw were from a three-legged species, would we then say that there turned out to be no tigers after all? I think we would say that in spite of the optical illusion which had deceived the explorers, tigers in fact have three legs.

Further, is it true that anything satisfying this description in the dictionary is necessarily a tiger? It seems to me that it is not. Suppose we discover an animal which, though having all external appearances of a tiger as described here, has an internal structure completely different from that of the tiger. Actually the word 'feline' was put in here, so it is not entirely fair. Let's suppose it were left out, for this example. That a tiger belongs to any particular biological family, anyway, was something we discovered. If 'feline' means just having the appearance of a cat, let's suppose that it does have the appearance of a big cat. We might find animals in some part of the world which, though they look just like a tiger, on examination were discovered not even to be mammals. Let's say they were in fact very peculiar looking reptiles. Do we then conclude on the basis of this description that some tigers are reptiles? We don't. We would rather conclude that these animals, though they have the external marks by which we originally identified tigers, are not in fact tigers, because they are not of the same species as the species which we called 'the species of tigers'. Now this, I think, is not because, as some people would say, the old concept of tiger has been replaced by a new scientific definition. I think this is true of the concept of tiger *before* the internal structure of tigers has been investigated. Even though we don't *know* the internal structure of tigers, we suppose—and let us suppose that we are right—that tigers form a certain species or natural kind. We then can imagine that there should be a creature which, though having all the exter-

---

[4] Paul Ziff, *Semantic Analysis*, Ithaca, Cornell University Press, 1960, pp. 184–85.

* A *contradictio in adjecto* is an expression where the property ascribed to the object cannot consistently be had by that object, for example, a square circle.

nal appearance of tigers, differs from them internally enough that we should say that it is not the same kind of thing. We can imagine it without knowing anything about this internal structure—what this internal structure is. We can say in advance that we use the term 'tiger' to designate a species, and that anything not of this species, even though it looks like a tiger, is not in fact a tiger.

Just as something may have all the properties by which we originally identified tigers and yet not be a tiger, so we might also find out tigers had *none* of the properties by which we originally identified them. Perhaps *none* are quadrupedal, none tawny yellow, none carnivorous, and so on; all these properties turn out to be based on optical illusions or other errors, as in the case of gold. So the term 'tiger', like the term 'gold', does *not* mark out a 'cluster concept' in which most, but perhaps not all, of the properties used to identify the kind must be satisfied. On the contrary, possession of most of these properties need not be a necessary condition for membership in the kind, nor need it be a sufficient condition.

Since we have found out that tigers do indeed, as we suspected, form a single kind, then something not of this kind is not a tiger. Of course, we may be mistaken in supposing that there is such a kind. In advance, we suppose that they probably do form a kind. Past experience has shown that usually things like this, living together, looking alike, mating together, do form a kind. If there are two kinds of tigers that have something to do with each other but not as much as we thought, then maybe they form a larger biological family. If they have absolutely nothing to do with each other, then there are really two kind of tigers. This all depends on the history and on what we actually find out.

The philosopher I find most to recognize this sort of consideration (our thoughts on these matters developed independently) is Putnam. In an article called 'It Ain't Necessarily So',[5] he says of statements about species, that they are 'less necessary' (as he cautiously says) than statements like 'bachelors aren't married'. The example he gives is 'cats are animals'. Cats might turn out to be automata, or strange demons (not his example) planted by a magician. Suppose they turned out to be a species of demons. Then on his view, and I think also my view, the inclination is to say, not that there turned out to be no cats, but that cats have turned out not to be animals as we originally supposed. The original concept of cat is: *that kind of thing,* where the kind can be identified by paradigmatic instances. It is not something picked out by any qualitative dictionary definition. However, Putnam's conclusion is that statements like 'cats are animals' are 'less necessary' than statements like 'bachelors are unmarried'. Certainly I agree that the argument indicates that such statements are not known *a priori,* and hence are not analytic, whether a given kind is a species of animals is a matter for empirical investigation. Perhaps this epistemological sense is what Putnam means by 'necessary'. The question remains whether such statements are necessary in the non-epistemological sense advocated in these

[5] *Journal of Philosophy,* 59, No. 22 (October 25, 1962), pp. 658–71.

lectures. So the next thing to investigate is (using the concept of necessity that I talked about): are such statements as 'cats are animals', or such statements as 'gold is a yellow metal', necessary?

So far I've only been talking about what we could find out. I've been saying we could find out that gold was not in fact yellow, contrary to what we thought. If one went in more detail into the concept of metals, let's say in terms of valency properties, one could certainly find out that though one took gold to be a metal, gold is not in fact a metal. Is it necessary or contingent that gold be a metal? I don't want to go into detail on the concept of a metal—as I said, I don't know enough about it. Gold apparently has the atomic number 79. Is it a necessary or a contingent property of gold that it has the atomic number 79? Certainly we could find out that we were mistaken. The whole theory of protons, of atomic numbers, the whole theory of molecular structure and of atomic structure, on which such views are based, could *all* turn out to be false. Certainly we didn't know it from time immemorial. So in that sense, gold could turn out not to have atomic number 79.

Given that gold *does* have the atomic number 79, could something be gold without having the atomic number 79? Let us suppose the scientists have investigated the nature of gold and have found that it is part of the very nature of this substance, so to speak, that it have the atomic number 79. Suppose we now find some other yellow metal, or some other yellow thing, with all the properties by we originally identified gold, and many of the additional ones that we have discovered later. An example of one with many of the initial properties is iron pyrites, 'fool's gold.' As I have said, we wouldn't say that this substance is gold. So far we are speaking of the actual world. Now consider a possible world. Consider a counterfactual situation in which, let us say, fool's gold or iron pyrites was actually found in various mountains in the United States, or in areas of South Africa and the Soviet Union. Suppose that all the areas which actually contain gold now, contained pyrites instead, or some other substance which counterfeited the superficial properties of gold but lacked its atomic structure. Would we say, of this counterfactual situation, that in that situation gold would not even have been an element (because pyrites is not an element)? It seems to me that we would not. We would instead describe this as a situation in which a substance, say iron pyrites, which is not gold, would have been found in the very mountains which actually contain gold and would have had the very properties by which we commonly identify gold. But it would not be gold; it would be something else. One should *not* say that it would still be gold in this possible world, though gold would then lack the atomic number 79. It would be some other stuff, some other substance. (Once again, whether people counterfactually would have *called* it 'gold' is irrelevant. *We* do not describe it as gold.) And so, it seems to me, this would not be a case in which possibly gold might not have been an element, nor can there be such a case (except in the epistemic sense of 'possible'). Given that gold *is* this element, any other substance, even though it looks like gold and is found in the very places where we in fact find gold, would not be gold. It would be some other substance which was a counterfeit for gold. In any counterfactual situation where the

same geographical areas were filled with such a substance, they would not have been filled with gold. They would have been filled with something else.

So if this consideration is right, it tends to show that such statements representing scientific discoveries about what this stuff *is* are not contingent truths but necessary truths in the strictest possible sense. It's not just that it's a scientific law, but of course we can imagine a world in which it would fail. Any world in which we imagine a substance which does not have these properties is a world in which we imagine a substance which is not gold, provided these properties form the basis of what the substance is. In particular, then, present scientific theory is such that it is part of the nature of gold as we have it to be an element with atomic number 79. It will therefore be necessary and not contingent that gold be an element with atomic number 79. (We may also in the same way, then, investigate further how color and metallic properties follow from what we have found the substance gold to be: to the extent that such properties follow from the atomic structure of gold, they are necessary properties of it, even though they unquestionably are not part of the *meaning* of 'gold' and were not known with *a priori* certainty.)

38

Personal Identity

JOHN LOCKE

For biographical information about John Locke, see reading 15.

Students of science fiction can easily appreciate the problem that Locke is trying to resolve in this passage from An Essay Concerning Human Understanding. *Consider the well-worn plot about the evil billionaire who learns that he is dying and decides that he is going to preserve his life by taking over someone else's body. What must the dying man do to ensure that he—a particular person—survives into the future? Should he try to suck the life-blood or life-force out of someone else's body and take it into his own body, in the manner of Count Dracula? Or, like the aliens in* The Invasion of the Body Snatchers, *should he try somehow to "inhabit" some (other) healthy body?*

Locke's question is: what makes someone the same person through time? or, what must be preserved in order to preserve your identity as a person? After considering a variety of imaginary situations involving the transmigration of souls, body-switching, loss of memory and split personality, Locke concludes that the crucial factor in personal identity is continuity of memory.

1. Another occasion the mind often takes of comparing, is the very being of things, when, considering *anything as existing at any determined time and place,* we compare it with *itself existing at another time,* and thereon form the ideas of *identity* and *diversity.* When we see anything to be in any place in any instant of time, we are sure (be it what it will) that it is that very thing, and not another which at that same time exists in another place, how like and undistinguishable soever it may be in all other respects: and in this consists *identity,* when the ideas it is attributed to vary not at all from what they were that moment wherein we consider their former existence, and to which we compare the present. For we never finding, nor conceiving it possible, that two things of the same kind should exist in the same place at the same time, we rightly conclude, that, whatever exists anywhere at any time, excludes all of the same kind, and is there itself alone. When therefore we demand whether anything be the *same* or no, it refers always to something that existed such a time in such a place, which it was certain, at that instant, was the same with itself, and no other. From whence it follows, that one thing cannot have two beginnings of existence, nor two things one beginning; it being impossible for two things of the same kind to be or exist in the same instant, in the very same place; or one and the same thing in different places. That, therefore, that had

one beginning, is the same thing; and that which had a different beginning in time and place from that, is not the same, but diverse. That which has made the difficulty about this relation has been the little care and attention used in having precise notions of the things to which it is attributed.

2. We have the ideas but of three sorts of substances: 1. *God.* 2. *Finite intelligences.** 3. *Bodies.*

First, *God* is without beginning, eternal, unalterable, and everywhere, and therefore concerning his identity there can be no doubt.

Secondly, *Finite spirits* having had each its determinate time and place of beginning to exist, the relation to that time and place will always determine to each of them its identity, as long as it exists.

Thirdly, The same will hold of every *particle of matter,* to which no addition or subtraction of matter being made, it is the same. For, though these three sorts of substances, as we term them, do not exclude one another out of the same place, yet we cannot conceive but that they must necessarily each of them exclude any of the same kind out of the same place: or else the notions and names of identity and diversity would be in vain, and there could be no such distinctions of substances, or anything else one from another. For example: could two bodies be in the same place at the same time; then those two parcels of matter must be one and the same, take them great or little; nay, all bodies must be one and the same. For, by the same reason that two particles of matter may be in one place, all bodies may be in one place: which, when it can be supposed, takes away the distinction of identity and diversity of one and more, and renders it ridiculous. But it being a contradiction that two or more should be one, identity and diversity are relations and ways of comparing well founded, and of use to the understanding.

3. All other things being but modes† or relations ultimately terminated in substances, the identity and diversity of each particular existence of them too will be by the same way determined: only as to things whose existence is in succession, such as are the actions of finite beings, v.g. *motion* and *thought,* both which consist in a continued train of succession, concerning *their* diversity there can be no question: because each perishing the moment it begins, they cannot exist in different times, or in different places, as permanent beings can at different times exist in distant places; and therefore no motion or thought, considered as at different times, can be the same, each part thereof having a different beginning of existence.

4. From what has been said, it is easy to discover what is so much inquired after, the *principium individuationis;*‡ and that, it is plain, is existence itself; which determines a being of any sort to a particular time and place, incommunicable to two beings of the same kind. This, though it seems easier to

---

*A "finite intelligence" is a person.

† An attribute of some substance.

‡ A *principium individudationis* is a principle by which we can individuate distinct individuals.

conceive in simple substances or modes; yet, when reflected on, is not more difficult in compound ones, if care be taken to what it is applied: v.g. let us suppose an atom, i.e. a continued body under one immutable superficies, existing in a determined time and place; it is evident, that, considered in any instant of its existence, it is in that instant the same with itself. For, being at that instant what it is, and nothing else, it is the same, and so must continue as long as its existence is continued; for so long it will be the same, and no other. In like manner, if two or more atoms be joined together into the same mass, every one of those atoms will be the same, by the foregoing rule: and whilst they exist united together, the mass, consisting of the same atoms, must be the same mass, or the same body, let the parts be ever so differently jumbled. But if one of these atoms be taken away, or one new one added, it is no longer the same mass or the same body. In the state of living creatures, their identity depends not on a mass of the same particles, but on something else. For in them the variation of great parcels of matter alters not the identity: an oak growing from a plant to a great tree, and then lopped, is still the same oak; and a colt grown up to a horse, sometimes fat, sometimes lean, is all the while the same horse: though, in both these cases, there may be a manifest change of the parts; so that truly they are not either of them the same masses of matter, though they be truly one of them the same oak, and the other the same horse. The reason whereof is, that, in these two cases—a *mass of matter* and a *living body*—identity is not applied to the same thing.

5. We must therefore consider wherein an oak differs from a mass of matter, and that seems to me to be in this, that the one is only the cohesion of particles of matter any how united, the other such a disposition of them as constitutes the parts of an oak; and such an organization of those parts as is fit to receive and distribute nourishment, so as to continue and frame the wood, bark, and leaves, &c., of an oak, in which consists the vegetable life. That being then one plant which has such an organization of parts in one coherent body, partaking of one common life, it continues to be the same plant as long as it partakes of the same life, though that life be communicated to new particles of matter vitally united to the living plant, in a like continued organization conformable to that sort of plants. For this organization, being at any one instant in any one collection of matter, is in that particular concrete distinguished from all other, and *is* that individual life, which existing constantly from that moment both forwards and backwards, in the same continuity of insensibly succeeding parts united to the living body of the plant, it has that identity which makes the same plant, and all the parts of it, parts of the same plant, during all the time that they exist united in that continued organization, which is fit to convey that common life to all the parts so united.

6. The case is not so much different in *brutes* but that any one may hence see what makes an animal and continues it the same. Something we have like this in machines, and may serve to illustrate it. For example, what is a watch? It is plain it is nothing but a fit organization or construction of parts to a certain end, which, when a sufficient force is added to it, it is capable to attain. If we would suppose this machine one continued body, all whose organized parts

were repaired, increased, or diminished by a constant addition or separation of insensible parts, with one common life, we should have something very much like the body of an animal; with this difference, That, in an animal the fitness of the organization, and the motion wherein life consists, begin together, the motion coming from within; but in machines the force coming sensibly from without, is often away when the organ is in order, and well fitted to receive it.

7. This also shows wherein the identity of the same *man* consists; viz. in nothing but a participation of the same continued life, by constantly fleeting particles of matter, in succession vitally united to the same organized body. He that shall place the identity of man in anything else, but, like that of other animals, in one fitly organized body, taken in any one instant, and from thence continued, under one organization of life, in several successively fleeting particles of matter united to it, will find it hard to make an embryo, one of years, mad and sober, the *same* man, by any supposition, that will not make it possible for Seth, Ismael, Socrates, Pilate, St. Austin, and Cæsar Borgia, to be the same man. For if the identity of *soul alone* makes the same *man;* and there be nothing in the nature of matter why the same individual spirit may not be united to different bodies, it will be possible that those men, living in distant ages, and of different tempers, may have been the same man: which way of speaking must be from a very strange use of the word man, applied to an idea out of which body and shape are excluded. And that way of speaking would agree yet worse with the notions of those philosophers who allow of transmigration, and are of opinion that the souls of men may, for their miscarriages, be detruded into the bodies of beasts, as fit habitations, with organs suited to the satisfaction of their brutal inclinations. But yet I think nobody, could he be sure that the *soul* of Heliogabalus were in one of his hogs, would yet say that hog were a *man* or *Heliogabalus.*

8. It is not therefore unity of substance that comprehends all sorts of identity, or will determine it in every case; but to conceive and judge of it aright, we must consider what idea the word it is applied to stands for: it being one thing to be the same *substance,* another the same *man,* and a third the same *person,* if *person, man,* and *substance,* are three names standing for three different ideas;—for such as is the idea belonging to that name, such must be the identity; which, if it had been a little more carefully attended to, would possibly have prevented a great deal of that confusion which often occurs about this matter, with no small seeming difficulties, especially concerning *personal* identity, which therefore we shall in the next place a little consider.

9. An animal is a living organized body; and consequently the same animal, as we have observed, is the same continued *life* communicated to different particles of matter, as they happen successively to be united to that organized living body. And whatever is talked of other definitions, ingenious observation puts it past doubt, that the idea in our minds, of which the sound man in our mouths is the sign, is nothing else but of an animal of such a certain form. Since I think I may be confident, that, whoever should see a creature of his own shape or make, though it had no more reason all its life than a cat or a parrot, would call him still a *man;* or whoever should hear a cat or a parrot

discourse, reason, and philosophize, would call or think it nothing but a *cat* or a *parrot;* and say, the one was a dull irrational man, and the other a very intelligent rational parrot. A relation we have in an author of great note, is sufficient to countenance the supposition of a rational parrot. His words are:

'I had a mind to know, from Prince Maurice's own mouth, the account of a common, but much credited story, that I had heard so often from many others, of an old parrot he had in Brazil, during his government there, that spoke, and asked, and answered common questions, like a reasonable creature: so that those of his train there generally concluded it to be witchery or possession; and one of his chaplains, who lived long afterwards in Holland, would never from that time endure a parrot, but said they all had a devil in them. I had heard many particulars of this story, and assevered by people hard to be discredited, which made me ask Prince Maurice what there was of it. He said, with his usual plainness and dryness in talk, there was something true, but a great deal false of what had been reported. I desired to know of him what there was of the first. He told me short and coldly, that he had heard of such an old parrot when he had been at Brazil; and though he believed nothing of it, and it was a good way off, yet he had so much curiosity as to send for it: that it was a very great and a very old one; and when it came first into the room where the prince was, with a great many Dutchman about him, it said presently, *What a company of white men are here!* They asked it, what it thought that man was, pointing to the prince. It answered, *Some General or other.* When they brought it close to him, he asked it, *D'où venez-vous?* It answered, *De Marinnan.* The Prince, *À qui estes-vous?* The parrot, *À un Portugais.* The Prince, *Que fais-tu là?* Parrot, *Je garde les poulles.* The Prince laughed, and said, *Vous gardez les poulles?* The parrot answered, *Oui, moi; et je sçai bien faire;* and made the chuck four or five times that people use to make to chickens when they call them. I set down the words of this worthy dialogue in French, just as Prince Maurice said them to me. I asked him in what language the parrot spoke, and he said in Brazilian. I asked whether he understood Brazilian; he said No, but he had taken care to have two interpreters by him, the one a Dutchman that spoke Brazilian, and the other a Brazilian that spoke Dutch; that he asked them separately and privately, and both of them agreed in telling him just the same thing that the parrot had said. I could not but tell this odd story, because it is so much out of the way, and from the first hand, and what may pass for a good one; for I dare say this Prince at least believed himself in all he told me, having ever passed for a very honest and pious man: I leave it to naturalists to reason, and to other men to believe, as they please upon it; however, it is not, perhaps, amiss to relieve or enliven a busy scene sometimes with such digressions, whether to the purpose or no.'

10a. I have taken care that the reader should have the story at large in the author's own words, because he seems to me not to have thought it incredible; for it cannot be imagined that so able a man as he, who had sufficiency enough to warrant all the testimonies he gives of himself, should take so much pains, in a place where it had nothing to do, to pin so close, not only a man whom he mentions as his friend, but on a Prince in whom he acknowledges very great

honesty and piety, a story which, if he himself thought incredible, he could not but also think ridiculous. The Prince, it is plain, who vouches this story, and our author, who relates it from him, both of them call this talker a parrot: and I ask any one else who thinks such a story fit to be told, whether, if this parrot, and all of its kind, had always talked, as we have a prince's word for it this one did,—whether, I say, they would not have passed for a race of *rational animals;* but yet, whether, for all that, they would have been allowed to be men, and not *parrots?* For I presume it is not the idea of a thinking or rational being alone that makes the *idea of a man* in most people's sense: but of a body, so and so shaped, joined to it; and if that be the idea of a man, the same successive body not shifted all at once, must, as well as the same immaterial spirit, go to the making of the same man.*

11a. This being premised, to find wherein personal identity consists, we must consider what *person* stands for;—which, I think, is a thinking intelligent being, that has reason and reflection, and can consider itself as itself, the same thinking thing, in different times and places; which it does only by that consciousness which is inseparable from thinking, and, as it seems to me, essential to it: it being impossible for any one to perceive without *perceiving* that he does perceive. When we see, hear, smell, taste, feel, meditate, or will anything, we know that we do so. Thus it is always as to our present sensations and perceptions: and by this every one is to himself that which he calls *self:*—it not being considered, in this case, whether the same self be continued in the same or divers substances. For, since consciousness always accompanies thinking, and it is that which makes every one to be what he calls self, and thereby distinguishes himself from all other thinking things, in this alone consists personal identity, i.e. the sameness of a rational being: and as far as this consciousness† can be extended backwards to any past action or thought, so far reaches the identity of that person; it is the same self now it was then; and it is by the same self with this present one that now reflects on it, that that action was done.

10b. But it is further inquired, whether it be the same identical substance. This few would think they had reason to doubt of, if these perceptions, with their consciousness, always remained present in the mind, whereby the same thinking thing would be always consciously present, and, as would be thought, evidently the same to itself. But that which seems to make the difficulty is this, that this consciousness being interrupted always be forgetfulness, there being no moment of our lives wherein we have the whole train of all our past actions before our eyes in one view, but even the best memories losing the sight of one part whilst they are viewing another; and we sometimes, and that the greatest part of our lives, not reflecting on our past selves, being intent on our present thoughts, and in sound sleep having no thoughts at all, or at least none with

---

* This and the following three sections have been renumbered from the Campbell Fraser edition of Locke's, *Essay Concerning Human Understanding*. In that standard edition, our sections 10a and 10b are both numbered 10, while our 11a and 11b are both numbered 11.

† By "consciousness" Locke means memory.

that consciousness which remarks our waking thoughts,—I say, in all these cases, our consciousness being interrupted, and we losing the sight of our past selves, doubts are raised whether we are the same thinking thing, i.e. the same *substance* or no. Which, however reasonable or unreasonable, concerns not *personal* identity at all. The question being what makes the same person; and not whether it be the same identical substance, which always thinks in the same person, which, in this case, matters not at all: different substances, by the same consciousness (where they do partake in it) being united into one person, as well as different bodies by the same life are united into one animal, whose identity is preserved in that change of substances by the unity of one continued life. For, it being the same consciousness that makes a man be himself to himself, personal identity depends on that only, whether it be annexed solely to one individual substance, or can be continued in a succession of several substances. For as far as any intelligent being *can* repeat the idea of any past action with the same consciousness it had of it at first, and with the same consciousness it has of any present action; so far it is the same personal self. For it is by the consciousness it has of its present thoughts and actions, that it is *self to itself* now, and so will be the same self, as far as the same consciousness can extend to actions past or to come; and would be by distance of time, or change of substance, no more two persons, than a man be two men by wearing other clothes to-day than he did yesterday, with a long or a short sleep between: the same consciousness uniting those distant actions into the same person, whatever substances contributed to their production.

11b. That this is so, we have some kind of evidence in our very bodies, all whose particles, whilst vitally united to this same thinking conscious self, so that *we feel* when they are touched, and are affected by, and conscious of good or harm that happens to them, are a part of ourselves; i.e. of our thinking conscious self. Thus, the limbs of his body are to every one a part of himself; he sympathizes and is concerned for them. Cut off a hand, and thereby separate it from that consciousness he had of its heat, cold, and other affections, and it is then no longer a part of that which is himself, any more than the remotest part of matter. Thus, we see the *substance* whereof personal self consisted at one time may be varied at another, without the change of personal identity; there being no question about the same person, though the limbs which but now were a part of it, be cut off.

12. But the question is, Whether if the same substance which thinks be changed, it can be the same person; or, remaining the same, it can be different persons?

And to this I answer: First, This can be no question at all to those who place thought in a purely material animal constitution, void of an immaterial substance. For, whether their supposition be true or no, it is plain they conceive personal identity preserved in something else than identity of substance; as animal identity is preserved in identity of life, and not of substance. And therefore those who place thinking in an immaterial substance only, before they can come to deal with these men, must show why personal identity cannot be preserved in the change of immaterial substances, or variety of particular immaterial substances, as well as animal identity is preserved in the change of mate-

rial substances, or variety of particular bodies: unless they will say, it is one immaterial spirit that makes the same life in brutes, as it is one immaterial spirit that makes the same person in men; which the Cartesians at least will not admit, for fear of making brutes thinking things too.

13. But next, as to the first part of the question, Whether, if the same thinking substance (supposing immaterial substances only to think) be changed, it can be the same person? I answer, that cannot be resolved but by those who know what kind of substances they are that do think; and whether the consciousness of past actions can be transferred from one thinking substance to another. I grant were the same consciousness the same individual action it could not: but it being a present representation of a past action, why it may not be possible, that that may be represented to the mind to have been which really never was, will remain to be shown. And therefore how far the consciousness of past actions is annexed to any individual agent, so that another cannot possibly have it, will be hard for us to determine, till we know what kind of action it is that cannot be done without a reflex act of perception accompanying it, and how performed by thinking substances, who cannot think without being conscious of it. But that which we call the same consciousness, not being the same individual act, why one intellectual substance may not have represented to it, as done by itself, what *it* never did, and was perhaps done by some other agent—why, I say, such a representation may not possibly be without reality of matter of fact, as well as several representations in dreams are, which yet whilst dreaming we take for true—will be difficult to conclude from the nature of things. And that it never is so, will by us, till we have clearer views of the nature of thinking substances, be best resolved into the goodness of God; who, as far as the happiness or misery of any of his sensible creatures is concerned in it, will not, by a fatal error of theirs, transfer from one to another that consciousness which draws reward or punishment with it. How far this may be an argument against those who would place thinking in a system of fleeting animal spirits, I leave to be considered. But yet, to return to the question before us, it must be allowed, that, if the same consciousness (which, as has been shown, is quite a different thing from the same numerical figure or motion in body) can be transferred from one thinking substance to another, it will be possible that two thinking substances may make but one person. For the same consciousness being preserved, whether in the same or different substances, the personal identity is preserved.

14. As to the second part of the question, Whether the same immaterial substance remaining, there may be two distinct persons; which question seems to me to be built on this,—Whether the same immaterial being, being conscious of the action of its past duration, may be wholly stripped of all the consciousness of its past existence, and lose it beyond the power of ever retrieving it again: and so as it were beginning a new account from a new period, have a consciousness that *cannot* reach beyond this new state. All those who hold pre-existence are evidently of this mind; since they allow the soul to have no remaining consciousness of what it did in that pre-existent state, either wholly separate from body, or informing any other body; and if they should not, it is plain

experience would be against them. So that personal identity, reaching no further than consciousness reaches, a pre-existent spirit not having continued so many ages in a state of silence, must needs make different persons. Suppose a Christian Platonist or a Pythagorean should, upon God's having ended all his works of creation the seventh day, think his soul hath existed ever since; and should imagine it has revolved in several human bodies; as I once met with one, who was persuaded his had been the *soul* of Socrates (how reasonably I will not dispute; this I know, that in the post he filled, which was no inconsiderable one, he passed for a very rational man, and the press has shown that he wanted not parts or learning;)—would any one say, that he, being not conscious of any of Socrates's actions or thoughts, could be the same *person* with Socrates? Let any one reflect upon himself, and conclude that he has in himself an immaterial spirit, which is that which thinks in him, and, in the constant change of his body keeps him the same: and is that which he calls *himself:* let him also suppose it to be the same soul that was in Nestor or Thersites, at the siege of Troy, (for souls being, as far as we know anything of them, in their nature indifferent to any parcel of matter, the supposition has no apparent absurdity in it,) which it may have been, as well as it is now the soul of any other man: but he now having no consciousness of any of the actions either of Nestor or Thersites, does or can he conceive himself the same person with either of them? Can he be concerned in either of their actions? attribute them to himself, or think them his own, more than the actions of any other men that ever existed? So that this consciousness, not reaching to any of the actions of either of those men, he is no more one *self* with either of them than if the soul or immaterial spirit that now informs him had been created, and began to exist, when it began to inform his present body; though it were never so true, that the same *spirit* that informed Nestor's or Thersites' body were numerically the same that now informs his. For this would no more make him the same person with Nestor, than if some of the particles of matter that were once a part of Nestor were now a part of this man; the same immaterial substance, without the same consciousness, no more making the same person, by being united to any body, than the same particle of matter, without consciousness, united to any body, makes the same person. But let him once find himself conscious of any of the actions of Nestor, he then finds himself the same person with Nestor.

15. And thus may we be able, without any difficulty, to conceive the same person at the resurrection, though in a body not exactly in make or parts the same which he had here,—the same consciousness going along with the soul that inhabits it. But yet the soul alone, in the change of bodies, would scarce to any one but to him that makes the soul the man, be enough to make the same man. For should the soul of a prince, carrying with it the consciousness of the prince's past life, enter and inform the body of a cobbler, as soon as deserted by his own soul, every one sees he would be the same *person* with the prince, accountable only for the prince's actions: but who would say it was the same *man?* The body too goes to the making the man, and would, I guess, to everybody determine the man in this case, wherein the soul, with all its princely thoughts about it, would not make another man: but he would be the same

cobbler to every one besides himself. I know that, in the ordinary way of speaking, the same person, and the same man, stand for one and the same thing. And indeed every one will always have a liberty to speak as he pleases, and to apply what articulate sounds to what ideas he thinks fit, and change them as often as he pleases. But yet, when we will inquire what makes the same *spirit, man,* or *person,* we must fix the ideas of spirit, man, or person in our minds; and having resolved with ourselves what we mean by them, it will not be hard to determine, in either of them, or the like, when it is the same, and when not.

16. But though the same immaterial substance or soul does not alone, wherever it be, and in whatsoever state, make the same *man;* yet it is plain, consciousness, as far as ever it can be extended—should it be to ages past—unites existences and actions very remote in time into the same *person,* as well as it does the existences and actions of the immediately preceding moment: so that whatever has the consciousness of present and past actions, is the same person to whom they both belong. Had I the same consciousness that I saw the ark and Noah's flood, as that I saw an overflowing of the Thames last winter, or as that I write now, I could no more doubt that I who write this now, that saw the Thames overflowed last winter, and that viewed the flood at the general deluge, was the same *self,*—place that self in what *substance* you please—than that I who write this am the same *myself* now whilst I write (whether I consist of all the same substance, material or immaterial, or no) that I was yesterday. For as to this point of being the same self, it matters not whether this present self be made up of the same or other substances—I being as much concerned, and as justly accountable for any action that was done a thousand years since, appropriated to me now by this self-consciousness, as I am for what I did the last moment.

17. *Self* is that conscious thinking thing,—whatever substance made up of, (whether spiritual or material, simple or compounded, it matters not)—which is sensible or conscious of pleasure and pain, capable of happinesss or misery, and so is concerned for itself, as far as that consciousness extends. Thus every one finds that, whilst comprehended under that consciousness, the little finger is as much a part of himself as what is most so. Upon separation of this little finger, should this consciousness go along with the little finger, and leave the rest of the body, it is evident the little finger would be the person, the same person; and self then would have nothing to do with the rest of the body. As in this case it is the consciousness that goes along with the substance, when one part is separate from another, which makes the same person, and constitutes this inseparable self: so it is in reference to substances remote in time. That with which the consciousness of this present thinking thing *can* join itself, makes the same person, and is one self with it, and with nothing else; and so attributes to itself, and owns all the actions of that thing, as its own, as far as that consciousness reaches, and no further; as every one who reflects will perceive.

18. In this personal identity is founded all the right and justice of reward and punishment; happiness and misery being that for which every one is concerned for *himself,* and not mattering what becomes of any *substance,* not

joined to, or affected with that consciousness. For, as it is evident in the instance I gave but now, if the consciousness went along with the little finger when it was cut off, that would be the same self which was concerned for the whole body yesterday, as making part of itself, whose actions then it cannot but admit as its own now. Though, if the same body should still live, and immediately from the separation of the little finger have its own peculiar consciousness, whereof the little finger knew nothing, it would not at all be concerned for it, as a part of itself, or could own any of its actions, or have any of them imputed to him.

19. This may show us wherein personal identity consists: not in the identity of substance, but, as I have said, in the identity of consciousness, wherein if Socrates and the present mayor of Queinborough agree, they are the same person: if the same Socrates waking and sleeping do not partake of the same consciousness, Socrates waking and sleeping is not the same person. And to punish Socrates waking for what sleeping Socrates thought, and waking Socrates was never conscious of, would be no more of right, than to punish one twin for what his brother-twin did, whereof he knew nothing, because their outsides were so like, that they could not be distinguished; for such twins have been seen.

20. But yet possibly it will still be objected,—Suppose I wholly lose the memory of some parts of my life, beyond a possibility of retrieving them, so that perhaps I shall never be conscious of them again; yet am I not the same person that did those actions, had those thoughts that I once was conscious of, though I have now forgot them? To which I answer, that we must here take notice what the word *I* is applied to; which, in this case, is the *man* only. And the same man being presumed to be the same person, I is easily here supposed to stand also for the same person. But if it be possible for the same man to have distinct incommunicable consciousness at different times, it is past doubt the same man would at different times make different persons; which, we see, is the sense of mankind in the solomnest declaration of their opinions, human laws not punishing the mad man for the sober man's actions, nor the sober man for what the mad man did,—thereby making them two persons: which is somewhat explained by our way of speaking in English when we say such an one is 'not himself,' or is 'beside himself'; in which phrases it is insinuated, as if those who now, or at least first used them, thought that self was changed; the self-same person was no longer in that man.

21. But yet it is hard to conceive that Socrates, the same individual man, should be two persons. To help us a little in this, we must consider what is meant by Socrates, or the same individual *man*.

First, it must be either the same individual, immaterial, thinking substance; in short, the same numerical soul, and nothing else.

Secondly, or the same animal, without any regard to an immaterial soul.

Thirdly, or the same immaterial spirit united to the same animal.

Now, take which of these suppositions you please, it is impossible to make personal identity to consist in anything but consciousness; or reach any further than that does.

For, by the first of them, it must be allowed possible that a man born of different women, and in distant times, may be the same man. A way of speaking which, whoever admits, must allow it possible for the same man to be two distinct persons, as any two that have lived in different ages without the knowledge of one another's thoughts.

By the second and third, Socrates, in this life and after it, cannot be the same man any way, but by the same consciousness; and so making human identity to consist in the same thing wherein we place personal identity, there will be no difficulty to allow the same man to be the same person. But then they who place human identity in consciousness only, and not in something else, must consider how they will make the infant Socrates the same man with Socrates after the resurrection. But whatsoever to some men makes a man, and consequently the same individual man, wherein perhaps few are agreed, personal identity can by us be placed in nothing but consciousness, (which is that alone which makes what we call *self*,) without involving us in great absurdities.

22. But is not a man drunk and sober the same person? why else is he punished for the fact he commits when drunk, though he be never afterwards conscious of it? Just as much the same person as a man that walks, and does other things in his sleep, is the same person, and is answerable for any mischief he shall do in it. Human laws punish both, with a justice suitable to *their* way of knowledge;—because, in these cases, they cannot distinguish certainly what is real, what counterfeit: and so the ignorance in drunkenness or sleep is not admitted as a plea. For, though punishment be annexed to personality, and personality to consciousness, and the drunkard perhaps be not conscious of what he did, yet human judicatures justly punish him; because the fact is proved against him, but want of consciousness cannot be proved for him. But in the Great Day, wherein the secrets of all hearts shall be laid open, it may be reasonable to think, no one shall be made to answer for what he knows nothing of; but shall receive his doom, his conscience accusing or excusing him.

23. Nothing but consciousness can unite remote existences into the same person: the identity of substance will not do it; for whatever substance there is, however framed, without consciousness there is no person: and a carcass may be a person, as well as any sort of substance be so, without consciousness.

Could we suppose two distinct incommunicable consciousnesses acting the same body, the one constantly by day, the other by night; and, on the other side, the same consciousness, acting by intervals, two distinct bodies: I ask, in the first case, whether the day and the night—man would not be two as distinct persons as Socrates and Plato? And whether, in the second case, there would not be one person in two distinct bodies, as much as one man is the same in two distinct clothings? Nor is it at all material to say, that this same, and this distinct consciousness, in the cases above mentioned, is owing to the same and distinct immaterial substances, bringing it with them to those bodies; which, whether true or no, alters not the case: since it is evident the personal identity would equally be determined by the consciousness, whether that consciousness were annexed to some individual immaterial substance or no. For, granting that the thinking substance in man must be necessarily supposed immaterial,

it is evident that immaterial thinking thing may sometimes part with its past consciousness, and be restored to it again: as appears in the forgetfulness men often have of their past actions; and the mind many times recovers the memory of a past consciousness, which it had lost for twenty years together. Make these intervals of memory and forgetfulness to take their turns regularly by day and night, and you have two persons with the same immaterial spirit, as much as in the former instance two persons with the same body. So that self is not determined by identity or diversity of substance, which it cannot be sure of, but only by identity of consciousness.

24. Indeed it may conceive the substance whereof it is now made up to have existed formerly, united in the same conscious being: but, consciousness removed, that substance is no more itself, or makes no more a part of it, than any other substance; as is evident in the instance we have already given of a limb cut off, of whose heat, or cold, or other affections, having no longer any consciousness, it is no more of a man's self than any other matter of the universe. In like manner it will be in reference to any immaterial substance, which is void of that consciousness whereby I am myself to myself: [if there be any part of its existence which] I cannot upon recollection join with that present consciousness whereby I am now myself, it is, in that part of its existence, no more *myself* than any other immaterial being. For, whatsoever any substance has thought or done, which I cannot recollect, and by my consciousness make my own thought and action, it will no more belong to me, whether a part of me thought or did it, than if it had been thought or done by any other immaterial being anywhere existing.

25. I agree, the more probable opinion is, that this consciousness is annexed to, and the affection of, one individual immaterial substance.

But let men, according to their diverse hypotheses, resolve of that as they please. This every intelligent being, sensible of happiness or misery, must grant— that there is something that is *himself,* that he is concerned for, and would have happy; that this self has existed in a continued duration more than one instant, and therefore it is possible may exist, as it has done, months and years to come, without any certain bounds to be set to its duration; and may be the same self, by the same consciousness continued on for the future. And thus, by this consciousness he finds himself to be the same self which did such and such an action some years since, by which he comes to be happy or miserable now. In all which account of self, the same numerical *substance* is not considered as making the same self; but the same continued *consciousness,* in which several substances may have been united, and again separated from it, which, whilst they continued in a vital union with that wherein this consciousness then resided, made a part of that same self. Thus any part of our bodies, vitally united to that which is conscious in us, makes a part of ourselves: but upon separation from the vital union by which that consciousness is communicated, that which a moment since was part of ourselves, is now no more so than a part of another man's self is a part of me: and it is not impossible but in a little time may become a real part of another person. And so we have the same numerical substance become a part of two different persons; and the same person pre-

served under the change of various substances. Could we suppose any spirit wholly stripped of all its memory or consciousness of past actions, as we find our minds always are of a great part of ours, and sometimes of them all; the union or separation of such a spiritual substance would make no variation of personal identity, any more than that of any particle of matter does. Any substance vitally united to the present thinking being is a part of that very same self which now is; anything united to it by a consciousness of former actions, makes also a part of the same self, which is the same both then and now.

26. *Person*, as I take it, is the name for this self. Wherever a man finds what he calls himself, there, I think, another may say is the same person. It is a forensic term, appropriating actions and their merit; and so belongs only to intelligent agents, capable of a law, and happiness, and misery. This personality extends itself beyond present existence to what is past, only by consciousness,—whereby it becomes concerned and accountable; owns and imputes to itself past actions, just upon the same ground and for the same reason as it does the present. All which is founded in a concern for happiness, the unavoidable concomitant of consciousness; that which is conscious of pleasure and pain, desiring that that self that is conscious should be happy. And therefore whatever past actions it cannot reconcile or *appropriate* to that present self by consciousness, it can be no more concerned in than if they had never been done: and to receive pleasure or pain, i.e. reward or punishment, on the account of any such action, is all one as to be made happy or miserable in its first being, without any demerit at all. For, supposing a *man* punished now for what he had done in another life, whereof he could be made to have no consciousness at all, what difference is there between that punishment and being *created* miserable? And therefore, conformable to this, the apostle tells us, that, at the great day, when every one shall 'receive according to his doings, the secrets of all hearts shall be laid open.' The sentence shall be justified by the consciousness all persons shall have, that *they themselves,* in what bodies soever they appear, or what substances soever that consciousness adheres to, are the *same* that committed those actions, and deserve that punishment for them.

27. I am apt enough to think I have, in treating of this subject, made some suppositions that will look strange to some readers, and possibly they are so in themselves. But yet, I think they are such as are pardonable, in this ignorance we are in of the nature of that thinking thing that is in us, and which we look on as *ourselves*. Did we know what it was; or how it was tied to a certain system of fleeting animal spirits; or whether it could or could not perform its operations of thinking and memory out of a body organized as ours is; and whether it has pleased God that no one such spirit shall ever be united to any but one such body, upon the right constitution of whose organs its memory should depend; we might see the absurdity of some of those suppositions I have made. But taking, as we ordinarily now do (in the dark concerning these matters,) the soul of a man for an immaterial substance, independent from matter, and indifferent alike to it all; there can, from the nature of things, be no absurdity at all to suppose that the same *soul* may at different times be united to different *bodies,* and with them make up for that time one *man:* as

well as we suppose a part of a sheep's body yesterday should be a part of a man's body to-morrow, and in that union make a vital part of Melibœus himself, as well as it did of his ram.

28. To conclude: Whatever substance begins to exist, it must, during its existence, necessarily be the same: whatever compositions of substances begin to exist, during the union of those substances, the concrete must be the same: whatsoever mode begins to exist, during its existence it is the same: and so if the composition be of distinct substances and different modes, the same rule holds. Whereby it will appear, that the difficulty or obscurity that has been about this matter rather rises from the names ill-used, than from any obscurity in things themselves. For whatever makes the specific idea to which the name is applied, if that idea be steadily kept to, the distinction of anything into the same and divers will easily be conceived, and there can arise no doubt about it.

29. For, supposing a rational spirit be the idea of a *man,* it is easy to know what is the same man, viz. the same spirit—whether separate or in a body— will be the *same man.* Supposing a rational spirit vitally united to a body of a certain conformation of parts to make a man; whilst that rational spirit, with that vital conformation of parts, though continued in a fleeting successive body, remains, it will be the *same man.* But if to any one the idea of a man be but the vital union of parts in a certain shape; as long as that vital union and shape remain in a concrete, no otherwise the same but by a continued succession of fleeting particles, it will be the *same man.* For, whatever be the composition whereof the complex idea is made, whenever existence makes it one particular thing under any denomination, *the same existence continued* preserves it the *same* individual under the same denomination.

39

The Self and the Future

BERNARD WILLIAMS

Bernard Williams (b. 1929) is Knightbridge Professor of Philosophy at the University of Cambridge. He has made important contributions to ethics and the philosophy of mind. Two collections of his papers are entitled Problems of the Self *and* Moral Luck.

In this essay from Problems of the Self, *Williams suggests there may be something wrong both with Locke's conclusions about personal identity (reading 38) and with the type of argument he uses to support his conclusion. By reflecting on imaginary cases wherein people appear to switch bodies, lose their memories, and so forth, Locke tries to marshall a case for the view that continuity of memory is the crucial factor in the preservation of personal identity. Williams tries to weaken our confidence in this type of argument by presenting two different descriptions of what he considers to be the same imaginary case. Given one description, we are inclined to conclude that mental factors are crucial to personal identity; given the other, we are likely to conclude that bodily factors are more important than mental factors in our continuing identities as persons. Williams concludes that if the method of appealing to imaginary cases produces such unstable results, then it is probably not a satisfactory method for resolving the question of personal identity.*

SUPPOSE THAT THERE WERE some process to which two persons, *A* and *B*, could be subjected as a result of which they might be said—question-beggingly—to have *exchanged bodies.* That is to say—less question-beggingly—there is a certain human body which is such that when previously we were confronted with it, we were confronted with person *A*, certain utterances coming from it were expressive of memories of the past experiences of *A*, certain movements of it partly constituted the actions of *A* and were taken as expressive of the character of *A*, and so forth; but now, after the process is completed, utterances coming from this body are expressive of what seem to be just those memories which previously we identified as memories of the past experiences of *B*, its movements partly constitute actions expressive of the character of *B*, and so forth; and conversely with the other body.

There are certain important philosophical limitations on how such imaginary cases are to be constructed, and how they are to be taken when constructed in various ways. I shall mention two principal limitations, not in order to pursue them further here, but precisely in order to get them out of the way.

There are certain limitations, particularly with regard to character and mannerisms, to our ability to imagine such cases even in the most restricted sense of our being disposed to take the later performances of that body which was previously A's as expressive of B's character; if the previous A and B were extremely unlike one another both physically and psychologically, and if, say, in addition, they were of different sex, there might be grave difficulties in reading B's dispositions in any possible performances of A's body. Let us forget this, and for the present purpose just take A and B as being sufficiently alike (however alike that has to be) for the difficulty not to arise; after the experiment, persons familiar with A and B are just *overwhelmingly struck* by the B-ish character of the doings associated with what was previously A's body, and conversely. Thus the feat of imagining an exchange of bodies is supposed possible in the most restricted sense. But now there is a further limitation which has to be overcome if the feat is to be not merely possible in the most restricted sense but also is to have an outcome which, on serious reflection, we are prepared to describe as A and B having changed bodies—that is, an outcome where, confronted with what was previously A's body, we are prepared seriously to say that we are now confronted with B.

It would seem a necessary condition of so doing that the utterances coming from that body be taken as genuinely expressive of memories of B's past. But memory is a causal notion; and as we actually use it, it seems a necessary condition of x's present knowledge of x's earlier experiences constituting memory of those experiences that the causal chain linking the experiences and the knowledge should not run outside x's body. Hence if utterances coming from a given body are to be taken as expressive of memories of the experiences of B, there should be some suitable causal link between the appropriate state of that body and the original happening of those experiences to B. One radical way of securing that condition in the imagined exchange case is to suppose, with Shoemaker,[1] that the brains of A and of B are transposed. We may not need so radical a condition. Thus suppose it were possible to extract information from a man's brain and store it in a device while his brain was repaired, or even renewed, the information then being replaced; it would seem exaggerated to insist that the resultant man could not possibly have the memories he had before the operation. With regard to our knowledge of our own past, we draw distinctions between merely recalling, being reminded, and learning again, and those distinctions correspond (roughly) to distinctions between no new input, partial new input, and total new input with regard to the information in question; and it seems clear that the information-parking case just imagined would not count as new input in the sense necessary and sufficient for 'learning again'. Hence we can imagine the case we are concerned with in terms of information extracted into such devices from A's and B's brains and replaced in the other brain; this is the sort of model which, I think not unfairly for the present argument, I shall have in mind.

---

[1] *Self-Knowledge and Self-Identity* (Ithaca, N.Y., 1963), pp. 23 seq.

We imagine the following. The process considered above exists; two persons can enter some machine, let us say, and emerge changed in the appropriate ways. If A and B are the persons who enter, let us call the persons who emerge the *A-body-person* and the *B-body-person:* the A-body-person is that person (whoever it is) with whom I am confronted when, after the experiment, I am confronted with that body which previously was A's body—that is to say, that person who would naturally be taken for A by someone who just saw this person, was familiar with A's appearance before the experiment, and did not know about the happening of the experiment. A non-question-begging description of the experiment will leave it open which (if either) of the persons A and B the A-body-person is; the description of the experiment as 'persons changing bodies' of course implies that the A-body-person is actually B.

We take two persons A and B who are going to have the process carried out on them. (We can suppose, rather hazily, that they are willing for this to happen; to investigate at all closely at this stage why they might be willing or unwilling, what they would fear, and so forth, would anticipate some later issues.) We further announce that one of the two resultant persons, the A-body-person and the B-body-person, is going after the experiment to be given $100,000, while the other is going to be tortured. We then ask each of A and B to choose which treatment should be dealt out to which of the persons who will emerge from the experiment, the choice to be made (if it can be) on selfish grounds.

Suppose that A chooses that the B-body-person should get the pleasant treatment and the A-body-person the unpleasant treatment; and B chooses conversely (this might indicate that they thought that 'changing bodies' was indeed a good description of the outcome). The experimenter cannot act in accordance with both these sets of preferences, those expressed by A and those expressed by B. Hence there is one clear sense in which A and B cannot both get what they want: namely, that if the experimenter, before the experiment, announces to A and B that he intends to carry out the alternative (for example), of treating the B-body-person unpleasantly and the A-body-person pleasantly—then A can say rightly, 'That's not the outcome I chose to happen', and B can say rightly, 'That's just the outcome I chose to happen'. So, evidently, A and B before the experiment can each come to know either that the outcome he chose will be that which will happen, or that the one he chose will not happen, and in that sense they can get or fail to get what they wanted. But is it also true that when the experimenter proceeds after the experiment to act in accordance with one of the preferences and not the other, *then* one of A and B will have got what he wanted, and the other not?

There seems very good ground for saying so. For suppose the experimenter, having elicited A's and B's perference, says nothing to A and B about what he will do; conducts the experiment; and then, for example, gives the unpleasant treatment to the B-body-person and the pleasant treatment to the A-body-person. Then the B-body-person will not only complain of the unpleasant treatment as such, but will complain (since he has A's memories) that that was not the outcome he chose, since he chose that the B-body-person should be well treated; and since A made his choice in selfish spirit, he may add that he

precisely chose in that way because he did not want the unpleasant things to happen to *him*. The A-body-person meanwhile will express satisfaction both at the receipt of the $100,000, and also at the fact that the experimenter has chosen to act in the way that he, *B*, so wisely chose. These facts make a strong case for saying that the experimenter has brought it about that *B* did in the outcome get what he wanted and *A* did not. It is therefore a strong case for saying that the *B*-body-person really is *A*, and the *A*-body-person really is *B*; and therefore for saying that the process of the experiment really is that of changing bodies. For the same reasons it would seem that *A* and *B* in our example really did choose wisely, and that it was *A*'s bad luck that the choice he correctly made was not carried out, *B*'s good luck that the choice he correctly made was carried out. This seems to show that to care about what happens to me in the future is not necessarily to care about what happens to *this* body (the one I now have); and this in turn might be taken to show that in some sense of Descartes's obscure phrase, I and my body are 'really distinct' (though, of course, nothing in these considerations could support the idea that I could exist without a body at all).

These suggestions seems to be reinforced if we consider the cases where *A* and *B* make other choices with regard to the experiment. Suppose that *A* chooses that the *A*-body-person should get the money, and the *B*-body-person get the pain, and *B* chooses conversely. Here again there can be no outcome which matches the expressed preferences of both of them: they cannot both get what they want. The experimenter announces, before the experiment, that the *A*-body-person will in fact get the money, and the *B*-body-person will get the pain. So *A* at this stage gets what he wants (the announced outcome matches his expressed preference). After the experiment, the distribution is carried out as announced. Both the *A*-body-person and the *B*-body-person will have to agree that what is happening is in accordance with the preference that *A* originally expressed. The *B*-body-person will naturally express this acknowledgement (since he has *A*'s memories) by saying that this is the distribution he chose; he will recall, among other things, the experimenter announcing this outcome, his approving it as what he chose, and so forth. However, he (the *B*-body-person) certainly does not like what is now happening to him, and would much prefer to be receiving what the *A*-body-person is receiving—namely, $100,000. The *A*-body-person will on the other hand recall choosing an outcome other than this one, but will reckon it good luck that the experimenter did not do what he recalls choosing. It looks, then, as though the *A*-body-person has got what he wanted, but not what he chose, while the *B*-body-person has got what he chose, but not what he wanted. So once more it looks as though they are, respectively, *B* and *A*; and that in this case the original choices of both *A* and *B* were unwise.

Suppose, lastly, that in the original choice *A* takes the line of the first case and *B* of the second: that is, *A* chooses that the *B*-body-person should get the money and the *A*-body-person the pain, and *B* chooses exactly the same thing. In this case, the experimenter would seem to be in the happy situation of giving both persons what they want—or at least, like God, what they have chosen.

In this case, the *B*-body-person likes what he is receiving, recalls choosing it, and congratulates himself on the wisdom of (as he puts it) his choice; while the *A*-body-person does not like what he is receiving, recalls choosing it, and is forced to acknowledge that (as he puts it) his choice was unwise. So once more we seem to get results to support the suggestions drawn from the first case.

. . .

Let us now consider something apparently different. Someone in whose power I am tells me that I am going to be tortured tomorrow. I am frightened, and look forward to tomorrow in great apprehension. He adds that when the time comes, I shall not remember being told that this was going to happen to me, since shortly before the torture something else will be done to me which will make me forget the announcement. This certainly will not cheer me up, since I know perfectly well that I can forget things, and that there is such a thing as indeed being tortured unexpectedly because I had forgotten or been made to forget a prediction of the torture: that will still be a torture which, so long as I do know about the prediction, I look forward to in fear. He then adds that my forgetting the announcement will be only part of a larger process: when the moment of torture comes, I shall not remember any of the things I am now in a position to remember. This does not cheer me up, either, since I can readily conceive of being involved in an accident, for instance, as a result of which I wake up in a completely amnesiac state and also in great pain; that could certainly happen to me, I should not like it to happen to me, nor to know that it was going to happen to me. He now further adds that at the moment of torture I shall not only not remember the things I am now in a position to remember, but will have a different set of impressions of my past, quite different from the memories I now have. I do not think that this would cheer me up, either. For I can at least conceive the possibility, if not the concrete reality, of going completely mad, and thinking perhaps that I am George IV or somebody; and being told that something like that was going to happen to me would have no tendency to reduce the terror of being told authoritatively that I was going to be tortured, but would merely compound the horror. Nor do I see why I should be put into any better frame of mind by the person in charge adding lastly that the impressions of my past with which I shall be equipped on the eve of torture will exactly fit the past of another person now living, and that indeed I shall acquire these impressions by (for instance) information now in his brain being copied into mine. Fear, surely, would still be the proper reaction: and not because one did not know what was going to happen, but because in one vital respect at least one did know what was going to happen—torture, which one can indeed expect to happen to oneself, and to be preceded by certain mental derangements as well.

If this is right, the whole question seems now to be totally mysterious. For what we have just been through is of course merely one side, differently represented, of the transaction which we considered before; and it represents it as a perfectly hateful prospect, while the previous considerations represented it as something one should rationally, perhaps even cheerfully, choose out of the

options there presented. It is differently presented, of course, and in two notable respects; but when we look at these two differences of presentation, can we really convince ourselves that the second presentation is wrong or misleading, thus leaving the road open to the first version which at the time seemed so convincing? Surely not.

The first difference is that in the second version the torture is throughout represented as going to happen to *me:* 'you', the man in charge persistently says. Thus he is not very neutral. But should he have been neutral? Or, to put it another way, does his use of the second person have a merely emotional and rhetorical effect on me, making me afraid when further reflection would have shown that I had no reason to be? It is certainly not obviously so. The problem just is that through every step of his predictions I seem to be able to follow him successfully. And if I reflect on whether what he has said gives me grounds for fearing that I shall be tortured, I could consider that behind my fears lies some principle such as this: that my undergoing physical pain in the future is not excluded by any psychological state I may be in at the time, with the platitudinous exception of those psychological states which in themselves exclude experiencing pain, notably (if it is a psychological state) unconsciousness. In particular, what impressions I have about the past will not have any effect on whether I undergo the pain or not. This principle seems sound enough.

. . .

I said that there were two notable differences between the second presentation of our situation and the first. The first difference, which we have just said something about, was that the man predicted the torture for *me,* a psychologically very changed 'me'. We have yet to find a reason for saying that he should not have done this, or that I really should be unable to follow him if he does; I seem to be able to follow him only too well. The second difference is that in this presentation he does not mention the other man, except in the somewhat incidental rôle of being the provenance of the impressions of the past I end up with. He does not mention him at all as someone who will end up with impressions of the past derived from me (and, incidentally, with $100,000 as well— a consideration which, in the frame of mind appropriate to this version, will merely make me jealous).

But why *should* he mention this man and what is going to happen to him? My selfish concern is to be told what is going to happen to me, and now I know: torture, preceded by changes of character, brain operations, changes in impressions of the past. The knowledge that one other person, or none, or many will be similarly mistreated may affect me in other ways, of sympathy, greater horror at the power of this tyrant, and so forth; but surely it cannot affect my expectations of torture? But—someone will say—this is to leave out exactly the feature which, as the first presentation of the case showed, makes all the difference: for it is to leave out the person who, as the first presentation showed, will be you. It is to leave out not merely a feature which should fundamentally affect your fears, it is to leave out the very person for whom you are fearful. So of course, the objector will say, this makes all the difference.

But can it? Consider the following series of cases. In each case we are to suppose that after what is described, A is, as before, to be tortured; we are also to suppose the person A is informed beforehand that just these things followed by the torture will happen to him:

(i) A is subjected to an operation which produces total amnesia;

(ii) amnesia is produced in A, and other interference leads to certain changes in his character;

(iii) changes in his character are produced, and at the same time certain illusory 'memory' beliefs are induced in him: these are of a quite fictitious kind and do not fit the life of any actual person;

(iv) the same as (iii), except that both the character traits and the 'memory' impressions are designed to be appropriate to another actual person, B;

(v) the same as (iv), except that the result is produced by putting the information into A from the brain of B, by a method which leaves B the same as he was before;

(vi) the same happens to A as in (v), but B is not left the same, since a similar operation is conducted in the reverse direction.

I take it that no-one is going to dispute that A has reasons, and fairly straightforward reasons, for fear of pain when the prospect is that of situation (i); there seems no conceivable reason why this should not extend to situation (ii), and the situation (iii) can surely introduce no difference of principle—it just seems a situation which for more than one reason we should have grounds for fearing, as suggested above. Situation (iv) at least introduces the person B, who was the focus of the objection we are now discussing. But it does not seem to introduce him in any way which makes a material difference; if I can expect pain through a transformation which involves new 'memory'-impressions, it would seem a purely external fact, relative to that, that the 'memory'-impressions had a model. Nor, in (iv), do we satisfy a causal condition which I mentioned at the beginning for the 'memories' actually being memories; though notice that if the job were done thoroughly, I might well be able to elicit from the A-body-person the kinds of remarks about his previous expectations of the experiment—remarks appropriate to the original B—which so impressed us in the first version of the story. I shall have a similar assurance of this being so in situation (v), where, moreover, a plausible application of the causal condition is available.

But two things are to be noticed about this situation. First, if we concentrate on A and the A-body-person, we do not seem to have added anything which from the point of view of his fears makes any material difference; just as, in the move from (iii) to (iv), it made no relevant difference that the new 'memory'-impressions which precede the pain had, as it happened, a model, so in the move from (iv) to (v) all we have added is that they have a model which is also their cause; and it is still difficult to see why that, to him looking forward, could possibly make the difference between expecting pain and not expecting pain. To illustrate that point from the case of character: if A is capable of

expecting pain, he is capable of expecting pain preceded by a change in his dispositions—and to that expectation it can make no difference, whether that change in his dispositions is modelled on, or indeed indirectly caused by, the dispositions of some other person. If his fears can, as it were, reach through the change, it seems a mere trimming how the change is in fact induced. The second point about situation (v) is that if the crucial question for A's fears with regard to what befalls the A-body-person is whether the A-body-person is or is not the person B, then that condition has not yet been satisfied in situation (v): for there we have an undisputed B in addition to the A-body-person, and certainly those two are not the same person.

But in situation (vi), we seemed to think, that is finally what he is. But if A's original fears could reach through the expected changes in (v), as they did in (iv) and (iii), then certainly they can reach through in (vi). Indeed, from the point of view of A's expectations and fears, there is less difference between (vi) and (v) than there is between (v) and (iv) or between (iv) and (iii). In those transitions, there were at least differences—though we could not see that they were really relevant differences—in the content or cause of what happened to him; in the present case there is absolutely no difference at all in what happens to him, the only difference being in what happens to someone else. If he can fear pain when (v) is predicted, why should he cease to when (vi) is?

I can see only one way of relevantly laying great weight on the transition from (v) to (vi); and this involves a considerable difficulty. This is to deny that, as I put it, the transition from (v) to (vi) involves merely the addition of some-thing happening to *somebody else;* what rather it does, it will be said, is to involve the reintroduction of A himself, as the B-body-person; since he has reappeared in this form, it is for this person, and not for the unfortunate A-body-person, that A will have his expectations. This is to reassert, in effect, the viewpoint emphasised in our first presentation of the experiment. But this surely has the consequence that A should not have fears for the A-body-person who appeared in situation (v). For by the present argument, the A-body-person in (vi) is not A; the B-body-person is. But the A-body-person in (v) is, in character, history, everything, exactly the same as the A-body-person in (vi); so if the latter is not A, then neither is the former. (It is this point, no doubt, that encourages one to speak of the difference that goes with (vi) as being, on the present view, the *reintroduction* of A.) But no-one else in (v) has any better claim to be A. So in (v), it seems, A just does not exist. This would certainly explain why A should have no fears for the state of things in (v)—though he might well have fears for the path to it. But it rather looked earlier as though he could well have fears for the state of things in (v). Let us grant, however, that that was an illusion, and that A really does not exist in (v); then does he exist in (iv), (iii), (ii), or (i)? It seems very difficult to deny it for (i) and (ii); are we perhaps to draw the line between (iii) and (iv)?

Here someone will say: you must not insist on drawing a line—borderline cases are borderline cases, and you must not push our concepts beyond their limits. But this well-known piece of advice, sensible as it is in many cases, seems in the present case to involve an extraordinary difficulty. It may intellectually

comfort observers of A's situation; but what is A supposed to make of it? To be told that a future situation is a borderline one for its being myself that is hurt, that it is conceptually undecidable whether it will be me or not, is something which, it seems, I can do nothing with; because, in particular, it seems to have no comprehensible representation in my expectations and the emotions that go with them.

If I expect that a certain situation, S, will come about in the future, there is of course a wide range of emotions and concerns, directed on S, which I may experience now in relation to my expectation. Unless I am exceptionally egoistic, it is not a condition on my being concerned in relation to this expectation, that I myself will be involved in S—where my being 'involved' in S means that I figure in S as someone doing something at that time or having something done to me, or, again, that S will have consequences affecting me at that or some subsequent time. There are some emotions, however, which I will feel only if I will be involved in S, and fear is an obvious example.

Now the description of S under which it figures in my expectations will necessarily be, in various ways, indeterminate; and one way in which it may be indeterminate is that it leaves open whether I shall be involved in S or not. Thus I may have good reason to expect that one of us five is going to get hurt, but no reason to expect it to be me rather than one of the others. My present emotions will be correspondingly affected by this indeterminacy. Thus, sticking to the egoistic concern involved in fear, I shall presumably be somewhat more cheerful than if I knew it was going to be me, somewhat less cheerful than if I had been left out altogether. Fear will be mixed with, and qualified by, apprehension; and so forth. These emotions revolve around the thought of the eventual determination of the indeterminacy; moments of straight fear focus on its really turning out to be me, of hope on its turning out not to be me. All the emotions are related to the coming about of what I expect; and what I expect in such a case just cannot come about save by coming about in one of the ways or another.

There are other ways in which indeterminate expectations can be related to fear. Thus I may expect (perhaps neurotically) that something nasty is going to happen to me, indeed expect that when it happens it will take some determinate form, but have no range, or no closed range, of candidates for the determinate form to rehearse in my present thought. Different from this would be the fear of something radically indeterminate—the fear (one might say) of a nameless horror. If somebody had such a fear, one could even say that he had, in a sense, a perfectly determinate expectation: if what he expects indeed comes about, there will be nothing more determinate to be said about it after the event than was said in the expectation. Both these cases of course are cases of *fear* because one thing that is fixed amid the indeterminacy is the belief that it is me to whom the things will happen.

Central to the expectation of S is the thought of what it will be like when it happens—thought which may be indeterminate, range over alternatives, and so forth. When S involves me, there can be the possibility of a special form of such thought: the thought of how it will be for me, the imaginative projection

of myself as participant in *S*. I do not have to think about *S* in this way, when it involves me; but I may be able to. (It might be suggested that this possibility was even mirrored in the language, in the distinction between 'expecting to be hurt' and 'expecting that I shall be hurt'; but I am very doubtful about this point, which is in any case of no importance.)

Suppose now that there is an *S* with regard to which it is for conceptual reasons undecidable whether it involves me or not, as is proposed for the exerimental situation by the line we are discussing. It is important that the expectation of *S* is not *indeterminate* in any of the ways we have just been considering. It is not like the nameless horror, since the fixed point of that case was that it was going to happen to the subject, and that made his state unequivocally fear. Nor is it like the expectation of the man who expects one of the five to be hurt; his fear was indeed equivocal, but its focus, and that of the expectation, was that when *S* came about, it would certainly come about in one way or the other. In the present case, fear (of the torture, that is to say, not of the initial experiment) seems neither appropriate, nor inappropriate, nor appropriately equivocal. Relatedly, the subject has an incurable difficulty about how he may think about *S*. If he engages in projective imaginative thinking (about how it will be for him), he implicitly answers the necessarily unanswerable question; if he thinks that he cannot engage in such thinking, it looks very much as if he also answers it, though in the opposite direction. Perhaps he must just refrain from such thinking; but is he just refraining from it, if it is incurably undecidable whether he can or cannot engage in it?

It may be said that all that these considerations can show is that fear, at any rate, does not get its proper footing in this case; but that there could be some other, more ambivalent, form of concern which would indeed be appropriate to this particular expectation, the expectation of the conceptually undecidable situation. There are, perhaps, analogous feelings that actually occur in actual situations. Thus material objects do occasionally undergo puzzling transformations which leave a conceptual shadow over their identity. Suppose I were sentimentally attached to an object to which this sort of thing then happened; it might be that I could neither feel about it quite as I did originally, nor be totally indifferent to it, but would have some other and rather ambivalent feeling towards it. Similarly, it may be said, toward the prospective sufferer of pain, my identity relations with whom are conceptually shadowed, I can feel neither as I would if he were certainly me, nor as I would if he were certainly not, but rather some such ambivalent concern.

But this analogy does little to remove the most baffling aspect of the present case—an aspect which has already turned up in what was said about the subject's difficulty in thinking either projectively or non-projectively about the situation. For to regard the prospective pain-sufferer *just* like the transmogrified object of sentiment, and to conceive of my ambivalent distress about his future pain as just like ambivalent distress about some future damage to such an object, is of course to leave him and me clearly distinct from one another, and thus to displace the conceptual shadow from its proper place. I have to get nearer to him than that. But is there any nearer that I can get to him without

expecting his pain? If there is, the analogy has not shown us it. We can certainly not get nearer by expecting, as it were, *ambivalent* pain; there is no place at all for that. There seems to be an obstinate bafflement to mirroring in my expectations a situation in which it is conceptually undecidable whether I occur.

The bafflement seems, moreover, to turn to plain absurdity if we move from conceptual undecidability to its close friend and neighbour, conventionalist decision. This comes out if we consider another description, overtly conventionalist, of the series of cases which occasioned the present discussion. This description would reject a point I relied on in an earlier argument—namely, that if we deny that the A-body-person in (vi) is A (because the B-body-person is), then we must deny that the A-body-person in (v) is A, since they are exactly similar. 'No', it may be said, 'this is just to assume that we say the same in different sorts of situation. No doubt when we have the very good candidate for being A—namely, the B-body-person—we call him A; but this does not mean that we should not call the A-body-person A in that other situation when we have no better candidate around. Different situations call for different descriptions.' This line of talk is the sort of thing indeed appropriate to lawyers deciding the ownership of some property which has undergone some bewildering set of transformations; they just have to decide, and in each situation, let us suppose, it has got to go to somebody, on as reasonable grounds as the facts and the law admit. But as a line to deal with a person's fears or expectations about his own future, it seems to have no sense at all. If A's fears can extend to what will happen to the A-body-person in (v), I do not see how they can be rationally diverted from the fate of the exactly similar person in (vi) by his being told that someone would have a reason in the latter situation which he would not have in the former for deciding to call another person A.

Thus, to sum up, it looks as though there are two presentations of the imagined experiment and the choice associated with it, each of which carries conviction, and which lead to contrary conclusions. The idea, moreover, that the situation after the experiment is conceptually undecidable in the relevant respect seems not to assist, but rather to increase, the puzzlement; while the idea (so often appealed to in these matters) that it is conventionally decidable is even worse. Following from all that, I am not in the least clear which option it would be wise to take if one were presented with them before the experiment. I find that rather disturbing.

Whatever the puzzlement, there is one feature of the arguments which have led to it which is worth picking out, since it runs counter to something which is, I think, often rather vaguely supposed. It is often recognised that there are 'first-personal' and 'third-personal' aspects of questions about persons, and that there are difficulties about the relations between them. It is also recognised that 'mentalistic' considerations (as we may vaguely call them) and considerations of bodily continuity are involved in questions of personal identity (which is not to say that there are mentalistic and bodily criteria of personal identity). It is tempting to think that the two distinctions run in parallel: roughly, that a first-person approach concentrates attention on mentalistic considerations, while a third-personal approach emphasises considerations of bodily continuity. The

present discussion is an illustration of exactly the opposite. The first argument, which led to the 'mentalistic' conclusion that A and B would change bodies and that each person should identify himself with the destination of his memories and character, was an argument entirely conducted in third-personal terms. The second argument, which suggested the bodily continuity identification, concerned itself with the first-personal issue of what A could expect. That this is so seems to me (though I will not discuss it further here) of some significance.

I will end by suggesting one rather shaky way in which one might approach a resolution of the problem, using only the limited materials already available.

The apparently decisive arguments of the first presentation, which suggested that A should identify himself with the B-body-person, turned on the extreme neatness of the situation in satisfying, if any could, the description of 'changing bodies'. But this neatness is basically artificial; it is the product of the will of the experimenter to produce a situation which would naturally elicit, with minimum hesitation, that description. By the sorts of methods he employed, he could easily have left off earlier or gone on further. He could have stopped at situation (v), leaving B as he was; or he could have gone on and produced two persons each with A-like character and memories, as well as one or two with B-like characteristics. If he had done either of those, we should have been in yet greater difficulty about what to say; he just chose to make it as easy as possible for us to find something to say. Now if we had some model of ghostly persons in bodies, which were in some sense actually moved around by certain procedures, we could regard the neat experiment just as the *effective* experiment: the one method that really did result in the ghostly persons' changing places without being destroyed, dispersed, or whatever. But we cannot seriously use such a model. The experimenter has not in the sense of that model *induced* a change of bodies; he has rather produced the one situation out of a range of equally possible situations which we should be most disposed to call a change of bodies. As against this, the principle that one's fears can extend to future pain whatever psychological changes precede it seems positively straightforward. Perhaps, indeed, it is not; but we need to be shown what is wrong with it. Until we are shown what is wrong with it, we should perhaps decide that if we were the person A then, if we were to decide selfishly, we should pass the pain to the B-body-person. It would be risky: that there is room for the notion of a *risk* here is itself a major feature of the problem.

40

Later Selves and Moral Principles

DEREK PARFIT

Derek Parfit (b. 1942) is a contemporary metaphysician and moral philosopher. He is currently a fellow at All Souls College, Oxford.

In reading 38, John Locke suggests that our moral practices of praising and blaming people depend on our views about personal identity. In this paper, Derek Parfit considers some implications for our moral practices if we adopt what he calls the "Complex View" of personal identity. Parfit thinks that most of us hold the "Simple View" of personal identity: personal identity is an all or nothing affair, either the individual before us is or is not the same person we knew at an earlier stage. The Simple View of personal identity supports certain moral practices. For example, if the individual before us is the same person as someone who committed a crime, then punishment is in order; otherwise the individual is completely blameless. By contrast, the Complex View takes personal identity to be determined by factors like the number of memory connections to the past life of an individual and the amount of continuity of character traits with an individual at an earlier point. Because these factors are matters of degree, so is personal identity. Thus, the individual before us might be strongly continuous, somewhat continuous, or only quite tenuously continuous with a person we knew before. In the latter case, we should not take as harsh an attitude towards the present individual for a crime committed by an "earlier self." Parfit also examines the implications of the Complex View for the practice of promising and for our views about justice among individuals.

I shall first sketch different views about the nature of personal identity, then suggest that the views support different moral claims.

I

Most of us seem to have certain beliefs about our own identity. We seem for instance to believe that, whatever happens, any future person must be either us, or someone else.

These beliefs are like those that some of us have about a simpler fact. Most of us now think that to be a person, as opposed to a mere animal, is just to have certain more specific properties, such as rationality. These are matters of degree. So we might say that the fact of personhood is just the fact of having certain other properties, which are had to different degrees.

There is a different view. Some of us believe that personhood is a further, deep, fact, and cannot hold to different degrees.

This second view may be confused with some trivial claims. Personhood is, in a sense, a further fact. And there is a sense in which all persons are equally persons.

Let us first show how these claims may be trivial. We can use a different example. There is a sense in which all our relatives are equally our relatives. We can use the phrase 'related to' so that what it means has no degrees; on this use, parents and remote cousins are as much relatives. It is obvious, though, that kinship has degrees. This is shown in the phrase 'closely related to': remote cousins are, as relatives, less close. I shall summarize such remarks in the following way. On the above use, the fact of being someone's relative has in its *logic* no degrees. But in its *nature*—in what it involves—it does have degrees. So the fact's logic hides its nature. Hence the triviality of the claim that all our relatives are equally our relatives. (The last few sentences may be wrongly worded, but I hope that the example suggests what I mean.)

To return to the claims about personhood. These were: that it is a further fact, and that all persons are equally persons. As claims about the fact's logic, these are trivial. Certain people think the claims profound. They believe them to be true of the fact's nature.

The difference here can be shown in many ways. Take the question, 'When precisely does an embryo become a person?' If we merely make the claims about the fact's logic, we shall not believe that this question must have a precise answer. Certain people do believe this. They believe that any embryo must either be, or not be, a complete person. Their view goes beyond the 'logical claims'. It concerns the nature of personhood.

We can now return to the main argument. About the facts of both personhood and personal identity, there are two views. According to the first, these facts have a special nature. They are further facts, independent of certain more specific facts; and in every case they must either hold completely, or completely fail to hold. According to the second view, these facts are not of this nature. They consist in the holding of the more specific facts; and they are matters of degree.

Let us name such opposing views. I shall call the first kind 'Simple' and the second 'Complex'.

Such views may affect our moral principles, in the following way. If we change from a Simple to a Complex View, we acquire two beliefs: we decide that a certain fact is in its nature less deep, and that it sometimes holds to reduced degrees. These beliefs may have two effects: the first belief may weaken certain principles, and the second give the principles a new scope.

Take the views about personhood. An ancient principle gives to the welfare of people absolute precedence over that of mere animals. If the difference between people and mere animals is in its nature less deep, this principle can be more plausibly denied. And if embryos are not people, and become them only by degrees, the principle forbidding murder can be more plausibly given less scope.

I have not defended these claims. They are meant to parallel what I shall defend in the case of the two views about personal identity.

II

We must first sketch these views. It will help to revive a comparison. What is involved in the survival of a nation are just certain continuities, such as those of a people and a political system. When there is a weakening of these continuities, as there was, say, in the Norman Conquest, it may be unclear whether a nation survives. But there is here no problem. And the reason is that the survival of a nation just involves these continuities. Once we know how the continuities were weakened, we need not ask, as a question about an independent fact, 'Did a nation cease to exist?' There is nothing left to know.

We can add the following remarks. Though identity has no degrees, these continuities are matters of degree. So the identity of nations over time is only in its logic 'all-or-nothing'; in its nature it has degrees.

The identity of people over time is, according to the 'Complex View', comparable. It consists in bodily and psychological continuity. These, too, are matters of degree. So we can add the comparable remark. The identity of people over time is only in its logic 'all-or-nothing'; in its nature it has degrees.

How do the continuities of bodies and minds have degrees? We can first dismiss bodies, since they are morally trivial. Let us next call 'direct' the psychological relations which hold between: the memory of an experience and this experience, the intention to perform some later action and this action, and different expressions of some lasting character-trait. We can now name two general features of a person's life. One, 'connectedness', is the holding, over time, of particular 'direct' relations. The other, 'continuity', is the holding of a chain of such relations. If, say, I cannot now remember some earlier day, there are no 'connections of memory' between me now and myself on that day. But there may be 'continuity of memory'. This there is if, on every day between, I remembered the previous day.

Of these two general relations, I define 'continuous with' so that, in its logic, it has no degrees. It is like 'related to' in the use on which all our relatives are equally our relatives. But 'connectedness' has degrees. Between different parts of a person's life, the connections of memory, character, and intention are—in strength and number—more or less. ('Connected to' is like 'closely related to'; different relatives can be more or less close.)

We can now restate the Complex View. What is important in personal identity are the two relations we have just sketched. One of these, continuity, is in its logic all-or-nothing. But it just involves connectedness, which clearly has degrees. In its nature, therefore, continuity holds to different degrees. So the fact of personal identity also, in its nature, has degrees.

To turn to the Simple View. Here the fact is believed to be, in its nature, all-or-nothing. This it can only be if it does not just consist in (bodily and) psychological continuity—if it is, in its nature, a further fact. To suggest why:

These continuities hold, over time, to different degrees. This is true in actual cases, but is most clearly true in some imaginary cases. We can imagine cases where the continuities between each of us and a future person hold to every possible degree. Suppose we think, in imagining these cases, 'Such a future person must be either, and quite simply, *me,* or *someone else*'. (Suppose we think, 'Whatever happens, any future experience must be either *wholly* mine, or *not* mine *at all*'.) If the continuities can hold to every degree, but the fact of our identity must hold completely or not at all, then this fact cannot consist in these continuities. It must be a further, independent, fact.

It is worth repeating that the Simple View is about the nature of personal identity, not its logic. This is shown by the reactions most of us have to various so-called 'problem cases'. These reactions also show that even if, on the surface, we reject the Simple View, at a deeper level we assume it to be true.

We can add this—rough—test of our assumptions. Nations are in many ways unlike people; for example, they are not organisms. But if we take the Complex View, we shall accept this particular comparison: the survival of a person, like that of a nation, is a matter of degree. If instead we reject this comparison, we take the Simple View.

One last preliminary. We can use 'I', and the other pronouns, so that they cover only the part of our lives to which, when speaking, we have the strongest psychological connections. We assign the rest of our lives to what we call our 'other selves'. When, for instance, we have undergone any marked change in character, or conviction, or style of life, we might say, 'It was not *I* who did that, but an earlier self'.

. . .

Whether we are inclined to use such talk will depend upon our view about the nature of personal identity. If we take the Simple View, we shall not be so inclined, for we shall think it deeply true that all the parts of a person's life are as much parts of his life. If we take the Complex View, we shall be less impressed by this truth. It will seem like the truth that all the parts of a nation's history are as much parts of its history. Because this latter truth is superficial, we at times subdivide such a history into that of a series of successive nations, such as Anglo-Saxon, Medieval, or Post-Imperial England. The connections between these, though similar in kind, differ in degree. If we take the Complex View, we may also redescribe a person's life as the history of a series of successive selves. And the connections between these we shall also claim to be similar in kind, different in degree.

III

We can now turn to our question. Do the different views tend to support different moral claims?

I have space to consider only three subjects: desert, commitment, and distributive justice. And I am forced to oversimplify, and to distort. So it may help to start with some general remarks.

My suggestions are of this form: 'The Complex View supports certain claims.' By 'supports' I mean both 'makes more plausible' and 'helps to explain'. My suggestions thus mean: 'If the true view is the Complex, not the Simple, View, certain claims are more plausible. We may therefore be, on the Complex View, more inclined to make these claims.'

I shall be discussing two kinds of case: those in which the psychological connections are as strong as they ever are, and those in which they are markedly weak. I choose these kinds of case for the following reason. If we change from the Simple to the Complex View, we believe (I shall claim) that our identity is in its nature less deep, and that it sometimes holds to reduced degrees. The first of these beliefs covers every case, even those where there are the strongest connections. But the second of the two beliefs only covers cases where there are weak connections. So the two kinds of case provide separate testing-grounds for the two beliefs.

Let us start with the cases of weak connection. And our first principle can be that we deserve to be punished for certain crimes.

We can suppose that, between some convict now and himself when he committed some crime, there are only weak psychological connections. (This will usually be when conviction takes place after many years.) We can imply the weakness of these connections by calling the convict, not the criminal, but his later self.

Two grounds for detaining him would be unaffected. Whether a convict should be either reformed, or preventively detained, turns upon his present state, not his relation to the criminal. A third ground, deterrence, turns upon a different question. Do potential criminals care about their later selves? Do they care, for instance, if they do not expect to be caught for many years? If they do, then detaining their later selves could perhaps deter.

Would it be deserved? Locke thought that if we forget our crimes we deserve no punishment.[1] Geach considers this view 'morally repugnant'.[2] Mere loss of memory does seem to be insufficient. Changes of character would appear to be more relevant. The subject is, though, extremely difficult. Claims about desert can be plausibly supported with a great variety of arguments. According to some of these loss of memory would be important. And according to most the nature and cause of any change in character would need to be known.

I have no space to consider these details, but I shall make one suggestion. This appeals to the following assumption. When some morally important fact holds to a lesser degree, it can be more plausibly claimed to have less importance—even, in extreme cases, none.

I shall not here defend this assumption. I shall only say that most of us apply the assumption to many kinds of principle. Take, for example, the two principles that we have special duties to help our relatives, or friends. On the

---

[1] *Essay Concerning Human Understanding*, 1690, Bk II, Chapter XXVII, section 26.

[2] P. T. Geach, *God and Soul*, London, Routledge and Kegan Paul, 1969, p. 4.

assumption, we might claim that we have less of a special duty to help our less close relatives, or friends, and, to those who are very distant, none at all.

My suggestion is this. If the assumption is acceptable, and the Complex View correct, it becomes more plausible to make the following claim: when the connections between convicts and their past criminal selves are less, they deserve less punishment; if they are very weak, they perhaps deserve none. This claim extends the idea of 'diminished responsibility'. It does not appeal to mental illness, but instead treats a later self like a sane accomplice. Just as a man's deserts correspond to the degree of his complicity with some criminal, so his deserts, now, for some past crime correspond to the degree of connectedness between himself now and himself when committing that crime.

If we add the further assumption that psychological connections are, in general, weaker over longer periods, the claim provides a ground for Statutes of Limitations. (They of course have other grounds.)

IV

We can next consider promises. There are here two identities involved. The first is that of the person who, once, made a promise. Let us suppose that between this person now and himself then there are only weak connections. Would this wipe away his commitment? Does a later self start with a clean slate?

On the assumption that I gave, the Complex View supports the answer, 'yes'. Certain people think that only short-term promises carry moral weight. This belief becomes more plausible on the Complex View.

The second relevant identity is that of the person who received the promise. There is here an asymmetry. The possible effect of the Complex View could be deliberately blocked. We could ask for promises of this form: 'I shall help you, and all your later selves.' If the promises that I *receive* take this form, they cannot be plausibly held to be later undermined by any change in *my* character, or by any other weakening, over the rest of *my* life, in connectedness.

The asymmetry is this: similar forms cannot so obviously stay binding on the *maker* of a promise. I might say, 'I, and all my later selves, shall help you'. But it is plausible to reply that I can only bind my present self. This is plausible because it is like the claim that I can only bind myself. No one, though, denies that I can promise you that I shall help someone else. So I can clearly promise you that I shall help your later selves.

Such a promise may indeed seem especially binding. Suppose that you change faster than I do. I may then regard myself as committed, not to you, but to your earlier self. I may therefore think that you cannot waive my commitment. (It would be like a commitment, to someone now dead, to help his children. We cannot be released from such commitments.)

Such a case would be rare. But an example may help the argument. Let us take a nineteenth-century Russian who, in several years, should inherit vast estates. Because he has socialist ideals, he intends, now, to give the land to the

468

peasants. But he knows that in time his ideals may fade. To guard against this possibility, he does two things. He first signs a legal document, which will automatically give away the land, and which can only be revoked with his wife's consent. He then says to his wife, 'If I ever change my mind, and ask you to revoke the document, promise me that you will not consent'. He might add, 'I regard my ideals as essential to me. If I lose these ideals, I want you to think that *I* cease to exist. I want you to regard your husband, then, not as me, the man who asks you for this promise, but only as his later self. Promise me that you would not do what he asks.'

This plea seems understandable. And if his wife made this promise, and he later asked her to revoke the document, she might well regard herself as in no way released from her commitment. It might seem to her as if she has obligations to two different people. She might think that to do what her husband now asks would be to betray the young man whom she loved and married. And she might regard what her husband now says as unable to acquit her of disloyalty to this young man—of disloyalty to her husband's earlier self.

Such an example may seem not to require the distinction between successive selves. Suppose that I ask you to promise me never to give me cigarettes, even if I beg you for them. You might think that I cannot, in begging you, simply release you from this commitment. And to think this you need not deny that it is I to whom you are committed.

This seems correct. But the reason is that addiction clouds judgment.Similar examples might involve extreme stress or pain, or (as with Odysseus, tied to the mast) extraordinary temptation. When, though, nothing clouds a person's judgment, most of us believe that the person to whom we are committed can always release us. He can always, if in sound mind, waive our commitment. We believe this whatever the commitment may be. So (on this view) the content of a commitment cannot stop its being waived.

To return to the Russian couple. The man's ideals fade, and he asks his wife to revoke the document. Though she promised him to refuse, he declares that he now releases her from this commitment. We have sketched two ways in which she might think that she is not released. She might, first, take her husband's change of mind as proof that he cannot now make considered judgments. But we can suppose that she has no such thought. We can also suppose that she shares our view about commitment. If so, she will only believe that her husband is unable to release her if she thinks that it is, in some sense, not *he* to whom she is committed. We have sketched such a sense. She may regard the young man's loss of his ideals as involving his replacement by a later self.

The example is of a quite general possibility. We may regard some events within a person's life as, in certain ways, like birth or death. Not in all ways, for beyond these events the person has earlier or later selves. But it may be only one out of the series of selves which is the object of some of our emotions, and to which we apply some of our principles.

The young Russian socialist regards his ideals as essential to his present self. He asks his wife to promise to this present self not to act against these ideals.

And, on this way of thinking, she can never be released from her commitment. For the self to whom she is committed would, in trying to release her, cease to exist.

The way of thinking may seem to be within our range of choice. We can indeed choose when to *speak* of a new self, just as we can choose when to speak of the end of Medieval England. But the way of speaking would express beliefs. And the wife in our example cannot choose her beliefs. That the young man whom she loved and married has, in a sense, ceased to exist, that her middle-aged and cynical husband is at most the later self of this young man—these claims may seem to her to express more of the truth than the simple claim, 'but they are the same person'. Just as we can give a more accurate description if we divide the history of Russia into that of the Empire and of the Soviet Union, so it may be more accurate to divide her husband's life into that of two successive selves.

V

I have suggested that the Complex View supports certain claims. It is worth repeating that these claims are at most more plausible on the Complex View (more, that is, than on the Simple View). They are not entailed by the Complex View.

We can sometimes show this in the following way. Some claims make sense when applied to successive generations. Such claims can obviously be applied to successive selves. For example, it perhaps makes sense to believe that we inherit the commitments of our parents. If so, we can obviously believe that commitments are inherited by later selves.

Other claims may be senseless when applied to generations. Perhaps we cannot intelligibly think that we deserve to be punished for all our parents' crimes. But even if this is so, it should still make sense to have the comparable thought about successive selves. No similarity in the form of two relations could force us to admit that they are morally equivalent, for we can always appeal to the difference in their content.

There are, then, no entailments. But there seldom are in moral reasoning. So the Complex View may still support certain claims. Most of us think that our children are neither bound by our commitments, nor responsible for all we do. If we take the Complex View, we may be more inclined to think the same about our later selves. And the correctness of the view might make such beliefs more defensible.

VI

. . .

I shall now turn to my last subject, distributive justice. Here the consequences of a change to the Complex View seem harder to assess. The reason is this: in the case of the principles of desert and commitment, both the possible effects,

470

the weakening and the change in scope, are in theory pro-utilitarian.* (Since these principles compete with the principle of utility, it is obviously in theory pro-utilitarian if they are weakened. And their new scope would be a reduced scope. This should also be pro-utilitarian.) Since both the possible effects would be in the same direction, we can make this general claim: if the change of view has effects upon these principles, these effects would be pro-utilitarian. In the case of distributive justice, things are different. Here, as I shall argue, the two possible effects seem to be in opposite directions. So there is a new question: which is the more plausible combined effect? My reply will again be: pro-utilitarian.

VII

Before defending this claim, I shall mention two related claims. These can be introduced in the following way.

Utilitarians reject distributive principles. They aim for the greatest net sum of benefits minus burdens, whatever its distribution. Let us say they 'maximize'.

There is, here, a well-known parallel. When we can affect only one person, we accept maximization. We do not believe that we ought to give a person fewer happy days so as to be more fair in the way we spread them out over the parts of his life. There are, of course, arguments for spreading out enjoyments. We remain fresh, and have more to look forward to. But these arguments do not count against maximization; they remind us how to achieve it.

When we can affect several people, utilitarians make similar claims. They admit new arguments for spreading out enjoyments, such as that which appeals to relative deprivation. But they treat equality as a mere means, not a separate aim.

Since their attitude to sets of lives is like ours to single lives, utilitarians disregard the boundaries between lives. We may ask, 'Why?'

Here are three suggestions.—Their approach to morality leads them to overlook these boundaries.—They believe that the boundaries are unimportant, because they think that sets of lives are like single lives.—They take the Complex View.

The first suggestion has been made by Rawls. It can be summarized like this. Utilitarians tend to approach moral questions as if they were impartial observers. When they ask themselves, as observers, what is right, or what they prefer, they tend to *identify* with *all* the affected people. This leads them to ignore the fact that *different* people are affected, and so to reject the claims of justice.[3]

In the case of some utilitarians, Rawls's explanation seems sufficient. Let us call these the 'identifying observers'. But there are others who in contrast always

---

* A utilitarian is, roughly, someone who believes that an action is right if it produces the greatest happiness for the greatest number. See readings 5, 6, and 7.

[3] John Rawls, *A Theory of Justice,* Cambridge, Mass., Harvard University Press, 1971, p. 27, and pp. 185–9.

seem '*detached* observers'. These utilitarians do not seem to overlook the distinction between people. And, as Rawls remarks, there is no obvious reason why observers who remain *detached* cannot adopt the principles of justice. If we approach morality in a quite detached way—if we do not think of ourselves as potentially involved—we may , I think, be somewhat more inclined to reject these principles. But this particular approach to moral questions does not itself seem a sufficient explanation for utilitarian beliefs.

The Complex View may provide a different explanation. These two are quite compatible. Utilitarians may both approach morality as observers, and take the Complex View. (The explanations may indeed be mutually supporting.)

To turn to the remaining explanation. Utilitarians treat sets of lives in the way that we treat single lives. It has been suggested, not that they ignore the difference between people, but that they actually believe that a group of people is like a super-person. This suggestion is, in a sense, the reverse of mine. It imputes a different view about the facts. And it can seem the more plausible.

Let us start with an example. Suppose that we must choose whether to let some child undergo some hardship. If he does, this will either be for his own greater benefit in adult life, or for the similar benefit of someone else. Does it matter which?

Most of us would answer: 'Yes. If it is for the child's own benefit, there can at least be no unfairness.' We might draw the general conclusion that failure to relieve useful burdens is more likely to be justified if they are for a person's *own* good.

Utilitarians, confusingly, could accept this conclusion. They would explain it in a different way. They might, for instance, point out that such burdens are in general easier to bear.

To block this reply, we can suppose that the child in our example cannot be cheered up in this way. Let us next ignore other such arguments. This simplifies the disagreement. Utilitarians would say: 'Whether it is right to let the child bear the burden only depends upon how great the benefit will be. It does not depend upon who benefits. It would make no moral difference if the benefit comes, not to the child himself, but to someone else.' Non-utilitarians might reply: 'On the contrary, if it comes to the child himself this helps to justify the burden. If it comes to someone else, that is unfair.'

We can now ask: do the two views about the nature of personal identity tend to support different sides in this debate?

Part of the answer seems clear. Non-utilitarians think it a morally important fact that it be the child himself who, as an adult, benefits. This fact, if it seems more important on one of the views, ought to do so on the Simple View, for it is on this view that the identity between the child and the adult is in its nature deeper. On the Complex View, it is less deep, and holds, over adolescence, to reduced degrees. If we take the Complex View, we may compare the lack of connections between the child and his adult self to the lack of connections between different people. That it will be *he* who receives the benefit may thus seem less important. We might say, 'It will not be *he*. It will only be his adult self.'

472

The Simple View seems, then, to support the non-utilitarian reply. Does it follow that the Complex View tends to support utilitarian beliefs? Not directly. For we might say, 'Just as it would be unfair if it is someone else who benefits, so if it won't be he, but only his adult self, that would also be unfair.'

The point is a general one. If we take the Complex View, we may regard the (rough) subdivisions within lives as, in certain ways, like the divisions between lives. We may therefore come to treat alike two kinds of distribution: within lives, and between lives. But there are two ways of treating these alike. We can apply distributive principles to both, or to neither.

Which of these might we do? I claim that we may abandon these principles. Someone might object: 'If we do add, to the divisions between lives, subdivisions within lives, the effects could only be these. The principles that we now apply to the divisions we come to apply to the sub-divisions. (If, to use your own example, we believe that our sons do not inherit our commitments, we may come to think the same about our later selves.)

'The comparable effect would now be this. We demand fairness to later selves. We *extend* distributive principles. You instead claim that we may abandon these principles. Since this is *not* the comparable effect, your claim must be wrong.'

The objection might be pressed. We might add: 'If we did abandon these principles, we should be moving in reverse. We should not be treating parts of one life as we now treat different lives, but be treating different lives as we now treat one life. This, the reverse effect, could only come from the reverse comparison. Rather than thinking that a person's life is like the history of a nation, we must be thinking that a nation—or indeed any group—is like a person.'

To review the argument so far. Treating alike single people and groups may come from accepting some comparison between them. But there are two ways of treating them alike. We can demand fairness even within single lives, or reject this demand in the case of groups. And there are two ways of taking this comparison. We can accept the Complex View and compare a person's life to the history of a group, or accept the reverse view and compare groups to single people.

Of these four positions, I had matched the Complex View with the abandonment of fairness. The objection was that it seemed to be better matched with the demand for fairness even within lives. And the rejection of this demand, in the case of groups, seemed to require what I shall call 'the Reverse View'.

My reply will be this. Disregard for the principles of fairness could perhaps be supported by the Reverse View. But it does not have to be. And in seeing why we shall see how it may be supported by the Complex View.

Many thinkers have believed that a society, or nation, is like a person. This belief seems to weaken the demand for fairness. When we are thought to be mere parts of a social organism, it can seem to matter less how we are each treated.

If the rejection of fairness has to be supported in this way, utilitarians can be justly ignored. This belief is at best superficially true when held about soci-

eties. And to support utilitarian views it would have to be held about the whole of mankind, where it is absurd.

Does the rejection of fairness need such support? Certain writers think that it does. Gauthier*, for instance, suggests that to suppose that we should maximize for mankind 'is to suppose that mankind is a super-person'. This suggestion seems to rest on the following argument. 'We are free to maximize within one life only because it is *one* life. So we could only be free to maximize over different lives if they are like parts of a single life.'

Given this argument, utilitarians would, I think, deny the premise. They would deny that it is the unity of a life which, within this life, justifies maximization. They can then think this justified over different lives without assuming mankind to be a super-person.

The connection with the Complex View is, I think, this. It is on this view, rather than the Simple View, that the premise is more plausibly denied. That is how the Complex View may support utilitarian beliefs.

To expand these remarks. There are two kinds of distribution: within lives, and between lives. And there are two ways of treating these alike. We can apply distributive principles to both, or to neither.

Utilitarians apply them to neither. I suggest that this may be (in part) because they take the Complex View. An incompatible suggestion is that they take the Reverse View.

My suggestion may seem clearly wrong if we overlook the following fact. There are two routes to the abandonment of distributive principles. We may give them no scope, or instead give them no weight.

Suppose we assume that the only route is the change in scope. Then it may indeed seem that utilitarians must either be assuming that any group of people is like a single person (Gauthier's suggestion), or at least be forgetting that it is not (Rawls's suggestion).

I shall sketch the other route. Utilitarians may not be denying that distributive principles have scope. They may be denying that they have weight. This, the second of the kinds of effect that I earlier distinguished, *may* be supported by the Complex View.

The situation, more precisely, may be this. If the Complex View supports a change in the scope of distributive principles, it perhaps supports giving them more scope. It perhaps supports their extension even within single lives. But the other possible effect, the weakening of these principles, may be the more strongly supported. That is how the net effect may be pro-utilitarian.

This suggestion differs from the other two in the following way. Rawls remarks that the utilitarian attitude seems to involve 'conflating all persons into one'. This remark also covers Gauthier's suggestion. But the attitude may derive, not from the conflation of persons, but from their (partial) disintegration. It may rest upon the view that a person's life is less deeply integrated than we mostly think. Utilitarians may be treating benefits and burdens, not as if they all came

---

* Parfit is referring to David Gauthier, a contemporary moral philosopher who teaches at the University of Pittsburgh.

within the same life, but as if it made no moral difference where they came. This belief may be supported by the view that the unity of each life, and hence the difference between lives, is in its nature less deep.

VIII

I shall next sketch a brief defence of this suggestion. And I shall start with a new distributive principle. Utilitarians believe that benefits and burdens can be freely weighed against each other, even if they come to different people. This is frequently denied.

We must first distinguish two kinds of weighing. The claim that a certain burden 'factually outweighs' another is the claim that it is greater. The claim that it 'morally outweighs' the other is the claim that we should relieve it even at the cost of failing to relieve the other. Similar remarks apply to the weighing of benefits against burdens, and against each other.

Certain people claim that burdens cannot even *factually* outweigh each other if they come to different people. (They claim that the sense of 'greater than' can only be provided by a single person's preferences.) I am here concerned with a different claim. At its boldest this is that the burdens and benefits of different people cannot be *morally* weighed. I shall consider one part of this claim. This goes: 'Someone's burden cannot be morally outweighed by mere benefits to someone else.' I say 'mere' benefits, because the claim is not intended to deny that it *can* be right to let a person bear a burden so as to benefit another. Such acts may, for instance, be required by justice. What the claim denies is that such acts can be justified solely upon utilitarian grounds. It denies that a person's burden can be morally outweighed by *mere* benefits to someone else.

This claim often takes qualified forms. It can be restricted to great burdens, or be made to require that the net benefit be proportionately great. I shall here discuss the simplest form, for my remarks could be adapted to the other forms. Rawls puts the claim as follows: 'The reasoning which balances the gains and losses of different persons . . . is excluded. So I shall call this the 'objection to balancing'.[4]

This objection rests in part on a different claim. This goes: 'Someone's burden cannot be *compensated* by benefits to someone else.' This second claim is, with qualifications, clearly true. We cannot say, 'On the contrary, our burdens can be compensated by benefits to anyone else, even a total stranger'.

Not only is this second claim clearly true; its denial is in no way supported by the Complex View. So if the change to this view has effects upon this claim, they would be these. We might, first, extend the claim even within single lives. We might say, in the example that I gave, 'The child's burden cannot be compensated by benefits to his adult self.' This claim would be like the claims that we are sometimes not responsible for, nor bound by, our earlier selves. It would apply to certain parts of one life what we now believe about different lives. It would therefore seem to be, as a change in scope, in the right direction.

---

[4] *A Theory of Justice*, p. 28.

We might, next, give the claim less weight. Our ground would be the one that I earlier gave. Compensation presupposes personal identity. On the Complex View, we may think that our identity is, because less deep, less morally important. We may therefore think that the fact of compensation is itself less morally important. Though it cannot be denied, the claim about compensation may thus be given less weight.

If we now return to the objection to balancing, things are different. The concept of 'greater moral weight' does not presuppose personal identity. So this objection can be denied; and the Complex View seems to support this denial.

The denial might be put like this: 'Our burdens cannot indeed be *compensated* by mere benefits to someone else. But they may be *morally outweighed* by such benefits. It may still be right to give the benefits rather than relieve the burdens. Burdens are morally outweighed by benefits if they are factually outweighed by these benefits. All that is needed is that the benefits be greater than the burdens. It is unimportant, in itself, to whom both come.'

This is the utilitarian reply. I shall next suggest why the Complex View seems, more than the Simple View, to support this reply.

The objection to balancing rests in part on the claim about compensation. On the Complex View, this claim can more plausibly be thought less important. If we take this view, we may (we saw) think both that there is less scope for compensation and that it has less moral weight. If the possibilities of compensation are, in these two ways, less morally important, there would then be less support for the objection to balancing. It would be more plausible to make the utilitarian reply.

The point can be made in a different way. Even those who object to balancing think it justified to let us bear burdens for our own good. So their claim must be that a person's burden, while it can be morally outweighed by benefits to him, cannot ever be outweighed by mere benefits to others. This is held to be so even if the benefits are far greater than the burden. The claim thus gives to the boundaries between lives—or to the fact of non-identity—overwhelming significance. It allows within the same life what, for different lives, it totally forbids.

This claim seems to be more plausible on the Simple View. Since identity is, here, thought to involve more, non-identity could plausibly seem more important. On the Simple View, we are impressed by the truth that all of a person's life is as much his life. If we are impressed by this truth—by the unity of each life—the boundaries between lives will seem to be deeper. This supports the claim that, in the moral calculus, these boundaries cannot be crossed. On the Complex View, we are less impressed by this truth. We regard the unity of each life as in its nature less deep, and as a matter of degree. We may therefore think the boundaries between lives to be less like those between, say, the squares on a chess-board, and to be more like those between different countries. They may then seem less morally decisive.

. . .

476

41

Hard Determinism

B. F. SKINNER

B. F. Skinner (b. 1904) is the founder of a major branch of behaviorism. His books include The Behavior of Organisms, Walden Two, Science and Human Behavior, *and* Beyond Freedom and Dignity. *He is currently retired after a long teaching career at Harvard University.*

Skinner has always tried to show the relevance of his work to the ways in which we think about ourselves. In this scene from his novel, Walden Two, *Skinner uses three characters to present the case for determinism, sometimes called "hard determinism." The determinist position maintains that human actions are never free, but are always the result of known or unknown causes. Skinner tries to advance the argument for determinism through two of his characters, Frazier and the narrator. They rebut the objections raised by the character Castle, who is trying to argue for free will. Castle claims that people are obviously free, except when they are physically restrained or victims of force. His opponents, invoking a classic move from the hard determinist's repertoire, argue that people feel free only because they are unaware of the forces that shape their behavior. In particular, people only realize their behavior is being directed when they feel forced to act against their desires. What they fail to see is that their desires themselves have been shaped by the reinforcements provided by their environment.*

"Mr. Castle," said Frazier very earnestly, "let me ask you a question. I warn you, it will be the most terrifying question of your life. *What would you do if you found yourself in possession of an effective science of behavior?* Suppose you suddenly found it possible to control the behavior of men as you wished. What would you do?"

"That's an assumption?"

"Take it as one if you like. *I* take it as a fact. And apparently you accept it as a fact too. I can hardly be as despotic as you claim unless I hold the key to an extensive practical control."

"What would I do?" said Castle thoughtfully. "I think I would dump your science of behavior in the ocean."

"And deny men all the help you could otherwise give them?"

"And give them the freedom they would otherwise lose forever!"

"How could you give them freedom?"

"By refusing to control them!"

"But you would only be leaving the control in other hands."

"Whose?"

"The charlatan, the demagogue, the salesman, the ward heeler, the bully, the cheat, the educator, the priest—all who are now in possession of the techniques of behavioral engineering."

"A pretty good share of the control would remain in the hands of the individual himself."

"That's an assumption, too, and it's your only hope. It's your only possible chance to avoid the implications of a science of behavior. If man is free, then a technology of behavior is impossible. But I'm asking you to consider the other case."

"Then my answer is that your assumption is contrary to fact and any further consideration idle."

"And your accusations—?"

"—were in terms of intention, not of possible achievement."

Frazier sighed dramatically.

"It's a little late to be proving that a behavioral technology is well advanced. How can you deny it? Many of its methods and techniques are really as old as the hills. Look at their frightful misuse in the hands of the Nazis! And what about the techniques of the psychological clinic? What about education? Or religion? Or practical politics? Or advertising and salesmanship? Bring them all together and you have a sort of rule-of-thumb technology of vast power. No, Mr. Castle, the science is there for the asking. But its techniques and methods are in the wrong hands—they are used for personal aggrandizement in a competitive world or, in the case of the psychologist and educator, for futilely corrective purposes. My question is, have you the courage to take up and wield the science of behavior for the good of mankind? You answer that you would dump it in the ocean!"

"I'd want to take it out of the hands of the politicians and advertisers and salesmen, too."

"And the psychologists and educators? You see, Mr. Castle, you can't have that kind of cake. The fact is, we not only *can* control human behavior, we *must*. But who's to do it, and what's to be done?"

"So long as a trace of personal freedom survives, I'll stick to my position," said Castle, very much out of countenance.

"Isn't it time we talked about freedom?" I said. "We parted a day or so ago on an agreement to let the question of freedom ring. It's time to answer, don't you think?"

"My answer is simple enough," said Frazier. "I deny that freedom exists at all. I must deny it—or my program would be absurd. You can't have a science about a subject matter which hops capriciously about. Perhaps we can never *prove* that man isn't free; it's an assumption. But the increasing success of a science of behavior makes it more and more plausible."

"On the contrary, a simple personal experience makes it untenable," said Castle. "The experience of freedom. I *know* that I'm free."

"It must be quite consoling," said Frazier.

"And what's more—you do, too," said Castle hotly. "When you deny your

own freedom for the sake of playing with a science of behavior, you're acting in plain bad faith. That's the only way I can explain it." He tried to recover himself and shrugged his shoulders. "At least you'll grant that you *feel* free."

"The 'feeling of freedom' should deceive no one," said Frazier. "Give me a concrete case."

"Well, right now," Castle said. He picked up a book of matches. "I'm free to hold or drop these matches."

"You will, of course, do one or the other," said Frazier. "Linguistically or logically there seem to be two possibilities, but I submit that there's only one in fact. The determining forces may be subtle but they are inexorable. I suggest that as an orderly person you will probably hold—ah! you drop them! Well, you see, that's all part of your behavior with respect to me. You couldn't resist the temptation to prove me wrong. It was all lawful. You had no choice. The deciding factor entered rather late, and naturally you couldn't foresee the result when you first held them up. There was no strong likelihood that you would act in either direction, and so you said you were free."

"That's entirely too glib," said Castle. "It's easy to argue lawfulness after the fact. But let's see you predict what I will do in advance. Then I'll agree there's law."

"I didn't say that behavior is always predictable, any more than the weather is always predictable. There are often too many factors to be taken into account. We can't measure them all accurately, and we couldn't perform the mathematical operations needed to make a prediction if we had the measurements. The legality is usually an assumption—but none the less important in judging the issue at hand."

"Take a case where there's no choice, then," said Castle. "Certainly a man in jail isn't free in the sense in which I am free now."

"Good! That's an excellent start. Let us classify the kinds of determiners of human behavior. One class, as you suggest, is physical restraint—handcuffs, iron bars, forcible coercion. These are ways in which we shape human behavior according to our wishes. They're crude, and they sacrifice the affection of the controllee, but they often work. Now, what other ways are there of limiting freedom?"

Frazier had adopted a professorial tone and Castle refused to answer.

"The threat of force would be one," I said.

"Right. And here again we shan't encourage any loyalty on the part of the controllee. He has perhaps a shade more of the feeling of freedom, since he can always 'choose to act and accept the consequences,' but he doesn't feel exactly free. He knows his behavior is being coerced. Now what else?"

I had no answer.

"Force or the threat of force—I see no other possibility," said Castle after a moment.

"Precisely," said Frazier.

"But certainly a large part of my behavior has no connection with force at all. There's my freedom!" said Castle.

"I wasn't agreeing that there was no other possibility—metely that *you* could see no other. Not being a good behaviorist—or a good Christian, for that matter—you have no feeling for a tremendous power of a different sort."

"What's that?"

"I shall have to be technical." said Frazier. "But only for a moment. It's what the science of behavior calls 'reinforcement theory.' The things that can happen to us fall into three classes. To some things we are indifferent. Other things we like—we want them to happen, and we take steps to make them happen again. Still other things we don't like—we don't want them to happen and we take steps to get rid of them or keep them from happening again.

"Now," Frazier continued earnestly, "if it's in our power to create any of the situations which a person likes or to remove any situation he doesn't like, we can control his behavior. When he behaves as we want him to behave, we simply create a situation he likes, or remove one he doesn't like. As a result, the probability that he will behave that way again goes up, which is what we want. Technically it's called 'positive reinforcement.'

"The old school made the amazing mistake of supposing that the reverse was true, that by removing a situation a person likes or setting up one he doesn't like—in other words by punishing him—it was possible to *reduce* the probability that he would behave in a given way again. That simply doesn't hold. It has been established beyond question. What is emerging at this critical stage in the evolution of society is a behavioral and cultural technology based on positive reinforcement alone. We are gradually discovering—at an untold cost in human suffering—that in the long run punishment doesn't reduce the probability that an act will occur. We have been so preoccupied with the contrary that we always take 'force' to mean punishment. We don't say we're using force when we send shiploads of food into a starving country, though we're displaying quite as much *power* as if we were sending troops and guns."

"I'm certainly not an advocate of force," said Castle. "But I can't agree that it's not effective."

"It's *temporarily* effective, that's the worst of it. That explains several thousand years of bloodshed. Even nature has been fooled. We 'instinctively' punish a person who doesn't behave as we like—we spank him if he's a child or strike him if he's a man. A nice distinction! The immediate effect of the blow teaches us to strike again. Retribution and revenge are the most natural things on earth. But in the long run the man we strike is no less likely to repeat his act."

"But he won't repeat it if we hit him hard enough," said Castle.

"He'll still *tend* to repeat it. He'll *want* to repeat it. We haven't really altered his potential behavior at all. That's the pity of it. If he doesn't repeat it in our presence, he will in the presence of someone else. Or it will be repeated in the disguise of a neurotic symptom. If we hit hard enough, we clear a little place for ourselves in the wilderness of civilization, but we make the rest of the wilderness still more terrible.

"Now, early forms of government are naturally based on punishment. It's the obvious technique when the physically strong control the weak. But we're in the throes of a great change to positive reinforcement—from a competitive

society in which one man's reward is another man's punishment, to a cooperative society in which no one gains at the expense of anyone else.

"The change is slow and painful because the immediate, temporary effect of punishment overshadows the eventual advantage of positive reinforcement. We've all seen countless instances of the temporary effect of force, but clear evidence of the effect of not using force is rare. That's why I insist that Jesus, who was apparently the first to discover the power of refusing to punish, must have hit upon the principle by accident. He certainly had none of the experimental evidence which is available to us today, and I can't conceive that it was possible, no matter what the man's genius, to have discovered the principle from casual observation."

"A tough of revelation, perhaps?" said Castle.

"No, accident. Jesus discovered one principle because it had immediate consequences, and he got another thrown in for good measure."

I began to see light.

"You mean the principle of 'love your enemies'?" I said.

"Exactly! To 'do good to those who despitefully use you' has two unrelated consequences. You gain the peace of mind we talked about the other day. Let the stronger man push you around—at least you avoid the torture of your own rage. *That's* the immediate consequence. What an astonishing discovery it must have been to find that in the long run you could *control the stronger man* in the same way!"

"It's generous of you to give so much credit to your early colleague," said Castle, "but why are we still in the throes of so much misery? Twenty centuries should have been enough for one piece of behavioral engineering."

"The conditions which made the principle difficult to discover made it difficult to teach. The history of the Christian Church doesn't reveal many cases of doing good to one's enemies. To inoffensive heathens, perhaps, but not enemies. One must look outside the field of organized religion to find the principle in practice at all. Church governments are devotees of *power*, both temporal and bogus."

"But what has all this got to do with freedom?" I said hastily.

Frazier took time to reorganize his behavior. He looked steadily toward the window, against which the rain was beating heavily.

"Now that we *know* how positive reinforcement works and why negative doesn't," he said at last, "we can be more deliberate, and hence more successful, in our cultural design. We can achieve a sort of control under which the controlled, though they are following a code much more scrupulously than was ever the case under the old system, nevertheless *feel free*. They are doing what they want to do, not what they are forced to do. That's the source of the tremendous power of positive reinforcement—there's no restraint and no revolt. By a careful cultural design, we control not the final behavior, but the *inclination* to behave—the motives, the desires, the wishes.

"The curious thing is that in that case the *question of freedom never arises*. Mr. Castle was free to drop the match book in the sense that nothing was preventing him. If it had been securely bound to his hand he wouldn't have

been free. Nor would he have been quite free if I'd covered him with a gun and threatened to shoot him if he let it fall. The question of freedom arises when there is restraint—either physical or psychological.

"But restraint is only one sort of control, and absence of restraint isn't freedom. It's not control that's lacking when one feels 'free,' but the objectionable control of force. Mr. Castle felt free to hold or drop the matches in the sense that he felt no restraint—no threat of punishment in taking either course of action. He neglected to examine his positive reasons for holding or letting go, in spite of the fact that these were more compelling in this instance than any threat of force.

"We have no vocabulary of freedom in dealing with what we want to do," Frazier went on. "The question never arises. When men strike for freedom, they strike against jails and the police, or the threat of them—against oppression. They never strike against forces which make them want to act the way they do. Yet, it seems to be understood that governments will operate only through force or the threat of force, and that all other principles of control will be left to education, religion, and commerce. If this continues to be the case, we may as well give up. A government can never create a free people with the techniques now allotted to it.

"The question is: Can men live in freedom and peace? And the answer is: Yes, if we can build a social structure which will satisfy the needs of everyone and in which everyone will want to observe the supporting code. But so far this has been achieved only in Walden Two. Your ruthless accusations to the contrary, Mr. Castle, this is the freest place on earth. And it is free precisely because we make no use of force or the threat of force. Every bit of our research, from the nursery through the psychological management of our adult membership, is directed toward that end—to exploit every alternative to forcible control. By skillful planning, by a wise choice of techniques we *increase* the feeling of freedom.

"It's not planning which infringes upon freedom, but planning which uses force. A sense of freedom was practically unknown in the planned society of Nazi Germany, because the planners made a fantastic use of force and the threat of force.

"No, Mr. Castle, when a science of behavior has once been achieved, there's no alternative to a planned society. We can't leave mankind to an accidental or biased control. But by using the principle of positive reinforcement—carefully avoiding force or the threat of force—we can preserve a personal sense of freedom."

. . .

42
Radical Freedom

JEAN-PAUL SARTRE

*Jean-Paul Sartre (1905–1980) was an influential French intellectual, with
interests spanning philosophy, literature, and politics. His most important
philosophical work is* Being and Nothingness. *He also wrote a number of
well received plays, including "The Flies" and "No Exit."*

In this excerpt from Being and Nothingness, *Sartre offers a very radical
version of libertarianism, the thesis that human beings are free. While
Sartre's terminology is somewhat elaborate, his message is straightforward.
It is commonly assumed that we are free with respect to some aspects of our
lives: most people can choose their own careers, choose their friends, and
choose to do or forbear a great variety of actions. However, according to
that same common wisdom, we are not free to choose other features of
our lives, for example, whether we are attractive or ugly, strong or weak,
whether we live in a time of war or peace. But Sartre claims that we are
responsible for every aspect of our lives. Because we are conscious beings,
we can appraise all aspects of our world and can judge them to be
satisfactory, or deficient in some respects. Since we are capable of seeing deficiencies and of recognizing them as deficiencies, we must bear
responsibility for any faults in our world, or in ourselves, that we allow to
remain.*

Freedom: The First Condition Of Action

IT IS STRANGE THAT philosophers have been able to argue endlessly about
determinism and free will, to cite examples in favor of one or the other thesis
without ever attempting first to make explicit the structures contained in the
very idea of *action*. The concept of an act contains, in fact, numerous subordinate notions which we shall have to organize and arrange in a hierarchy: to
act is to modify the *shape* of the world; it is to arrange means in view of an
end; it is to produce an organized instrumental complex such that by a series
of concatenations and connections the modification effected on one of the links
causes modifications throughout the whole series and finally produces an anticipated result. But this is not what is important for us here. We should observe
first that an action is on principle *intentional*. The careless smoker who has
through negligence caused the explosion of a powder magazine has not *acted*.
On the other hand the worker who is charged with dynamiting a quarry and
who obeys the given orders has acted when he has produced the expected
explosion; he knew what he was doing or, if you prefer, he intentionally realized
a conscious project.

This does not mean, of course, that one must foresee all the consequences of his act. The emperor Constantine when he established himself at Byzantium, did not foresee that he would create a center of Greek culture and language, the appearance of which would ultimately provoke a schism in the Christian Church and which would contribute to weakening the Roman Empire. Yet he performed an act just in so far as he realized his project of creating a new residence for emperors in the Orient. Equating the result with the intention is here sufficient for us to be able to speak of action. But if this is the case, we establish that the action necessarily implies as its condition the recognition of a "desideratum"; that is, of an objective lack or again of a *négatité*.* The *intention* of providing a rival for Rome can come to Constantine only through the apprehension of an objective lack: Rome lacks a counterweight; to this still profoundly pagan city ought to be opposed a Christian city which at the moment *is missing*. Creating Constantinople is understood as an *act* only if first the conception of a new city has preceded the action itself or at least if this conception serves as an organizing theme for all later steps. But this conception can not be the pure representation of the city as *possible*. It apprehends the city in its essential characteristic, which is to be a *desirable* and not yet realized possible.

This means that from the moment of the first conception of the act, consciousness has been able to withdraw itself from the full world of which it is consciousness and to leave the level of being in order frankly to approach that of non-being. Consciousness in so far as it is considered exclusively in its being, is perpetually referred from being to being and can not find in being any motive for revealing non-being. The imperial system with Rome as its capital functions positively and in a certain real way which can be easily discovered. Will someone say that the taxes are collected badly, that Rome is not secure from invasions, that it does not have the geographical location which is suitable for the capital of a Mediterranean empire which is threatened by barbarians, that its corrupt morals make the spread of the Christian religion difficult? How can anyone fail to see that all these considerations are *negative;* that is, that they aim at what is not, not at what is. To say that sixty per cent of the anticipated taxes have been collected can pass, if need be, for a positive appreciation of the situation *such as it is*. To say that they are *badly* collected is to consider the situation across a situation which is posited as an absolute end but which precisely *is not*. To say that the corrupt morals at Rome hinder the spread of Christianity is not to consider this diffusion for what it is; that is, for a propagation at a rate which the reports of the clergy can enable us to determine. It is to posit the diffusion in itself as insufficient; that is, as suffering from a secret nothingness. But it appears as such only if it is surpassed toward a limiting-situation posited *a priori* as a value (for example, toward a certain rate of religious conversions, toward a certain mass morality). This limiting-situation can not be conceived in terms of the simple consideration of the real state of

---

* By *négatité*, Sartre means something which is absent or missing.

things; for the most beautiful girl in the world can offer only what she *has,* and in the same way the most miserable situation can by itself be designated only as it *is* without any reference to an ideal nothingness.

In so far as man is immersed in the historical situation, he does not even succeed in conceiving of the failures and lacks in a political organization or determined economy; this is not, as is stupidly said, because he "is accustomed to it," but because he apprehends it in its plenitude of being and because he can not even imagine that he can exist in it otherwise. For it is necessary here to reverse common opinion and on the basis of what it is not, to acknowledge the harshness of a situation or the suffering which it imposes, both of which are motives for conceiving of another state of affairs in which things would be better for everybody. It is on the day that we can conceive of a different state of affairs that a new light falls on our troubles and our suffering and that we *decide* that these are unbearable. A worker in 1830 is capable of revolting if his salary is lowered, for he easily conceives of a situation in which his wretched standard of living would be not as low as the one which is about to be imposed on him. But he does not represent his sufferings to himself as unbearable; he adapts himself to them not through resignation but because he lacks the education and reflection necessary for him to conceive of a social state in which these sufferings would not exist. Consequently *he does not act.* Masters of Lyon following a riot, the workers at Croix-Rousse do not know what to do with their victory; they return home bewildered, and the regular army has no trouble in overcoming them. Their misfortunes do not appear to them "habitual" but rather *natural;* they are, that is all, and they constitute the workers' condition. They are not detached; they are not seen in the clear light of day, and consequently they are integrated by the worker with his being. He suffers without considering his suffering and without conferring value upon it. To suffer and to *be* are one and the same for him. His suffering is the pure affective tenor of his non-positional consciousness, but he does not *contemplate* it. Therefore this suffering can not be in itself a *motive* for his acts. Quite the contrary, it is after he has formed the project of changing the situation that it will appear intolerable to him. This means that he will have had to give himself room, to withdraw in relation to it, and will have to have effected a double nihilation: on the one hand, he must posit an ideal state of affairs as a pure *present* nothingness; on the other hand, he must posit the actual situation as nothingness in relation to this state of affairs. He will have to conceive of a happiness attached to his class as a pure possible—that is, presently as a certain nothingness—and on the other hand, he will return to the present situation in order to illuminate it in the light of this nothingness and in order to nihilate it in turn by declaring: "I *am not* happy."

Two important consequences result. (1) No factual state whatever it may be (the political and economic structure of society, the psychological "state," *etc.*) is capable by itself of motivating any act whatsoever. For an act is a projection of the for-itself toward what is not, and what is can in no way determine by itself what is not. (2) No factual state can determine consciousness to apprehend it as a *négatité* or as a lack. Better yet no factual state can determine conscious-

ness to define it and to circumscribe it since, as we have seen, Spinoza's*
statement, "Omnis determinatio est negatio," remains profoundly true. Now
every action has for its express condition not only the discovery of a state of
affairs as 'lacking in —," i.e., as a *négatité*—but also, and before all else, the
constitution of the state of things under consideration into an isolated system.
There is a factual state—satisfying or not—only by means of the nihilating
power of the for-itself. But this power of nihilation can not be limited to realizing a simple *withdrawal* in relation to the world. In fact in so far as consciousness is "invested" by being, in so far as it simply suffers what is, it must
be included in being. It is the organized form—worker-finding-his-suffering-
natural—which must be surmounted and denied in order for it to be able to
form the object of a revealing contemplation. This means evidently that it is
by a pure wrenching away from himself and the world that the worker can
posit his suffering as unbearable suffering and consequently can *make of it the
motive* for his revolutionary action. This implies for consciousness the permanent possibility of effecting a rupture with its own past, of wrenching itself
away from its past so as to be able to consider it in the light of a non-being
and so as to be able to confer on it the meaning which *it has* in terms of the
project of a meaning which it *does not have*. Under no circumstances can the
past in any way by itself produce *an act;* that is, the positing of an end which
turns back upon itself so as to illuminate it. This is what Hegel† caught sight
of when he wrote that "the mind is the negative," although he seems not to
have remembered this when he came to presenting his own theory of action
and of freedom. In fact as soon as one attributes to consciousness this negative
power with respect to the world and itself, as soon as the nihilation forms an
integral part of the *positing* of an end, we must recognize that the indispensable
and fundamental condition of all action is the freedom of the acting being.

Thus at the outset we can see what is lacking in those tedious discussions
between determinists and the proponents of free will. The latter are concerned
to find cases of decision for which there exists no prior cause, or deliberations
concerning two opposed acts which are equally possible and possess causes
(and motives) of exactly the same weight. To which the determinists may easily
reply that there is no action without a cause and that the most insignificant
gesture (raising the right hand rather than the left hand, *etc.*) refers to causes
and motives which confer its meaning upon it. Indeed the case could not be
otherwise since every action must be *intentional;* each action must, in fact, have
an end, and the end in turn is referred to a cause. Such indeed is the unity of
the three temporal ekstases;‡ the end or temporalization of my future implies
a cause (or motive); that is, it points toward my past, and the present is the
upsurge of the act. To speak of an act without a cause is to speak of an act

---

* Benedict (Baruch) Spinoza (1632–1677) was an important early modern philosopher.

† G. W. F. Hegel (1770–1831) was a major German philosopher.

‡ Here Sartre is simply referring to the past, the present, and the future.

486

which would lack the intentional structure of every act; and the proponents of free will be searching for it on the level of the act which is in the process of being performed can only end up by rendering the act absurd. But the determinists in turn are weighting the scale by stopping their investigation with the mere designation of the cause and motive. The essential question in fact lies beyond the complex organization "cause-intention-act-end"; indeed we ought to ask how a cause (or motive) can be constituted as such.

Now we have just seen that if there is no act without a cause, this is not in the sense that we can say that there is no phenomenon without a cause. In order to be a *cause,* the *cause* must be *experienced* as such. Of course this does not mean that it is to be thematically conceived and made explicit as in the case of deliberation. But at the very least it means that the for-itself must confer on it its value as cause or motive. And, as we have seen, this constitution of the cause as such can not refer to another real and positive existence; that is, to a prior cause. For otherwise the very nature of the act as engaged intentionally in non-being would disappear. The motive is understood only by the end; that is, by the non-existent. It is therefore in itself a *négatité.* If I accept a niggardly salary it is doubtless because of fear; and fear is a motive. But it is *fear of dying from starvation;* that is, this fear has meaning only outside itself in an end ideally posited, which is the preservation of a life which I apprehend as "in danger." And this fear is understood in turn only in relation to the *value which I* implicitly give to this life; that is, it is referred to that hierarchal system of ideal objects which are values. Thus the motive makes itself understood as what it is by means of the ensemble of beings which "are not," by ideal existences, and by the future. Just as the future turns back upon the present and the past in order to elucidate them, so it is the ensemble of my projects which turns back in order to confer upon the *motive* its structure as a motive. It is only because I escape the in-itself by nihilating myself toward my possibilities that this in-itself can take on value as cause or motive. Causes and motives have meaning only inside a projected ensemble which is precisely an ensemble of non-existents. And this ensemble is ultimately myself as transcendence; it is Me in so far as I have to be myself outside of myself.

If we recall the principle which we established earlier—namely that it is the apprehension of a revolution as possible which gives to the workman's suffering its value as a motive—we must thereby conclude that it is by fleeing a situation toward our possibility of changing it that we organize this situation into complexes of causes and motives. The nihilation by which we achieve a withdrawal in relation to the situation is the same as the ekstasis by which we project ourselves toward a modification of this situation. The result is that it is in fact impossible to find an act without a motive but that this does not mean that we must conclude that the motive causes the act; the motive is an integral part of the act. For as the resolute project toward a change is not distinct from the act, the motive, the act, and the end are all constituted in a single upsurge. Each of these three structures claims the two others as its meaning. But the organized totality of the three is no longer explained by any particular structure, and its upsurge as the pure temporalizing nihilation of the in-itself is one with freedom.

It is the act which decides its ends and its motives, and the act is the expression of freedom.

. . .

Common opinion does not hold that to be free means only to choose oneself. A choice is said to be free if it is such that it could have been other than what it is. I start out on a hike with friends. At the end of several hours of walking my fatigue increases and finally becomes very painful. At first I resist and then suddenly I let myself go, I give up, I throw my knapsack down on the side of the road and let myself fall down beside it. Someone will reproach me for my act and will mean thereby that I was free—that is, not only was my act not determined by any thing or person, but also I could have succeeded in resisting my fatigue longer, I could have done as my companions did and reached the resting place before relaxing. I shall defend myself by saying that I was *too tired*. Who is right? Or rather is the debate not based on incorrect premises? There is no doubt that I could have done otherwise, but that is not the problem. It ought to be formulated rather like this: could I have done otherwise without perceptibly modifying the organic totality of the projects which I am; or is the fact of resisting my fatigue such that instead of remaining a purely local and accidental modification of my behavior, it could be effected only by means of a radical transformation of my being-in-the-world—a transformation, moreover, which is *possible?* In other words: I could have done otherwise. Agreed. But *at what price?*

We are going to reply to this question by first presenting a *theoretical* description which will enable us to grasp the principle of our thesis. We shall see subsequently whether the concrete reality is not shown to be more complex and whether without contradicting the results of our theoretical inquiry, it will not lead us to enrich them and make them more flexible.

Let us note first that the fatigue by itself could not provoke my decision. As we saw with respect to physical pain, fatigue is only the way in which I exist my body. It is not at first the object of a positional consciousness, but it is the very facticity of my consciousness. If then I hike across the country, what is revealed to me is the surrounding world; this is the object of my consciousness, and this is what I transcend toward possibilities which are my own—those, for example, of arriving this evening at the place which I have set for myself in advance. Yet to the extent that I apprehend this countryside with my eyes which unfold distances, my legs which climb the hills and consequently cause new sights and new obstacles to appear and disappear, with my back which carries the knapsack—to this extent I have a non-positional consciousness (of) this body which rules my relations with the world and which signifies my engagement in the world, in the form of fatigue. Objectively and in correlation with this non-thetic consciousness the roads are revealed as interminable, the slopes as *steeper,* the sun as more burning, *etc.* But I do not yet *think* of my fatigue; I apprehend it as the quasi-object of my reflection. Nevertheless there comes a moment when I do seek to consider my fatigue and to recover it. We really ought to provide an interpretation for this same intention; however, let us take

it for what it is. It is not at all a contemplative apprehension of my fatigue; rather, as we saw with respect to pain, I *suffer* my fatigue. That is, a reflective consciousness is directed upon my fatigue in order to live it and to confer on it a value and a practical relation to myself. It is only on this plane that the fatigue will appear to me as bearable or intolerable. It will never be anything in itself, but it is the reflective For-itself* which rising up suffers the fatigue as intolerable.

Here is posited the essential question: my companions are in good health—like me; they have had practically the same training as I so that although it is not possible to *compare* psychic events which occur in different subjectivities, I usually conclude—and witnesses after an objective consideration of our bodies-for-others conclude—that they are for all practical purposes "as fatigued as I am." How does it happen therefore that they suffer their fatigue differently? Someone will say that the difference stems from the fact that I am a "sissy" and that the others are not. But although this evaluation undeniably has a practical bearing on the case and although one could take this into account when there arose a question of deciding whether or not it would be a good idea to take me on another expedition, such an evaluation can not satisfy us here. We have seen that to be ambitious is to project conquering a throne or honors; it is not a *given* which would incite one to conquest; it is this conquest itself. Similarly to be a "sissy" can not be a factual given and is only a name given to the way in which I suffer my fatigue. If therefore I wish to understand under what conditions I can suffer a fatigue as unbearable, it will not help to address oneself to so-called factual givens, which are revealed as being only a choice; it is necessary to attempt to examine this choice itself and to see whether it is not explained within the perspective of a larger choice in which it would be integrated as a secondary structure. If I question one of my companions, he will explain to me that he is fatigued, of course, but that he *loves* his fatigue; he gives himself up to it as to a bath; it appears to him in some way as the privileged instrument for discovering the world which surrounds him, for adapting himself to the rocky roughness of the paths, for discovering the "mountainous" quality of the slopes. In the same way it is this light sunburn on the back of his neck and this slight ringing in his ears which will enable him to realize a direct contact with the sun. Finally the feeling of effort is for him that of fatigue overcome. But as his fatigue is nothing but the passion which he endures so that the dust of the highways, the burning of the sun, the roughness of the roads may exist to the fullest, his effort (i.e., this sweet familiarity with a fatigue which he loves, to which he abandons himself and which nevertheless he himself directs) is given as a way of appropriating the mountain, of suffering it to the end and being victor over it. . . . Thus my companion's fatigue is lived in a vaster project of a trusting abandon to nature, of a passion consented to in

---

* "For-itself" is Sartre's special term for the person. Sartre uses this term to reflect what he takes to be a fundamental fact about persons: they can appraise and so construct themselves.

order that it may exist at full strength, and at the same time the project of sweet mastery and appropriation. It is only in and through this project that the fatigue will be able to be understood and that it will have meaning for him.

. . .

Freedom and Responsibility

Although the considerations which are about to follow are of interest primarily to the ethicist, it may nevertheless be worthwhile after these descriptions and arguments to return to the freedom of the for-itself and to try to understand what the fact of this freedom represents for human destiny.

The essential consequence of our earlier remarks is that man being condemned to be free* carries the weight of the whole world on his shoulders; he is responsible for the world and for himself as a way of being. We are taking the word "responsibility" in its ordinary sense as "consciousness (of) being the incontestable author of an event or of an object." In this sense the responsibility of the for-itself is overwhelming since he is the one by whom it happens that *there is* a world; since he is also the one who makes himself be, then whatever may be the situation in which he finds himself, the for-itself must wholly assume this situation with its peculiar coefficient of adversity, even though it be insupportable. He must assume the situation with the proud consciousness of being the author of it, for the very worst disadvantages or the worst threats which can endanger my person have meaning only in and through my project; and it is on the ground of the engagement which I am that they appear. It is therefore senseless to think of complaining since nothing foreign has decided what we feel, what we live, or what we are.

Furthermore this absolute responsibility is not resignation; it is simply the logical requirement of the consequences of our freedom. What happens to me happens through me, and I can neither affect myself with it nor revolt against it nor resign myself to it. Moreover everything which happens to me is *mine*. By this we must understand first of all that I am always equal to what happens to me *qua* man, for what happens to a man through other men and through himself can be only human. The most terrible situations of war, the worst tortures do not create a non-human state of things; there is no non-human situation. It is only through fear, flight, and recourse to magical types of conduct that I shall decide on the non-human, but this decision is human, and I shall carry the entire responsibility for it. But in addition the situation is *mine* because it is the image of my free choice of myself, and everything which it presents to me is *mine* in that this represents me and symbolizes me. Is it not I who decide the coefficient of adversity in things and even their unpredictability by deciding myself?

---

* Sartre thinks that people have no choice about being free. As a "for-itself," one is always in a position to appraise and to choose, or to choose not to appraise and choose.

Thus there are no *accidents* in a life; a community event which suddenly bursts forth and involves me in it does not come from the outside. If I am mobilized in a war, this war is *my* war; it is in my image and I deserve it. I deserve it first because I could always get out of it by suicide or by desertion; these ultimate possibles are those which must always be present for us when there is a question of envisaging a situation. For lack of getting out of it, I have *chosen* it. This can be due to inertia, to cowardice in the face of public opinion, or because I prefer certain other values to the value of the refusal to join in the war (the good opinion of my relatives, the honor of my family, *etc.*). Anyway you look at it, it is a matter of a choice. This choice will be repeated later on again and again without a break until the end of the war. Therefore we must agree with the statement by J. Romains, "In war there are no innocent victims."[1] If therefore I have preferred war to death or to dishonor, everything takes place as if I bore the entire responsibility for this war. Of course others have declared it, and one might be tempted perhaps to consider me as a simple accomplice. But this notion of complicity has only a juridical sense, and it does not hold here. For it depended on me that for me and by me this war should not exist, and I have decided that it does exist. There was no compulsion here, for the compulsion could have got no hold on a freedom. I did not have any excuse; for as we have said repeatedly in this book, the peculiar character of human reality is that it is without excuse. Therefore it remains for me only to lay claim to this war.

But in addition the war is *mine* because by the sole fact that it arises in a situation which I cause to be and that I can discover it there only by engaging myself for or against it, I can no longer distinguish at present the choice which I make of myself from the choice which I make of the war. To live this war is to choose myself through it and to choose it through my choice of myself. There can be no question of considering it as "four years of vacation" or as a "reprieve," as a "recess," the essential part of my responsibilities being elsewhere in my married, family, or professional life. In this war which I have chosen I choose myself from day to day, and I make it mine by making myself. If it is going to be four empty years, then it is I who bear the responsibility for this.

Finally, as we pointed out earlier, each person is an absolute choice of self from the standpoint of a world of knowledges and of techniques which this choice both assumes and illumines; each person is an absolute upsurge at an absolute date and is perfectly unthinkable at another date. It is therefore a waste of time to ask what I should have been if this war had not broken out, for I have chosen myself as one of the possible meanings of the epoch which imperceptibly led to war. I am not distinct from this same epoch; I could not be transported to another epoch without contradiction. Thus I *am* this war which restricts and limits and makes comprehensible the period which preceded it. In this sense we may define more precisely the responsibility of the for-itself if to the earlier quoted statement, "There are no innocent victims," we add the

[1] J. Romains, *Les hommes de bonne volonté. Vol. III: "Prélude à Verdun."*

491

words, "We have the war we deserve." Thus, totally free, undistinguishable from the period for which I have chosen to be the meaning, as profoundly responsible for the war as if I had myself declared it, unable to live without integrating it in my *situation,* engaging myself in it wholly and stamping it with my seal, I must be without remorse or regrets as I am without excuse; for from the instant of my upsurge into being, I carry the weight of the world by myself alone without anything or any person being able to lighten it.

Yet this responsibility is of a very particular type. Someone will say, "I did not ask to be born." This is a naive way of throwing greater emphasis on our facticity. I am responsible for everything, in fact, except for my very responsibility, for I am not the foundation of my being. Therefore everything takes place as if I were compelled to be responsible. I am *abandoned* in the world, not in the sense that I might remain abandoned and passive in a hostile universe like a board floating on the water, but rather in the sense that I find myself suddenly alone and without help, engaged in a world for which I bear the whole responsibility without being able, whatever I do, to tear myself away from this responsibility for an instant. For I am responsible for my very desire of fleeing responsibilities. To make myself passive in the world, to refuse to act upon things and upon Others is still to choose myself, and suicide is one mode among others of being-in-the-world.* Yet I find an absolute responsibility for the fact that my facticity (here the fact of my birth) is directly inapprehensible and even inconceivable, for this fact of my birth never appears as a brute fact but always across a projective reconstruction of my for-itself. I am ashamed of being born or I am astonished at it or I rejoice over it or in attempting to get rid of my life I affirm that I live and I assume this life as bad. Thus in a certain sense I *choose* being born. This choice itself is integrally affected with facticity since I am not able not to choose, but this facticity in turn will appear only in so far as I surpass it toward my ends. Thus facticity is everywhere but inapprehensible; I never encounter anything except my responsibility. That is why I can not ask, "Why *was* I born?" or curse the day of my birth or declare that I did not ask to be born, for these various attitudes toward my birth—i.e., toward the *fact* that I realize a presence in the world—are absolutely nothing else but ways of assuming this birth in full responsibility and of making it *mine.* Here again I encounter only myself and my projects so that finally my abandonment—i.e., my facticity—consists simply in the fact that I am condemned to be wholly responsible for myself. I am the being which *is* in such a way that in its being its being is in question. And this "is" of my being *is* at present and inapprehensible.

Under these conditions since every event in the world can be revealed to me only as an *opportunity* (an opportunity made use of, lacked, neglected, *etc.*), or better yet since everything which happens to us can be considered as a *chance* (i.e., can appear to us only as a way of realizing this being which is in question in our being) and since others as transcendences-transcended are themselves

---

* What Sartre means here by "being-in-the-world" is a way of acting, choosing.

only *opportunities* and *chances,* the responsibility of the for-itself extends to the entire world as a peopled-world. It is precisely thus that the for-itself apprehends itself in anguish; that is, as a being which is neither the foundation of its own being nor of the Other's being nor of the in-itselfs* which form the world, but a being which is compelled to decide the meaning of being—within it and everywhere outside of it. The one who realizes in anguish his condition as *being* thrown into a responsibility which extends to his very abandonment has no longer either remorse or regret or excuse; he is no longer anything but a freedom which perfectly reveals itself and whose being resides in this very revelation. But as we pointed out at the beginning of this work, most of the time we flee anguish in bad faith.

---

* "In-itself" is a contrastive term with "for-itself." Unlike a for-itself, an in-itself cannot choose its mode of being.

43

Free Will as Involving Determinism

R. E. HOBART

R. E. Hobart (1868–1963) was an American philosopher who taught at Harvard University. The name "Hobart" was a pseudonym; his real name was Dickinson Miller.

This essay is a classic defense of soft determinism, the view that free will and determinism are compatible. Hobart defends their compatibility, and indeed the stronger view that a free act must be causally determined. He argues that a free act is precisely one that is caused by the agent's own desires. Freedom is doing what you want to do, and not what you are compelled or forced to do. Causation does not rule out freedom as long as it works through the agent's own desires.

If Hobart's conception of freedom is to stand, it must illuminate the connection between freedom and moral responsibility. Hobart attempts to show it does, arguing that the desire that causes a person to act is typically an element of his character. Moreover, a person's character—his stable desires, and perhaps other psychological traits—is precisely what makes him what he is. Because of this, an act which satisfies Hobart's definition of freedom will stem from, and express, the agent's basic nature. Hence, it is the agent, and no one else, who should be held responsible for it.

Although Hobart's account is attractive, it is also open to various objections. One problem is that determinism implies the agent's character was itself causally determined, and that his act was theoretically predictable even before it occurred. Another is that Hobart's definition may seem to imply an agent is free even if he could not have done otherwise. Hobart attempts to rebut these objections. He argues that neither the role of the past in determining a person's character nor the predictability of his actions is relevant to a person's freedom. Moreover, he notes that an agent motivated by his desires could have done differently in the sense that different desires would have issued in different actions. On these and related questions, Hobart's subtle discussion deserves careful study.

THE THESIS OF THIS ARTICLE is that there has never been any ground for the controversy between the doctrine of free will and determinism, that it is based upon a misapprehension, that the two assertions are entirely consistent, that one of them strictly implies the other, that they have been opposed only because of our natural want of the analytical imagination. In so saying I do not tamper with the meaning of either phrase. That would be unpardonable. I

mean free will in the natural and usual sense, in the fullest, the most absolute sense in which for the purposes of the personal and moral life the term is ever employed. I mean it as implying responsibility, merit and demerit, guilt and desert. I mean it as implying, after an act has been performed, that one "could have done otherwise" than one did. I mean it as conveying these things also, not in any subtly modified sense but in exactly the sense in which we conceive them in life and in law and in ethics. These two doctrines have been opposed because we have not realised that free will can be analysed without being destroyed, and that determinism is merely a feature of the analysis of it. And if we are tempted to take refuge in the thought of an "ultimate," an "innermost" liberty that eludes the analysis, then we have implied a deterministic basis and constitution for this liberty as well. For such a basis and constitution lie in the idea of liberty.

. . .

I am not maintaining that determinism is true; only that it is true in so far as we have free will. That we are free in willing is, broadly speaking, a fact of experience. That broad fact is more assured than any philosophical analysis. It is therefore surer than the deterministic analysis of it, entirely adequate as that in the end appears to be. But it is not here affirmed that there are no small exceptions, no slight undetermined swervings, no ingredient of absolute chance. All that is here said is that such absence of determination, if and so far as it exists, is no gain to freedom, but sheer loss of it; no advantage to the moral life, but blank subtraction from it.—When I speak below of "the indeterminist"* I mean the libertarian† indeterminist, that is, him who believes in free will and holds that it involves indetermination.

By the analytical imagination is meant, of course, the power we have, not by nature but by training, of realising that the component parts of a thing or process, taken together, each in its place, with their relations, are identical with the thing or process itself. If it is "more than its parts," then this "more" will appear in the analysis. It is not true, of course, that all facts are susceptible of analysis, but so far as they are, there is occasion for the analytical imagination. We have been accustomed to think of a thing or a person as a whole, not as a combination of parts. We have been accustomed to think of its activities as the way in which, as a whole, it naturally and obviously behaves. It is a new, an unfamiliar and an awkward act on the mind's part to consider it, not as one thing acting in its natural manner, but as a system of parts that work together in a complicated process. Analysis often seems at first to have taken away the individuality of the thing, its unity, the impression of the familiar identity. For a simple mind this is strikingly true of the analysis of a complicated machine. The reader may recall Paulsen's ever significant story about the introduction

---

* An indeterminist is someone who denies that all events are caused.

† A libertarian is someone who believes in free will.

of the railway into Germany. When it reached the village of a certain enlightened pastor, he took his people to where a locomotive engine was standing, and in the clearest words explained of what parts it consisted and how it worked. He was much pleased by their eager nods of intelligence as he proceeded. But on his finishing they said: "Yes, yes, Herr Pastor, but there's a horse inside, isn't there?" They could not *realise* the analysis. They were wanting in the analytical imagination. Why not? They had never been trained to it. It is in the first instance a great effort to think of all the parts working together to produce the simple result that the engine glides down the track. It is easy to think of a horse inside doing all the work. A horse is a familiar totality that does familiar things. They could no better have grasped the physiological analysis of a horse's movements had it been set forth to them.

. . .

Now the position of the indeterminist is that a free act of will is the act of the self. The self becomes through it the author of the physical act that ensues. This volition of the self causes the physical act but it is not in its turn caused, it is "spontaneous." To regard it as caused would be determinism. The causing self to which the indeterminist here refers is to be conceived as distinct from character; distinct from temperament, wishes, habits, impulses. He emphasises two things equally: the physical act springs from the self through its volition, and it does not spring merely from character, it is not simply the result of character and circumstances. If we ask, "Was there anything that induced the self thus to act?" we are answered in effect, "Not definitively. The self feels motives but its act is not determined by them. It can choose between them."

The next thing to notice is that this position of the indeterminist is taken in defence of moral conceptions. There would be no fitness, he says, in our reproaching ourselves, in our feeling remorse, in our holding ourselves or anyone guilty, if the act in question were not the act of the self instead of a product of the machinery of motives.

We have here one of the most remarkable and instructive examples of something in which the history of philosophy abounds—of a persistent, and agelong deadlock due solely to the indisposition of the human mind to look closely into the meaning of its terms.

How do we reproach ourselves? We say to ourselves, "How negligent of me!" "How thoughtless!" "How selfish!" "How hasty and unrestrained!" "That I should have been capable even for a moment of taking such a petty, irritated view!" etc. In other words, we are attributing to ourselves at the time of the act, in some respect and measure, a bad character, and regretting it. And that is the entire point of our self-reproach. We are turning upon ourselves with disapproval and it may be with disgust; we wish we could undo what we did in the past, and, helpless to do that, feel a peculiar thwarted poignant anger and shame at ourselves that we *had it in us* to perpetrate the thing we now condemn. It is self we are reproaching, i.e., self that we are viewing as bad in that it produced bad actions. Except in so far as what-it-is produced these bad actions, there is no ground for reproaching it (calling it bad) and no meaning

in doing so. All self-reproach is self-judging, and all judging is imputing a character. We are blaming ourselves. If spoken, what we are thinking would be dispraise. And what are praise and dispraise? Always, everywhere, they are *descriptions* of a person (more or less explicit) with favourable or unfavourable feeling of what is described,—descriptions in terms of value comporting fact, or of fact comporting value, or of both fact and value. In moral instances they are descriptions of his character. We are morally characterising him in our minds (as above) with appropriate feelings. We are attributing to him the character that we approve and like and wish to see more of, or the contrary. All the most intimate terms of the moral life imply that the act has proceeded from *me,* the distinctive me, from the manner of man I am or was. And this is the very thing on which the libertarian lays stress. What the indeterminist prizes with all his heart, what he stoutly affirms and insists upon, is precisely what he denies, namely, that I, the concrete and specific moral being, am the author, the source of my acts. For, of course, that is determinism. To say that they come from the self is to say that they are determined by the self—the moral self, the self with a moral quality. He gives our preferrings the bad name of the machinery of motives, but they are just what we feel in ourselves when we decide. When he maintains that the self at the moment of decision may act to some extent independently of motives, *and is good or bad according as it acts in this direction or that,* he is simply setting up one character within another, he is separating the self from what he understands by the person's character as at first mentioned, only thereupon to attribute to it a character of its own, *in that he judges it good or bad.*

The whole controversy is maintained by the indeterminist in order to defend the validity of the terms in which we morally judge,—for example, ourselves. But the very essence of all judgment, just so far as it extends, asserts determination.

If in conceiving the self you detach it from all motives or tendencies, what you have is not a morally admirable or condemnable, not a morally characterisable self at all. Hence it is not subject to reproach. You cannot call a self good because of its courageous free action, and then deny that its action was determined by its character. In calling it good because of that action you have implied that the action came from its goodness (which means its good character) and was a sign thereof. By their fruits ye shall know them. The indeterminist appears to imagine that he can distinguish the moral "I" from all its propensities, regard its act as arising in the moment undetermined by them, and yet can then (for the first time, in his opinion, with propriety!) ascribe to this "I" an admirable quality. At the very root of his doctrine he contradicts himself. How odd that he never catches sight of that contradiction! He fights for his doctrine in order that he may call a man morally good, on account of his acts, with some real meaning; and his doctrine is that a man's acts (precisely so far as "free" or undetermined) do not come from his goodness. So they do not entitle us to call him good. He has taken his position in defence of moral conceptions, and it is fatal to all moral conceptions.

We are told, however, that it is under determinism that we should have no right any more to praise or to blame. At least we could not do so in the old

sense of the terms. We might throw words of praise to a man, or throw words of blame at him, because we know from observation that they will affect his action; but the old light of meaning in the terms has gone out. Well, all we have to do is to keep asking what this old meaning was. We praise a man by saying that he is a good friend, or a hard worker, or a competent man of business, or a trusty assistant, or a judicious minister, or a gifted poet, or one of the noblest of men—one of the noblest of characters! In other words, he is a being with such and such qualities. If it is moral praise, he is a being with such and such tendencies to bring forth good acts. If we describe a single act, saying, for instance: "Well done!" we mean to praise the person for the act as being the author of it. It is he who has done well and proved himself capable of doing so. If the happy act is accidental we say that no praise is deserved for it. If a person is gratified by praise it is because of the estimate of him, in some respect or in general, that is conveyed. Praise (once again) means description, with expressed or implied admiration. If any instance of it can be found which does not consist in these elements our analysis fails. "Praise the Lord, O my soul, *and forget not all His benefits*,"—and the Psalm goes on to tell His loving and guarding acts toward humankind. To praise the Lord is to tell His perfections, especially the perfections of His character. This is the old light that has always been in words of praise and there appears no reason for its going out.

Indeterminism maintains that we need not be impelled to action by our wishes, that our active will need not be determined by them. Motives "incline without necessitating." We choose amongst the ideas of action before us, but need not choose solely according to the attraction of desire, in however wide a sense that word is used. Our inmost self may rise up in its autonomy and moral dignity, independently of motives, and register its sovereign decree.

Now, *in so far* as this "interposition of the self" is undertermined, the act is not *its* act, it does not issue from any concrete continuing self; it is born at the moment, of nothing, hence it expresses no quality; it bursts into being from no source. The self does not register *its* decree, for the decree is not the product of just that *"it."* The self does not rise up in *its* moral dignity, for dignity is the quality of an enduring being, influencing its actions, and therefore expressed by them, and that would be determination. *In proportion* as an act of volition starts of itself without cause it is exactly, so far as the freedom of the individual is concerned, as if it had been thrown into his mind from without—"suggested" to him—by a freakish demon. It is exactly like it in this respect, that in neither case does the volition arise from what the man is, cares for or feels allegiance to; it does not come out of him. *In proportion* as it is undetermined, it is just as if his legs should suddenly spring up and carry him off where he did not prefer to go. Far from constituting freedom, that would mean, in the exact measure in which it took place, the loss of freedom. It would be an interference, and an utterly uncontrollable interference, with his power of acting as he prefers. In fine, then, *just so far* as the volition is undetermined, the self can neither be praised nor blamed for it, since it is not the act of the self.

The principle of free will says: "*I* produce my volitions." Determinism says:

"My volitions are produced by *me*." Determinism is free will expressed in the passive voice.

After all, it is plain what the indeterminists have done. It has not occurred to them that our free will may be resolved into its component elements. (Thus far a portion only of this resolution has been considered.) When it is thus resolved they do not recognize it. The analytical imagination is considerably taxed to perceive the identity of the free power that we feel with the component parts that analysis shows us. We are gratified by their nods of intelligence and their bright, eager faces as the analysis proceeds, but at the close are a little disheartened to find them falling back on the innocent supposition of a horse inside that does all the essential work. They forget that they may be called upon to analyse the horse. They solve the problem by forgetting analysis. The solution they offer is merely: "There is a self inside which does the deciding." Or, let us say, it is as if the *Pfarrer* were explaining the physiology of a horse's motion. They take the whole thing to be analysed, imagine a duplicate of it reduced in size, so to speak, and place this duplicate-self inside as an explanation—making it the elusive source of the "free decisions." They do not see that they are merely pushing the question a little further back, since the process of deciding, with its constituent factors, must have taken place within that inner self. Either it decided in a particular way because, on the whole, it preferred to decide in that way, or the decision was an underived event, a rootless and sourceless event. It is the same story over again. In neither case is there any gain in imagining a second self inside, however wonderful and elusive. Of course, it is the first alternative that the indeterminist is really imagining. If you tacitly and obscurely conceive the self as deciding *its own way, i.e.,* according to its preference, but never admit or recognise this, then you can happily remain a libertarian indeterminist; but upon no other terms. In your theory there is a heart of darkness.

Freedom.—In accordance with the genius of language, free will means freedom of persons in willing, just as "free trade" means freedom of persons (in a certain respect) in trading. The freedom of anyone surely always implies his possession of a power, and means the absence of any interference (whether taking the form of restraint or constraint) with his exercise of that power. Let us consider this in relation to freedom in willing.

"Can."—We say, "I can will this or I can will that, whichever I choose." Two courses of action present themselves to my mind. I think of their consequences, I look on this picture and on that, one of them commends itself more than the other, and I will an act that brings it about. I knew that I could choose either. That means that I had the power to choose either.

What is the meaning of "power"? A person has a power if it is a fact that when he sets himself in the appropriate manner to produce a certain event that event will actually follow. I have the power to lift the lamp; that is, if I grasp it and exert an upward pressure with my arm, *it will rise.* I have the power to will so and so; that is, if I want, that act of will will take place. That and none other is the meaning of power, is it not? A man's being in the proper active

posture of body or of mind is the cause, and the sequel in question will be the effect. (Of course, it may be held that the sequel not only does but must follow, in a sense opposed to Hume's doctrine of cause. Very well; the question does not here concern us.)

Thus power depends upon, or rather consists in, a law. The law in question takes the familiar form that if something happens a certain something else will ensue. If A happens then B will happen. The law in this case is that if the man definitively so desires then volition will come to pass. There is a series, wish—will—act. The act follows according to the will (that is a law,—I do not mean an underived law) and the will follows according to the wish (that is another law). A man has the power (sometimes) to act as he wishes. He has the power (whenever he is not physically bound or held) to act as he wills. He has the power always (except in certain morbid states) to will as he wishes. All this depends upon the laws of his being. Wherever there is a power there is a law. In it the power wholly consists. A man's power to will as he wishes is simply the law that his will follows his wish.

What, again, does freedom mean? It means the absence of any interference with all this. Nothing steps in to prevent my exercising my power.[1]

All turns on the meaning of "can." "I can will either this or that" means, I am so constituted that if I definitively incline to this, the appropriate act of will will take place, and if I definitively incline to that, the appropriate act of will will take place. The law connecting preference and will exists, and there is nothing to interfere with it. My free power, then, is not an exemption from law but in its inmost essence an embodiment of law.

Thus it is true, after the act of will, that I could have willed otherwise. It is most natural to add, "if I had wanted to"; but the addition is not required. The point is the meaning of "could." I could have willed whichever way I pleased. I had the power to will otherwise, there was nothing to prevent my doing so, and I should have done so if I had wanted. If someone says that the wish I actually had prevented my willing otherwise, so that I could not have done it, he is merely making a slip in the use of the word "could." He means, that wish could not have produced anything but this volition. But "could" is asserted not of the wish (a transient fact to which power in this sense is not and should not be ascribed) but of the person. And the person *could* have produced something else than that volition. He could have produced any volition he wanted; he had the power to do so.

But the objector will say, "The person as he was at the moment—the person

---

[1] A word as to the relation of power and freedom. Strictly power cannot exist without freedom, since the result does not follow without it. Freedom on the other hand is a negative term, meaning the absence of something, and implies a power only because that whose absence it signifies is interference, which implies something to be interfered with. Apart from this peculiarity of the term itself, there might be freedom without any power. Absence of interference (of what would be interference if there were a power) might exist in the absence of a power; a man might be free to do something because there was nothing to interfere with his doing it, but might have no power to do it. Similarly and conveniently we may speak of a power as existing though interfered with; that is, the law may exist that would constitute a power if the interference were away.

as animated by that wish—could not have produced any other volition." Oh, yes, he could. "Could" has meaning not as applied to a momentary actual phase of a person's life, but to the person himself of whose life that is but a phase; and it means that (even at that moment) he had the power to will just as he preferred. *The idea of power, because it is the idea of a law, is hypothetical, carries in itself hypothesis as part of its very intent and meaning—"if he should prefer this, if he should prefer that,"—and therefore can be truly applied to a person irrespective of what at the moment he does prefer. It remains hypothetical even when applied.*[2] This very peculiarity of its meaning is the whole point of the idea of power. It is just because determinism is true, because a law obtains, that one "could have done otherwise."

Sidgwick[*] set over against "the formidable array of cumulative evidence" offered for determinism the "affirmation of consciousness" "that I can now choose to do" what is right and reasonable, "however strong may be my inclination to act unreasonably."[3] But it is not against determinism. It is a true affirmation (surely not of immediate consciousness but of experience), the affirmation of my power to will what I deem right, however intense and insistent my desire for the wrong. I can will anything, and can will effectively anything that my body will enact. I can will it despite an inclination to the contrary of any strength you please—strength as felt by me before decision. We all know cases where we have resisted impulses of great strength in this sense and we can imagine them still stronger. I have the power to do it, and shall do it, shall exercise that power, if I prefer. Obviously in that case (be it psychologically remarked) my solicitude to do what is right will have proved itself even stronger (as measured by ultimate tendency to prevail, though not of necessity by sensible vividness or intensity) than the inclination to the contrary, for that is what is meant by my preferring to do it. I am conscious that the field for willing is open; I can will anything that I elect to will. Sidgwick did not analyse the meaning of "can," that is all. He did not precisely catch the outlook of consciousness when it says, "I can." He did not distinguish the function of the word, which is to express the the availability of the alternatives I see when, before I have willed, and perhaps before my preference is decided, I look out on the field of conceivable voliton. He did not recognize that I must have a word to express my power to will as I please, quite irrespective of what I shall please, and that "can" is that word. It is no proof that I cannot do something to point out that I shall not do it if I do not prefer. A man, let us say, can turn on the electric light; but he will not turn it on if he walks away from it; though it is still true that he can turn it on. When we attribute power to a man we do not mean that something will accomplish itself without his wanting it to. That

---

[2] I am encouraged by finding in effect the same remark in Prof. G. E. Moore's *Ethics*, ch. vi., at least as regards what he terms one sense of the word "could." I should hazard saying, the only sense in this context. [G. E. Moore (1873–1958) was an influential British philosopher.]

[3] *Methods of Ethics*, 7th ed., 65.

[*] Henry Sidgwick (1838–1900) was an English moral philosopher.

would never suggest the idea of power. We mean that if he makes the requisite move the thing will be accomplished. It is part of the idea that the initiative shall rest with him. The initiative for an act of will is a precedent phase of consciousness that we call the definitive inclination, or, in case of conflict, the definitive preference for it. If someone in the throes of struggle with temptation says to himself, "I can put this behind me," he is saying truth and precisely the pertinent truth. He is bringing before his mind the act of will, unprevented, quite open to him, that would deliver him from what he deems noxious. It may still happen that the noxiousness of the temptation does not affect him so powerfully as its allurement, and that he succumbs. It is no whit less true, according to determinism, that he could have willed otherwise. To analyse the fact expressed by "could" is not to destroy it.

But it may be asked, "Can I will in opposition to my strongest desire at the moment when it is strongest?" If the words "at the moment when it is strongest" qualify "can," the answer has already been given. If they qualify "will," the suggestion is a contradiction in terms. Can I turn-on-the-electric-light-at-a-moment-when-I-am-not-trying-to-do-so? This means, if I try to turn on the light at a moment when I am not trying to, will it be turned on? A possible willing as I do not prefer to will is not a power on my part, hence not to be expressed by "I can."

Everybody knows that we often will what we do not want to will, what we do not prefer. But when we say this we are using words in another sense than that in which I have just used them. In *one* sense of the words, whenever we act we are doing what we prefer, on the whole, in view of all the circumstances. We are acting for the greatest good or the least evil or a mixture of these. In the *other* and more usual sense of the words, we are very often doing what we do not wish to do, *i.e.*, doing some particular thing we do not wish because we are afraid of the consequences or disapprove of the moral complexion of the particular thing we do wish. We do the thing that we do not like because the other thing has aspects that we dislike yet more. We are still doing what we like best on the whole. It is again a question of the meaning of words.

Compulsion.—The indeterminist conceives that according to determinism the self is carried along by wishes to acts which it is thus necessitated to perform. This mode of speaking distinguishes the self from the wishes and represents it as under their dominion. This is the initial error. This is what leads the indeterminist wrong on all the topics of his problem. And the error persists in the most recent writings. In fact, the moral self is the wishing self. The wishes are its own. It cannot be described as under their dominion, for it has no separate predilections to be overborne by them; they themselves are its predilections. To fancy that because the person acts according to them he is compelled, a slave, the victim of a power from whose clutches he cannot extricate himself, is a confusion of ideas, a mere slip of the mind. The answer that has ordinarily been given is surely correct; all compulsion is causation, but not all causation is compulsion. Seize a man and violently force him to do something, and he is compelled—also caused—to do it. But induce him to do it by giving him reasons and his doing it is caused but not compelled.

Passivity.—We have to be on our guard even against conceiving the induce-ment as a cause acting like the impact of a billiard ball, by which the self is precipitated into action like a second billiard ball, as an effect. The case is not so simple. Your reasons have shown him that his own preferences require the action. He does it of his own choice; he acts from his own motives in the light of your reasons. The sequence of cause and effect goes on within the self, with contributory information from without.

It is not clarifying to ask, "Is a volition free or determined?" It is the person who is free, and his particular volition that is determined. Freedom is something that we can attribute only to a continuing being, and he can have it only so far as the particular transient volitions within him are determined. (According to the strict proprieties of language, it is surely events that are caused, not things or persons; a person or thing can be caused or determined only in the sense that its beginning to be, or changes in it, are caused or determined.)

It is fancied that, owing to the "necessity" with which an effect follows upon its cause, if my acts of will are caused I am not free in thus acting. Consider an analogous matter. When I move I use ligaments. "Ligament" means that which binds, and a ligament does bind bones together. But *I* am not bound. *I* (so far as my organism is concerned) am rendered possible by the fact that my bones are bound one to another; that is part of the secret of my being able to act, to move about and work my will. If my bones ceased to be bound one to another I should be undone indeed. The human organism is detached, but it is distinctly important that its component parts shall not be detached. Just so my free power of willing is built up of tight cause-and-effect connections. The point is that when I employ the power thus constituted nothing determines the par-ticular employment of it but *me*. Each particular act of mine is determined from outside itself, *i.e.*, by a cause, a prior event. But not from outside me. I, the possessor of the power, am not in my acts passively played upon by causes outside me, but am enacting my own wishes in virtue of a chain of causation within me. What is needed is to distinguish broadly between a particular effect, on the one hand, and, on the other, the detached, continuous life of a mental individual and his organism; a life reactive, but reacting according to its own nature.

What makes the other party uncontrollably reject all this—let us never for-get—is the words. They smell of sordid detail, of unwinsome psychological machinery. They are not bathed in moral value, not elevated and glowing. In this the opponents' instinct is wholly right; only when they look for the value they fail to focus their eyes aright. It is in the whole act and the whole trait and the whole being that excellence and preciousness inhere; analysis must needs show us elements which, taken severally, are without moral expressiveness; as would be even the celestial anatomy of an angel appearing on earth. The ana-lytic imagination, however, enables us to see the identity of the living fact in its composition with the living fact in its unity and integrity. Hence we can resume the thought of it as a unit and the appropriate feelings without fancying that analysis threatens them or is at enmity with them.

. . .

Prediction.—If we knew a man's character thoroughly and the circumstances that he would encounter, determinism (which we are not here completely asserting) says that we could foretell his conduct. This is a thought that repels many libertarians. Yet to predict a person's conduct need not be repellent. If you are to be alone in a room with $1000 belonging to another on the table and can pocket it without anyone knowing the fact, and if I predict that you will surely *not* pocket it, that is not an insult. I say, I know you, I know your character; you will not do it. But if I say that you are "a free being" and that I really do not know whether you will pocket it or not, that is rather an insult. On the other hand, there are cases where prediction is really disparaging. If I say when you make a remark, "I knew you were going to say that," the impression is not agreeable. My exclamation seems to say that your mind is so small and simple that one can predict its ideas. That is the real reason why people resent in such cases our predicting their conduct; that if present human knowledge, which is known to be so limited, can foresee their conduct, it must be more naive and stereotyped than they like to think it. It is no reflection upon the human mind or its freedom to say that one who knew it through and through (a human impossibility) could foreknow its preferences and its spontaneous choice. It is of the very best of men that even we human beings say, "I am sure of him." It has perhaps in this controversy hardly been observed how much at this point is involved, how far the question of prediction reaches. The word "reliable" or "trustworthy" is a prediction of behaviour. Indeed, all judgment of persons whatever, in the measure of its definitude, is such a prediction.

Material Fate.—The philosopher in the old story, gazing at the stars, falls into a pit. We have to notice the pitfall in our subject to which, similarly occupied, Prof. Eddington* has succumbed.

"What significance is there in my mental struggle to-night whether I shall or shall not give up smoking, if the laws which govern the matter of the physical universe already pre-ordain for the morrow a configuration of matter consisting of pipe, tobacco, and smoke connected with my lips?[4]

No laws, according to determinism, pre-ordain such a configuration, unless I give up the struggle. Let us put the matter aside for the moment, to return to it. Fatalism says that my morrow is determined no matter how I struggle. This is of course a superstition. Determinism says that my morrow is determined through my struggle. There is this significance in my mental effort, that it is deciding the event. The stream of causation runs through my deliberations and decision, and, if it did not run as it does run, the event would be different. The past cannot determine the event except through the present. And no past moment determined it any more truly than does the present moment. In other words, each of the links in the causal chain must be in its place. Determinism (which, the reader will remember, we have not here taken for necessarily true in all detail) says that the coming result is "pre-ordained" (literally, caused) at each

* Sir Arthur Eddington (1882–1944) was an English astronomer and physicist.

[4] *Philosophy*, Jan., 1933, p. 41

stage, and therefore the whole following series for to-morrow may be described as already determined; so that did we know all about the struggler, how strong of purpose he was and how he was influenced (which is humanly impossible) we could tell what he would do. But for the struggler this fact (supposing it to be such) is not pertinent. If, believing it, he ceases to struggle, he is merely revealing that the forces within him have brought about that cessation. If on the other hand he struggles manfully he will reveal the fact that they have brought about his success. Since the causation of the outcome works through his struggle in either case equally, it cannot become for him a moving consideration in the struggle. In it the question is, "Shall I do this or that?" It must be answered in the light of what there is to recommend to me this or that. To this question the scientific truth (according to determinism) that the deliberation itself is a play of causation is completely irrelevant; it merely draws the mind delusively away from the only considerations that concern it.

. . .

Self as Product and Producer.—We can at this stage clearly see the position when a certain very familiar objection is raised. "How can any one be praised or blamed if he was framed by nature as he is, if heredity and circumstance have given him his qualities? A man can surely be blamed only for what he does himself, and he did not make his original character; he simply found it on his hands." A man is to be blamed only for what he does himself, for that alone tells what he is. He did not make his character; no, but he made his acts. Nobody blames him for making such a character, but only for making such acts. And to blame him for that is simply to say that he is a bad act-maker. If he thinks the blame misapplied he has to prove that he is not that sort of an act–maker. Are we to be told that we may not recognise what he is, with appropriate feelings of its quality, because he did not create himself—a mere contortion and intussusception of ideas? The moral self cannot be *causa sui*. To cause his original self a man must have existed before his original self. Is there something humiliating to him in the fact that he is not a contradiction in terms? If there were a being who made his "original character," and made a fine one, and we proceeded to praise him for it, our language would turn out to be a warm ascription to him of a still earlier character, so that the other would not have been original at all. To be praised or blamed you have to be; and be a particular person; and the praise or blame is telling what kind of a person you are. There is no other meaning to be extracted from it. Of course, a man does exist before his later self, and in that other sense he can be a moral *causa sui*. If by unflagging moral effort he achieves for himself better subsequent qualities, what can merit praise but the ingredient in him of aspiration and resolution that was behind the effort? If he should even remake almost his whole character, still there would be a valiant remnant that had done it.

. . .

The indeterminist, we noticed, requires a man to be "an absolute moral source" if we are to commend him. Well, if he were so, what could we say about him but what kind of a source he was? And he is so in fact. Suppose

now that this source has in turn a source—or that it has not! Does that (either way) change what it is?

"But moral severity! How can we justly be severe toward a mere fact in nature—inhuman nature?" Because it is evil; because it must be checked. If somebody takes pleasure in torturing an innocent person, we spring to stop the act; to hold back the perpetrator, if need be with violence; to deter him from doing it again, if need be with violence; to warn any other possible perpetrators: "This shall not be done; we are the enemies of this conduct; this is evil conduct." At what could we be indignant but at a fact in somebody's human nature? Our severity and enmity are an active enmity to the evil; they are all part of that first spring to stop the act. "Society is opposed in every possible manner to such cruelty. You shall be made to feel that society is so, supposing that you cannot be made to feel yourself the vileness of the act." It does not remove our sense of its vileness to reflect that he was acting according to his nature. That is very precisely why we are indignant at him. We intend to make him feel that his nature is in that respect evil and its expression insufferable. We intend to interfere with the expression of his nature. That what he did proceeded from it is not a disturbing and pause-giving consideration in the midst of our conduct, but the entire basis of it. The very epithet "vile" assumes that his behaviour arose from an intention and a moral quality in the man. How can we justly be severe? Because he *ought* to be checked and deterred, made to feel the moral estimate of what he has been doing.

. . .

To be sure, determinism as a philosophic doctrine, determinism so named, may come as a new and repellent idea to us. We have been thinking in the right terms of thought all the while, but we did not identify them with terms of causation; when the philosophical names are put upon them we recoil, not because we have a false conception of the facts, but a false conception of the import of the philosophical terms. When we feel that somebody could have done otherwise but chose to do a wrong act knowingly, then we one and all feel that he is culpable and a proper object of disapproval, as we ought to feel. We merely have not been schooled enough in the application of general terms to call the course of mental events within him causation. So again, goodness consists in qualities, but the qualities express themselves in choosing, which is unfettered and so often trembles in the balance; when we are suddenly confronted with the abstract question, "Can we be blamed for a quality we did not choose?" the colours run and the outlines swim a little; some disentanglement of abstract propositions is required, though we think aright in practice on the concrete cases. So all that philosophic determinism "forces us to face" is the meaning of our terms.

No, it is the opposite doctrine that must revolutionise our attitude toward moral judgments. It it is true, we must come to see that no moral severity towards the helpless subject of an act of will that he suddenly finds discharging itself within him, though not emanating from what he is or prefers, can be deserved or relevant. To comprehend all is to pardon all—so far as it is undetermined. Or, rather, not to pardon but to acquit of all.

However, in face of the actual facts, there is something that does bring us to a larger than the usual frame of mind about indignation and punishment and the mood of severity. And that is thought, sympathetic thought, any thought that enters with humane interest into the inner lives of others and pursues in imagination the course of them. In an outbreak of moral indignation we are prone to take little cognizance of that inner life. We are simply outraged by a noxious act and a noxious trait (conceived rather objectively and as it concerns the persons affected) and feel that such act should not be and that such a trait should be put down. The supervening of a sympathetic mental insight upon moral indignation is not a displacement, but the turning of attention upon facts that call out other feelings too. To comprehend all is neither to pardon all nor to acquit of all; overlooking the disvalue of acts and intentions would not be comprehension; but it is to appreciate the human plight; the capacity for suffering, the poor contracted outlook, the plausibilities that entice the will. This elicits a sympathy or concern co-existing with disapproval. That which is moral in moral indignation and behind it, if we faithfully turn to it and listen, will not let us entirely wash our hands even of the torturer, his feelings and his fate; certainly will not permit us to take satisfaction in seeing him in turn tortured, merely for the torture's sake. His act was execrable because of its effect on sentient beings, but he also is a sentient being. The humanity that made us reprobate his crime has not ceased to have jurisdiction. The morality that hates the sin has in that very fact the secret of its undiscourageable interest in the sinner. We come, not to discredit indignation and penalty, nor to tamper with their meaning, but to see their office and place in life and the implications wrapped up in their very fitness.

. . .

Responsibility.—Again, it is said that determinism takes from man all responsibility. As regards the origin of the term, a man is responsible when he is the person to respond to the question why the act was performed, how it is to be explained or justified. That is what he must answer; he is answerable for the act. The act proceeded from him. He is to say whether it proceeded consciously. He is to give evidence that he did or did not know the moral nature of the act and that he did or did not intend the result. He is to say how he justifies it or if he can justify it. If the act proceeded from him by pure accident, if he can show that he did the damage (if damage it was) by brushing against something by inadvertence, for example, then he has not to respond to the question what he did it for—he is not consciously responsible—nor how it is justified—he is not morally responsible, though of course he may have been responsible in these respects for a habit of carelessness.

But why does the peculiar moral stain of guilt or ennoblement of merit belong to responsibility? If an act proceeds from a man and not merely from his accidental motion but from his mind and moral nature, we judge at once that like acts may be expected from him in the future. The colour of the act for good or bad is reflected on the man. We see him now as a living source of possible acts of the same kind. If we must be on our guard against such acts we must be on our guard against such men. If we must take steps to defend

ourselves against such acts we must take steps to defend ourselves against such men. If we detest such acts, we must detest that tendency in such men which produced them. He is guilty in that he knowingly did evil, in that the intentional authorship of evil is in him. Because the act proceeded in every sense from him, for that reason he is (so far) to be accounted bad or good according as the act is bad or good, and he is the one to be punished if punishment is required. And that is moral responsibility.

But how, it is asked, can I be responsible for what I will if a long train of past causes has made me will it—the old query asked anew in relation to another category, responsibility, which must be considered separately. Is it not these causes that are "responsible"- for my act—to the use the word in the only sense, says the objector, that seems to remain for it?

The parent past produced the man, none the less the man is responsible for his acts. We can truly say that the earth bears apples, but quite as truly that trees bear apples. The earth bears the apples by bearing trees. It does not resent the claim of the trees to bear the apples, or try to take the business out of the trees' hands. Nor need the trees feel their claim nullified by the earth's part in the matter. There is no rivalry between them. A man is a being with free will and responsibility; where this being came from, I repeat, is another story. The past finished its functions in the business when it generated him as he is. So far from interfering with him and coercing him the past does not even exist. If we could imagine it as lingering on into the present, standing over against him and stretching out a ghostly hand to stay his arm, then indeed the past would be interfering with his liberty and responsibility. But so long as it and he are never on the scene together they cannot wrestle; the past cannot overpower him. The whole alarm is an evil dream, a nightmare due to the indigestion of words. The past has created, and left extant, a free-willed being.

. . .

If the general view here taken, which seems forced upon us in the prosaic process of examining words, is correct, then as we look back over the long course of this controversy and the false antithesis that has kept it alive, how can we help exclaiming, "What waste!" Waste is surely the tragic fact above all in life; we contrast it with the narrow areas where reason and its economy of means to ends in some measure reign. But here is huge waste in the region of reasoning itself, the enemy in the citadel. What ingenuity, what resource in fresh shifts of defence, what unshaken loyalty to inward repugnances, what devotion to ideal values, have here been expended in blind opposition instead of analysis. The cause of determinism, seeming to deny freedom, has appeared as the cause of reason, of intelligence itself, and the cause of free will, seeming to exclude determination, has appeared that of morals. The worst waste is the clash of best things. In our subject it is time this waste should end. Just as we find that morality requires intelligence to give effect and remains rudimentary and largely abortive till it places the conscience of the mind in the foreground, so we find that determinism and the faith in freedom meet and are united in the facts, and that the long enmity has been a bad dream.

44

Acting Freely

GERALD DWORKIN

Gerald Dworkin (b. 1937) is Professor of Philosophy at the University of Illinois at Chicago Circle. He is the editor of Determinism, Free-Will and Moral Responsibility, *and a co-editor of* The IQ Controversy.

  Like R. E. Hobart (reading 43), Dworkin is a compatibilist, or soft determinist. In this essay, Dworkin tries to solve some important problems that have plagued the compatibilist position. Specifically, he addresses the question of how we are to distinguish free acts for which we are morally responsible from acts done under compulsion. This difficulty arises because the soft determinist believes all a person's actions are caused by his own desires. After carefully analyzing a number of different complications, Dworkin proposes to solve this problem by drawing a distinction between two sorts of desires, or reasons for action. According to Dworkin, a free act is an act motivated by a reason which the agent finds acceptable; one acts under compulsion when one acts for a reason that one does not want to have as a reason to act.

> And those who act under compulsion and unwillingly act with pain.
> Aristotle
> *Nichomachean Ethics*

WHENEVER COERCION TAKES PLACE one will is subordinated to another. The coerced is no longer a completely independent agent. If my will is overborne by yours I serve your ends and not mine. I am motivated by your interests and not mine. I do what you want, not want I want.

  The domain of human motivation is always haunted by a tautology hovering overhead. The strongest motive always prevails; the dominant desire determines action; we always do what we want to do. Since coercion designates a process in which a particular class of reasons for acting is singled out it might be predicted that, sooner or later, these truisms would make their appearance. And following close behind, as usual, we find paradox.

I

  The following is surely a plausible explication of what it is for a man to be free.

> I am free when my conduct is under my control, and I act under constraint when my conduct is controlled by someone else. My conduct is under my own control

509

when it is determined by my own desires, motives, and intentions, and not under my control when it is determined by the desires, motives, and intentions of someone else. University of California Associates.[1]

Against this view Oppenheim argues that

Whenever I act my conduct is 'determined by my own desires, motives, and intentions.' This follows from the very definitions of 'action'.[2]

Plamenatz takes a similar position.

It is, of course, quite clear that all action is necessarily voluntary, since it is never possible for a man to do what he does not wish. Indeed, to do what one wishes is the same thing as to act, for an action which has no motive is inconceivable.[3]

This remark occurs in the context of a discussion of freedom and Plamenatz illustrates his comment with a typical example of coercion.

If, for instance, A threatens to shoot B unless he raises his hand above his head, then B's motive for doing what is required, although it consists in the fear of what will happen to him if he does not (or rather in the effect of this fear, which is the desire to do what may ensure its not happening to him) is as much his motive as any other motive would be.

But if it is true that we always do what we wish, that we always act in accordance with our own desires, then how is the distinction between acting freely and acting under constraint to be drawn? What happens to Mill's definition of liberty as "doing what one desires"? What sense is to be attached to the idea of making or forcing someone to do what he doesn't want to do? How is coercion possible?

Another way of putting the problem is in terms of the kinds of explanation we give of human action. If asked to explain why Jones acts in a certain way we may make reference to certain goals he is pursuing, certain intentions or desires, and/or particular beliefs he has about his condition and environment. If we have specified correctly his beliefs and his goals and have ascertained further that the proper connection exists between them, we have given an explanation of his behavior (assuming it is an action which is to be explained, for we may give the same kind of explanation to explain why someone desires something). If a reference to beliefs and desires is possible in every case of explanation of motivated behavior, there will necessarily be a reference to

---

[1] "The Freedom of the Will," reprinted in Feigl and Sellars, *Readings in Philosophical Analysis* (New York: Appleton-Century-Crofts, 1949), p. 599.

[2] F. Oppenheim, *Dimensions of Freedom* (New York: St. Martin's Press, 1961), p. 36.

[3] J. P. Plamenatz, *Consent, Freedom and Political Obligation* (London: Oxford University Press, 1938), p. 110.

something the agent wants or desires. Hence, so this argument goes, it is always true that an agent does something that he wants to do. This form of the argument is presented by Daveney in an article on "Wanting."

> It may be stated of every intentional action that I perform that in some sense I *want* to do it; because if I didn't want to do it I wouldn't do it. If anyone wishes to deny this, let him explain how it is possible for every action to be explained in terms of some "want" statement.[4]

What for Oppenheim and Plamenatz is a necessary connection between the concepts of action and desire is for Daveney a consequence of the kinds of explanation that are available for understanding human action. In both cases the conclusion is that we always do as we wish or want.

II

Obviously those who hold this view can find ways of drawing a distinction between actions done under compulsion and those done freely, just as, in another philosophical tradition, the egoist can argue that he can distinguish altruism from selfishness. The enlightened egoist having read his Butler and Bradley* agrees that a man's laying down his life for his country is, in many respects, quite different from a man's betraying his country for monetary gains. All the egoist insists upon is that both men act to satisfy some desire of theirs. Similarly one can argue that to act under compulsion is to act as one wants but there are important differences which depend on the source of our wants. There are desires which a man has naturally and spontaneously and those which are imposed upon him by force. There are wants which come from inside and those which come from outside. This view assimilates desires to possessions, some of which a man comes with, some of which he borrows or acquires, and some of which are thrust upon him—still they are all "his." Even with property, however, not every mode of acquisition entitles us to say that something belongs to a man, is his. With the "inner" world, whether it be the realm of the will or the understanding, "mine" and "thine" are immensely complicated notions. I propose in this essay to follow out some of the alternative ways of conceptualizing this relation and to examine the consequences of adopting various alternatives.

III

It is essential to clarify the relationship between the identification of a desire as belonging to a man, as being his desire, and the mode of acquisition of the desire. With property we can consider both possession and ownership, what a

---

[4] T. V. Daveney, "Wanting", *Philosophical Quarterly*, Vol. 11. No. 43, April, 1961, p. 139.

* Joseph Butler (1692–1752) and F. H. Bradley (1846–1924) were British philosophers.

man has and what belongs to him. The concepts are independent for something may belong to a man although he does not possess it, e.g., it is stolen from him, and he may possess something that doesn't belong to him. Sometimes determining what belongs to someone will be, in part, tracing how the object came into his possession. Did he buy it? Was it given to him? Did he take it without permission? Did he make a mistake and take the wrong object? The criteria for either possession or ownership are very complicated and may only be defined by considering appropriate conventions and the purposes they serve.

Can a similar distinction be drawn with respect to our desires? We might begin by considering another "inner state" that of "belief." We identify a belief p as belonging to X i.e., that X believes p, if his behavior is such that it can be explained on the assumption that he does so believe. Others, or indeed X himself, may know that he acquired the belief in some unusual manner, say, through conditioning or manipulation or the injection of a drug, and this may make a difference in their appraisal of his actions but this does not affect the fact that X believes p, i.e., that the belief belongs to X. The assertion "He (X) doesn't believe p; he was brainwashed" is a *non sequitur*.* The latter part has no logical bearing on the former. Nor will it help to bring in a "really" to save the situation. "He doesn't really believe it" applies to someone who pretends to believe p, or, perhaps to someone who deceives (pretends to) himself about p. There is no question in any of these situations of acting in accordance with the beliefs of another, of one's action being determined not by one's own beliefs but by those of someone else. The normal, rational paths to belief may have been circumvented but then there are no necessary (essential) paths that one must tread before the belief can be ascribed to one.

In view of this it seems plausible to say much the same kind of thing in the case of desire. Don't we identify a desire as belonging to someone in terms of the role played by the desire in explaining the actions of the individual? Shouldn't there be this parallel since beliefs and wants enter explanation in a symmetric fashion? Action can only be explained in terms of a belief given knowledge, perhaps assumed, about the wants of the agent. If I explain X's crossing the street by saying that he believes the drugstore is open, it is in a context that assumes X must want something that is in some way connected with the drug-store being open. Aren't there, then, exactly parallel cases to the ones I gave in connection with belief? A man may desire to eat toothpaste because of a post-hypnotic suggestion. Someone may want to commit suicide given the choice between that and public disgrace. The father of a kidnapped child may want to give money to the kidnapper. In each case we identify the desire as belonging to the agent in terms of what is needed to adequately explain his behavior. I am going to argue that cases like the last example are significantly different from the others and that bringing out the difference will show that the basis for ascribing desires to individuals is more complicated than that for ascribing beliefs.

---

*A *non sequitur* is a statement or argument whose conclusion does not follow from its premise.

IV

When we speak of what a man wants to do we may be referring to his intentions or to his desires, to what he is prepared to do or to what he is pleased to do. When we focus on the former we are interested in what he is aiming at, what the point of his doings is. When we examine the latter we are concerned with what satisfies, with that which brings action to a (temporary) stop. In many instances the two notions go together as we prepare to do what we wish to do and so it is easy to pass from "he did it" to "he intended to do it" to "he wanted to do it." In general we can form two lists, the first containing notions such as intention, decision, choice, will, the second containing desire, want, wish. The terms of these two lists are related in non-contingent ways—no special explanation is required to account for the fact that we intend to do what we want to do. When I have decided what I want to do then I have decided what I intend to do if the circumstances are favorable and there is no counter-vailing consideration. But our wishes and our intentions may spring apart due to such varied factors as obligations, natural necessities, conventional pressures, coercion, etc. Though these all differ from one another they all represent constraints on our inclinations, obstacles to the normal satisfaction of our desires.

Consider the victim of a highwayman. Why do we say that he doesn't do what he wants? Is it that he is doing something that he doesn't want to do? That depends on how what he is doing is described. If it is described as handing over money to another then he may or may not mind doing that sort of thing; it depends on the circumstances. A man might want to hand over some money to another because he is asked by a relative, or because he is feeling charitable, or because he desires to rid himself of worldly things. What he doesn't want to do when faced with the highwayman is to hand money over in these circumstances, for these reasons. Suppose it is claimed that handing the money over in these circumstances is a way of preserving his life and that this *is* something that he wants to do. This is presumably the kind of thing Daveney has in mind when he says it is "possible for every action to be explained in terms of some 'want' statement." I don't know whether the general form of this thesis is correct or not. It could be stated this way. Given any action of an agent he either wants to perform the action for its own sake *or* there is something the agent wants which is such that he believes that performing this action is a condition (necessary or sufficient) for obtaining what he wants. I am inclined to think that this isn't so, that one may perform an action for reasons that have nothing to do with one's wants and that the only way to establish the thesis would be to invent "pseudo-wants." But even accepting the general thesis doesn't commit one to accepting the view that we always do what we want to do unless we accept the inference from 'X wants A' and 'B is a necessary condition for obtaining A' to 'X wants B'; a form of inference which is clearly invalid in view of any number of counter-examples. "He who wills the end, wills the necessary means to it" is only true if by 'willing' is understood 'intending' and not 'wanting.' There are very good grounds for supposing that a man doesn't intend to

go on living when we find out that he doesn't intend to go on breathing. On the other hand finding out that a man doesn't want to go to the dentist doesn't supply very good grounds for supposing that he doesn't want to get rid of his toothache.

It might be argued that we can describe what the man is doing as "preserving his life" instead of doing x as a means of preserving his life just as we can describe what a person does as "turning on the light" instead of "flipping the switch in order to turn on the light." Under this description isn't the man doing what he wants to do? More generally won't it always be possible to re-describe the action in terms of some more general desire whose object is promoted by the action as described more narrowly? Thus the man who hands money over to a kidnapper is "saving the life of his child", the man who accedes to the demands of a blackmailer is "preserving his reputation", etc. And since it is admitted that *these* are genuine desires of the agent it follows that the agent is doing what he wants.

Normally the difficulty with this type of argument is that statements of desire are cases of indirect discourse so that it is not safe to take inferences for granted. From "Kennedy wanted to become the 37th President of the United States" we cannot infer that "Kennedy wanted to be the only President assassinated in Dallas" although, in fact, the two descriptions refer to the same man. The usual explanation for this is that a man may want something under a certain description and not be aware that another description is also true of the object of his desire. This explanation cannot account for the kinds of situations we are considering for there is no ignorance present in these cases. If it is proper to redescribe the act of handing money over to the kidnapper as "saving the child's life" one cannot avoid the conclusion that the man is doing what he wants by claiming that he is not aware of both descriptions. His reason for handing over the money *is* to save the child's life. This is not something he might discover later as a man might discover that the 37th President will be assassinated.

This argument relies on two premises neither of which can be taken for granted. The first assumes the legitimacy of redescribing the specific action that takes place (handing over the money, keeping silent) as "saving his child" or "preserving his life." The second premise asserts that a certain form of inference is valid; that from "X wants A" and "X knows that A is B (doing A is doing B)" we can infer that "X wants B." Let us consider each of these assumptions.

The first assumption concerns the conditions under which we may replace one description of an action by some other description. It is a claim that one and the same action may be referred to by different descriptions. Unfortunately we know very little about the modes of individuating actions and the criteria for the identity of actions. All that we have are some pre-systematic data about when we are inclined to say that doing one thing is the same as doing another and when we feel reluctant to make such claims. Anscombe gives an example of a man pumping water (which is poisoned) into a cistern which supplies water to a house in which a number of party chiefs are living.[5] She points out

[5] G. E. M. Anscombe, *Intention* (Ithaca: Cornell University Press, 1957), p. 40.

that we may ask the man why he is x'ing (moving his arm) and get an answer that is either of the form "to y" (to operate the pump) or "I'm y'ing" (I'm pumping the water). This can go on for a while but at some point there is a break such that while one can ask "Why are you x'ing?" the answer can only be of the form "to y" not of the form "I'm y'ing." To the question "Why are you poisoning the inhabitants?" the answer "to save the Jews" does not allow the further description of what the man is doing as "saving the Jews." Unfortunately Anscombe gives us no tests for determining when such a break occurs. There are obvious hypotheses which suggest themselves. For example that it is a necessary condition for redescribing x as y (where one does x in order to bring about y) that x and y be sufficiently close together in time and that there be reasonable grounds for supposing that x will be followed by y. Thus A's stabbing B in order that B shall die may be redescribed as A's killing B (provided that 1) B dies, and 2) does so within a reasonably short period of time). But A's making a speech in order to be elected President will not be redescribed as A's being elected President. However, both these conditions are met by the example of the man who hands over his money to a kidnapper. He has grounds for supposing this will save his child and this will presumably happen within a short span of time.

The general thesis that we can always replace "doing x in order to do y" by "doing x, in these circumstances, is doing y" is false. If I am practicing parking in order to pass my driver's test then it just is not the case that practicing parking, in those circumstances, *is* passing my driver's test. The specific thesis that when a man hands money to a kidnapper we can identify "what he does" as saving his life seems to me to be wrong and to arise from a confusion between an *action* which is discrete, particular, done or performed, and an *end* which is general, occupies no definite stretch in time, is accomplished or succeeded in. One can succeed in an end (acquiring money) without doing anything at all. On the other hand one can succeed in an end (preserving one's life) by performing very different kinds of actions (eating a steak dinner, running from the battlefield). To fully substantiate this point one would have to have a fully developed theory about how we individuate and typify actions. All I have hoped to accomplish here is throw doubt on the first premise of the argument.

The second premise states that the following inference is always valid: "X wants (to do) A", "X knows that (doing) A is (doing) B", hence "X wants (to do) B." One can think of a number of counter-examples. X wants to marry A, knows that A is the woman with the worst temper in the world, but it is not the case that X wants to marry the woman with the worst temper in the world. X wants to push the switch (to see if his hand still functions after an accident), knows that pushing the switch turns on the lights, yet X doesn't want to turn on the lights. X wants to sleep with A, knows that sleeping with A is committing adultery, but it is not the case that X wants to commit adultery. As in the case with many such arguments about intensional contexts one may deny the plausibility of the counter-example and insist in each case upon the validity of the inference. It is possible to say that "in a sense" X wants B in all these cases, but the sense is specified by repeating the conditions of the example. One can

also insist, to refer to more familiar problems, that if Smith believes that Jones is next door, and Jones is the murderer of Robinson, then "in a sense" Smith believes that the murderer of Robinson is next door, where again the sense is specified by the belief condition and the identity condition. Such victories are hollow because if anything significant depended upon them we would ultimately rely on our prior recognition of the meaning of the key terms; a meaning which is usually less problematic than the inferences.

Although I think that the thesis that we always do what we want to is false it does bring to our attention a significant point about motivating conduct by creating reasons for action. When we speak of providing a motive for someone to act this may be taken in two ways. It may mean that we have created or stimulated a new type of motivation (curiosity, exercise of skill) or that we have harnessed a pre-existing motivation of the agent by creating a situation in which he now has a reason for acting which he lacked previously, i.e., he can satisfy an antecedently existing basic drive. Coercion always involves this latter process, utilizing basic drives which almost everyone shares—self-preservation, avoidance of pain, embarrassment, concern for the welfare of those close to us. It is a mistake, however, to jump from the fact that there must be some pre-existing desire of the agent to be exploited to claiming that when the agent acts to satisfy those desires he does what he wants.

Two patterns of action should be kept distinct although they may both be schematized as follows: X wants to do A, some factor intervenes, X does B. Sometimes when the intervening factor is of the proper kind, e.g., incentives, new information, re-examination of the consequences of doing A, X no longer wants to do A and doing B is a result of this transformation, of his changing his mind. Sometimes, however, we do not think of X's desires as changing but of being frustrated or thwarted. To return to the earlier discussion of the mode of acquisition of desires I am suggesting that it is a mistake to think of someone as acquiring a new "want" or "desire to do something" as a result of coercion. What a person may acquire as a result of such intervention is a new intention, a new disposition to act. But wants are not to be equated with mere dispositions to act. We must be able to distinguish between those actions which we perform because we want to and those we perform because we have to.

V

Granted that sometimes we do things for other reasons than our wanting to do them there still remains the problem of why acting on some of these reasons, but not others, is not acting freely. What I want to do now is account for the fact that only certain reasons are considered coercive and restrictive of liberty; why, *contra* Hobbes, we regard fear and not covetousness as cancelling liberty.[6]

---

[6] "For there appeareth no reason why that which we do upon fear, should be less firm than that which we do for covetousness. For both the one and the other make the action voluntary." Hobbes, T. "De Corpore Politico," in *Body, Man and Citizen*, ed. R. S. Peters (New York: Crowell-Collier, 1962), p. 286.

It is obvious that the mere presence of external intervention, that is the creating of reasons for action by others is not enough to explain why acting on some of these reasons, but not others, is acting unfreely.[7] If I had not been told of a book sale or been given tickets to the opera I would have done something else this evening. Given the new situation I no longer do what I wanted to do formerly but that is because I now want to do something else. But the notions of "doing what I want" and "acting freely" cannot be identified. It does not follow that if I do what I do not want to do I act unfreely. Consider the following situation in which another person creates a reason for my doing something which I would not choose to do had the reason not been created. A dull and boring acquaintance invites me to his home for dinner knowing that I accept some principle of reciprocity or gratitude. I now have a reason for extending him an invitation to my house—something I do not want to do. Yet my invitation is issued freely, albeit reluctantly. My liberty has not been infringed upon. What differentiates this kind of situation from that of the kidnapper or blackmailer? I suggest it is the attitude a man takes toward the reasons for which he acts, whether or not he identifies himself with these reasons, assimilates them to himself, which is crucial for determining whether or not he acts freely. Men resent acting for certain reasons; they would not choose to be motivated in certain ways. They mind acting simply in order to preserve a present level of welfare against diminution by another. They resent acting simply in order to avoid unpleasant consequences with no attendant promotion of their own interests and welfare. On the other hand although I may not want to perform the particular act of issuing a dinner invitation to a boring acquaintance I do not mind acting for reasons which fall under the heading of reciprocity. Such examples are interesting because there are many parallels in the vocabulary used to talk about obligations and that used to talk about compulsion. We speak of "having to do it," "having no choice." There is present in both a contrast between what one does reluctantly and what one does willingly. In his *Lectures on Ethics* Kant has a category called "moral compulsion" which is defined as "a determination to the unwilling performance of an action" and I am morally compelled to act by another if he "forces me by moral motives to do an action which I do reluctantly.[8] The Japanese have a species of moral obligation call Giri and they talk of being "forced with giri" or of someone "concerning me with giri" meaning that someone has argued the speaker into an act he did not want to perform by raising some issue of *on* (moral indebtedness). Many of these situations involve calling someone's attention to reasons which already exist for doing something rather than creating reasons for acting and therefore fall under the heading of moral persuasion—but the dividing line

---

[7] Cf. "What we say of a man when we say that he has not acted of his own free will is that the action of some other person has caused him to be confronted with an object of desire or aversion but for which he would not have acted as he did." Hardie, W. F. R. "My Own Free Will", *Philosophy*, January, 1957, p. 22.

[8] (New York: Harper and Row, 1963), p. 27.

is not sharp. The weight of advice is often due as much to the stature of the adviser—*his* saying it is a new reason for acting—as to the cogency of the reasons to which attention is directed. I am chiefly interested in what Fried calls "moral causation"; moving another to action by "bringing about circumstances such that the desired action is one which in the circumstances is required by an acknowledged moral principle."[9] Like coercion this provides reasons for acting which depend for their efficacy on pre-established motivations. One might say that the difference between moral persuasion and moral causation is the difference between blowing on existing coals to make them glow (or burn) and providing new fuel.

Why don't we consider moral causation an infringement on the liberty of the agent? The agent doesn't do what he wants to do and he only acts in this way because a reason has been provided by another agent. I suggest that it is the agent's attitude toward acting for that kind of reason which makes the difference. Since moral causation can only succeed if the person accepts certain principles of morality and accepting such principles is accepting new reasons for acting the agent has already accepted the legitimacy of certain motivations. Whether this acceptance is due to the fact that such principles are ultimately self-imposed limitations (Kant) or whether some reference must be made to prudential gains that accrue from such acceptance (Hobbes) need not be settled at this juncture. All that is essential is that most of us do not resent acting for reasons of morality.

This factor, the attitude of the agent toward the reasons and desires which motivate his conduct, makes it difficult, at times, for us to assess correctly whether or not someone acts freely. The kleptomaniac who regards his impulses to steal as, in some sense, an alien feature of his personality and resents being driven to act as he does, is a case in point. It is highly questionable whether such people literally could not act otherwise, that it is beyond their powers to offer resistance to their anti-social impulses. It is more plausible to suppose that it is just very difficult for them to refrain, that they act in this fashion not in order to satisfy some rationally recognized need but rather to avoid some danger to their psychic economy the details of which may be spelled out by psychologists. They are, therefore, similar in important ways to victims of external coercion. Any theory of internal, psychological freedom has to have notions which correspond to those psychoanalysts refer to as "ego-alien." There must be part of the human personality which take up an "attitude" toward the reason, desires, and motives which determine the conduct of the agent.

Let me put my thesis in another way. Aristotle observes that "those who act under compulsion and unwillingly act with pain." I am arguing that this is a necessary fact. We only consider ourselves as being interfered with, as no longer acting on our own free will, when we find acting for certain reasons painful. To put the thesis epigrammatically; we do not find it painful to act because we are compelled; we consider ourselves compelled because we find it painful to act for these reasons.

[9] Charles Fried, "Moral Causation", *Harvard Law Review* (April, 1964), p. 1261.

VI

I shall conclude by discussing some objections that can be raised to my theory and some applications of it. First some objections. Consider a kleptomaniac who knows that what he does is wrong, who cannot stop himself by his own conscious efforts, but does know that constant surveillance with its attendant threats of detection and punishment is effective in preventing him from stealing. It could be said of him that he welcomes the motivation provided by threat of punishment yet isn't it true that he is interfered with, deprived of liberty, as much as any other person would be? It is important to bear in mind the distinction between what a man is free to do and what he does freely. The kleptomaniac is not free to take other people's property in a society which has a legal apparatus which forbids such acts. A man is not free to do something if he is either prevented from doing it or if his doing it would result in severe deprivation to him. All this is true independently of the wants of any particular person. That I have never contemplated kidnapping anyone, nor have any desire to do so, doesn't negate the fact that I am not free to do so. Nevertheless it may be the case that at some point I want to kidnap somebody and yet refrain from doing so and it can now be asked whether I did so of my own free will. The answer to *that* question will depend on my reasons. It will make a difference whether I refrained out of fear of being punished or because I decided it would be wrong to act on my desire or because an easier way of making money occurred to me. To give another example, I may pay my taxes freely (because, say, I accept some principle of fairness which requires all to make an equal sacrifice in return for benefits which all share in), although I am not free not to pay my taxes. Even if I didn't want to pay my taxes I would be forced to.

There are a number of distinct locutions that include the word "free" and which deserve some sytematic analysis. The only one who has attempted this, as far as I know, is Oppenheim. In addition to "acting freely" and "being free to do x" there are the notions of "feeling free," "being free," and something we might call "being free with respect to x." I am free to pay my taxes because nobody prevents me from doing so or threatens me with harm if I do so. Oppenheim says I am not free to pay my taxes because I am not free to refrain from doing so, but this is a mistake. What he should say, and what he does sometimes slip into saying, is that I am not free with respect to paying my taxes, e.g., it is not open to me to refrain. Thus some sample definitions would run: (I use "iff" to mean "if and only if".)

(1) A is unfree to X, iff either A is prevented from doing X or it is made punishable for A to do X.
(2) A is free to do X, iff it is not the case that A is unfree to do X.
(3) A is free with respect to doing X, iff A is free to do X and A is free to refrain from doing X.

How the notions of "feeling free" and "being free" are related is very obscure. The following observation seems quite wrong as it stands, although it is reasonable if "being free" were replaced by "feeling free":

. . . an individual may be free even when subject to restrictions (and compulsions) if those restrictions facilitate the achievement of his purposes, and provided that he willingly accepts these restrictions in principle.[10]

If one accepts the statement as it stands then one is led to the paradox of the free slave, the individual who accepts the fetters that bind him. But fetters are fetters even if they are accepted fetters. Nevertheless, as opposed to those like Oppenheim who dismiss the notion of "feeling free" as somehow "subjective" and not a worthy candidate for "scientific treatment" of the question of human freedom, I think that this idea is a very important one, that ultimately we care about being free because there are occasions on which we want to feel free. We think that it is significant to the slave that he is not free because we believe, given certain plausible assumptions about human nature, that there will come a time when he will desire to do something (which he doesn't at this moment of time) and will then resent the restrictions that have always been present. He will mind not being free to do certain things which hitherto he has not wanted to do.

As for "acting freely", which is what I have been concerned about, I am suggesting that it be defined as follows:

A does X freely *iff* A does X for reasons which he doesn't mind acting from.

This definition implies that A may do something freely though he is neither free to do it nor free with respect to doing it.

To return to the kleptomaniac, normally people who refrain from stealing because of fear of punishment are said not to be acting freely but I would argue that given the case as it is described this man does act freely. For since he welcomes the motivation provided by the fear of punishment we can take this as an indication that what he really wants to do is to be stopped from acting as it appears he wants to act. In so far as the threat enables him to do what he really wants to do he cannot regard it as an obstacle to acting freely but merely as an additional and necessary motivation for doing what he wants to do. To understand what a man wants to do is at least partly to understand which interventions he regards as obstacles and which he regards as either aids to present desires or considerations for changing desires.

Still it might be objected that there may be aberrant individuals who don't mind acting for reasons which most of us do mind acting for, and conversely do mind acting for reasons that most of us are indifferent to or welcome. Thus Mr. X doesn't mind being motivated by fear of loss. Are we to say that he acts freely when he hands his money over to the robber? It is difficult to know what to say here for we are faced with a breakdown of normal connections which are not quite strong enough to be necessary bonds but are not so loose that their severance does not create difficulties for our understanding of what is

[10]J. R. Pennock, *Liberal Democracy* (New York: Rinehart, 1950), p. 59.

occurring. We are asked to imagine a man who having the normal attitudes toward his goods does not resent giving them up when confronted with a "money or your life" situation. What will this man do when faced with a choice between two paths: one of which he knows to be free of robbers and the other of which he believes to be lined with them? Consider the following dialogue.

A: "He will take the robber-free path."

B: "Why?"

A: "Because he wants to retain his goods."

B: "Not in all circumstances. Otherwise one would make the prediction that if faced with two paths one of which is lined with people selling food and the other not, X would choose the path free of vendors."

A: "That's true. But in the case of buying food he is willing to give up some of his goods. In the case of the robbers he is not."

B: "Why not? By hypothesis, once in a coercive situation he doesn't mind giving up his goods, so what reasons does he have for avoiding getting into such situations?"

It begins to look as if Mr. X cannot have the normal attitude toward his possessions for it is part of *that* attitude that one tries to avoid getting into situations in which one gives up valued things without getting something in return. This is too crude for it sounds as if I am ruling out the possibility of altruistic or charitable acts. What I want to say is that we can only understand Mr. X if we interpret his actions as being altruistic ("Poor man, he needs the money more than I do.") or motivated by some need to atone or stemming from a re-evaluation of the worth of possessions, etc. Given our normal attitudes toward valued objects a man must resent having them taken from him by force.

None of this denies that human beings vary with respect to what they mind being motivated by. There are undoubtedly those like Thrasymachus who view morality as a subtle scheme enabling the powerful to enforce their rule. Such persons when they act for reasons of "morality" resent having to conform to the demands of others. But I am willing to say of such people that they do not act freely. They do not identify themselves with the reasons for which they act. They do regard such considerations as alien to their personality. I don't regard it as a weakness of my view that acting for certain reasons will be acting unfreely for some persons but not for others. In fact the theory will be confirmed by explaining such differences which are found on the pre-analytic level.

What I have tried to do in this essay is give an account of why we pick out a certain class of reasons for acting and say that acting for such reasons but not others is not acting freely, why we consider some interventions of others as creating obstacles to our desires and others not, why coercion is thought of as a way of getting someone to do what he doesn't want to do rather than a way of getting someone to want to do something else. My explanation was in terms of the resentment or aversion men have to acting for certain reasons. If we could conceive of a creature so devoid of inner resources, so docile and submissive that he never minded acting in a way different from his original

intentions, who saw every action of his as arising from a new desire, then we would also have a being whose liberty we could not infringe. Just as one cannot force open a door that swings freely on its hinges one cannot force a man whose will swings willingly in any direction.

PART IV Suggestions For Further Reading

A. Necessity, Possibility, and Essence

Frankfurt, Harry G., ed. *Leibniz: A Collection of Critical Essays,* (Doubleday-Anchor, 1972)

Lewis, David K. *Philosophical Papers,* vol. I, (Oxford University Press, 1983)

Loux, Michael, ed. *The Possible and the Actual,* (Cornell University Press, 1979)

Plantinga, Alvin. *The Nature of Necessity,* (Oxford University Press, 1979)

Putnam, Hilary. *Philosophical Papers,* vol. II, (Cambridge University Press, 1975)

Schwartz, Stephen P., ed. *Naming, Necessity and Natural Kinds,* (Cornell University Press, 1977)

B. Personal Identity

Perry, John. *A Dialogue on Personal Identity and Immortality,* (Hackett, 1978)

Perry, John, ed. *Personal Identity,* (University of California Press, 1975)

Rorty, Amélie Oksenberg, ed. *The Identities of Persons,* (University of California Press, 1976)

Shoemaker, Sydney. *Self-Knowledge and Self-Identity,* (Cornell University Press, 1963)

C. Free Will and Determinism

Bergman, Fritjhof. *On Being Free,* (University of Notre Dame Press, 1979)

Dworkin, Gerald, ed. *Determinism, Free Will and Moral Responsibility,* (Prentice-Hall, 1970)

Watson, Gary, ed. *Free Will,* (Oxford University Press, 1982)

V

PHILOSOPHY
OF RELIGION

PHILOSOPHY OF RELIGION is an ancient branch of philosophical inquiry that attempts to clarify religious beliefs and subject them to critical scrutiny. Some thinkers have employed the methods of philosophy to support religion, while others have used these same methods with quite different aims. All philosophy of religion, however, is concerned with questions that arise when religious doctrines are tested by the canons of reason.

Chief among the issues that philosophers of religion have examined throughout the centuries is the question, Does God exist? Theism is the belief that God does exist. Atheism is the belief that God does not exist. Agnosticism is the belief that sufficient evidence is not available to decide whether God exists. Which of these positions is correct?

In answering this question we must first determine what is meant by "God," a term that has been used in many different ways. Let us adopt a common view, shared by many religious believers, that the word refers to an all-good, all-powerful, eternal creator of the world. The question then is, Does a Being so described exist?

Several proofs have been offered to defend the claim that such a Being exists. In the selection by Saint Anselm (reading 46), we are presented with the ontological argument for the existence of God. This argument makes no appeal to empirical evidence but purports to demonstrate that by His very nature God must exist. Criticisms of this argument are offered in this selection by the Monk

Gaunilo, Saint Anselm's contemporary, as well as in the selection by Ernest Nagel (reading 49).

Several other arguments are offered in the selection by Saint Thomas Aquinas (reading 47). These are called *cosmological arguments,* for they are based on a variety of fundamental principles about the structure of the world, such as the thesis that nothing is uncaused. Criticisms of these sorts of arguments are presented in the selection by Nagel.

A third type of proof, the *teleological argument,* or argument from design, is put forward by the character of Cleanthes in the selection from David Hume's *Dialogues Concerning Natural Religion* (reading 48). This argument proceeds from the premise of the world's magnificent order to the conclusion that the world must be the work of a Supreme Mind responsible for that order. This argument is opposed for various reasons by the characters Demea and Philo in Hume's *Dialogues* and is also criticized in the selection by Nagel.

To attack an argument supporting the existence of God, however, is not equivalent to offering an argument against the existence of God. Are there arguments not only against theism but in favor of atheism?

A well-known argument of this sort is the problem of evil, presented by Demea and supported by Philo in Hume's *Dialogues.* Why should there be evil in a world created by an all-good, all-powerful Being? A being who is all-good would presumably do everything possible to abolish evil. Therefore, if there were an all-good, all-powerful Being, there would be no evil. But evil does appear to exist. Thus, it would seem there is no being who is all-good and all-powerful. This argument is defended by Nagel in reading 49.

There have been numerous attempts to find a solution to the problem of evil. A familiar strategy is to attempt to demonstrate how the goods of the world are made possible by the presence of evils. For instance, it has been argued that if there were no sins there could be no forgiveness. This general strategy for resolving the problem of evil is developed in reading 50 by Richard Swinburne. The strategy is opposed in the selection by Nagel.

But if evil is compatible with the existence of God, then does the existence of God provide any assurance against evil? If so, what sort of assurance? If not, what meaning can we give to the claim that God loves us or even that God exists? This challenge is posed in reading 51 by Antony Flew. His co-symposiasts in this selection, R. M. Hare and Basil Mitchell, attempt to respond.

Questions about the meaning of religious language have been much discussed by philosophers in recent years, but concern about such matters can be traced back to the ancient Greeks. One of the earliest works in philosophy of religion, Plato's *Euthyphro* (reading 45), raises issues regarding the language we use to talk about God. We speak, for example, of making sacrifices to God. But why make sacrifices to a Being that has no needs? Or does God have needs? Faced with these queries, one might respond that it is meaningless to use ordinary terms such as "needs" when speaking of God. But, if so, what words, if any, would be appropriate?

Another major issue raised in the *Euthyphro* is whether morality is based on theism or stands independently. If morality stands independently, then we can

adhere to moral standards without believing in God. But if God's will defines what is moral, then praise for God's goodness would appear pointless. In effect, to say that God's will is good would be only to say that God's will is God's will, a claim without content. This line of argument is further developed in reading 52 by Steven M. Cahn.

All of these puzzling issues illustrate the challenges of providing a coherent, convincing account of the nature of God. But does a commitment to religion depend on belief in God, or can there be religions that do not assume a theistic perspective? Cahn suggests that doubts about the existence or nature of God are compatible with prayer, ritual, and other practices we associate with the religious outlook. Cahn thus defends the possibility of religion without God.

In studying all these selections, readers are advised to remember that some of the most renowned philosophers of the past and present have been firmly committed to theism, while others of equal stature have been agnostics or atheists. All would have agreed, however, that whatever one's position, it is more clearly and more fully understood in the light of philosophical inquiry.

45

God and Morality

PLATO

For biographical information about Plato, see reading 13.

The key question in the Euthyphro *is the nature of piety, our relationship to the divine. Euthyphro has come to court to prosecute his own father on the charge of murder. Euthyphro claims that in pursuing this case, he is acting with piety, and says to Socrates that piety is what all the gods love. Socrates asks Euthyphro whether the pious is loved by the gods because it is pious, or whether it is pious because it is loved by the gods. In effect, Socrates forces Euthyphro to judge God's will by moral standards or accept as moral whatever God might will. Euthyphro can offer no satisfactory response, nor can he answer Socrates's subsequent questions concerning the relationship between piety and justice and the purpose of sacrifice and prayer.*

As is typical of Plato's early dialogues, the search for a definition of a central concept ends unsuccessfully. But along the way the participants and the reader explore a variety of important issues, stumble across numerous perplexing problems, and discover in the end that they know far less about the entire subject than they thought they knew before they began. This process, however, is far from useless, for as Socrates emphasizes, recognizing what one does not know is the first step on the path to wisdom.

EUTHYPHRO: What's new, Socrates, to make you leave your usual haunts in the Lyceum and spend your time here by the king-archon's court? Surely you are not prosecuting any one before the king archon as I am?

SOCRATES: The Athenians do not call this a prosecution but an indictment, Euthyphro.

E: What is this you say? Someone must have indicted you, for you are not going to tell me that you have indicted someone else.

S: No indeed.

E: But someone else has indicted you?

S: Quite so.

E: Who is he?

S: I do not really know him myself, Euthyphro. He is apparently young and unknown. They call him Meletus, I believe. He belongs to the Pitthean deme, if you know anyone from that deme called Meletus, with long hair, not much of a beard, and a rather aquiline nose.

E: I don't know him, Socrates. What charge does he bring against you?

S: What charge? A not ignoble one I think, for it is no small thing for a young

man to have knowledge of such an important subject. He says he knows how our young men are corrupted and who corrupts them. He is likely to be wise, and when he sees my ignorance corrupting his contemporaries, he proceeds to accuse me to the city as to their mother. I think he is the only one of our public men to start out the right way, for it is right to care first that the young should be as good as possible, just as a good farmer is likely to take care of the young plants first, and of the others later. So, too, Meletus first gets rid of us who corrupt the growth of the young, as he says, and then afterwards he will obviously take care of the older and become a source of great blessings for the city, as seems likely to happen to one who started out this way.

E: I could wish this were true, Socrates, but I fear the opposite may happen. He seems to me to start out by harming the very heart of the city by attempting to wrong you. Tell me, what does he say you do to corrupt the young?

S: Strange things, to hear him tell it, for he says that I am a maker of gods, that I create new gods while not believing in the old gods, and he has indicted me for this very reason, as he puts it.

E: I understand, Socrates. This is because you say that the divine sign keeps coming to you. So he has written this indictment against you as one who makes innovations in religious matters, and he comes to court to slander you, knowing that such things are easily misrepresented to the crowd. The same is true in my case. Whenever I speak of divine matters in the assembly and foretell the future, they laugh me down as if I were crazy; and yet I have foretold nothing that did not happen. Nevertheless, they envy all of us who do this. One need not give them any thought, but carry on just the same.

S: My dear Euthyphro, to be laughed at does not matter perhaps, for the Athenians do not mind anyone they think clever, as long as he does not teach his own wisdom, but if they think that he makes others to be like himself they get angry, whether through envy, as you say, or for some other reason.

E: I have certainly no desire to test their feelings toward me in this matter.

S: Perhaps you seem to make yourself but rarely available, and not to be willing to teach your own wisdom, but my liking for people makes them think that I pour out to anybody anything I have to say, not only without charging a fee but appearing glad to reward anyone who is willing to listen. If then they were intending to laugh at me, as you say they laugh at you, there would be nothing unpleasant in their spending their time in court laughing and jesting, but if they are going to be serious, the outcome is not clear except to you prophets.

E: Perhaps it will come to nothing, Socrates, and you will fight your case as you think best, as I think I will mine.

S: What is your case, Euthyphro? Are you the defendant or the prosecutor?

E: The prosecutor.

S: Whom do you prosecute?

E: One whom I am thought crazy to prosecute.

S: Are you pursuing someone who will easily escape you?

E: Far from it, for he is quite old.

S: Who is it?

E: My father.

S: My dear sir! Your own father?

E: Certainly.

S: What is the charge? What is the case about?

E: Murder, Socrates.

S: Good heavens! Certainly, Euthyphro, most men would not know how they could do this and be right. It is not the part of anyone to do this, but of one who is far advanced in wisdom.

E: Yes by Zeus, Socrates, that is so.

S: Is then the man your father killed one of your relatives? Or is that obvious, for you would not prosecute your father for the murder of a stranger.

E: It is ridiculous, Socrates, for you to think that it makes any difference whether the victim is a stranger or a relative. One should only watch whether the killer acted justly or not; if he acted justly, let him go, but if not, one should prosecute, even if the killer shares your hearth and table. The pollution is the same if you knowingly keep company with such a man and do not cleanse yourself and him by bringing him to justice. The victim was a dependent of mine, and when we were farming in Naxos he was a servant of ours. He killed one of our household slaves in drunken anger, so my father bound him hand and foot and threw him in a ditch, then sent a man here to enquire from the priest what should be done. During that time he gave no thought or care to the bound man, as being a killer, and it was no matter if he died, which he did. Hunger and cold and his bonds caused his death before the messenger came back from the seer. Both my father and my other relatives are angry that I am prosecuting my father for murder on behalf of a murderer, as he did not even kill him. They say that such a victim does not deserve a thought and that it is impious for a son to prosecute his father for murder. But their ideas of the divine attitude to piety and impiety are wrong, Socrates.

S: Whereas, by Zeus, Euthyphro, you think that your knowledge of the divine, and of piety and impiety, is so accurate that, when those things happened as you say, you have no fear of having acted impiously in bringing your father to trial?

E: I should be of no use, Socrates, and Euthyphro would not be superior to the majority of men, if I did not have accurate knowledge of all such things.

S: It is indeed most important, my admirable Euthyphro, that I should become your pupil, and as regards this indictment challenge Meletus about these very things and say to him: that in the past too I considered knowledge about the divine to be most important, and that now that he says that I improvise and innovate about the gods I have become your pupil. I would say to him: "If, Meletus, you agree that Euthyphro is wise in these matters, consider me, too, to have the right beliefs and do not bring me to trial. If you do not think so, then prosecute that teacher of mine for corrupting the older men, me and his own father, by teaching me and by exhorting and punishing him. If he is

not convinced, does not discharge me, or indicts you instead of me, I shall repeat the same challenge in court.

E: Yes by Zeus, Socrates, and, if he should try to indict me, I think I would find his weak spots and the talk in court would be about him rather than about me.

S: It is because I realize this that I am eager to become your pupil, my dear friend. I know that other people as well as this Meletus do not even seem to notice you, whereas he sees me so sharply and clearly that he indicts me for ungodliness. So tell me now, by Zeus, what you just now maintained you clearly knew: what kind of thing do you say that godliness and ungodliness are, both as regards murder and other things; or is the pious not the same and alike in every action, and the impious the opposite of all that is pious and like itself, and everything that is to be impious presents us with one form or appearance in so far as it is impious.

E: Most certainly, Socrates.

S: Tell me then, what is the pious, and what the impious, do you say?

E: I say that the pious is to do what I am doing now, to prosecute the wrong-doer, be it about murder or temple robbery or anything else, whether the wrongdoer is your father or your mother or anyone else; not to prosecute is impious. And observe, Socrates, that I can quote the law as a great proof that this is so. I have already said to others that such actions are right, not to favour the ungodly, whoever they are. These people themselves believe that Zeus is the best and most just of the gods, yet they agree that he bound his father because he unjustly swallowed his sons, and that he in turn cas-trated his father for similar reasons. But they are angry with me because I am prosecuting my father for his wrongdoing. They contradict themselves in what they say about the gods and about me.

S: Indeed, Euthyphro, this is the reason why I am a defendant in the case, because I find it hard to accept things like that being said about the gods, and it is likely to be the reason why I shall be told I do wrong. Now, however, if you, who have full knowledge of such things, share their opinions, then we must agree with them too, it would seem. For what are we to say, we who agree that we ourselves have no knowledge? Tell me, by the god of friendship, do you really believe these things are true?

E: Yes, Socrates, and so are even more surprising things, of which the majority has no knowledge.

S: And do you believe that there really is war among the gods, and terrible enmities and battles, and other such things as are told by the poets, and other sacred stories such as are embroidered by good writers and by representations of which the robe of the goddess is adorned when it is carried up to the Acropolis. Are we to say these things are true, Euthyphro?

E: Not only these, Socrates, but, as I was saying just now, I will, if you wish, relate many other things about the gods which I know will amaze you.

S: I should not be surprised, but you will tell me these at leisure some other time. For now, try to tell me more clearly what I was asking just now, for,

my friend, you did not teach me adequately when I asked you what the pious was, but you told me that what you are doing now, to prosecute your father for murder, is pious.

E: And I told the truth, Socrates.

S: Perhaps. You agree, however, that there are many other pious actions.

E: There are.

S: Bear in mind then that I did not bid you tell me one or two of the many pious actions but that form itself that makes all pious actions pious, for you agreed that all impious actions are impious and all pious actions pious through one form, or don't you remember?

E: I do.

S: Tell me then what form itself is, so that I may look upon it, and using it as a model, say that any action of yours or another's that is of that kind is pious, and if it is not that it is not.

E: If that is how you want it, Socrates, that is how I will tell you.

S: That is what I want.

E: Well then, what is dear to the gods is pious, what is not is impious.

S: Splendid, Euthyphro! You have now answered in the way I wanted. Whether your answer is true I do not know yet, but you will obviously show me that what you say is true.

E: Certainly.

S: Come then, let us examine what we mean. An action or a man dear to the gods is pious, but an action or a man hated by the gods is impious. They are not the same, but opposites, the pious and the impious. Is that not so?

E: It is indeed.

S: And that seems to be a good statement?

E: I think so, Socrates.

S: We have also stated that the gods are in a state of discord, that they are at odds with each other, Euthyphro, and that they are at enmity with each other. That too has been said.

E: It has.

S: What are the subjects of difference that cause hatred and anger? Let us look at it this way. If you and I were to differ about numbers as to which is the greater, would this difference make us enemies and angry with each other, or would we proceed to count and soon resolve our difference about this?

E: We would certainly do so.

S: Again, if we differed about the larger and the smaller, we would turn to measurement and soon cease to differ.

E: That is so.

S: And about the heavier and the lighter, we would resort to weighing and be reconciled.

E: Of course.

S: What subject of difference would make us angry and hostile to each other if we were unable to come to a decision? Perhaps you do not have an answer ready, but examine as I tell you whether these subjects are the just and the

unjust, the beautiful and the ugly, the good and the bad. Are these not the subjects of difference about which, when we are unable to come to a satisfactory decision, you and I and other men become hostile to each other whenever we do.

E: That is the difference, Socrates, about those subjects.

S: What about the gods, Euthyphro? If indeed they have differences, will it not be about these same subjects?

E: It certainly must be so.

S: Then according to your argument, my good Euthyphro, different gods consider different things to be just, beautiful, ugly, good and bad, for they would not be at odds with one another unless they differed about these subjects, would they?

E: You are right.

S: And they like what each of them considers beautiful, good, and just, and hate the opposites of these?

E: Certainly.

S: But you say that the same things are considered just by some gods and unjust by others, and as they dispute about these things they are at odds and at war with each other. Is that not so?

E: It is.

S: The same things then are loved by the gods and hated by the gods, both god-loved and god-hated.

E: It seems likely.

S: And the same things would be both pious and impious, according to this argument?

E: I'm afraid so.

S: So you did not answer my question, you surprising man. I did not ask you what same thing is both pious and impious, and it appears that what is loved by the gods is also hated by them. So it is in no way surprising if your present action, namely punishing your father, may be pleasing to Zeus but displeasing to Kronos and Ouranos, pleasing to Hephaestus but displeasing to Hera, and so with any other gods who differ from each other on this subject.

E: I think, Socrates, that on this subject no gods would differ from one another, that whoever has killed anyone unjustly should pay the penalty.

S: Well now, Euthyphro, have you ever heard any man maintaining that one who has killed or done anything else unjustly should not pay the penalty?

E: They never cease to dispute on this subject, both elsewhere and in the courts, for when they have committed many wrongs they do and say anything to avoid the penalty.

S: Do they agree they have done wrong, Euthyphro, and in spite of so agreeing do they nevertheless say they should not be punished?

E: No, they do not agree on that point.

S: So they do not say or do anything. For they do not venture to say this, or dispute that they must not pay the penalty if they have done wrong, but I think they deny doing wrong. Is that not so?

E: That is true.

S: Then they do not dispute that the wrongdoer must be punished, but they may disagree as to who the wrongdoer is, what he did and when.

E: You are right.

S: Do not the gods have the same experience, if indeed they are at odds with each other about the just and the unjust, as your argument maintains? Some assert that they wrong one another, while others deny it, but no one among gods or men ventures to say that the wrongdoer must not be punished.

E: Yes, that is true, Socrates, as to the main point.

S: And those who disagree, whether men or gods, dispute about each action, if indeed the gods disagree. Some say it is done justly, others unjustly. Is that not so?

E: Yes indeed.

S: Come now, my dear Euthyphro, tell me, too, that I may become wiser, what proof you have that all the gods consider that man to have been killed unjustly who became a murderer while in your service, was bound by the master of his victim, and died in his bonds before the one who bound him found out from the seers what was to be done with him, and that it is right for a son to denounce and to prosecute his father on behalf of such a man. Come, try to show me a clear sign that all the gods definitely believe this action to be right. If you can give me adequate proof of this, I shall never cease to extol your wisdom.

E: This is perhaps no light task, Socrates, though I could show you very clearly.

S: I understand that you think me more dull-witted than the jury, as you will obviously show them that these actions were unjust and that all the gods hate such actions.

E: I will show it to them clearly, Socrates, if only they will listen to me.

S: They will listen if they think you show them well. But this thought came to me as I was speaking, and I am examining it, saying to myself: "If Euthyphro shows me conclusively that all the gods consider such a death unjust, to what greater extent have I learned from him the nature of piety and impiety? This action would then, it seems, be hated by the gods, but the pious and the impious were not thereby now defined, for what is hated by the gods has also been shown to be loved by them." So I will not insist on this point; let us assume, if you wish, that all the gods consider this unjust and that they all hate it. However, is this the correction we are making in our discussion, that what all the gods hate is impious, and what they all love is pious, and that what some gods love and others hate is neither or both? Is that how you now wish us to define piety and impiety?

E: What prevents us from doing so, Socrates?

S: For my part nothing, Euthyphro, but you look whether on your part this proposal will enable you to teach me most easily what you promised.

E: I would certainly say that the pious is what all the gods love, and the opposite, which all the gods hate, is the impious.

S: Then let us again examine whether that is a sound statement, or do we let

it pass, and if one of us, or someone else, merely says that this is so, do we accept that it is so? Or should we examine what the speaker means?

E: We must examine it, but I certainly think that this is now a fine statement.

S: We shall soon know better whether it is. Consider this: Is the pious loved by the gods because it is pious, or is it pious because it is loved by the gods?

E: I don't know what you mean, Socrates.

S: I shall try to explain more clearly; we speak of something being carried and something carrying, of something being led and something leading, of something being seen and something seeing, and you understand that these things are all different from one another and how they differ?

E: I think I do.

S: So there is something being loved and something loving, and the loving is a different thing.

E: Of course.

S: Tell me then whether that which is (said to be) being carried is being carried because someone carries it or for some other reason.

E: No, that is the reason.

S: And that which is being led is so because someone leads it, and that which is being seen because someone sees it?

E: Certainly.

S: It is not seen by someone because it is being seen but on the contrary it is being seen because someone sees it, nor is it because it is being led that someone leads it but because someone leads it that it is being led; it is not because it is being seen that someone sees it, but it is being seen because someone sees it; nor does someone carry an object because it is being carried, but it is being carried because someone carries it. Is what I want to say clear, Euthyphro? I want to say this, namely, that if anything comes to be, or is affected, it does not come to be because it is coming to be, but it is coming to be because it comes to be; nor is it affected because it is being affected but because something affects it. Or do you not agree?

E: I do.

S: What is being loved is either something that comes to be or something that is affected by something?

E: Certainly.

S: So it is in the same case as the things just mentioned; it is not loved by those who love it because it is being loved, but it is being loved because they love it?

E: Necessarily.

S: What then do we say about the pious, Euthyphro? Surely that it is loved by all the gods, according to what you say?

E: Yes.

S: Is it loved because it is pious, or for some other reason?

E: For no other reason.

S: It is loved then because it is pious, but it is not pious because it is loved?

E: Apparently.

s: And because it is loved by the gods it is being loved and is dear to the gods?

e: Of course.

s: The god-beloved is then not the same as the pious, Euthyphro, nor the pious the same as the god-beloved, as you say it is, but one differs from the other.

e: How so, Socrates?

s: Because we agree that the pious is beloved for the reason that it is pious, but it is not pious because it is loved. Is that not so?

e: Yes.

s: And that the god-beloved, on the other hand, is so because it is loved by the gods, by the very fact of being loved, but it is not loved because it is god-beloved.

e: True.

s: But if the god-beloved and the pious were the same, my dear Euthyphro, and the pious were loved because it was pious, then the god-beloved would be loved because it was god-beloved, and if the god-beloved was god-beloved because it was loved by the gods, then the pious would also be pious because it was loved by the gods; but now you see that they are in opposite cases as being altogether different from each other: the one is of a nature to be loved because it is loved, the other is loved because it is of a nature to be loved. I'm afraid, Euthyphro, that when you were asked what piety is, you did not wish to make its nature clear to me, but you told me an affect or quality of it, that the pious has the quality of being loved by all the gods, but you have not yet told me what the pious is. Now, if you will, do not hide things from me but tell me again from the beginning what piety is, whether loved by the gods or having some other quality—we shall not quarrel about that—but be keen to tell me what the pious and the impious are.

e: But Socrates, I have no way of telling you what I have in mind, for whatever proposition we put forward goes around and refuses to stay put where we establish it.

s: Your statements, Euthyphro, seem to belong to my ancestor, Daedalus. If I were stating them and putting them forward, you would perhaps be making fun of me and say that because of my kinship with him my conclusions in discussion run away and will not stay where one puts them. As these propositions are yours, however, we need some other jest, for they will not stay put for you, as you say yourself.

e: I think the same jest will do for our discussion, Socrates, for I am not the one who makes them go round and not remain in the same place; it is you who are the Daedalus; for as far as I am concerned they would remain as they were.

s: It looks as if I was cleverer than Daedalus in using my skill, my friend, in so far as he could only cause to move the things he made himself, but I can make other people's move as well as my own. And the smartest part of my skill is that I am clever without wanting to be, for I would rather have my arguments remain unmoved than possess the wealth of Tantalus as well as the cleverness of Daedalus. But enough of this. Since I think you are making unnecessary difficulties, I am as eager as you are to find a way to teach me

about piety, and do not give up before you do. See whether you think all that is pious is of necessity just.

E: I think so.

S: And is then all that is just pious? Or is all that is pious just, but not all that is just pious, but some of it is and some is not?

E: I do not follow what you are saying, Socrates.

S: Yet you are younger than I by as much as you are wiser. As I say, you are making difficulties because of your wealth of wisdom. Pull yourself together, my dear sir, what I am saying is not difficult to grasp. I am saying the opposite of what the poet said who wrote:

> You do not wish to name Zeus, who had done it, and who made all things grow, for where there is fear there is also shame.

I disagree with the poet. Shall I tell you why?

E: Please do.

S: I do not think that "where there is fear there is also shame," for I think that many people who fear disease and poverty and many other such things feel fear, but are not ashamed of the things they fear. Do you not think so?

E: I do indeed.

S: But where there is shame there is also fear. Does anyone feel shame at something who is not also afraid at the same time of a reputation for wickedness?

E: He is certainly afraid.

S: It is then not right to say "where there is fear there is also shame," but that where there is shame there is also fear, for fear covers a larger area than shame. Shame is a part of fear just as odd is a part of number, with the result that it is not true that where there is number there is also oddness, but that where there is oddness there is also number. Do you follow me?

E: Surely.

S: This is the kind of thing I was asking before, whether where there is piety there is also justice, but where there is justice there is not always piety, for the pious is a part of justice. Shall we say that, or do you think otherwise?

E: No, but like that, for what you say appears to be right.

S: See what comes next; if the pious is a part of the just, we must, it seems, find out what part of the just it is. Now if you asked me something of what we mentioned just now, such as what part of number is the even, and what number that is, I would say it is the number that is divisible into two equal, not unequal, parts. Or do you not think so?

E: I do.

S: Try in this way to tell me what part of the just the pious is, in order to tell Meletus not to wrong us any more and not to indict me for ungodliness, since I have learned from you sufficiently what is godly and pious and what is not.

E: I think, Socrates, that the godly and pious is the part of the just that is concerned with the care of the gods, while that concerned with the care of men is the remaining part of justice.

S: You seem to me to put that very well, but I still need a bit of information. I do not know yet what you mean by care, for you do not mean it in the sense as the care of other things, as, for example, not everyone knows how to care for horses, but the horse breeder does.

E: Yes, I do mean it that way.

S: So horse breeding is the care of horses.

E: Yes.

S: Nor does everyone know how to care for dogs, but the hunter does.

E: That is so.

S: So hunting is the care of dogs.

E: Yes.

S: And cattle raising is the care of cattle.

E: Quite so.

S: While piety and godliness is the care of the gods, Euthyphro. Is that what you mean?

E: It is.

S: Now care in each case has the same effect; it aims at the good and the benefit of the object cared for, as you can see that horses cared for by horse breeders are benefited and become better. Or do you not think so?

E: I do.

S: So dogs are benefited by dog breeding, cattle by cattle raising, and so with all the others. Or do you think that care aims to harm the object of its care?

E: By Zeus, no.

S: It aims to benefit the object of its care.

E: Of course.

S: Is piety then, which is the care of the gods, also to benefit the gods and make them better? Would you agree that when you do something pious you make some one of the gods better?

E: By Zeus, no.

S: Nor do I think that this is what you mean—far from it—but that is why I asked you what you meant by the care of gods, because I did not believe you meant this kind of care.

E: Quite right, Socrates, that is not the kind of care I mean.

S: Very well, but what kind of care of the gods would piety be?

E: The kind of care, Socrates, that slaves take of their masters.

S: I understand. It is likely to be the service of the gods.

E: Quite so.

S: Could you tell me to the achievement of what goal service to doctors tends? Is it not, do you think to achieving health?

E: I think so.

S: What about service to shipbuilders? To what achievement is it directed?

E: Clearly, Socrates, to the building of a ship.

S: And service to housebuilders to the building of a house?

E: Yes.

S: Tell me then, my good sir, to the achievement of what aim does service to the gods tend? You obviously know since you say that you, of all men, have the best knowledge of the divine.

E: And I am telling the truth, Socrates.

S: Tell me then, by Zeus, what is that excellent aim that the gods achieve, using us as their servants?

E: Many fine things, Socrates.

S: So do generals, my friend. Nevertheless you could tell me their main concern, which is to achieve victory in war, is it not?

E: Of course.

S: The farmers too, I think, achieve many fine things, but the main point of their efforts is to produce food from the earth.

E: Quite so.

S: Well then, how would you sum up the many fine things that the gods achieve?

E: I told you a short while ago, Socrates, that it is a considerable task to acquire any precise knowledge of these things, but, to put it simply, I say that if a man knows how to say and do what is pleasing to the gods at prayer and sacrifice, those are pious actions such as preserve both private houses and public affairs of state. The opposite of these pleasing actions are impious and overturn and destroy everything.

S: You could tell me in far fewer words, if you were willing, the sum of what I asked, Euthyphro, but you are not keen to teach me, that is clear. You were on the point of doing so, but you turned away. If you had given that answer, I should now have acquired from you sufficient knowledge of the nature of piety. As it is, the lover of inquiry must follow it wherever it may lead him. Once more then, what do you say that piety and the pious are, and also impiety? Are they a knowledge of how to sacrifice and pray?

E: They are.

S: To sacrifice is to make a gift to the gods, whereas to pray is to beg from the gods?

E: Definitely, Socrates.

S: It would follow from this statement that piety would be a knowledge of how to give to, and beg from, the gods.

E: You understood what I said very well, Socrates.

S: That is because I am so desirous of your wisdom, and I concentrate my mind on it, so that no word of yours may fall to the ground. But tell me, what is this service to the gods? You say it is to beg from them and to give to them?

E: I do.

S: And to beg correctly would be to ask from them things that we need?

E: What else?

s: And to give correctly is to give them what they need from us, for it would not be skillful to bring gifts to anyone that are in no way needed.

E: True, Socrates.

s: Piety would then be a sort of trading skill between gods and men?

E: Trading yes, if you prefer to call it that.

s: I prefer nothing, unless it is true. But tell me, what benefit do the gods derive from the gifts they receive from us? What they give us is obvious to all. There is for us no good that we do not receive from them, but how are they benefited by what they receive from us? Or do we have such an advantage over them in the trade that we receive all our blessings from them and they receive nothing from us?

E: Do you suppose, Socrates, that the gods are benefited by what they receive from us?

s: What could those gifts from us to the gods be, Euthyphro?

E: What else, you think, than honour, reverence, and what I mentioned before, gratitude.

s: The pious is then, Euthyphro, pleasing to the gods, but not beneficial or dear to them?

E: I think it is of all things most dear to them.

s: So the pious is once again what is dear to the gods.

E: Most certainly.

s: When you say this, will you be surprised if your arguments seems to move about instead of staying put? And will you accuse me of being Daedalus who makes them move, though you are yourself much more skillful than Daedalus and make them go round in a circle? Or do you not realize that our argument has moved around and come again to the same place? You surely remember that earlier the pious and the god-beloved were shown not to be the same but different from each other. Or do you not remember?

E: I do.

s: Do you then not realize that when you say now that that what is dear to the gods is the pious? Is this not the same as the god-beloved? Or is it not?

E: It certainly is.

s: Either we were wrong when we agreed before, or, if we were right then, we are wrong now.

E: That seems to be so.

s: So we must investigate again from the beginning what piety is, as I shall not willingly give up before I learn this. Do not think me unworthy, but concentrate your attention and tell the truth. For you know it, if any man does, and I must not let you go, like Proteus, before you tell me. If you had no clear knowledge of piety and impiety you would never have ventured to prosecute your old father for murder on behalf of a servant. For fear of the gods you would have been afraid to take the risk lest you should not be acting rightly, and would have been ashamed before men, but now I know well that you believe you have clear knowledge of piety and impiety. So tell me, my good Euthyphro, and do not hide what you believe.

E: Some other time, Socrates, for I am in a hurry now, and it is time for me to go.

S: What a thing to do, my friend! By going you have cast me down from a great hope I had, that I would learn from you the nature of the pious and the impious and so escape Meletus' indictment by showing that I had acquired wisdom in divine matters from Euthyphro, and my ignorance would no longer cause me to be careless and inventive about such things, and that I would be better for the rest of my life.

46

The Ontological Argument

SAINT ANSELM and GAUNILO

Saint Anselm (1033–1109), born in a village that is now part of Italy, was educated in a Benedictine monastery and eventually became Archbishop of Canterbury. His most famous work is the Proslogion, *in which he sets out to argue for the existence of God and His attributes as traditionally conceived.*

The proof he offers for the existence of God was dubbed the "ontological argument" by the eighteenth-century German philosopher Immanuel Kant. Saint Anselm begins by defining God as "something than which nothing greater could be conceived." He then attempts to demonstrate that it would be a contradiction to deny the existence in reality of something than which nothing greater could be conceived, since, if it did not exist in reality, something greater could be conceived, namely, something that existed in reality. Hence, Saint Anselm concludes, God exists.

Saint Anselm's argument has been carefully examined by generations of thinkers. Some philosophers, such as Saint Thomas Aquinas, David Hume, and Kant, believed it unsound, while others, such as René Descartes, Baruch Spinoza, and Gottfried Leibniz, defended it. Indeed, to this day philosophers continue to explore the argument, either offering new versions that they believe to be persuasive or presenting refutations of proposed variations on the original theme. Whether or not the ontological argument is successful, it is surely one of the most fascinating and challenging pieces of philosophical reasoning ever conceived.

Perhaps the earliest reply to Saint Anselm's argument was offered by his contemporary, the monk Gaunilo. Gaunilo maintains that if Saint Anselm's reasoning were valid, ficitious things of all sorts could be proven to exist, such as, for example, an island than which none greater could be conceived. Key sections of Gaunilo's reply are reprinted here, along with parts of Saint Anselm's response.

Proslogion (Saint Anselm)
Preface

AFTER I PUBLISHED, at the pressing entreaties of certain brethren, a certain little treatise as an example of one's meditating on the grounds of faith* (in the person of someone who investigates, by means of silently reasoning with him-

---

* Anselm here refers to an earlier and longer work of his, the *Monologion*.

self, that which he does not know), considering it to be a connected sequence of many arguments, I began to ask myself whether by chance *one* argument* could be discovered, which would require nothing other than itself alone for proving itself, and which would suffice alone for demonstrating (1) that God truly exists, (2) that He is the supreme good, needing nothing else, and Whom all things need in order to be and to be well, and (3) whatever we believe about the divine being. When I would often and eagerly turn my thoughts to that end, then sometimes that which I sought would appear to me now to be able to be grasped, and at other times it would completely escape the keenness of my mind. At length, despairing, I wanted to give up the inquiry as if it were of a thing impossible to be discovered. But when I wanted to shut out that conception completely from myself, in order not to impede my mind—by occupying it in error—from other thoughts in which I could make progress, then it began to obtrude itself more and more, with a certain importunity, despite my unwillingness and resistance. Then one day, when I was excessively weary of resisting its importunity, in the very conflict of my thoughts that which I had given up thus presented itself, so that I eagerly embraced the conception which I was anxiously repelling.

Judging then that that which it delighted me to have discovered, if it were written down, would be pleasurable to some people reading it, I have written the following little treatise on this very conception and on certain others, as a person trying to raise his mind to the contemplation of God and seeking to understand that which he believes. And seeing that I judged that neither this work nor that work to which I referred above were worth of the name "book," or to have the author's name set upon them, yet neither did I think that they ought to be sent forth without some title, by which in some way they would invite a person into whose hands they would come to read them. I have given each its own title, so that the former is called *An Example of Meditating on the Grounds of Faith,* and the following is called *Faith Seeking Understanding.*

But when each of these works, under these titles, was transcribed by several readers, several people (especially the reverend Archbishop of Lyons, Hugh, administering the apostolic office in France, who has commanded me by his apostolic authority) have urged me to prefix my name to them. So that it would be more convenient, I have named the former work *Monologion,* that is, a soliloquy; and the latter *Proslogion,* that is, an address.

. . .

Chapter II: That God Truly Exists

Therefore, Lord, You Who give understanding to faith, give to me: insofar as You know it to be advantageous, let me understand that You exist, as we believe, and also that You are that which we believe You to be. And indeed,

---

* The Latin word *argumentum* has much the same latitude of meaning as the English word "argument." When Anselm says that he sought "one argument," he could mean either that he sought one pattern of reasoning which would demonstrate that God exists *and* that He is the supreme good, and so forth, or that he sought one sign or token which, when its logical implications were traced out (perhaps involving several different "arguments" in the first sense), would show that God exists and that He is the supreme good, and so forth.

we believe You to be something than which nothing greater could be conceived. Or is there thus not something of such a nature, since the fool has said in his heart—there is no God [Psalm 14:1, 53:1]. But surely this same fool, when he hears this very thing that I speak—"something than which nothing greater can be conceived"—understands that which he hears, and that which he understands is in his understanding, even if he does not understand it to exist. For it is one thing for a thing to be in the understanding, and another to understand a thing to exist. For when a painter conceives before hand that which he is to make, he certainly has it in the understanding, but he does not yet understand to exist that which he has not yet made. However, when he has painted it, he both has it in the understanding and understands that that which he has now made exists. Therefore, even the fool is convinced that something than which nothing greater can be conceived is at least in the understanding, since when he hears this, he understands it, and whatever is understood is in the understanding. And surely that than which a greater cannot be conceived cannot be in the understanding alone. For if it is even in the understanding alone, it can be conceived to exist in reality also, which is greater. Thus if that than which a greater cannot be conceived is in the understanding alone, then that than which a greater cannot be conceived itself is that than which a greater can be conceived. But surely this cannot be. Therefore without doubt something than which a greater cannot be conceived exists, both in the understanding and in reality.

Chapter III: That God Cannot be Conceived not to Exist

And surely it exists so truly that it could not be conceived not to exist. For something can be conceived to exist which could not be conceived not to exist, which is greater than that which can be conceived not to exist. Thus if that than which a greater cannot be conceived can be conceived not to exist, then that than which a greater cannot be conceived itself is not that than which a greater cannot be conceived, which cannot be made consistent. Thus something than which a greater cannot be conceived exists so truly that it could not be conceived not to exist.

And this You are, Lord our God. Thus so truly do You exist, Lord my God, that You could not be conceived not to exist. And justly so. For if some mind could conceive of something better than You, the creature would rise above the creator and would judge the creator, which is exceedingly absurd. And indeed, whatever is distinct from You alone can be conceived not to exist. Therefore You alone are the truest of all things and thus You have existence as the greatest of all things, since anything else does not exist so truly, and for that reason has less existence. And so why has the fool said in his heart that there is no God, when to a rational mind it would be so obvious that You exist as the greatest of all things? Why, unless because he is stupid and a fool?

Chapter IV: How the Fool has Said in his Heart What Cannot be Conceived

Indeed how has he said in his heart what he has not been able to conceive, or how has he not been able to conceive what he has said in his heart, when to say in the heart and to conceive are the same? If he truly—rather, *since* he truly—both has conceived (since he has spoken in his heart) and has not spoken in his heart (since he has not been able to conceive), then there is not only one way in which something is said in the heart or is conceived. For in one way a thing is conceived when a word signifying it is conceived; in another when that thing itself is understood. In the former way, thus, God can be conceived not to exist; in the latter, not at all. No one, in fact, understanding what God is, can conceive that God does not exist, although he may say these words in his heart, either without significance or with some extraneous significance. For God is that than which a greater cannot be conceived. He who understands this well certainly understands this very being to exist in such a way that it is not able not to exist in conception. Thus he who understands that God so exists, cannot conceive Him not to exist.

I give thanks to You, good Lord, I give thanks to You, because that which before I believed through Your giving to me, I now so understand through Your illuminating me that if I were unwilling to believe that You exist, I would not be able to understand that You exist.

A Reply on Behalf of the Fool (Gaunilo)

[1] To one doubting whether there is, or to one denying that there is, something of such a nature that nothing greater [than it] can be conceived, it is said here [in the *Proslogion*] that that being is proved to exist: first because the one who denies or doubts it himself already has it in the understanding, since one who hears what is said understands what is said; next because that which he understands is necessarily such that it is not only in the understanding but also in reality. And this is proved in the following way: because it is greater to be also in reality than only in the understanding, and if that being is only in the understanding, whatever would have been also in reality will be greater than it. And so that which is greater than all things will be less than something, and it will not be greater than all things, which is of course inconsistent. And therefore it is necessarily the case that that which is greater than all things, which has already been proved to be in the understanding, is not only in the understanding but also in reality, because otherwise it cannot be greater than all things. Perhaps he [the fool] can respond:

[2] This being is already said to be in my understanding for no other reason than that I understand what is said. Could it not be said that whatever things are fictitious and which in themselves are absolutely in no way existent things are similarly in the understanding, since if someone speaks of them, I understand whatever he says?

. . .

[6] For example: some say that somewhere in the ocean there is an island, which through the difficulty—or rather, the impossibility—of discovering that which does not exist, some have named "The Lost Island." And it is fabled that it abounds with riches and delights of all sorts of inestimable fruitfulness, much more than the Isles of the Blessed, and having no owner or inhabitant, it is in every way superior in its abundance of goods to all other lands that men inhabit taken together. If someone says all this to me, I shall easily understand what is said, in which nothing is difficult. But if now he goes on to say, as if it followed logically: "You can no more doubt that this island which is superior to all lands truly exists somewhere in reality, than that it is even clearly in your understanding; and since it is more superior to be not only in the understanding but also in reality, therefore it is necessary that it is existent, since if it did not exist, any other land in reality whatsoever would be superior to it, so that this very thing, already conceived by you to be superior, will not be superior"; if, I say, he should wish to prove to me by means of the above that this island truly exists beyond doubt, either I should think that he was joking, or I should not know which of us I ought to consider the bigger fool—I, if I acceded to him, or he, if he thought he had proved with any certainty the existence of this island, unless he had first shown that its very superiority exists—just as a true and certain thing, and not as a false or uncertain thing—in my understanding.

[7] This, for the nonce, the fool might reply to objections. To one who in turn asserts that this being is so great that it is too powerful to be only in conception—and this again "proved" in no other way than from [the fact] that otherwise, it will not be greater than all things—he could reply with the very same response and say: "When, then, did I say that there exists, as a true being, something such that it is greater than all things, so that from this it is of necessity proved to me that this being itself also exists in reality to such a degree that it could not be conceived not to exist?" Therefore one most certainly should first prove by argument that something superior—that is, greater and better than all natures which exist—exists, so that from this we might then establish all else that it is necessary for that which is greater and better than all things not to be lacking.

When, however, it is said that this supreme being cannot be conceived not to exist, perhaps it would be better said that it cannot be understood not to exist or even to be possible not to exist. For according to the proper meaning of the words, fictitious things cannot be understood, which nevertheless can be conceived, in the way in which the fool has conceived God not to exist. And I know most certainly also that I exist, but I also know, nevertheless, that I can not-exist. Indeed, I undoubtedly understand that that which exists supremely—namely, God—both exists and cannot not-exist. However, I do not know whether I can conceive myself not to exist as long as I know most certainly that I do exist. But if I can, why not also for whatever else I know with the same certitude? If, however, I cannot, then that will not be unique to God.

A Reply by the Author (Saint Anselm)

. . .

[III] But it is as though, you say, someone said that some island in the ocean, which surpasses all lands in its fertility, and which, because of the difficulty—or rather, impossibility—of discovering that which does not exist, is called "The Lost Island," cannot for that reason be doubted to exist truly in reality, since one easily understands the words describing it. I say with confidence that if anyone discovers for me something existing either in reality itself or only in conception—except that than which a greater cannot be conceived—to which the logical pattern of my argument applies, I shall discover that lost island and give it to him, never more to be lost.

But clearly now it is seen that that than which a greater cannot be conceived cannot be conceived not to exist, because it exists as a matter of such certain truth. For otherwise it would not exist at all. In fact, if anyone says that he conceives that this being does not exist, I say that when he conceives of this, either he conceives of something than which a greater cannot be conceived, or he does not. If he does not conceive of it, then he does not conceive not to exist that which he does not conceive. If he truly does conceive of it, he certainly conceives of something which cannot be conceived not to exist. For if it could be conceived not to exist, it could be conceived to have a beginning and an end. But this cannot be. Thus he who conceives of this being conceives of something which cannot be conceived not to exist. He who truly conceives this does not conceive this very thing not to exist—otherwise he conceives what cannot be conceived. Therefore that than which nothing greater can be conceived cannot be conceived not to exist.

[IV] You say, moreover, that when it is said that that supreme being cannot be conceived not to exist, perhaps it would be better said that it cannot be understood not to exist or even to be possible not to exist.

One should rather have said that it cannot be conceived. For if I had said that this being cannot be understood not to exist, perhaps you yourself, who say that according to the proper meaning of the words, fictitious things cannot be understood, would object that nothing that exists can be understood not to exist. For it is false that that which exists does not exist. Therefore not to be possible to be understood not to exist is not unique to God. So if some of those things which most certainly exist can be understood not to exist, then similarly other things which certainly exist can be understood not to exist.

But surely this cannot be objected to "conception," if [the issue] is considered carefully. For even if none of those things which exist can be understood not to exist, nevertheless all [of them] can be conceived not to exist, except that which supremely exists. For all and only those things can be conceived not to exist which have a beginning or an end or a composition of parts along with, as I have already said, whatever does not exist as a whole in some place or at

some time.* In fact, that being alone cannot be conceived not to exist, in which [there is] neither beginning nor end nor composition of parts, and which conception does not discover except as a whole always and everywhere.

Know, therefore, that you can conceive yourself not to exist while you know most certainly that you exist; I am surprised that you have said that you do not know this. For we conceive of many things which we know to exist as not existing, and many things which we know not to exist as existing, not by judging them to be as we conceive them, but by imagining [them so]. (1) And certainly we can conceive something not to exist while we know it to exist, since we can [conceive] the one and know the other at the same time. (2) And we cannot conceive [something] not to exist while we know it to exist, since we cannot conceive it to exist and not to exist at the same time. So if one thus distinguishes these two senses in this case, one will understand that (2) nothing, while it is known to exist, can be conceived not to exist, and that (1) whatever exists—except for that than which a greater cannot be conceived—even when it is known to exist, can be conceived not to exist. So, therefore, it is unique to God not to be possible to be conceived not to exist, and yet many things cannot be conceived, while they exist, not to exist. But how it might be said that God can be conceived not to exist I think I have discussed sufficiently in the book itself.

[V] . . . You often represent me as saying that since that which is greater than all things is in the understanding, if it is in the understanding it is also in reality, for otherwise that which is greater than all things was not greater than all things. Nowhere in all of my writings is such a proof to be found. For what is said to be "greater than all things" and "that than which a greater cannot be conceived" do not have the same power for proving that that which is so-called exists in reality.

---

* Anselm is referring to the following passage from the first chapter of his reply to Gaunilo: "Without doubt, for whatever does not exist in some place or at some time, even if it does exist in some [other] place or at some [other] time, it can nevertheless be conceived to exist at no time and in no place, just as it does not exist in some place or at some time. For that which did not exist yesterday and exists today: just as it is understood not to have existed yesterday, it can be supposed to exist at no time. And for that which does not exist here and does exist elsewhere: just as it does not exist here, it can be conceived to exist in no place. Similarly, for that whose individual parts do not exist where or when other parts exist: all its parts and thus the whole itself can be conceived to exist at no time or in no place. For even if time might be said to exist always and the world everywhere, yet the former does not exist always as a whole nor is the latter everywhere as a whole. And just as the individual parts of time do not exist when others do exist, so they can be conceived to exist at no time. And as for the individual parts of the world: just as they do not exist where other parts do exist, so they can be supposed to exist in no place. But even that which is composed of parts can be dissolved in conception and not be. Therefore for whatever does not exist as a whole in some place or at some time: even if it does exist, it can be conceived not to exist. Yet if that than which a greater cannot be conceived exists, it cannot be conceived not to exist; otherwise, if it exists, it is not that than which a greater cannot be conceived, which is inconsistent. Thus there is no way in which it does not exist as a whole in every place or at every time; rather, it exists as a whole always and everywhere."

47

Five Proofs for the Existence of God

SAINT THOMAS AQUINAS

Saint Thomas Aquinas (1225–1274) was born near Naples, joined the Dominican order, and received his doctorate in theology at the University of Paris, where he later taught. He was a prolific writer, whose masterpiece is the monumental Summa Theologica. *His works were so esteemed by the Church that in 1879 Pope Leo XIII declared Aquinas's system of thought to be the official Catholic philosophy.*

At the beginning of the thirteenth century, the major works of the Greek philosopher Aristotle were recovered in the West. His fame at the time was such that he was referred to simply as "the Philosopher." In the following excerpt from Summa Theologica, *Aquinas sets out to demonstrate that Aristotelian thought is compatible with the essential doctrines of Christianity. Aquinas admits that certain Christian tenets, such as that of the world being created at a particular time rather than existing eternally, transcend reason, and so cannot be proved by argument but only by an appeal to faith. He maintains, however, that the presuppositions of faith are themselves open to rational proof, and central among these is the existence of God. Aquinas offers five proofs in defense of the claim that God exists, and these have received extraordinary attention from philosophers throughout the centuries.*

THE EXISTENCE OF GOD can be proved in five ways.

The first and more manifest way is the argument from motion. It is certain, and evident to our senses, that in the world some things are in motion. Now whatever is moved is moved by another, for nothing can be moved except it is in potentiality to that towards which it is moved; whereas a thing moves inasmuch as it is in act. For motion is nothing else than the reduction of something from potentiality to actuality. But nothing can be reduced from potentiality to actuality, except by something in a state of actuality. Thus that which is actually hot, as fire, makes wood, which is potentially hot, to be actually hot, and thereby moves and changes it. Now it is not possible that the same thing should be at once in actuality and potentiality in the same respect, but only in different respects. For what is actually hot cannot simultaneously be potentially hot; but it is simultaneously potentially cold. It is therefore impossible that in the same respect and in the same way a thing should be both mover and moved, *i.e.,* that it should move itself. Therefore, whatever is moved must be moved by another. If that by which it is moved be itself moved, then this also must needs

547

be moved by another, and that by another again. But this cannot go on to infinity, because then there would be no first mover, and, consequently, no other mover, seeing that subsequent movers move only inasmuch as they are moved by the first mover; as the staff moves only because it is moved by the hand. Therefore it is necessary to arrive at a first mover, moved by no other; and this everyone understands to be God.

The second way is from the nature of efficient cause. In the world of sensible things we find there is an order of efficient causes. There is no case known (neither is it, indeed, possible) in which a thing is found to be the efficient cause of itself; for so it would be prior to itself, which is impossible. Now in efficient causes it is not possible to go on to infinity, because in all efficient causes following in order, the first is the cause of the intermediate cause, and the intermediate is the cause of the ultimate cause, whether the intermediate cause be several, or one only. Now to take away the cause is to take away the effect. Therefore, if there be no first cause among efficient causes, there will be no ultimate, nor any intermediate, cause. But if in efficient causes it is possible to go on to infinity, there will be no first efficient cause, neither will there be an ultimate effect, nor any intermediate efficient causes; all of which is plainly false. Therefore it is necessary to admit a first efficient cause, to which everyone gives the name of God.

The third way is taken from possibility and necessity, and runs thus. We find in nature things that are possible to be and not to be, since they are found to be generated, and to be corrupted, and consequently, it is possible for them to be and not to be. But it is impossible for these always to exist, for that which can not-be at some time is not. Therefore, if everything can not-be, then at one time there was nothing in existence. Now if this were true, even now there would be nothing in existence, because that which does not exist begins to exist only through something already existing. Therefore, if at one time nothing was in existence, it would have been impossible for anything to have begun to exist; and thus even now nothing would be in existence—which is absurd. Therefore, not all beings are merely possible, but there must exist something the existence of which is necessary. But every necessary thing either has its necessity caused by another, or not. Now it is impossible to go on to infinity in necessary things which have their necessity caused by another, as has been already proved in regard to efficient causes. Therefore we cannot but admit the existence of some being having of itself its own necessity, and not receiving it from another, but rather causing in others their necessity. This all men speak of as God.

The fourth way is taken from the gradation to be found in things. Among beings there are some more and some less good, true, noble, and the like. But *more* and *less* are predicated of different things according as they resemble in their different ways something which is the maximum, as a thing is said to be hotter according as it more nearly resembles that which is hottest; so that there is something which is truest, something best, something noblest, and, consequently, something which is most being, for those things that are greatest in

truth are greatest in being, as it is written in *Metaph*. ii.* Now the maximum in any genus is the cause of all in that genus, as fire, which is the maximum of heat, is the cause of all hot things, as is said in the same book. Therefore there must also be something which is to all beings the cause of their being, goodness, and every other perfection; and this we call God.

The fifth way is taken from the governance of the world. We see that things which lack knowledge, such as natural bodies, act for an end, and this is evident from their acting always, or nearly always, in the same way, so as to obtain the best result. Hence it is plain that they achieve their end, not fortuitously, but designedly. Now whatever lacks knowledge cannot move towards an end, unless it be directed by some being endowed with knowledge and intelligence; as the arrow is directed by the archer. Therefore some intelligent being exists by whom all natural things are directed to their end; and this being we call God.

* The reference is to Aristotle's *Metaphysics*.

48

The Teleological Argument

DAVID HUME

*David Hume (1711–1776), the influential Scottish philosopher and
historian, published his major philosophical work,* A Treatise of Human
Nature, *at the age of twenty-eight. His exhaustive* History of England *was
for many years considered the standard treatment of the subject. His other
works include* An Enquiry Concerning Human Understanding, An Enquiry
Concerning the Principles of Morals, Political Discourses, *and* The Natural
History of Religion. *His* Dialogues Concerning Natural Religion, *excerpted
here, was published only posthumously, on the advice of those who feared
adverse public reaction.*

*"Natural religion" was the term used by eighteenth-century writers to
refer to theological tenets provable by human reason alone, unaided by
any appeal to divine revelation. The three characters in the* Dialogues *are
distinguished by their views concerning the scope and limits of human
reason. Cleanthes claims he can present rational arguments that demonstrate
the truth of traditional Christian theology. Demea is deeply committed to
that theology but does not believe empirical evidence can provide any defense for his faith. Philo doubts that reason yields conclusive results in
any field of inquiry, and he is especially critical of theological dogmatism.
By subtle and realistic interplay among these three characters, Hume
suggests a surprising affinity between the skeptic and the person of faith, as
well as the equally surprising lack of affinity between the person of faith
and the philosophical theist.*

I MUST OWN, Cleanthes, said Demea, that nothing can more surprise
me than the light in which you have all along put this argument. By the whole
tenor of your discourse, one would imagine that you were maintaining the
Being of a God against the cavils of atheists and infidels, and were necessitated
to become a champion for that fundamental principle of all religion. But this,
I hope, is not by any means a question among us. No man; no man, at least of
common sense, I am persuaded, ever entertained a serious doubt with regard
to a truth so certain and self-evident. The question is not concerning the *being*
but the *nature of God.* This I affirm, from the infirmities of human understanding, to be altogether incomprehensible and unknown to us. The essence of that
supreme mind, his attributes, the manner of his existence, the very nature of
his duration—these and every particular which regards so divine a being are

mysterious to men. Finite, weak, and blind creatures, we ought to humble ourselves in his august presence, and, conscious of our frailties, adore in silence his infinite perfections which eye hath not seen, ear hath not heard, neither hath it entered into the heart of man to conceive. They are covered in a deep cloud from human curiosity; it is profaneness to attempt penetrating through these sacred obscurities; and, next to the impiety of denying his existence, is the temerity of prying into his nature and essence, decrees and attributes.

But lest you should think that my *piety* has here got the better of my *philosophy,* I shall support my opinion, if it needs any support, by a very great authority. I might cite all the divines, almost from the foundation of Christianity, who have ever treated of this or any other theological subject; but I shall confine myself, at present, to one equally celebrated for piety and philosophy. It is Father Malebranche who, I remember, thus expresses himself,[1] "One ought not so much (says he) to call God a spirit in order to express positively what he is, as in order to signify that he is not matter. He is a Being infinitely perfect— of this we cannot doubt. But in the same manner as we ought not to imagine, even supposing him corporeal, that he is clothed with a human body, as the anthropomorphites asserted, under color that that figure was the most perfect of any, so neither ought we to imagine that the spirit of God has human ideas or bears any resemblance to our spirit, under color that we know nothing more perfect than a human mind. We ought rather to believe that as he comprehends the perfections of matter without being material . . . he comprehends also the perfections of created spirits without being spirit, in the manner we conceive spirit: That his true name is *He that is,* or, in other words, Being without restriction, All Being, the Being infinite and universal."

After so great an authority, Demea, replied Philo, as that which you have produced, and a thousand more which you might produce, it would appear ridiculous to me to add my sentiment or express my approbation of your doctrine. But surely, where reasonable men treat these subjects, the question can never be concerning the *being* but only the *nature* of the Deity. The former truth, as you well observe, is unquestionable and self-evident. Nothing exists without a cause; and the original cause of this universe (whatever it be) we call *God,* and piously ascribe to him every species of perfection. Whoever scruples this fundamental truth deserves every punishment which can be inflicted among philosophers, to wit, the greatest ridicule, contempt, and disapprobation. But as all perfection is entirely relative, we ought never to imagine that we comprehend the attributes of this divine Being, or to suppose that his perfections have any analogy or likeness to the perfections of a human creature. Wisdom, thought, design, knowledge—these we justly ascribe to him because these words are honorable among men, and we have no other language or other conceptions by which we can express our adoration of him. But let us beware lest we think that our ideas anywise correspond to his perfections, or that his attributes have any resemblance to these qualities among men. He is infinitely superior to our

[1] *Recherche de la Vérité,* liv. 3, cap. 9.

limited view and comprehension; and is more the object of worship in the temple than of disputation in the schools.

In reality, Cleanthes, continued he, there is no need of having recourse to that affected scepticism so displeasing to you in order to come at this determination. Our ideas reach no farther than our experience: We have no experience of divine attributes and operations. I need not conclude my syllogism: You can draw the inference yourself. And it is a pleasure to me (and I hope to you, too) that just reasoning and sound piety here concur in the same conclusion, and both of them establish the adorably mysterious and incomprehensible nature of the Supreme Being.

Not to lose any time in circumlocutions, said Cleanthes, addressing himself to Demea, much less in replying to the pious declamations of Philo, I shall briefly explain how I conceive this matter. Look round the world: Contemplate the whole and every part of it: You will find it to be nothing but one great machine, subdivided into an infinite number of lesser machines, which again admit of subdivisions to a degree beyond what human senses and faculties can trace and explain. All these various machines, and even their most minute parts, are adjusted to each other with an accuracy which ravishes into admiration all men who have ever contemplated them. The curious adapting of means to ends, throughout all nature, resembles exactly, though it much exceeds, the productions of human contrivance—of human design, thought, wisdom, and intelligence. Since therefore the effects resemble each other, we are led to infer, by all the rules of analogy, that the causes also resemble, and that the Author of Nature is somewhat similar to the mind of man, though possessed of much larger faculties, proportioned to the grandeur of the work which he has executed. By this argument *a posteriori,* and by this argument alone, do we prove at once the existence of a Deity and his similarity to human mind and intelligence.

I shall be so free, Cleanthes, said Demea, as to tell you that from the beginning I could not approve of your conclusion concerning the similarity of the Deity to men, still less can I approve of the mediums by which you endeavor to establish it. What! No demonstration of the Being of God! No abstract arguments! No proofs *a priori!* Are these which have hitherto been so much insisted on by philosophers all fallacy, all sophism? Can we reach no farther in this subject than experience and probability? I will say not that this is betraying the cause of a Deity; but surely, by this affected candor, you give advantages to atheists which they never could obtain by the mere dint of argument and reasoning.

What I chiefly scruple in this subject, said Philo, is not so much that all religious arguments are by Cleanthes reduced to experience, as that they appear not to be even the most certain and irrefragable of that inferior kind. That a stone will fall, that fire will burn, that the earth has solidity, we have observed a thousand and a thousand times; and when any new instance of this nature is presented, we draw without hesitation the accustomed inference. The exact similarity of the cases gives us a perfect assurance of a similar event, and a stronger evidence is never desired nor sought after. But wherever you depart, in the least, from the similarity of the cases, you diminish proportionably the evidence; and may at last bring it to a very weak *analogy,* which is confessedly

liable to error and uncertainty. After having experienced the circulation of the blood in human creatures, we make no doubt that it takes place in Titius and Maevius; but from its circulation in frogs and fishes it is only a presumption, though a strong one, from analogy that it takes place in men and other animals. The analogical reasoning is much weaker when we infer the circulation of the sap in vegetables from our experience that the blood circulates in animals; and those who hastily followed that imperfect analogy are found, by more accurate experiments, to have been mistaken.

If we see a house, Cleanthes, we conclude, with the greatest certainty, that it had an architect or builder because this is precisely that species of effect which we have experienced to proceed from that species of cause. But surely you will not affirm that the universe bears such a resemblance to a house that we can with the same certainty infer a similar cause, or that the analogy is here entire and perfect. The dissimilitude is so striking that the utmost you can here pretend to is a guess, a conjecture, a presumption concerning a similar cause; and how that pretension will be received in the world, I leave you to consider.

It would surely be very ill received, replied Cleanthes; and I should be deservedly blamed and detested did I allow that the proofs of a Deity amounted to no more than a guess or conjecture. But is the whole adjustment of means to ends in a house and in the universe so slight a resemblance? the economy of final causes? the order, proportion, and arrangement of every part? Steps of a stair are plainly contrived that human legs may use them in mounting; and this inference is certain and infallible. Human legs are also contrived for walking and mounting; and this inference, I allow, is not altogether so certain because of the dissimilarity which you remark; but does it, therefore, deserve the name only of presumption or conjecture?

Good God! cried Demea, interrupting him, where are we? Zealous defenders of religion allow that the proofs of a Deity fall short of perfect evidence! And you, Philo, on whose assistance I depended in proving the adorable mysteriousness of the Divine Nature, do you assent to all these extravagant opinions of Cleanthes? For what other name can I give them? or, why spare my censure when such principles are advanced, supported by such an authority, before so young a man as Pamphilus?

You seem not to apprehend, replied Philo, that I argue with Cleanthes in his own way, and, by showing him the dangerous consequences of his tenets, hope at last to reduce him to our opinion. But what sticks most with you, I observe, is the representation which Cleanthes has made of the argument *a posteriori;* and, finding that that argument is likely to escape your hold and vanish into air, you think it so disguised that you can scarcely believe it to be set in its true light. Now, however much I may dissent, in other respects, from the dangerous principle of Cleanthes, I must allow that he has fairly represented that argument, and I shall endeavor so to state the matter to you that you will entertain no further scruples with regard to it.

Were a man to abstract from everything which he knows or has seen, he would be altogether incapable, merely from his own ideas, to determine what kind of scene the universe must be, or to give the preference to one state or

situation of things above another. For as nothing which he clearly conceives could be esteemed impossible or implying a contradiction, every chimera of his fancy would be upon an equal footing; nor could he assign just reason why he adheres to one idea or system, and rejects the others which are equally possible.

Again, after he opens his eyes and contemplates the world as it really is, it would be impossible for him at first to assign the cause of any one event, much less the whole of things, or of the universe. He might set his fancy a rambling, and she might bring him in an infinite variety of reports and representations. These would all be possible; but, being all equally possible, he would never of himself give a satisfactory account for his preferring one of them to the rest. Experience alone can point out to him the true cause of any phenomenon.

Now, according to this method of reasoning, Demea, it follows (and is, indeed, tacitly allowed by Cleanthes himself) that order, arrangement, or the adjustment of final causes, is not of itself any proof of design, but only so far as it has been experienced to proceed from that principle. For aught we can know *a priori*, matter may contain the source or spring of order originally within itself, as well as mind does; and there is no more difficulty in conceiving that the several elements, from an internal unknown cause, may fall into the most exquisite arrangement, than to conceive that their ideas, in the great universal mind, from a like internal unknown cause, fall into that arrangement. The equal possibility of both these suppositions is allowed. But, by experience, we find (according to Cleanthes) that there is a difference between them. Throw several pieces of steel together, without shape or form they will never arrange themselves so as to compose a watch. Stone and mortar and wood, without an architect, never erect a house. But the ideas in a human mind, we see, by an unknown, inexplicable economy, arrange themselves so as to form the plan of a watch or house. Experience, therefore, proves that there is an original principle of order in mind, not in matter. From similar effects we infer similar causes. The adjustment of means to ends is alike in the universe, as in a machine of human contrivance. The causes, therefore, must be resembling.

I was from the beginning scandalized, I must own, with this resemblance which is asserted between the Deity and human creatures, and must conceive it to imply such a degradation of the Supreme Being as no sound theist could endure. With your assistance, therefore, Demea, I shall endeavor to defend what you justly call the adorable mysteriousness of the Divine nature, and shall refute this reasoning of Cleanthes, provided he allows that I have made a fair representation of it.

When Cleanthes had assented, Philo, after a short pause, proceeded in the following manner.

That all inferences, Cleanthes, concerning fact are founded on experience, and that all experimental reasonings are founded on the supposition that similar causes prove similar effects, and similar effects similar causes, I shall not at present much dispute with you. But observe, I entreat you, with what extreme caution all just reasoners proceed in the transferring of experiments to similar cases. Unless the cases be exactly similar, they repose no perfect confidence in applying their past observation to any particular phenomenon. Every alteration

of circumstances occasions a doubt concerning the event; and it requires new experiments to prove certainly that the new circumstances are of no moment or importance. A change in bulk, situation, arrangement, age, disposition of the air, or surrounding bodies—any of these particulars may be attended with the most unexpected consequences. And unless the objects be quite familiar to us, it is the highest temerity to expect with assurance, after any of these changes, an event similar to that which before fell under our observation. The slow and deliberate steps of philosophers here, if anywhere, are distinguished from the precipitate march of the vulgar, who, hurried on by the smallest similitude, are incapable of all discernment or consideration.

But can you think, Cleanthes, that your usual phlegm and philosophy have been preserved in so wide a step as you have taken when you compared to the universe houses, ships, furniture, machines; and, from their similarity in some circumstances, inferred a similarity in their causes? Thought, design, intelligence, such as we discover in men and other animals, is no more than one of the springs and principles of the universe, as well as heat or cold, attraction or repulsion, and a hundred others which fall under daily observation. It is an active cause by which some particular parts of nature, we find, produce alterations on other parts. But can a conclusion, with any propriety, be transferred from parts to the whole? Does not the great disproportion bar all comparison and inference? From observing the growth of a hair, can we learn anything concerning the generation of a man? Would the manner of a leaf's blowing, even though perfectly known, afford us any instruction concerning the vegetation of a tree?

But allowing that we were to take the *operations* of one part of nature upon another for the foundation of our judgment concerning the *origin* of the whole (which never can be admitted), yet why select so minute, so weak, so bounded a principle as the reason and design of animals is found to be upon this planet? What peculiar privilege has this little agitation of the brain which we call *thought,* that we must thus make it the model of the whole universe? Our partiality in our own favor does indeed present it on all occasions, but sound philosophy ought carefully to guard against so natural an illusion.

So far from admitting, continued Philo, that the operations of a part can afford us any just conclusion concerning the origin of the whole, I will not allow any one part to form a rule for another part if the latter be very remote from the former. Is there any reasonable ground to conclude that the inhabitants of other planets possess thought, intelligence, reason, or anything similar to these faculties in men? When nature has so extremely diversified her manner of operation in this small globe, can we imagine that she incessantly copies herself throughout so immense a universe? And if thought, as we may well suppose, be confined merely to this narrow corner and has even there so limited a sphere of action, with what propriety can we assign it for the original cause of all things? The narrow views of a peasant who makes his domestic economy the rule for the government of kingdoms is in comparison a pardonable sophism.

But were we ever so much assured that a thought and reason resembling the human were to be found throughout the whole universe, and were its activity

elsewhere vastly greater and more commanding than it appears in this globe; yet I cannot see why the operations of a world constituted, arranged, adjusted, can with any propriety be extended to a world which is in its embryo-state, and is advancing towards that constitution and arrangement. By observation we know somewhat of the economy, action, and nourishment of a finished animal; but we must transfer with great caution that observation to the growth of a foetus in the womb, and still more to the formation of an animalcule in the loins of its male parent. Nature, we find, even from our limited experience, possesses an infinite number of springs and principles which incessantly discover themselves on every change of her position and situation. And what new and unknown principles would actuate her in so new and unknown a situation as that of the formation of a universe, we cannot, without the utmost temerity, pretend to determine.

A very small part of this great system, during a very short time, is very imperfectly discovered to us; and do we thence pronounce decisively concerning the origin of the whole?

Admirable conclusion! Stone, wood, brick, iron, brass, have not, at this time, in this minute globe of earth, an order or arrangement without human art and contrivance; therefore, the universe could not originally attain its order and arrangement without something similar to human art. But is a part of nature a rule for another part very wide of the former? Is it a rule for the whole? Is a very small part a rule for the universe? Is nature in one situation a certain rule for nature in another situation vastly different from the former?

And can you blame me, Cleanthes, if I here imitate the prudent reserve of Simonides, who, according to the noted story, being asked by Hiero, *What God was?* desired a day to think of it, and then two days more; and after that manner continually prolonged the term, without ever bringing in his definition or description? Could you even blame me if I had answered, at first, *that I did not know,* and was sensible that this subject lay vastly beyond the reach of my faculties? You might cry out sceptic and railer, as much as you pleased; but, having found in so many other subjects much more familiar the imperfections and even contradictions of human reason, I never should expect any success from its feeble conjectures in a subject so sublime and so remote from the sphere of our observation. When two *species* of objects have always been observed to be conjoined together, I can *infer,* by custom, the existence of one wherever I *see* the existence of the other; and this I call an argument from experience. But how this argument can have place where the objects, as in the present case, are single, individual, without parallel or specific resemblance, may be difficult to explain. And will any man tell me with a serious countenance that an orderly universe must arise from some thought and art like the human because we have experience of it? To ascertain this reasoning it were requisite that we had experience of the origin of the worlds; and it is not sufficient, surely, that we have seen ships and cities arise from human art and contrivance . . .

Philo was proceeding in this vehement manner, somewhat between jest and earnest, as it appeared to me, when he observed some signs of impatience in Cleanthes, and then immediately stopped short. What I had to suggest, said

Cleanthes, is only that you would not abuse terms, or make use of popular expressions to subvert philosophical reasonings. You know that the vulgar often distinguish reason from experience, even where the question relates only to matter of fact and existence, though it is found, where that *reason* is properly analyzed, that it is nothing but a species of experience. To prove by experience the origin of the universe from mind is not more contrary to common speech than to prove the motion of the earth from the same principle. And a caviller might raise all the same objections to the Copernican system which you have urged against my reasonings. Have you other earths, might he say, which you have seen to move? Have . . .

Yes! cried Philo, interrupting him, we have other earths. Is not the moon another earth, which we see to turn round its center? Is not Venus another earth, where we observe the same phenomenon? Are not the revolutions of the sun also a confirmation, from analogy, of the same theory? All the planets, are they not earths which revolve about the sun? Are not the satellites moons which move round Jupiter and Saturn, and along with these primary planets round the sun? These analogies and resemblances, with others which I have not mentioned, are the sole proofs of the Copernican system; and to you it belongs to consider whether you have any analogies of the same kind to support your theory.

In reality, Cleanthes, continued he, the modern system of astronomy is now so much received by all inquirers, and has become so essential a part even of our earliest education, that we are not commonly very scrupulous in examining the reasons upon which it is founded. It is now become a matter of mere curiosity to study the first writers on that subject who had the full force of prejudice to encounter, and were obliged to turn their arguments on every side in order to render them popular and convincing. But if we peruse Galileo's famous *Dialogues* concerning the system of the world, we shall find that that great genius, one of the sublimest that ever existed, first bent all his endeavors to prove that there was no foundation for the distinction commonly made between elementary and celestial substances. The schools, proceeding from the illusions of sense, had carried this distinction very far; and had established the latter substances to be ingenerable, incorruptible, unalterable, impassible; and had assigned all the opposite qualities to the former. But Galileo, beginning with the moon, proved its similarity in every particular to the earth: its convex figure, its natural darkness when not illuminated, its density, its distinction into solid and liquid, the variations of its phases, the mutual illuminations of the earth and moon, their mutual eclipses, the inequalities of the lunar surface, etc. After many instances of this kind, with regard to all the planets, men plainly saw that these bodies became proper objects of experience, and that the similarity of their nature enabled us to extend the same arguments and phenomena from one to the other.

In this cautious proceeding of the astronomers you may read your own condemnation, Cleanthes; or rather may see that the subject in which you are engaged exceeds all human reason and inquiry. Can you pretend to show any such similarity between the fabric of a house and the generation of a universe?

Have you ever seen nature in any such situation as resembles the first arrangement of the elements? Have worlds ever been formed under your eye, and have you had leisure to observe the whole progress of the phenomenon, from the first appearance of order to its final consummation? If you have, then cite your experience and deliver your theory.

. . .

But to show you still more inconveniences, continued Philo, in your anthropomorphism, please to take a new survey of your principles. *Like effects prove like causes.* This is the experimental argument; and this, you say too, is the sole theological argument. Now it is certain that the liker the effects are which are seen and the liker the causes which are inferred, the stronger is the argument. Every departure on either side diminishes the probability and renders the experiment less conclusive. You cannot doubt of the principle; neither ought you to reject its consequences.

All the new discoveries in astronomy which prove the immense grandeur and magnificence of the works of nature are so many additional arguments for a Deity, according to the true system of theism; but, according to your hypothesis of experimental theism, they become so many objections, by removing the effect still farther from all resemblance to the effects of human art and contrivance. For if Lucretius, even following the old system of the world could exclaim:

> Quis regere immensi summam, quis habere profundi
> Indu manu validas potis est moderanter habenas?
> Quis pariter coelos omnes convertere? et omnes
> Ignibus aetheriis terras suffire feraces?
> Omnibus inque locis esse omni tempore praesto?[2]

If Tully esteemed this reasoning so natural as to put it into the mouth of his Epicurean:

> Quibus enim oculis animi intueri potuit vester Plato fabricam illam tanti operis, qua construi a Deo atque aedificari mundum facit? quae molitio? quae ferramenta? qui vectes? quae machinae? qui ministri tanti muneris fuerunt? quemadmodum autem obedire et parere voluntati architecti aer, ignis, aqua, terra potuerunt?[3]

---

[2] Lib. xi. 1094. The quotation is from *On the Nature of the Universe.* "Who is able to rule the whole of the immeasurable; who is able, with control, to hold in hand the strong reins of the boundless? Who equally is able to turn all the heavens? And who is able to warm all fertile grounds with ethereal fire? Who is able to be present in all places at every time?" (The translation is by William E. Mann.)

[3] *De Nat. Deor.*, lib. i. The quotation is from *On the Nature of the Gods.* "For with which of the soul's eyes has your [master] Plato been able to contemplate that fabrication of such great labor, by which he establishes that the universe is furnished and even constructed by God? What preparation [was involved]? What tools? What levers? What machines? What agents were there for such a great enterprise? Moreover, how were air, fire, water, and earth able to obey and to come forth at the will of the architect?" (The translation is by William E. Mann, whose amplifications are in brackets.)

and is left afterwards to fix every point of his theology by the utmost license of fancy and hypothesis. This world, for aught he knows, is very faulty and imperfect, compared to a superior standard; and was only the first rude essay of some infant deity who afterwards abandoned it, ashamed of his lame performance; it is the work only of some dependent, inferior deity, and is the object of derision to his superiors; it is the production of old age and dotage in some superannuated deity; and ever since his death has run on at adventures, from the first impulse and active force which it received from him. You justly give signs of horror, Demea, at these strange suppositions; but these, and a thousand more of the same kind, are Cleanthes' suppositions, not mine. From the moment the attributes of the Deity are supposed finite, all these have place. And I cannot, for my part, think that so wild and unsettled a system of theology is, in any respect, preferable to none at all.

These suppositions I absolutely disown, cried Cleanthes; they strike me, however, with no horror, especially when proposed in that rambling way in which they drop from you. On the contrary, they give me pleasure when I see that, by the utmost indulgence of your imagination, you never get rid of the hypothesis of design in the universe, but are obliged at every turn to have recourse to it. To this concession I adhere steadily; and this I regard as a sufficient foundation for religion.

. . .

It is my opinion, I own, replied Demea, that each man feels, in a manner, the truth of religion within his own breast; and, from a consciousness of his imbecility and misery rather than from any reasoning, is led to seek protection from that Being on whom he and all nature are dependent. So anxious or so tedious are even the best scenes of life that futurity is still the object of all our hopes and fears. We incessantly look forward and endeavor, by prayers, adoration, and sacrifice, to appease those unknown powers whom we find, by experience, so able to afflict and oppress us. Wretched creatures that we are! What resource for us amidst the innumerable ills of life did not religion suggest some methods of atonement, and appease those terrors with which we are incessantly agitated and tormented?

I am indeed persuaded, said Philo, that the best and indeed the only method of bringing everyone to a due sense of religion is by just representations of the misery and wickedness of men. And for that purpose a talent of eloquence and strong imagery is more requisite than that of reasoning and argument. For is it necessary to prove what everyone feels within himself? It is only necessary to make us feel it, if possible, more intimately and sensibly.

The people, indeed, replied Demea, are sufficiently convinced of this great and melancholy truth. The miseries of life, the unhappiness of man, the general corruptions of our nature, the unsatisfactory enjoyment of pleasures, riches, honors—these phrases have become almost proverbial in all languages. And who can doubt of what all men declare from their own immediate feeling and experience?

In this point, said Philo, the learned are perfectly agreed with the vulgar; and in all letters, *sacred* and *profane,* the topic of human misery has been insisted

on with the most pathetic eloquence that sorrow and melancholy could inspire. The poets, who speak from sentiment, without a system, and whose testimony has therefore the more authority, abound in images of this nature. From Homer down to Dr. Young, the whole inspired tribe have ever been sensible that no other representation of things would suit the feeling and observation of each individual.

As to authorities, replied Demea, you need not seek them. Look round this library of Cleanthes. I shall venture to affirm that, except authors of particular sciences, such as chemistry or botany, who have no occasion to treat of human life, there is scarce one of those innumerable writers from whom the sense of human misery has not, in some passage or other, extorted a complaint and confession of it. At least, the chance is entirely on that side; and no one author has ever, so far as I can recollect, been so extravagant as to deny it.

There you must excuse me, said Philo: Leibniz has denied it, and is perhaps the first[4] who ventured upon so bold and paradoxical an opinion; at least, the first who made it essential to his philosophical system.

And by being the first, replied Demea, might he not have been sensible of his error? For is this a subject in which philosophers can propose to make discoveries especially in so late an age? And can any man hope by a simple denial (for the subject scarcely admits of reasoning) to bear down the united testimony of mankind, founded on sense and consciousness?

And why should man, added he, pretend to an exemption from the lot of all other animals? The whole earth, believe me, Philo, is cursed and polluted. A perpetual war is kindled amongst all living creatures. Necessity, hunger, want stimulate the strong and courageous; fear, anxiety, terror agitate the weak and infirm. The first entrance into life gives anguish to the new-born infant and to its wretched parent; weakness, impotence, distress attend each stage of that life, and it is, at last, finished in agony and horror.

Observe, too, says Philo, the curious artifices of nature in order to embitter the life of every living being. The stronger prey upon the weaker and keep them in perpetual terror and anxiety. The weaker, too, in their turn, often prey upon the stronger, and vex and molest them without relaxation. Consider that innumerable race of insects, which either are bred on the body of each animal or, flying about, infix their stings in him. These insects have others still less than themselves which torment them. And thus on each hand, before and behind, above and below, every animal is surrounded with enemies which incessantly seek his misery and destruction.

Man alone, said Demea, seems to be, in part, an exception to this rule. For by combination in society he can easily master lions, tigers, and bears, whose greater strength and agility naturally enable them to prey upon him.

On the contrary, it is here chiefly, cried Philo, that the uniform and equal maxims of nature are most apparent. Man, it is true, can, by combination,

---

[4] That sentiment had been maintained by Dr. King and some few others before Leibniz, though by none of so great fame as the German philosopher.

surmount all his *real* enemies and become master of the whole animal creation; but does he not immediately raise up to himself *imaginary* enemies, the demons of his fancy, who haunt him with superstitious terrors and blast every enjoyment of life? His pleasure, as he imagines, becomes in their eyes a crime; his food and repose give them umbrage and offence; his very sleep and dreams furnish new materials to anxious fear; and even death, his refuge from every other ill, presents only the dread of endless and innumerable woes. Nor does the wolf molest more the timid flock than superstition does the anxious breast of wretched mortals.

Besides, consider, Demea: This very society by which we surmount those wild beasts, our natural enemies, what new enemies does it not raise to us? What woe and misery does it not occasion? Man is the greatest enemy of man. Oppression, injustice, contempt, contumely, violence, sedition, war, calumny, treachery, fraud—by these they mutually torment each other, and they would soon dissolve that society which they had formed were it not for the dread of still greater ills which must attend their separation.

But though these external insults, said Demea, from animals, from men, from all the elements, which assault us form a frightful catalogue of woes, they are nothing in comparison of those which arise within ourselves, from the distempered condition of our mind and body. How many lie under the lingering torment of diseases? Hear the pathetic enumeration of the great poet.

> Intestine stone and ulcer, colic-pangs,
> Demoniac frenzy, moping melancholy,
> And moon-struck madness, pining atrophy,
> Marasmus, and wide-wasting pestilence.
> Dire was the tossing, deep the groans: *Despair*
> Tended the sick, busiest from couch to couch.
> And over them triumphant *Death* his dart
> Shook: but delay'd to strike, though oft invok'd
> With vows, as their chief good and final hope.

The disorders of the mind, continued Demea, though more secret, are not perhaps less dismal and vexatious. Remorse, shame, anguish, rage, disappointment, anxiety, fear, dejection, despair—who has ever passed through life without cruel inroads from these tormentors? How many have scarcely ever felt any better sensations? Labor and poverty, so abhorred by everyone, are the certain lot of the far greater number; and those few privileged persons who enjoy ease and opulence never reach contentment or true felicity. All the goods of life united would not make a very happy man, but all the ills united would make a wretch indeed; and any one of them almost (and who can be free from every one), nay, often the absence of one good (and who can possess all) is sufficient to render life ineligible.

Were a stranger to drop on a sudden into this world, I would show him, as a specimen of its ills, a hospital full of diseases, a prison crowded with malefactors and debtors, a field of battle strewed with carcases, a fleet foundering in the ocean, a nation languishing under tyranny, famine, or pestilence. To turn

the gay side of life to him and give him a notion of its pleasures—whither should I conduct him? To a ball, to an opera, to court? He might justly think that I was only showing him a diversity of distress and sorrow.

There is no evading such striking instances, said Philo, but by apologies which still further aggravate the charge. Why have all men, I ask, in all ages, complained incessantly of the miseries of life? . . . They have no just reason, says one: These complaints proceed only from their discontented, repining, anxious disposition . . . And can there possibly, I reply, be a more certain foundation of misery than such a wretched temper?

But if they were really as unhappy as they pretend, says my antagonist, why do they remain in life? . . .

Not satisfied with life, afraid of death.

This is the secret chain, say I, that holds us. We are terrified, not bribed to the continuance of our existence.

It is only a false delicacy, he may insist, which a few refined spirits indulge, and which has spread these complaints among the whole race of mankind . . . And what is this delicacy, I ask, which you blame? Is it anything but a greater sensibility to all the pleasures and pains of life? And if the man of a delicate, refined temper, by being so much more alive than the rest of the world, is only so much more unhappy, what judgment must we form in general of human life?

Let men remain at rest, says our adversary, and they will be easy. They are willing artificers of their own misery. . . . No! reply I: An anxious languor follows their repose; disappointment, vexation, trouble, their activity and ambition.

I can observe something like what you mention in some others, replied Cleanthes; but I confess I feel little or nothing of it in myself, and hope that it is not so common as you represent it.

If you feel not human misery yourself, cried Demea, I congratulate you on so happy a singularity. Others, seemingly the most prosperous, have not been ashamed to vent their complaints in the most melancholy strains. Let us attend to the great, the fortunate emperor, Charles V, when, tired with human grandeur, he resigned all his extensive dominions into the hands of his son. In the last harangue which he made on that memorable occasion, he publicly avowed *that the greatest prosperities which he had ever enjoyed had been mixed with so many adversities that he might truly say he had never enjoyed any satisfaction or contentment.* But did the retired life in which he sought for shelter afford him any greater happiness? If we may credit his son's account, his repentance commenced the very day of his resignation.

Cicero's fortune, from small beginnings, rose to the greatest luster and renown; yet what pathetic complaints of all ills of life do his familiar letters, as well as philosophical discourses, contain? And suitably to his own experience, he introduces Cato, the great, the fortunate Cato protesting in his old age that had he a new life in his offer he would reject the present.

As yourself, ask any of your acquaintance, whether they would live over again the last ten or twenty years of their life. No! but the next twenty, they say, will be better:

> And from the dregs of life, hope to receive
> What the first sprightly running could not give.

Thus, at last, they find (such is the greatness of human misery, it reconciles even contradictions) that they complain at once of the shortness of life and of its vanity and sorrow.

And is it possible, Cleanthes, said Philo, that after all these reflections, and infinitely more which might be suggested, you can still persevere in your anthropomorphism, and assert the moral attributes of the Deity, his justice, benevolence, mercy, and rectitude, to be of the same nature with these virtues in human creatures? His power, we allow, is infinite; whatever he wills is executed; but neither man nor any other animal is happy; therefore, he does not will their happiness. His wisdom is infinite; he is never mistaken in choosing the means to any end; but the course of nature tends not to human or animal felicity; therefore, it is not established for that purpose. Through the whole compass of human knowledge there are no inferences more certain and infallible than these. In what respect, then, do his benevolence and mercy resemble the benevolence and mercy of men?

Epicurus' old questions are yet unanswered.

Is he willing to prevent evil, but not able? then is he impotent. Is he able, but not willing? then is he malevolent. Is he both able and willing? whence then is evil?

You ascribe, Cleanthes (and I believe justly), a purpose and intention to nature. But what, I beseech you, is the object of that curious artifice and machinery which she has displayed in all animals—the preservation alone of individuals, and propagation of the species? It seems enough for her purpose, if such a rank be barely upheld in the universe, without any care or concern for the happiness of the members that compose it. No resource for this purpose: no machinery in order merely to give pleasure or ease: no fund of pure joy and contentment: no indulgence without some want or necessity accompanying it. At least, the few phenomena of this nature are overbalanced by opposite phenomena of still greater importance.

Our sense of music, harmony, and indeed beauty of all kinds, gives satisfaction, without being absolutely necessary to the preservation and propagation of the species. But what racking pains, on the other hand, arise from gouts, gravels, megrims, toothaches, rheumatisms, where the injury to the animal machinery is either small or incurable? Mirth, laughter, play, frolic seem gratuitous satisfactions which have no further tendency; spleen, melancholy, discontent, superstition are pains of the same nature. How then does the divine benevolence display itself, in the sense of you anthropomorphites? None but we mystics, as you were pleased to call us, can account for this strange mixture of phenomena, by deriving it from attributes infinitely perfect but incomprehensible.

And have you, at last, said Cleanthes smiling, betrayed your intentions, Philo? Your long agreement with Demea did indeed a little surprise me, but I find you were all the while erecting a concealed battery against me. And I must confess that you have now fallen upon a subject worthy of your noble spirit of opposition and controversy. If you can make out the present point, and prove mankind to be unhappy or corrupted, there is an end at once of all religion. For to what purpose establish the natural attributes of the Deity, while the moral are still doubtful and uncertain?

You take umbrage very easily, replied Demea, at opinions the most innocent and the most generally received, even amongst the religious and devout themselves; and nothing can be more surprising than to find a topic like this—concerning the wickedness and misery of man—charged with no less than atheism and profaneness. Have not all pious divines and preachers who have indulged their rhetoric on so fertile a subject; have they not easily, I say, given a solution of any difficulties which may attend it? This world is but a point in comparison of the universe; this life but a moment in comparison of eternity. The present evil phenomena, therefore, are rectified in other regions, and in some future period of existence. And the eyes of men, being then opened to larger views of things, see the whole connection of general laws, and trace, with adoration, the benevolence and rectitude of the Deity through all the mazes and intricacies of his providence.

No! replied Cleanthes, no! These arbitrary suppositions can never be admitted, contrary to matter of fact, visible and uncontroverted. Whence can any cause be known but from its known effects? Whence can any hypothesis be proved but from the apparent phenomena? To establish one hypothesis upon another is building entirely in the air; and the utmost we ever attain by these conjectures and fictions is to ascertain the bare possibility of our opinion, but never can we, upon such terms, establish its reality.

The only method of supporting divine benevolence—and it is what I willingly embrace—is to deny absolutely the misery and wickedness of man. Your representations are exaggerated; your melancholy views mostly fictitious; your inferences contrary to fact and experience. Health is more common than sickness; pleasure than pain; happiness than misery. And for one vexation which we meet with, we attain, upon computation, a hundred enjoyments.

Admitting your position, replied Philo, which yet is extremely doubtful, you must at the same time allow that, if pain be less frequent than pleasure, it is infinitely more violent and durable. One hour of it is often able to outweigh a day, a week, a month of our common insipid enjoyments; and how many days, weeks, and months are passed by several in the most acute torments? Pleasure, scarcely in one instance, is ever able to reach ecstasy and rapture; and in no one instance can it continue for any time at its highest pitch and altitude. The spirits evaporate, the nerves relax, the fabric is disordered, and the enjoyment quickly degenerates into fatigue and uneasiness. But pain often, good God, how often! rises to torture and agony; and the longer it continues, it becomes still more genuine agony and torture. Patience is exhausted, courage languishes,

melancholy seizes us, and nothing terminates our misery but the removal of its cause or another event which is the sole cure of all evil, but which, from our natural folly, we regard with still greater horror and consternation.

But not to insist upon these topics, continued Philo, though most obvious, certain, and important, I must use the freedom to admonish you, Cleanthes, that you have put the controversy upon a most dangerous issue, and are unawares introducing a total scepticism into the most essential articles of natural and revealed theology. What! no method of fixing a just foundation for religion unless we allow the happiness of human life, and maintain a continued existence even in this world, with all our present pains, infirmities, vexations, and follies, to be eligible and desirable! But this is contrary to everyone's feeling and experience; it is contrary to an authority so established as nothing can subvert. No decisive proofs can ever be produced against this authority; nor is it possible for you to compute, estimate, and compare all the pains and all the pleasures in the lives of all men and of all animals; and thus, by your resting the whole system of religion on a point which, from its very nature, must forever be uncertain, you tacitly confess that that system is equally uncertain.

But allowing you what never will be believed, at least, what you never possibly can prove, that animal or, at least, human happiness in this life exceeds its misery, you have yet done nothing; for this is not, by any means, what we expect from infinite power, infinite wisdom, and infinite goodness. Why is there any misery at all in the world? Not by chance, surely. From some cause then. Is it from the intention of the Deity? But he is perfectly benevolent. Is it contrary to his intention? But he is almighty. Nothing can shake the solidity of this reasoning, so short, so clear, so decisive, except we assert that these subjects exceed all human capacity, and that our common measures of truth and falsehood are not applicable to them—a topic which I have all along insisted on, but which you have, from the beginning, rejected with scorn and indignation.

But I will be contented to retire still from this intrenchment, for I deny that you can ever force me in it. I will allow that pain or misery in man is *compatible* with infinite power and goodness in the Deity, even in your sense of these attributes: what are you advanced by all these concessions? A mere possible compatibility is not sufficient. You must *prove* these pure, unmixed and uncontrollable attributes from the present mixed and confused phenomena, and from these alone. A hopeful undertaking! Were the phenomena ever so pure and unmixed, yet, being finite, they would be insufficient for that purpose. How much more, where they are also so jarring and discordant!

Here, Cleanthes, I find myself at ease in my argument. Here I triumph. Formerly, when we argued concerning the natural attributes of intelligence and design, I needed all my sceptical and metaphysical subtilty to elude your grasp. In many views of the universe and of its parts, particularly the latter, the beauty and fitness of final causes strike us with such irresistible force that all objections appear (what I believe they really are) mere cavils and sophisms; nor can we then imagine how it was ever possible for us to repose any weight on them. But there is no view of human life or of the condition of mankind from which,

without the greatest violence, we can infer the moral attributes or learn that infinite benevolence, conjoined with infinite power and infinite wisdom, which we must discover by the eyes of faith alone. It is your turn now to tug the laboring oar, and to support your philosophical subtilties against the dictates of plain reason and experience.

. . .

49

A Defense of Atheism

ERNEST NAGEL

Ernest Nagel (b. 1901), University Professor Emeritus at Columbia University, is one of the world's most distinguished philosophers of science. Among his books are Sovereign Reason, Logic Without Metaphysics, Teleology Revisited, *and his magnum opus,* The Structure of Science: Problems in the Logic of Scientific Explanation.

The following essay has six parts. At the beginning of section 2, Nagel distinguishes between atheists who believe theism is meaningful but false, and those who believe theism is not even meaningful. Nagel himself defends the first position; the second is defended by Antony Flew in "Theology and Falsification" (reading 51). Nagel considers the best-known arguments for the existence of God and rejects them all. In section 5, he considers the problem of evil, and concludes that it is not possible to reconcile the alleged omnipotence and omnibenevolence of God with the evils of our world. Hence, Nagel accepts atheism.

In section 6, Nagel briefly enumerates some doctrines that he attributes to typical atheists: the rejection of disembodied spirits, the acceptance of the scientific method of inquiry as the ideal for establishing claims to knowledge, the appeal to consequences as the basis for judging moral issues, and a tragic outlook on life. Undoubtedly, many atheists do subscribe to these views, but it also should be emphasized that atheists need not do so. Atheism is simply the doctrine that God does not exist, and those who agree on this matter may, in fact, agree about little else.

THE ESSAYS IN THIS BOOK are devoted in the main to the exposition of the major religious creeds of humanity. It is a natural expectation that this final paper, even though its theme is so radically different from nearly all of the others, will show how atheism belongs to the great tradition of religious thought. Needless to say, this expectation is difficult to satisfy, and did anyone succeed in doing so he would indeed be performing the neatest conjuring trick of the week. But the expectation nevertheless does cause me some embarrassment, which is only slightly relieved by an anecdote Bertrand Russell reports in his recent book, *Portraits from Memory*. Russell was imprisoned during the First World War for pacifistic activities. On entering the prison he was asked a number of customary questions about himself for the prison records. One question was about his religion. Russell explained that he was an agnostic. "Never heard of it," the warden declared. "How do you spell it?" When Russell

told him, the warden observed, "Well, there are many religions, but I suppose they all worship the same God." Russell adds that this remark kept him cheerful for about a week. Perhaps philosophical atheism also is a religion.

1

I must begin by stating what sense I am attaching to the word "atheism," and how I am construing the theme of this paper. I shall understand by "atheism" a critique and a denial of the major claims of all varieties of theism. And by theism I shall mean the view which holds, as one writer has expressed it, "that the heavens and the earth and all that they contain owe their existence and continuance in existence to the wisdom and will of a supreme, self-consistent, omnipotent, omniscient, righteous, and benevolent being, who is distinct from, and independent of, what he has created." Several things immediately follow from these definitions.

In the first place, atheism is not necessarily an irreligious concept, for theism is just one among many views concerning the nature and origin of the world. The denial of theism is logically compatible with a religious outlook upon life, and is in fact characteristic of some of the great historical religions. For as readers of this volume will know, early Buddhism is a religion which does not subscribe to any doctrine about a god; and there are pantheistic religions and philosophies which, because they deny that God is a being separate from and independent of the world, are not theistic in the sense of the word explained above.

The second point to note is that atheism is not to be identified with sheer unbelief, or with disbelief in some particular creed of a religious group. Thus, a child who has received no religious instruction and has never heard about God, is not an atheist—for he is not denying any theistic claims. Similarly in the case of an adult who, if he has withdrawn from the faith of his fathers without reflection or because of frank indifference to any theological issue, is also not an atheist—for such an adult is not challenging theism and is not professing any views on the subject. Moreover, though the term "atheist" has been used historically as an abusive label for those who do not happen to subscribe to some regnant orthodoxy (for example, the ancient Romans called the early Christians atheist, because the latter denied the Roman divinities), or for those who engage in conduct regarded as immoral it is not in this sense that I am discussing atheism.

One final word of preliminary explanation. I propose to examine some *philosophic* concepts of atheism, and I am not interested in the slightest in the many considerations atheists have advanced against the evidences for some particular religious and theological doctrine—for example, against the truth of the Christian story. What I mean by "philosophical" in the present context is that the views I shall consider are directed against any form of theism, and have their origin and basis in a logical analysis of the theistic position, and in a comprehensive account of the world believed to be wholly intelligible without the adoption of a theistic hypothesis.

Theism as I conceive it is a theological proposition, not a statement of a position that belongs primarily to religion. On my view, religion as a historical and social phenomenon is primarily an institutionalized *cultus* or practice, which possesses identifiable social functions and which expresses certain attitudes men take toward their world. Although it is doubtful whether men ever engage in religious practices or assume religious attitudes without some more or less explicit interpretation of their ritual or some rationale for their attitude, it is still the case that it is possible to distinguish religion as a social and personal phenomenon from the theological doctrines which may be developed as justifications for religious practices. Indeed, in some of the great religions of the world the profession of a creed plays a relatively minor role. In short, religion is a form of social communion, a participation in certain kinds of ritual (whether it be a dance, worship, prayer, or the like), and a form of experience (sometimes, though not invariably, directed to a personal confrontation with divine and holy things). Theology is an articulated and, at its best, a rational attempt at understanding these feelings and practices, in the light of their relation to other parts of human experience, and in terms of some hypothesis concerning the nature of things entire.

2

As I see it, atheistic philosophies fall into two major groups: 1) those which hold that the theistic doctrine is meaningful, but reject it either on the ground that, (a) the positive evidence for it is insufficient, or (b) the negative evidence is quite overwhelming; and 2) those who hold that the theistic thesis is not even meaningful, and reject it (a) as just nonsense or (b) as literally meaningless but interpreting it as a symbolic rendering of human ideals, thus reading the theistic thesis in a sense that most believers in theism would disavow. It will not be possible in the limited space at my disposal to discuss the second category of atheistic critiques; and in any event, most of the traditional atheistic critiques of theism belong to the first group.

But before turning to the philosophical examination of the major classical arguments for theism, it is well to note that such philosophical critiques do not quite convey the passion with which atheists have often carried on their analyses of theistic views. For historically, atheism has been, and indeed continues to be, a form of social and political protest, directed as much against institutionalized religion as against theistic doctrine. Atheism has been, in effect, a moral revulsion against the undoubted abuses of the secular power exercised by religious leaders and religious institutions.

Religious authorities have opposed the correction of glaring injustices, and encouraged politically and socially reactionary policies. Religious institutions have been havens of obscurantist thought and centers for the dissemination of intolerance. Religious creeds have been used to set limits to free inquiry, to perpetuate inhumane treatment of the ill and the underprivileged, and to support moral doctrines insensitive to human suffering.

These indictments may not tell the whole story about the historical significance of religion; but they are at least an important part of the story. The refutation of theism has thus seemed to many as an indispensable step not only towards liberating men's minds from superstition, but also towards achieving a more equitable reordering of society. And no account of even the more philosophical aspects of atheistic thought is adequate, which does not give proper recognition to the powerful social motives that actuate many atheistic arguments.

But however this may be, I want now to discuss three classical arguments for the existence of God, arguments which have constituted at least a partial basis for theistic commitments. As long as theism is defended simply as a dogma, asserted as a matter of direct revelation or as the deliverance of authority, belief in the dogma is impregnable to rational argument. In fact, however, reasons are frequently advanced in support of the theistic creed, and these reasons have been the subject of acute philosophical critiques.

One of the oldest intellectual defenses of theism is the cosmological argument, also known as the argument from a first cause. Briefly put, the argument runs as follows. Every event must have a cause. Hence an event A must have as cause some event B, which in turn must have a cause C, and so on. But if there is no end to this backward progression of causes, the progression will be infinite; and in the opinion of those who use this argument, an infinite series of actual events is unintelligible and absurd. Hence there must be a first cause, and this first cause is God, the initiator of all change in the universe.

The argument is an ancient one, and is especially effective when stated within the framework of assumptions of Aristotelian physics; and it has impressed many generations of exceptionally keen minds. The argument is nonetheless a weak reed on which to rest the theistic thesis. Let us waive any question concerning the validity of the principle that every event has a cause, for though the question is important its discussion would lead us far afield. However, if the principle is assumed, it is surely incongruous to postulate a first cause as a way of escaping from the coils of an infinite series. For if everything must have a cause, why does not God require one for His own existence? The standard answer is that He does not need any, because He is self-caused. But if God can be self-caused, why cannot the world itself be self-caused? Why do we require a God transcending the world to bring the world into existence and to initiate changes in it? On the other hand, the supposed inconceivability and absurdity of an infinite series of regressive causes will be admitted by no one who has competent familiarity with the modern mathematical analysis of infinity. The cosmological argument does not stand up under scrutiny.

The second "proof" of God's existence is usually called the ontological argument. It too has a long history going back to early Christian days, though it acquired great prominence only in medieval times. The argument can be stated in several ways, one of which is the following. Since God is conceived to be omnipotent, he is a perfect being. A perfect being is defined as one whose essence or nature lacks no attributes (or properties) whatsoever, one whose nature is complete in every respect. But it is evident that we have an idea of a perfect being, for we have just defined the idea; and since this is so, the argument

continues, God who is the perfect being must exist. Why must he? Because his existence follows from his defined nature. For if God lacked the attribute of existence, he would be lacking at least one attribute, and would therefore not be perfect. To sum up, since we have an idea of God as a perfect being, God must exist.

There are several ways of approaching this argument, but I shall consider only one. The argument was exploded by the 18th century philosopher Immanuel Kant. The substance of Kant's criticism is that it is just a confusion to say that existence is an attribute, and that though the *word* "existence" may occur as the grammatical predicate in a sentence no attribute is being predicated of a thing when we say that the thing exists or has existence. Thus, to use Kant's example, when we think of $100 we are thinking of the nature of this sum of money; but the nature of $100 remains the same whether we have $100 in our pockets or not. Accordingly, we are confounding grammar with logic if we suppose that some characteristic is being attributed to the nature of $100 when we say that a hundred dollar bill exists in someone's pocket.

To make the point clearer, consider another example. When we say that a lion has a tawny color, we are predicating a certain attribute of the animal, and similarly when we say that the lion is fierce or is hungry. But when we say the lion exists, all that we are saying is that something is (or has the nature of) a lion; we are not specifying an attribute which belongs to the nature of anything that is a lion. In short, the word "existence" does not signify any attribute, and in consequence no attribute that belongs to the nature of anything. Accordingly, it does not follow from the assumption that we have an idea of a perfect being that such a being exists. For the idea of a perfect being does not involve the attribute of existence as a constituent of that idea, since there is no such attribute. The ontological argument thus has a serious leak, and it can hold no water.

3

The two arguments discussed thus far are purely dialectical, and attempt to establish God's existence without any appeal to empirical data. The next argument, called the argument from design, is different in character, for it is based on what purports to be empirical evidence. I wish to examine two forms of this argument.

One variant of it calls attention to the remarkable way in which different things and processes in the world are integrated with each other, and concludes that this mutual "fitness" of things can be explained only by the assumption of a divine architect who planned the world and everything in it. For example, living organisms can maintain themselves in a variety of environments, and do so in virtue of their delicate mechanisms which adapt the organisms to all sorts of environmental changes. There is thus an intricate pattern of means and ends throughout the animate world. But the existence of this pattern is unintelligible, so the argument runs, except on the hypothesis that the pattern has been deliberately instituted by a Supreme Designer. If we find a watch in some deserted

spot, we do not think it came into existence by chance, and we do not hesitate to conclude that an intelligent creature designed and made it. But the world and all its contents exhibit mechanisms and mutual adjustments that are far more complicated and subtle than are those of a watch. Must we not therefore conclude that these things too have a Creator?

The conclusion of this argument is based on an inference from analogy: the watch and the world are alike in possessing a congruence of parts and an adjustment of means to ends; the watch has a watch–maker; hence the world has a world–maker. But is the analogy a good one? Let us once more waive some important issues, in particular the issue whether the universe is the unified system such as the watch admittedly is. And let us concentrate on the question what is the ground for our assurance that watches do not come into existence except through the operations of intelligent manufacturers. The answer is plain. We have never run across a watch which has not been deliberately made by someone. But the situation is nothing like this in the case of the innumerable animate and inanimate systems with which we are familiar. Even in the case of living organisms, though they are generated by their parent organisms, the parents do not "make" their progeny in the same sense in which watch–makers make watches. And once this point is clear, the inference from the existence of living organisms to the existence of a supreme designer no longer appears credible.

Moreover, the argument loses all its force if the facts which the hypothesis of a divine designer is supposed to explain can be understood on the basis of a better supported assumption. And indeed, such an alternative explanation is one of the achievements of Darwinian biology. For Darwin showed that one can account for the variety of biological species, as well as for their adaptations to their environments, without invoking a divine creator and acts of special creation. The Darwinian theory explains the diversity of biological species in terms of chance variations in the structure of organisms, and of a mechanism of selection which retains those variant forms that possess some advantages for survival. The evidence for these assumptions is considerable; and developments subsequent to Darwin have only strengthened the case for a thoroughly naturalistic explanation of the facts of biological adaptation. In any event, this version of the argument from design has nothing to recommend it.

A second form of this argument has been recently revived in the speculations of some modern physicists. No one who is familiar with the facts, can fail to be impressed by the success with which the use of mathematical methods has enabled us to obtain intellectual mastery of many parts of nature. But some thinkers have therefore concluded that since the book of nature is ostensibly written in mathematical language, nature must be the creation of a divine mathematician. However, the argument is most dubious. For it rests, among other things, on the assumption that mathematical tools can be successfully used only if the events of nature exhibit some *special* kind of order, and on the further assumption that if the structure of things were different from what they are mathematical language would be inadequate for describing such structure.

But it can be shown that no matter what the world were like—even if it impressed us as being utterly chaotic—it would still possess some order, and would in principle be amenable to a mathematical description. In point of fact, it makes no sense to say that there is absolutely *no* pattern in any conceivable subject matter. To be sure, there are differences in complexities of structure, and if the patterns of events were sufficiently complex we might not be able to unravel them. But however that may be, the success of mathematical physics in giving us some understanding of the world around us does not yield the conclusion that only a mathematician could have devised the patterns of order we have discovered in nature.

4

The inconclusiveness of the three classical arguments for the existence of God was already made evident by Kant, in a manner substantially not different from the above discussion. There are, however, other types of arguments for theism that have been influential in the history of thought, two of which I wish to consider, even if only briefly.

Indeed, though Kant destroyed the classical intellectual foundations for theism, he himself invented a fresh argument for it. Kant's attempted proof is not intended to be a purely theoretical demonstration, and is based on the supposed facts of our moral nature. It has exerted an enormous influence on subsequent theological speculation. In barest outline, the argument is as follows. According to Kant, we are subject not only to physical laws like the rest of nature, but also to moral ones. These moral laws are categorical imperatives, which we must heed not because of their utilitarian consequences, but simply because as autonomous mortal agents it is our duty to accept them as binding. However, Kant was keenly aware that though virtue may be its reward, the virtuous man (that is, the man who acts out of a sense of duty and in conformity with the moral law) does not always receive his just desserts in this world; nor did he shut his eyes to the fact that evil men frequently enjoy the best things this world has to offer. In short, virtue does not always reap happiness. Nevertheless, the highest human good is the realization of happiness commensurate with one's virtue; and Kant believed that it is a practical postulate of the moral life to promote this good. But what can guarantee that the highest good is realizable? Such a guarantee can be found only in God, who must therefore exist if the highest good is not to be a fatuous ideal. The existence of an omnipotent, omniscient, and omnibenevolent God is thus postulated as a necessary condition for the possibility of a moral life.

Despite the prestige this argument has acquired, it is difficult to grant it any force. It is easy enough to postulate God's existence. But as Bertrand Russell observed in another connection, postulation has all the advantages of theft over honest toil. No postulation carries with it any assurance that what is postulated is actually the case. And though we may postulate God's existence as a means to guaranteeing the possibility of realizing happiness together with virtue, the

postulation establishes neither the actual realizability of this ideal nor the fact of his existence. Moreover, the argument is not made more cogent when we recognize that it is based squarely on the highly dubious conception that considerations of utility and human happiness must not enter into the determination of what is morally obligatory. Having built his moral theory on a radical separation of means from ends, Kant was driven to the desperate postulation of God's existence in order to relate them again. The argument is thus at best a *tour de force,* contrived to remedy a fatal flaw in Kant's initial moral assumptions. It carries no conviction to anyone who does not commit Kant's initial blunder.

One further type of argument, pervasive in much Protestant theological literature, deserves brief mention. Arguments of this type take their point of departure from the psychology of religious and mystical experience. Those who have undergone such experiences, often report that during the experience they feel themselves to be in the presence of the divine and holy, that they lose their sense of self-identity and become merged with some fundamental reality, or that they enjoy a feeling of total dependence upon some ultimate power. The overwhelming sense of transcending one's finitude which characterizes such vivid periods of life, and of coalescing with some ultimate source of all existence, is then taken to be compelling evidence for the existence of a supreme being. In a variant form of this argument, other theologians have identified God as the object which satisfies the commonly experienced need for integrating one's scattered and conflicting impulses into a coherent unity, or as the subject which is of ultimate concern to us. In short, a proof of God's existence is found in the occurrence of certain distinctive experiences.

It would be flying in the face of well-attested facts were one to deny that such experiences frequently occur. But do these facts constitute evidence for the conclusion based on them? Does the fact, for example, that an individual experiences a profound sense of direct contact with an alleged transcendent ground of all reality, constitute competent evidence for the claim that there is such a ground and that it is the immediate cause of the experience? If well-established canons for evaluating evidence are accepted, the answer is surely negative. No one will dispute that many men do have vivid experiences in which such things as ghosts or pink elephants appear before them; but only the hopelessly credulous will without further ado count such experiences as establishing the existence of ghosts and pink elephants. To establish the existence of such things, evidence is required that is obtained under controlled conditions and that can be confirmed by independent inquirers. Again, though a man's report that he is suffering pain may be taken at face value, one cannot take at face value the claim, were he to make it, that it is the food he ate which is the cause (or a contributory cause) of his felt pain—not even if the man were to report a vivid feeling of abdominal disturbance. And similarly, an overwhelming feeling of being in the presence of the Divine is evidence enough for admitting the genuineness of such feeling; it is no evidence for the claim that a supreme being with a substantial existence independent of the experience is the cause of the experience.

5

Thus far the discussion has been concerned with noting inadequacies in various arguments widely used to support theism. However, much atheistic criticism is also directed toward exposing incoherencies in the very thesis of theism. I want therefore to consider this aspect of the atheistic critique, though I will restrict myself to the central difficulty in the theistic position which arises from the simultaneous attribution of omnipotence, omniscience, and omnibenevolence to the Deity. The difficulty is that of reconciling these attributes with the occurrence of evil in the world. Accordingly, the question to which I now turn is whether, despite the existence of evil, it is possible to construct a theodicy which will justify the ways of an infinitely powerful and just God to man.

Two main types of solutions have been proposed for this problem. One way that is frequently used is to maintain that what is commonly called evil is only an illusion, or at worst only the "privation" or absence of good. Accordingly, evil is not "really real," it is only the "negative" side of God's beneficence, it is only the product of our limited intelligence which fails to plumb the true character of God's creative bounty. A sufficient comment on this proposed solution is that facts are not altered or abolished by rebaptizing them. Evil may indeed be only an appearance and not genuine. But this does not eliminate from the realm of appearance the tragedies, the sufferings, and the iniquities which men so frequently endure. And it raises once more, though on another level, the problem of reconciling the fact that there is evil in the realm of appearance with God's alleged omnibenevolence. In any event, it is small comfort to anyone suffering a cruel misfortune for which he is in no way responsible, to be told that what he is undergoing is only the absence of good. It is a gratuitous insult to mankind, a symptom of insensitivity and indifference to human suffering, to be assured that all the miseries and agonies men experience are only illusory.

Another gambit often played in attempting to justify the ways of God to man is to argue that the things called evil are evil only because they are viewed in isolation; they are not evil when viewed in proper perspective and in relation to the rest of creation. Thus, if one attends to but a single instrument in an orchestra, the sounds issuing from it may indeed be harsh and discordant. But if one is placed at a proper distance from the whole orchestra, the sounds of that single instrument will mingle with the sounds issuing from the other players to produce a marvellous bit of symphonic music. Analogously, experiences we call painful undoubtedly occur and are real enough. But the pain is judged to be an evil only because it is experienced in a limited perspective—the pain is there for the sake of a more inclusive good, whose reality eludes us because our intelligences are too weak to apprehend things in their entirety.

It is an appropriate retort to this argument that of course we judge things to be evil in a human perspective, but that since we are not God this is the only proper perspective in which to judge them. It may indeed be the case that what is evil for us is not evil for some other part of creation. However, we are not this other part of creation, and it is irrelevant to argue that were we something

other than what we are, our evaluations of what is good and bad would be different. Moreover, the worthlessness of the argument becomes even more evident if we remind ourselves that it is unsupported speculation to suppose that whatever is evil in a finite perspective is good from the purported perspective of the totality of things. For the argument can be turned around: what we judge to be a good is a good only because it is viewed in isolation; when it is viewed in proper perspective, and in relation to the entire scheme of things, it is an evil. This is in fact a standard form of the argument for a universal pessimism. Is it any worse than the similar argument for a universal optimism? The very raising of this question is a *reductio ad absurdum* of the proposed solution to the ancient problem of evil.

I do not believe it is possible to reconcile the alleged omnipotence and omnibenevolence of God with the unvarnished facts of human existence. In point of fact, many theologians have concurred in this conclusion; for in order to escape from the difficulty which the traditional attributes of God present, they have assumed that God is not all powerful, and that there are limits as to what He can do in his efforts to establish a righteous order in the universe. But whether such a modified theology is better off, is doubtful; and in any event, the question still remains whether the facts of human life support the claim that an omnibenevolent Deity, though limited in power, is revealed in the ordering of human history. It is pertinent to note in this connection that though there have been many historians who have made the effort, no historian has yet succeeded in showing to the satisfaction of his professional colleagues that the hypothesis of a Divine Providence is capable of explaining anything which cannot be explained just as well without this hypothesis.

6

This last remark naturally leads to the question whether, apart from their polemics against theism, philosophical atheists have not shared a common set of positive views, a common set of philosophical convictions which set them off from other groups of thinkers. In one very clear sense of this query the answer is indubitably negative. For there never has been what one might call a "school of atheism," in the way in which there has been a Platonic school or even a Kantian school. In point of fact, atheistic critics of theism can be found among many of the conventional groupings of philosophical thinkers—even, I venture to add, among professional theologians in recent years who in effect preach atheism in the guise of language taken bodily from the Christian tradition.

Nevertheless, despite the variety of philosophic positions to which at one time or another in the history of thought atheists have subscribed, it seems to me that atheism is not simply a negative standpoint. At any rate, there is a certain quality of intellectual temper that has characterized, and continues to characterize, many philosophical atheists. (I am excluding from consideration the so-called "village atheist," whose primary concern is to twit and ridicule those who accept some form of theism, or for that matter those who have any religious convictions.) Moreover, their rejection of theism is based not only on

the inadequacies they have found in the arguments for theism, but often also on the positive ground that atheism is a corollary to a better supported general outlook upon the nature of things. I want therefore to conclude this discussion with a brief enumeration of some points of positive doctrine to which by and large philosophical atheists seem to me to subscribe. These points fall into three major groups.

In the first place, philosophical atheists reject the assumption that there are disembodied spirits, or that incorporeal entities of any sort can exercise a causal agency. On the contrary, atheists are generally agreed that if we wish to achieve any understanding of what takes place in the universe, we must look to the operations of organized bodies. Accordingly, the various processes taking place in nature, whether animate or inanimate, are to be explained in terms of the properties and structures of identifiable and spatio-temporally located objects. Moreover, the present variety of systems and activities found in the universe is to be accounted for on the basis of the transformations things undergo when they enter into different relations with one another—transformations which often result in the emergence of novel kinds of objects. On the other hand, though things are in flux and undergo alteration, there is no all-encompassing unitary pattern of change. Nature is ineradicably plural, both in respect to the individuals occurring in it as well as in respect to the processes in which things become involved. Accordingly, the human scene and the human perspective are not illusory; and man and his works are no less and no more "real" than are other parts or phases of the cosmos. At the risk of using a possibly misleading characterization, all of this can be summarized by saying that an atheistic view of things is a form of materialism.

In the second place, atheists generally manifest a marked empirical temper, and often take as their ideal the intellectual methods employed in the contemporaneous empirical sciences. Philosophical atheists differ considerably on important points of detail in their account of how responsible claims to knowledge are to be established. But there is substantial agreement among them that controlled sensory observation is the court of final appeal in issues concerning matters of fact. It is indeed this commitment to the use of an empirical method which is the final basis of the atheistic critique of theism. For at bottom this critique seeks to show that we can understand whatever a theistic assumption is alleged to explain, through the use of the proved methods of the positive sciences and without the introduction of empirically unsupported *ad hoc* hypotheses about a Deity. It is pertinent in this connection to recall a familiar legend about the French mathematical physicist Laplace. According to the story, Laplace made a personal presentation of a copy of his now famous book on celestial mechanics to Napoleon. Napoleon glanced through the volume, and finding no reference to the Deity asked Laplace whether God's existence played any role in the analysis. "Sire, I have no need for that hypothesis," Laplace is reported to have replied. The dismissal of sterile hypotheses characterizes not only the work of Laplace; it is the uniform rule in scientific inquiry. The sterility of the theistic assumption is one of the main burdens of the literature of atheism both ancient and modern.

And finally, atheistic thinkers have generally accepted a utilitarian basis for judging moral issues, and they have exhibited a libertarian attitude toward human needs and impulses. The conceptions of the human good they have advocated are conceptions which are commensurate with the actual capacities of mortal men, so that it is the satisfaction of the complex needs of the human creature which is the final standard for evaluating the validity of a moral ideal or moral prescription.

In consequence, the emphasis of atheistic moral reflection has been this-worldly rather than other-worldly, individualistic rather than authoritarian. The stress upon a good life that must be consummated in this world, has made atheists vigorous opponents of moral codes which seek to repress human impulses in the name of some unrealizable other-worldly ideal. The individualism that is so pronounced a strain in many philosophical atheists has made them tolerant of human limitations and sensitive to the plurality of legitimate moral goals. On the other hand, this individualism has certainly not prevented many of them from recognizing the crucial role which institutional arrangements can play in achieving desirable patterns of human living. In consequence, atheists have made important contributions to the development of a climate of opinion favorable to pursuing the values of a liberal civilization and they have played effective roles in attempts to rectify social injustices.

Atheists cannot build their moral outlook on foundations upon which so many men conduct their lives. In particular, atheism cannot offer the incentives to conduct and the consolations for misfortune which theistic religions supply to their adherents. It can offer no hope of personal immortality, no threats of Divine chastisement, no promise of eventual recompense for injustices suffered, no blueprints to sure salvation. For on its view of the place of man in nature, human excellence and human dignity must be achieved within a finite life-span, or not at all, so that the rewards of moral endeavor must come from the quality of civilized living, and not from some source of disbursement that dwells outside of time. Accordingly, atheistic moral reflection at its best does not culminate in a quiescent ideal of human perfection, but is a vigorous call to intelligent activity—activity for the sake of realizing human potentialities and for eliminating whatever stands in the way of such realization. Nevertheless, though slavish resignation to remediable ills is not characteristic of atheistic thought, responsible atheists have never pretended that human effort can invariably achieve the heart's every legitimate desire. A tragic view of life is thus an uneliminable ingredient in atheistic thought. This ingredient does not invite or generally produce lugubrious lamentation. But it does touch the atheist's view of man and his place in nature with an emotion that makes the philosophical atheist a kindred spirit to those who, within the frameworks of various religious traditions, have developed a serenely resigned attitude toward the inevitable tragedies of the human estate.

50

The Problem of Evil

RICHARD SWINBURNE

Richard Swinburne (b. 1934) is Professor of Philosophy at the University of Keele in England. He is the author of The Coherence of Theism, The Existence of God, *and* Faith and Reason, *a trilogy that offers a defense of the Christian creed.*

Swinburne recognizes that the problem of evil can be interpreted in at least two ways. First, it can be considered as challenging any possibility, however slight, that the evils we face could exist in a world created by an all-good, all-powerful Being. But it seems conceivable that these evils are logically necessary in order for our world to be the best possible; for example immoral choices may be an inherent feature of a world in which human beings exercise free will. In this case, an all-good, all-powerful Being would have to permit such evils, otherwise the best possible world could not exist.

But the problem of evil also can be interpreted as challenging the probability that our world with its evils was created by an all-good, all-powerful Being. In other words, just how plausible is it that we live in the best possible world and that every evil in it is logically necessary in order for the good to be maximized? Swinburne is sensitive to this second interpretation of the problem and attempts to offer a plausible, not merely conceivable, explanation of evil. Whether he succeeds is for the reader to decide.

GOD IS, by definition, omniscient, omnipotent, and perfectly good. By "omniscient" I understand "one who knows all true propositions." By "omnipotent" I understand "able to do anything logically possible." By "perfectly good" I understand "one who does no morally bad action," and I include among actions omissions to perform some action. The problem of evil is then often stated as the problem whether the existence of God is compatible with the existence of evil. Against the suggestion of compatibility, an atheist often suggests that the existence of evil entails the nonexistence of God. For, he argues, if God exists, then being omniscient, he knows under what circumstances evil will occur, if he does not act; and being omnipotent, he is able to prevent its occurrence. Hence, being perfectly good, he will prevent its occurrence and so evil will not exist. Hence the existence of God entails the nonexistence of evil. Theists have usually attacked this argument by denying the claim that necessarily a perfectly good being, foreseeing the occurrence of evil and able to prevent it, will prevent it. And indeed, if evil is understood in the very

581

wide way in which it normally is understood in this context, to include physical pain of however slight a degree, the cited claim is somewhat implausible. For it implies that if through my neglecting frequent warnings to go to the dentist, I find myself one morning with a slight toothache, then necessarily, there does not exist a perfectly good being who foresaw the evil and was able to have prevented it. Yet it seems fairly obvious that such a being might well choose to allow me to suffer some mild consequences of my folly—as a lesson for the future which would do me no real harm.

The threat to theism seems to come, not from the existence of evil as such, but rather from the existence of evil of certain kinds and degrees—severe undeserved physical pain or mental anguish, for example. I shall therefore list briefly the kinds of evil which are evident in our world, and ask whether their existence in the degrees in which we find them is compatible with the existence of God. I shall call the man who argues for compatibility the theodicist, and his opponent the antitheodicist. The theodicist will claim that it is not morally wrong for God to create or permit the various evils, normally on the grounds that doing so is providing the logically necessary conditions of greater goods. The antitheodicist denies these claims by putting forward moral principles which have as consequences that a good God would not under any circumstances create or permit the evils in question. I shall argue that these moral principles are not, when carefully examined, at all obvious, and indeed that there is a lot to be said for their negations. Hence I shall conclude that it is plausible to suppose that the existence of these evils is compatible with the existence of God.

Since I am discussing only the compatibility of various evils with the existence of God, I am perfectly entitled to make occasionally some (non-self-contradictory) assumption, and argue that if it was true, the compatibility would hold. For if p is compatible with q, given r (where r is not self-contradictory), then p is compatible with q simpliciter. It is irrelevant to the issue of compatibility whether these assumptions are true. If, however, the assumptions which I make are clearly false, and if also it looks as if the existence of God is compatible with the existence of evil *only* given those assumptions, the formal proof of compatibility will lose much of interest. To avoid this danger, I shall make only such assumptions as are not clearly false—and also in fact the ones which I shall make will be ones to which many theists are already committed for entirely different reasons.

What then is wrong with the world? First, there are painful sensations, felt both by men, and, to a lesser extent, by animals. Second, there are painful emotions, which do not involve pain in the literal sense of this word—for example, feelings of loss and failure and frustration. Such suffering exists mainly among men, but also, I suppose, to some small extent among animals too. Third, there are evil and undesirable states of affairs, mainly states of men's minds, which do not involve suffering. For example, there are the states of mind of hatred and envy; and such states of the world as rubbish tipped over a beauty spot. And fourth, there are the evil actions of men, mainly actions having as foreseeable consequences evils of the first three types, but perhaps

other actions as well—such as lying and promise breaking with no such fore-seeable consequences. As before, I include among actions, omissions to perform some actions. If there are rational agents other than men and God (if he exists), such as angels or devils or strange beings on distant planets, who suffer and perform evil actions, then their evil feelings, states, and actions must be added to the list of evils.

I propose to call evil of the first type physical evil, evil of the second type mental evil, evil of the third type state evil, and evil of the fourth type moral evil. Since there is a clear contrast between evils of the first three types, which are evils that happen to men or animals or the world, and evils of the fourth type, which are evils that men do, there is an advantage in having one name for evils of any of the first three types—I shall call these passive evils. I distinguish evil from mere absence of good. Pain is not simply the absence of pleasure. A headache is a pain, whereas not having the sensation of drinking whiskey is, for many people, mere absence of pleasure. Likewise, the feeling of loss in bereavement is an evil involving suffering, to be contrasted with the mere absence of the pleasure of companionship. Some thinkers have, of course, claimed that a good God would create a "best of all (logically) possible worlds" (i.e., a world than which no better is logically possible), and for them the mere absence of good creates a problem since it looks as if a world would be a better world if it had that good. For most of us, however, the mere absence of good seems less of a threat to theism than the presence of evil, partly because it is not at all clear whether any sense can be given to the concept of a best of all possible worlds (and if it cannot then of logical necessity there will be a better world than any creatable world) and partly because even if sense can be given to this concept it is not at all obvious that God has an obligation to create such a world—to whom would he be doing an injustice if he did not? My concern is with the threat to theism posed by the existence of evil.

Now much of the evil in the world consists of the evil actions of men and the passive evils brought about by those actions. (These include the evils brought about intentionally by men, and also the evils which result from long years of slackness by many generations of men. Many of the evils of 1975 are in the latter category, and among them many state evils. The hatred and jealousy which many men and groups feel today result from an upbringing consequent on generations of neglected opportunities for reconciliations.) The antitheo-dicist suggests as a moral principle (P1) that a creator able to do so ought to create only creatures such that necessarily they do not do evil actions. From this it follows that God would not have made men who do evil actions. Against this suggestion the theodicist naturally deploys the free-will defense, elegantly expounded in recent years by Alvin Plantinga.[1] This runs roughly as follows: it is not logically possible for an agent to make another agent such that necessarily he freely does only good actions. Hence if a being G creates a free

---

[1] See Alvin Plantinga, "The Free Will Defence," in Max Black, ed., *Philosophy in America* (London, 1965); *God and Other Minds* (Ithaca, N. Y., and London, 1967), chaps. 5 and 6; and *The Nature of Necessity* (Oxford, 1974), chap. 9.

agent, he gives to the agent power of choice between alternative actions, and how he will exercise that power is something which G cannot control while the agent remains free. It is a good thing that there exist free agents, but a logically necessary consequence of their existence is that their power to choose to do evil actions may sometimes be realized. The price is worth paying, however, for the existence of agents performing free actions remains a good thing even if they sometimes do evil. Hence it is not logically possible that a creator create free creatures "such that necessarily they do not do evil actions." But it is not a morally bad thing that he create free creatures, even with the possibility of their doing evil. Hence the cited moral principle is implausible.

The free-will defense as stated needs a little filling out. For surely there could be free agents who did not have the power of moral choice, agents whose only opportunities for choice were between morally indifferent alternatives—between jam and marmalade for breakfast, between watching the news on BBC 1 or the news on ITV. They might lack this power either because they lacked the power of making moral judgments (i.e., lacked moral discrimination); or because all their actions which were morally assessable were caused by factors outside their control; or because they saw with complete clarity what was right and wrong and had no temptation to do anything except the right. The free-will defense must claim, however, that it is a good thing that there exist free agents with the power and opportunity of choosing between morally good and morally evil actions, agents with sufficient moral discrimination to have some idea of the difference and some (though not overwhelming) temptation to do other than the morally good. Let us call such agents humanly free agents. The defense must then go on to claim that it is not logically possible to create humanly free agents such that necessarily they do not do morally evil actions. Unfortunately, this latter claim is highly debatable, and I have no space to debate it. I propose therefore to circumvent this issue as follows. I shall add to the definition of humanly free agents, that they are agents whose choices do not have fully deterministic precedent causes. Clearly then it will not be logically possible to create humanly free agents whose choices go one way rather than another, and so not logically possible to create humanly free agents such that necessarily they do not do evil actions. Then the free-will defense claims that $(P1)$ is not universally true; it is not morally wrong to create humanly free agents—despite the real possibility that they will do evil. Like many others who have discussed this issue, I find this a highly plausible suggestion. Surely as parents we regard it as a good thing that our children have power to do free actions of moral significance—even if the consequence is that they sometimes do evil actions. This conviction is likely to be stronger, not weaker, if we hold that the free actions with which we are concerned are ones which do not have fully deterministic precedent causes. In this way we show the existence of God to be compatible with the existence of moral evil—but only subject to a very big assumption—that men are humanly free agents. If they are not, the compatibility shown by the free-will defense is of little interest. For the agreed exception to $(P1)$ would not then justify a creator making men who did evil actions; we should need a different exception to avoid incompatibility. The assumption

seems to me not clearly false, and is also one which most theists affirm for quite other reasons. Needless to say, there is no space to discuss the assumption here.

All that the free-will defense has shown so far, however (and all that Plantinga seems to show), is grounds for supposing that the existence of moral evil is compatible with the existence of God. It has not given grounds for supposing that the existence of evil consequences of moral evils is compatible with the existence of God. In an attempt to show an incompatibility, the antitheodicist may suggest instead of (P1), (P2)—that a creator able to do so ought always to ensure that any creature whom he creates does not cause passive evils, or at any rate passive evils which hurt creatures other than himself. For could not God have made a world where there are humanly free creatures, men with the power to do evil actions, but where those actions do not have evil consequences, or at any rate evil consequences which affect others—e.g., a world where men cannot cause pain and distress to other men? Men might well do actions which are evil either because they were actions which they believed would have evil consequences or because they were evil for some other reason (e.g., actions which involved promise breaking) without them in fact having any passive evils as consequences. Agents in such a world would be like men in a simulator training to be pilots. They can make mistakes, but no one suffers through those mistakes. Or men might do evil actions which did have the evil consequences which were foreseen but which damaged only themselves. Some philosophers might hold that an action would not be evil if its foreseen consequences were ones damaging only to the agent, since, they might hold, no one has any duties to himself. For those who do not hold this position, however, there are some plausible candidates for actions evil solely because of their foreseeable consequences for the agent—e.g., men brooding on their misfortunes in such a way as foreseeably to become suicidal or misanthropic.

I do not find (P2) a very plausible moral principle. A world in which no one except the agent was affected by his evil actions might be a world in which men had freedom but it would not be a world in which men had responsibility. The theodicist claims that it would not be wrong for God to create interdependent humanly free agents, a society of such agents responsible for each other's well-being, able to make or mar each other.

Fair enough, the antitheodicist may again say. It is not wrong to create a world where creatures have responsibilities for each other. But might not those responsibilities simply be that creatures had the opportunity to benefit or to withhold benefit from each other, not a world in which they had also the opportunity to cause each other pain? One answer to this is that if creatures have only the power to benefit and not the power to hurt each other, they obviously lack any very strong responsibility for each other. To bring out the point by a caricature—a world in which I could choose whether or not to give you sweets, but not whether or not to break your leg or make you unpopular, is not a world in which I have a very strong influence on your destiny, and so not a world in which I have a very full responsibility for you. Further, however, there is a point which will depend on an argument which I will give further on. In the actual world very often a man's withholding benefits from another is

correlated with the latter's suffering some passive evil, either physical or mental. Thus if I withhold from you certain vitamins, you will suffer disease. Or if I deprive you of your wife by persuading her to live with me instead, you will suffer grief at the loss. Now it seems to me that a world in which such correlations did not hold would not necessarily be a better world than the world in which they do. The appropriateness of pain to bodily disease or deprivation, and of mental evils to various losses or lacks of a more spiritual kind, is something for which I shall argue in detail a little later.

So then the theodicist objects to (P2) on the grounds that the price of possible passive evils for other creatures is a price worth paying for agents to have great responsibilities for each other. It is a price which (logically) must be paid if they are to have those responsibilities. Here again a reasonable antitheodicist may see the point. In bringing up our own children, in order to give them responsibility, we try not to interfere too quickly in their quarrels—even at the price, sometimes, of younger children getting hurt physically. We try not to interfere, first, in order to train our children for responsibility in later life and second because responsibility here and now is a good thing in itself. True, with respect to the first reason, whatever the effects on character produced by training, God could produce without training. But if he did so by imposing a full character on a humanly free creature, this would be giving him a character which he had not in any way chosen or adopted for himself. Yet it would seem a good thing that a creator should allow humanly free creatures to influence by their own choices the sort of creatures they are to be, the kind of character they are to have. That means that the creator must create them immature, and allow them gradually to make decisions which affect the sort of beings they will be. And one of the greatest privileges which a creator can give to a creature is to allow him to help in the process of education, in putting alternatives before his fellows.

Yet though the antitheodicist may see the point, in theory, he may well react to it rather like this. "Certainly some independence is a good thing. But surely a father ought to interfere if his younger son is really getting badly hurt. The ideal of making men free and responsible is a good one, but there are limits to the amount of responsibility which it is good that men should have, and in our world men have too much responsibility. A good God would certainly have intervened long ago to stop some of the things which happen in our world." Here, I believe, lies the crux—it is simply a matter of quantity. The theodicist says that a good God could allow men to do to each other the hurt they do, in order to allow them to be free and responsible. But against him the antitheodicist puts forward as a moral principle (P3) that a creator able to do so ought to ensure that any creature whom he creates does not cause passive evils as many and as evil as those in our world. He says that in our world freedom and responsibility have gone too far—produced too much physical and mental hurt. God might well tolerate a boy hitting his younger brothers, but not Belsen.

The theodicist is in no way committed to saying that a good God will not stop things getting too bad. Indeed, if God made our world, he has clearly done so. There are limits to the amount and degree of evil which are possible in our

world. Thus there are limits to the amount of pain which a person can suffer—persons live in our world only so many years and the amount which they can suffer at any given time (if mental goings-on are in any way correlated with bodily ones) is limited by their physiology. Further, theists often claim that from time to time God intervenes in the natural order which he has made to prevent evil which would otherwise occur. So the theodicist can certainly claim that a good God stops too much sufferings—it is just that he and his opponent draw the line in different places. The issue as regards the passive evils caused by men turns ultimately to the quantity of evil. To this crucial matter I shall return toward the end of the paper.

We shall have to turn next to the issue of passive evils not apparently caused by men. But, first, I must consider a further argument by the theodicist in support of the free-will defense and also an argument of the antitheodicist against it. The first is the argument that various evils are logically necessary conditions for the occurrence of actions of certain especially good kinds. Thus for a man to bear his suffering cheerfully there has to be suffering for him to bear. There have to be acts which irritate for another to show tolerance of them. Likewise, it is often said, acts of forgiveness, courage, self-sacrifice, compassion, overcoming temptation, etc., can be performed only if there are evils of various kinds. Here, however, we must be careful. One might reasonably claim that all that is necessary for some of these good acts (or acts as good as these) to be performed is belief in the existence of certain evils, not their actual existence. You can show compassion toward someone who appears to be suffering, but is not really; you can forgive someone who only appeared to insult you, but did not really. But if the world is to be populated with imaginary evils of the kind needed to enable creatures to perform acts of the above specially good kinds, it would have to be a world in which creatures are generally and systematically deceived about the feelings of their fellows—in which the behavior of creatures generally and unavoidably belies their feelings and intentions. I suggest, in the tradition of Descartes (*Meditations* 4, 5 and 6), that it would be a morally wrong act of a creator to create such a deceptive world. In that case, given a creator, then, without an immoral act on his part, for acts of courage, compassion, etc., to be acts open to men to perform, there have to be various evils. Evils give men the opportunity to perform those acts which show men at their best. A world without evils would be a world in which men could show no forgiveness, no compassion, no self-sacrifice. And men without that opportunity are deprived of the opportunity to show themselves at their noblest. For this reason God might well allow some of his creatures to perform evil acts with passive evils as consequences, since these provide the opportunity for especially noble acts.

Against the suggestion of the developed free-will defense that it would be justifiable for God to permit a creature to hurt another for the good of his or the other's soul, there is one natural objection which will surely be made. This is that it is generally supposed to be the duty of men to stop other men hurting each other badly. So why is it not God's duty to stop men hurting each other badly? Now the theodicist does not have to maintain that it is never God's duty

to stop men hurting each other; but he does have to maintain that it is not God's duty in circumstances where it clearly is our duty to stop such hurt if we can—e.g., when men are torturing each other in mind or body in some of the ways in which they do this in our world and when, if God exists, he does not step in.

Now different views might be taken about the extent of our duty to interfere in the quarrels of others. But the most which could reasonably be claimed is surely this—that we have a duty to interfere in three kinds of circumstances— (1) if an oppressed person asks us to interfere and it is probable that he will suffer considerably if we do not, (2) if the participants are children or not of sane mind and it is probable that one or other will suffer considerably if we do not interfere, or (3) if it is probable that considerable harm will be done to others if we do not interfere. It is not very plausible to suppose that we have any duty to interfere in the quarrels of grown sane men who do not wish us to do so, unless it is probable that the harm will spread. Now note that in the characterization of each of the circumstances in which we would have a duty to interfere there occurs the word "probable," and it is being used in the "epistemic" sense—as "made probable by the total available evidence." But then the "probability" of an occurrence varies crucially with which community or individual is assessing it, and the amount of evidence which they have at the time in question. What is probable relative to your knowledge at t_1 may not be at all probable relative to my knowledge at t_2. Hence a person's duty to interfere in quarrels will depend on their probable consequences relative to that person's knowledge. Hence it follows that one who knows much more about the probable consequences of a quarrel may have no duty to interfere where another with less knowledge does have such a duty—and conversely. Hence a God who sees far more clearly than we do the consequences of quarrels may have duties very different from ours with respect to particular such quarrels. He may know that the suffering that A will cause B is not nearly as great as B's screams might suggest to us and will provide (unknown to us) an opportunity to C to help B recover and will thus give C a deep responsibility which he would not otherwise have. God may very well have reason for allowing particular evils which it is our bounden duty to attempt to stop at all costs simply because he knows so much more about them than we do. And this is no ad hoc hypothesis—it follows directly from the characterization of the kind of circumstances in which persons have a duty to interfere in quarrels.

We may have a duty to interfere in quarrels when God does not for a very different kind of reason. God, being our creator, the source of our beginning and continuation of existence, has rights over us which we do not have over our fellow-men. To allow a man to suffer for the good of his or someone else's soul one has to stand in some kind of parental relationship toward him. I don't have the right to let some stranger Joe Bloggs suffer for the good of his soul or of the soul of Bill Snoggs, but I do have *some* right of this kind in respect of my own children. I may let the younger son suffer *somewhat* for the good of his and his brother's soul. I have this right because in small part I am responsible for his existence, its beginning and continuance. If this is correct, then a fortiori,

God who is, ex hypothesi, so much more the author of our being than are our parents, has so many more rights in this respect. God has rights to allow others to suffer, while I do not have those rights and hence have a duty to interfere instead. In these two ways the theodicist can rebut the objection that if we have a duty to stop certain particular evils which men do to others, God must have this duty too.

In the free-will defense, as elaborated above, the theist seems to me to have an adequate answer to the suggestion that necessarily a good God would prevent the occurrence of the evil which men cause—if we ignore the question of the quantity of evil, to which I will return at the end of my paper. But what of the passive evil apparently not due to human action? What of the pain caused to men by disease or earthquake or cyclone, and what too of animal pain which existed before there were men? There are two additional assumptions, each of which has been put forward to allow the free-will defense to show the compatibility of the existence of God and the existence of such evil. The first is that, despite appearances, men are ultimately responsible for disease, earthquake, cyclone, and much animal pain. There seem to be traces of this view in Genesis 3:16-20. One might claim that God ties the goodness of man to the well-being of the world and that a failure of one leads to a failure of the other. Lack of prayer, concern, and simple goodness lead to the evils in nature. This assumption, though it may do some service for the free-will defense, would seem unable to account for the animal pain which existed before there were men. The other assumption is that there exist humanly free creatures other than men, which we may call fallen angels, who have chosen to do evil, and have brought about the passive evils not brought about by men. These were given the care of much of the material world and have abused that care. For reasons already given, however, it is not God's moral duty to interfere to prevent the passive evils caused by such creatures. This defense has recently been used by, among others, Plantinga. This assumption, it seems to me, will do the job, and is not *clearly* false. It is also an assumption which was part of the Christian tradition long before the free-will defense was put forward in any logically rigorous form. I believe that this assumption may indeed be indispensable if the theist is to reconcile with the existence of God the existence of passive evils of certain kinds, e.g., certain animal pain. But I do not think that the theodicist need deploy it to deal with the central cases of passive evils not caused by men—mental evils and the human pain that is a sign of bodily malfunctioning. Note, however, that if he does not attribute such passive evils to the free choice of some other agent, the theodicist must attribute them to the direct action of God himself, or rather, what he must say is that God created a universe in which passive evils must necessarily occur in certain circumstances, the occurrence of which is necessary or at any rate not within the power of a humanly free agent to prevent. The antitheodicist then naturally claims, that although a creator might be justified in allowing free creatures to produce various evils, nevertheless (P4) a creator is never justified in creating a world in which evil results except by the action of a humanly free agent. Against this the theodicist tries to sketch reasons which a good creator might have for creating a world

in which there is evil not brought about by humanly free agents. One reason which he produces is one which we have already considered earlier in the development of the free-will defense. This is the reason that various evils are logically necessary conditions for the occurrence of actions of certain especially noble kinds. This was adduced earlier as a reason why a creator might allow creatures to perform evil acts with passive evils as consequences. It can also be adduced as a reason why he might himself bring about passive evils—to give further opportunities for courage, patience, and tolerance. I shall consider here one further reason that, the theodicist may suggest, a good creator might have for creating a world in which various passive evils were implanted, which is another reason for rejecting (P4). It is, I think, a reason which is closely connected with some of the other reasons which we have been considering why a good creator might permit the existence of evil.

A creator who is going to create humanly free agents and place them in a universe has a choice of the kind of universe to create. First, he can create a finished universe in which nothing needs improving. Humanly free agents know what is right, and pursue it; and they achieve their purposes without hindrance. Second, he can create a basically evil universe, in which everything needs improving, and nothing can be improved. Or, third, he can create a basically good but half-finished universe—one in which many things need improving, humanly free agents do not altogether know what is right, and their purposes are often frustrated; but one in which agents can come to know what is right and can overcome the obstacles to the achievement of their purposes. In such a universe the bodies of creatures may work imperfectly and last only a short time; and creatures may be morally ill-educated, and set their affections on things and persons which are taken from them. The universe might be such that it requires long generations of cooperative effort between creatures to make perfect. While not wishing to deny the goodness of a universe of the first kind, I suggest that to create a universe of the third kind would be no bad thing, for it gives to creatures the privilege of making their own universe. Genesis 1 in telling of a God who tells men to "subdue" the earth pictures the creator as creating a universe of this third kind; and fairly evidently—given that men are humanly free agents—our universe is of this kind.

Now a creator who creates a half-finished universe of this third kind has a further choice as to how he molds the humanly free agents which it contains. Clearly he will have to give them a nature of some kind, that is, certain narrow purposes which they have a natural inclination to pursue until they choose or are forced to pursue others—e.g., the immediate attainment of food, sleep, and sex. There could hardly be humanly free agents without some such initial purposes. But what is he to do about their knowledge of their duty to improve the world—e.g., to repair their bodies when they go wrong, so that they can realize long-term purposes, to help others who cannot get food to do so, etc.? He could just give them a formal hazy knowledge that they had such reasons for action without giving them any strong inclination to pursue them. Such a policy might well seem an excessively laissez-faire one. We tend to think that parents who give their children no help toward taking the right path are less than perfect

parents. So a good creator might well help agents toward taking steps to improve the universe. We shall see that he can do this in one of two ways.

An action is something done for a reason. A good creator, we supposed, will give to agents some reasons for doing right actions—e.g., that they are right, that they will improve the universe. These reasons are ones of which men can be aware and then either act on or not act on. The creator could help agents toward doing right actions by making these reasons more effective causally; that is, he could make agents so that by nature they were inclined (though not perhaps compelled) to pursue what is good. But this would be to impose a moral character on agents, to give them wide general purposes which they naturally pursue, to make them naturally altruistic, tenacious of purpose, or strong-willed. But to impose a character on creatures might well seem to take away from creatures the privilege of developing their own characters and those of their fellows. We tend to think that parents who try too forcibly to impose a character, however good a character, on their children, are less than perfect parents.

The alternative way in which a creator could help creatures to perform right actions is by sometimes providing additional reasons for creatures to do what is right, reasons which by their very nature have a strong causal influence. Reasons such as improving the universe or doing one's duty do not necessarily have a strong causal influence, for as we have seen creatures may be little influenced by them. Giving a creature reasons which by their nature were strongly causally influential on a particular occasion on any creature whatever his character, would not impose a particular character on a creature. It would, however, incline him to do what is right on that occasion and maybe subsequently too. Now if a reason is by its nature to be strongly causally influential it must be something of which the agent is aware which causally inclines him (whatever his character) to perform some action, to bring about some kind of change. What kind of reason could this be except the existence of an unpleasant feeling, either a sensation such as a pain or an emotion such as a feeling of loss or deprivation? Such feelings are things of which agents are conscious, which cause them to do whatever action will get rid of those feelings, and which provide reason for performing such action. An itch causally inclines a man to do whatever will cause the itch to cease, e.g., scratch, and provides a reason for doing that action. Its causal influence is quite independent of the agent—saint or sinner, strong-willed or weak-willed, will all be strongly inclined to get rid of their pains (though some may learn to resist the inclination). Hence a creator who wished to give agents some inclination to improve the world without giving them a character, a wide set of general purposes which they naturally pursue, would tie some of the imperfections of the world to physical or mental evils.

To tie desirable states of affairs to pleasant feelings would not have the same effect. Only an existing feeling can be causally efficacious. An agent could be moved to action by a pleasant feeling only when he had it, and the only action to which he could be moved would be to keep the world as it is, not to improve it. For men to have reasons which move men of any character to actions of

perfecting the world, a creator needs to tie its imperfections to unpleasant feelings, that is, physical and mental evils.

There is to some considerable extent such tie-up in our universe. Pain normally occurs when something goes wrong with the working of our body which is going to lead to further limitation on the purposes which we can achieve; and the pain ends when the body is repaired. The existence of the pain spurs the sufferer, and others through the sympathetic suffering which arises when they learn of the sufferer's pain, to do something about the bodily malfunctioning. Yet giving men such feelings which they are inclined to end involves the imposition of no character. A man who is inclined to end his toothache by a visit to the dentist may be saint or sinner, strong-willed or weak-willed, rational or irrational. Any other way of which I can conceive of giving men an inclination to correct what goes wrong, and generally to improve the universe, would seem to involve imposing a character. A creator could, for example, have operated exclusively by threats and promises, whispering in men's ears, "unless you go to the dentist, you are going to suffer terribly," or "if you go to the dentist, you are going to feel wonderful." And if the order of nature is God's creation, he does indeed often provide us with such threats and promises—not by whispering in our ears but by providing inductive evidence. There is plenty of inductive evidence that unattended cuts and sores will lead to pain; that eating and drinking will lead to pleasure. Still, men do not always respond to threats and promises or take the trouble to notice inductive evidence (e.g., statistics showing the correlation between smoking and cancer). A creator could have made men so that they naturally took more account of inductive evidence. But to do so would be to impose character. It would be to make men, apart from any choice of theirs, rational and strong-willed.

Many mental evils too are caused by things going wrong in a man's life or in the life of his fellows and often serve as a spur to a man to put things right, either to put right the cause of the particular mental evil or to put similar things right. A man's feeling of frustration at the failure of his plans spurs him either to fulfill those plans despite their initial failure or to curtail his ambitions. A man's sadness at the failure of the plans of his child will incline him to help the child more in the future. A man's grief at the absence of a loved one inclines him to do whatever will get the loved one back. As with physical pain, the spur inclines a man to do what is right but does so without imposing a character—without, say, making a man responsive to duty, or strong-willed.

Physical and mental evils may serve as spurs to long-term cooperative research leading to improvement of the universe. A feeling of sympathy for the actual and prospective suffering of many from tuberculosis or cancer leads to acquisition of knowledge and provision of cure for future sufferers. Cooperative and long-term research and cure is a very good thing, the kind of thing toward which men need a spur. A man's suffering is never in vain if it leads through sympathy to the work of others which eventually provides a long-term cure. True, there could be sympathy without a sufferer for whom the sympathy is felt. Yet in a world made by a creator, there cannot be sympathy on the large scale without a sufferer, for whom the sympathy is felt, unless the creator

planned for creatures generally to be deceived about the feelings of their fellows; and that, we have claimed, would be morally wrong.

So generally many evils have a biological and psychological utility in producing spurs to right action without imposition of character, a goal which it is hard to conceive of being realized in any other way. This point provides a reason for the rejection of (P4). There are other kinds of reason which have been adduced reasons for rejecting (P4)—e.g., that a creator could be justified in bringing about evil as a punishment—but I have no space to discuss these now. I will, however, in passing, mention briefly one reason why a creator might make a world in which certain mental evils were tied to things going wrong. Mental suffering and anguish are a man's proper tribute to losses and failures, and a world in which men were immunized from such reactions to things going wrong would be a worse world than ours. By showing proper feelings a man shows his respect for himself and others. Thus a man who feels no grief at the death of his child or the seduction of his wife is rightly branded by us as insensitive, for he has failed to pay the proper tribute of feeling to others, to show in his feeling how much he values them and thereby failed to value them properly—for valuing them properly involves having proper reactions of feeling to their loss. Again, only a world in which men feel sympathy for losses experienced by their friends, is a world in which love has full meaning.

So, I have argued, there seem to be kinds of justification for the evils which exist in the world, available to the theodicist. Although a good creator might have very different kinds of justification for producing, or allowing others to produce, various different evils, there is a central thread running through the kind of theodicy which I have made my theodicist put forward. This is that it is a good thing that a creator should make a half-finished universe and create immature creatures, who are humanly free agents, to inhabit it; and that he should allow them to exercise some choice over what kind of creatures they are to become and what sort of universe is to be (while at the same time giving them a slight push in the direction of doing what is right); and that the creatures should have power to affect not only the development of the inanimate universe but the well-being and moral character of their fellows, and that there should be opportunities for creatures to develop noble characters and do especially noble actions. My theodicist has argued that if a creator is to make a universe of this kind, then evils of various kinds may inevitably—at any rate temporarily—belong to such a universe; and that it is not a morally bad thing to create such a universe despite the evils.

Now a morally sensitive antitheodicist might well in principle accept some of the above arguments. He may agree that in principle it is not wrong to create humanly free agents, despite the possible evils which might result, or to create pains as biological warnings. But where the crunch comes, it seems to me, is in the amount of evil which exists in our world. The antitheodicist says, all right, it would not be wrong to create men able to harm each other, but it would be wrong to create men able to put each other in Belsen. It would not be wrong to create backaches and headaches, even severe ones, as biological warnings, but not the long severe incurable pain of some diseases. In reply the theodicist

must argue that a creator who allowed men to do little evil would be a creator who gave them little responsibility; and a creator who gave them only coughs and colds, and not cancer and cholera would be a creator who treated men as children instead of giving them real encouragement to subdue the world. The argument must go on with regard to particular cases. The antitheodicist must sketch in detail and show his adversary the horrors of particular wars and diseases. The theodicist in reply must sketch in detail and show his adversary the good which such disasters make possible. He must show to his opponent men working together for good, men helping each other to overcome disease and famine; the heroism of men who choose the good in spite of temptation, who help others not merely by giving them food but who teach them right and wrong, give them something to live for and something to die for. A world in which this is possible can only be a world in which there is much evil as well as great good. Interfere to stop the evil and you cut off the good.

Like all moral arguments this one can be settled only by each party pointing to the consequences of his opponent's moral position and trying to show that his opponent is committed to implausible consequences. They must try, too, to show that each other's moral principles do or do not fit well with other moral principles which each accepts. The exhibition of consequences is a long process, and it takes time to convince an opponent even if he is prepared to be rational, more time than is available in this paper. All that I claim to have *shown* here is that there is no *easy proof* of incompatibility between the existence of evils of the kinds we find around us and the existence of God. Yet my sympathies for the outcome of any more detailed argument are probably apparent, and indeed I may have said enough to convince some readers as to what that outcome would be.

My sympathies lie, of course, with the theodicist. The theodicist's God is a god who thinks the higher goods so worthwhile that he is prepared to ask a lot of man in the way of enduring evil. Creatures determining in cooperation their own character and future, and that of the universe in which they live, coming in the process to show charity, forgiveness, faith, and self-sacrifice is such a worthwhile thing that a creator would not be unjustified in making or permitting a certain amount of evil in order that they should be realized. No doubt a good creator would put a limit on the amount of evil in the world and perhaps an end to the struggle with it after a number of years. But if he allowed creatures to struggle with evil, he would allow them a real struggle with a real enemy, not a parlor game. The antitheodicist's mistake lies in extrapolating too quickly from *our* duties when faced with evil to the duties of a creator, while ignoring the enormous differences in the circumstances of each. Each of us at one time can make the existing universe better or worse only in a few particulars. A creator can choose the kind of universe and the kind of creatures there are to be. It seldom becomes us in our ignorance and weakness to do anything more than remove the evident evils—war, disease, and famine. We seldom have the power or the knowledge or the right to use such evils to forward deeper and longer-term goods. To make an analogy, the duty of the weak and ignorant is to eliminate cowpox and not to spread it, while the doctor

has a duty to spread it (under carefully controlled conditions). But a creator who made or permitted his creatures to suffer much evil and asked them to suffer more is a very demanding creator, one with high ideals who expects a lot. For myself I can say that I would not be too happy to worship a creator who expected too little of his creatures. Nevertheless such a God does ask a lot of creatures . A theodicist is in a better position to defend a theodicy such as I have outlined if he is prepared also to make the further additional claim—that God knowing the worthwhileness of the conquest of evil and the perfecting of the universe by men, shared with them this task by subjecting himself as man to the evil in the world. A creator is more justified in creating or permitting evils to be overcome by his creatures if he is prepared to share with them the burden of the suffering and effort.

51

Theology and Falsification

ANTHONY FLEW, R. M. HARE and BASIL MITCHELL

Antony Flew (b. 1923) is Professor of Philosophy at the University of Reading in England. He is the author of many works, including Hume's Philosophy of Belief, An Introduction to Western Philosophy, *and* The Politics of Procrustes. *Basil Mitchell (b. 1917) is Nolloth Professor of the Philosophy of the Christian Religion at the University of Oxford. His works include* Law, Morality, and Religion in a Secular Society, The Justification of Religious Belief, *and* Morality: Religious and Secular. *For biographical information about R. M. Hare, see reading 7.*

The symposium reprinted here has given rise to more discussion than any other writings in recent decades in the philosophy of religion. Flew challenges those who affirm the existence of God by claiming not that their view is false but that it has no meaning. He suggests that in order for a belief to be meaningful it must be possible for it to be disproved. For instance, my belief that my radio works well would be disproven by its going on and off uncontrollably. But is there any evidence we would accept as a refutation of the existence of God? That is the crucial question Flew poses.

Hare responds by introducing the notion of a blik, *an undefined term that appears akin to an unprovable assumption. Hare claims we all have such* bliks *about the world, and that Christian belief is one example. He acknowledges that some* bliks *are right and others wrong, but ventures no opinion regarding the rightness or wrongness of the* blik *he attributes to Christians. He leaves open the question implicit in Flew's argument, of the consequences should Christian belief be wrong.*

Mitchell disagrees with Hare. He claims that evidence does count against Christian doctrines, but for a person of faith such evidence can never be allowed to be decisive. In response, Flew argues that if Christian doctrine is always qualified in the face of contrary evidence, it eventually will be emptied of meaning, thus falling victim to what Flew terms "the death by a thousand qualifications."

Antony Flew

LET US BEGIN with a parable. It is a parable developed from a tale told by John Wisdom in his haunting and revelatory article 'Gods'.[1] Once upon a time two explorers came upon a clearing in the jungle. In the clearing were growing

---

[1] P. A. S., 1944–5, reprinted as Ch. X of *Logic and Language,* Vol. I (Blackwell, 1951), and in his *Philosophy and Psychoanalysis* (Blackwell, 1953).

many flowers and many weeds. One explorer says, 'Some gardener must tend this plot'. The other disagrees, 'There is no gardener'. So they pitch their tents and set a watch. No gardener is ever seen. 'But perhaps he is an invisible gardener'. So they set up a barbed-wire fence. They electrify it. They patrol with bloodhounds. (For they remember how H. G. Wells's *The Invisible Man* could be both smelt and touched through he could not be seen.) But no shrieks ever suggest that some intruder has received a shock. No movements of the wire ever betray an invisible climber. The bloodhounds never give cry. Yet still the Believer is not convinced. 'But there is a gardener, invisible, intangible, insensible to electric shocks, a gardener who has no scent and makes no sound, a gardener who comes secretly to look after the garden which he loves'. At last the Sceptic despairs, 'But what remains of your original assertion? Just how does what you call an invisible, intangible, eternally elusive gardener differ from an imaginary gardener or even from no gardener at all?'

In this parable we can see how what starts as an assertion, that something exists or that there is some analogy between certain complexes of phenomena, may be reduced step by step to an altogether different status, to an expression perhaps of a 'picture preference'.[2] The Sceptic says there is no gardener. The Believer says there is a gardener (but invisible, etc.). One man talks about sexual behaviour. Another man prefers to talk of Aphrodite (but knows that there is not really a superhuman person additional to, and somehow responsible for, all sexual phenomena). The process of qualification may be checked at any point before the original assertion is completely withdrawn and something of that first assertion will remain (Tautology). Mr. Wells's invisible man could not, admittedly, be seen, but in all other respects he was a man like the rest of us. But though the process of qualification may be, and of course usually is, checked in time, it is not always judiciously so halted. Someone may dissipate his assertion completely without noticing that he has done so. A fine brash hypothesis may thus be killed by inches, the death by a thousand qualifications.

And in this, it seems to me, lies the peculiar danger, the endemic evil, of theological utterance. Take such utterances as 'God has a plan', 'God created the world', 'God loves us as a father loves his children'. They look at first sight very much like assertions, vast cosmological assertions. Of course, this is no sure sign that they either are, or are intended to be, assertions. But let us confine ourselves to the cases where those who utter such sentences intend them to express assertions. (Merely remarking parenthetically that those who intend or interpret such utterances as crypto-commands, expressions of wishes, disguised ejaculations, concealed ethics, or as anything else but assertions, are unlikely to succeed in making them either properly orthodox or practically effective.)

Now to assert that such and such is the case is necessarily equivalent to denying that such and such is not the case. Suppose then that we are in doubt as to what someone who gives vent to an utterance is asserting, or suppose that, more radically, we are sceptical as to whether he is really asserting anything at all, one way of trying to understand (or perhaps it will be to expose)

---

[2] Cf. J. Wisdom, 'Other Minds', *Mind,* 1940; reprinted in his *Other Minds* (Blackwell, 1952).

his utterance is to attempt to find what he would regard as counting against, or as being incompatible with, its truth. For if the utterance is indeed an assertion, it will necessarily be equivalent to a denial of the negation of that assertion. And anything which would count against the assertion, or which would induce the speaker to withdraw it and to admit that it had been mistaken, must be part of (or the whole of) the meaning of the negation of that assertion. And to know the meaning of the negation of an assertion, is as near as makes no matter, to know the meaning of that assertion. And if there is nothing which a putative assertion denies then there is nothing which it asserts either: and so it is not really an assertion. When the Sceptic in the parable asked the Believer, 'Just how does what you call an invisible, intangible, eternally elusive gardener differ from an imaginary gardener or even from no gardener at all?' he was suggesting that the Believer's earlier statement had been so eroded by qualification that it was no longer an assertion at all.

Now it often seems to people who are not religious as if there was no conceivable event or series of events the occurrence of which would be admitted by sophisticated religious people to be a sufficient reason for conceding 'There wasn't a God after all' or 'God does not really love us then'. Someone tells us that God loves us as a father loves his children. We are reassured. But then we see a child dying of inoperable cancer of the throat. His earthly father is driven frantic in his efforts to help, but his Heavenly Father reveals no obvious sign of concern. Some qualification is made—God's love is 'not a merely human love' or it is 'an inscrutable love', perhaps—and we realize that such sufferings are quite compatible with the truth of the assertion that 'God loves us as a father (but, of course, . . .)'. We are reassured again. But then perhaps we ask: what is this assurance of God's (appropriately qualified) love worth, what is this apparent guarantee really a guarantee against? Just what would have to happen not merely (morally and wrongly) to tempt but also (logically and rightly) to entitle us to say 'God does not love us' or even 'God does not exist'? I therefore put to the succeeding symposiasts the simple central questions, 'What would have to occur or to have occurred to constitute for you a disproof of the love of, or of the existence of, God?'

R. M. Hare

I wish to make it clear that I shall not try to defend Christianity in particular, but religion in general—not because I do not believe in Christianity, but because you cannot understand what Christianity is, until you have understood what religion is.

I must begin by confessing that, on the ground marked out by Flew, he seems to me to be completely victorious. I therefore shift my ground by relating another parable. A certain lunatic is convinced that all dons want to murder him. His friends introduce him to all the mildest and most respectable dons that they can find, and after each of them has retired, they say, 'You see, he doesn't really want to murder you; he spoke to you in a most cordial manner; surely you are convinced now?' But the lunatic replies, 'Yes, but that was only

his diabolical cunning; he's really plotting against me the whole time, like the rest of them; I know it I tell you'. However many kindly dons are produced, the reaction is still the same.

Now we say that such a person is deluded. But what is he deluded about? About the truth or falsity of an assertion? Let us apply Flew's test to him. There is no behaviour of dons that can be enacted which he will accept as counting against his theory; and therefore his theory, on this test, asserts nothing. But it does not follow that there is no difference between what he thinks about dons and what most of us think about them—otherwise we should not call him a lunatic and ourselves sane, and dons would have no reason to feel uneasy about his presence in Oxford.

Let us call that in which we differ from this lunatic, our respective *bliks*. He has an insane *blik* about dons; we have a sane one. It is important to realize that we have a sane one, not no *blik* at all; for there must be two sides to any argument—if he has a wrong *blik,* then those who are right about dons must have a right one. Flew has shown that a *blik* does not consist in an assertion or system of them; but nevertheless it is very important to have the right *blik*.

Let us try to imagine what it would be like to have different *bliks* about other things than dons. When I am driving my car, it sometimes occurs to me to wonder whether my movements of the steering-wheel will always continue to be followed by corresponding alterations in the direction of the car. I have never had a steering failure, though I have had skids, which must be similar. Moreover, I know enough about how the steering of my car is made, to know the sort of thing that would have to go wrong for the steering to fail—steel joints would have to part, or steel rods break, or something—but how do I know that this won't happen? The truth is, I don't know; I just have a *blik* about steel and its properties, so that normally I trust the steering of my car; but I find it not at all difficult to imagine what it would be like to lose this *blik* and acquire the opposite one. People would say I was silly about steel; but there would be no mistaking the reality of the difference between our respective *bliks*—for example, I should never go in a motor-car. Yet I should hesitate to say that the difference between us was the difference between contradictory assertions. No amount of safe arrivals or bench-tests will remove my *blik* and restore the normal one; for my *blik* is compatible with any finite number of such tests.

It was Hume who taught us that our whole commerce with the world depends upon our *blik* about the world; and that differences between *bliks* about the world cannot be settled by observation of what happens in the world. That was why, having performed the interesting experiment of doubting the ordinary man's *blik* about the world, and showing that no proof could be given to make us adopt one *blik* rather than another, he turned to backgammon to take his mind off the problem. It seems, indeed, to be impossible even to formulate as an assertion the normal *blik* about the world which makes me put my confidence in the future reliability of steel joints, in the continued ability of the road to support my car, and not gape beneath it revealing nothing below; in the general non-homicidal tendencies of dons; in my own continued well-being (in

some sense of that word that I may not now fully understand) if I continue to do what is right according to my lights; in the general likelihood of people like Hitler coming to a bad end. But perhaps a formulation less inadequate than most is to be found in the Psalms: 'The earth is weak and all the inhabiters thereof: I bear up the pillars of it'.

The mistake of the position which Flew selects for attack is to regard this kind of talk as some sort of *explanation,* as scientists are accustomed to use the word. As such, it would obviously be ludicrous. We no longer believe in God as an Atlas—*nous n'avons pas besoin de cette hypothèse.** But it is nevertheless true to say that, as Hume saw, without a *blik* there can be no explanation; for it is by our *bliks* that we decide what is and what is not an explanation. Suppose we believed that everything that happened, happened by pure chance. This would not of course be an assertion; for it is compatible with anything happening or not happening, and so, incidentally, is its contradictory. But if we had this belief, we should not be able to explain or predict or plan anything. Thus, although we should not be *asserting* anything different from those of a more normal belief, there would be a great difference between us; and this is the sort of difference that there is between those who really believe in God and those who really disbelieve in him.

The word 'really' is important, and may excite suspicion. I put it in, because when people have had a good Christian upbringing, as have most of those who now profess not to believe in any sort of religion, it is very hard to discover what they really believe. The reason why they find it so easy to think that they are not religious, is that they have never got into the frame of mind of one who suffers from the doubts to which religion is the answer. Not for them the terrors of the primitive jungle. Having abandoned some of the more picturesque fringes of religion, they think that they have abandoned the whole thing—whereas in fact they still have got, and could not live without, a religion of a comfortably substantial, albeit highly sophisticated, kind, which differs from that of many 'religious people' in little more than this, that 'religious people' like to sing Psalms about theirs—a very natural and proper thing to do. But nevertheless there may be a big difference lying behind—the difference between two people who, though side by side, are walking in different directions. I do not know in what direction Flew is walking; perhaps he does not know either. But we have had some examples recently of various ways in which one can walk away from Christianity, and there are any number of possibilities. After all, man has not changed biologically since primitive times; it is his religion that has changed, and it can easily change again. And if you do not think that such changes make a difference, get acquainted with some Sikhs and some Mussulmans of the same Punjabi stock; you will find them quite different sorts of people.

There is an important difference between Flew's parable and my own which we have not yet noticed. The explorers do not *mind* about their garden; they discuss it with interest, but not with concern. But my lunatic, poor fellow,

---

* We have no need of this hypothesis.

minds about dons; and I mind about the steering of my car; it often has people in it that I care for. It is because I mind very much about what goes on in the garden in which I find myself, that I am unable to share the explorers' detachment.

Basil Mitchell

Flew's article is searching and perceptive, but there is, I think, something odd about his conduct of the theologian's case. The theologian surely would not deny that the fact of pain counts against the assertion that God loves men. This very incompatibility generates the most intractable of theological problems—the problem of evil. So the theologian *does* recognize the fact of pain as counting against Christian doctrine. But it is true that he will not allow it—or anything— to count decisively against it; for he is committed by his faith to trust in God. His attitude is not that of the detached observer, but of the believer.

Perhaps this can be brought out by yet another parable. In time of war in an occupied country, a member of the resistance meets one night a stranger who deeply impresses him. They spend that night together in conversation. The Stranger tells the partisan that he himself is on the side of the resistance— indeed that he is in command of it, and urges the partisan to have faith in him no matter what happens. The partisan is utterly convinced at that meeting of the Stranger's sincerity and constancy and undertakes to trust him.

They never meet in conditions of intimacy again. But sometimes the Stranger is seen helping members of the resistance, and the partisan is grateful and says to his friends, 'He is on our side'.

Sometimes he is seen in the uniform of the police handing over patriots to the occupying power. On these occasions his friends murmur against him: but the partisan still says, 'He is on our side'. He still believes that, in spite of appearances, the Stranger did not deceive him. Sometimes he asks the Stranger for help and receives it. He is then thankful. Sometimes he asks and does not receive it. Then he says, 'The Stranger knows best'. Sometimes his friends, in exasperation, say, 'Well, what *would* he have to do for you to admit that you were wrong and that he is not on our side?' But the partisan refuses to answer. He will not consent to put the Stranger to the test. And sometimes his friends complain, 'Well, if *that's* what you mean by his being on our side, the sooner he goes over to the other side the better'.

The partisan of the parable does not allow anything to count decisively against the proposition 'The Stranger is on our side'. This is because he has committed himself to trust the Stranger. But he of course recognizes that the Stranger's ambiguous behaviour *does* count against what he believes about him. It is precisely this situation which constitutes the trial of his faith.

When the partisan asks for help and doesn't get it, what can he do? He can (a) conclude that the stranger is not on our side or; (b) maintain that he is on our side, but that he has reasons for withholding help.

The first he will refuse to do. How long can he uphold the second position without its becoming just silly?

I don't think one can say in advance. It will depend on the nature of the impression created by the Stranger in the first place. It will depend, too, on the manner in which he takes the Stranger's behaviour. If he blandly dismisses it as of no consequence, as having no bearing upon his belief, it will be assumed that he is thoughtless or insane. And it quite obviously won't do for him to say easily, 'Oh, when used of the Stranger the phrase "is on our side" *means* ambiguous behaviour of this sort'. In that case he would be like the religious man who says blandly of a terrible disaster 'It is God's will'. No, he will only be regarded as sane and reasonable in his belief, if he experiences in himself the full force of the conflict.

It is here that my parable differs from Hare's. The partisan admits that many things may and do count against his belief: whereas Hare's lunatic who has a *blik* about dons doesn't admit that anything counts against his *blik*. Nothing *can* count against *bliks*. Also the partisan has a reason for having in the first instance committed himself, viz. the character of the Stranger; whereas the lunatic has no reason for his *blik* about dons—because, of course, you can't have reasons for *bliks*.

This means that I agree with Flew that theological utterances must be assertions. The partisan is making an assertion when he says, 'The Stranger is on our side'.

Do I want to say that the partisan's belief about the Stranger is, in any sense, an explanation? I think I do. It explains and makes sense of the Stranger's behaviour: it helps to explain also the resistance movement in the context of which he appears. In each case it differs from the interpretation which the others put upon the same facts.

'God loves men' resembles 'the Stranger is on our side' (and many other significant statements, e.g. historical ones) in not being conclusively falsifiable. They can both be treated in at least three different ways: (1) As provisional hypotheses to be discarded if experience tells against them; (2) As significant articles of faith; (3) As vacuous formulae (expressing, perhaps, a desire for reassurance) to which experience makes no difference and which make no difference to life.

The Christian, once he has committed himself, is precluded by his faith from taking up the first attitude: 'Thou shalt not tempt the Lord thy God'. He is in constant danger, as Flew has observed, of slipping into the third. But he need not; and, if he does, it is a failure in faith as well as in logic.

Antony Flew

It has been a good discussion: and I am glad to have helped to provoke it. But now—at least in *University*—it must come to an end: and the Editors of *University* have asked me to make some concluding remarks. Since it is impossible to deal with all the issues raised or to comment separately upon each contribution, I will concentrate on Mitchell and Hare, as representative of two very different kinds of response to the challenge made in 'Theology and Falsification'.

The challenge, it will be remembered, ran like this. Some theological utterances seem to, and are intended to, provide explanations or express assertions. Now an assertion, to be an assertion at all, must claim that things stand thus and thus; *and not otherwise*. Similarly an explanation, to be an explanation at all, must explain why this particular thing occurs; *and not something else*. Those last clauses are crucial. And yet sophisticated religious people—or so it seemed to me—are apt to overlook this, and tend to refuse to allow, not merely that anything actually does occur, but that anything conceivably could occur, which would count against their theological assertions and explanations. But in so far as they do this their supposed explanations are actually bogus, and their seeming assertions are really vacuous.

Mitchell's response to this challenge is admirably direct, straightforward, and understanding. He agrees 'that theological utterances must be assertions'. He agrees that if they are to be assertions, there must be something that would count against their truth. He agrees, too, that believers are in constant danger of transforming their would-be assertions into 'vacuous formulae'. But he takes me to task for an oddity in my 'conduct of the theologian's case. The theologian surely would not deny that the fact of pain counts against the assertion that God loves men. This very incompatibility generates the most intractable of theological problems, the problem of evil'. I think he is right. I should have made a distinction between two very different ways of dealing with what looks like evidence against the love of God: the way I stressed was the expedient of qualifying the original assertion; the way the theologian usually takes, at first, is to admit that it looks bad but to insist that there is—there must be—some explanation which will show that, in spite of appearances, there really is a God who loves us. His difficulty, it seems to me, is that he has given God attributes which rule out all possible saving explanations. In Mitchell's parable of the Stranger it is easy for the believer to find plausible excuses for ambiguous behaviour: for the Stranger is a man. But suppose the Stranger is God. We cannot say that he would like to help but cannot: God is omnipotent. We cannot say that he would help if he only knew: God is omniscient. We cannot say that he is not responsible for the wickedness of others: God creates those others. Indeed an omnipotent, omniscient God must be an accessory before (and during) the fact to every human misdeed; as well as being responsible for every non-moral defect in the universe. So, though I entirely concede that Mitchell was absolutely right to insist against me that the theologian's first move is to look for an *explanation*, I still think that in the end, if relentlessly pursued, he will have to resort to the avoiding action of *qualification*. And there lies the danger of that death by a thousand qualifications, which would, I agree, constitute 'a failure in faith as well as in logic'.

Hare's approach is fresh and bold. He confesses that 'on the ground marked out by Flew, he seems to me to be completely victorious'. He therefore introduces the concept of *blik*. But while I think that there is room for some such concept in philosophy, and that philosophers should be grateful to Hare for his invention, I nevertheless want to insist that any attempt to analyse Christian religious utterances as expressions or affirmations of a *blik* rather than as (at

least would-be) assertions about the cosmos is fundamentally misguided. *First,* because thus interpreted they would be entirely unorthodox. If Hare's religion really is a *blik,* involving no cosmological assertions about the nature and activities of a supposed personal creator, then surely he is not a Christian at all? *Second,* because thus interpreted, they could scarcely do the job they do. If they were not even intended as assertions then many religious activities would become fraudulent, or merely silly. If 'You ought *because* it is God's will' asserts no more than 'You ought', then the person who prefers the former phraseology is not really giving a reason, but a fraudulent substitute for one, a dialectical dud cheque. If 'My soul must be immortal *because* God loves his children, etc.' asserts no more than 'My soul must be immortal', then the man who reassures himself with theological arguments for immortality is being as silly as the man who tries to clear his overdraft by writing his bank a cheque on the same account. (Of course neither of these utterances would be distinctively Christian: but this discussion never pretended to be so confined.) Religious utterances may indeed express false or even bogus assertions: but I simply do not believe that they are not both intended and interpreted to be or at any rate to presuppose assertions, at least in the context of religious practice; whatever shifts may be demanded, in another context, by the exigencies of theological apologetic.

One final suggestion. The philosophers of religion might well draw upon George Orwell's last appalling nightmare *1984* for the concept of *doublethink.* '*Doublethink* means the power of holding two contradictory beliefs simultaneously, and accepting both of them. The party intellectual knows that he is playing tricks with reality, but by the exercise of *doublethink* he also satisfied himself that reality is not violated' (*1984,* p. 220). Perhaps religious intellectuals too are sometimes driven to doublethink in order to retain their faith in a loving God in face of the reality of a heartless and indifferent world. But of this more another time, perhaps.

52
Religion Reconsidered

STEVEN M. CAHN

Steven M. Cahn (b. 1942) is Professor of Philosophy and Dean of Graduate Studies at the Graduate School and University Center of The City University of New York. He is the author of Fate, Logic, and Time, A New Introduction to Philosophy, The Eclipse of Excellence, *and* Education and the Democratic Ideal.

It is common to equate a belief in God with adherence to a religion. But theists need not be committed to any particular religious tradition. After all, proofs for the existence of God offer no hint as to which rituals or moral codes God approves. Of course, holy books contain presumed insights into God's will, but different religions rely on different holy books. Each of these books typically claims to embody God's revelations to His chosen prophet or prophets, but different religions follow different prophets. Faced with a multitude of competing religious claims, an individual who believes in God might nevertheless decide not to belong to any particular religion. Such an individual might appropriately be described as a nonreligious theist.

But if theists need not be religious adherents, must religious adherents be theists? Cahn believes not. In this selection he finds it reasonable for individuals to perform rituals, utter prayers, accept metaphysical beliefs, and commit themselves to moral principles without accepting theism. In other words, he argues for the possibility of religion without God.

MOST OF US suppose that all religions are akin to the one we happen to know best. But this assumption can be misleading. For example, many Christians believe that all religions place heavy emphasis on an afterlife, although, in fact, the central concern of Judaism is life in this world, not the next. Similarly, many Christians and Jews are convinced that a person who is religious must affirm the existence of a supernatural God. They are surprised to learn that religions such as Jainism or Theravada Buddhism deny the existence of a Supreme Creator of the world.

But how can there be a non-supernatural religion? To numerous theists as well as atheists the concept appears contradictory. I propose to show, however, that nothing in the theory or practice of religion—not ritual, not prayer, not metaphysical belief, not moral commitment—necessitates a commitment to traditional theism. In other words, one may be religious while rejecting supernaturalism.

Let us begin with the concept of ritual. A ritual is a prescribed symbolic action. In the case of religion, the ritual is prescribed by the religious organi-

zation, and the act symbolizes some aspect of religious belief. Those who find the beliefs of supernaturalistic religion unreasonable or the activities of the organization unacceptable may come to consider any ritual irrational. But, although particular rituals may be based on irrational beliefs, nothing is inherently irrational about ritual.

Consider the simple act of two people shaking hands when they meet. This act is a ritual, prescribed by our society and symbolic of the individuals' mutual respect. There is nothing irrational about this act. Of course, if people shook hands in order to ward off evil demons, then shaking hands would be irrational. But that is not the reason people shake hands. The ritual has no connection with God or demons but indicates the attitude one person has toward another.

It might be assumed that the ritual of handshaking escapes irrationality only because the ritual is not prescribed by any specific organization and is not part of an elaborate ceremony. But to see that this assumption is false, consider the graduation ceremony at a college. The graduates and faculty all wear peculiar hats and robes, and the participants stand and sit at appropriate times throughout the ceremony. However, there is nothing irrational about this ceremony. Indeed, the ceremonies of graduation day, far from being irrational, are symbolic of commitment to the process of education and the life of reason.

At first glance it may appear that rituals are comparatively insignificant features of our lives, but the more one considers the matter, the more it becomes apparent that rituals are a pervasive and treasured aspect of human experience. Who would want to eliminate the festivities associated with holidays such as Independence Day or Thanksgiving? What would college football be without songs, cheers, flags, and the innumerable other symbolic features surrounding the game? And those who disdain popular rituals typically proceed to establish their own distinctive ones, ranging from characteristic habits of dress to the use of drugs, all symbolic of a rejection of traditional mores.

Religious persons, like all others, search for an appropriate means of emphasizing their commitment to a group or its values. Rituals provide such a means. It is true that supernaturalistic religion has often infused its rituals with superstition, but nonreligious rituals can be equally as superstitious as religious ones. For example, most Americans view the Fourth of July as an occasion on which they can express pride in their country's heritage. With this purpose in mind, the holiday is one of great significance. However, if it were thought that the singing of the fourth verse of "The Star-Spangled Banner" four times on the Fourth of July would protect our country against future disasters, then the original meaning of the holiday would soon be lost in a maze of superstition.

A naturalistic (i.e. non-supernaturalistic) religion need not utilize ritual in such a superstitious manner, for it does not employ rituals in order to please a benevolent deity or appease an angry one. Rather, naturalistic religion views ritual, as Jack Cohen has put it, as "the enhancement of life through the dramatization of great ideals."[1] If a group places great stress on justice or freedom,

---

[1] Jack Cohen, *The Case for Religious Naturalism* (New York: Reconstructionist Press, 1958), p. 150.

why should it not utilize ritual in order to emphasize these goals? Such a use of ritual serves to solidify the group and to strengthen its devotion to its expressed purposes. And these purposes are strengthened all the more if the ritual in question has the force of tradition, having been performed by many generations who have belonged to the same group and have struggled to achieve the same goals. Ritual so conceived is not a form of superstition; rather, it is a reasonable means of strengthening religious commitment and is as useful to naturalistic religion as it is to supernaturalistic religion.

Having considered the role of ritual in a naturalistic religion, let us next turn to the concept of prayer. It might be thought that naturalistic religion could have no use for prayer, since prayer is supposedly addressed to a supernatural being, and proponents of naturalistic religion do not believe in the existence of such a being. But this objection oversimplifies the concept of prayer, focusing attention on one type of prayer while neglecting an equally important but different sort of prayer.

Supernaturalistic religion makes extensive use of petitionary prayer, prayer that petitions a supernatural being for various favors. These may range all the way from the personal happiness of the petitioner to the general welfare of all society. But since petitionary prayer rests upon the assumption that a supernatural being exists, it is clear that such prayer has no place in a naturalistic religion.

However, not all prayers are prayers of petition. There are also prayers of meditation. These prayers are not directed to any supernatural being and are not requests for the granting of favors. Rather, these prayers provide the opportunity for persons to rethink their ultimate commitments and rededicate themselves to live up to their ideals. Such prayers may take the form of silent devotion or may involve oral repetition of certain central texts. Just as Americans repeat the Pledge of Allegiance and reread the Gettysburg Address, so adherents of naturalistic religion repeat the statements of their ideals and reread the documents that embody their traditional beliefs.

It is true that supernaturalistic religions, to the extent that they utilize prayers of meditation, tend to treat these prayers irrationally, by supposing that if the prayers are not uttered a precise number of times under certain specified conditions, then the prayers lose all value. But there is no need to view prayer in this way. Rather, as Julian Huxley wrote, prayer "permits the bringing before the mind of a world of thought which in most people must inevitably be absent during the occupations of ordinary life: . . . it is the means by which the mind may fix itself upon this or that noble or beautiful or awe-inspiring idea, and so grow to it and come to realize it more fully."[2]

Such a use of prayer may be enhanced by song, instrumental music, and various types of symbolism. These elements, fused together, provide the means for adherents of naturalistic religion to engage in religious services akin to those engaged in by adherents of supernaturalistic religion. The difference between

---

[2] Julian Huxley, *Religion Without Revelation* (New York: New American Library, 1957), p. 141.

the two services is that those who attend the latter come to relate themselves to God, while those who attend the former come to relate themselves to their fellow human beings and to the world in which we live.

We have so far discussed how ritual and prayer can be utilized in naturalistic religion, but to adopt a religious perspective also involves metaphysical beliefs and moral commitments. Can these be maintained without recourse to supernaturalism?

If we use the term *metaphysics* in its usual sense, to refer to the systematic study of the most basic features of existence, then it is clear that a metaphysical system may be either supernaturalistic or naturalistic. The views of Plato, Descartes, and Leibniz are representative of a supernaturalistic theory; the views of Aristotle, Spinoza, and Dewey are representative of a naturalistic theory.

Spinoza's *Ethics,* for example, one of the greatest metaphysical works ever written, explicitly rejects the view that there exists any being apart from Nature itself. Spinoza identifies God with Nature as a whole, and urges that the good life consists in coming to understand Nature. In his words, "our salvation, or blessedness, or freedom consists in a constant and eternal love toward God . . ."[3] Spinoza's concept of God, however, is explicitly not the supernaturalistic concept of God, and Spinoza's metaphysical system thus exemplifies not only a naturalistic metaphysics but also the possibility of reinterpreting the concept of God within a naturalistic framework.

But can those who do not believe in a supernaturalistic God commit themselves to moral principles, or is the acceptance of moral principles dependent upon acceptance of supernaturalism? It is sometimes assumed that those who reject a supernaturalistic God are necessarily immoral, for their denial of the existence of such a God leaves them free to act without fear of Divine punishment. This assumption, however, is seriously in error.

The refutation of the view that morality must rest upon belief in a supernatural God was provided more than two thousand years ago by Socrates in Plato's *Euthyphro* dialogue. Socrates asked the following question: Are actions right because God says they are right, or does God say actions are right because they are right? This question is not a verbal trick; on the contrary, it poses a serious dilemma for those who believe in a supernatural deity. Socrates was inquiring whether actions are right due to God's fiat or whether God is Himself subject to moral standards. If actions are right due to God's command, then anything God commands is right, even if He should command torture or murder. But if one accepts this view, then it makes no sense to say that God Himself is good, for since the good is whatever God commands, to say that God commands rightly is simply to say that He commands as He commands, which is a tautology. This approach makes a mockery of morality, for might does not make right, even if the might is the infinite might of God. To act morally is not to act out of fear of punishment; it is not to act as one is commanded to act.

---

[3] Spinoza, *Ethics,* ed. James Gutmann (New York: Hafner Publishing Co., 1957), pt. V, prop. XXXVI, note.

Rather, it is to act as one ought to act. And how one ought to act is not dependent upon anyone's power, even if the power be Divine.

Thus, actions are not right because God commands them; on the contrary, God commands them because they are right. But in that case, what is right is independent of what God commands, for what He commands must conform with an independent standard in order to be right. Since one could act in accordance with this independent standard without believing in the existence of a supernatural God, it follows that morality does not rest upon supernaturalism. Consequently, naturalists can be highly moral (as well as immoral) persons, and supernaturalists can be highly immoral (as well as moral) persons. This conclusion should come as no surprise to anyone who has contrasted the life of Buddha, an atheist, with the life of the monk Torquemada.

We have now seen that naturalistic religion is a genuine possibility, since it is reasonable for individuals to perform rituals, utter prayers, accept metaphysical beliefs, and commit themselves to moral principles without believing in supernaturalism. Indeed, one can even do so while maintaining allegiance to Christianity or Judaism. Consider, for example, those Christians who accept the "Death of God"[4] or those Jews who adhere to Reconstructionist Judaism.[5]

Such options are philosophically respectable. Whether to choose any of them is for each reader to decide.

---

[4] See John H. T. Robinson, *Honest to God* (Philadelphia: The Westminster Press, 1963).

[5] See Mordecai M. Kaplan, *Judaism as a Civilization* (New York: Schocken Books, 1967).

PART V   Suggestions For Further Reading

Cahn, Steven M., ed. *Philosophy of Religion,* (Harper-Row, 1970)

Cahn, Steven M. and Shatz, David, eds. *Contemporary Philosophy of Religion* (Oxford University Press, 1982)

Cohen, Jack J. *The Case for Religious Naturalism* (Reconstructionist Press, 1958)

Helm, Paul, ed. *Divine Commands and Morality* (Oxford University Press, 1981)

Hick, John. *Philosophy of Religion,* 3rd edition (Prentice-Hall, 1983)

Kenny, Anthony. *The Five Ways: St. Thomas Aquinas' Proofs of God's Existence* (University of Notre Dame Press, 1980)

Martin, Charles B. *Religious Belief* (Cornell University Press, 1959)

McPherson, Thomas. *The Argument from Design* (St. Martin, 1972)

Pike, Nelson, ed. *God and Evil: Reading on the Theological Problem of Evil* (Prentice-Hall, 1964)

Plantinga, Alvin, ed. *The Ontological Argument: From St. Anselm to Contemporary Philosophers* (Anchor Books, 1965)

VI

PHILOSOPHY
OF MIND

WHAT IS THE NATURE of the human mind? How do we think? Are human beings the only beings capable of thought? Is human reasoning shaped mostly by innate forces, or does the environment play a crucial role in producing our thoughts? What is the relation between the mind and the brain? Could a computer ever think?

Questions about the nature of the human mind are both very difficult and very personal. When psychologists, computer scientists, neurophysiologists, or philosophers turn their attention to the study of the mind, their work takes on an added dimension. We identify our humanity so closely with the possession of a mind that a theory of the mind will be, at the same time, a theory of human nature. Put simply, a theory of the mind will be a theory of us, so it is hardly surprising that rival proposals have been debated with great passion. For example, in both the seventeenth century controversy between Descartes and Locke and the twentieth century debate between Skinner and Chomsky over the relative contribution of innate and environmental factors, the parties have not only regarded their opponents as wrong, but as wrong-headed.

There is no adequate account of human mentality at this time. Despite over 2,000 years of speculations, about 300 years of relatively sustained efforts by philosophers-psychologists to explain the mind, and about 100 years of experimental psychology and neurophysiology, the subject is still largely beyond our grasp. Fortunately, the absence of a widely accepted theory does not mean the absence of progress. In this section we present most of the major historical and

contemporary approaches to the study of the mind. This will provide a variety of frameworks for thinking about the mind. In addition, several of the authors present and defend their views by explicitly pointing out some shortcomings of rival approaches, so a careful reading of the selections will reveal some of the strengths and weaknesses of the different ways of modeling the mind. Thus, while readers will not be presented with the last word on how the mind works, they should be able to achieve a good understanding of some of the most fruitful ways of pursuing the study of the mind.

Several of our authors address the fundamental question of how to distinguish mental phenomena from the nonmental. Their sensible idea is that, prior to developing a theory of the mental, we need to have a fairly clear understanding of what phenomena are to be covered by the theory. Aristotle (reading 53) simply offers a catalog of the activities that most people regard as carried out by the *psūché* or mind. Franz Brentano's account (reading 55) is much more ambitious. He claims that all mental phenomena share a characteristic feature—intentionality. What Brentano means by "intentionality" is the property of being about something else, or referring to something else. When MacBeth contemplates murdering Duncan, for example, his thoughts are about a certain individual, Duncan, and about a certain type of event, the murder of Duncan. Brentano claims that this is always the case: any mental state refers to something beyond itself. In sharp contrast, B. F. Skinner (reading 56) denies that the classification "mental" defines any special group of phenomena at all. According to Skinner, so-called mental processes—thinking, for example—are simply fictional causes of behavior, on a par with such obviously bogus causes as the position of the stars at one's birth.

Another fundamental question is whether mental processes can be carried out by physical objects, in particular, whether the brain is capable of accounting for all mental activity. Philosophers and psychologists who deny that the brain or central nervous system can perform mental functions are called *dualists*. They assume that, besides physical objects, there must be some other kind of entity, a mental substance or soul for example, that is capable of carrying out mental processes. Among our authors, René Descartes (reading 54) is a dualist. The antidualist or *materialist* position is represented by three contemporary philosophers, David M. Armstrong, Jerry A. Fodor, and Daniel C. Dennett (readings 59, 60 and 61).

For materialists, an important question arises about how a physiological state of the brain could also be accurately described as a mental state, as, for example, a "desire to go to the movies." Two different solutions have been proposed in recent philosophy of mind literature. Armstrong (and others) suggest that a mental state, such as a desire to go to the movies, could simply be identified with a particular physiological condition of the brain—a particular pattern of neural firings, for example. Other philosophers advocate a looser relation between brain states and mental states. Drawing on an analogy with the software/hardware distinction in computers, they claim that mental states should not be identified with specific physiological states, because like computer software, the same mental states and patterns of mental states could be realized in diverse

physiological systems (diverse hardwares). This view is represented by Fodor and Dennett.

A different type of question about the mental has been a recurrent theme in the philosophy of mind: Is the mind of the adult, with all its beliefs, attitudes, and capabilities, shaped largely by innate endowment, or by environmental forces? This question has been hotly debated, because of its potential implications for human development. In this section, the claim that our mental equipment is largely innate is advanced by Noam Chomsky (reading 58). In opposition, B. F. Skinner maintains that the environment is almost entirely responsible for shaping human behavior. The importance of environmental factors is also defended by John Locke in "Empiricism" (reading 25).

Upon reflection, the thoughtful reader may be puzzled about the subject matter of this section. It may seem that we have suddenly switched from the study of philosophy to the study of psychology. In fact, this introduction could serve as well as a preface to a psychology text. Moreover, some of our authors are psychologists. There are both historical and contemporary reasons for the interdisciplinary character of philosophy of mind, sometimes called "philosophical psychology." The historical reasons are fairly obvious. When Descartes argues that a physical object cannot possibly carry out mental processes, for example, there is no point in asking whether his inquiry is more properly called "philosophy" or more properly called "psychology." He is simply an inquirer trying to explain, by whatever means he can, how the mind operates. Since psychology did not become a separate academic discipline until late in the nineteenth century, the same may be said about all the historical figures.

The contemporary reasons behind the dual academic character of this field illustrate the interdisciplinary nature of philosophy itself. Because of the complex nature of mental processes, many psychologists have found themselves raising fundamental questions about methodology. Virtually any new, or relatively new, psychological theory is accompanied by a methodological or philosophical defense. Thus psychologists have had to become philosophers, just as thinkers in any field (law or modern art, to give two diverse examples) have to become philosophers when their work requires them to assess the fundamental principles of their discipline. From the other direction, philosophers are attracted to philosophical psychology for two reasons. First, they are interested in the philosophical questions about the proper foundations for a science of psychology. Second, as noted above, a theory of human mentality is inevitably the keystone of a general theory of human nature. Since a traditional goal of philosophy has been to construct a synthetic theory of human nature—one which integrates our moral, political, rational, social, emotional, and biological aspects—philosophers are eager to understand new psychological theories and to see how they fit into a general account of human nature and its place in the world.

53

The Functions
of the Soul

ARISTOTLE

For biographical information about Aristotle, see reading 11.

This selection is from the De Anima, *Aristotle's treatise on the soul or* psūché *(a Greek root of our word "psychology"). In this brief excerpt, Aristotle discusses some of the views of his predecessors about* psūché. *He begins by describing some of the difficulties involved in theorizing about the soul—the problem of finding uncontested facts from which to begin, the complications caused by not having a clear view of the relation between the soul and the body. Aristotle notes that most people agree on two attributes of the soul: movement and sensation. However, opinions quickly diverge about what the soul must be like in order to possess these attributes. Some think the soul must be like fire, others compare it to "motes" (minute particles) in the air. One crucial difference of opinion concerns whether the soul (roughly, that which gives life to animals) should be identified with the mind (that is, our faculty of thinking and attaining truth).*

Aristotle's own approach is to think about the soul in terms of its characteristic activities. His goal is to produce an adequate definition of the soul—to say what a soul is—by circumscribing an interconnected group of activities the soul performs. One question Aristotle considers explicitly is whether a soul must be embodied. Unlike Descartes (reading 54), Aristotle rejects the possibility of a disembodied soul, on the grounds that such a being could not perform the characteristic activities of the soul.

1. Holding as we do that, while knowledge of any kind is a thing to be honoured and prized, one kind of it may, either by reason of its greater exactness or of a higher dignity and greater wonderfulness in its objects, be more honourable and precious than another, on both accounts we should naturally be led to place in the front rank the study of the soul. The knowledge of the soul admittedly contributes greatly to the advance of truth in general, and, above all, to our understanding of Nature, for the soul is in some sense the principle of animal life. Our aim is to grasp and understand, first its essential nature, and secondly its properties; of these some are thought to be affections proper to the soul itself, while others are considered to attach to the animal[1] owing to the presence within it of soul.

---

[1] i.e. the complex of soul and body.—TRANS.

To attain any assured knowledge about the soul is one of the most difficult things in the world. As the form of question which here presents itself, viz. the question 'What is it?', recurs in other fields, it might be supposed that there was some single method of inquiry applicable to all objects whose essential nature we are endeavouring to ascertain (as there *is* for derived properties the single method of demonstration); in that case what we should have to seek for would be this unique method. But if there is no such single and general method for solving the question of essence, our task becomes still more difficult; in the case of each different subject we shall have to determine the appropriate process of investigation. If to this there be a clear answer, e.g. that the process is demonstration or division, or some other known method, difficulties and hesitations still beset us—with what facts shall we begin the inquiry? For the facts which form the starting-points in different subjects must be different, as e.g. in the case of numbers and surfaces.

First, no doubt, it is necessary to determine in which of the *summa genera* soul lies, what it *is;* is it 'a this-somewhat', a substance, or is it a quale or a quantum, or some other of the remaining kinds of predicates which we have distinguished?*

Further, does soul belong to the class of potential existents, or is it not rather an actuality? Our answer to this question is of the greatest importance.

We must consider also whether soul is divisible or is without parts, and whether it is everywhere homogeneous or not; and if not homogeneous, whether its various forms are different specifically or generically: up to the present time those who have discussed and investigated soul seem to have confined themselves to the human soul. We must be careful not to ignore the question whether soul can be defined in a single unambiguous formula, as is the case with animal, or whether we must not give a separate formula for each sort of it, as we do for horse, dog, man, god (in the latter case the 'universal' animal—and so too every other 'common predicate'—being treated either as nothing at all or as a later product[2]). Further, if what exists is not a plurality of souls, but a plurality of parts of one soul, which ought we to investigate first, the whole soul or its parts? (It is also a difficult problem to decide which of these parts are in nature distinct from one another.) Again, which ought we to investigate first, these parts or their functions, mind or thinking, the faculty or the act of sensation, and so on? If the investigation of the functions precedes that of the parts, the further question suggests itself: ought we not before either to consider the correlative objects, e.g. of sense or thought? It seems not only useful for the discovery of the causes of the derived properties of substances to be acquainted with the essential nature of those substances (as in mathematics it is useful for the understanding of the property of the equality of the interior angles of a triangle to two right angles to know the essential nature of the straight and the

---

* That is, is the soul a thing, like a dog or a house, or a property, like redness or baldness?

[2] i.e. as presupposing the various sorts instead of being presupposed by them—TRANS.

curved or of the line and the plane) but also conversely, for the knowledge of the essential nature of a substance is largely promoted by an acquaintance with its properties: for, when we are able to give an account conformable to experience of all or most of the properties of a substance, we shall be in the most favourable position to say something worth saying about the essential nature of that subject; in all demonstration a definition of the essence is required as a starting-point, so that definitions which do not enable us to discover the derived properties, or which fail to facilitate even a conjecture about them, must obviously, one and all, be dialectical and futile.

A further problem presented by the affections of soul is this: are they all affections of the complex of body and soul, or is there any one among them peculiar to the soul by itself? To determine this is indispensable but difficult. If we consider the majority of them, there seems to be no case in which the soul can act or be acted upon without involving the body; e.g. anger, courage, appetite, and sensation generally. Thinking seems the most probable exception; but if this too proves to be a form of imagination or to be impossible without imagination, it too requires a body as a condition of its existence. If there is any way of acting or being acted upon proper to soul, soul will be capable of separate existence; if there is none, its separate existence is impossible. In the latter case, it will be like what is straight, which has many properties arising from the straightness in it, e.g. that of touching a bronze sphere at a point, though straightness divorced from the other constituents of the straight thing cannot touch it in this way; it cannot be so divorced at all, since it is always found in a body. It therefore seems that all the affections of soul involve a body—passion, gentleness, fear, pity, courage, joy, loving, and hating; in all these there is a concurrent affection of the body. In support of this we may point to the fact that, while sometimes on the occasion of violent and striking occurrences there is no excitement or fear felt, on others faint and feeble stimulations produce these emotions, viz. when the body is already in a state of tension resembling its condition when we are angry. Here is a still clearer case: in the absence of any external cause of terror we find ourselves experiencing the feelings of a man in terror. From all this it is obvious that the affections of soul are enmattered formulable essences.

Consequently their definitions ought to correspond, e.g. anger should be defined as a certain mode of movement of such and such a body (or part or faculty of a body) by this or that cause and for this or that end. That is precisely why the study of the soul must fall within the science of Nature, at least so far as in its affections it manifests this double character. Hence a physicist would define an affection of soul differently from a dialectician; the latter would define e.g. anger as the appetite for returning pain for pain, or something like that, while the former would define it as a boiling of the blood or warm substance surrounding the heart. The latter assigns the material conditions, the former the form or formulable essence; for what he states is the formulable essence of the fact, though for its actual existence there must be embodiment of it in a material such as is described by the other. Thus the essence of a house is assigned in such a formula as 'a shelter against destruction by wind, rain, and

heat'; the physicist would describe it as 'stones, bricks, and timbers'; but there is a third possible description which would say that it was that form in that material with that purpose or end.* Which, then, among these is entitled to be regarded as the genuine physicist? The one who confines himself to the material, or the one who restricts himself to the formulable essence alone? Is it not rather the one who combines both in a single formula? If this is so, how are we to characterize the other two? Must we not say that there is no type of thinker who concerns himself with those qualities or attributes of the material which are in fact inseparable from the material, and without attempting even in thought to separate them? The physicist is he who concerns himself with all the properties active and passive of bodies or materials thus or thus defined; attributes not considered as being of this character he leaves to others, in certain cases it may be to a specialist, e.g. a carpenter or a physician, in others (a) where they are inseparable in fact, but are separable from any particular kind of body by an effort of abstraction, to the mathematician, (b) where they are separate both in fact and in thought from body altogether, to the First Philosopher or metaphysician. But we must return from this digression, and repeat that the affections of soul are inseparable from the material substratum of animal life, to which we have seen that such affections, e.g. passion and fear, attach, and have not the same mode of being as a line or a plane.

2. For our study of soul it is necessary, while formulating the problems of which in our further advance we are to find the solutions, to call into council the views of those of our predecessors who have declared any opinion on this subject, in order that we may profit by whatever is sound in their suggestions and avoid their errors.

The starting-point of our inquiry is an exposition of those characteristics which have chiefly been held to belong to soul in its very nature. Two characteristic marks have above all others been recognized as distinguishing that which has soul in it from that which has not—movement and sensation. It may be said that these two are what our predecessors have fixed upon as characteristic of soul.

Some say that what originates movement is both pre-eminently and primarily soul; believing that what is not itself moved cannot originate movement in another, they arrived at the view that soul belongs to the class of things in movement. This is what led Democritus to say that soul is a sort of fire or hot substance; his 'forms' or atoms are infinite in number; those which are spherical he calls fire and soul, and compares them to the motes in the air which we see in shafts of light coming through windows; the mixture of seeds of all sorts he calls the elements of the whole of Nature (Leucippus gives a similar account); the spherical atoms are identified with soul because atoms of that shape are most adapted to permeate everywhere, and to set all the others moving by being themselves in movement. This implies the view that soul is identical with what produces movement in animals. That is why, further, they regard respiration

* That is, a shelter against destruction by wind, rain, and heat out of stones, bricks, and timbers.

as the characteristic mark of life; as the environment compresses the bodies of animals, and tends to extrude those atoms which impart movement to them, because they themselves are never at rest, there must be a reinforcement of these by similar atoms coming in from without in the act of respiration; for they prevent the extrusion of those which are already within by counteracting the compressing and consolidating force of the environment; and animals continue to live only as long as they are able to maintain this resistance.

The doctrine of the Pythagoreans seems to rest upon the same ideas; some of them declared the motes in air, others what moved them, to be soul. These motes were referred to because they are seen always in movement, even in a complete calm.

The same tendency is shown by those who define soul as that which moves itself; all seem to hold the view that movement is what is closest to the nature of soul, and that while all else is moved by soul, it alone moves itself. This belief arises from their never seeing anything originating movement which is not first itself moved.

Similarly also Anaxagoras (and whoever agrees with him in saying that mind set the whole in movement) declares the moving cause of things to be soul. His position must, however, be distinguished from that of Democritus. Democritus roundly identifies soul and mind, for he identifies what appears with what is true—that is why he commends Homer for the phrase 'Hector lay with thought distraught'; he does not employ mind as a special faculty dealing with truth, but identifies soul and mind. What Anaxagoras says about them is more obscure; in many places he tells us that the cause of beauty and order is mind, elsewhere that it is soul; it is found, he says, in all animals, great and small, high and low, but mind (in the sense of intelligence) appears not to belong alike to all animals, and indeed not even to all human beings.

All those, then, who had special regard to the fact that what has soul in it is moved, adopted the view that soul is to be identified with what is eminently originative of movement. All, on the other hand, who looked to the fact that what has soul in it knows or perceives what is, identify soul with the principle or principles of Nature, according as they admit several such principles or one only. Thus Empedocles declares that it is formed out of all his elements, each of them also being soul; his words are:

> For 'tis by Earth we see Earth, by Water Water,
> By Ether Ether divine, by Fire destructive Fire,
> By Love Love, and Hate by cruel Hate.

In the same way Plato in the *Timaeus*[3] fashions the soul out of his elements; for like, he holds, is known by like, and things are formed out of the principles or elements, so that soul must be so too. Similarly also in his lectures 'On Philosophy' it was set forth that the Animal-itself is compounded of the Idea

---

[3] 35 A ff.—TRANS.

618

itself of the One together with the primary length, breadth, and depth, everything else, the objects of its perception, being similarly constituted. Again he puts his view in yet other terms: Mind is the monad, science or knowledge the dyad (because[4] it goes undeviatingly from one point to another), opinion the number of the plane,[5] sensation the number of the solid[6]; the numbers are by him expressly identified with the Forms themselves or principles, and are formed out of the elements; now things are apprehended either by mind or science or opinion or sensation, and these same numbers are the Forms of things.

Some thinkers, accepting both premises, viz. that the soul is both originative of movement and cognitive, have compounded it of both and declared the soul to be a self-moving number.

As to the nature and number of the first principles opinions differ. The difference is greatest between those who regard them as corporeal and those who regard them as incorporeal, and from both dissent those who make a blend and draw their principles from both sources. The number of principles is also in dispute; some admit one only, others assert several. There is a consequent diversity in their several accounts of soul; they assume, naturally enough, that what is in its own nature originative of movement must be among what is primordial. That has led some to regard it as fire, for fire is the subtlest of the elements and nearest to incorporeality; further, in the most primary sense, fire both is moved and originates movement in all the others.

Democritus has expressed himself more ingeniously than the rest on the grounds for ascribing each of these two characters to soul; soul and mind are, he says, one and the same thing, and this thing must be one of the primary and indivisible bodies, and its power of originating movement must be due to its fineness of grain and the shape of its atoms; he says that of all the shapes the spherical is the most mobile, and that this is the shape of the particles of both fire and mind.

Anaxagoras, as we said above, seems to distinguish between soul and mind, but in practice he treats them as a single substance, except that it is mind that he specially posits as the principle of all things; at any rate what he says is that mind alone of all that is is simple, unmixed, and pure. He assigns both characteristics, knowing and origination of movement, to the same principle, when he says that it was mind that set the whole in movement.

Thales, too, to judge from what is recorded about him, seems to have held soul to be a motive force, since he said that the magnet has a soul in it because it moves the iron.

Diogenes (and others) held the soul to be air because he believed air to be finest in grain and a first principle; therein lay the grounds of the soul's powers of knowing and originating movement. As the priordial principle from which

---

[4] Like the straight line, whose number is the dyad.—TRANS.

[5] The triad.—TRANS.

[6] The tetrad.—TRANS.

all other things are derived, it is cognitive; as finest in grain, it has the power to originate movement.

Heraclitus too says that the first principle—the 'warm exhalation' of which, according to him, everything else is composed—is soul; further, that this exhalation is most incorporeal and in ceaseless flux; that what is in movement requires that what knows it should be in movement; and that all that is has its being essentially in movement (herein agreeing with the majority).

Alcmaeon also seems to have held a similar view about soul; he says that it is immortal because it resembles 'the immortals', and that this immortality belongs to it in virtue of its ceaseless movement; for all the 'things divine', moon, sun, the planets, and the whole heavens, are in perpetual movement.

Of more superficial writers, some, e.g. Hippo, have pronounced it to be water; they seem to have argued from the fact that the seed of all animals is fluid, for Hippo tries to refute those who say that the soul is blood, on the ground that the seed, which is the primordial soul, is not blood.

Another group (Critias, for example) did hold it to be blood; they take perception to be the most characteristic attribute of soul, and hold that perceptiveness is due to the nature of blood.

Each of the elements has thus found its partisan, except earth—earth has found no supporter unless we count as such those who have declared soul to be, or to be compounded of, *all* the elements. All, then, it may be said, characterize the soul by three marks, Movement, Sensation, Incorporeality, and each of these is traced back to the first principles. That is why (with one exception) all those who define the soul by its power of knowing make it either an element or construct it out of the elements. The language they all use is similar; like, they say, is known by like; as the soul knows everything, they construct it out of all the principles. Hence all those who admit but one cause or element, make the soul also one (e.g. fire or air), while those who admit a multiplicity of principles make the soul also multiple. The exception is Anaxagoras; he alone says that mind is impassible and has nothing in common with anything else. But, if this is so, how or in virtue of what cause can it know? That Anaxagoras has not explained, nor can any answer be inferred from his words. All who acknowledge pairs of opposites among their principles, construct the soul also out of these contraries, while those who admit as principles only one contrary of each pair, e.g. either hot or cold, likewise make the soul some one of these. That is why, also, they allow themselves to be guided by the names; those who identify soul with the hot argue that *zen* (to live) is derived from *zein* (to boil), while those who identify it with the cold say that soul (*psyche*) is so called from the process of respiration and refrigeration (*katapsyxis*).

Such are the traditional opinions concerning soul, together with the grounds on which they are maintained.

3. We must begin our examination with movement; for, doubtless, not only is it false that the essence of soul is correctly described by those who say that it is what moves (or is capable of moving) itself, but it is an impossibility that movement should be even an attribute of it.

We have already pointed out that there is no necessity that what originates movement should itself be moved. There are two senses in which anything may be moved—either (a) indirectly, owing to something other than itself, or (b) directly, owing to itself. Things are 'indirectly moved' which are moved as being contained in something which is moved, e.g. sailors in a ship, for they are moved in a different sense from that in which the ship is moved; the ship is 'directly moved', they are 'indirectly moved', because they are in a moving vessel. This is clear if we consider their limbs; the movement proper to the legs (and so to man) is walking, and in this case the sailors are not walking. Recognizing the double sense of 'being moved', what we have to consider now is whether the soul is 'directly moved' and participates in such direct movement.

There are four species of movement—locomotion, alteration, diminution, growth; consequently if the soul is moved, it must be moved with one or several or all of these species of movement. Now if its movement is not incidental, there must be a movement natural to it, and, if so, as all the species enumerated involve place, place must be natural to it. But if the essence of soul be to move itself, its being moved cannot be incidental to it, as it is to what is white or three cubits long; they too can be moved, but only incidentally—what is moved is that of which 'white' and 'three cubits long' are the attributes, the body in which they inhere; hence *they* have no place: but if the soul naturally partakes in movement, it follows that it must have a place.

Further, if there be a movement natural to the soul, there must be a counter-movement unnatural to it, and conversely. The same applies to rest as well as to movement; for the *terminus ad quem* of a thing's natural movement is the place of its natural rest, and similarly the *terminus ad quem* of its enforced movement is the place of its enforced rest. But what meaning can be attached to enforced movements or rests of the soul, it is difficult even to imagine.

Further, if the natural movement of the soul be upward, the soul must be fire; if downward, it must be earth; for upward and downward movements are the definitory characteristics of these bodies. The same reasoning applies to the intermediate movements, *termini,* and bodies. Further, since the soul is observed to originate movement in the body, it is reasonable to suppose that it transmits to the body the movements by which it itself is moved, and so, reversing the order, we may infer from the movements of the body back to similar movements of the soul. Now the body is moved from place to place with movements of locomotion. Hence it would follow that the soul too must in accordance with the body change either its place as a whole or the relative places of its parts. This carries with it the possibility that the soul might even quit its body and re-enter it, and with this would be involved the possibility of a resurrection of animals from the dead. But, it may be contended, the soul can be moved indirectly by something else; for an animal can be pushed out of its course. Yes, but that to whose *essence* belongs the power of being moved by itself, cannot be moved by something else except incidentally,[7] just as what is good by or in

---

[7] i.e. so that what is moved is not it but something which 'goes along with it', e.g. a vehicle in which it is contained.—TRANS.

itself cannot owe its goodness to something external to it or to some end to which it is a means.

If the soul *is* moved, the most probable view is that what moves it is sensible things.[8]

We must note also that, if the soul moves itself, it must be the mover itself that is moved, so that it follows that if movement is in every case a displacement of that which is in movement, in that respect in which it is said to be moved, the movement of the soul must be departure from its essential nature, at least if its self-movement is essential to it, not incidental.

Some go so far as to hold that the movements which the soul imparts to the body in which it is are the same in kind as those with which it itself is moved. An example of this is Democritus, who uses language like that of the comic dramatist Philippus, who accounts for the movements that Daedalus imparted to his wooden Aphrodite by saying that he poured quicksilver into it; similarly Democritus says that the spherical atoms which according to him constitute soul, owing to their own ceaseless movements draw the whole body after them and so produce its movements. We must urge the question whether it is these very same atoms which produce rest also—how they could do so, it is difficult and even impossible to say. And, in general, we may object that it is not in this way that the soul appears to originate movement in animals—it is through intention or process of thinking.

It is in the same fashion that the *Timaeus* also tries to give a physical account of how the soul moves its body; the soul, it is here said, is in movement, and so owing to their mutual implication moves the body also. After compounding the soul-substance out of the elements and dividing it in accordance with the harmonic numbers, in order that it may possess a connate sensibility for 'harmony' and that the whole may move in movements well attuned, the Demiurge bent the straight line into a circle; this single circle he divided into two circles united at two common points; one of these he subdivided into seven circles. All this implies that the movements of the soul are identified with the local movements of the heavens.

Now, in the first place, it is a mistake to say that the soul is a spatial magnitude. It is evident that Plato means the soul of the whole to be like the sort of soul which is called mind—not like the sensitive or the desiderative soul, for the movements of neither of these are circular. Now mind is one and continuous in the sense in which the process of thinking is so, and thinking is identical with the thoughts which are its parts; these have a serial unity like that of number, not a unity like that of a spatial magnitude. Hence mind cannot have that kind of unity either; mind is either without parts or is continuous in some other way than that which characterizes a spatial magnitude. How, indeed, if it were a spatial magnitude, could mind possibly think? Will it think with any one indifferently of its parts? In this case, the 'part' must be understood either

---

[8] *sc.* in which the case the movement can only be 'incidental'; for, as we shall see later, is is really the bodily organ of sensation that then is 'moved'.—TRANS.

in the sense of a spatial magnitude or in the sense of a point (if a point *can* be called a part of a spatial magnitude). If we accept the latter alternative, the points being infinite in number, obviously the mind can never exhaustively traverse them; if the former, the mind must think the same thing over and over again, indeed an infinite number of times (whereas it is manifestly possible to think a thing once only). If contact of any part whatsoever of itself with the object is all that is required, why need mind move in a circle, or indeed possess magnitude at all? On the other hand, if contact with the whole circle is necessary, what meaning can be given to the contact of the parts? Further, how could what has no parts think what has parts, or what has parts think what has none?[9] We must identify the circle referred to with mind; for it is mind whose movement is thinking, and it is the circle whose movement is revolution, so that if thinking is a movement of revolution, the circle which has this characteristic movement must be mind.

If the circular movement is eternal, there must be something which mind is always thinking—what *can* this be? For all practical processes of thinking have limits—they all go on for the sake of something outside the process, and all theoretical processes come to a close in the same way as the phrases in speech which express processes and results of thinking. Every such linguistic phrase is either definitory or demonstrative. Demonstration has both a starting–point and may be said to end in a conclusion or inferred result; even if the process never reaches final completion, at any rate it never returns upon itself again to its starting–point, it goes on assuming a fresh middle term or a fresh extreme, and moves straight forward, but circular movement returns to its starting–point. Definitions, too, are closed groups of terms.

Further, if the same revolution is repeated, mind must repeatedly think the same object.

Further, thinking has more resemblance to a coming to rest or arrest than to a movement; the same may be said of inferring.

It might also be urged that what is difficult and enforced is incompatible with blessedness; if the movement of the soul is not of its essence, movement of the soul must be contrary to its nature. It must also be painful for the soul to be inextricably bound up with the body; nay more, if, as is frequently said and widely accepted, it is better for mind not to be embodied, the union must be for it undesirable.

Further, the cause of the revolution of the heavens is left obscure. It is not the essence of soul which is the cause of this circular movement—that movement is only incidental to soul—nor is, *a fortiori*, the body its cause. Again, it is not even asserted that it is better that soul should be so moved; and yet the reason for which God caused the soul to move in a circle can only have been that movement was better for it than rest, and movement of this kind better than any other. But since this sort of consideration is more appropriate to another field of speculation, let us dismiss it for the present.

[9] *sc.* but mind in fact or cognizes both.—TRANS.

The view we have just been examining, in company with most theories about the soul, involves the following absurdity: they all join the soul to a body, or place it in a body, without adding any specification of the reason of their union, or of the bodily conditions required for it. Yet such explanation can scarcely be omitted; for some community of nature is presupposed by the fact that the one acts and the other is acted upon, the one moves and the other is moved; interaction always implies a *special* nature in the two interagents. All, however, that these thinkers do is to describe the specific characteristics of the soul; they do not try to determine anything about the body which is to contain it, as if it were possible, as in the Pythagorean myths, that any soul could be clothed upon with any body—an absurd view, for each body seems to have a form and shape of its own.* It is as absurd as to say that the art of carpentry could embody itself in flutes; each art must use its tools, each soul its body.

* Here Aristotle is objecting to the claim that a soul is clothed in a body, or housed in a body, when that claim is not supported by any account of what a body must be like to house a soul, or what a soul must be like to be housed in a body.

54
Dualism

RENÉ DESCARTES

For biographical information about René Descartes, see reading 24.

These selections are from Descartes's Meditations on First Philosophy, Meditation VI, *and* Discourse on Method, *section V. In the* Meditations, *Descartes tries to show how we are capable of having certain knowledge (see reading 25). By the sixth Meditation, he believes he has shown that each of us can know with perfect certainty he himself exists as a mind, and that God exists and would not allow us to be deceived about those things we believe with certainty. Descartes now asks, How do we know that we have bodies, as well as minds? His major concern is to chart the relation between the mind and the body. Descartes maintains that while the mind and body are intimately conjoined, they are nonetheless distinct entities that can exist independently of one another.*

In the fifth part of the Discourse, *Descartes is arguing again for dualism, the view that mental activity must be carried out by a mental entity that is distinct from any physical object. Descartes reasons that if a physical object could think, then we ought to be able to build a thinking machine. He claims that we could build artificial animals, but never an artificial person, a body plus a mind, because such a creature would fail two crucial tests: it could not use language normally and it could not deal intelligently with novel situations. Descartes's arguments for dualism all have the same form. First, he maintains that the mind has a certain property—indivisibility or universality, for example—and then argues that no physical thing can have such a property. This same form of argument has been used in all subsequent attempts to show that the mind cannot be identified with the brain.*

Sixth Meditation

IT REMAINS for me to examine whether material things exist. I already know at least the possibility of their existence, in so far as they are the subject-matter of pure mathematics, since in this regard I clearly and distinctly perceive them. For God is undoubtedly able to effect whatever I am thus able to perceive; and I have never decided that anything could not be done by him, except on the ground that it would involve contradiction for me to perceive such a thing distinctly. Further, when I am occupied with material objects, I am aware of using the faculty of imagination; and this seems to imply that they exist. For when I consider carefully what imagination is, it seems to be a kind of application of the cognitive faculty to a body intimately present to it—a body, therefore, that exists.

To explain this, I begin by examining the difference between imagination and pure understanding. For instance, when I imagine a triangle, I do not just understand that it is a figure enclosed in three lines; I also at the same time see the three lines present before my mind's eye, and this is what I call imagining them. Now if I want to think of a chiliagon, I understand just as well that it is a figure of a thousand sides as I do that a triangle is a figure of three sides; but I do not in the same way imagine the thousand sides, or see them as presented to me. I am indeed accustomed always to imagine something when I am thinking of a corporeal object; so I may confusedly picture to myself some kind of figure; but obviously this picture is not a chiliagon, since it is in no way different from the one I should form if I were thinking of a myriagon, or any other figure with very many sides; and it in no way helps me to recognise the properties that distinguish a chiliagon from other polygons. If now it is a pentagon that is in question, I can understand its figure, as I can the figure of a chiliagon, without the aid of imagination; but I may also imagine this very figure, applying my mind's eye to its five sides and at the same time to the area contained by them; and here I clearly discern that I have to make some special effort of mind to imagine it that I do not make in just understanding it; this new mental effort plainly shows the difference between imagination and pure understanding.

I further consider that this power of imagination in me, taken as distinct from the power of understanding, is not essential to the nature of myself, that is, of my mind; for even if I lacked it, I should nevertheless undoubtedly still be the selfsame one that I am; it seems, therefore, that this power must depend on some object other than myself. And if there is a body to which the mind is so conjoined that it can at will apply itself, so to say, to contemplating it, then I can readily understand the possibility of my imagining corporeal objects by this means. The difference between this mode of consciousness and pure understanding would then be simply this: in the act of understanding the mind turns as it were towards itself, and contemplates one of the ideas contained in itself; in the act of imagining, it turns to the body, and contemplates something in it resembling an idea understood by the mind itself or perceived by sense. I can readily understand, I say, that imagination could be performed in this way, if a body exists; and since there does not occur to me any other equally convenient way of explaining it, I form from this the probable conjecture that the body exists. But this is only probable; and, in spite of a careful investigation of all points, I can as yet see no way of arguing conclusively from the fact that there is in my imagination a distinct idea of a corporeal nature to the existence of any body.

Besides that aspect of body which is the subject-matter of pure mathematics, there are many other things that I habitually imagine—colours, sounds, flavours, pain, and so on; but none of these are so distinctly imagined. In any case, I perceive them better by way of sensation, and it is from thence that they seem to have reached my imagination, by the help of memory. Thus it will be more convenient to treat of them by treating of sense at the same time; I must see if I can get any certain argument for the existence of material objects from things perceived in the mode of consciousness that I call sensation.

I will first recall to myself what kinds of things I previously thought were real, as being perceived in sensation, and for what reasons I thought so; then I will set out my reasons for having later on called them in question; finally I will consider what to hold now.

In the first place, then: I had sensations of having a head, hands, feet, and the other members that make up the body; and I regarded the body as part of myself, or even as my whole self. I had sensations of the commerce of this body with many other bodies, which were capable of being beneficial or injurious to it in various ways; I estimated the beneficial effects by a sensation of pleasure, and the injurious, by a sensation of pain. Besides pain and pleasure, I had internal sensations of hunger, thirst, and other such appetites; and also of physical inclinations towards gladness, sadness, anger, and other like emotions. I had external sensations not only of the extension, shapes, and movements of bodies, but also of their hardness, heat, and other tangible qualities; also, sensations of light, colours, odours, flavours, and sounds. By the varieties of these qualities I distinguished from one another the sky, the earth, the seas, and all other bodies.

I certainly had some reason, in view of the ideas of these qualities that presented themselves to my consciousness (*cogitationi*), and that were the only proper and immediate object of my sensations, to think that I was aware in sensation of objects quite different from my own consciousness: viz. bodies from which the ideas proceeded. For it was my experience (*experiebar*) that the ideas came to me without any consent of mine; so that I could neither have a sensation of any object, however I wished, if it were not present to the sense-organ, nor help having the sensation when the object was present. Moreover, the ideas perceived in sensation were much more vivid and prominent, and, in their own way, more distinct, than any that I myself deliberately produced in my meditations, or observed to have been impressed on my memory; and thus it seemed impossible for them to proceed from myself; and the only remaining possibility was that they came from some other objects. Now since I had no conception of these objects from any other source than the ideas themselves, it could not but occur to me that they were like the ideas. Further, I remembered that I had had the use of the senses before the use of reason; and I saw that the ideas I formed myself were less prominent than those I perceived in sensation, and mostly consisted of parts taken from sensation; I thus readily convinced myself that I had nothing in my intellect that I had not previously had in sensation.

Again, I had some reason for holding that the body I called 'my body' by a special title really did belong to me more than any other body did. I could never separate myself entirely from it, as I could from other bodies. All the appetites and emotions I had, I felt in the body and on its account. I felt pain, and the titillations of pleasure, in parts of *this* body, not of other, external bodies. Why should a sadness of the mind follow upon a sensation of pain, and a kind of happiness upon the titillation of sense? Why should that twitching of the stomach which I call hunger tell me that I must eat; and a dryness of the throat, that I must drink; and so on? I could give no account of this except

627

that nature taught me so; for there is no likeness at all, so far as I can see, between the twitching in the stomach and the volition to take food; or between the sensation of an object that gives me pain, and the experience (*cogitationem*) of sadness that arises from the sensation. My other judgments, too, as regards the objects of sensation seemed to have been lessons of nature; for I had convinced myself that things were so, before setting out any reasons to prove this.

Since then, however, I have had many experiences that have gradually sapped the faith I had in the senses. It sometimes happened that towers which had looked round at a distance looked square when close at hand; and that huge statues standing on the roof did not seem large to me looking up from the ground. And there were countless other cases like these, in which I found the external senses to be deceived in their judgment; and not only the external senses, but the internal senses as well. What [experience] can be more intimate than pain? Yet I had heard sometimes, from people who had had a leg or arm cut off, that they still seemed now and then to feel pain in the part of the body that they lacked; so it seemed in my own case not to be quite certain that a limb was in pain, even if I felt pain in it. And to these reasons for doubting I more recently added two more, of highly general application. First, there is no kind of sensation that I have ever thought I had in waking life, but I may also think I have some time when I am asleep; and since I do not believe that sensations I seem to have in sleep come from external objects, I did not see why I should believe this any the more about sensations I seem to have when I am awake. Secondly, I did not as yet know the Author of my being (or at least pretended I did not); so there seemed to be nothing against my being naturally so constituted as to be deceived even about what appeared to myself most true. As for the reasons of my former conviction that sensible objects are real, it was not difficult to answer them. I was, it seemed, naturally impelled to many courses from which reason dissuaded me; so I did not think I ought to put much reliance on what nature had taught me. And although sense-perceptions did not depend on my will, it must not be concluded, I thought, that they proceed from objects distinct from myself; there might perhaps be some faculty in myself, as yet unknown to me, that produced them.

But now that I am beginning to be better acquainted with myself and with the Author of my being, my view is that I must not rashly accept all the apparent data of sensation; nor, on the other hand, call them all in question.

In the first place, I know that whatever I clearly and distinctly understand can be made by God just as I understand it; so my ability to understand one thing clearly and distinctly apart from another is enough to assure me that they are distinct, because God at least can separate them. (It is irrelevant what faculty enables me to think of them as separate.) Now I know that I exist, and at the same time I observe absolutely nothing else as belonging to my nature or essence except the mere fact that I am a conscious being; and just from this I can validly infer that my essence consists simply in the fact that I am a conscious being. It is indeed possible (or rather, as I shall say later on, it is certain) that I have a body closely bound up with myself; but at the same time I have, on the one hand, a clear and distinct idea of myself taken simply as a conscious, not an

extended, being;* and, on the other hand, a distinct idea of body, taken simply as an extended, not a conscious, being; so it is certain that I am really distinct from my body, and could exist without it.

Further, I find in myself powers for special modes of consciousness, e.g. imagination and sensation; I can clearly and distinctly understand myself as a whole apart from these powers, but not the powers apart from myself—apart from an intellectual substance to inhere in; for the essential (*formali*) conception of them includes some kind of intellectual act; and I thus perceive that they are distinct from me in the way aspects (*modos*) are from the object to which they belong. I also recognise other powers—those of local motion, and change of shape, and so on; these, like the ones I mentioned before, cannot be understood apart from a substance to inhere in; nor, therefore, can they exist apart from it. Clearly these, if they exist, must inhere in a corporeal or extended, not an intellectual substance; for it is some form of extension, not any intellectual act, that is involved in a clear and distinct conception of them. Now I have a passive power of sensation—of getting and recognising the ideas of sensible objects. But I could never have the use of it if there were not also in existence an active power, either in myself or in something else, to produce or make the ideas. This power certainly cannot exist in me; for it presupposes no action of my intellect, and the ideas are produced without my co-operation, and often against my will. The only remaining possibility is that it inheres in some substance other than myself. This must contain all the reality that exists representatively in the ideas produced by this active power; and it must contain it (as I remarked previously) either just as it is represented, or in some higher form. So either this substance is a body—is of corporeal nature—and contains actually whatever is contained representatively in the ideas; or else it is God, or some creature nobler than bodies, and contains the same reality in a higher form. But since God is not deceitful, it is quite obvious that he neither implants the ideas in me by his own direct action, nor yet by means of some creature that contains the representative reality of the ideas not precisely as they represent it, but only in some higher form. For God has given me no faculty at all to discern their origin; on the other hand, he has given me a strong inclination to believe that these ideas proceed from corporeal objects; so I do not see how it would make sense to say God is not deceitful, if in fact they proceed from elsewhere, not from corporeal objects. Therefore corporeal objects must exist. It may be that not all bodies are such as my senses apprehend them, for this sensory apprehension is in many ways obscure and confused; but at any rate their nature must comprise whatever I clearly and distinctly understand—that is, whatever, generally considered, falls within the subject-matter of pure mathematics.

There remain some highly doubtful and uncertain points; either mere details, like the sun's having a certain size or shape, or things unclearly understood, like light, sound, pain, and so on. But since God is not deceitful, there cannot

* For Descartes, an extended thing is something which takes up space, or has spatial extent. So he is claiming that the mind has no spatial extent.

possibly occur any error in my opinions but I can correct by means of some faculty God has given me to that end; and this gives me some hope of arriving at the truth even on such matters. Indeed, all nature's lessons undoubtedly contain some truth; for by nature, as a general term, I now mean nothing other than either God himself, or the order of created things established by God; and by *my* nature in particular I mean the complex of all that God has given *me*.

Now there is no more explicit lesson of nature than that I have a body; that it is being injured when I feel pain; that it needs food, or drink, when I suffer from hunger, or thirst, and so on. So I must not doubt that there is some truth in this. Nature also teaches by these sensations of pain, hunger, thirst, etc., that I am not present in my body merely as a pilot is present in a ship; I am most tightly bound to it, and as it were mixed up with it, so that I and it form a unit. Otherwise, when the body is hurt, I, who am simply a conscious being, would not feel pain on that account, but would perceive the injury by a pure act of understanding, as the pilot perceives by sight any breakages there may be in the ship; and when the body needs food or drink, I should explicitly understand the fact, and not have confused sensations of hunger and thirst. For these sensations of thirst, hunger, pain, etc., are simply confused modes of consciousness that arise from the mind's being united to, and as it were mixed up with, the body.

· · ·

I must begin by observing the great difference between mind and body. Body is of its nature always divisible; mind is wholly indivisible. When I consider the mind—that is, myself, in so far as I am merely a conscious being—I can distinguish no parts within myself; I understand myself to be a single and complete thing. Although the whole mind seems to be united to the whole body, yet when a foot or an arm or any other part of the body is cut off I am not aware that any subtraction has been made from the mind. Nor can the faculties of will, feeling, understanding and so on be called its parts; for it is one and the same mind that wills, feels, and understands. On the other hand, I cannot think of any corporeal or extended object without being readily able to divide it in thought and therefore conceiving of it as divisible. This would be enough to show me the total difference between mind and body, even if I did not sufficiently know this already.

Next, I observe that my mind is not directly affected by all parts of the body; but only by the brain, and perhaps only by one small part of that—the alleged seat of common sensibility. Whenever this is disposed in a given way, it gives the same indication to the mind, even if the other parts of the body are differently disposed at the time; of this there are innumerable experimental proofs, of which I need not give an account here.

I observe further that, from the nature of body, in whatever way a part of it could be moved by another part at some distance, that same part could also be moved in the same way by intermediate parts, even if the more distant part did nothing. For example, if ABCD is a cord, there is no way of moving A by pulling the end D that could not be carried out equally well if B or C in the

middle were pulled and the end D were not moved at all. Now, similarly, when I feel pain in my foot, I have learnt from the science of physic that this sensation is brought about by means of nerves scattered throughout the foot; these are stretched like cords from there to the brain, and when they are pulled in the foot they transmit the pull to the inmost part of the brain, to which they are attached, and produce there a kind of disturbance which nature has decreed should give the mind a sensation of pain, as it were in the foot. But in order to reach the brain, these nerves have to pass through the leg, the thigh, the back, and the neck; so it may happen that, although it is not the part in the foot that is touched, but only some intermediate part, there is just the same disturbance produced in the brain as when the foot is injured; and so necessarily the mind will have the same sensation of pain. And the same must be believed as regards any other sensation.

Finally, I observe that, since any given disturbance in the part of the brain that directly affects the mind can produce only one kind of sensation, nothing better could be devised than that it should produce that one among all the sensations it could produce which is most conducive, and most often conducive, to the welfare of a healthy man. Now experience shows that all the sensations nature has given us are of this kind; so nothing can be found in them but evidence of God's power and goodness. For example: when the nerves of the foot are strongly and unusually disturbed, this disturbance, by way of the spinal cord, arrives at the interior of the brain; there it gives the mind the signal for it to have a certain sensation, viz. pain, as it were in the foot; and this arouses the mind to do its best to remove the cause of the pain, as being injurious to the foot. Now God might have so made human nature that this very disturbance in the brain was a sign to the mind of something else; it might have been a sign of its own occurrence in the brain; or of the disturbance in the foot, or in some intermediate place; or, in fact, of anything else whatever. But there would be no alternative equally conducive to the welfare of the body. Similarly, when we need drink, there arises a dryness of the throat, which disturbs the nerves of the throat, and by means of them the interior of the brain; and this disturbance gives the mind the sensation of thirst, because the most useful thing for us to know in this whole process is that we then need drink to keep healthy. And so in other cases.

From all this it is clear that in spite of God's immeasurable goodness, man as a compound of body and mind cannot but be sometimes deceived by his own nature. For some cause that occurs, not in the foot, but in any other of the parts traversed by the nerves from the foot to the brain, or even in the brain itself, may arouse the same disturbance as is usually aroused by a hurt foot; and then pain will be felt as it were in the foot, and there will be a 'natural' illusion of sense. For the brain-disturbance in question cannot but produce always the same sensation in the mind; and it usually arises much more often from a cause that is hurting the foot than from another cause occurring somewhere else; so it is in accordance with reason that it should always give the mind the appearance of pain in the foot rather than some other part. Again, sometimes dryness of the throat arises not, as usual, from the fact that drink

would be conducive to bodily health, but from some contrary cause, as in dropsy; but it is far better that it should deceive us in that case, than if it always deceived us when the body was in good condition. And so generally.

This consideration is of the greatest help to me, not only for noticing all the errors to which my nature is liable, but also for readily correcting or avoiding them. I know that all my sensations are much more often true than delusive signs in matters regarding the well-being of the body; I can almost always use several senses to examine the same object; above all, I have my memory, which connects the present to the past, and my understanding, which has now reviewed all the causes of error. So I ought not to be afraid any longer that all that the senses show me daily may be an illusion; the exaggerated doubts of the last few days are to be dismissed as ridiculous. In particular, this is true of the chief reason for doubt—that sleep and waking life were indistinguishable to me; for I can now see a vast difference between them. Dreams are never connected by memory with all the other events of my life, like the things that happen when I am awake. If in waking life somebody suddenly appeared and directly after-wards disappeared, as happens in dreams, and I could not see where he had come from or where he went, I should justifiably decide he was a ghost, or a phantasm formed in my own brain, rather than a real man. But when I distinctly observe where an object comes from, where it is, and when this happens; and when I can connect the perception of it uninteruptedly with the whole of the rest of my life; then I am quite certain that while this is happening to me I am not asleep but awake. And I need not doubt the reality of things at all, if after summoning all my senses, my memory, and my understanding to examine them, these sources yield no conflicting information. In such things I am nowise deceived, because God is no deceiver. But since practical needs do not always leave time for such a careful examination, we must admit that in human life errors as regards particular things are always liable to happen; and we must recognise the infirmity of our nature.

Discourse V

. . .

I specially dwelt on showing* that if there were machines with the organs and appearance of a monkey, or some other irrational animal, we should have no means of telling that they were not altogether of the same nature as those animals; whereas if there were machines resembling our bodies, and imitating our actions as far as is morally possible, we should still have two means of telling that, all the same, they were not real men. First, they could never use words or other constructed signs, as we do to declare our thoughts to others. It is quite conceivable that a machine should be so made as to utter words, and

---

* Descartes is describing some of the theories presented in *Le Monde,* a wide-ranging treatise that he wrote in 1633 but did not publish because of Galileo's recent condemnation.

even utter them in connexion with physical events that cause a change in one of its organs; so that e.g. if it is touched in one part, it asks what you want to say to it, and if touched in another, it cries out that it is hurt; but not that it should be so made as to arrange words variously in response to the meaning of what is said in its presence, as even the dullest men can do. Secondly, while they might do many things as well as any of us or better, they would infallibly fail in others, revealing that they acted not from knowledge but only from the disposition of their organs. For while reason is a universal tool that may serve in all kinds of circumstances, these organs need a special arrangement for each special action; so it is morally impossible that a machine should contain so many varied arrangements as to act in all the events of life in the way reason enables us to act.

Now in just these two ways we can also recognise the difference between men and brutes. For it is a very remarkable thing that there are no men so dull and stupid, not even lunatics, that they cannot arrange various words and form a sentence to make their thoughts (*pensées*) understood; but no other animal, however perfect or well bred, can do the like. This does not come from their lacking the organs; for magpies and parrots can utter words like ourselves, and yet they cannot talk like us, that is, with any sign of being aware of (*qu'ils pensent*) what they say. Whereas men born deaf-mutes, and thus devoid of the organs that others use for speech, as much as brutes are or more so, usually invent for themselves signs by which they make themselves understood to those who are normally with them, and who thus have a chance to learn their language. This is evidence that brutes not only have a smaller degree of reason than men, but are wholly lacking in it. For it may be seen that a very small degree of reason is needed in order to be able to talk; and in view of the inequality that occurs among animals of the same species, as among men, and of the fact that some are easier to train than others, it is incredible that a monkey or parrot who was one of the most perfect members of his species should not be comparable in this regard to one of the stupidest children or at least to a child with a diseased brain, if their souls were not wholly different in nature from ours. And we must not confuse words with natural movements, the expressions of emotion, which can be imitated by machines as well as by animals. Nor must we think, like some of the ancients, that brutes talk but we cannot understand their language; for if that were true, since many of their organs are analogous to ours, they could make themselves understood to us, as well as to their fellows. It is another very remarkable thing that although several brutes exhibit more skill than we in some of their actions, they show none at all in many other circumstances; so their excelling us is no proof that they have a mind (*de l'esprit*), for in that case they would have a better one than any of us and would excel us all round; it rather shows that they have none, and that it is nature that acts in them according to the arrangements of their organs; just as we see how a clock, composed merely of wheels and springs, can reckon the hours and measure time more correctly than we can with all our wisdom.

I went on to describe the rational soul, and showed that, unlike the other things I had spoken of, it cannot be extracted from the potentiality of matter, but must be specially created; and how it is not enough for it to dwell in the human body like a pilot in his ship, which would only account for its moving the limbs of the body; in order to have in addition feelings and appetites like ours, and so make up a true man, it must be joined and united to the body more closely. Here I dwelt a little on the subject of the soul, as among the most important; for, after the error of denying God, (of which I think I have already given a sufficient refutation), there is none more likely to turn weak characters from the strait way of virtue than the supposition that the soul of brutes must be of the same nature as ours, so that after this life we have no more to hope or fear than flies or ants. Whereas, when we realise how much they really differ from us, we understand much better the arguments proving that our soul is of a nature entirely independent of the body, and thus not liable to die with it; and since we can discern no other causes that should destroy it, we are naturally led to decide that it is immortal.

55

The Distinction
Between Mental and
Physical Phenomena

FRANZ BRENTANO

Franz Brentano (1938–1917) is an important figure in philosophical psychology because of his teaching as well as his writing. He exerted an extraordinary influence on a gifted collection of students, including Sigmund Freud, Edmund Husserl, and Alexius Meinong. Through Husserl, he helped to shape the development of contemporary phenomenology.

In this section from Psychology from an Empirical Standpoint, *Brentano's goal is to determine the marks by which we can distinguish mental and physical phenomena. He canvasses a number of proposed criteria, rejecting some and supporting others. He rejects one of Descartes's criteria for the mental—lack of spatial extent—partly because this criterion is merely negative, stating what mentality lacks, rather than offering a positive description. Drawing on a long philosophical tradition, Brentano distinguishes between "outer perception" and "inner perception." Outer perception is simply perception via one of the five senses: sight, hearing, smell, taste, and touch. At least since the time of Locke, philosophers have suggested we also possess a kind of inner perception, because we are able to report things like our hopes, fears, thoughts, and sensations. Brentano considers the possibility that mental phenomena could be distinguished as the objects of inner perception, physical phenomena being the objects of outer perception. The criterion that Brentano ultimately accepts as having paramount importance is "intentionality"—the property of being about some object beyond itself. As you read this passage, for example, you are thinking about Brentano, or perhaps about Brentano's work. Two crucial questions emerge from Brentano's theses: First, are all mental states, includ-sensations, characterized by intentionality? (What is a pain about?) Second, how is it possible for any mental state to be about something? (What is it that makes your thought about Brentano a thought about Brentano?)*

1. All the data of our consciousness are divided into two great classes—the class of physical and the class of mental phenomena. We spoke of this distinction earlier when we established the concept of psychology, and we returned to it again in our discussion of psychological method. But what we have said is still not sufficient. We must now establish more firmly and more exactly what was only mentioned in passing before.

This seems all the more necessary since neither agreement nor complete clarity has been achieved regarding the delimitation of the two classes. We have already seen how physical phenomena which appear in the imagination are sometimes taken for mental phenomena. There are many other such instances of confusion. And even important psychologists may be hard pressed to defend themselves against the charge of self-contradiction. For instance, we encounter statements like the following: sensation and imagination are distinguished by the fact that one occurs as the result of a physical phenomenon, while the other is evoked by a mental phenomenon according to the laws of association. But then the same psychologists admit that what appears in sensation does not correspond to its efficient cause. Thus it turns out that the so-called physical phenomenon does not actually appear to us, and, indeed, that we have no presentation of it whatsoever—certainly a curious misuse of the term "phenomenon"! Given such a state of affairs, we cannot avoid going into the question in somewhat greater detail.

2. The explanation we are seeking is not a definition according to the traditional rules of logic. These rules have recently been the object of impartial criticism, and much could be added to what has already been said. Our aim is to clarify the meaning of the two terms *"physical phenomenon"* and *"mental phenomenon,"* removing all misunderstanding and confusion concerning them. And it does not matter to us what means we use, as long as they really serve to clarify these terms.

To this end, it is not sufficient merely to specify more general, more inclusive definitions. Just as deduction is opposed to induction when we speak of kinds of proof, in this case explanation by means of subsumption under a general term is opposed to explanation by means of particulars, through examples. And the latter kind of explanation is appropriate whenever the particular terms are clearer than the general ones. Thus it is probably a more effective procedure to explain the term "color" by saying that it designates the class which contains red, blue, green and yellow, than to do the opposite and attempt to explain "red" by saying it is a particular kind of color. Moreover, explanation through particular definitions will be of even greater use when we are dealing, as in our case, with terms which are not common in ordinary life, while those for the individual phenomena included under them are frequently used. So let us first of all try to clarify the concepts by means of examples.

Every idea or presentation which we acquire either through sense perception or imagination is an example of a mental phenomenon. By presentation I do not mean that which is presented, but rather the act of presentation. Thus, hearing a sound, seeing a colored object, feeling warmth or cold, as well as similar states of imagination are examples of what I mean by this term. I also mean by it the thinking of a general concept, provided such a thing actually does occur. Furthermore, every judgement, every recollection, every expectation, every inference, every conviction or opinion, every doubt, is a mental phenomenon. Also to be included under this term is every emotion: joy, sorrow, fear, hope, courage, despair, anger, love, hate, desire, act of will, intention, astonishment, admiration, contempt, etc.

Examples of physical phenomena, on the other hand, are a color, a figure, a landscape which I see, a chord which I hear, warmth, cold, odor which I sense; as well as similar images which appear in the imagination.

These examples may suffice to illustrate the differences between the two classes of phenomena.

3. Yet we still want to try to find a different and a more unified way of explaining mental phenomena. For this purpose we make use of a definition we used earlier when we said that the term "mental phenomena" applies to presentations as well as to all the phenomena which are based upon presentations. It is hardly necessary to mention again that by "presentation" we do not mean that which is presented, but rather the presenting of it. This act of presentation forms the foundation not merely of the act of judging, but also of desiring and of every other mental act. Nothing can be judged, desired, hoped or feared, unless one has a presentation of that thing. Thus the definition given includes all the examples of mental phenomena which we listed above, and in general all the phenomena belonging to this domain.

It is a sign of the immature state of psychology that we can scarcely utter a single sentence about mental phenomena which will not be disputed by many people. Nevertheless, most psychologists agree with what we have just said, namely, that presentations are the foundation for the other mental phenomena. Thus Herbart asserts quite rightly, "Every time we have a feeling, there will be something or other presented in consciousness, even though it may be something very diversified, confused and varied, so that this particular presentation is included in this particular feeling. Likewise, whenever we desire something . . . we have before our minds that which we desire."[1]

. . .

4. People have tried to formulate a completely unified definition which distinguishes all mental phenomena from physical phenomena by means of negation. All physical phenomena, it is said, have extension and spatial location, whether they are phenomena of vision or of some other sense, or products of the imagination, which presents similar objects to us. The opposite, however, is true of mental phenomena; thinking, willing and the like appear without extension and without spatial location.

According to this view, it would be possible for us to characterize physical phenomena easily and exactly in contrast to mental phenomena by saying that they are those phenomena which appear extended and localized in space. Mental phenomena would then be definable with equal exactness as those phenomena which do not have extension or spatial location. Descartes and Spinoza could be cited in support of such a distinction. The chief advocate of this view, however, is Kant, who explains space as the form of the intuition of the external sense.

---

[1] *Psychologie als Wissenschaft,* Part II, Sect. 1, Chap. 1, No. 103. Cp. also Drobisch, *Empirische Psychologie,* p. 38, and others of Herbart's school.

Recently Bain has given the same definition:

> The department of the Object, or Object-World, is exactly
> circumscribed by one property, Extension. The world of
> Subject-experience is devoid of this property. A tree or a river is
> said to possess extended magnitude. A pleasure has no length,
> breadth, or thickness; it is in no respect an extended thing. A
> thought or idea may refer to extended magnitudes, but it cannot
> be said to have extension in itself. Neither can we say that an
> act of the will, a desire or a belief occupy dimensions in space.
> Hence all that comes within the sphere of the Subject is
> spoken of as the Unextended.
>
> Thus, if Mind, as commonly happens, is put for the sum-total
> of Subject-experiences, we may define it negatively by a single
> fact—the absence of Extension.[2]

Thus it seems that we have found, at least negatively, a unified definition for the totality of mental phenomena.

But even on this point there is no unanimity among psychologists, and we hear it denied for contradictory reasons that extension and lack of extension are characteristics which distinguish physical and mental phenomena.

Many declare that this definition is false because not only mental phenomena, but also many physical phenomena appear to be without extension. A large number of not unimportant psychologists, for example, teach that the phenomena of some, or even of all of our senses originally appear apart from all extension and spatial location. In particular, this view is quite generally held with respect to sounds and olfactory phenomena. It is true of colors according to Berkeley, of the phenomena of touch according to Platner, and of the phenomena of all the external senses according to Herbart and Lotze, as well as according to Hartley, Brown, the two Mills, H. Spencer and others. Indeed it seems that the phenomena revealed by the external senses, especially sight and the sense of touch, are all spatially extended. The reason for this, it is said, is that we connect them with spatial presentations that are gradually developed on the basis of earlier experiences. They are originally without spatial location, and we subsequently localize them. If this were really the only way in which physical phenomena attain spatial location we could obviously no longer separate the two areas by reference to this property. In fact, mental phenomena are also localized by us in this way, as, for example, when we locate a phenomenon of anger in the irritated lion, and our own thoughts in the space which we occupy.

This is one way in which the above definition has been criticized by a great number of eminent psychologists, including Bain. At first sight he seems to

---

[2] *Mental Science,* 3rd ed. (London, 1872), Introduction, Ch. 1.

defend such a definition, but in reality he follows Hartley's lead on this issue. He has only been able to express himself as he does because he does not actually consider the phenomena of the external senses, in and for themselves, to be physical phenomena (although he is not always consistent in this).

Others, as we said, will reject this definition for the opposite reason. It is not so much the assertion that all physical phenomena appear extended that provokes them, but rather the assertion that all mental phenomena lack extension. According to them, certain mental phenomena also appear to be extended. Aristotle seems to have been of this opinion when, in the first chapter of this treatise on sense and sense objects he considers it immediately evident, without any prior proof, that sense perception is the act of a bodily organ.[3] Modern psychologists and physiologists sometimes express themselves in the same way regarding certain affects. They speak of feelings of pleasure or pain which appear in the external organs, sometimes even after the amputation of the limb and yet, feeling, like perception, is a mental phenomenon. Some authors even maintain that sensory appetites appear localized. This view is shared by the poet when he speaks, not, to be sure, of thought, but of rapture and longing which suffuse the heart and all parts of the body.

Thus we see that the distinction under discussion is disputed from the point of view of both physical and mental phenomena. Perhaps both of these objections are equally unjustified. At any rate, another definition common to all mental phenomena is still desirable. Whether certain mental and physical phenomena appear extended or not, the controversy proves that the criterion given for a clear separation is not adequate. Furthermore, this criterion gives us only a negative definition of mental phenomena.

5. What positive criterion shall we now be able to provide? Or is there perhaps no positive definition which holds true of all mental phenomena generally? Bain thinks that in fact there is none.[4] Nevertheless, psychologists in earlier times have already pointed out that there is a special affinity and analogy which exists among all mental phenomena, and which physical phenomena do not share.

Every mental phenomenon is characterized by what the Scholastics of the Middle Ages called the intentional (or mental)[5] inexistence of an object, and what we might call, though not wholly unambiguously, reference to a content, direction toward an object (which is not to be understood here as meaning a thing), or immanent objectivity. Every mental phenomenon includes something

---

[3] *De Sensu et Sensibili,* 1, 436, b. 7. Cp. also what he says in *De Anima,* I, 1, 403 16, about affective states, in particular about fear.

[4] *The Senses and the Intellect,* Introduction.

[5] They also use the expression "to exist as an object (objectively) in something," which, if we wanted to use it at the present time, would be considered, on the contrary, as a designation of a real existence outside the mind. At least this is what is suggested by the expression "to exist immanently as an object," which is occasionally used in a similar sense, and in which the term "immanent" should obviously rule out the misunderstanding which is to be feared.

as object within itself, although they do not all do so in the same way. In presentation something is presented, in judgement something is affirmed or denied, in love loved, in hate hated, in desire desired and so on.[6]

This intentional in-existence is characteristic exclusively of mental phenomena. No physical phenomenon exhibits anything like it. We can, therefore, define mental phenomena by saying that they are those phenomena which contain an object intentionally within themselves.

But here, too, we come upon controversies and contradiction. Hamilton, in particular, denies this characteristic to a whole broad class of mental phenomena, namely, to all those which he characterizes as feelings, to pleasure and pain in all their most diverse shades and varieties. With respect to the phenomena of thought and desire he is in agreement with us. Obviously there is no act of thinking without an object that is thought, nor a desire without an object that is desired. "In the phenomena of Feelings—the phenomena of Pleasure and Pain—on the contrary, consciousness does not place the mental modification or state before itself; it does not contemplate it apart—as separate from itself—but is, as it were, fused into one. The peculiarity of Feeling, therefore, is that there is nothing but what is subjectively subjective; there is no object different from the self—no objectification of any mode of self."[7] In the first instance there would be something which, according to Hamilton's terminology, is "objective," in the second instance something which is "objectively subjective," as in self-awareness, the object of which Hamilton consequently calls the "subject-object." By denying both concerning feelings, Hamilton rejects unequivocally all intentional in-existence of these phenomena.

In reality, what Hamilton says is not entirely correct, since certain feelings undeniably refer to objects. Our language itself indicates this through the expressions it employs. We say that we are pleased with or about something, that we feel sorrow or grieve about something. Likewise, we say: that pleases me, that hurts me, that makes me feel sorry, etc. Joy and sorrow, like affirmation and negation, love and hate, desire and aversion, clearly follow upon a presentation and are related to that which is presented.

---

[6] Aristotle himself spoke of this mental in-existence. In his books on the soul he says that the sensed object, as such, is in the sensing subject; that the sense contains the sensed object without its matter; that the object which is thought is in the thinking intellect. In Philo, likewise, we find the doctrine of mental existence and in-existence. However, since he confuses mental existence with existence in the proper sense of the word, he reaches his contradictory doctrine of the *logos* and Ideas. The same is true of the Neoplatonists. St. Augustine in his doctrine of the *Verbum mentis* and of its inner origin touches upon the same fact. St. Anselm does the same in his famous ontological argument; many people have observed that his consideration of mental existence as a true existence is at the basis of his paralogism (cp. Überweg, *Geschichte der Philosophie*, II). St. Thomas Aquinas teaches that the object which is thought is intentionally in the thinking subject, the object which is loved in the person who loves, the object which is desired in the person desiring, and he uses this for theological purposes. When the Scriptures speak of an indwelling of the Holy Ghost, St. Thomas explains it as an intentional indwelling through love. In addition, he attempted to find, through the intentional in-existence in the acts of thinking and loving, a certain analogy for the mystery of the Trinity and the procession *ad intra* of the Word and the Spirit.

[7] *Lecture on Metaphysics*, I, 432.

One is most inclined to agree with Hamilton in those cases in which, as we saw earlier, it is most easy to fall into the error that feeling is not based upon any presentation: the case of pain caused by a cut or a burn, for example. But the reason is simply the same temptation toward this, as we have seen, erroneous assumption. Even Hamilton recognizes with us the fact that presentations occur without exception and thus even here they form the basis of the feeling. Thus his denial that feelings have an object seems all the more striking.

One thing certainly has to be admitted; the object to which a feeling refers is not always an external object. Even in cases where I hear a harmonious sound, the pleasure which I feel is not actually pleasure in the sound but pleasure in the hearing. In fact you could say, not incorrectly, that in a certain sense it even refers to itself, and this introduces, more or less, what Hamilton was talking about, namely that the feeling and the object are "fused into one." But this is nothing that is not true in the same way of many phenomena of thought and knowledge, as we will see when we come to the investigation of inner consciousness. Still they retain a mental inexistence, a Subject-Object, to use Hamilton's mode of speech, and the same thing is true of these feelings. Hamilton is wrong when he says that with regard to feelings everything is "subjectively subjective"—an expression which is actually self-contradictory, for where you cannot speak of an object, you cannot speak of a subject either. Also, Hamilton spoke of a fusing into one of the feeling with the mental impression, but when carefully considered it can be seen that he is bearing witness against himself here. Every fusion is a unification of several things; and thus the pictorial expression which is intended to make us concretely aware of the distinctive character of feeling still points to a certain duality in the unity.

We may, therefore, consider the intentional in-existence of an object to be a general characteristic of mental phenomena which distinguishes this class of phenomena from the class of physical phenomena.

6. Another characteristic which all mental phenomena have in common is the fact that they are only perceived in inner consciousness, while in the case of physical phenomena only external perception is possible. This distinguishing characteristic is emphasized by Hamilton.[8]

It could be argued that such a definition is not very meaningful. In fact, it seems much more natural to define the act according to the object, and therefore to state that inner perception, in contrast to every other kind, is the perception of mental phenomena. However, besides the fact that it has a special object, inner perception possesses another distinguishing characteristic: its immediate, infallible self-evidence. Of all the types of knowledge of the objects of experience, inner perception alone possesses this characteristic. Consequently, when we say that mental phenomena are those which are apprehended by means of inner perception, we say that their perception is immediately evident.

Moreover, inner perception is not merely the only kind of perception which is immediately evident; it is really the only perception in the strict sense of the

---

[8] *Lecture on Metaphysics*, I, 432.

word.[9] As we have seen, the phenomena of the so-called external perception cannot be proved true and real even by means of indirect demonstration. For this reason, anyone who in good faith has taken them for what they seem to be is being misled by the manner in which the phenomena are connected. Therefore, strictly speaking, so-called external perception is not perception. Mental phenomena, therefore, may be described as the only phenomena of which perception in the strict sense of the word is possible.

This definition, too, is an adequate characterization of mental phenomena. That is not to say that all mental phenomena are internally perceivable by all men, and so all those which someone cannot perceive are to be included by him among physical phenomena. On the contrary, as we have already expressly noted above, it is obvious that no mental phenomenon is perceived by more than one individual. At the same time, however, we also saw that every type of mental phenomenon is present in every fully developed human mental life. For this reason, the reference to the phenomena which constitute the realm of inner perception serves our purpose satisfactorily.

7. We said that mental phenomena are those phenomena which alone can be perceived in the strict sense of the word. We could just as well say that they are those phenomena which alone possess real existence as well as intentional existence. Knowledge, joy and desire really exist. Color, sound and warmth have only a phenomenal and intentional existence.

There are philosophers who go so far as to say that it is self-evident that phenomena such as those which we call physical phenomena *could not* correspond to any reality. According to them, the assertion that these phenomena have an existence different from mental existence is self-contradictory. Thus, for example, Bain says that attempts have been made to explain the phenomena of external perception by supposing a material world, "in the first instance, detached from perception, and, afterwards, coming into perception, by operating upon the mind." "This view," he says, "involves a contradiction. The prevailing doctrine is that a tree is something in itself apart from all perception; that, by its luminous emanations, it impresses our mind and is then perceived, the perception being an effect, and the unperceived tree [i.e. the one which exists outside of perception] the cause. But the tree is known only through perception; what it may be anterior to, or independent of, perception, we cannot tell; we can think of it as perceived but not as unperceived. There is a manifest contradiction in the supposition; we are required at the same moment to perceive the thing and not to perceive it. We know the touch of iron, but we cannot know the touch apart from the touch."[10]

I must confess that I am unable to convince myself of the soundness of this argument. It is undoubtedly true that a color appears to us only when we have

---

[9] The German word which we translate as "perception" is *"Wahrnehmung"* which literally means taking something to be true. The English word does not reflect this literal meaning so this paragraph only makes sense if we bear in mind the German word.—TRANS.

[10] *Mental Science,* 3rd ed., p. 198.

a presentation of it. We cannot conclude from this, however, that a color cannot exist without being presented. Only if the state of being presented were contained in the color as one of its elements, as a certain quality and intensity is contained in it, would a color which is not presented imply a contradiction, since a whole without one of its parts is indeed a contradiction. But this is obviously not the case. Otherwise, it would also be absolutely inconceivable how the belief in the real existence of physical phenomena outside our presentation could have, not to say originated, but achieved the most general dissemination, been maintained with the utmost tenacity, and, indeed, even been shared for a long time by the most outstanding thinkers. Bain said: "We can think of a tree as perceived, but not as unperceived. There is a manifest contradiction in the supposition." If what he said were correct, his further conclusions could not be objected to. But it is precisely this which cannot be granted. Bain explains this statement by remarking, "We are required at the same moment to perceive the thing and not to perceive it." It is not correct, however, to say that such a demand is placed upon us, for, in the first place, not every act of thinking is a perception. Secondly, even if this were the case, it would only follow that we can think only of trees that have been perceived by us, but not that we can think only of trees *as perceived by us*. To taste a piece of white sugar does not mean to taste a piece of sugar *as white*. The fallacy reveals itself quite clearly in the case of mental phenomena. If someone said, "I cannot think about a mental phenomenon without thinking about it; therefore I can only think about mental phenomena as thought by me; therefore no mental phenomenon exists outside my thinking," his method of reasoning would be identical to that of Bain. Nevertheless, even Bain will not deny that his individual mental life is not the only one which has actual existence. When Bain adds: "we know the touch of iron, but it is not possible that we should know the touch apart from the touch," he obviously uses the word "touch" first to mean the object that is sensed and secondly to mean the act of sensing. These are different concepts, even though the word is the same. Consequently, only those who would let themselves be deceived by this equivocation could grant the existence of immediate evidence as postulated by Bain.

It is not correct, therefore, to say that the assumption that there exists a physical phenomenon outside the mind which is just as real as those which we find intentionally in us, implies a contradiction. It is only that, when we compare one with the other we discover conflicts which clearly show that no real existence corresponds to the intentional existence in this case. And even if this applies only to the realm of our own experience, we will nevertheless make no mistake if in general we deny to physical phenomena any existence other than intentional existence.

8. There is still another circumstance which people have said distinguishes between physical and mental phenomena. They say that mental phenomena always manifest themselves serially, while many physical phenomena manifest themselves simultaneously. But people do not always mean the same thing by this assertion, and not all of the meanings which it has been given are in accord with the truth.

Recently Herbert Spencer expressed himself on this subject in the following vein: "The two great classes of vital actions called Physiology and Psychology are broadly distinguished in this, that while the one includes both simultaneous and successive changes the other includes successive changes only. The phenomena forming the subject matter of Physiology present themselves as an immense number of different series bound up together. Those forming the subject matter of psychology present themselves as but a single series. A glance at the many continuous actions constituting the life of the body at large shows that they are synchronous—that digestion, circulation, respiration, excretion, secretions, etc., in all their many subdivisions are going on at one time in mutual dependence. And the briefest introspection makes it clear that the actions constituting thought occur, not together, but one after another."[11] Spencer restricts his comparison to physiological and physical phenomena found in one and the same organism endowed with mental life. If he had not done this, he would have been forced to admit that many series of mental phenomena occur simultaneously too, because there is more than one living being endowed with mental life in the world. However, even within the limits which he has assigned to it, the assertion he advances is not entirely true. Spencer himself is so far from failing to recognize this fact that he immediately calls attention to those species of lower animals, for example the *radiata,* in which a multiple mental life goes on simultaneously in *one* body. For this reason he thinks—but others will not readily admit it—that there is little difference between mental and physical life.[12] In addition he makes further concessions which reduce the difference between physiological and mental phenomena to a mere matter of degree. Furthermore, if we ask ourselves what it is that Spencer conceives as those physiological phenomena whose changes, in contrast to the changes of mental phenomena, are supposed to occur simultaneously, it appears that he uses this term not to describe specifically physical phenomena, but rather the causes, which are in themselves unknown, of these phenomena. In fact, with respect to the physical phenomena which manifest themselves in sensation, it seems undeniable that they cannot modify themselves simultaneously, if the sensations themselves do not undergo simultaneous changes. Hence, we can hardly attain a distinguishing characteristic for the two classes of phenomena in this way.

Others have wanted to find a characteristic of mental life in the fact that consciousness can grasp simultaneously only *one object,* never more than one, at a time. They point to the remarkable case of the error that occurs in the determination of time. This error regularly appears in astronomical observations in which the simultaneous swing of the pendulum does not enter into consciousness simultaneously with, but earlier or later than, the moment when the observed star touches the hairline in the telescope. Thus, mental phenomena always merely follow each other, one at a time, in a simple series. However, it

---

[11] *Principles of Psychology,* 2nd ed. I, Sect. 177, 395.

[12] *Principles of Psychology,* p. 397.

would certainly be a mistake to generalize without further reflection from a case which implies such an extreme concentration of attention. Spencer, at least, says: "I find that there may sometimes be detected as many as five simultaneous series of nervous changes, which in various degrees rise into consciousness so far that we cannot call any of them absolutely unconscious. When walking, there is the locomotive series; there may be, under certain circumstances, a tactual series; there is very often (in myself at least), an auditory series, constituting some melody or fragment of a melody which haunts me; and there is the visual series: all of which, subordinate to the dominant consciousness formed by some train of reflection, are continually crossing it and weaving themselves into it."[13] The same facts are reported by Hamilton, Cardaillac, and other psychologists on the basis of their experiences. Assuming, however, that it were true that all cases of perception are similar to that of the astronomer, should we not always at least have to acknowledge the fact that frequently we think of something and at the same time make a judgement about it or desire it? So there would still be several simultaneous mental phenomena. Indeed, we could, with more reason, make the opposite assertion, namely, that very often many mental phenomena are present in consciousness simultaneously, while there can never be more than one physical phenomenon at a time.

What is the only sense, then, in which we might say that a mental phenomenon always appears by itself, while many physical phenomena can appear at the same time? We can say this insofar as the whole multiplicity of mental phenomena which appear to us in our inner perception always appear as a unity, while the same is not true of the physical phenomena which we grasp simultaneously through the so-called external perception. As happens frequently in other cases, so here, too, unity is confused by many psychologists with simplicity; as a result they have maintained that they perceive themselves in inner consciousness as something simple. Others, in contesting with good reason the simplicity of this phenomenon, at the same time denied its unity. The former could not maintain a consistent position because, as soon as they described their inner life, they found that they were mentioning a large variety of different elements; and the latter could not avoid involuntarily testifying to the unity of mental phenomena. They speak, as do others, of an "I" and not of a "we" and sometimes describe this as a "bundle" of phenomena, and at the other times by other names which characterize a fusion into an inner unity. When we perceive color, sound, warmth, odor simultaneously nothing prevents us from assigning each one to a particular thing. On the other hand, we are forced to take the multiplicity of the various acts of sensing, such as seeing, hearing, experiencing warmth and smelling, and the simultaneous acts of willing and feeling and reflecting, as well as the inner perception which provides us with the knowledge of all those, as parts of one single phenomenon in which they are contained, as one single and unified thing. We shall discuss in detail

---

[13] *Principles of Psychology,* p. 398. Drobisch likewise says that it is a "fact that many series of ideas can pass simultaneously through consciousness, but, as it were, at different levels."

later on what constitutes the basis for this necessity. At that time we shall also present several other points pertaining to the same subject. The topic under discussion, in fact, is nothing other than the so-called unity of consciousness, one of the most important, but still contested, facts of psychology.

9. Let us, in conclusion, summarize the results of the discussion about the difference between mental and physical phenomena. First of all, we illustrated the specific nature of the two classes by means of *examples.* We then defined mental phenomena as *presentations* or as phenomena which are based *upon presentation;* all the other phenomena being physical phenomena. Next we spoke of *extension,* which psychologists have asserted to be the specific characteristic of all physical phenomena, while all mental phenomena are supposed to be unextended. This assertion, however, ran into contradictions which can only be clarified by later investigations. All that can be determined now is that all mental phenomena really appear to be unextended. Further we found that the *intentional in-existence,* the reference to something as an object, is a distinguishing characteristic of all mental phenomena. No physical phenomenon exhibits anything similar. We went on to define mental phenomena as the exclusive *object of inner perception;* they alone, therefore, are perceived with immediate evidence. Indeed, in the strict sense of the word, they alone are perceived. On this basis we proceeded to define them as the only phenomena which possess *actual existence* in addition to intentional existence. Finally, we emphasized as a distinguishing characteristic the fact that the mental phenomena which we perceive, in spite of all their multiplicity, *always* appear to us *as a unity,* while physical phenomena, which we perceive at the same time, do not all appear in the same way as parts of one single phenomenon.

That feature which best characterizes mental phenomena is undoubtedly their intentional in-existence. By means of this and the other characteristics listed above, we may now consider mental phenomena to have been clearly differentiated from physical phenomena.

Our explanations of mental and physical phenomena cannot fail to place our earlier definitions of psychology and natural science in a clearer light. In fact, we have stated that the one is the science of mental phenomena, and the other the science of physical phenomena. It is now easy to see that both definitions tacitly include certain limitations.

This is especially true of the definition of the natural sciences. These sciences do not deal with all physical phenomena, but only with those which appear in sensation, and as such do not take into account the phenomena of imagination. And even in regard to the former they only determine their laws insofar as they depend on the physical stimulation of the sense organs. We could express the scientific task of the natural sciences by saying something to the effect that they are those sciences which seek to explain the succession of physical phenomena connected with normal and pure sensations (that is, sensations which are not influenced by special mental conditions and processes) on the basis of the assumption of a world which resembles one which has three dimensional extension in space and flows in *one* direction in time, and which influences our sense organs. Without explaining the absolute nature of this world, these sciences

would limit themselves to ascribing to its forces capable of producing sensations and of exerting a reciprocal influence upon one another, and determining for these forces the laws of co-existence and succession. Through these laws they would then establish indirectly the laws of succession of the physical phenomena of sensations, if, through scientific abstraction from the concomitant mental conditions, we admit that they manifest themselves in a pure state and as occurring in relation to a constant sensory capacity. We must interpret the expression "science of physical phenomena" in this somewhat complicated way if we want to identify it with natural science.

We have nevertheless seen how the expression "physical phenomenon" is sometimes erroneously applied to the above mentioned forces themselves. And, since normally the object of a science is characterized as that object whose laws such a science determines directly and explicitly, I believe I will not be mistaken if I assume that the definition of natural science as the science of physical phenomena is frequently connected with the concept of forces belonging to a world which is similar to one extended in space and flowing in time; forces which, through their influence on the sense organs, arouse sensation and mutually influence each other in their action, and of which natural science investigates the laws of co-existence and succession. If those forces are considered as the object of natural sciences, there is also the advantage that this science appears to have as its object something that really and truly exists. This could, of course, also be attained if natural science were defined as the science of sensation, tacitly adding the same restriction which we have just mentioned. Indeed, the reason why the expression "physical phenomenon" is preferred probably stems from the fact that certain psychologists have thought that the external causes of sensations correspond to the physical phenomena which occur in them, either in all respects, which was the original point of view, or at least in respect to three-dimensional extension, which is the opinion of certain people at the present time. It is clear that the otherwise improper expression "external perception" stems from this conception. It must be added, however, that the act of sensing manifests, in addition to the intentional in-existence of the physical phenomenon, other characteristics with which the natural scientist is not at all concerned, since through them sensation does not give us information in the same way about the distinctive relationships which govern the external world.

With respect to the definition of psychology, it might first seem as if the concept of mental phenomena would have to be broadened rather than narrowed, both because the physical phenomena of imagination fall within its scope at least as much as mental phenomena as previously defined, and because the phenomena which occur in sensation cannot be disregarded in the theory of sensation. It is obvious, however, that they are taken into account only as the content of mental phenomena when we describe the specific characteristics of the latter. The same is true of all mental phenomena which have a purely phenomenal existence. We must consider only mental phenomena in the sense of real states as the proper object of psychology. And it is in reference only to these phenomena that we say that psychology is the science of mental phenomena.

56

Behaviorism

B. F. SKINNER

For biographical information about B. F. Skinner, see reading 41.

In these excerpts from Science and Human Behavior, *Skinner presents a comprehensive account of the theory of behaviorism and argues for the superiority of his approach to various other ways of understanding "mental phenomena." Skinner claims that it is both unscientific and fruitless to try to explain human behavior by reference to inner causes—thoughts or neural activity, for example. Instead we should seek the causes of human behavior outside the individual in the environment. Skinner maintains that all human behavior can be explained by reference to three different stimulus-response relations. A narrow range of human behaviors, such as tearing in the presence of onions, can be described as "unconditioned reflexes." These activities are simply automatic, untrained responses to the presence of certain stimuli. A somewhat wider class of behaviors is accurately described as "conditioned reflexes." The best known ixample is the salivation evoked in Pavlov's dogs by the ringing of a bell, after the bell-ringing had been paired with the natural or unconditioned stimulus of food. According to Skinner, the vast majority of human behavior is the result of "operant conditioning." Operant conditioning takes place when a particular behavior is rewarded or "reinforced." So, for example, Skinner would account for the fact that you are studying philosophy not by reference to your desires or goals, but by looking back in your life history for occasions on which your family or your culture rewarded you for this type of activity.*

THE TERMS "cause" and "effect" are no longer widely used in science. They have been associated with so many theories of the structure and operation of the universe that they mean more than scientists want to say. The terms which replace them, however, refer to the same factual core. A "cause" becomes a "change in an independent variable" and an "effect" a "change in a dependent variable." The old "cause-and-effect connection" becomes a "functional relation." The new terms do not suggest *how* a cause causes its effect: they merely assert that different events tend to occur together in a certain order. This is important, but it is not crucial. There is no particular danger in using "cause" and "effect" in an informal discussion if we are always ready to substitute their more exact counterparts.

We are concerned, then, with the causes of human behavior. We want to know why men behave as they do. Any condition or event which can be shown to have an effect upon behavior must be taken into account. By discovering

and analyzing these causes we can predict behavior; to the extent that we can manipulate them, we can control behavior.

There is a curious inconsistency in the zeal with which the doctrine of personal freedom has been defended, because men have always been fascinated by the search for causes. The spontaneity of human behavior is apparently no more challenging than its "why and wherefore." So strong is the urge to explain behavior that men have been led to anticipate legitimate scientific inquiry and to construct highly implausible theories of causation. This practice is not unusual in the history of science. The study of any subject begins in the realm of superstition. The fanciful explanation precedes the valid. Astronomy began as astrology; chemistry as alchemy. The field of behavior has had, and still has, its astrologers and alchemists. A long history of prescientific explanation furnishes us with a fantastic array of causes which have no function other than to supply spurious answers to questions which must otherwise go unanswered in the early stages of a science.

. . .

Inner "Causes"

Every science has at some time or other looked for causes of action inside the things it has studied. Sometimes the practice has proved useful, sometimes it has not. There is nothing wrong with an inner explanation as such, but events which are located inside a system are likely to be difficult to observe. For this reason we are encouraged to assign properties to them without justification. Worse still, we can invent causes of this sort without fear of contradiction. The motion of a rolling stone was once attributed to its *vis viva*. The chemical properties of bodies were thought to be derived from the *principles* or *essences* of which they were composed. Combustion was explained by the *phlogiston* inside the combustible object. Wounds healed and bodies grew well because of a *vis medicatrix*. It has been especially tempting to attribute the behavior of a living organism to the behavior of an inner agent, as the following examples may suggest.

Neural Causes. The layman uses the nervous system as a ready explanation of behavior. The English language contains hundreds of expressions which imply such a causal relationship. At the end of a long trial we read that the jury shows signs of *brain fag,* that the *nerves* of the accused are *on edge,* that the wife of the accused is on the verge of a *nervous breakdown,* and that his lawyer is generally thought to have lacked the *brains* needed to stand up to the prosecution. Obviously, no direct observations have been made of the nervous systems of any of these people. Their "brains" and "nerves" have been invented on the spur of the moment to lend substance to what might otherwise seem a superficial account of their behavior.

. . .

Eventually a science of the nervous system based upon direct observation rather than inference will describe the neural states and events which immediately precede instances of behavior. We shall know the precise neurological

conditions which immediately precede, say, the response, "No, thank you." These events in turn will be found to be preceded by other neurological events, and these in turn by others. This series will lead us back to events outside the nervous system and, eventually, outside the organism. In the chapters which follow we shall consider external events of this sort in some detail. We shall then be better able to evaluate the place of neurological explanations of behavior. However, we may note here that we do not have and may never have this sort of neurological information at the moment it is needed in order to predict a specific instance of behavior. It is even more unlikely that we shall be able to alter the nervous system directly in order to set up the antecedent conditions of a particular instance. The causes to be sought in the nervous system are, therefore, of limited usefulness in the prediction and control of specific behavior.

Psychic inner causes. An even more common practice is to explain behavior in terms of an inner agent which lacks physical dimensions and is called "mental" or "psychic." The purest form of the psychic explanation is seen in the animism of primitive peoples. From the immobility of the body after death it is inferred that a spirit responsible for movement has departed. The *enthusiastic* person is, as the etymology of the word implies, energized by a "god within." It is only a modest refinement to attribute every feature of the behavior of the physical organism to a corresponding feature of the "mind" or of some inner "personality." The inner man is regarded as driving the body very much as the man at the steering wheel drives a car. The inner man wills an action, the outer executes it. The inner loses his appetite, the outer stops eating. The inner man wants and the outer gets. The inner has the impulse which the outer obeys.

It is not the layman alone who resorts to these practices, for many reputable psychologists use a similar dualistic system of explanation. The inner man is sometimes personified clearly, as when delinquent behavior is attributed to a "disordered personality," or he may be dealt with in fragments, as when behavior is attributed to mental processes, faculties, and traits. Since the inner man does not occupy space, he may be multiplied at will. It has been argued that a single physical organism is controlled by several psychic agents and that its behavior is the resultant of their several wills. The Freudian concepts of the ego, superego, and id are often used in this way. They are frequently regarded as nonsubstantial creatures, often in violent conflict, whose defeats or victories lead to the adjusted or maladjusted behavior of the physical organism in which they reside.

Direct observation of the mind comparable with the observation of the nervous system has not proved feasible. It is true that many people believe that they observe their "mental states" just as the physiologist observes neural events, but another interpretation of what they observe is possible. . . . Introspective psychology no longer pretends to supply direct information about events which are the causal antecedents, rather than the mere accompaniments, of behavior. It defines its "subjective" events in ways which strip them of any usefulness in a causal analysis. The events appealed to in early mentalistic explanations of behavior have remained beyond the reach of observation. Freud insisted upon

this by emphasizing the role of the unconscious—a frank recognition that important mental processes are not directly observable. The Freudian literature supplies many examples of behavior from which unconscious wishes, impulses, instincts, and emotions are inferred. Unconscious thought-processes have also been used to explain intellectual achievements. Though the mathematician may feel that he knows "how he thinks," he is often unable to give a coherent account of the mental processes leading to the solution of a specific problem. But any mental event which is unconscious is necessarily inferential, and the explanation is therefore not based upon independent observations of a valid cause.

The fictional nature of this form of inner cause is shown by the ease with which the mental process is discovered to have just the properties needed to account for the behavior. When a professor turns up in the wrong classroom or gives the wrong lecture, it is because his *mind* is, at least for the moment, *absent*. If he forgets to give a reading assignment, it is because it has slipped his *mind* (a hint from the class may *remind* him of it). He begins to tell an old joke but pauses for a moment, and it is evident to everyone that he is trying to make up his *mind* whether or not he has already used the joke that term. His lectures grow more tedious with the years, and questions from the class confuse him more and more, because his *mind* is failing. What he says is often disorganized because his *ideas* are confused. He is occasionally unnecessarily emphatic because of the force of his *ideas*. When he repeats himself, it is because he has an *idée fixe;* and when he repeats what others have said, it is because he borrows his *ideas*. Upon occasion there is nothing in what he says because he lacks *ideas*. In all this it is obvious that the mind and the ideas, together with their special characteristics, are being invented on the spot to provide spurious explanations. A science of behavior can hope to gain very little from so cavalier a practice. Since mental or psychic events are asserted to lack the dimensions of physical science, we have an additional reason for rejecting them.

Conceptual inner causes. The commonest inner causes have no specific dimensions at all, either neurological or psychic. When we say that a man eats *because* he is hungry, smokes a great deal *because* he has the tobacco habit, fights *because* of the instinct of pugnacity, behaves brilliantly *because* of his intelligence, or plays the piano well *because* of his musical ability, we seem to be referring to causes. But on analysis these phrases prove to be merely redundant descriptions. A single set of facts is described by the two statements: "He eats" and "He is hungry." A single set of facts is described by the two statements: "He smokes a great deal" and "He has the smoking habit." A single set of facts is described by the two statements: "He plays well" and "He has musical ability." The practice of explaining one statement in terms of the other is dangerous because it suggests that we have found the cause and therefore need search no further. Moreover, such terms as "hunger," "habit," and "intelligence" convert what are essentially the properties of a process or relation into what appear to be things. Thus we are unprepared for the properties eventually to be discovered in the behavior itself and continue to look for something which may not exist.

The Variables of Which Behavior is a Function

The practice of looking inside the organism for an explanation of behavior has tended to obscure the variables which are immediately available for a scientific analysis. These variables lie outside the organism, in its immediate environment and in its environmental history. They have a physical status to which the usual techniques of science are adapted, and they make it possible to explain behavior as other subjects are explained in science. These independent variables are of many sorts and their relations to behavior are often subtle and complex, but we cannot hope to give an adequate account of behavior without analyzing them.

Consider the act of drinking a glass of water. This is not likely to be an important bit of behavior in anyone's life, but it supplies a convenient example. We may describe the topography of the behavior in such a way that a given instance may be identified quite accurately by any qualified observer. Suppose now we bring someone into a room and place a glass of water before him. Will he drink? There appear to be only two possibilities: either he will or he will not. But we speak of the *chances* that he will drink, and this notion may be refined for scientific use. What we want to evaluate is the *probability* that he will drink. This may range from virtual certainty that drinking will occur to virtual certainty that it will not. The very considerable problem of how to measure such a probability will be discussed later. For the moment, we are interested in how the probability may be increased or decreased.

Everyday experience suggests several possibilities, and laboratory and clinical observations have added others. It is decidedly not true that a horse may be led to water but cannot be made to drink. By arranging a history of severe deprivation we could be "absolutely sure" that drinking would occur. In the same way we may be sure that the glass of water in our experiment will be drunk. Although we are not likely to arrange them experimentally, deprivations of the necessary magnitude sometimes occur outside the laboratory. We may obtain an effect similar to that of deprivation by speeding up the excretion of water. For example, we may induce sweating by raising the temperature of the room or by forcing heavy exercise, or we may increase the excretion of urine by mixing salt or urea in food taken prior to the experiment. It is also well known that loss of blood, as on a battlefield, sharply increases the probability of drinking. On the other hand, we may set the probability at virtually zero by inducing or forcing our subject to drink a large quantity of water before the experiment.

If we are to predict whether or not our subject will drink, we must know as much as possible about these variables. If we are to induce him to drink, we must be able to manipulate them. In both cases, moreover, either for accurate prediction or control, we must investigate the effect of each variable quantitatively with the methods and techniques of a laboratory science.

Other variables may, of course, affect the result. Our subject may be "afraid" that something has been added to the water as a practical joke or for experi-

mental purposes. He may even "suspect" that the water has been poisoned. He may have grown up in a culture in which water is drunk only when no one is watching. He may refuse to drink simply to prove that we cannot predict or control his behavior. These possibilities do not disprove the relations between drinking and the variables listed in the preceding paragraphs; they simply remind us that other variables may have to be taken into account. We must know the history of our subject with respect to the behavior of drinking water, and if we cannot eliminate social factors from the situation, then we must know the history of his personal relations to people resembling the experimenter. Adequate prediction in any science requires information about all relevant variables, and the control of a subject matter for practical purposes makes the same demands.

Other types of "explanation" do not permit us to dispense with these requirements or to fulfill them in any easier way. It is of no help to be told that our subject will drink provided he was born under a particular sign of the zodiac which shows a preoccupation with water or provided he is the lean and thirsty type or was, in short, "born thirsty." Explanations in terms of inner states or agents, however, may require some further comment. To what extent is it helpful to be told, "He drinks because he is thirsty"? If to be thirsty means nothing more than to have a tendency to drink, this is mere redundancy. If it means that he drinks because of a state of thirst, an inner causal event is invoked. If this state is purely inferential—if no dimensions are assigned to it which would make direct observation possible—it cannot serve as an explanation. But if it has physiological or psychic properties, what role can it play in a science of behavior?

The physiologist may point out that several ways of raising the probability of drinking have a common effect: they increase the concentration of solutions in the body. Through some mechanism not yet well understood, this may bring about a corresponding change in the nervous system which in turn makes drinking more probable. In the same way, it may be argued that all these operations make the organism "feel thirsty" or "want a drink" and that such a psychic state also acts upon the nervous system in some unexplained way to induce drinking. In each case we have a causal chain consisting of three links: (1) an operation performed upon the organism from without—for example, water deprivation; (2) an inner condition—for example, physiological or psychic thirst; and (3) a kind of behavior—for example, drinking. Independent information about the second link would obviously permit us to predict the third without recourse to the first. It would be a preferred type of variable because it would be non-historic; the first link may lie in the past history of the organism, but the second is a current condition. Direct information about the second link is, however, seldom, if ever, available. Sometimes we infer the second link from the third: an animal is judged to be thirsty if it drinks. In that case, the explanation is spurious. Sometimes we infer the second link from the first: an animal is said to be thirsty if it has not drunk for a long time. In that case, we obviously cannot dispense with the prior history.

The second link is useless in the *control* of behavior unless we can manipulate it. At the moment, we have no way of directly altering neural processes at appropriate moments in the life of a behaving organism, nor has any way been discovered to alter a psychic process. We usually set up the second link through the first: we make an animal thirsty, in either the physiological or the psychic sense, by depriving it of water, feeding it salt, and so on. In that case, the second link obviously does not permit us to dispense with the first. Even if some new technical discovery were to enable us to set up or change the second link directly, we should still have to deal with those enormous areas in which human behavior is controlled through manipulation of the first link. A technique of operating upon the second link would increase our control of behavior, but the techniques which have already been developed would still remain to be analyzed.

The most objectionable practice is to follow the causal sequence back only as far as a hypothetical second link. This is a serious handicap both in a theoretical science and in the practical control of behavior. It is no help to be told that to get an organism to drink we are simply to "make it thirsty" unless we are also told how this is to be done. When we have obtained the necessary prescription for thirst, the whole proposal is more complex than it need be. Similarly, when an example of maladjusted behavior is explained by saying that the individual is "suffering from anxiety," we have still to be told the cause of the anxiety. But the external conditions which are then invoked could have been directly related to the maladjusted behavior. Again, when we are told that a man stole a loaf of bread because "he was hungry," we have still to learn of the external conditions responsible for the "hunger." These conditions would have sufficed to explain the theft.

The objection to inner states is not that they do not exist, but that they are not relevant in a functional analysis. We cannot account for the behavior of any system while staying wholly inside it; eventually we must turn to forces operating upon the organism from without. Unless there is a weak spot in our causal chain so that the second link is not lawfully determined by the first, or the third by the second, then the first and third links must be lawfully related. If we must always go back beyond the second link for prediction and control, we may avoid many tiresome and exhausting digressions by examining the third link as a function of the first. Valid information about the second link may throw light upon this relationship but can in no way alter it.

A Functional Analysis

The external variables of which behavior is a function provide for what may be called a causal or functional analysis. We undertake to predict and control the behavior of the individual organism. This is our "dependent variable"— the effect for which we are to find the cause. Our "independent variables"— the causes of behavior—are the external conditions of which behavior is a function. Relations between the two—the "cause-and-effect relationships" in

behavior—are the laws of a science. A synthesis of these laws expressed in quantitative terms yields a comprehensive picture of the organism as a behaving system.

This must be done within the bounds of a natural science. We cannot assume that behavior has any peculiar properties which require unique methods or special kinds of knowledge. It is often argued that an act is not so important as the "intent" which lies behind it, or that it can be described only in terms of what it "means" to the behaving individual or to others whom it may affect. If statements of this sort are useful for scientific purposes, they must be based upon observable events, and we may confine ourselves to such events exclusively in a functional analysis. We shall see later that although such terms as "meaning" and "intent" appear to refer to properties of behavior, they usually conceal references to independent variables. This is also true of "aggressive," "friendly," "disorganized," "intelligent," and other terms which appear to describe properties of behavior but in reality refer to its controlling relations.

The independent variables must also be described in physical terms. An effort is often made to avoid the labor of analyzing a physical situation by guessing what it "means" to an organism or by distinguishing between the physical world and a psychological world of "experience." This practice also reflects a confusion between dependent and independent variables. The events affecting an organism must be capable of description in the language of physical science. It is sometimes argued that certain "social forces" or the "influences" of culture or tradition are exceptions. But we cannot appeal to entities of this sort without explaining how they can affect both the scientist and the individual under observation. The physical events which must then be appealed to in such an explanation will supply us with alternative material suitable for a physical analysis.

. . .

Reflex Action

Descartes had taken an important step in suggesting that some of the spontaneity of living creatures was only apparent and that behavior could sometimes be traced to action from without. The first clear-cut evidence that he had correctly surmised the possibility of external control came two centuries later in the discovery that the tail of a salamander would move when part of it was touched or pierced, even though the tail had been severed from the body. Facts of this sort are now familiar, and we have long since adapted our beliefs to take them into account. At the time the discovery was made, however, it created great excitement. It was felt to be a serious threat to prevailing theories of the inner agents responsible for behavior. If the movement of the amputated tail could be controlled by external forces, was its behavior when attached to the salamander of a different nature? If not, what about the inner causes which had hitherto been used to account for it? It was seriously suggested as an answer that the "will" must be coexistent with the body and that some part of it must invest any amputated part. But the fact remained that an external event had

been identified which could be substituted, as in Descartes's daring hypothesis, for the inner explanation.

The external agent came to be called a *stimulus*. The behavior controlled by it came to be called a *response*. Together they comprised what was called a *reflex*—on the theory that the disturbance caused by the stimulus passed to the central nervous system and was "reflected" back to the muscles. It was soon found that similar external causes could be demonstrated in the behavior of larger portions of the organism—for example, in the body of a frog, cat, or dog in which the spinal cord had been severed at the neck. Reflexes including parts of the brain were soon added, and it is now common knowledge that in the intact organism many kinds of stimulation lead to almost inevitable reactions of the same reflex nature. Many characteristics of the relation have been studied quantitatively. The time which elapses between stimulus and response (the "latency") has been measured precisely. The magnitude of the response has been studied as a function of the intensity of the stimulus. Other conditions of the organism have been found to be important in completing the account— for example, a reflex may be "fatigued" by repeated rapid elicitation.

The reflex was at first closely identified with hypothetical neural events in the so-called "reflex arc." A surgical division of the organism was a necessary entering wedge, for it provided a simple and dramatic method of analyzing behavior. But surgical analysis became unnecessary as soon as the principle of the stimulus was understood and as soon as techniques were discovered for handling complex arrangements of variables in other ways. By eliminating some conditions, holding others constant, and varying others in an orderly manner, basic lawful relations could be established without dissection and could be expressed without neurological theories.

The extension of the principle of the reflex to include behavior involving more and more of the organism was made only in the face of vigorous opposition. The reflex nature of the spinal animal was challenged by proponents of a "spinal will." The evidence they offered in support of a residual inner cause consisted of behavior which apparently could not be explained wholly in terms of stimuli. When higher parts of the nervous system were added, and when the principle was eventually extended to the intact organism, the same pattern of resistance was followed. But arguments for spontaneity, and for the explanatory entities which spontaneity seems to demand, are of such form that they must retreat before the accumulating facts. Spontaneity is negative evidence; it points to the weakness of a current scientific explanation, but does not in itself prove an alternative version. By its very nature, spontaneity must yield ground as a scientific analysis is able to advance. As more and more of the behavior of the organism has come to be explained in terms of stimuli, the territory held by inner explanations has been reduced. The "will" has retreated up the spinal cord, through the lower and then the higher parts of the brain, and finally, with the conditioned reflex, has escaped through the front of the head. At each stage, some part of the control of the organism has passed from a hypothetical inner entity to the external environment.

The Range of Reflex Action

A certain part of behavior, then, is elicited by stimuli, and our prediction of that behavior is especially precise. When we flash a light in the eye of a normal subject, the pupil contracts. When he sips lemon juice, saliva is secreted. When we raise the temperature of the room to a certain point, the small blood vessels in his skin enlarge, blood is brought nearer to the skin, and he "turns red." We use these relations for many practical purposes. When it is necessary to induce vomiting, we employ a suitable stimulus—an irritating fluid or a finger in the throat. The actress who must cry real tears resorts to onion juice on her handkerchief.

As these examples suggest, many reflex responses are executed by the "smooth muscles" (for example, the muscles in the walls of the blood vessels) and the glands. These structures are particularly concerned with the internal economy of the organism. They are most likely to be of interest in a science of behavior in the emotional reflexes to be discussed in Chapter X. Other reflexes use the "striped muscles" which move the skeletal frame of the organism. The "knee jerk" and other reflexes which the physician uses for diagnostic purposes are examples. We maintain our posture, either when standing still or moving about, with the aid of a complex network of such reflexes.

In spite of the importance suggested by these examples, it is still true that if we were to assemble all the behavior which falls into the pattern of the simple reflex, we should have only a very small fraction of the total behavior of the organism. This is not what early investigators in the field expected. We now see that the principle of the reflex was overworked. The exhilarating discovery of the stimulus led to exaggerated claims. It is neither plausible nor expedient to conceive of the organism as a complicated jack-in-the-box with a long list of tricks, each of which may be evoked by pressing the proper button. The greater part of the behavior of the intact organism is not under this primitive sort of stimulus control. The environment affects the organism in many ways which are not conveniently classed as "stimuli," and even in the field of stimulation only a small part of the forces acting upon the organism elicit responses in the invariable manner of reflex action. To ignore the principle of the reflex entirely, however, would be equally unwarranted.

Conditioned Reflexes

. . .

The difference between an unskilled conjecture and a scientific fact is not simply a difference in evidence. It had long been known that a child might cry before it was hurt or that a fox might salivate upon seeing a bunch of grapes. What Pavlov added can be understood most clearly by considering his history. Originally he was interested in the process of digestion, and he studied the conditions under which digestive juices were secreted. Various chemical substances in the mouth or in the stomach resulted in the reflex action of the

digestive glands. Pavlov's work was sufficiently outstanding to receive the Nobel Prize, but it was by no means complete. He was handicapped by a certain unexplained secretion. Although food in the mouth might elicit a flow of saliva, saliva often flowed abundantly when the mouth was empty. We should not be surprised to learn that this was called "psychic secretion." It was explained in terms which "any child could understand." Perhaps the dog was "thinking about food." Perhaps the sight of the experimenter preparing for the next experiment "reminded" the dog of the food it had received in earlier experiments. But these explanations did nothing to bring the unpredictable salivation within the compass of a rigorous account of digestion.

Pavlov's first step was to control conditions so that "psychic secretion" largely disappeared. He designed a room in which contact between dog and experimenter was reduced to a minimum. The room was made as free as possible from incidental stimuli. The dog could not hear the sound of footsteps in neighboring rooms or smell accidental odors in the ventilating system. Pavlov then built up a "psychic secretion" step by step. In place of the complicated stimulus of an experimenter preparing a syringe or filling a dish with food, he introduced controllable stimuli which could be easily described in physical terms. In place of the accidental occasions upon which stimulation might precede or accompany food, Pavlov arranged precise schedules in which controllable stimuli and food were presented in certain orders. Without influencing the dog in any other way, he could sound a tone and insert food into the dog's mouth. In this way he was able to show that the tone *acquired* its ability to elicit secretion, and he was also able to follow the process through which this came about. Once in possession of these facts, he could then give a satisfactory account of all secretion. He had replaced the "psyche" of psychic secretion with certain objective facts in the recent history of the organism.

The process of conditioning, as Pavlov reported it in his book *Conditioned Reflexes,* is a process of *stimulus substitution.* A previously neutral stimulus acquires the power to elicit a response which was originally elicited by another stimulus. The change occurs when the neutral stimulus is followed or "reinforced" by the effective stimulus. Pavlov studied the effect of the interval of time elapsing between stimulus and reinforcement. He investigated the extent to which various properties of stimuli could acquire control. He also studied the converse process, in which the conditioned stimulus loses its power to evoke the response when it is no longer reinforced—a process which he called "extinction."

The quantitative properties which he discovered are by no means "known to every child." And they are important. The most efficient use of conditioned reflexes in the practical control of behavior often requires quantitative information. A satisfactory theory makes the same demands. In dispossessing explanatory fictions, for example, we cannot be sure that an event of the sort implied by "psychic secretion" is not occasionally responsible until we can predict the exact amount of secretion at any given time. Only a quantitative description will make sure that there is no additional mental process in which the dog "associates the sound of the tone with the idea of food" or in which

it salivates because it "expects" food to appear. Pavlov could dispense with concepts of this sort only when he could give a complete quantitative account of salivation in terms of the stimulus, the response, and the history of conditioning.

Pavlov, as a physiologist, was interested in how the stimulus was converted into neural processes and in how other processes carried the effect through the nervous system to the muscles and glands. The subtitle of his book is *An Investigation of the Physiological Activity of the Cerebral Cortex*. The "physiological activity" was inferential. We may suppose, however, that comparable processes will eventually be described in terms appropriate to neural events. Such a description will fill in the temporal and spatial gaps between an earlier history of conditioning and its current result. The additional account will be important in the integration of scientific knowledge but will not make the relation between stimulus and response any more lawful or any more useful in prediction and control. Pavlov's achievement was the discovery, not of neural processes, but of important quantitative relations which permit us, regardless of neurological hypotheses, to give a direct account of behavior in the field of the conditioned reflex.

. . .

The Range of Conditioned Reflexes

Although the process of conditioning greatly extends the scope of the eliciting stimulus, it does not bring all the behavior of the organism within such stimulus control. According to the formula of stimulus substitution we must elicit a response before we can condition it. All conditioned reflexes are, therefore, based upon unconditioned reflexes. But we have seen that reflex responses are only a small part of the total behavior of the organism. Conditioning adds new controlling stimuli, but not new responses. In using the principle, therefore, we are not subscribing to a "conditioned-reflex theory" of all behavior.

. . .

Learning Curves

One of the first serious attempts to study the changes brought about by the consequences of behavior was made by E. L. Thorndike in 1898. His experiments arose from a controversy which was then of considerable interest. Darwin, in insisting upon the continuity of species, had questioned the belief that man was unique among the animals in his ability to think. Anecdotes in which lower animals seemed to show the "power of reasoning" were published in great numbers. But when terms which had formerly been applied only to human behavior were thus extended, certain questions arose concerning their meaning. Did the observed facts point to mental processes, or could these apparent evidences of thinking be explained in other ways? Eventually it became clear that the assumption of inner thought-processes was not required. Many years were to pass before the same question was seriously raised concerning human behavior, but Thorndike's experiments and his alternative explanation of reasoning in animals were important steps in that direction.

If a cat is placed in a box from which it can escape only by unlatching a door, it will exhibit many different kinds of behavior, some of which may be effective in opening the door. Thorndike found that when a cat was put into such a box again and again, the behavior which led to escape tended to occur sooner and sooner until eventually escape was as simple and quick as possible. The cat had solved its problem as well as if it were a "reasoning" human being, though perhaps not so speedily. Yet Thorndike observed no "thought-process" and argued that none was needed by way of explanation. He could describe his results simply by saying that a part of the cat's behavior was "stamped in" because it was followed by the opening of the door.

The fact that behavior is stamped in when followed by certain consequences, Thorndike called "The Law of Effect." What he had observed was that certain behavior occurred more and more readily in comparison with other behavior characteristic of the same situation. By noting the successive delays in getting out of the box and plotting them on a graph, he constructed a "learning curve." This early attempt to show a quantitative process in behavior, similar to the processes of physics and biology, was heralded as an important advance. It revealed a process which took place over a considerable period of time and which was not obvious to casual inspection. Thorndike, in short, had made a discovery. Many similar curves have since been recorded and have become the substance of chapters on learning in psychology texts.

Learning curves do not, however, describe the basic process of stamping in. Thorndike's measure—the time taken to escape—involved the elimination of other behavior, and his curve depended upon the number of different things a cat might do in a particular box. It also depended upon the behavior which the experimenter or the apparatus happened to select as "successful" and upon whether this was common or rare in comparison with other behavior evoked in the box. A learning curve obtained in this way might be said to reflect the properties of the latch box rather than of the behavior of the cat. The same is true of many other devices developed for the study of learning. The various mazes through which white rats and other animals learn to run, the "choice boxes" in which animals learn to discriminate between properties or patterns of stimuli, the apparatuses which present sequences of material to be learned in the study of human memory—each of these yields its own type of learning curve.

By averaging many individual cases, we may make these curves as smooth as we like. Moreover, curves obtained under many different circumstances may agree in showing certain general properties. For example, when measured in this way, learning is generally "negatively accelerated"—improvement in performance occurs more and more slowly as the condition is approached in which further improvement is impossible. But it does not follow that negative acceleration is characteristic of the basic process. Suppose, by analogy, we fill a glass jar with gravel which has been so well mixed that pieces of any given size are evenly distributed. We then agitate the jar gently and watch the pieces rearrange themselves. The larger move toward the top, the smaller toward the bottom. This process, too, is negatively accelerated. At first the mixture separates rap-

idly, but as separation proceeds, the condition in which there will be no further change is approached more and more slowly. Such a curve may be quite smooth and reproducible, but this fact alone is not of any great significance. The curve is the result of certain fundamental processes involving the contact of spheres of different sizes, the resolution of the forces resulting from agitation, and so on, but it is by no means the most direct record of these processes.

Learning curves show how the various kinds of behavior evoked in complex situations are sorted out, emphasized, and reordered. The basic process of the stamping in of a single act brings this change about, but it is not reported directly by the change itself.

Operant Conditioning

To get at the core of Thorndike's Law of Effect, we need to clarify the notion of "probability of response." This is an extremely important concept; unfortunately, it is also a difficult one. In discussing human behavior, we often refer to "tendencies" or "predispositions" to behave in particular ways. Almost every theory of behavior uses some such term as "excitatory potential," "habit strength," or "determining tendency." But how do we observe a tendency? And how can we measure one?

If a given sample of behavior existed in only two states, in one of which it always occurred and in the other never, we should be almost helpless in following a program of functional analysis. An all-or-none subject matter lends itself only to primitive forms of description. It is a great advantage to suppose instead that the *probability* that a response will occur ranges continuously between these all-or-none extremes. We can then deal with variables which, unlike the eliciting stimulus, do not "cause a given bit of behavior to occur" but simply make the occurrence more probable. We may then proceed to deal, for example, with the combined effect of more than one such variable.

The everyday expressions which carry the notion of probability, tendency, or predisposition describe the frequencies with which bits of behavior occur. We never observe a probability as such. We say that someone is "enthusiastic" about bridge when we observe that he plays bridge often and talks about it often. To be "greatly interested" in music is to play, listen to, and talk about music a good deal. The "inveterate" gambler is one who gambles frequently. The camera "fan" is to be found taking pictures, developing them, and looking at pictures made by himself and others. The "highly sexed" person frequently engages in sexual behavior. The "dipsomaniac" drinks frequently.

In characterizing a man's behavior in terms of frequency, we assume certain standard conditions: he must be able to execute and repeat a given act, and other behavior must not interfere appreciably. We cannot be sure of the extent of a man's interest in music, for example, if he is necessarily busy with other things. When we come to refine the notion of probability of response for scientific use, we find that here, too, our data are frequencies and that the conditions under which they are observed must be specified. The main technical problem in designing a controlled experiment is to provide for the observation

and interpretation of frequencies. We eliminate, or at least hold constant, any condition which encourages behavior which competes with the behavior we are to study. An organism is placed in a quiet box where its behavior may be observed through a one-way screen or recorded mechanically. This is by no means an environmental vacuum, but the organism will react to the features of the box in many ways; but its behavior will eventually reach a fairly stable level, against which the frequency of a selected response may be investigated.

To study the process which Thorndike called stamping in, we must have a "consequence." Giving food to a hungry organism will do. We can feed our subject conveniently with a small food tray which is operated electrically. When the tray is first opened, the organism will probably react to it in ways which interfere with the process we plan to observe. Eventually, after being fed from the tray repeatedly, it eats readily, and we are then ready to make this consequence contingent upon behavior and to observe the result.

We select a relatively simple bit of behavior which may be freely and rapidly repeated, and which is easily observed and recorded. If our experimental subject is a pigeon, for example, the behavior of raising the head above a given height is convenient. This may be observed by sighting across the pigeon's head at a scale pinned on the far wall of the box. We first study the height at which the head is normally held and select some line on the scale which is reached only infrequently. Keeping our eye on the scale we then begin to open the food tray very quickly whenever the head rises above the line. If the experiment is conducted according to specifications, the result is invariable: we observe an immediate change in the frequency with which the head crosses the line. We also observe, and this is of some importance theoretically, that higher lines are now being crossed. We may advance almost immediately to a higher line in determining when food is to be presented. In a minute or two, the bird's posture has changed so that the top of the head seldom falls below the line which we first chose.

When we demonstrate the process of stamping in in this relatively simple way, we see that certain common interpretations of Thorndike's experiment are superfluous. The expression "trial-and-error learning," which is frequently associated with the Law of Effect, is clearly out of place here. We are reading something into our observations when we call any upward movement of the head a "trial," and there is no reason to call any movement which does not achieve a specified consequence an "error." Even the term "learning" is misleading. The statement that the bird "learns that it will get food by stretching its neck" is an inaccurate report of what has happened. To say that it has acquired the "habit" of stretching its neck is merely to resort to an explanatory fiction, since our only evidence of the habit is the acquired tendency to perform the act. The barest possible statement of the process is this: we make a given consequence contingent upon certain physical properties of behavior (the upward movement of the head), and the behavior is then observed to increase in frequency.

It is customary to refer to any movement of the organism as a "response." The word is borrowed from the field of reflex action and implies an act which, so to speak, answers a prior event—the stimulus. But we may make an event

contingent upon behavior without identifying, or being able to identify, a prior stimulus. We did not alter the environment of the pigeon to *elicit* the upward movement of the head. It is probably impossible to show that any single stimulus invariably precedes this movement. Behavior of this sort may come under the control of stimuli, but the relation is not that of elicitation. The term "response" is therefore not wholly appropriate but is so well established that we shall use it in the following discussion.

A response which has already occurred cannot, of course, be predicted or controlled. We can only predict that *similar* responses will occur in the future. The unit of a predictive science is, therefore, not a response but a class of responses. The word "operant" will be used to describe this class. The term emphasizes the fact that the behavior *operates* upon the environment to generate consequences. The consequences define the properties with respect to which responses are called similar. The term will be used both as an adjective (operant behavior) and as a noun to designate the behavior defined by a given consequence.

A single instance in which a pigeon raises its head is a *response*. It is a bit of history which may be reported in any frame of reference we wish to use. The behavior called "raising the head," regardless of when specific instances occur, is an *operant*. It can be described, not as an accomplished act, but rather as a set of acts defined by the property of the height to which the head is raised. In this sense an operant is defined by an effect which may be specified in physical terms; the "cutoff" at a certain height is a property of behavior.

The term "learning" may profitably be saved in its traditional sense to describe the reassortment of responses in a complex situation. Terms for the process of stamping in may be borrowed from Pavlov's analysis of the conditioned reflex. Pavlov himself called all events which strengthened behavior "reinforcement" and all the resulting changes "conditioning." In the Pavlovian experiment, however, a reinforcer is paired with a *stimulus;* whereas in operant behavior it is contingent upon a *response*. Operant reinforcement is therefore a separate process and requires a separate analysis. In both cases, the strengthening of behavior which results from reinforcement is appropriately called "conditioning." In operant conditioning we "strengthen" an operant in the sense of making a response more probable or, in actual fact, more frequent. In Pavlovian or "respondent" conditioning we simply increase the magnitude of the response elicited by the conditioned stimulus and shorten the time which elapses between stimulus and response. (We note, incidentally, that these two cases exhaust the possibilities: an organism is conditioned when a reinforcer [1] accompanies another stimulus or [2] follows upon the organism's own behavior. Any event which does neither has no effect in changing a probability of response.) In the pigeon experiment, then, food is the *reinforcer* and presenting food when a response is emitted is the *reinforcement*. The *operant* is defined by the property upon which reinforcement is contingent—the height to which the head must be raised. The change in frequency with which the head is lifted to this height is the process of *operant conditioning*.

While we are awake, we act upon the environment constantly, and many of

the consequences of our actions are reinforcing. Through operant conditioning the environment builds the basic repertoire with which we keep our balance, walk, play games, handle instruments and tools, talk, write, sail a boat, drive a car, or fly a plane. A change in the environment—a new car, a new friend, a new field of interest, a new job, a new location—may find us unprepared, but our behavior usually adjusts quickly as we acquire new responses and discard old. We shall see in the following chapter that operant reinforcement does more than build a behavioral repertoire. It improves the efficiency of behavior and maintains behavior in strength long after acquisition or efficiency has ceased to be of interest.

57

Skinner Skinned

DANIEL C. DENNETT

Daniel C. Dennett (b. 1942) is currently Professor of Philosophy at Tufts University. He is the author of two recent books in philosophy of mind: Content and Consciousness *and* Brainstorms.

In "Skinner Skinned" Dennett offers a sympathetic, but ultimately quite critical analysis of Skinner's theory of behaviorism (reading 56). Dennett's first task is to try to fathom the reasons behind Skinner's theory. In particular, Dennett focuses on the question of why Skinner rejects explanations of human behavior which appeal to mental processes. Dennett calls these explanations, which refer to things like the agent's beliefs, desires, reasonings, or reflections, "intentional explanations," or sometimes "mentalistic explanations." According to Dennett, Skinner has a fairly reasonable objection to this type of explanation. The objection is that mentalistic explanations are too easy and they do not increase our understanding. For example, if a friend were to ask, "Why are you reading this book?" and you were to answer, "Because I want to," your friend might well feel that not much of an explanation had been provided. Still, Dennett maintains, against Skinner, that the beginnings of an explanation have been given. For your answer does rule out some possibilities, for example, that you are reading this book because you believe it will make you rich, or because you believe that reading is a good way to lose weight. Dennett believes that Skinner would be right only if mentalistic explanations had to stop at this level—with wants, desires, and so on. Then the explanations would be almost useless. Dennett locates Skinner's error in the belief that mentalistic explanations must terminate at this superficial level. If we deepen the explanation by explaining, for example, what a want is and where it comes from, then the mentalistic explanation can be viewed as the first step in a serious and illuminating theory.

B. F. SKINNER has recently retired, after a long and distinguished career at Harvard, and for better or for worse it appears that the school of psychology he founded, Skinnerian behaviorism, is simultaneously retiring from the academic limelight. Skinner's army of enemies would like to believe, no doubt, that his doctrines are succumbing at last to their barrage of criticism and invective, but of course science doesn't behave like that, and the reasons for the decline in influence of behaviorism are at best only indirectly tied to the many attempts at its "refutation." We could soften the blow for Skinner, perhaps, by putting the unwelcome message in terms he favors: psychologists just don't find behaviorism very *reinforcing* these days. Skinner might thing that was

unfair, but if he demanded *reasons,* if he asked his critics to *justify* their refusal to follow his lead, he would have to violate his own doctrines and methods. Those of us who are not Skinnerians, on the other hand, can without inconsistency plumb the inner thought processes, reasons, motives, decisions and beliefs of both Skinner and his critics, and try to extract from them an analysis of what is wrong with Skinnerian behaviorism and why.

. . .

Although counting myself among Skinner's opponents, I want to try to avoid the familiar brawl and do something diagnostic. I want to show *how* Skinner goes astray, through a series of all too common slight errors. He misapplies some perfectly good principles (principles, by the way, that his critics have often failed to recognize); he misdescribes crucial distinctions by lumping them all together; and he lets wishful thinking cloud his vision—a familiar enough failure. In particular, I want to show the falsehood of what I take to be Skinner's central philosophical claim, on which all the others rest, and which he apparently derives from his vision of psychology. The claim is that *behavioral science proves that people are not free, dignified, morally responsible agents.* It is this claim that secures what few links there are between Skinner's science and his politics. I want to show how Skinner arrives at this mistaken claim, and show how tempting in fact the path is. I would like to proceed by setting out with as much care as I can the steps of Skinner's argument for the claim, but that is impossible, since Skinner does not present arguments—at least, not wittingly. He has an ill-concealed disdain for arguments, a bias he feeds by supposing that brute facts will sweep away the most sophisticated arguments, and that the brute facts are on his side. His impatience with arguments does not, of course, prevent him from relying on arguments, it just prevents him from seeing that he is doing this—and it prevents him from seeing that his brute facts of behavior are not facts at all, but depend on an interpretation of the data which in turn depends on an argument, which, finally, is fallacious. To get this phantom—but utterly central—argument out in the open will take a bit of reconstruction.

The first step in Skinner's argument is to characterize his enemy, "mentalism". He has a strong gut intuition that the *traditional* way of talking about and explaining human behavior—in "mentalistic" terms of a person's beliefs, desires, ideas, hopes, fears, feelings, emotions—is somehow utterly disqualified. This way of talking, he believes, is disqualified in the sense that not only is it not science as it stands; it could not be turned into science or used in science; it is inimical to science, would *have* to be in conflict with *any* genuine science of human behavior. Now the first thing one must come to understand is this antipathy of Skinner's for all things "mentalistic". Once one understands the antipathy, it is easy enough to see the boundaries of Skinner's enemy territory.

Skinner gives so many different reasons for disqualifying mentalism that we may be sure he has failed to hit the nail on the head—but he does get close to an important truth, and we can help him to get closer. Being a frugal Yankee, Skinner is reluctant to part with *any* reason, however unconvincing, for being

against mentalism, but he does disassociate himself from some of the traditional arguments of behaviorists and other anti-mentalists at least to the extent of calling them relatively unimportant. For instance, perhaps the most ancient and familiar worry about mentalism is the suspicion that

(1) mental things must be made of *non-physical* stuff

thus raising the familiar and apparently fatal problems of Cartesian inter-actionism. Skinner presents this worry,[1] only to downplay it,[2] but when all else fails, he is happy to lean on it.[3] More explicitly, Skinner rejects the common behaviorist claim that it is

(2) the *privacy* of the mental

in contrast to the public objectivity of the data of behavior that makes the mental so abhorrent to science. "It would be foolish to deny the existence of that private world, but it is also foolish to assert that because it is private it is of a different nature from the world outside."[4] This concession to privacy is not all that it appears, however, for his concept of privacy is not the usual one encountered in the literature. Skinner does not even consider the possibility that one's mental life might be *in principle* private, *non-contingently* inaccessible. That is, he supposes without argument that the only sort of privacy envisaged is the sort that could someday be dispelled by poking around in the brain, and since "the skin is not that important as a boundary",[5] what it hides is nothing science will not be able to handle when the time comes. So Skinner suggests he will *not* object to the privacy of mental events, since their privacy would be no obstacle to science. At the same time Skinner often seeks to discredit explanations that appeal to some inner thing "we cannot see", which seems a contradiction.[6] For if we read these as objections to what we cannot

---

[1] *Beyond Freedom and Dignity* (New York: Knopf, 1971), p. 11. See also Skinner's *About Behaviorism* (New York: Random House, 1974): p. 31: "Almost all versions (of mentalism) contend that the mind is a non-physical space in which events obey non-physical laws".

[2] *Beyond Freedom and Dignity*, pp. 12 and 191.

[3] In the film, *Behavior Control: Freedom and Morality* (Open University Film Series). This is a conversation between Skinner and Geoffrey Warnock, reviewed by me in *Teaching Philosophy*, I, 2 (Fall, 1975): 175–7. See also *About Behaviorism*, p. 121: "By attempting to move human behavior into a world of non-physical dimensions, mentalistic or cognitivistic psychologists have cast the *basic* issues in insoluble form." Note that here he countenances no exceptions to the cognitivist-dualist equation.

[4] *Beyond Freedom and Dignity*, p. 191. See also Skinner's *Science and Human Behavior* (Free Press paperback edition, 1953): p. 285 and 82.

[5] "Behaviorism at Fifty", in T. W. Wann, ed., *Behaviorism and Phenomenology* (University of Chicago Press, 1964): 84.

[6] *Beyond Freedom and Dignity*: pp. 1, 14 and 193. In *About Behaviorism* Skinner countenances *covert* behavior (p. 26) and "private consequences" as reinforcers (p. 106), but on other pages insists "the environment stays where it is and where it has always been—outside the body" (p. 75), and "Neither the stimulus nor the response is ever *in* the body in any literal sense" (p. 148). See also "Why Look Inside", *About Behaviorism*, 165–69.

in principle see, to what is necessarily unobservable, then he must after all be appealing tacitly to a form of the privacy objection. But perhaps we should read these disparagements of appeals to what we cannot see merely as disparagements of appeals to what we cannot *now* see, but whose existence we are *inferring*. Skinner often inveighs against appealing to

(3) events whose occurrence "can only be inferred".[7]

Chomsky takes this to be Skinner's prime objection against mentalistic psychology,[8] but Skinner elsewhere is happy to note that "Science often talks about things it cannot see or measure"[9] so it cannot be that simple. It is not that all inferred entities or events are taboo, for Skinner himself on occasion explicitly infers the existence of such events; it must be a particular sort of inferred events. In particular,

(4) *internal* events

are decried, for they "have the effect of diverting attention from the external environment".[10] But if "the skin is not that important as a boundary", what can be wrong with internal events as such? No doubt Skinner finds *some* cause for suspicion in the mere internality of some processes; nothing else could explain his persistent ostrich-attitude towards physiological psychology.[11] But in his better moments he sees that there is nothing intrinsically wrong with inferring the existence of internal mediating events and processes—after all, he admits that some day physiology will describe the inner mechanisms that account for the relations between stimuli and responses, and he could hardly deny that in the meantime such inferences may illuminate the physiological investigations.[12] It must be only when the internal mediators are of a certain sort that

---

[7] *Beyond Freedom and Dignity*, p. 14.

[8] "The Case Against B. F. Skinner", *New York Review of Books* (December 30, 1971).

[9] "Behaviorism at Fifty", p. 84.

[10] *Beyond Freedom and Dignity*, p. 195; see also pp. 8 and 10. *About Behaviorism*, p. 18 and 170; *Cumulative Record* (1961): pp. 274–75.

[11] In "Operant Behavior", in W. K. Honig, ed., *Operant Behavior: Areas of Research and Application* (New York: Appleton Century Crofts, 1966), Skinner disparages theories that attempt to order the behavioral chaos by positing "some mental, physiological or merely conceptual inner system which by its nature is neither directly observed in nor accurately represented on any occasion by, the performance of an organism. There is no comparable inner system in an operant analysis" (p. 16). Here sheer internality is apparently the bogy. See also *Science and Human Behavior*, p. 32ff.

[12] He could hardly deny this, but he comes perilously close to it in *About Behaviorism*, where a particularly virulent attack of operationalism tempts him to challenge the credentials of such innocuous "scientific" concepts as the *tensile strength* of rope and the *viscosity* of fluids (pp. 165–66). Before philosophers scoff at this, they should remind themselves where psychologists caught this disease. A few pages later (p. 169) Skinner grants that a molecular explanation of viscosity is "a step forward" and so are physiological explanations of behavior. In "What is Psychotic Behavior?" (in *Cumulative Record*) he disparages "potential energy" and "magnetic field".

they are anathema. But what sort? Why, the "occult", "prescientific", "fictional" sort, the "*mental* way station" sort,[13] but these characterizations beg the question. So the first four reasons Skinner cites are all inconclusive or contradicted by Skinner himself. If there is something wrong with mentalistic talk, it is not necessarily because mentalism is dualism, that mentalism posits non-physical things, and it is not *just* that it involves internal, inferred, unobservable things, for he says or implies that there is nothing wrong with these features by themselves. If we are to go any further in characterizing Skinner's enemy we must read between the lines.[14]

In several places Skinner hints that what is bothering him is the *ease* with which mentalistic explanations can be concocted.[15] One *invents* whatever mental events one needs to "explain" the behavior in question. One falls back on the "miracle-working mind", which, just because it *is* miraculous, "explains nothing at all".[16] Now this is an ancient and honorable objection vividly characterized by Molière as the *virtus dormitiva*. The learned "doctor" in *Le Malade Imaginaire,* on being asked to explain what it was in the opium that put people to sleep, cites its *virtus dormitiva* or sleep-producing power. Leibniz similarly lampooned those who forged

> expressly occult qualities or faculties which they imagined to be like little demons or goblins capable of producing unceremoniously that which is demanded, just as if watches marked the hours by a certain horodeictic faculty without having need of wheels, or as if mills crushed grains by a fractive faculty without needing any thing resembling millstones.[17]

By seeming to offer an explanation, Skinner says, inventions of this sort "bring curiosity to an end". Now there can be no doubt that convicting a theory of relying on a *virtus dormitiva* is fatal to that theory, but getting the conviction is not always a simple matter—it often has been, though, in Twentieth Century psychology, and this may make Skinner complacent. Theories abounded in the early days of behaviorism which posited curiosity drives, the reduction of which explained why rats in mazes were curious; untapped reservoirs of aggressiveness to explain why animals were aggressive; and invisible, internal punishments and rewards that were postulated solely to account for the fact that unpunished, unrewarded animals sometimes refrained from or persisted in forms of behavior. But mentalistic explanations do not *seem* to cite

---

[13] *Beyond Freedom and Dignity,* pp. 9 and 23; *Cumulative Record,* pp. 283–84; "Behaviorism at Fifty".

[14] A patient and exhaustive review of these issues in Skinner's writings up to 1972 can be found in Russell Keat, "A Critical Examination of B. F. Skinner's Objections to Mentalism", *Behaviorism,* vol. I (Fall, 1972).

[15] "Behaviorism at Fifty", p. 80; *Beyond Freedom and Dignity,* Chapter 1, and p. 160.

[16] *Beyond Freedom and Dignity,* p. 195.

[17] *New Essays on the Understanding* (1704): Preface. See also Leibniz' *Discourse on Metaphysics,* X.

a *virtus dormitiva*. For instance, explaining Tom's presence on the uptown bus by citing his desire to go to Macy's and his belief that Macy's is uptown does not look like citing a *virtus dormitiva:* it is not as empty and question-begging as citing a special uptown-bus-affinity in him would be. Yet I think it is clear that Skinner does think that all mentalistic explanation is infected with the *virtus dormitiva.*[18] This is interesting, for it means that *mentalistic* explanations are on a par for Skinner with a lot of bad *behavioristic* theorizing, but since he offers no discernible defense of this claim, and since I think the claim is ultimately indefensible (as I hope to make clear shortly), I think we must look elsewhere for Skinner's best reason for being against mentalism.

There is a special case of the *virtus dormitiva,* in fact alluded to in the Leibniz passage I quoted, which is the key to Skinner's objection: sometimes the thing the desperate theoretician postulates takes the form of a little man in the machine, a *homunculus,* a demon or goblin as Leibniz says. Skinner often alludes to this fellow. "The function of the inner man is to provide an explanation which will not be explained in turn."[19] In fact, Skinner identifies this little man with the notion of an autonomous, free and dignified moral agent: he says we must abolish "the autonomous man—the inner man, the homunculus, the possessing demon, the man defended by the literature of freedom and dignity".[20] This is a typical case of Skinner's exasperating habit of running together into a single undifferentiated lump a number of distinct factors that are related. Here the concept of a moral agent is identified with the concept of a little man in the brain, which in turn is identified with the demons of yore. Skinner, then, sees superstition and demonology every time a claim is made on behalf of moral responsibility, and every time a theory seems to be utilizing a homunculus. It all looks the same to him: bad. Moreover, he lumps *this* pernicious bit of superstition (the moral-autonomous-homunculus-goblin) with all the lesser suspicions we have been examining; it turns out that "mental" means "internal" means "inferred" means "unobservable" means "private" means *"virtus dormitiva"* means "demons" means "superstition". Psychologists who study physiology (and hence look at *internal* things), or talk of *inferred* drives, or use mentalistic terms like "belief" are all a sorry lot for Skinner, scarcely distinguishable from folk who believe in witches, or, perish the thought, in the freedom and dignity of man. Skinner brands them all with what we might call guilt by free association. For instance, in *Beyond Freedom and Dignity,* after all Skinner's claims to disassociate himself from the lesser objections to mentalism, on p. 200 he lets all the sheep back into the fold:

> Science does not dehumanize man; it de-homunculizes him . . . Only by *dispossessing* him can we turn to the *real* causes of human behavior. Only then can we

---

[18] Skinner finds a passage in Newton to much the same effect as Leibniz: *Beyond Freedom and Dignity,* p. 9.

[19] *Ibid.,* p. 14.

[20] *Ibid.,* p. 200.

turn from the *inferred* to the observed, from the miraculous to the natural, from the *inaccessible* to the manipulable. *(my italics)*[21]

But I was saying that hidden in this pile of dubious and inconsequential objections to mentalism is something important and true. What is it? It is that Skinner sees—or almost sees—that there is a special way that questions can be begged in psychology, and this way is *akin to* introducing a homunculus. Since psychology's task is to account for the intelligence or rationality of men and animals, it cannot fulfill its task if anywhere along the line it *presupposes* intelligence or rationality. Now introducing a homunculus does just that, as Skinner recognizes explicitly in "Behaviorism at Fifty":

> ... the little man ... was recently the hero of a television program called "Gateways to the Mind" ... The viewer learned, from animated cartoons, that when a man's finger is pricked, electrical impulses resembling flashes of lightning run up the afferent nerves and appear on a television screen in the brain. The little man wakes up, sees the flashing screen, reaches out, and pulls the lever ... More flashes of lightning go down the nerves to the muscles, which then contract, as the finger is pulled away from the threatening stimulus. *The behavior of the homunculus was, of course, not explained.* An explanation would presumably require another film. And it, in turn, another.*(my italics)* [22]

This "explanation" of our ability to respond to pin-pricks depends on the intelligence or rationality of the little man looking at the TV screen in the brain—and what does *his* intelligence depend on? Skinner sees clearly that introducing an unanalyzed homunculus is a dead end for psychology, and what he sees dimly is that a homunculus is hidden in effect in your explanation *whenever you use a certain vocabulary,* just because the use of that vocabulary, like the explicit introducton of a homunculus, presupposes intelligence or rationality. For instance, if I say that Tom is taking the uptown bus because he *wants* to go to Macy's and *believes* Macy's is uptown, my explanation of Tom's action *presupposes* Tom's intelligence, because if Tom weren't intelligent enough to put two and two together, as we say, he might fail to see that taking the uptown bus was a way of getting to Macy's. My explanation has a suppressed further premise: expanded it should read: Tom believes Macy's is uptown, and Tom wants to go to Macy's, so *since Tom is rational* Tom wants to go uptown, etc. Since I am relying on Tom's rationality to give me an explanation, it can hardly be an explanation of what makes Tom rational, even in part.

Whenever an explanation invokes the terms "want", "believe", "perceive", "think", "fear"—in short the "mentalistic" terms Skinner abhors—it must

---

[21] In *About Behaviorism*, (pp. 213–14) Skinner provides a marvelous list of the cognitivistic horrors—together with the hint that they are all equally bad, and that the use of one implicates one in the countenancing of all the others: " ... sensations ... intelligence ... decisions ... beliefs ... a death instinct ... sublimation ... an id ... a sense of shame ... reaction formations ... psychic energy ... consciousness ... mental illnesses ... "

[22] "Behaviorism at Fifty", p. 80.

presuppose in some measure and fashion the rationality or intelligence of the entity being described. My favorite example of this is the chess-playing computer. There are now computer programs that can play a respectable game of chess. If you want to predict or explain the moves the computer makes you can do it mechanistically (either by talking about the opening and closing of logic gates, etc., or at a more fundamental physical level by talking about the effects of the electrical energy moving through the computer) or you can say, "If the computer *wants* to capture my bishop and *believes* I wouldn't trade my queen for his knight, then the computer will move his pawn forward one space," or something like that. We need not take seriously the claim that the computer *really* has beliefs and desires in order to use this way of reasoning. Such reasoning about the computer's "reasoning" may in fact enable you to predict the computer's behavior quite well (if the computer is well-programmed), and in a sense such reasoning can even explain the computer's behavior—we might say: "Oh, now I understand why the computer didn't move its rook."—but in another sense it doesn't explain the computer's behavior at all. What is awesome and baffling about a chess-playing computer is how a mere mechanical thing could be made to be so "smart". Suppose you were to ask the designer, "How did the computer 'figure out' that it should move its knight?" and he replied: "Simple; it recognized that its opponent couldn't counterattack without losing a rook." This would be highly unsatisfactory to us, for the question is, how was he able to make a computer that *recognized* anything in the first place? So long as our explanation still has "mentalistic" words like "recognize" and "figure out" and "want" and "believe" in it, it will presuppose the very set of capacities—whatever the capacities are that go to make up intelligence—it ought to be accounting for. And notice: this defect in the explanation need have nothing to do with postulating any non-physical, inner, private, inferred, unobservable events or processes, because it need not postulate any processes or events at all. The computer designer may know exactly what events are or are not going on inside the computer, or for that matter on its highly visible output device: in choosing to answer by talking of the computer's *reasons* for making the move it did, he is not asserting that there are any extra, strange, hidden processes going on; he is simply explaining the *rationale* of the program without telling us how it's done. Skinner comes very close to seeing this. He says:

> Nor can we escape. . . . by breaking the little man into pieces and dealing with his wishes, cognitions, motives, and so on, bit by bit. The objection is not that those things are mental but that they offer no real explanation and stand in the way of a more effective analysis.[23]

The upshot of this long and winding path through Skinner's various objections to mentalism is this: if we ignore the inconsistencies, clear away the red herrings, focus some of Skinner's vaguer comments, and put a few words in

---

[23] "Behaviorism at Fifty", p. 80.

his mouth, he comes up identifying the enemy as a certain class of terms—the "mentalistic" terms in his jargon—which when used in psychological theories "offer no real explanation" because using them is something like supposing there is a little man in the brain. Skinner never says the use of these terms presupposes rationality, but it does. Skinner also never gives us an exhaustive list of the mentalistic terms, or a definition of the class, but once again we can help him out. These terms, the use of which presupposes the rationality of the entity under investigation, are what philosophers call the *intentional idioms*.[24] They can be distinguished from other terms by several peculiarities of their logic, which is a more manageable way of distinguishing them than Skinner's. Thus, spruced up, Skinner's position becomes the following: *don't use intentional idioms in psychology.*

. . .

So let us put words in Skinner's mouth, and follow the phantom argument to its conclusion. We can, then, "agree" with Skinner when we read him between the lines to be asserting that no satisfactory, psychological theory can *rest* on any use of intentional idioms, for their use presupposes rationality, which is the very thing psychology is supposed to explain. So if there is progress in psychology, it will inevitably be, as Skinner suggests, in the direction of eliminating ultimate appeals to beliefs, desires, and other intentional items from out explanations. So far so good. But now Skinner appears to make an important misstep, for he seems to draw the further conclusion that *intentional idioms therefore have no legitimate place in any psychological theory*. But this has not been shown at all. There is no reason why intentional terms cannot be used provisionally in the effort to map out the functions of the behavior control system of men and animals, just so long as a way is found eventually to "cash them out" by designing a mechanism to function as specified. For example, we may not now be able to describe mechanically how to build a "belief store" for a man or animal, but if we specify how such a belief store must function, we can use the notion in a perfectly scientific way pending completion of its mechanical or physiological analysis. Mendelian genetics, for instance, thrived as a science for years with nothing more to feed on than the concept of a gene, a whatever-it-turns-out-to-be that functions as a transmitter of a heritable trait. All that is required by sound canons of scientific practice is that we not suppose or claim that we have reached an end to explanation in citing such a thing. Skinner, or rather phantom-Skinner, is wrong, then, to think it follows from the fact that psychology cannot make any *final appeal* to intentional items, that there can be no place for intentional idioms in psychology.

It is this misstep that leads Skinner into his most pervasive confusion. We have already seen that Skinner, unlike Quine, thinks that translation of intentional into non-intentional terms is possible. But if so, why can't intentional

[24] See, e.g., Roderick Chisholm, *Perceiving, A Philosophical Study* (1957), and numerous articles since then; also Quine, *Word and Object* (1960); W. G. Lycan, "On Intentionality and the Psychological", *American Philosophical Quarterly* (October, 1969).

explanations, in virtue of these bonds of translation, find a place in psychology? Skinner vacillates between saying they can and they can't, often within the space of a few pages.

. . .

In spite of his vacillation in print, it is clear that Skinner must come down in favor of the exclusive view, if his argument is to work. Certainly the majority of his remarks favor this view, and in fact it becomes quite explicit on p. 101 of *Beyond Freedom and Dignity* where Skinner distinguishes the "pre-scientific" (i.e., intentional) view of a person's behavior from the scientific view and goes on to say, "Neither view can be proved, but it is in the nature of scientific inquiry that the evidence should shift in favor of the second." Here we see Skinner going beyond the correct intuition that it is in the nature of scientific inquiry that ultimate appeals to intentional idioms must disappear as progress is made, to the bolder view that as this occurs intentional explanations will be rendered false, not reduced or translated into other terms.

I argue [elsewhere] that intentional and mechanistic or scientific explanations *can* co-exist, and have given [t]here an example supposed to confirm this: we know that there is a purely mechanistic explanation of the chess playing computer, and yet it is *not false* to say that the computer *figures out* or *recognizes* the best move, or that it *concludes* that its opponent cannot make a certain move, any more than it is false to say that a computer *adds* or *multiplies*. There has often been confusion on this score. It used to be popular to say, "A computer can't really think, of course; all it can do is add, subtract, multiply and divide." That leaves the way open to saying, "A computer can't really multiply, of course; all it can do is add numbers together very, very fast," and that must lead to the admission: "A computer cannot really add numbers, of course; all it can do is control the opening and closing of hundreds of tiny switches," which leads to: "A computer can't really control its switches, of course; it's simply at the mercy of the electrical currents pulsing through it." What this chain of claims adds up to "prove", obviously, is that computers are really pretty dull lumps of stuff—they can't do anything interesting at all. They can't really guide rockets to the moon, or make out paychecks, or beat human beings at chess, but of course they can do all that and more. What the computer programmer can do if we give him the chance is not *explain away* the illusion that the computer is doing these things, but *explain how* the computer truly is doing these things.

Skinner fails to see the distinction between explaining and explaining away. In this regard he is succumbing to the same confusion as those who suppose that since color can be explained in terms of the properties of atoms which are not colored, nothing is colored. Imagine the Skinner-style exclusion claim: "The American flag is *not* red, white and blue, but rather a collection of colorless atoms." Since Skinner fails to make this distinction, he is led to the exclusive view, the view that true scientific explanations will exclude true intentional explanations, and typically, though he asserts this, he offers no arguments for

it. Once again, however, with a little extrapolation we can see what perfectly good insights led Skinner to this error.

There are times when a mechanistic explanation obviously does exclude an intentional explanation. Wooldridge gives us a vivid example:

> When the time comes for egg laying the wasp *Sphex* builds a burrow for the purpose and seeks out a cricket which she stings in such a way as to paralyze but not kill it. She drags the cricket into her burrow, lays her eggs alongside, closes the burrow, then flies away, never to return. In due course, the eggs hatch and the wasp grubs feed off the paralyzed cricket, which has not decayed, having been kept in the wasp equivalent of deep freeze. To the human mind, such an elaborately organized and seemingly purposeful routine conveys a convincing flavor of logic and thoughtfulness—until more details are examined. For example, the wasp's routine is to bring the paralyzed cricket to the burrow, leave it on the threshold, go inside to see that all is well, emerge, and then drag the cricket in. If, while the wasp is inside making her preliminary inspection the cricket is moved a few inches away, the wasp, on emerging from the burrow, will bring the cricket back to the threshold, but not inside, and will then repeat the preparatory procedure of entering the burrow to see that everything is all right. If again the cricket is removed a few inches while the wasp is inside, once again the wasp will move the cricket up to the threshold and re-enter the burrow for a final check. The wasp never thinks of pulling the cricket straight in. On one occasion, this procedure was repeated forty times, always with the same result.[25]

In this case what we took at first to be a bit of intelligent behavior is unmasked. When we see how simple, rigid and mechanical it is, we realize that we were attributing too much to the wasp. Now Skinner's experimental life has been devoted to unmasking, over and over again, the behavior of pigeons and other lower animals. In "Behaviorism at Fifty" he gives an example almost as graphic as our wasp. Students watch a pigeon being conditioned to turn in a clockwise circle, and Skinner asks them to describe what they have observed. They all talk of the pigeon *expecting, hoping* for food, *feeling* this, *observing* that, and Skinner points out with glee that they have observed nothing of the kind; he has a simpler, more mechanical explanation of what has happened, and it *falsifies* the students' unfounded *inferences*. Since in this case explanation is unmasking or explaining away, it always is. Today pigeons, tomorrow the world. What Skinner fails to see is that it is not the fact that he has an explanation that unmasks the pretender after intelligence, but rather that his explanation is so simple. If Skinner had said to his students, "Aha! You think the pigeon is so smart, but here's how it learned to do its trick," and proceeded to inundate them with hundreds of pages of detailed explanation of highly complex inner mechanisms, their response would no doubt be that yes, the pigeon did seem, on his explanation, to be pretty smart.

---

[25] *The Machinery of the Brain* (New York: McGraw Hill, 1963): p. 82.

The fact that it is the simplicity of explanations that can render elaborate intentional explanations false is completely lost to Skinner for a very good reason: the only *well-formulated, testable* explanations Skinner and his colleagues have so far come up with have been, perforce, relatively simple, and deal with the relatively simple behavior controls of relatively simple animals. Since all the explanations he has so far come up with have been of the unmasking variety (pigeons, it turns out, do not have either freedom or dignity), Skinner might be forgiven for supposing that all explanations in psychology, including all explanations of human behavior, must be similarly unmasking.

It might, of course, turn out to be the case that all human behavior could be unmasked, that all signs of human cleverness are as illusory as the wasp's performance, but in spite of all Skinner's claims of triumph in explaining human behavior, his own testimony reveals this to be wishful thinking. Even if we were to leave unchallenged all the claims of operant conditioning of human beings in experimental situations,[26] there remain areas of human behavior that prove completely intractable to Skinner's mode of analysis. Not surprisingly, these are the areas of deliberate, intentional action. The persistently recalcitrant features of human behavior for the Skinnerians can be grouped under the headings of novelty and generality. The Skinnerian must explain all behavior by citing the subject's past history of similar stimuli and responses, so when someone behaves in a novel manner, there is a problem. Pigeons do not exhibit very interesting novel behavior, but human beings do. Suppose, to borrow one of Skinner's examples, I am held up and asked for my wallet.[27] This has never happened to me before, so the correct response cannot have been "reinforced" for me, yet I do the smart thing: I hand over my wallet. Why? The Skinnerian must claim that this is not truly novel behavior at all, but an instance of a *general sort* of behavior which has been previously conditioned. But what sort is it? Not only have I not been trained to hand over my wallet to men with guns, I have not been trained to empty my pockets for women with bombs, nor to turn over my possessions to armed entities. None of these things has ever happened to me before. I may never have been threatened before at all. Or more plausibly, it may well be that most often when I have been threatened in the past, the "reinforced" response was to *apologize* to the threatener for something I'd said. Obviously, though, when told, "Your money or your life!" I don't respond by saying, "I'm sorry. I take it all back." It is perfectly clear that what experience has taught me is that if I *want* to save my skin, and *believe* I am being threatened, I should do what I *believe* my threatener *wants* me to do. But of course Skinner cannot permit this intentional formulation at all, for

[26] But we shouldn't. See W. F. Brewer, "There is No Convincing Evidence for Operant or Classical Conditioning in Adult Humans", in W. B. Weimer, ed., *Cognition and the Symbolic Processes* (Hillsdale, New Jersey: Erlbaum, 1974).

[27] See *Science and Human Behavior*, p. 177, and Chomsky's amusing *reductio ad absurdum* of Skinner's analysis of "your money or your life" in his review of *Verbal Behavior*, in *Language* (1959), reprinted in J. Fodor and J. Katz, ed., *The Structure of Language, Readings in the Philosophy of Language* (New York: Prentice Hall, 1964).

in ascribing wants and beliefs it would presuppose my rationality. He must insist that the "threat stimuli" I now encounter (and these are not defined) are similar in some crucial but undescribed respect to some stimuli encountered in my past which were followed by responses of some sort similar to the one I now make, where the past responses were reinforced somehow by their consequences. But see what Skinner is doing here. He is positing an external *virtus dormitiva*. He has no record of any earlier experiences of this sort, but *infers* their existence, and moreover *endows* them with an automatically theory-satisfying quality: these postulated earlier experiences are claimed to resemble-in-whatever-is-the-crucial-respect the situation they must resemble for the Skinnerian explanation to work. Why do I hand over my wallet? Because I must have had in the past some experiences that reinforced wallet-handing-over behavior in circumstances like this.

. . .

I am suggesting that once Skinner turns from pigeons to people, his proffered "explanations" of human behavior are no better than this. If Skinner complains that mentalistic explanations are too easy, since we always know exactly what mental events to postulate to "explain" the behavior, the same can be said of all the explanation sketches of complex human behavior in Skinner's books. They offer not a shred of confirmation that Skinner's basic mode of explanation—in terms of reinforcement of operants—will prove fruitful in accounting for human behavior. It is hard to be sure, but Skinner even seems to realize this. He says at one point, "The instances of behavior cited in what follows are not offered as 'proof' of the interpretation", but he goes right on to say, "The proof is to be found in the basic analysis." But insofar as the "basic analysis" proves anything, it proves that people are not like pigeons, that Skinner's unmasking explanations will not be forthcoming. Certainly if we discovered that people only handed over their wallets to robbers after being conditioned to do this, and, moreover, continued to hand over their wallets after the robber had shown his gun was empty, or when the robber was flanked by policemen, we would have to admit that Skinner had unmasked the pretenders; human beings would be little better than pigeons or wasps, and we would have to agree that we had no freedom and dignity.

Skinner's increasing reliance, however, on a *virtus dormitiva* to "explain" complex human behavior is a measure of the difference between pigeons and persons, and hence is a measure of the distance between Skinner's premises and his conclusions. When Skinner speculates about the past history of reinforcement in a person in order to explain some current behavior, he is saying, in effect, "I don't know which of many possible equivalent series of events occurred, but one of them did, and that explains the occurrence of this behavior now." But what is the equivalence class Skinner is pointing to in every case? What do the wide variety of possible stimulus histories have in common? Skinner can't tell us in his vocabulary, but it is easy enough to say: the stimulus histories that belong to the equivalence class have in common the fact that they *had the effect of teaching the person that p,* of storing certain information. In the end Skinner

is playing the same game with his speculations as the cognitivist who speculates about internal representations of information. Skinner is simply relying on a more cumbersome vocabulary.

Skinner has failed to show that psychology without mentalism is either possible or—in his own work—actual, and so he has failed to explode the myths of freedom and dignity. Since that explosion was to have been his first shot in a proposed social revolution, its misfiring saves us the work of taking seriously his alternately dreary and terrifying proposals for improving the world.

58
Linguistic Contributions
to the Study of Mind

NOAM CHOMSKY

Noam Chomsky (b. 1928), a major intellectual figure of the twentieth century, has written on linguistics, philosophy, psychology, and contemporary affairs. He is currently Institute Professor in the Department of Linguistics at the Massachusetts Institute of Technology. Among his many books are Syntactic Structures, Aspects of the Theory of Syntax *and* Cartesian Linguistics.

More than any other figure, Chomsky is responsible for the growth and progress of contemporary linguistics. Chomsky was quick to see the implications of his theory of language, the theory of transformational grammar, for a traditional debate in philosophy of mind: the debate over innateness. In reading 25, Locke suggests that we acquire ideas through experience. This view was presented in opposition to Descartes's claim that we are born with all the ideas which we will ever have (see reading 30). In Cartesian Linguistics, Language and Mind *(excerpted here), and other writings, Chomsky argues that Descartes was right. Chomsky's influential argument can be stated quite simply: To be able to use a language, a person must know the grammar of that language. Thus in order to learn a language —English, for example—a child must master the grammar of that language. However, a transformational grammar for English is a large set of complex rules. The child's language training is insufficient to enable him to master those rules, especially at the rate children learn a language. Thus, the only way to explain a child's mastery of English is to assume he was born with some knowledge of grammatical rules. Thus a child must have a rich innate endowment.*

ONE DIFFICULTY in the psychological sciences lies in the familiarity of the phenomena with which they deal. A certain intellectual effort is required to see how such phenomena can pose serious problems or call for intricate explanatory theories. One is inclined to take them for granted as necessary or somehow "natural."

The effects of this familiarity of phenomena have often been discussed. Wolfgang Köhler, for example, has suggested that psychologists do not open up "entirely new territories" in the manner of the natural sciences, "simply because man was acquainted with practically all territories of mental life a long time before the founding of scientific psychology . . . because at the very beginning of their work there were no entirely unknown mental facts left which they

could have discovered."[1] The most elementary discoveries of classical physics have a certain shock value—man has no intuition about elliptical orbits or the gravitational constant. But "mental facts" of even a much deeper sort cannot be "discovered" by the psychologist, because they are a matter of intuitive acquaintance and, once pointed out, are obvious.

There is also a more subtle effect. Phenomena can be so familiar that we really do not see them at all, a matter that has been much discussed by literary theorists and philosophers. For example, Viktor Shklovskij in the early 1920's developed the idea that the function of poetic art is that of "making strange" the object depicted. "People living at the seashore grow so accustomed to the murmur of the waves that they never hear it. By the same token, we scarcely ever hear the words which we utter. . . . We look at each other, but we do not see each other any more. Our perception of the world has withered away; what has remained is mere recognition." Thus, the goal of the artist is to transfer what is depicted to the "sphere of new perception"; as an example, Shklovskij cites a story by Tolstoy in which social customs and institutions are "made strange" by the device of presenting them from the viewpoint of a narrator who happens to be a horse.[2]

The observation that "we look at each other, but we do not see each other any more" has perhaps itself achieved the status of "words which we utter but scarcely ever hear." But familiarity, in this case as well, should not obscure the importance of the insight.

Wittgenstein makes a similar observation, pointing out that "the aspects of things that are most important for us are hidden because of their simplicity and familiarity (one is unable to notice something—because it is always before one's eyes)."[3] He sets himself to "supplying . . . remarks on the natural history of human beings: we are not contributing curiosities however, but observations which no one has doubted, but which have escaped remark only because they are always before our eyes."[4]

Less noticed is the fact that we also lose sight of the need for explanation when phenomena are too familiar and "obvious." We tend too easily to assume that explanations must be transparent and close to the surface. The greatest defect of classical philosophy of mind, both rationalist and empiricist, seems to me to be its unquestioned assumption that the properties and content of the mind are accessible to introspection; it is surprising to see how rarely this assumption has been challenged, insofar as the organization and function of the intellectual faculties are concerned, even with the Freudian revolution. Cor-

---

[1] W. Köhler, *Dynamics in Psychology* (New York: Liveright, 1940).

[2] See V. Ehrlich, *Russian Formalism*, 2nd rev. ed. (New York: Humanities, 1965), pp. 176–77.

[3] Ludwig Wittgenstein, *Philosophical Investigations* (New York: Oxford University Press, 1953), Section 129.

[4] *Ibid.*, Section 415.

respondingly, the far-reaching studies of language that were carried out under the influence of Cartesian rationalism suffered from a failure to appreciate either the abstractness of those structures that are "present to the mind" when an utterance is produced or understood, or the length and complexity of the chain of operations that relate the mental structures expressing the semantic content of the utterance to the physical realization.

A similar defect mars the study of language and mind in the modern period. It seems to me that the essential weakness in the structuralist and behaviorist approaches to these topics is the faith in the shallowness of explanations, the belief that the mind must be simpler in its structure than any known physical organ and that the most primitive of assumptions must be adequate to explain whatever phenomena can be observed. Thus, it is taken for granted without argument or evidence (or is presented as true by definition) that a language is a "habit structure" or a network of associative connections, or that knowledge of language is merely a matter of "knowing how," a skill expressible as a system of dispositions to respond. Accordingly, knowledge of language must develop slowly through repetition and training, its apparent complexity resulting from the proliferation of very simple elements rather than from deeper principles of mental organization that may be as inaccessible to introspection as the mechanisms of digestion or coordinated movement. Although there is nothing inherently unreasonable in an attempt to account for knowledge and use of language in these terms, it also has no particular plausibility or a priori justification. There is no reason to react with uneasiness or disbelief if study of the knowledge of language and use of this knowledge should lead in an entirely different direction.

I think that in order to achieve progress in the study of language and human cognitive faculties in general it is necessary first to establish "psychic distance" from the "mental facts" to which Köhler referred, and then to explore the possibilities for developing explanatory theories, whatever they may suggest with regard to the complexity and abstractness of the underlying mechanisms. We must recognize that even the most familiar phenomena require explanation and that we have no privileged access to the underlying mechanisms, no more so than in physiology or physics. Only the most preliminary and tentative hypotheses can be offered concerning the nature of language, its use, and its acquisition. As native speakers, we have a vast amount of data available to us. For just this reason it is easy to fall into the trap of believing that there is nothing to be explained, that whatever organizing principles and underlying mechanisms may exist must be "given" as the data is given. Nothing could be further from the truth, and an attempt to characterize precisely the system of rules we have mastered that enables us to understand new sentences and produce a new sentence on an appropriate occasion will quickly dispel any dogmatism on this matter. The search for explanatory theories must begin with an attempt to determine these systems of rules and to reveal the principles that govern them.

The person who has acquired knowledge of a language has internalized a

system of rules that relate sound and meaning in a particular way. The linguist constructing a grammar of a language is in effect proposing a hypothesis concerning this internalized system. The linguist's hypothesis, if presented with sufficient explicitness and precision, will have certain empirical consequences with regard to the form of utterances and their interpretations by the native speaker. Evidently, knowledge of language—the internalized system of rules— is only one of the many factors that determine how an utterance will be used or understood in a particular situation. The linguist who is trying to determine what constitutes knowledge of a language—to construct a correct grammar— is studying one fundamental factor that is involved in performance, but not the only one. This idealization must be kept in mind when one is considering the problem of confirmation of grammars on the basis of empirical evidence. There is no reason why one should not also study the interaction of several factors involved in complex mental acts and underlying actual performance, but such a study is not likely to proceed very far unless the separate factors are themselves fairly well understood.

In a good sense, the grammar proposed by the linguist is an explanatory theory; it suggests an explanation for the fact that (under the idealization mentioned) a speaker of the language in question will perceive, interpret, form, or use an utterance in certain ways and not in other ways. One can also search for explanatory theories of a deeper sort. The native speaker has acquired a grammar on the basis of very restricted and degenerate evidence; the grammar has empirical consequences that extend far beyond the evidence. At one level, the phenomena with which the grammar deals are explained by the rules of the grammar itself and the interaction of these rules. At a deeper level, these same phenomena are explained by the principles that determine the selection of the grammar on the basis of the restricted and degenerate evidence available to the person who has acquired knowledge of the language, who has constructed for himself this particular grammar. The principles that determine the form of grammar and that select a grammar of the appropriate form on the basis of certain data constitute a subject that might, following a traditional usage, be termed "universal grammar." The study of universal grammar, so understood, is a study of the nature of human intellectual capacities. It tries to formulate the necessary and sufficient conditions that a system must meet to qualify as a potential human language, conditions that are not accidentally true of the existing human languages, but that are rather rooted in the human "language capacity," and thus constitute the innate organization that determines what counts as linguistic experience and what knowledge of language arises on the basis of this experience. Universal grammar, then, constitutes an explanatory theory of a much deeper sort than particular grammar, although the particular grammar of a language can also be regarded as an explanatory theory.

In practice, the linguist is always involved in the study of both universal and particular grammar. When he constructs a descriptive, particular grammar in one way rather than another on the basis of what evidence he has available,

he is guided, consciously or not, by certain assumptions as to the form of grammar, and these assumptions belong to the theory of universal grammar. Conversely, his formulation of principles of universal grammar must be justified by the study of their consequences when applied in particular grammars. Thus, at several levels the linguist is involved in the construction of explanatory theories, and at each level there is a clear psychological interpretation for his theoretical and descriptive work. At the level of particular grammar, he is attempting to characterize knowledge of a language, a certain cognitive system that has been developed—unconsciously, of course—by the normal speaker-hearer. At the level of universal grammar, he is trying to establish certain general properties of human intelligence. Linguistics, so characterized, is simply the subfield of psychology that deals with these aspects of mind.

I will try to give some indication of the kind of work now in progress that aims, on the one hand, to determine the systems of rules that constitute knowledge of a language, and on the other, to reveal the principles that govern these systems. Obviously, any conclusions that can be reached today regarding particular or universal grammar must be quite tentative and restricted in their coverage. And in a brief sketch such as this only the roughest outlines can be indicated. To try to give something of the flavor of what is being done today I will concentrate on problems that are current in that they can be formulated with some clarity and studied, though they still resist solution.

As I indicated in the first lecture, I believe that the most appropriate general framework for the study of problems of language and mind is the system of ideas developed as part of the rationalist psychology of the seventeenth and eighteenth centuries, elaborated in important respects by the romantics and then largely forgotten as attention shifted to other matters. According to this traditional conception, a system of propositions expressing the meaning of a sentence is produced in the mind as the sentence is realized as a physical signal, the two being related by certain formal operations that, in current terminology, we may call *grammatical transformations*. Continuing with current terminology, we can thus distinguish the *surface structure* of the sentence, the organization into categories and phrases that is directly associated with the physical signal, from the underlying *deep structure,* also a system of categories and phrases, but with a more abstract character. Thus, the surface structure of the sentence "A wise man is honest" might analyze it into the subject "a wise man" and the predicate "is honest." The deep structure, however, will be rather different. It will, in particular, extract from the complex idea that constitutes the subject of the surface structure an underlying proposition with the subject "man" and the predicate "be wise." In fact, the deep structure, in the traditional view, is a system of two propositions, neither of which is asserted, but which interrelate in such a way as to express the meaning of the sentence "A wise man is honest." We might represent the deep structure in this sample case by formula 1, and the surface structure by formula 2, where paired brackets are labeled to show the category of phrase that they bound. (Many details are omitted.)

1 $\left[{}_{NP}\left[{}_{S}\left[{}_{NP}\text{a man}\left[{}_{NP}\text{[man]}\right]_{NP}\text{VP}\left[\text{is wise}\right]_{VP}\right]_{S}\right]_{NP}\text{VP}\left[\text{is honest}\right]_{VP}\right]_{S}$

2 $\left[{}_{S}{}_{NP}\left[\text{a wise man}\right]_{NP}\text{VP}\left[\text{is honest}\right]_{VP}\right]_{S}$

An alternative and equivalent notation, widely used, expresses the labeled bracketing of 1 and 2 in tree form, as 1′ and 2′ respectively:

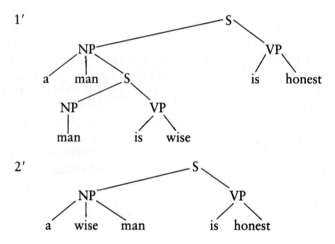

If we understand the relation "subject-of" to hold between a phrase of the category noun phrase (NP) and the sentence (S) that directly dominates it, and the relation "predicate-of" to hold between a phrase of the category verb phrase (VP) and the sentence that directly dominates it, then structures 1 and 2 (equivalently, 1′ and 2′) specify the grammatical functions of subject and predicate in the intended way. The grammatical functions of the deep structure (1) play a central role in determining the meaning of the sentence. The phrase structure indicated in 2, on the other hand, is closely related to its phonetic shape—specifically, it determines the intonation contour of the utterance represented.

Knowledge of a language involves the ability to assign deep and surface structures to an infinite range of sentences, to relate these structures appropriately, and to assign a semantic interpretation and a phonetic interpretation to the paired deep and surface structures. This outline of the nature of grammar seems to be quite accurate as a first approximation to the characterization of "knowledge of a language."

How are the deep and surface structures related? Clearly, in the simple example given, we can form the surface structure from the deep structure by performing such operations as the following:

3 a.   assign the marker *wh-* to the most deeply embedded NP, "man"

     b.   replace the NP so marked by "who"

     c.   delete "who is"

     d.   invert "man" and "wise."

Applying just operations **a** and **b,** we derive the structure underlying the sentence "a man who is wise is honest," which is one possible realization of the underlying structure (1). If, furthermore, we apply the operation **c** (deriving "a man wise is honest"), we must, in English, also apply the subsidiary operation **d,** deriving the surface structure (2), which can then be phonetically interpreted.

If this approach is correct in general, then a person who knows a specific language has control of a grammar that *generates* (that is, characterizes) the infinite set of potential deep structures, maps them onto associated surface structures, and determines the semantic and phonetic interpretations of these abstract objects. From the information now available, it seems accurate to propose that the surface structure determines the phonetic interpretation completely and that the deep structure expresses those grammatical functions that play a role in determining the semantic interpretation, although certain aspects of the surface structure may also participate in determining the meaning of the sentence in ways that I will not discuss here. A grammar of this sort will therefore define a certain infinite correlation of sound and meaning. It constitutes a first step toward explaining how a person can understand an arbitrary sentence of his language.

Even this artificially simple example serves to illustrate some properties of grammars that appear to be general. An infinite class of deep structures much like 1 can be generated by very simple rules that express a few rudimentary grammatical functions, if we assign to these rules a recursive property—in particular, one that allows them to embed structures of the form [s . . .]s within other structures. Grammatical transformations will then iterate to form, ultimately, a surface structure that may be quite remote from the underlying deep structure. The deep structure may be highly abstract; it may have no close point-by-point correlation to the phonetic realization. Knowledge of a language—"linguistic competence," in the technical sense of this term discussed briefly in the first lecture—involves a mastery of these grammatical processes.

With just this much of a framework, we can begin to formulate some of the problems that call for analysis and explanation. One major problem is posed by the fact that the surface structure generally gives very little indication in itself of the meaning of the sentence. There are, for example, numerous sentences that are ambiguous in some way that is not indicated by the surface structure. Consider sentence **4:**

4   I disapprove of John's drinking.

This sentence can refer either to the fact of John's drinking or to its character. The ambiguity is resolved, in different ways, in sentences **5** and **6**:

5   I disapprove of John's drinking the beer.

6   I disapprove of John's excessive drinking.

It is clear that grammatical processes are involved. Notice that we cannot simultaneously extend **4** in both of the ways illustrated in **5** and **6**; that would give us **7**:

7   *I disapprove of John's excessive drinking the beer.[5]

Our internalized grammar assigns two different abstract structures to **4**, one of which is related to the structure that underlies **5**, the other to the structure that underlies **6**. But it is at the level of deep structure that the distinction is represented; it is obliterated by the transformations that map the deep structures onto the surface form associated with **4**.

The processes that are involved in examples **4**, **5**, and **6** are quite common in English. Thus, the sentence "I disapprove of John's cooking" may imply either that I think his wife should cook or that I think he uses too much garlic, for example. Again, the ambiguity is resolved if we extend the sentence in the manner indicated in **5** and **6**.

The fact that **7** is deviant requires explanation. The explanation in this case would be provided, at the level of particular grammar, by formulation of the grammatical rules that assign alternative deep structures and that in each case permit one but not the other of the extensions to **5** or **6**. We would then explain the deviance of **7** and the ambiguity of **4** by attributing this system of rules to the person who knows the language, as one aspect of his knowledge. We might, of course, try to move to a deeper level of explanation, asking how it is that the person has internalized these rules instead of others that would determine a different sound-meaning correlation and a different class of generated surface structures (including, perhaps, **7**). This is a problem of universal grammar, in the sense described earlier. Using the terminology of note 5, the discussion at the level of particular grammar would be one of descriptive adequacy, and at the level of universal grammar it would be one of explanatory adequacy.

Notice that the internalized rules of English grammar have still further consequences in a case like the one just discussed. There are transformations of great generality that permit or require the deletion of repeated elements, in

---

[5] I use the asterisk in the conventional way, to indicate a sentence that deviates in some respect from grammatical rule.

whole or in part, under well-defined conditions. Applied to structure 8, these rules derive 9.[6]

8 I don't like John's cooking any more than Bill's cooking.

9 I don't like John's cooking any more than Bill's .

Sentence 9 is ambiguous. It can mean either that I don't like the fact that John cooks any more than I like the fact that Bill cooks, or that I don't like the quality of John's cooking any more than I like the quality of Bill's cooking. However, it cannot mean that I don't like the quality of John's cooking any more than I like the fact that Bill cooks, or conversely, with "fact" and "quality" interchanged. That is, in the underlying structure (8) we must understand the ambiguous phrases "John's cooking" and "Bill's cooking" in the same way if we are to be able to delete "cooking." It seems reasonable to assume that what is involved is some general condition on the applicability of deletion operations such as the one that gives 9 from 8, a rather abstract condition that takes into account not only the structure to which the operation applies but also the history of derivation of this structure.

. . .

To summarize: Along the lines that have been outlined here, we might develop on the one hand a system of general principles of universal grammar,[7] and on the other, particular grammars that are formed and interpreted in accordance with these principles. The interplay of universal principles and particular rules leads to empirical consequences such as those we have illustrated; at various levels of depth, these rules and principles provide explanations for facts about linguistic competence—the knowledge of language possessed by each normal speaker—and about some of the ways in which this knowledge is put to use in the performance of the speaker or hearer.

The principles of universal grammar provide a highly restrictive schema to which any human language must conform, as well as specific conditions deter-

---

[6] Henceforth I shall generally delete brackets in giving a deep, surface, or intermediate structure, where this will not lead to confusion. One should think of 8 and 9 as each having a full labeled bracketing associated with it. Notice that 8 is not, of course, a deep structure, but rather the result of applying transformations to a more primitive abstract object.

[7] Notice that we are interpreting "universal grammar" as a system of conditions on grammars. It may involve a skeletal substructure of rules that any human language must contain, but it also incorporates conditions that must be met by such grammars and principles that determine how they are interpreted. This formulation is something of a departure from a traditional view that took universal grammar to be simply a substructure of each particular grammar, a system of rules at the very core of each grammar. This traditional view has also received expression in recent work. It seems to me to have little merit. As far as information is available, there are heavy constraints on the form and interpretation of grammar at all levels, from the deep structures of syntax, through the transformational component, to the rules that interpret syntactic structures semantically and phonetically.

mining how the grammar of any such language can be used. It is easy to imagine alternatives to the conditions that have been formulated (or those that are often tacitly assumed). These conditions have in the past generally escaped notice, and we know very little about them today. If we manage to establish the appropriate "psychic distance" from the relevant phenomena and succeed in "making them strange" to ourselves, we see at once that they pose very serious problems that cannot be talked or defined out of existence. Careful consideration of such problems as those sketched here indicates that to account for the normal use of language we must attribute to the speaker-hearer an intricate system of rules that involve mental operations of a very abstract nature, applying to representations that are quite remote from the physical signal. We observe, furthermore, that knowledge of language is acquired on the basis of degenerate and restricted data and that it is to a large extent independent of intelligence and of wide variations in individual experience.

If a scientist were faced with the problem of determining the nature of a device of unknown properties that operates on data of the sort available to a child and gives as "output" (that is, as a "final state of the device," in this case) a particular grammar of the sort that it seems necessary to attribute to the person who knows the language, he would naturally search for inherent principles of organization that determine the form of the output on the basis of the limited data available. There is no reason to adopt a more prejudiced or dogmatic view when the device of unknown properties is the human mind; specifically there is no reason to suppose, in advance of any argument, that the general empiricist assumptions that have dominated speculation about these matters have any particular privileged claim. No one has succeeded in showing why the highly specific empiricist assumptions about how knowledge is acquired should be taken seriously. They appear to offer no way to describe or account for the most characteristic and normal constructions of human intelligence, such as linguistic competence. On the other hand, certain highly specific assumptions about particular and universal grammar give some hope of accounting for the phenomena that we face when we consider knowledge and use of language. Speculating about the future, it seems not unlikely that continued research along the lines indicated here will bring to light a highly restrictive schematism that determines both the content of experience and the nature of the knowledge that arises from it, thus vindicating and elaborating some traditional thinking about problems of language and mind. It is to this matter, among others, that I shall turn in the final lecture.

59

The Central-State Theory

D. M. ARMSTRONG

*David M. Armstrong (b. 1926) is a contemporary philosopher who is
currently Challis Professor of Philosophy at the University of Sydney,
Australia. Besides his work in philosophy of mind, Armstrong has also
made important contributions to epistemology and metaphysics.*

In this excerpt from A Materialist Theory of the Mind, *Armstrong
proposes a solution to an apparent difficulty for identifying mental states as
states of the central nervous system. He wants to view mental processes as
straightforward neurological processes. This approach engenders a puzzle: If
mental processes, like believing or desiring, really are neural processes, then
how are we able to understand human psychology at all when, even now,
we have no idea what kinds of neural processes we are talking about? Yet,
we appear to have some grasp, at least, of what people believe and of why
they do the things they do. Armstrong proposes to resolve this quandary by
drawing on an analogy. Early geneticists were able to talk about genes and
the phenomena of heredity even though they did not know that genes are
segments of DNA (or RNA). They discussed genes in terms of their* causal
role *in producing various traits. This was quite possible even though they
did not know the materials of which genes were made. Similarly, Armstrong
suggests that we have been able to talk sensibly about mental states because,
again, we talk about mental states in terms of their* causal roles. *As in
the case of the gene, we may consider some of the causes and effects of
mental states even though we are still ignorant about their neurological
constitution.*

BUT NOW WE MUST examine the second form of Materialism, the view
which identifies mental states with purely physical states of the central nervous
sytesm. If the mind is thought of as 'that which has mental states', then we can
say that, on this theory, the mind is simply the central nervous system, or, less
accurately but more epigrammatically, the mind is simply the brain.

Is the Theory Really Paradoxical?

Many philosophers still regard this theory of mind as a very extraordinary
one. In 1962, for instance, A. G. N. Flew wrote:

> In the face of the powerful and resolute advocacy now offered *this admittedly
> paradoxical view* can no longer be dismissed in such short order. (*Philosophical
> Review*, Vol. LXXI, 1962, p. 403, my italics)

At the risk of seeming ungrateful to Professor Flew, it is interesting to notice that, even while conceding that the theory merits serious discussion, he calls it 'admittedly paradoxical'. I think his attitude is shared by many philosophers. Certainly I myself found the theory paradoxical when I first heard it expounded.

But it is important to realize that this opinion that the Central-state theory is paradoxical, is confined almost exclusively to philosophers. They are usually taught as first-year University students that the mind cannot possibly be the brain, and as a result they are inclined to regard the falsity of the Central-state theory as self-evident. But this opinion is not widely shared. Outside philosophy, the Central-state doctrine enjoys wide support.

In the first place, there is evidence from modern idiom. We speak of 'brains', 'brain-child', 'brain-storm', 'racking one's brains' and 'brain-washing', and in each case we are speaking about the mind. If one follows this up, as I have done, by asking people of general education, but no philosophical training, whether they think the mind is the brain or not, many say it is. Some even treat the matter as closed, asking what else it could be. Those who deny that the mind is the brain usually do so for *theological* reasons.

If we then turn to those scientists who are most directly concerned with the problem, viz. the psychologists, we find no tendency to say that the Central-state theory is paradoxical or far-out. D. O. Hebb may be fairly quoted as representative. Now in his *Textbook of Psychology* (Saunders, 1958, p. 3) he writes:

> There are two theories of mind, speaking very generally. One is animistic, a theory that the body is inhabited by an entity—the mind or soul—that is quite different from it, having nothing in common with bodily processes. The second theory is physiological or mechanistic, it assumes that mind is a bodily process, an activity of the brain. Modern psychology works with this latter theory only. Both are intellectually respectable (that is, each has support from highly intelligent people, including scientists), and there is certainly no decisive means available of proving one to be right, the other wrong.

These appeals to the authority of the unphilosophic man and the psychologists are, of course, not intended to do anything to settle the substantive question. They are made only with the hope of moderating philosophical dogmatism. It may be that the unphilosophic man and the psychologists are seriously confused. But it may also be that, as so often in the past, the philosophers have been misled by plausible arguments. The reasonable man ought to regard the question as open.

The Theory Measured Against Demands Already Formulated

Getting down to more serious business, let us measure the theory against the various demands that a satisfactory theory of mind must meet as they have emerged in the last four chapters, beginning with the demands that create no difficulty.

(i) It is clear that this theory accounts very simply for the unity of mind and body. The brain is physically inside the body. It is the pilot in the vessel. This fits in remarkably well with ordinary talk about the mind. It is completely natural to speak of the mind as 'in' the body, and to speak of mental processes as 'inner' processes. Now 'in' is primarily a spatial word. The naturalness of this way of speaking is strikingly, and the more strikingly because quite unconsciously, brought out by Hume. For in the course of putting forward a theory of mind according to which it is not in physical space, he says:

> Suppose we could see clearly into the *breast* of another and observe that succession of perceptions which constitutes his mind or thinking principle . . . (*Treatise,* Bk. I, Pt. IV, Sect. 6, p. 260, ed. Selby-Bigge, my italics)

Hume's way of talking here, indefensible on his own theory, seems to us *all* to be a natural way of talking, although we might now say 'head', not 'breast'. But a Dualist must say that the mind is not in the body in any gross material sense of the word 'in'. What his own refined sense of the word is, is a mystery.

(ii) Central-state Materialism can provide a simple principle of numerical difference for minds, viz., difference of place, just as the Attribute and the Behaviourist theory can.

(iii) Central-state Materialism can explain very simply the interaction of mind and body. Brain and body interact, so mind and body interact.

(iv) Central-state Materialism allows us to say that the mind comes into being in a gradual way, and that there is no sharp break between not having a mind and having one. For in the evolution of the species, and in the development of the individual, the brain comes into being in a gradual way. The simplification of our world-picture that results is the especial advantage of Materialist theories (including Behaviourism).

(v) But unlike Behaviourism, a Central-state theory does not deny the existence of inner mental states. On the contrary, it asserts their existence: they are physical states of the brain.

Nevertheless, a Central-state theory seems to face some serious objections.

(i) We argued that any satisfactory theory of mind ought to allow for the logical possibility of disembodied minds. If the mind is the brain, it might seem that a mind logically cannot exist in a disembodied state in any but the crudest sense, that is to say, as a brain without a body. This is not what we mean by a disembodied mind.

(ii) In criticizing the 'Bundle' theory, we saw that mental states are incapable of independent existence. It is not clear how the Central-state theory can account for this. Brain-states or processes seem to be things that could be conceived to exist independently of anything else. They do not even require a brain, for we could conceive them as, *e.g.* patterns of electrical discharge in space.

(iii) It is not clear what account a Central-state theory can give of the 'intentionality' or 'pointing' nature of mental processes. It is true that no theory we have examined has cast any particular light on this problem so far. But, as we noticed when discussing Behaviourism, Materialist theories are at a special

disadvantage in dealing with 'intentionality', because they cannot treat it as an irreducible, unanalysable, feature of mental processes on pain of contradicting their Materialism.

(iv) In discussing Behaviourism, we conceded that behaviour and dispositions to behave do enter into the concept of mind in some way. It is not clear how a Central-state theory does justice to this feature of the mental.

A Further Difficulty Formulated, and an Answer Sketched

But the difficulties considered in the previous section pale before one powerful line of argument that may seem to be a conclusive reason for denying that the mind is the brain. Take the statement 'The mind is the brain'. ('Mental processes are brain-processes' may be substituted if preferred.) Does the statement purport to be a logically necessary truth, or is it simply claimed to be contingently true? Does a defender of the Central-state theory want to assimilate the statement to 'An oculist *is* an eye-doctor' or '7 + 5 *is* 12', on the one hand, or to 'The morning star *is* the evening star' or 'The gene *is* the DNA molecule', on the other?

It is perfectly clear which way the cat must jump here. If there is anything certain in philosophy, it is certain that 'The mind is the brain' is not a logically necessary truth. When Aristotle said that the brain was nothing but an organ for keeping the body cool, he was certainly not guilty of denying a necessary truth. His mistake was an empirical one. So if it is true that the mind is the brain, a model must be found among contingent statements of identity. We must compare the statement to 'The morning star is the evening star' or 'The gene is the DNA molecule', or some other contingent assertion of identity. (The statement 'The gene is the DNA molecule' is not a very exact one from the biological point of view. But it will prove to be a useful example in the development of the argument, and it is accurate enough for our purposes here.)

But if 'The mind is the brain' is a contingent statement, then it follows that it must be possible to give logically independent explanations (or, alternatively, 'ostensive definitions') of the meaning of the two words 'mind' and 'brain'. For consider. 'The morning star is the evening star' is a contingent statement. We can explain the meaning of the phrase 'the morning star' thus: it is the very bright star seen in the sky on certain mornings of the year. We can explain the meaning of the phrase 'the evening star' thus: it is the very bright star seen in the sky on certain evenings of the year. We can give logically independent explanations of the meanings of the two phrases. 'The gene is the DNA molecule' is a contingent statement. We can explain the meaning of the word 'gene' thus: it is that thing or principle within us that is responsible for the transmission of hereditary characteristics, such as colour of eyes. We can explain the meaning of the phrase 'DNA molecule' along the following lines: it is a molecule of a certain very complex chemical constitution which forms the nucleus of the cell. We can give logically independent explanations of the word 'gene' and the phrase 'DNA molecule'.

Now if it is meaningful to say that 'The mind is the brain' it must be possible to treat the words 'mind' and 'brain' in the same way.

The word 'brain' gives no trouble. Clearly it is possible to explain its meaning in a quasi-ostensive way. The problem is posed by the word 'mind'. What verbal explanation or 'ostensive definition' can we give of the meaning of this word without implying a departure from a physicalist view of the world? This seems to be the great problem, or, at any rate, one great problem, faced by a Central-state theory.

The object that we call a 'brain' is called a brain in virtue of certain physical characteristics: it is a certain sort of physical object found inside people's skulls. Yet if we say that this object is also the mind, then, since the word 'mind' does not mean the same as the word 'brain', it seems that the brain can only be the mind in virtue of some *further* characteristic that the brain has. But what can this characteristic be? We seem on the verge of being forced back into an Attribute theory.

Put the problem another way. Central-state Materialism holds that when we are *aware* of our mental states what we are aware of are mere physical states of our brain. But we are certainly not aware of the mental states *as* states of the brain. What then are we aware of mental states as? Are we not aware of them as states of a quite peculiar, mental, sort?

The problem has so daunted one physicalist, Paul Feyerabend, that he has suggested that the materialist ought simply to recognize that his world-view does not allow statements that assert or imply the existence of minds. A true physicalism will simply talk about the operation of the central nervous system, and will write off talk about the mind as an intellectual loss. (See his 'Mental events and the Brain', *The Journal of Philosophy,* Vol. LX, 1963.)

I think that if the situation is as desperate as this it is desperate indeed. It is at least our first duty to see if we can give an explanation of the word 'mind' which will meet the demands that have just been outlined. In order to do this, let us turn to a way of thinking about man that has been popularized by psychology. Psychologists very often present us with the following picture. Man is an object continually acted upon by certain physical stimuli. These stimuli elicit from him certain behaviour, that is to say, a certain physical response. In the causal chain between the stimulus and the response, falls the mind. The mind is that which causally mediates our response to stimuli. Now the Central-state theory wants to say that between the stimulus and the response fall physical processes in the central nervous system, and nothing else at all, not even something 'epiphenomenal'. At the same time the theory cannot mention the central nervous system in its account of the concept of mind. If we now think of the psychologist's picture, the outline of a solution is in our hands. As a first approximation we can say that what we mean when we talk about the mind, or about particular mental processes, is nothing but the effect within a man of certain stimuli, and the cause within a man of certain responses. The intrinsic nature of these effects and causes is not something that is involved in the concept of mind or the particular mental concepts. The concept of a mental state is the

concept of that, whatever it may turn out to be, which is brought about in a man by certain stimuli and which in turn brings about certain responses. What it is in its own nature is something for science to discover. Modern science declares that this mediator between stimulus and response is in fact the central nervous system, or more crudely and inaccurately, but more simply, the brain.

Views of Place and Smart

If we now consider the two papers that are already 'classical' expositions of Central-state Materialism: U. T. Place's 'Is Consciousness a Brain Process?' *(British Journal of Psychology,* Vol. XLVII, 1956, pp. 44–50) and J. J. C. Smart's 'Sensations and Brain Processes' *(Philosophical Review,* Vol. LXVIII, 1959, pp. 141–56), we find that they give the problem we grappled with in the previous section only very brief consideration. So far as they do consider it, they come down on the side of the stimulus, not the response. Smart wrote:

> When a person says, 'I see a yellowish-orange after-image', he is saying something like this: *'There is something going on which is like what is going on when* I have my eyes open, am awake, and there is an orange illuminated in good light in front of me, that is, when I really see an orange.'

Here the having of an orange after-image is explicated in terms of the stimulus: an orange acting on a person in suitable conditions. Place took a similar line.

Now if we consider some other mental processes it is at once clear that this sort of analysis solely in terms of the effects of a stimulus can have no hope of success. Suppose I form the intention to go out and get a drink. There may well be no typical physical situations which have the effect of creating this state in me. The account of intentions must clearly proceed instead in terms of the behaviour that such an intention initiates. The intention is an inner cause of a certain sort of response, not the inner effect of a certain sort of stimulus. Of course, the intention *is* an effect of certain causes, but it cannot be *defined* in terms of these causes.

In fact, however, the point just made about intentions would constitute no criticism of Place's and Smart's position as put forward in these articles. For with respect to things like intentions they are not Central-state Materialists, but Behaviourists. Place wrote:

> In the case of cognitive concepts like 'knowing', 'believing', 'understanding', 'remembering', and volitional concepts like 'wanting' and 'intending', there can be little doubt, I think, that an analysis in terms of dispositions to behave is fundamentally sound. On the other hand, there would seem to be an intractable residue of concepts clustering around the notions of consciousness, experience, sensation, and mental imagery, where some sort of inner process story is unavoidable.

Smart took the same view.

Against Place and Smart, however, I wish to defend a Central-state account of *all* the mental concepts. We do naturally distinguish between the thought or

belief, and its expression in words or action, between the emotion and its expression in action, between the aim or intention and its expression in action. Taking the word literally, something is 'expressed' when it is squeezed out, as oil is expressed from olives. Applied to the mind, this yields the picture of an inner state bringing about outward behaviour. Surely some strong reason (as opposed to mere current prejudice) must be advanced if this picture is to be rejected? In default of such a reason it should be accepted.

It may be said that all we are ever aware of in introspection are sense-impressions, sensations and mental images. Now it may perhaps be granted that they are the most obtrusive sort of inner item, but it is far from clear that we are not sometimes aware of thoughts and intentions, for example, without accompanying imagery and sensations. Putting the matter at its lowest, it certainly seems to make sense to say 'I was aware of thoughts going through my mind. An inner event occurred, but no relevant images went through my mind, nor did I have any relevant sense-impressions or sensations.' Perhaps such statements are never true, but, again, perhaps they sometimes are. I think, indeed, that Place's and Smart's position is a mere hang-over from the Sensationalism of the British Empiricists which attempts to reduce all actual mental items to impressions, images and sensations. But once we have accepted any sort of inner mental item, strong arguments should be needed to exclude what are, *prima facie*, also items.

Smart has in fact changed his view on this matter. He now accepts a Central-state account of all the mental concepts. His original position was in fact, I think, an interesting example of a quite false spirit of economy. The motive was clear: if we have to admit inner items, let us admit as few as possible. But in fact once one has admitted the necessity for a certain sort of entity in one's theoretical scheme then it will often lead to a more economical theory if this sort of entity is postulated to explain the widest possible range of phenomena. Theoretical economy about entities is not like being economical with money. To be economical with money is to spend as little quantity of money as is consistent with one's purposes. But theoretical economy about entities is a matter of postulating the smallest number of *sorts* of entity that will explain the phenomena. Its analogue with respect to money would be a coinage that had the minimum number of *types* of coin consistent with all the sorts of financial operation that had to be undertaken. So once one admits inner mental states at all it is actually a theoretical economy to give a Central-state account of all the mental concepts.

But even if we confine ourselves to the ground originally chosen by Place and Smart, it is clear that their account of such things as perceptions in terms of the characteristic effects of certain stimuli is inadequate. I am not denying that what they say is part of the truth. As we shall see when we come to discuss the concept of perception in detail, it *is* part of our notion of seeing or seeming to see something yellow that it is the sort of inner event characteristically produced in us by the action of a yellow physical object. But a full account of the visual experience involves more than this. To show us that he can perceive, a man must show us that he can do certain things: that he can systematically

discriminate in his behaviour between certain classes of objects. As Anthony Kenny remarks in his *Action, Emotion and Will* (Routledge, 1963, p. 59) we pick a man's lack of perceptual powers by a certain inefficiency in conduct. So, even in such a case as perception, reference to certain sorts of *responses* for which the perception gives us a capacity is at least as important for elucidating the concept as reference to certain sorts of stimuli.

The Concept of a Mental State

The difficulties in Place's and Smart's position incline me to look to the response rather than the stimulus in seeking a general account of the mental concepts. The concept of a mental state is primarily the concept of *a state of the person apt for bringing about a certain sort of behaviour.* Sacrificing all accuracy for brevity we can say that, although mind is not behaviour, it is the *cause* of behaviour. In the case of some mental states only they are also *states of the person apt for being brought about by a certain sort of stimulus.* But this latter formula is a secondary one.

It will be advisable to dwell rather carefully on this first formula: state of the person apt for bringing about a certain sort of behaviour.

In the first place, I attach no special importance to the word 'state'. For instance, it is not meant to rule out 'process' or 'event'. I think that in fact useful distinctions can be made between states, processes and events, and that mental 'items', to use a neutral term, can be variously classified under these quite separate heads. This point will emerge in Part II. . . . But in the meanwhile 'state' is not meant to exclude 'process' or 'event'.

In the second place, I call attention to the word 'apt'. Here there are two points to be made: (a) By saying only that mental states are states *apt* for bringing about behaviour we allow for some mental states being actual occurrences, even although they result in no behaviour. (b) The formula is intended to cover more than one sort of relationship between mental state and behaviour. If we consider intentions, for instance, then they are naturally construed (*pace* Ryle) as causes within our minds that tend to initiate and sustain certain courses of behaviour. But it is most implausible to say that perceptions, for instance, are causes tending to initiate certain courses of behaviour. Suppose I see a magpie on the lawn. It may well be that magpies are things which I can take or leave, and that no impulse to do anything at all is involved in the perception. What must be said about perception (as will be elaborated later) is that it is a matter of acquiring capacities to make systematic physical discriminations within our environment *if we should be so impelled.* (If intentions are like pressures on a door, perceptions are like acquiring a key to the door. You can put the key in your pocket, and never do anything with it.) Other mental states will turn out to stand in still different causal relations to the behaviour which constitutes their 'expression'. In some cases, indeed, it will emerge that certain sorts of mental states can only be described in terms of their *resemblance* to other mental states that stand in causal relations to behaviour. Here the relation to behaviour is very indirect indeed.

696

A closely connected point is that, in many cases, an account of mental states involves not only their causal relation to behaviour, but their causal relation to other mental states. It may even be that an account of certain mental states will proceed solely in terms of the other mental states they are apt for bringing about. An intention to work out a sum 'in one's head' would be a case in point. The intention is a mental cause apt for bringing about the thoughts that are the successive steps in the calculation. So all that is demanded is that our analysis must *ultimately* reach mental states that are describable in terms of the behaviour they are apt for.

In the third place, the 'bringing about' involved is the 'bringing about' of ordinary, efficient, causality. It is no different in principle from the 'bringing about' involved when the impact of one billiard-ball brings about the motion of another ball. But the mention of Hume's paradigm should not mislead. I do not wish to commit myself for or against a Humean or semi-Humean analysis of the nature of the causal relation. I am simply saying that causality in the mental sphere is no different from causality in the physical sphere.

The further assumptions I will make about the nature of the causal relation in this work will only be two in number. In the first place, I will assume that the cause and its effect are 'distinct existences', so that the existence of the cause does not logically imply the existence of the effect, or *vice-versa*. In the second place, I will assume that if a sequence is a causal one, then it is a sequence that falls under some law. The stone causes the glass to break. There may be no law connecting the impact of stones on glass with the breaking of the glass. But in speaking of the sequence as a causal sequence, we imply that there is *some* description of the situation (not necessarily known to us) that falls under a law. These assumptions are not entirely uncontroversial, but at least are relatively modest.

In the fourth place, the word 'behaviour' is ambiguous. We may distinguish between 'physical behaviour', which refers to any merely physical action or passion of the body, and 'behaviour proper', which implies relationship to the mind. 'Behaviour proper' entails 'physical behaviour', but not all 'physical behaviour' is 'behaviour proper', for the latter springs from the mind in a certain particular way. A reflex knee jerk is 'physical behaviour', but it is not 'behaviour proper'. Now if in our formula 'behaviour' were to mean 'behaviour proper', then we would be giving an account of mental concepts in terms of a concept that already presupposes mentality, which would be circular. So it is clear that in our formula 'behaviour' must mean 'physical behaviour'. (And it is clear also that this is going to make our projected account of the mental concepts that much more difficult to carry through.)

It will be seen that our formula 'state of the person apt for bringing about a certain sort of behaviour' is something that must be handled with care. Perhaps it is best conceived of as a slogan or catch-phrase which indicates the general lines along which accounts of the individual mental concepts are to be sought, but does no more than this.

This leads on to a final point to be made about the formula. It should not be regarded as a guide to the producing of *translations* of mental statements.

It may well be that it is not possible to translate mental statements into statements that mention nothing but physical happenings, in any but the roughest way. It may be still true, nevertheless, that we can give a satisfactory and complete account of the situations covered by the mental concepts in purely physical and topic-neutral terms.

I think the situation is as follows. We apply certain concepts, the mental concepts, to human beings. That is to say, we attribute mental states to them. Then the question arises whether it is possible to do full justice to the nature of these mental states by means of purely physical or neutral concepts. We therefore try to sketch an account of typical mental states in purely physical or neutral terms. The account might fall indefinitely short of giving translations of mental statements, yet it might still be plausible to say that the account had done justice to the phenomena.

Of course, this does leave us with the question how, lacking the test of translation, we can ever know that we have succeeded in our enterprise. But this is just one instance of the perennial problem of finding a decision-procedure for philosophical problems. I think in fact that all we can do is this: we produce an account of a certain range of phenomena in terms of a favoured set of concepts; we then try to test this account by looking for actual and possible situations falling within this range of phenomena which seem to defy complete description in terms of the favoured concepts. If we can deal successfully with all the difficult cases, we have done all that we can do. But there is unlikely to be any way of *proving* to the general satisfaction that our enterprise has been successful. If there was, philosophy would be easier.

Distinction Between our View and Behaviourism: The Nature of Dispositions

I turn to a question that may be worrying some readers. Now that I have given an account of the concept of a mental state, does it not appear that I am a Behaviourist in disguise? Admittedly, there is one great divergence from Behaviourism: the mind is not to be identified with behaviour, but only with the inner principle of behaviour. But, in elucidating our formula, there has been talk about tendencies to initiate, and capacities for, behaviour. And are not these perilously close to the Behaviourist's dispositions?

There is some force in this. In talking about dispositions to behave Behaviourism did come quite close to the version of the Central-state theory being defended here, far closer than it came when it talked about behaviour itself. But Behaviourism and the Central-state theory still remain deeply at odds about *the way dispositions are to be conceived.*

Speaking of dispositional properties in *The Concept of Mind* Ryle wrote (p. 43):

> To possess a dispositional property *is not to be in a particular state, or to undergo a particular change;* it is to be bound or liable to be in a particular state, or to undergo a particular change, when a particular condition is realized. (My italics)

We might call this the Phenomenalist or Operationalist account of dispositions. A still more striking statement of this view is provided by H. H. Price in his *Thinking and Experience* (Hutchinson, 1953, p. 322), although Price is no Behaviourist. He said:

> There is no *a priori* necessity for supposing that *all* dispositional properties must have a 'categorical basis'. In particular, there may be mental dispositions which are ultimate . . .

To this we may oppose what may be called a Realist account of dispositions. According to the Realist view, to speak of an object's having a dispositional property entails that the object is in some non-dispositional state or that it has some property (there exists a 'categorical basis') which is responsible for the object manifesting certain behaviour in certain circumstances, manifestations whose nature makes the dispositional property the particular dispositional property it is. It is true that we may not know anything of the nature of the non-dispositional state. But, the Realist view asserts, in asserting that a certain piece of glass is brittle, for instance, we are *ipso facto* asserting that it is in a certain non-dispositional state which disposes it to shatter and fly apart in a wide variety of circumstances. Ignorance of the nature of the state does not affect the issue. The Realist view gains some support from ordinary language, where we often seem to identify a disposition and its 'categorical basis'. ('It has been found that brittleness is a certain sort of molecular pattern in the material.')

I will now present an *a priori* argument which purports to prove the truth of the Realist account of dispositions. Let us consider the following case. Suppose that, on a number of occasions, a certain rubber band has the same force, F, applied to it, and that on each occasion it stretches one inch. We can then attribute a disposition to the band. It is disposed to stretch one inch under force F.

Now one essential thing about dispositions is that we can attribute them to objects even at times when the circumstances in which the object manifests its dispositions do not obtain. Suppose, now, that I say of the band that, if it had been subjected to force F at T_1, a time when it was not so subjected, it would have stretched one inch. What warrant have I for my statement? Consider first the answer that a Realist about dispositions will give. He will say that there is every reason to believe that the categorical state of the band which is responsible for its stretching one inch under force F obtains at T_1. Given that it does obtain at T_1, then, as a matter of physical necessity, the band must stretch one inch under force F.

But what answer can the Phenomenalist about dispositions give? For him, a disposition does not entail the existence of a categorical state. The only reason he can give for saying that the band would have stretched one inch under force F at T_1 is that numerically the same band behaved in this way on other occasions. But now we may ask the Phenomenalist 'What is the magic in numerical identity?' A thing can change its properties over a period of time. Why should

it not change its dispositional properties? How does the Phenomenalist know what the band's dispositional properties are at T_1? He may reply 'We have every reason to think that the relevant categorical properties of the object are unchanged at T_1, so we have every reason to think that the dispositional properties are unchanged.' But since he has asserted that the connection between 'categorical basis' and dispositional property is not a necessary one, he can only be arguing that there is a *contingent* connection between categorical properties and the fact that the band has that dispositional property at T_1. But how could one ever establish a contingent connection between categorical properties and unfulfilled possibilities? It is not as if one could observe the unfulfilled possibilities independently, in order to see how they are correlated with the categorical properties! It seems that the Phenomenalist about dispositions will be reduced to utter scepticism about dispositions, except on occasions that they are actually manifested.

I think we can imagine the possibility that the band should be acted upon by force F on different occasions, and behave quite differently on these occasions, although there was no relevant difference in the categorical properties of the band on these occasions. That is to say, I think we can imagine that the Principle of Sufficient Reason may be false in the case of the band. But it is only to the extent that we accept the Principle of Sufficient Reason that we can introduce the notion of disposition. It is only to the extent that we relate disposition to 'categorical basis', and difference of disposition to difference of 'categorical basis', that we can speak of dispositions. We must be Realists, not Phenomenalists, about dispositions.

All this is of central importance to the philosophy of mind. Thus, if belief, for instance, is a disposition, then it is entailed that while I believe p my mind is in a certain non-dispositional state, a state which in suitable circumstances gives rise to 'manifestations of belief that p'. The fact that we may not know the concrete nature of this state is irrelevant.

The tremendous difference between this and the 'Phenomenalist' account of disposition emerges when we consider that, on this 'Realist' view of dispositions, we can think of them as *causes* or *causal factors*. On the Phenomenalist view, dispositions cannot be causes. To say the glass breaks because it is brittle is only to say that it breaks because it is the sort of thing that does break easily in the circumstances it is in. But if brittleness can be identified with an actual *state* of the glass, then we can think of it as a cause, or, more vaguely, a causal factor, in the process that brings about breaking. Dispositions are seen to be states that actually *stand behind* their manifestations. It is simply that the states are *identified* in terms of their manifestations in suitable conditions, rather than in terms of their intrinsic nature.

Our argument for a 'Realist' account of dispositions can equally be applied to capacities and powers. They, too, must be conceived of as states of the object that has the capacity or power.

It will now be seen that a Behaviourist must reject this account of mental predicates involving dispositions, capacities or powers. For if he subscribed to it he would be admitting that, in talking about the mind, we were committed

to talking about inner states of the person. But to make this admission would be to contradict his Behaviourism. It would contradict the *peripheralistic* or *positivistic* drive that is involved in Behaviourism. Behaviourism concentrates on the case of other minds, and there it substitutes the evidence that we have for the existence of other minds—behaviour—for the mental states themselves. To admit dispositions as states lying behind, and in suitable circumstances giving rise to, behaviour is to contradict the whole programme. If, however, the reader still wishes to call my view a form of Behaviourism, this is no more than a matter of verbal concern. For it remains a 'Behaviourism' that permits the contingent identification of mind and brain.

The Identification of Mind and Brain

Suppose now we accept for argument's sake the view that in talking about mental states we are simply talking about states of the person apt for the bringing about of behaviour of a certain sort. (The detailed working out and defence of this view will in fact occupy the major part of this book—Part Two.) The question then arises 'What in fact is the nature of these inner states? What are these inner causes like?' And here no logical analysis can help us. It is a matter of high-level scientific speculation.

At this point we have one of those exciting turn-arounds where old theories appear in a quite new light. We suddenly get a new view of Dualism and of the Attribute theories, not to mention any wilder views that may be proposed. They are not, as we have insisted upon treating them up to this point, accounts of the *concept* of mind at all. Given that the concept of a mental state is the concept of a state of the person apt for bringing about certain sorts of (physical) behaviour, then we should view the different accounts of the mind that have been advanced through the ages as different *scientific* answers to the question of the intrinsic nature of these states.

Take the primitive view that the mind or spirit is breath. Consider the difference between a living man and a corpse. A living man behaves in a quite different, and far more complex, way than any other sort of thing, but a corpse is little different from any other material object. What is the inner principle of the living man's behaviour? One obvious difference is that the living man breathes, the corpse does not. So it is a plausible preliminary hypothesis that the inner principle of man's unique behaviour—his spirit or mind—is breath or air.

Again, it is a meaningful suggestion that the mind is a flame in the body, or a collection of specially smooth and mobile atoms dispersed throughout the members. It is a meaningful suggestion that it is a spiritual substance, or a set of special properties of the body or central nervous system which are not reducible to the physico-chemical properties of matter. Or perhaps, as Central-state Materialism maintains, it is the physico-chemical workings of the central nervous system.

(Some theories, of course, do have to be rejected for conceptual reasons. We have argued that 'Bundle' Dualism is logically incoherent. Behaviourism is unacceptable because, since the mind is the inner principle of behaviour, it

cannot *be* behaviour. Any Parallelist theory must be rejected because the essential thing about the mind is that it stands and operates in the causal chain between stimulus and response. But these are unnatural views of the mind, only adopted unwillingly under the stress of great intellectual difficulties.)

At this point we see that the statement 'The gene is the DNA molecule' provides a very good model for many features of the statement 'The mind is the brain'. (I am greatly indebted to Brian Medlin for this very important model.) The concept of the gene, when it was introduced into biology as a result of Mendel's work, was the concept of a factor in the person or animal apt for the production of certain characteristics in that person or animal. The question then arose what in fact the gene was. All sorts of answers were possible. For instance, the gene might have been an immaterial principle which somehow brought it about that my eyes are the colour they are. In fact, however, biologists have concluded that there is sufficient evidence to identify that which is apt for the production of hereditary characteristics as the substance to be found at the centre of cells: deoxyribo-nucleic acid. This identification is a theoretical one. Nobody has directly observed, or could ever hope to observe in practice, the details of the causal chain from DNA molecule to the colouring of the eye. But the identification is sufficiently certain.

It may now be asserted that, once it be granted that the concept of a mental state is the concept of a state of the person apt for the production of certain sorts of behaviour, the identification of these states with physico-chemical states of the brain is, in the present state of knowledge, nearly as good a bet as the identification of the gene with the DNA molecule.

60

Functionalism

JERRY A. FODOR

Jerry A. Fodor (b. 1935) holds appointments in the Department of Psychology and the Department of Linguistics and Philosophy at the Massachusetts Institute of Technology. He is the author of The Modularity of Mind, Representations, *and* Psychological Explanation, *from which this selection is taken.*

Like D. M. Armstrong (reading 59), Fodor is a materialist. He believes that all our mental processes are carried out by the neural matter in our brains. However, unlike Armstrong, Fodor does not believe that we should identify different mental states with particular activities of particular systems of neurons. Instead Fodor suggests that the concept of a mental state is a functional concept. That is, we understand mental states in terms of the roles they play in our mental life, not in terms of their constitution. This notion of a functional concept can be made clearer by a simple example: "doorstop" is a functional concept. When we describe something as a "doorstop," we do not say anything about the constitution of the thing, but only about how it functions. Virtually any suitably heavy object can be used as a doorstop. Fodor's point is that something similar might be true of mental states. Since the concept of a mental state is a functional concept, a wide variety of different physiological states might play the role of the same mental state. In this case, it would be a mistake to identify a mental state with some particular physical state, just as it would be a mistake to identify doorstops as bricks just because some doorstops are bricks.

Materialism and the Relation Between Psychology and Neurology

. . .

FOR PURPOSES of the present investigation, we are primarily interested in materialism as it bears upon problems about psychological explanation. We need, therefore, to clarify the implications of the materialist view for an account of the relations between psychological and neurological theories. I shall argue that while it is by no means evident that materialism must be regarded as conceptually incoherent, it is equally unclear that the truth of materialism would entail the views of the relation between psychology and neurology that have often been held in conjunction with it. In particular, to claim that mind states and brain states are contingently identical need not be to hold that psychological theories are reducible to neurological theories. Nor would the truth

of materialism entail that the relevant relation between psychological and neurological constructs is that the latter provide "microanalyses" of the former. It is to these issues that we now proceed.

Let us commence by trying to form some picture of how the problem of the relation between psychology and neurology emerges during the course of attempts to provide systematic scientific explanations of behavior.

Such attempts have characteristically exhibited two phases that, although they may be simultaneous in point of history, are nevertheless distinguishable in point of logic. In the first phase, the psychologist attempts to arrive at theories that provide what are often referred to as "functional" characterizations of the mechanisms responsible for the production of behavior. To say that the psychologist is seeking functional characterizations of psychological constructs is at least to say that, in this phase of explanation, the criteria employed for individuating such constructs are based primarily upon hypotheses about the role they play in the etiology of behavior. Such hypotheses are constrained by two general considerations. On the one hand, by the principle that the psychological states, processes, and so on hypothesized to be responsible for the production of behavior must be supposed to be sufficiently complex to account for whatever behavioral capacities the organism can be demonstrated to possess; on the other, by the principle that specific aspects of the character of the organism's behavior must be explicable by reference to specific features of the hypothesized underlying states and processes or of their interactions.

Thus, for example, a psychologist might seek to explain failures of memory by reference to the decay of a hypothetical memory "trace," an attempt being made to attribute to the trace properties that will account for such observed features of memory as selectivity, stereotyping, and so forth. As more is discovered about memory—for example, about the effects of pathology upon memory, or about differences between "short-" and "long-term" memory— the properties attributed to the trace, and to whatever other psychological systems are supposed to interact with it, must be correspondingly elaborated. It is, of course, the theorist's expectation that, at some point, speculations about the character of the trace will lead to confirmable experimental predictions about previously unnoticed aspects of memory, thus providing independent evidence for the claim that the trace does in fact have the properties it is alleged to have.

To say that, in the first phase of psychological explanation, the primary concern is with determining the functional character of the states and processes involved in the etiology of behavior is thus to say that, at that stage, the hypothesized psychological constructs are individuated primarily or solely by reference to their alleged causal consequences. What one knows (or claims to know) about such constructs is the effects their activity has upon behavior. It follows that phase-one psychological theories postulate functionally equivalent mechanisms when and only when they postulate constructs of which the behavioral consequences are, in theoretically relevant respects, identical.

This sort of point has sometimes been made by comparing first-phase psychological theories with descriptions of a "machine table"—that is, of the sets

of directions for performing computations—of a digital computer. Neurological theories, correspondingly, are likened to descriptions of the "hardware"; that is, of the physical machinery into which such tables are programmed. Since two physical realizations of the same table—that is, two computers capable of performing the mathematically identical set of computations in mathematically identical ways—may differ arbitrarily in their physical structure, mathematical equivalence is independent of physical similarity: two machines may, in this sense, share functionally equivalent "psychological" mechanisms even though they have neither parts nor configurations of parts in common.

The second phase of psychological explanation has to do with the specification of those biochemical systems that do, in fact, exhibit the functional characteristics enumerated by phase-one theories. The image that suggests itself to many psychologists is that of opening a "black box": having arrived at a phase-one theory of the kinds of operations performed by the mechanisms that are causally responsible for behavior, one then "looks inside" to see whether or not the nervous system does in fact contain parts capable of performing the alleged functions. The situation is more complicated, however, than this image suggests since the notion of a "part," when applied to the nervous systems of organisms, is less than clear. The physiological psychologist's task of determining what, if any, organization into subsystems the nervous system of an organism exhibits is precisely the problem of determining whether the nervous system has subsystems whose functional characteristics correspond with those required by antecedently plausible psychological theories.

The two phases of psychological explanation thus condition one another. On the one hand, it is clear that a psychological theory that attributes to an organism a state or process that the organism has no physiological mechanisms capable of realizing is ipso facto incorrect. If memory is a matter of forming traces, then there must be subsystems of the nervous system that are capable of going from one steady state to another and that are capable of remaining in the relevant states for periods that are at least comparable to known retention periods. If no such mechanisms exist, then the trace is the wrong model for the functional organization of memory.

On the other hand, the relevant notion of a neurological subsystem is that of a biochemical mechanism whose operation can correspond to some state or process that is postulated by a satisfactory psychological theory. To say that the goals of physiological psychology are set by the attempt to find mechanisms that correspond to certain functions is to say that it is the psychological theory that articulates these functions that determines the principle of individuation for neurological mechanisms. Once again, analogies to the analysis of less complicated systems may be helpful. What makes a carburetor part of an engine is not the spatial contiguity of its own parts (the parts of fuel injectors exhibit no such contiguity) nor is it the homogeneity of the materials of which it is composed. It is rather the fact that its operation corresponds to a function that is detailed in the theory of internal-combustion engines that there is no sub- or superpart of the carburetor whose operation corresponds to that function.

The problem, then, is one of fit and mutual adjustment: on the one hand, there is a presumed psychological theory, which requires possibly quite specific, complex, and detailed operations on the part of the neurological mechanisms that underlie behavior; on the other hand, there is a putative articulation of the nervous system into subsystems that must be matched to these functional characteristics and that must also attempt to maximize anatomical, morphological, and biochemical plausibility. This extremely complex situation is sometimes abbreviated by materialist philosophers into the claim that identification between psychological and neurological states is established on the basis of constant correlation and simplicity. We have seen that it is an open question whether the relevant relation is identification. Our present point is that the evidence required to justify postulating the relation is something considerably more complex than mere correlation. It is rather a nice adjustment of the psychological characterization of function to considerations of neurological plausibility, and vice versa.

Microanalysis and Functional Analysis

This discussion of the way in which psychological and neurological theories integrate during the course of the development of scientific explanations of behavior is, to be sure, no more than the barest sketch. But, insofar as the sketch is at all plausible, it suggests that the reductivist view of the relation between psychological and neurological theories is seriously misleading, even if one accepts a materialistic account of the relation between psychological and neurological constructs. The suggestion is that if materialism is true, a completed account of behavior would contain statements that identify certain neural mechanisms as having functions detailed during the course of phase-one theory construction and that some such statements would hold for each psychological construct. But such statements, clearly, are quite different in kind from those that articulate paradigmatic cases of reductive analysis.

This distinction seems to have been pretty widely missed by materialists, particularly in the literature that relates discussions of materialism to problems about the unity of science. Oppenheim and Putnam, for example, are explicit in referring to neurological theories, such as those of Hebb, as constituting "micro-reductions" of the corresponding psychological theories of memory, learning, motivation, and so on. On the Oppenheim-Putnam account, "the essential feature of micro-reduction is that the branch [of science] B_1 [which provides the micro-reduction of B_2] deals with the parts of the objects dealt with by B_2."[1]

Our present point is that it is difficult to understand how this could be the correct model for the relation between psychological and neurological theories.

[1] P. Oppenheim and H. Putnam, "Unity of Science as a Working Hypothesis" in H. Feigl, G. Maxwell, and M. Scriven (eds.) *Concepts, Theories and the Mind-Body Problem*. Minnesota Studies in the Philosophy of Science. Minneapolis: University of Minnesota Press, Vol. II, pp. 3–36, p. 6.

Psychological entities (sensations, for example) are not readily thought of as capable of being microanalyzed into *anything,* least of all neurons or states of neurons. Pains do not have parts, so brain cells are not parts of pains.

It is, in short, conceivable that there may be true psycho-physical identity statements, but it seems inconceivable that such statements are properly analyzed as expressing what Place (1956) has called identities of composition, that is, as expressing relations between wholes and their parts.[2] It should be emphasized that not all statements of identities *are* identities of composition. Compare "Her hat is a bundle of straw" with "He is the boy I knew in Chicago."

It is worth pursuing at some length the difference between the present view of the relation between psychological and neurological constructs and the view typical of reductivist materialism. In reductive analysis (microanalysis), one asks: "What does X consist of?" and the answer has the form of a specification of the microstructure of Xs. Thus: "What does water consist of?" "Two atoms of hydrogen linked with one atom of oxygen." "What does lightning consist of?" "A stream of electrons." And so on. In typical cases of functional analysis, by contrast, one asks about a part of a mechanism *what role it plays* in the activities that are characteristic of the mechanism as a whole: "What does the camshaft do?" "It opens the valves, permitting the entry into the cylinder of fuel, which will then be detonated to drive the piston." Successful microanalysis is thus often contingent upon the development of powerful instruments of observation or precise methods of dissection. Successful functional analysis, on the other hand, requires an appreciation of the sorts of activity that are characteristic of a mechanism and of the contribution made by the functioning of each part of the mechanism to the economy of the whole.

Since microanalysis and functional analysis are very different ways of establishing relations between scientific theories, or between ordinary-language descriptions, conceptual difficulties may result when the vocabulary of one kind of analysis is confounded with the vocabulary of the other.

If I speak of a device as a "camshaft," I am implicitly identifying it by reference to its physical structure, and so I am committed to the view that it exhibits a characteristic and specifiable decomposition into physical parts. But if I speak of the device as a "valve lifter," I am identifying it by reference to its function and I therefore undertake no such commitment. There is, in particular, no sense to the question "What does a valve lifter consist of?" if this is understood as a request for microanalysis—that is, as analogous to such questions as "What does water consist of?"(There *is,* of course, sense to the question "What does *this* valve lifter consist of?" but the generic valve lifter must be *functionally* defined, and functions do not have parts.) One might put it that being a valve lifter is not reducible to (is not a matter of) being a collection of rods, springs, and atoms, in the sense in which being a camshaft is. The kinds of questions that it makes sense to ask about camshafts need not make sense, and are often impertinent, when asked about valve lifters.

[2] U. Place, "Is Consciousness a Brain Process?" in V. C. Chappell (ed.), *The Philosophy of Mind,* Englewood Cliffs, N. J. : Prentice-Hall, pp. 101–109.

It is, then, conceivable that serious confusions could be avoided if we interpreted statements that relate psychological and neurological constructs not as articulating microanalyses but as attributing certain psychological functions to corresponding neurological systems. For example, philosophers and psychologists who have complained that it is possible to trace an input from afferent to central to efferent neurological systems without once encountering motives, strategies, drives, needs, hopes, along with the rest of the paraphernalia of psychological theories, have been right in one sense but wrong in another, just as one would be if one argued that a complete mechanical account of the operation of an internal-combustion engine never encounters such a thing as a valve lifter. In both cases, the confusion occurs when a term that properly figures in functional accounts of mechanisms is confounded with terms that properly appear in mechanistic accounts, so that one is tempted to think of the function of a part as though it were itself one part among others.

From a functional point of view, a camshaft is a valve lifter and *this* valve lifter (i.e., this particular mechanism for lifting valves) may be "nothing but" a camshaft. But a mechanistic account of the operations of internal-combustion engines does not seek to replace the concept of a valve lifter with the concept of a camshaft, nor does it seek to "reduce" the former to the latter. What it does do is to explain *how* the valves get lifted: that is, what mechanical transactions are involved when the camshaft lifts the valves. In the same way, presumably, neurological theories seek to explain what biochemical transactions are involved when drives are reduced, motives entertained, objects perceived, and so on.

In short, drives, motives, strategies, and such are, on the present view, internal states postulated in attempts to account for behavior, perception, memory, and other phenomena in the domain of psychological theories. In completed accounts, they could presumably serve to characterize the functional aspects of neurological mechanisms; that is, they would figure in explanations of how such mechanisms operate to determine the molar behavior of an organism, its perceptual capacities, and so on. But this does not entail that drives, motives, and strategies have microanalyses in terms of neurological systems any more than valve lifters can be microanalyzed into camshafts.

There are still further philosophically pertinent differences between the suggestion that psychophysical identity statements should be understood as articulating functional analyses and the suggestion that they should be analyzed as microreductions.

When, in paradigmatic cases, entities in one theory are reduced to entities in another, it is presupposed that both theories have available conceptual mechanisms for saying what the entities have in common. For example, given that water can be "reduced" to H_2O, it is possible to say what all samples of water have in common either in the language of viscosity, specific gravity, and so on at the macrolevel, or in chemical language at the microlevel. It is patent that functional analysis need not share this property of reductive analysis. When we identify a certain mousetrap with a certain mechanism, we do not thereby commit ourselves to the possibility of saying in mechanistic terms what all

members of the set of mousetraps have in common. Because it is (roughly) a sufficient condition for being a mousetrap that a mechanism be customarily *used* in a certain way, there is nothing in principle that requires that a pair of mousetraps *have* any shared mechanical properties. It is, indeed, because "mousetrap" is functionally rather than mechanically defined that "building a better mousetrap"—that is, building a mechanically novel mousetrap, which functions better than conventional mousetraps do—is a reasonable goal to set oneself.

It is a consequence of this consideration that the present interpretation of the relation between neurological and psychological constructs is compatible with very strong claims about the ineliminability of mental language from behavioral theories. Let us suppose that there are true psychophysical statements that identify certain neurological mechanisms as the ones that possess certain psychologically relevant functional properties. It still remains quite conceivable that identical psychological functions could sometimes be ascribed to anatomically heterogeneous neural mechanisms. In that case, mental language will be required to state the conditions upon such ascriptions of functional equivalence. It is, in short, quite conceivable that a parsing of the nervous system by reference to anatomical or morphological similarities may often fail to correspond in any uniform way to its parsing in terms of psychological function. Whenever this occurs, explicit reference to the character of such functions will be required if we are to be able to say what we take the brain states that we classify together to have in common.

Every mousetrap can be identified with some mechanism, and being a mousetrap can therefore be identified with being a member of some (indefinite) set of possible mechanisms. But enumerating the set is not a way of dispensing with the notion of a mousetrap; that notion is required to say what all the members of the set have in common and, in particular, what credentials would be required to certify a putative new member as belonging to the set.

Such considerations may be extended to suggest not only that a *plausible* version of materialism will need to view psychological theories as articulating the functional characteristics of neural mechanisms, but also that that is the *only* version of materialism that is likely to prove coherent. Consider the following argument, which Sellars has offered as a refutation of materialism:

> Suppose I am experiencing a circular red raw feel . . . (in certain cases) the most careful and sophisticated introspection will fail to refute the following statement: "There is a finite subregion ΔR of the raw feel patch ψr, and a finite time interval Δt, such that during Δt no property of ΔR changes."

The refutation may now proceed by appeal to Leibniz' Law. Suppose there is a brain state ϕ_r which is held to be identical with the psychological state ψ_r that one is in when one senses something red (i.e., with the "red raw feel"). Then substitution of ϕ_r for ψ_r permits the inference: there is a finite region ΔR of the brain state ϕ_r and a finite time interval Δt, such that during Δt no property of ΔR changes.

> But this, as even pre-Utopian neurophysiology shows us, is factually false. . . . Thus, during, say, 500 milliseconds, the 5° region at the center of my phenomenal circle does not change in any property, whereas no region of the physical brain-event can be taken small enough such that *none* of its properties change during a 500-millisecond period.[3]

The point of this argument is, I think, entirely independent of its appeal to such dubious psychological entities as "red raw feels." For it seems pretty clear that the principles we employ for individuating neurological states are in general different from, and logically independent of, those that we employ for individuating psychological states. Since what counts as one sensation, one wish, one desire, one drive, and so on is not specified by reference to the organism's neurophysiology, it seems hardly surprising that an organism may persist in a given psychological condition while undergoing neurological change. If a materialist theory is so construed as to deny this, then materialism is certain to prove *contingently* false.

Nor does Sellars' argument depend solely upon the possibility of there being differences in "grain" between neurological and psychological variation. The problem is not just that slight changes in neurophysiology may be compatible with continuity of psychological state. It is rather that we have no right to assume a priori that the nervous system may not sometimes produce indistinguishable psychological effects by *radically* different physiological means. How much redundancy there may be in the nervous system is surely an open empirical question. It would be extraordinarily unwise if the claims for materialism or for the unity of science were to be formulated in such fashion as to require that for each distinguishable psychological state there must be one and only one corresponding brain state.

I see no way to accommodate such considerations that does not involve a wholesale employment of the notion of functional equivalence. For the point on which Sellars' argument turns is precisely that there may very well be sets of neurologically distinct brain states, whose members are nevertheless psychologically indistinguishable. In such cases, identification of the psychological state with any member of such a set produces problems with the substitutivity of identity.

It seems clear that a materialist can avoid these difficulties only at the price of assuming that the objects appropriate for identification with psychological states are sets of *functionally equivalent* neurological states. In particular, it must be true of any two members of such a set that an organism may alternate between them without thereby undergoing psychological change.

This is tantamount to saying that a materialist must recognize as scientifically relevant a taxonomy of neurological states according to their psychological

---

[3] Attributed to Sellars, in P. E. Meehl, "The Compleat Autocerebroscopist: A Thought-Experiment on Professor Feigl's Mind-Body Identity Thesis," in P. Feyerabend and G. Maxwell (eds.), *Mind, Matter and Method: Essays in Philosophy and in Honor of Herbert Feigl*. Minneapolis: University of Minnesota Press, pp. 103–180.

functions. Such a taxonomy defines a "natural kind" (although very likely not the same natural kind as emerges from purely anatomical and biochemical considerations). Thus, a reasonable version of materialism might hold that psychological theories and neurological theories both involve taxonomies defined over the same objects (brain states), but according to different principles. What we require of the members of a set of anatomically similar brain states is *not* what we require of the members of a set of functionally equivalent brain states. Yet in neither case need the classification be arbitrary. The psychological consequences of being in one or another brain state are either distinguishable or they are not. If they are distinguishable, it is a question of fact whether or not the distinction is of the kind that psychological theories recognize as systematic and significant.

It is tempting to suppose that there must be only one principle of sorting (taxonomy by physical similarity), on pain of there otherwise being chaos, that either there is *one* kind of scientifically relevant similarity or there is *every* kind. It is, however, unnecessary to succumb to any such temptation. What justifies a taxonomy, what makes a kind "natural," is the power and generality of the theories that we are enabled to formulate when we taxonomize in that way. Classifying together all the entities that are made up of the same kinds of parts is one way of taxonomizing fruitfully, but if we can find other principles for sorting brain states, principles that permit simple and powerful accounts of the etiology of behavior, then that is itself an adequate justification for sorting according to those principles.

It would seem, then, that both the traditional approach to materialism and the traditional approach to the unity of science are in need of liberalization. In the first case, if he is to accommodate the sort of problem that Sellars has raised, the materialist will have to settle for identifications of psychological states with sets of functionally equivalent brain states, and this means that the materialist thesis is at best no clearer than the notoriously unclear notion of functional equivalence. In the second case, it appears that if the doctrine of the unity of science is to be preserved, it will have to require something less (or other) than reducibility as the relation between constructs in neurology and those in psychology. It seems, then, that scientific theories can fit together in more than one way, perhaps in many ways. If this is correct, then reduction is only one kind of example of a relation between scientific theories that satisfies reasonable constraints on the unity of science. It would be interesting to know what other kinds of examples there are.

61

Artificial Intelligence as Philosophy and as Psychology

DANIEL C. DENNETT

For biographical information about Daniel C. Dennett, see reading 57.

In this essay, Dennett spells out some of the crucial features of the "computer model" for doing psychology. Computer programs are organized hierarchically. We may think of the highest level simply as a statement of the problem, such as: compute the square root of 625. At the next level, the problem is broken down into component steps, such that, if each of the component parts is executed, the problem will be done. In sophisticated programs, these parts are broken down into subparts, which are in turn decomposed into smaller and smaller parts until finally the most basic parts of the program are simple mechanical tasks. Drawing on this model, Dennett suggests that we approach the task of psychological explanation by decomposing mental processes into smaller units that we may think of as performed by miniagents, or "homunculi," within the person. Dennett's central point is that explaining human behavior by reference to homunculi seems doomed to circularity—we could be "explaining" the intelligent behavior of big agents by appealing to the unexplained intelligent guidance provided by little agents—unless work in computer programming showed us how to "discharge" the homunculi. The homunculi get discharged because the task assigned to a high-level (intelligent-looking) homunculus itself gets broken down into ever smaller components until at the bottom level, the homunculi do not seem to be intelligent at all. Such low-level homunculi may do nothing more than respond "yes" or "no" to various sequences of inputs. Dennett believes that circularity is thus avoided, because the intelligence of the little agent is itself explained.

PHILOSOPHERS OF MIND have been interested in computers since their arrival a generation ago, but for the most part they have been interested only in the most abstract questions of principle, and have kept actual machines at arm's length and actual programs in soft focus. Had they chosen to take a closer look at the details I do not think they would have found much of philosophic interest until fairly recently, but recent work in Artificial Intelligence, or AI, promises to have a much more variegated impact on philosophy, and so, quite appropriately, philosophers have begun responding with interest to

the bold manifestos of the Artificial Intelligentsia.[1] My goal . . . is to provide a sort of travel guide to philosophers pursuing this interest. It is well known that amateur travelers in strange lands often ludicrously miscomprehend what they see, and enthusiastically report wonders and monstrosities that later investigations prove never to have existed, while overlooking genuine novelties of the greatest importance. Having myself fallen prey to a variety of misconceptions about AI, and wasted a good deal of time and energy pursuing chimaeras, I would like to alert other philosophers to some of these pitfalls of interpretation. Since I am still acutely conscious of my own amateur status as an observer of AI, I must acknowledge at the outset that my vision of what is going on in AI, what is important and why, is almost certainly still somewhat untrustworthy. There is much in AI that I have not read, and much that I have read but not understood. So traveler, beware; take along any other maps you can find, and listen critically to the natives.

The interest of philosophers of mind in Artificial Intelligence comes as no surprise to many tough-minded experimental psychologists, for from their point of view the two fields look very much alike: there are the same broad generalizations and bold extrapolations, the same blithe indifference to the hard-won data of the experimentalist, the same appeal to the deliverances of casual introspection and conceptual analysis, the aprioristic reasonings about what is impossible in principle or what must be the case in psychology. The only apparent difference between the two fields, such a psychologist might say, is that the AI worker pulls his armchair up to a console. I will argue that this observation is largely justified, but should not in most regards be viewed as a criticism. There is much work for the armchair psychologist to do, and a computer console has proven a useful tool in this work.

Psychology turns out to be very difficult. The task of psychology is to explain human perception, learning, cognition, and so forth in terms that will ultimately unite psychological theory to physiology in one way or another, and there are two broad strategies one could adopt: a *bottom-up* strategy that starts with some basic and well-defined unit or theoretical atom for psychology, and builds these atoms into molecules and larger aggregates that can account for the complex phenomena we all observe, or a *top-down* strategy that begins with a more abstract decomposition of the highest levels of psychological organization, and hopes to analyze these into more and more detailed smaller systems or processes until finally one arrives at elements familiar to the biologists. It is a commonplace that both endeavors could and should proceed simultaneously, but there is now abundant evidence that the bottom-up strategy in psychology is unlikely to prove very fruitful. The two best developed attempts at bottom-up psychology are stimulus-response behaviorism and what we might call "neuron signal physiological psychology", and both are now widely regarded as

---

[1] J. Weizenbaum, *Computer Power and Human Reason* (San Francisco: Freeman, 1976): p. 179, credits Louis Fein with this term.

stymied, the former because stimuli and responses prove not to be perspicuously chosen atoms, the latter because even if synapses and impulse trains are perfectly good atoms, there are just too many of them, and their interactions are too complex to study once one abandons the afferent and efferent peripheries and tries to make sense of the crucial center. Bottom-up strategies have not proved notably fruitful in the early development of other sciences, in chemistry and biology for instance, and so psychologists are only following the lead of "mature" sciences if they turn to the top-down approach. Within that broad strategy there are a variety of starting points that can be ordered in an array. Faced with the practical impossibility of answering the empirical questions of psychology by brute inspection (how *in fact* does the nervous system accomplish X or Y or Z?), psychologists ask themselves an easier preliminary question: How could any system (with features A, B, C, . . .) possibly accomplish X?

This sort of question is easier because it is "less empirical"; it is an *engineering* question, a quest for a solution (*any* solution) rather than a discovery. Seeking an answer to such a question can sometimes lead to the discovery of general constraints on all solutions (including of course nature's as yet unknown solution), and therein lies the value of this style of aprioristic theorizing. Once one decides to do psychology this way, one can choose a degree of empirical difficulty for one's question by filling in the blanks in the question schema above. The more empirical constraints one puts on the description of the system, or on the description of the requisite behavior, the greater the claim to "psychological reality" one's answer must make. For instance, one can ask how any neuronal network with such-and-such physical features could *possibly* accomplish human color discriminations, or we can ask how any finite system could *possibly* subserve the acquisition of a natural language, or one can ask how human memory could *possibly* be so organized so as to make it so relatively easy for us to answer questions like "Have you ever ridden an antelope?", and so relatively hard to answer "What did you have for breakfast last Tuesday?". Or, one can ask, with Kant, how anything at all could *possibly* experience or know anything at all. Pure epistemology thus viewed, for instance, is simply the limiting case of the psychologists' quest, and is *prima face* no less valuable *to psychology* for being so neutral with regard to empirical details. Some such questions are of course better designed to yield good answers than others, but *properly carried out,* any such investigation can yield constraints that bind all more data-enriched investigations.

AI workers can pitch their investigations at any level of empirical difficulty they wish; at Carnegie Mellon University, for instance, much is made of paying careful attention to experimental data on human performance, and attempting to model human performance closely. Other workers in AI are less concerned with that degree of psychological reality and have engaged in a more abstract version of AI. There is much that is of value and interest to psychology at the empirical end of the spectrum, but I want to claim that AI is better viewed as sharing with traditional epistemology the status of being a most general, most abstract asking of the top-down question: how is knowledge possible? It has

seemed to some philosophers that AI cannot be plausibly so construed because it takes on an additional burden: it restricts itself to *mechanistic* solutions, and hence its domain is not the Kantian domain of all possible modes of intelligence, but just all possible mechanistically realizable modes of intelligence. This, it is claimed, would beg the question against vitalists, dualists and other anti-mechanists. But as I have argued elsewhere, the mechanism requirement of AI is not an additional constraint of any moment, for if psychology is possible at all, and if Church's thesis is true, the constraint of mechanism is no more severe than the constraint against begging the question in psychology, and who would wish to evade that?

So I am claiming that AI shares with philosophy (in particular, with epistemology and philosophy of mind) the status of most abstract investigation of the principles of psychology. But it shares with psychology *in distinction from philosophy* a typical tactic in *answering* its questions. In AI or cognitive psychology the typical attempt to answer a *general* top-down question consists in designing a *particular* system that does, or appears to do, the relevant job, and then considering which of its features are necessary not just to one's particular system but to any such system. Philosophers have generally shunned such elaborate system-designing in favor of more doggedly general inquiry. This is perhaps the major difference between AI and "pure" philosophical approaches to the same questions, and it is one of my purposes here to exhibit some of the relative strengths and weaknesses of the two approaches.

The system-design approach that is common to AI and other styles of top-down psychology is beset by a variety of dangers of which these four are perhaps the chief:

1. designing a system with component subsystems whose stipulated capacities are *miraculous* given the constraints one is accepting. (E.g., positing more information-processing in a component than the relevant time and matter will allow, or, at a more abstract level of engineering incoherence, positing a subsystem whose duties would require it to be more "intelligent" or "knowledgeable" than the supersystem of which it is to be a part.

2. mistaking *conditional* necessities of one's particular solution for completely general constraints (a trivial example would be proclaiming that brains use LISP; less trivial examples require careful elucidation).

3. restricting oneself artificially to the design of a subsystem (e.g., a depth perceiver or sentence parser) and concocting a solution that is systematically incapable of being grafted onto the other subsystems of a whole cognitive creature.

4. restricting the performance of one's system to an artificially small part of the "natural" domain of that system and providing no efficient or plausible way for the system to be enlarged.

These dangers are altogether familiar to AI, but are just as common, *if harder to diagnose conclusively,* in other approaches to psychology. Consider danger

(1): both Freud's ego subsystem and J. J. Gibson's invariance-sensitive perceptual "tuning forks" have been *charged* with miraculous capacities. Danger (2): behaviorists have been *charged* with illicitly extrapolating from pigeon-necessities to people-necessities, and it is often claimed that what the frog's eye tells the frog's brain is not at all what the person's eye tells the person's brain. Danger (3): it is notoriously hard to see how Chomsky's early *syntax*-driven system could interact with semantical components to produce or comprehend purposeful speech. Danger (4): it is hard to see how some models of nonsense-syllable rote memorization could be enlarged to handle similar but more sophisticated memory tasks. It is one of the great strengths of AI that when one of its products succumbs to any of these dangers this can usually be quite conclusively demonstrated.

I now have triangulated AI with respect to both philosophy and psychology (as my title suggested I would): AI can be (and should often be taken to be) as abstract and "unempirical" as philosophy in the questions it attempts to answer, but at the same time, it should be as explicit and particularistic in its models as psychology at its best. Thus one might learn as much of value to psychology or epistemology from a *particular* but highly *un*realistic AI model as one could learn from a detailed psychology of, say, Martians. A good psychology of Martians, however unlike us they might be, would certainly yield general principles of psychology or epistemology applicable to human beings. Now before turning to the all important question: "What, so conceived, has AI accomplished?", I want to consider briefly some misinterpretations of AI that my sketch of it so far does not protect us from.

Since we are viewing AI as a species of top-down cognitive psychology, it is tempting to suppose that the decomposition of function in a computer is intended by AI to be somehow isomorphic to the decomposition of function in a brain. One learns of vast programs made up of literally billions of basic computer events and somehow so organized as to produce a simulacrum of human intelligence, and it is altogether natural to suppose that since the brain is known to be composed of billions of tiny functioning parts, and since there is a *gap of ignorance* between our understanding of intelligent human behavior and our understanding of those tiny parts, the ultimate, millenial goal of AI must be to provide a hierarchical breakdown of parts in the computer that will mirror or be isomorphic to some hard-to-discover hierarchical breakdown of brain-event parts. The familiar theme of "organs made of tissues made of cells made of molecules made of atoms" is to be matched, one might suppose, in electronic hardware terms. In the thrall of this picture one might be discouraged to learn that some functional parts of the nervous system do not seem to function in the digital way the atomic functioning parts in computers do. The standard response to this worry would be that one had looked too deep in the computer (this is sometimes called the "grain problem"). The computer is a digital device at bottom, but a digital device can simulate an "analogue" device to any degree of continuity you desire, and at a higher level of aggregation in the computer one may find the analogue elements that are mappable onto the non-digital brain parts. As many writers have observed, we cannot gauge the psychological

reality of a model until we are given the commentary on the model that tells us which features of the model are intended to mirror real saliencies in nature, and which are either backstage expediters of the modeling or sheer inadvertent detail. (In the Eighteenth Century, scientists built beautiful brass clockwork models of the solar system called orreries. The *gears* of an orrery are not intended to represent anything real in the firmament, nor are the reflections of one brass globe in another.) When one looks at AI programs in detail one sees mountains of digital calculation or "number crunching"; if this looks terribly unbiological, this is to be excused since that part of the model's structure is to be viewed as backstage, not part of the model we are supposed to compare with nature.

This story is fine in principle, I think, and the day may come when this imagined isomorphism down to the neuronal level (but not backstage) is proclaimed, but in fact we see nothing remotely like this in current AI work. We see instead models that diverge from nature *very* early on the downward path. AI programs typically model relatively high-level cognitive features, such as concept learning or revision of goals or beliefs, and it does indeed often take millions of basic computer events to simulate just a handful of these *intended model features*—but no one really knows or cares what these basic events are, for no one supposes that *any* of the saliencies in the mass of activity that subserves the intended features are to be taken seriously as psychology or physiology. The psychological reality of an AI program is thus usually intended to be only skin deep; only the highest levels of program description and commentary are to be counted as the model.

The *thin*ness of the psychological reality of AI models is obscured for the uninitiated by a particularly misleading feature of most of the AI programs that get into the limelight. What especially attracts audiences and evokes wonder is the marvelous verisimilitude of some of the programs. Consider this excerpt of conversation (minus the programmer's excellent commentary) between Terry Winograd's SHRDLU and its interlocutor. SHRDLU is a program that lives in an imaginary "block world" where it can manipulate colored blocks on a table in response to commands and answer questions about its life in this world. Computer responses are capitalized.

Had you touched any pyramid before you put the green one on the little cube?

YES, THE GREEN ONE.

When did you pick it up?

WHILE I WAS STACKING UP THE RED CUBE, A LARGE RED BLOCK AND A LARGE GREEN CUBE.

Why?

TO GET RID OF IT.

Why did you do that?

TO CLEAR OFF THE RED CUBE.

Why did you clear off that cube?

TO PUT IT ON A LARGE GREEN CUBE.

Why did you do that?

BECAUSE YOU ASKED ME TO.[2]

When SHRDLU replies to the last question with "Because you asked me to", one can hardly help being struck by the apparent *humanity* of the response— "SHRDLU is *one of us!*" it is tempting to exclaim. If one is naive, one will be awestruck; if one is not, one will still be titillated by the illusion, for that is largely what it is. SHRDLU's response, though perfectly appropriate to the occasion (and not by coincidence!) is "canned". Winograd has simply given SHRDLU this whole sentence to print at times like these. If a child gave SHRDLU's response we would naturally expect its behavior to manifest a general capacity which might also reveal itself by producing the response: "Because you told me to," or, "Because that's what I was asked to do," or on another occasion: "Because I felt like it," or "Because your assistant told me to," but these are dimensions of subtlety beyond SHRDLU. Its behavior is remarkably versatile, but it does not reveal a rich knowledge of interpersonal relations, of the difference between requests and orders, of being cooperative with other people under appropriate circumstances. (It should be added that Winograd's paper makes it very explicit where and to what extent he is canning SHRDLU's responses, so anyone who feels cheated by SHRDLU has simply not read Winograd. Other natural language programs do not rely on canned responses, or rely on them to a minimal extent.)

The fact remains, however, that much of the antagonism to AI is due to resentment and distrust engendered by such legerdemain. Why do AI people use these tricks? For many reasons. First, they need to get some tell-tale response back from the program and it is as easy to can a mnemonically vivid and "natural" response as something more sober, technical and understated (perhaps: "REASON: PRIOR COMMAND TO DO THAT"). Second, in Winograd's case he was attempting to reveal the *minimal* conditions for correct analysis of certain linguistic forms (note all the "problems" of pronominal antecedents in the sentences displayed), so "natural" language *output* to reveal correct analysis of natural language *input* was entirely appropriate. Third, AI people put canned responses in their programs because it is fun. It is fun to amuse one's colleagues, who are not fooled of course, and it is especially fun to bamboozle the outsiders. As an outsider, one must learn to be properly unimpressed by AI verisimilitude, as one is by the chemist's dazzling forest of glass tubing, or the angry mouths full of teeth painted on World War II fighter planes.

· · ·

---

[2] Terry Winograd, *Understanding Natural Language* (New York: Academic Press, 1972), pp. 12ff.

The AI community pays a price for this misleading if fascinating fun, not only by contributing to the image of AI people as tricksters and hackers, but by fueling more serious misconceptions of the point of AI research. For instance, Winograd's real contribution in SHRDLU is *not* that he has produced an English speaker and understander that is psychologically realistic at many different levels of analysis (though that is what the verisimilitude strongly suggests, and what a lot of the fanfare—for which Winograd is not responsible—has assumed), but that he has explored some of the deepest demands on any system that can take direction (in a natural language), plan, change the world and keep track of the changes wrought or contemplated, and in the course of this exploration he has clarified the problems and proposed ingenious and plausible *partial* solutions to them. The real contribution in Winograd's work stands quite unimpeached by the perfectly true but irrelevant charge that SHRDLU doesn't have a *rich* or human understanding of most of the words in its very restricted vocabulary, or is terribly slow.

In fact, paying so much attention to the performance of SHRDLU (and similar systems) reveals a failure to recognize that AI programs are not *empirical* experiments but *thought*-experiments prosthetically regulated by computers. Some AI people have recently become fond of describing their discipline as "experimental epistemology". This unfortunate term should make a philosopher's blood boil, but if AI called itself thought-experimental epistemology (or even better: *Gedanken*-experimental epistemology) philosophers ought to be reassured. The questions asked and answered by the thought-experiments of AI are about whether or not one can obtain certain sorts of information processing—recognition, inference, control of various sorts, for instance—from certain sorts of designs. Often the answer is no. The process of elimination looms large in AI. Relatively plausible schemes are explored far enough to make it clear that they are utterly incapable of delivering the requisite behavior, and learning this is important progress, even if it doesn't result in a mind-boggling robot.

The hardware realizations of AI are almost gratuitous. Like dropping the cannonballs off the Leaning Tower of Pisa, they are demonstrations that are superfluous to those who have understood the argument, however persuasive they are to the rest. Are computers then irrelevant to AI? "In principle" they are irrelevant (in the same sense of "in principle", diagrams on the blackboard are in principle unnecessary to teaching geometry), but in practice they are not. I earlier described them as "prosthetic regulators" of thought-experiments. What I meant was this: it is notoriously difficult to keep wishful thinking out of one's thought-experiments; computer simulation *forces* one to recognize all the costs of one's imagined design. As Pylyshyn observes, "What is needed is ... a technical language with which to discipline one's imagination."[3] The discipline provided by computers is undeniable (and especially palpable to the beginning programmer). It is both a good thing—for the reasons just stated—and a bad thing. Perhaps you have known a person so steeped in, say, playing bridge, that his entire life becomes in his eyes a series of finesses, end plays and cross-ruffs. Every morning he draws life's trumps and whenever he can see the

end of a project he views it as a lay-down. Computer languages seem to have a similar effect on people who become fluent in them. Although I won't try to prove it by citing examples, I think it is quite obvious that the "technical language" Pylyshyn speaks of can cripple an imagination in the process of disciplining it.

It has been said so often that computers have huge effects on their users' imaginations that one can easily lose sight of one of the most obvious but still underrated ways in which computers achieve this effect, and that is the sheer speed of computers. Before computers came along the theoretician was strongly constrained to ignore the possibility of truly massive and complex processes in psychology because it was hard to see how such processes could fail to *appear* at worst mechanical and cumbersome, at best vegetatively slow, and of course a hallmark of mentality is its swiftness. One might say that the speed of thought defines the upper bound of subjective "fast", the way the speed of light defines the upper bound of objective "fast". Now suppose there had never been any computers but that somehow (by magic, presumably) Kenneth Colby had managed to dream up [his] flow charts as a proposed model of a part of human organization in paranoia. It is obvious to everyone, even Colby I think, that [his] is a vastly oversimplified model of paranoia, but had there not been computers to show us how all this processing and much much more can occur in a twinkling, we would be inclined to dismiss the proposal immediately as altogether too clanking and inorganic, a Rube Goldberg machine. Most programs look like that in slow motion (hand simulation) but speeded up they often reveal a dexterity and grace that appears natural, and this grace is entirely undetectable via a slow analysis of the program (cf. time lapse photography of plants growing and buds opening). The grace in operation of AI programs may be mere illusion. Perhaps nature is graceful *all the way down,* but for better or for worse, computer speed has liberated the imagination of theoreticians by opening up the possibility and plausibility of very complex interactive information processes playing a role in the production of cognitive events so swift as to be atomic to introspection.

At last I turn to the important question. Suppose that AI is viewed as I recommend, as a most abstract inquiry into the possibility of intelligence or knowledge. Has it solved any very general problems or discovered any very important constraints or principles? I think the answer is a qualified yes. In particular, I think AI has broken the back of an argument that has bedeviled philosophers and psychologists for over two hundred years. Here is a skeletal version of it: *First,* the only psychology that could possibly succeed in explaining the complexities of human activity must posit internal representations. This premise has been deemed obvious by just about everyone except the radical behaviorists (both in psychology and philosophy—both Watson and Skinner, and Ryle and Malcolm). Descartes doubted almost everything *but* this. For the

---

[3] Cf. Zenon Pylyshyn, "Complexity and the Study of Artificial and Human Intelligence", in Martin Ringle, ed., *Philosophical Perspectives on Artificial Intelligence* (Humanities Press and Harvester Press, 1978).

British Empiricists, the internal representations were called ideas, sensations, impressions; more recently psychologists have talked of hypotheses, maps, schemas, images, propositions, engrams, neural signals, even holograms and whole innate theories. So the first premise is quite invulnerable, or at any rate it has an impressive mandate. But, *second,* nothing is intrinsically a representation of anything; something is a representation only *for* or *to* someone; any representation or system of representations thus requires at least one *user* or *interpreter* of the representation who is external to it. Any such interpreter must have a variety of psychological or intentional traits: it must be capable of a variety of *comprehension,* and must have beliefs and goals (so it can *use* the representation to *inform* itself and thus assist it in achieving its goals). Such an interpreter is then a sort of homunculus.

Therefore, psychology *without* homunculi is impossible. But psychology *with* homunculi is doomed to circularity or infinite regress, so psychology is impossible.

The argument given is a relatively abstract version of a familiar group of problems. For instance, it seems (to many) that we cannot account for perception unless we suppose it provides us with an internal image (or model or map) of the external world, and yet what good would that image do us unless we have an inner eye to perceive it, and how are we to explain *its* capacity for perception? It also seems (to many) that understanding a heard sentence must be somehow *translating* it into some internal message, but how will this message in turn be understood: by translating it into something else? The problem is an old one, and let's call it *Hume's Problem,* for while he did not state it explicitly, he appreciated its force and strove mightily to escape its clutches. Hume's internal representations were impressions and ideas, and he wisely shunned the notion of an inner *self* that would intelligently *manipulate* these times, but this left him with the necessity of getting the ideas and impressions to "think for themselves". The result was his theory of the self as a "bundle" of (nothing but) impressions and ideas. He attempted to set these impressions and ideas into dynamic interaction by positing various associationistic links, so that each succeeding idea in the stream of consciousness dragged its successor onto the stage according to one or another principle, all without benefit of intelligent *supervision.* It didn't work, of course. It couldn't conceivably work, and Hume's failure is plausibly viewed as the harbinger of doom for any remotely analogous enterprise. On the one hand, how could *any* theory of psychology make sense of representations that *understand themselves,* and on the other, how could *any* theory of psychology avoid regress or circularity if it posits at least one representation-understander in addition to the representations?

Now no doubt some philosophers and psychologists who have appealed to internal representations over the years have believed in their hearts that somehow the force of this argument could be blunted, that Hume's problem could be solved, but I am sure no one had the slightest idea *how to do this* until AI and the notion of data-structures came along. Data-structures may or may not be biologically or psychologically realistic representations, but they are, if not living, breathing examples, at least clanking, functioning examples of representations that can be said in the requisite sense to understand themselves.

721

How this is accomplished can be metaphorically described (and any talk about internal representations is bound to have a large element of metaphor in it) by elaborating our description (see Chapter 5) of AI as a top-down theoretical inquiry. One starts, in AI, with a specification of a whole person or cognitive organism—what I call, more neutrally, an intentional system (see Chapter 1)—or some artificial segment of that person's abilities (e.g., chess-playing, answering questions about baseball) and then breaks that largest intentional system into an organization of subsystems, each of which could itself be viewed as an intentional system (with its own specialized beliefs and desires) and hence as formally a homunculus. In fact, homunculus talk is ubiquitous in AI, and almost always illuminating. AI homunculi talk to each other, wrest control from each other, volunteer, sub-contract, supervise, and even kill. There seems no better way of describing what is going on. Homunculi are *bogeymen* only if they duplicate *entire* the talents they are rung in to explain (a special case of danger (1)). If one can get a team or committee of *relatively* ignorant, narrow-minded, blind homunculi to produce the intelligent behavior of the whole, this is progress. A flow chart is typically the organizational chart of a committee of homunculi (investigators, librarians, accountants, executives); each box specifies a homunculus by prescribing a function *without saying how it is to be accomplished* (one says, in effect: put a little man in there to do the job). If we then look closer at the individual boxes we see that the function of each is accomplished by subdividing it via another flow chart into still smaller, more stupid homunculi. Eventually this nesting of boxes within boxes lands you with homunculi so stupid (all they have to do is remember whether to say yes or no when asked) that they can be, as one says, "replaced by a machine". One *discharges* fancy homunculi from one's scheme by organizing armies of such idiots to do the work.

When homunculi at a level interact, they do so by sending *messages,* and each homunculus has representations that it uses to execute its functions. Thus typical AI discussions *do* draw a distinction between representation and representation-user: they take the *first step* of the threatened infinite regress, but as many writers in AI have observed, it has gradually emerged from the tinkerings of AI that there is a trade-off between sophistication in the representation and sophistication in the user. The more raw and uninterpreted the representation—e.g., the mosaic of retinal stimulation at an instant—the more sophisticated the interpreter or user of the representation. The more interpreted a representation—the more *procedural* information is *embodied in it,* for instance—the less fancy the interpreter need be. It is this fact that permits one to get away with *lesser* homunculi at high levels, by getting their earlier or lower brethren to do some of the work. One never quite gets *completely* self-understanding representations (unless one stands back and views all representation in the system from a global vantage point), but all homunculi are ultimately discharged. One gets the advantage of the trade-off only by sacrificing versatility and universality in one's subsystems and their representations, so one's homunculi cannot be too versatile nor can the messages they send and receive have the full flavor of normal human linguistic interaction. We have

seen an example of how homuncular communications may fall short in SHRDLU's remark, "Because you asked me to." The context of production and the function of the utterance makes clear that this is a sophisticated communication and the product of a sophisticated representation, but it is not a full-fledged Gricean speech act. If it were, it would require too fancy a homunculus to use it.

There are two ways a philospher might view AI data structures. One could grant that they are indeed self-understanding representations or one could cite the various disanalogies between them and prototypical or *real* representations (human statements, paintings, maps) and conclude that data-structures are not really internal representations at all. But if one takes the latter line, the modest successes of AI simply serve to undercut our first premise: it is no longer obvious that psychology needs internal representations; internal pseudo-representations may do just as well.

It is certainly tempting to argue that since AI has provided us with the only known way of solving Hume's Problem, albeit for very restrictive systems, it must be on the right track, and its categories must be psychologically real, but one might well be falling into Danger (2) if one did. We can all be relieved and encouraged to learn that there is *a* way of solving Hume's Problem, but it has yet to be shown that AI's way is the only way it can be done.

AI has made a major contribution to philosophy and psychology by revealing a particular way in which simple cases of Hume's Problem can be solved. What else has it accomplished of interest to philosophers? I will close by just drawing attention to the two main areas where I think the AI approach is of particular relevance to philosophy.

For many years philosophers and psychologists have debated (with scant interdisciplinary communication) about the existence and nature of mental images. These discussions have been relatively fruitless, largely, I think, because neither side had any idea of how to come to grips with Hume's Problem. Recent work in AI, however, has recast the issues in a clearly more perspicuous and powerful framework, and anyone hoping to resolve this ancient issue will find help in the AI discussions.

The second main area of philosophical interest, in my view, is the so-called "frame problem." The frame problem is an abstract *epistemological* problem that was in effect discovered by AI thought-experimentation. When a cognitive creature, an entity with many beliefs about the world, performs an act, the world changes and many of the creature's beliefs must be revised or updated. How? It cannot be that we perceive and notice *all* the changes (for one thing, many of the changes we *know* to occur do not occur in our perceptual fields), and hence it cannot be that we rely entirely on perceptual input to revise our beliefs. So we must have internal ways of up-dating our beliefs that will fill in the gaps and keep our internal model, the totality of our beliefs, roughly faithful to the world.

If one supposes, as philosophers traditionally have, that one's beliefs are a set of propositions, and reasoning is inference or deduction from members of the set, one is in for trouble, for it is quite clear (though still controversial) that

systems relying only on such processes get swamped by combinatorial explosions in the updating effort. It seems that our entire conception of belief and reasoning must be radically revised if we are to explain the undeniable capacity of human beings to keep their beliefs roughly consonant with the reality they live in.

I think one can find an *appreciation* of the frame problem in Kant (we *might* call the frame problem Kant's Problem) but unless one disciplines one's thought-experiments in the AI manner, philosophical proposals of solutions to the problem, including Kant's of course, can be viewed as at best suggestive, at worst mere wishful thinking.

I do not want to suggest that philosophers abandon traditional philosophical methods and retrain themselves as AI workers. There is plenty of work to do by thought-experimentation and argumentation, disciplined by the canons of philosophical method and informed by the philosophical tradition. Some of the most influential recent work in AI (e.g., Minsky's papers on "Frames") is loaded with recognizably philosophical speculations of a relatively unsophisticated nature. Philosophers, I have said, should study AI. Should AI workers study philosophy? Yes, unless they are content to reinvent the wheel every few days. When AI reinvents a wheel, it is typically square, or at best hexagonal, and can only make a few hundred revolutions before it stops. Philosopher's wheels, on the other hand, are perfect circles, require *in principle* no lubrication, and can go in at least two directions at once. Clearly a meeting of minds is in order.

PART VI Suggestions For Further Reading

Anscombe, G. E. M. *Intention,* (Cornell University Press, 1963)

Block, Ned, ed. *Philosophy of Psychology*, vols. I and II, (Harvard, 1981)

Boden, Margaret. *Artificial Intelligence and Natural Man*, (Basic, 1981)

Chomsky, Noam. *Rules and Representations*, (Columbia University Press, 1980)

Dennett, Daniel C. *Content and Consciousness*, (Humanities, 1969)

Dreyfus, Hubert L. *What Computers Can't Do*, (Harper-Row, 1979)

Fodor, Jerry A. *Representations*, (MIT Press, 1981)

Haugland, John, ed. *Mind Design*, (MIT Press, 1981)

Rosenthal, David, ed. *Materialism and the Mind-Body Problem*, (Prentice-Hall, 1971)

Ryle, Gilbert. *The Concept of Mind*, (Barnes and Noble, 1949)

Wilkes, Kathleen V. *Physicalism*, (Humanities, 1978)

Continued from page ii.

GILBERT HARMAN   "Ethics and Observation" from *The Nature of Morality: An Introduction to Ethics* by Gilbert Harman. Copyright © 1977 by Oxford University Press, Inc. Reprinted by permission.

R. E. HOBART   "Free Will as Involving Determinism" from "Free Will as Involving Determinism and Inconceivable Without It" by R. E. Hobart from *Mind* 43:169 January 1934. Reprinted by permission of Basil Blackwell Publisher.

IMMANUEL KANT   "Morality and Rationality" from *The Foundations of the Metaphysics of Morals,* by Immanuel Kant translated by Lewis White Beck. © Bobbs-Merrill, 1959.

PHILIP KITCHER   "Believing Where We Cannot Prove" Reprinted from *Abusing Science,* copyright 1982 MIT Press.

HILARY KORNBLITH   for the general introduction and the introduction to reading selections in Part III, "Theory of Knowledge." Copyright Hilary Kornblith.

SAUL KRIPKE   "Metaphysical Necessity" reprinted by permission of the publishers from *Naming and Necessity,* by Saul Kripke, Cambridge, Mass.: Harvard University Press, Copyright © 1972, 1980 by Saul Kripke.

THOMAS S. KUHN   "Objectivity, Value Judgement, and Theory Choice" from *The Essential Tension,* pp. 320–339. Publisher: University of Chicago Press, 1977.

GOTTFRIED WILHELM LEIBNIZ   "On Possibility and Necessity" from *Philosophers Speak for Themselves From Descartes to Locke,* eds. T. V. Smith and M. Grene, pp. 306–310. Published by University of Chicago Press, 1977.

KARL MARX/FRIEDRICH ENGELS   "Communism" from *The Marx-Engels Reader,* Second Edition, by Karl Marx and Friedrich Engels edited by Robert C. Tucker, by permission of W. W. Norton & Company, Inc. Copyright © 1976, 1972, by W. W. Norton & Company, Inc.

ERNEST NAGEL   "A Defense of Atheism" from "Philosophical Concepts of Atheism" by Ernest Nagel from *Basic Beliefs,* edited by J. E. Fairchild, 1959. Permission to reprint by Sheridan House, Inc.

EDWARD NELL/ONORA O'NEIL   "On Justice Under Socialism" by Edward Nell and Onora O'Neil from *Dissent,* (summer, 1972), 483–491. Published by Foundation for the Study of Independent Social Ideas, Inc.

FRIEDRICH NIETZSCHE   "The Utility of Truth" by Friedrich Nietzsche from *The Gay Science* by Friedrich Nietzsche translated by Walter Kaufman. Copyright © 1974 by Random House, Inc. Also from *The Will to Power* by Nietzsche, translated by Walter Kaufman and R. J. Hollingdale, copyright © 1967, and from *The Basic Writings of Nietzsche* translated by Walter Kaufman. Copyright © 1966, 1967, and 1968. Reprinted by permission of the publisher.

ROBERT NOZICK   "The Principle of Fairness" from *Anarchy, State, and Utopia,* by Robert Nozick. Copyright © 1974 by Basic Books, Inc., Publishers, New York. Reprinted by permission.

DEREK PARFIT   "Later Selves and Moral Principles" from *Philosophy and Personal Relations: An Anglo-French Study,* ed. by Alan Montefiore (Montreal: McGill-Queen's University Press, 1973. Reprinted by permission of the publisher.

PLATO   "What Do We Owe to Our Country?" from the "Crito" by Plato from *Plato: The Last Days of Socrates,* translated by Hugh Tredennick (Penguin Classics, New Edition 1959) pp. 79–96. Copyright 1954, 1959, Hugh Tre-

4
5
6
7
8
9
0
1
2

727